A HISTORY OF WORLD SOCIETIES

FIFTH EDITION

A HISTORY OF WORLD SOCIETIES

VOLUME B   From 1100 to 1815

John P. McKay
University of Illinois at Urbana-Champaign

Bennett D. Hill
Georgetown University

John Buckler
University of Illinois at Urbana-Champaign

Patricia Buckley Ebrey
University of Washington

HOUGHTON MIFFLIN COMPANY

Boston   New York

Sponsoring Editor: Nancy Blaine
Development Editor: Dale Anderson
Senior Project Editor: Christina M. Horn
Editorial Assistant: Leah Y. Mehl
Production/Design Coordinator: Jennifer Meyer Dare
Manufacturing Manager: Florence Cadran
Senior Marketing Manager: Sandra McGuire

Credits   **Pages 635, 637:** Excerpts from *Equiano's Travels: The Interesting Narrative of the Life of Olaudah Equiano,* ed. P. Edwards (Heinemann, 1996), pp. 4, 23–26. Reprinted with permission.

Volume B Cover Image: *At the Fair,* by Boris Kustodiev (1878–1927). Oil painting. Superstock.
Cover Designer: Diana Coe/ko Design Studio; Tony Saizon
Photo Researcher: Linda Sykes

Printed in the U.S.A.

Library of Congress Catalog Card Number: 99-71939

ISBN: 0-395-94493-7

1 2 3 4 5 6 7 8 9-VH-03 02 01 00 99

About the Authors

John P. McKay Born in St. Louis, Missouri, John P. McKay received his B.A. from Wesleyan University (1961) and his Ph.D. from the University of California, Berkeley (1968). He began teaching history at the University of Illinois in 1966 and became a professor there in 1976. John won the Herbert Baxter Adams Prize for his book *Pioneers for Profit: Foreign Entrepreneurship and Russian Industrialization, 1885–1913* (1970). He has translated Jules Michelet's *The People* (1973) and has written *Tramways and Trolleys: The Rise of Urban Mass Transport in Europe* (1976), as well as more than a hundred articles, book chapters, and reviews, which have appeared in numerous publications. His research has been supported by fellowships from the Ford Foundation, the Guggenheim Foundation, the National Endowment for the Humanities, and IREX. Recently, he contributed extensively to C. Stewart and P. Fritzsche, eds., *Imagining the Twentieth Century* (1997), a study in world history.

Bennett D. Hill A native of Philadelphia, Bennett D. Hill earned advanced degrees from Harvard (A.M., 1958) and Princeton (Ph.D., 1963). He taught history at the University of Illinois at Urbana, where he was department chairman from 1978 to 1981. He has published *English Cistercian Monasteries and Their Patrons in the Twelfth Century* (1968), *Church and State in the Middle Ages* (1970), and articles in *Analecta Cisterciensia, The New Catholic Encyclopaedia, The American Benedictine Review,* and *The Dictionary of the Middle Ages.* His reviews have appeared in *The American Historical Review, Speculum,* and the *Journal of World History.* He has been a Fellow of the American Council of Learned Societies and served as Vice President of the American Catholic Historical Association (1995–1996). A Benedictine monk of St. Anselm's Abbey in Washington, D.C., he is also a Visiting Professor at Georgetown University.

John Buckler Born in Louisville, Kentucky, John Buckler received his B.A. (summa cum laude) from the University of Louisville in 1967. Harvard University awarded him the Ph.D. in 1973. From 1984 to 1986 he was an Alexander von Humboldt Fellow at the Institut für Alte Geschichte, University of Munich. He has lectured at the Fondation Hardt at the University of Geneva and at the University of Freiburg. He is currently a professor of Greek history at the University of Illinois. In 1980 Harvard University Press published his *Theban Hegemony, 371–362 B.C.* He has also published *Philip II and the Sacred War* (Leiden 1989) and co-edited *BOIOTIKA: Vorträge vom 5. Internationalen Böotien-Kolloquium* (Munich 1989). He has contributed articles to *The American Historical Association's Guide to Historical Literature* (Oxford 1995), *The Oxford Classical Dictionary* (Oxford 1996), and *Encyclopedia of Greece and the Hellenic Tradition* (London 1999).

Patricia Buckley Ebrey Born in Hasbrouck Heights, New Jersey, Patricia Ebrey received her A.B. from the University of Chicago in 1968 and her M.A. and Ph.D. from Columbia University in 1970 and 1975. Formerly a faculty member at the University of Illinois, she now teaches at the University of Washington. She has published widely on Chinese social history. Her books include *The Aristocratic Families of Early Imperial China* (1978), *Family and Property in Sung China* (1984), *Confucianism and Family Rituals in Imperial China* (1991), *The Inner Quarters: Marriage and the Lives of Chinese Women in the Sung Period* (1993), and *The Cambridge Illustrated History of China* (1996). *The Inner Quarters* was awarded the Levenson Prize of the Association for Asian Studies. She has also edited or coedited several important works, most notably *Chinese Civilization: A Sourcebook* (1981, 1993).

Contents in Brief

Chapter 13 Creativity and Crisis in the Central and Later Middle Ages 370

Chapter 14 Civilizations of the Americas, ca 400–1500 412

Chapter 15 Europe in the Renaissance and Reformation 442

Chapter 16 The Acceleration of Global Contact 490

Chapter 17 Absolutism and Constitutionalism in Europe, ca 1589–1725 526

Chapter 18 Toward a New World-View in the West 562

Chapter 19 The Changing Life of the People in Europe 590

Chapter 20 Africa and the World, ca 1400–1800 620

Chapter 21 West and South Asia: The Islamic World Powers,
ca 1450–1800 646

Chapter 22 Continuity and Change in East Asia, ca 1400–1800 678

Chapter 23 The Revolution in Western Politics, 1775–1815 714

Contents

Maps   xiii
Timelines   xv
Listening to the Past   xvii
Preface   xix

🜨 Chapter 13

Creativity and Crisis in the Central and Later Middle Ages   370

Medieval Universities   371

From Romanesque Gloom to "Uninterrupted Light"   372

Troubadour Poetry   374

Life in Christian Europe in the Central Middle Ages   375

Those Who Work 375 • Those Who Fight 383 • Those Who Pray 386

● Individuals in Society: *Jean Mouflet of Sens 379*

Crises of the Later Middle Ages   389

A Challenge to Religious Authority 389 • The Black Death 390 • The Hundred Years' War (ca 1337–1453) 393 • Religious Crisis 396

Marriage and the Parish in the Later Middle Ages   398

Peasant Revolts   400

Race and Ethnicity on the Frontiers   401

Vernacular Literature   403

Summary   405
Notes   405
Suggested Reading   407

❱ LISTENING TO THE PAST: Christine de Pisan (1363?–1434?)   410

🜨 Chapter 14

Civilizations of the Americas, ca 400–1500   412

The Geography and Peoples of the Americas   413

Mesoamerican Civilizations from the Olmecs to the Toltecs   415

The Olmecs 415 • The Maya of Central America 417 • Teotihuacán and Toltec Civilizations 420

● Individuals in Society: *Quetzalcoatl 421*

Aztec Society: Religion and War   422

Religion and Culture 423 • The Life of the People 425 • Gender, Culture, and Power 428 • The Cities of the Aztecs 430

The Incas of Peru   432

Inca Imperialism 433 • Inca Society 437

Summary   438
Notes   438
Suggested Reading   439

❱ LISTENING TO THE PAST: The Death of Inca Yupanque (Pachacuti Inca) in 1471   440

🜨 Chapter 15

Europe in the Renaissance and Reformation   442

Economic and Political Origins of the Italian Renaissance   443

Intellectual Hallmarks of the Renaissance   445

Individualism 445 • Humanism 445 • Secular Spirit 446 • Art and the Artist 447 • The Renaissance in the North 449

● Individuals in Society: *Gentile Bellini (ca 1431–1507) 450*

Social Change During the Renaissance   452

Education and Political Thought 452 •
Movable Type and the Spread of Literacy 453 •
Women 453 • Blacks 454

**Politics and the State in the Renaissance
(ca 1450–1521)**   455

France 456 • England 456 • Spain 457 •
Germany and the Habsburg Dynasty 458

**The Condition of the Church
(ca 1400–1517)**   459

Martin Luther and the Birth of Protestantism   461

Luther's Theology 461 • The Social Impact
of Luther's Beliefs 463 • The Political Impact
of Luther's Beliefs 465

The Growth of the Protestant Reformation   465

Calvinism 466 • The Anabaptists 467 •
The English Reformation 467

**The Catholic Reformation and the Counter-
Reformation**   469

The Council of Trent 470 • New Religious
Orders and the Inquisition 471

Politics, Religion, and War   471

The Origins of Difficulties in France
(1515–1559) 473 • Religious Riots and Civil
War in France (1559–1589) 474 • The Revolt
of the Netherlands and the Spanish Armada 475 •
The Thirty Years' War (1618–1648) 477

Changing Attitudes   480

The Status of Women 480

Literature, Art, and Music   482

Literature 482 • Baroque Art and Music 483

Summary   484
Notes   484
Suggested Reading   488

▌ LISTENING TO THE PAST: Calvin's Vision
for Christian Renewal   486

● **Chapter 16**

The Acceleration of Global Contact   490

The World of the Indian Ocean   491

Peoples and Cultures 491 • Religious
Revolutions 495 • Trade and Commerce 496

● **Individuals in Society:** *Zheng He (1373?–
1435) 498*

**European Discovery, Reconnaissance, and
Expansion**   499

Overseas Exploration and Conquest 499 •
Technological Stimuli to Exploration 501 •
The Explorers' Motives 503 • The Problem of
Christopher Columbus 505 • The Conquest of
Aztec Mexico and Inca Peru 506

Global Trade Networks   509

**The Chinese and Japanese Discovery
of the West**   512

The Impact of Contact   513

The Columbian Exchange 513 • The Native
American Holocaust 516 • Colonial
Administration 517 • Slavery and the Origins
of American Racism 517 • The Economic
Effects of Spain's Discoveries 520

Summary   521
Notes   522
Suggested Reading   523

▌ LISTENING TO THE PAST: Columbus
Describes His First Voyage   524

● **Chapter 17**

**Absolutism and Constitutionalism in
Europe, ca 1589–1725**   526

France: The Model of Absolute Monarchy   527

The Foundations of French Absolutism 527 •
The Monarchy of Louis XIV 529 • Economic
Management and Religious Policy 530 • French
Classicism 532 • The Wars of Louis XIV 532

**The Decline of Absolutist Spain in the
Seventeenth Century**   533

**Absolutism in Eastern Europe: Austria, Prussia,
and Russia**   535

Lords and Peasants 536 • Austria and the
Ottoman Turks 538 • The Emergence
of Prussia 540 • The Rise of Moscow 541 •
The Reforms of Peter the Great 545 •
Absolutism and the Baroque 547

● **Individuals in Society:** *Stenka Razin, Russian
Rebel 546*

England: The Triumph of Constitutional Monarchy 549

The Decline of Absolutism in England (1603–1660) 549 • The Restoration of the English Monarchy 552

The Dutch Republic in the Seventeenth Century 553

Summary 556

Notes 557

Suggested Reading 557

▌ LISTENING TO THE PAST: The Court at Versailles 558

Chapter 18

Toward a New World-View in the West 562

The Scientific Revolution 563

Scientific Thought in 1500 563 • The Copernican Hypothesis 564 • From Brahe to Galileo 565 • Newton's Synthesis 567 • Causes of the Scientific Revolution 567 • Some Consequences of the Scientific Revolution 570

The Enlightenment 570

The Emergence of the Enlightenment 570 • The Philosophes and the Public 572 • The Later Enlightenment 575 • Urban Culture and Public Opinion 576

The Enlightenment and Absolutism 578

Absolutism in Central and Eastern Europe 578 • Absolutism in France 583 • The Overall Influence of the Enlightenment 584

● Individuals in Society: *Moses Mendelssohn and the Jewish Enlightenment 580*

Summary 585

Notes 586

Suggested Reading 586

▌ LISTENING TO THE PAST: Voltaire on Religion 588

Chapter 19

The Changing Life of the People in Europe 590

Agriculture and Population 591

Working the Land 591 • The Balance of Numbers 593 • The Growth of Cottage Industry 594

Marriage and the Family 597

Extended and Nuclear Families 597 • Work Away from Home 598 • Premarital Sex and Community Controls 598 • New Patterns of Marriage and Illegitimacy 599

Children and Education 600

Child Care and Nursing 600 • Foundlings and Infanticide 601 • Attitudes Toward Children 602 • Schools and Popular Literature 603

Food and Medical Practice 604

Diets and Nutrition 604 • The Impact of Diet on Health 606 • Medical Practitioners 607 • Hospitals and Medical Experiments 610

● Individuals in Society: *Martha Ballard, American Midwife 609*

Religion and Popular Culture 611

The Institutional Church 612 • Protestant Revival 612 • Catholic Piety 614 • Leisure and Recreation 614

Summary 615

Notes 616

Suggested Reading 616

▌ LISTENING TO THE PAST: A New Way to Educate Children 618

Chapter 20

Africa and the World, ca 1400–1800 620

Senegambia and Benin 621

Women, Marriage, and Work 623 • Trade and Industry 626

The Sudan: Songhay, Kanem-Bornu, and Hausaland 626

Ethiopia 628

The Swahili City-States 629

The Slave Trade 631

The Atlantic Slave Trade 633 • Consequences Within Africa 639

● Individuals in Society: *Olaudah Equiano (1745–1797) 636*

Summary 641

Notes 642

Suggested Reading 643

▌ LISTENING TO THE PAST: Duarte Barbosa on the Swahili City-States 644

Chapter 21

West and South Asia: The Islamic
World Powers, ca 1450–1800   646

The Ottoman Turkish Empire   647

Evolution of the Ottoman State 647 •
Expansion and Foreign Policy 648 • Ottoman
Society 652 • Cultural Flowering 655 •
The Decline of Ottoman Power 657

● Individuals in Society: *Hürrem (ca 1505?–
1558) 654*

The Persian Theocratic State   659

**India, from Mughal Domination to British
Dominion (ca 1498–1805)**   663

The Rule of the Mughals 664 • Trade
and Commerce 670 • European Rivalry
for the Indian Trade 671 • Factory-Fort
Societies 671 • The Rise of the British East
India Company 672

Summary   673

Notes   674

Suggested Reading   675

▶ LISTENING TO THE PAST: The Weighing
of Shah Jahan on His Forty-Second Lunar
Birthday   676

Chapter 22

Continuity and Change in East Asia,
ca 1400–1800   678

**China, from the Ming to the Mid-Qing
(ca 1368–1795)**   679

Ming Government 680 • Economic, Social,
and Cultural Change 683 • Foreign
Relations 685 • Ming Decline 686 • Qing
Rule 687 • External Pressures 690 • The Life
of the People 692

Korea (Choson)   695

Political and Cultural Foundations 696 •
Economic and Social Change 696

Japan (ca 1400–1800)   698

Feudalism in Japan 698 • Nobunaga and
National Unification 699 • The Tokugawa
Regime 700 • Urbanization and
Commercialization 701 • The Life of
the People 703

● Individuals in Society: *Katsushika Hokusai
(1760–1849) 705*

Summary   709

Notes   709

Suggested Reading   712

▶ LISTENING TO THE PAST: The Qianlong
Emperor Responds to King George III   710

Chapter 23

The Revolution in Western Politics,
1775–1815   714

Liberty and Equality   715

The American Revolution (1775–1789)   717

The Origins of the Revolution 717 •
Independence 718 • Framing the
Constitution 719

The French Revolution (1789–1791)   720

The Breakdown of the Old Order 720 •
Legal Orders and Social Realities 721 •
The Formation of the National Assembly 722 •
The Revolt of the Poor and the Oppressed 724 •
A Limited Monarchy 725

**World War and Republican France
(1791–1799)**   727

Foreign Reactions and the Beginning of
War 727 • The Second Revolution 728 • Total
War and the Terror 730 • The Thermidorian
Reaction and the Directory (1794–1799) 733

The Napoleonic Era (1799–1815)   734

Napoleon's Rule of France 734 • Napoleon's
Wars and Foreign Policy 735

● Individuals in Society: *Jakob Walter, German
Draftee with Napoleon 740*

Summary   741

Notes   741

Suggested Reading   744

▶ LISTENING TO THE PAST: Revolution
and Women's Rights   742

Index   I-1

TIMELINE

A History of World Societies: A Brief Overview   I-22

Maps

13.1	The Course of the Black Death in Fourteenth-Century Europe	390
13.2	English Holdings in France During the Hundred Years' War	395
14.1	The Peoples of South America	414
14.2	The Maya World, A.D. 300–900	417
14.3	The Aztec Empire, 1519	422
14.4	The Inca Empire, 1463–1532	432
15.1	The European Empire of Charles V	460
15.2	The Protestant and the Catholic Reformations	473
15.3	The Netherlands, 1578–1609	476
15.4	Europe in 1648	479
16.1	Indian Ocean Trade Routes	492
16.2	European Exploration and Conquest, Fifteenth and Sixteenth Centuries	502
16.3	Seaborne Trading Empires in the Sixteenth and Seventeenth Centuries	510
16.4	The African Slave Trade	519
17.1	The Acquisitions of Louis XIV, 1668–1713	533
17.2	Europe in 1715	534
17.3	The Growth of Austria and Brandenburg-Prussia to 1748	539
17.4	The Expansion of Russia to 1725	544
17.5	Seventeenth-Century Dutch Commerce	555
19.1	Industry and Population in Eighteenth-Century Europe	596
20.1	West African Kingdoms and the Slave Trade, ca 1500 to 1800	622
20.2	East Africa in the Sixteenth Century	628
21.1	The Ottoman Empire at Its Height, 1566	649
21.2	The Safavid Empire	660
21.3	India, 1707–1805	669
22.1	The Qing Empire, 1759	689
22.2	Tokugawa Japan	702
23.1	Napoleonic Europe in 1810	738

Timelines

The Americas, ca 400–1500   431

Absolutism and Constitutionalism in Europe   537

The French Revolution   732

The Napoleonic Era   739

The comparative timeline *A History of World Societies: A Brief Overview* is located at the end of the book.

Listening to the Past

Chapter 13   Christine de Pisan (1363?–1434?)   410

Chapter 14   The Death of Inca Yupanque (Pachacuti Inca)
             in 1471   440

Chapter 15   Calvin's Vision for Christian Renewal   486

Chapter 16   Columbus Describes His First Voyage   524

Chapter 17   The Court at Versailles   558

Chapter 18   Voltaire on Religion   588

Chapter 19   A New Way to Educate Children   618

Chapter 20   Duarte Barbosa on the Swahili City-States   644

Chapter 21   The Weighing of Shah Jahan on His Forty-Second
             Lunar Birthday   676

Chapter 22   The Qianlong Emperor Responds to
             King George III   710

Chapter 23   Revolution and Women's Rights   742

Preface

In this age of a global environment and global warming, of a global economy and global banking, of global migration and rapid global travel, of global sports and global popular culture, the study of world history becomes more urgent. Surely, an appreciation of other, and earlier, societies helps us to understand better our own and to cope more effectively in pluralistic cultures worldwide. The large numbers of Turks living in Germany, of Italians, Hungarians and Slavic peoples living in Australia, of Japanese living in Peru and Argentina, and of Arabs, Mexicans, Chinese, and Filipinos living in the United States—to mention just a few obvious examples—represent diversity on a global scale. The movement of large numbers of peoples from one continent to another goes back thousands of years, at least as far back as the time when Asian peoples migrated across the Bering Strait to North America. Swift air travel and the Internet have accelerated these movements, and they testify to the incredible technological changes the world has experienced in the last half of the twentieth century.

For most peoples, the study of history has traditionally meant the study of their own national, regional, and ethnic pasts. Fully appreciating the great differences among various societies and the complexity of the historical problems surrounding these cultures, we have wondered if the study of local or national history is sufficient for people who will spend most of their lives in the twenty-first century on one small interconnected planet. The authors of this book believe the study of world history in a broad and comparative context is an exciting, important, and highly practical pursuit.

It is our conviction, based on considerable experience in introducing large numbers of students to the broad sweep of civilization, that a book reflecting current trends can excite readers and inspire a renewed interest in history and the human experience. Our strategy has been twofold.

First, we have made social history the core element of our work. We not only incorporate recent research by social historians but also seek to re-create the life of ordinary people in appealing human terms. A strong social element seems especially appropriate in a world history text, for identification with ordinary people of the past allows today's reader to reach an empathetic

understanding of different cultures and civilizations. At the same time we have been mindful of the need to give great economic, political, intellectual, and cultural developments the attention they deserve. We want to give individual students and instructors a balanced, integrated perspective so that they can pursue on their own or in the classroom those themes and questions that they find particularly exciting and significant.

Second, we have made every effort to strike an effective global balance. We are acutely aware of the great drama of our times—the passing of the era of Western dominance and the simultaneous rise of Asian and African peoples in world affairs. Increasingly, the whole world interacts, and to understand that interaction and what it means for today's citizens, we must study the whole world's history. Thus we have adopted a comprehensive yet manageable global perspective. We study all geographical areas and the world's main civilizations, conscious of their separate identities and unique contributions. We also stress the links among civilizations, for it is these links that have been transforming multicentered world history into the complex interactive process of different continents, peoples, and cultures that we see today.

CHANGES IN THE FIFTH EDITION

In preparing the fifth edition of this book we have worked hard to keep our book up-to-date and to strengthen our distinctive yet balanced approach.

Organizational Changes and New Author

In order to give greater depth to our world focus, major organizational changes proved essential. The fortunate addition of a distinguished Asian expert, Professor Patricia Buckley Ebrey, to our author team has enabled us not only to expand our coverage of Asian developments but also to concentrate that coverage on those historical problems scholars today consider most current. Thus, Chapter 4 considerably expands the treatment of early China; Chapter 7 contains new material on the Silk Road trade, Tang politics and culture, and the spread of Buddhism from India to China, Japan, and Korea; Chapter 11 has been largely rewritten, with fresh material on the Mongols, a new discussion on Islam in India and Muslim relations with local religions, and much revised coverage of Heian and Kamakura Japan. Chapter 16 likewise has been extensively rewritten, with new information on the culture of the Indian Ocean, on the impact of global trade on the Chinese and on the Spanish empire. Chapter 22 contains broadened treatment of the commerce of the Ming empire, introduces a new section on Korea, and explores the impact of urbanization and commercialization on Japan. Chapter 27 represents another major reorganization and revision, with new material on the Ottoman Empire under pressure, a more detailed appreciation of internal developments in eighteenth-century Africa before European imperialism, and new analysis of French and British imperialism in Asia. Chapter 32 has expanded the discussion of World War II in the Pacific, including the intensity of the fighting and the deep hostility between Americans and Japanese.

New "Individuals in Society" Feature

In each chapter of the fifth edition we have added a short study of a fascinating man or woman or group of people, which is carefully integrated into the main discussion in the text. This new "Individuals in Society" feature grows out of our long-standing focus on people's lives and the varieties of historical experience, and we believe that readers will empathize with these flesh-and-blood human beings as they themselves seek to define their own identities today. The spotlighting of individuals, both famous and obscure, carries forward the greater attention to cultural and intellectual developments that we used to invigorate our social history in the fourth edition, and it reflects changing interests within the historical profession as well as the development of "micro history."

The men and women we have selected represent a wide range of careers and personalities. Several are well-known historical figures, such as Aspasia, the famous Greek courtesan (Chapter 5); Theodora, the Byzantine empress (Chapter 8); Ibn Battuta, the Muslim world-traveler (Chapter 9); Olaudah Equiano, the black slave, entrepreneur, and navigator (Chapter 20); Rosa Luxemburg, the German socialist (Chapter 29); Vaclav Havel, the Czech poet-statesman (Chapter 33); and Mother Teresa of Calcutta, the Albanian-Indian nun and missionary (Chapter 36). Other individuals and groups, perhaps less well-known, illuminate aspects of their times: Lady Hao, a Chinese noblewoman (Chap-

ter 4); Mukhali, a Mongol army officer (Chapter 11); Zheng He, a Muslim Chinese admiral (Chapter 16); Hürrem, wife of Suleiman the Magnificent (Chapter 21); Martha Ballard, an obscure Maine midwife (Chapter 19); and the Protestant villagers who resisted Nazi evil in Le Chambon in southern France (Chapter 29). Creative artists and intellectuals include the ancient Egyptian scholar-bureaucrat Wen-Amon (Chapter 2); the Chinese poet Tao Qian (Chapter 7); the West African artist from Djenné (Chapter 10); the Jewish philosopher Moses Mendelssohn (Chapter 18); the prolific Japanese artist Hokusai (Chapter 22); and the influential romantic writer Germaine de Staël (Chapter 25).

Expanded Ethnic and Geographic Scope

In this fifth edition we have added significantly more discussion of groups and regions that are often short-changed in the general histories of world civilizations. This expanded scope is, we feel, an important improvement. It reflects the renewed awareness within the profession of the enormous diversity of the world's peoples, and of those peoples' efforts (or lack thereof) to understand others' regional, ethnic, and cultural identities. Examples of this enlarged scope include new material on Muslim attitudes toward blacks (Chapter 9) and on the Mongols and other peoples of Central Asia (Chapter 11); a broadened treatment of Europe's frontier regions—Iberia, Ireland, Scotland, eastern Europe, and the Baltic region (Chapter 12); the peoples of the Indian Ocean—of the Malay archipelago and the Philippines (Chapter 16); and a completely fresh discussion of twentieth-century eastern Europe (Chapters 29 and 33). Our broader treatment of Jewish history has been integrated in the text, with stimulating material on anti-Semitism during the Crusades (Chapter 12), during the Spanish Inquisition (Chapter 15), in tsarist Russia (Chapter 27), Jewish Enlightenment thought in Germany (Chapter 18), and the unfolding of the Holocaust during the Second World War (Chapter 32). Just as the fourth edition developed our treatment of the history of women and gender, so in this fifth edition significant issues of gender are explored with respect to Native American peoples (Chapter 14) and Indian Ocean peoples (Chapter 16). The overall length of the book has been slightly reduced, but an expanded treatment of non-European societies and cultures has been achieved by reducing detailed coverage of Europe in Chapters 5, 6, 8, 12, 13, 17, 19, 24, 26, 31, and 32.

Incorporation of Recent Scholarship

As in all of our previous revisions, we have made a con-
scientious effort to keep our book up-to-date with new
and significant scholarship. Because the authors are
committed to a balanced approach that reflects the true
value of history, we have continued to incorporate important new findings on political, cultural, and intellectual developments in this edition. Revisions of this
nature include a new interpretation of the religions of
India, showing the changes from Brahamanic religions
to Hinduism in Chapter 3; a new treatment of the character of Alexander the Great and on the Greeks in the
western Mediterranean in Chapter 5; significant new
research on Cairo as an international trading entrepôt
in Chapter 9; new material on Chinese economic progress in the early modern period in Chapter 11; a
new subsection on the importance of the Olmecs in
Chapter 14; an entirely new discussion in Chapter 20 of
women, marriage, and work in the West African kingdoms; the impact of the fall of communism on Europe
and the world in Chapter 33; and in Chapter 34 the
economic difficulties of Japan in the 1990s, national developments in Bangladesh, Rabin's assassination and
Israeli-Palestinian problems—with the goal of bringing Middle Eastern and Asian developments up to the
present.

Revised Full-Color Art and Map Program

Finally, the illustrative component of our work has been
carefully revised. We have added many new illustrations
to our extensive art program, which includes over three
hundred color reproductions, letting great art and important events come alive. Illustrations have been
selected to support and complement the text, and,
wherever possible, illustrations are contemporaneous
with the textual material discussed. Considerable research went into many of the captions in order to make
them as informative as possible. We have reflected on
the observation that "there are more valid facts and details in works of art than there are in history books,"
and we would modify it to say that art is "a history
book." Artwork remains an integral part of our book;
the past can speak in pictures as well as in words. The
use of full color serves to clarify the maps and graphs
and to enrich the textual material. The maps and map
captions have been updated to correlate directly to the
text, and several new maps have been added, as in
Chapters 7, 9, 16, and 28.

DISTINCTIVE FEATURES

In addition to the new "Individuals in Society" study,
distinctive features from earlier editions guide the
reader in the process of historical understanding. Many
of these features also show how historians sift through
and evaluate evidence. Our goal is to suggest how historians actually work and think. We want the reader to
think critically and to realize that history is neither a list
of cut-and-dried facts nor a senseless jumble of conflicting opinions. To help students and instructors realize
this goal, we have significantly expanded the discussion
of "what is history" in Chapter 1 of this edition.

Revised Primary-Source Feature

In the fourth edition we added a two-page excerpt from
a primary source at the end of each chapter. This important feature, entitled "Listening to the Past," extends and illuminates a major historical issue considered
in the chapter, and it has been well received by instructors and students. In the new edition we have reviewed
our selections and made judicious substitutions. For example, in Chapter 3 we use selections from the *Ra-
mayana,* the great Indian Sanskrit epic, to explore
Hinduism; In Chapter 5 the Greeks welcome the
Egyptian god Serapis to their pantheon of deities; in
Chapter 11 the *Pillow Book of Sei Shonagon* provides an
introduction to aspects of Asian sensuality; in Chapter
14 the death of Inca Yupanque offers students information on the complicated rituals related to imperial
death; in Chapter 20 the Portuguese Barbosa, through
his description of the African Swahili city-states, suggests cross-cultural attitudes in the fifteenth century; in
Chapter 21 the weighing of Shah Jahan reveals the fabulous wealth of Mughal India and the state's concern
for the poor; in Chapter 27 the daily lives of an ordinary
German soldier and of a Viennese woman on the home
front during World War I are revealed; and in Chapter
33 the Solidarity activist Adam Michnik defends nonvi-
olent resistance to communism from prison.

Each primary source opens with a problem-setting
introduction and closes with "Questions for Analysis"
that invite students to evaluate the evidence as historians would. Drawn from a range of writings addressing a
variety of social, cultural, political, and intellectual issues, these sources promote active involvement and
critical interpretation. Selected for their interest and importance and carefully fitted into their historical context, these sources do indeed allow the student to

"listen to the past" and to observe how history has been shaped by individual men and women, some of them great aristocrats, others ordinary folk.

Improved Chapter Features

Other distinctive features from earlier editions have been reviewed and improved in the fifth edition. To help guide the reader toward historical understanding, we pose specific historical questions at the beginning of each chapter. These questions are then answered in the course of each chapter, and each chapter concludes with a concise summary of its findings. All of the questions and summaries have been re-examined and frequently revised in order to maximize the usefulness of this popular feature.

In addition to posing chapter-opening questions and presenting more problems in historical interpretation, we have quoted extensively from a wide variety of primary sources in the narrative, demonstrating in our use of these quotations how historians evaluate evidence. Thus primary sources are examined as an integral part of the narrative as well as presented in extended form in the "Listening to the Past" chapter feature. We believe that such an extensive program of both integrated and separate primary source excerpts will help readers learn to interpret and think critically.

Each chapter concludes with carefully selected suggestions for further reading. These suggestions are briefly described to help readers know where to turn to continue thinking and learning about the world. Also, chapter bibliographies have been thoroughly revised and updated to keep them current with the vast amount of new work being done in many fields.

Revised Timelines

The timelines appearing in earlier editions have been revised in this edition. Once again we provide a unified timeline in an appendix at the end of the book. Comprehensive and easy to locate, this useful timeline allows students to compare simultaneous political, economic, social, cultural, intellectual, and scientific developments over the centuries.

Flexible Format

World history courses differ widely in chronological structure from one campus to another. To accommodate the various divisions of historical time into intervals that fit a two-quarter, three-quarter, or two-semester period, *A History of World Societies* is published in three versions that embrace the complete work:

- One-volume hardcover edition: *A History of World Societies*
- Two-volume paperback edition: *A History of World Societies,* Volume I, *To 1715* (Chapters 1–17), and Volume II, *Since 1500* (Chapters 16–36)
- Three-volume paperback edition: *A History of World Societies,* Volume A, *From Antiquity to 1500* (Chapters 1–14), Volume B, *From 1100 to 1815* (Chapters 13–23), and Volume C, *From 1775 to the Present* (Chapters 23–36)

Overlapping chapters in two-volume and three-volume editions facilitate matching the appropriate volume with the opening and closing dates of a specific course.

ANCILLARIES

Our learning and teaching ancillaries enhance the usefulness of the textbook:

- *GeoQuest World CD-ROM*
- *@history web site*
- *Study Guide*
- *Instructor's Resource Manual*
- *Test Items*
- *Computerized Test Items*
- *Map Transparencies*

A new CD-ROM, *GeoQuest World,* features thirty interactive maps that illuminate world history events from the days of the Persian Empire to the present. Each map is accompanied by exercises with answers and essay questions. The four different types of interactivity allow students to move at their own pace through each section.

Houghton Mifflin's @history web site provides the finest text-based materials available for students and instructors. For students, this site offers primary sources, text specific self-tests, and gateways to relevant history sites. Additional resources are provided for instructors.

The excellent *Study Guide* has been thoroughly revised by Professor James Schmiechen of Central Michigan University. Professor Schmiechen has been a tower of strength ever since he critiqued our initial prospectus, and he has continued to give us many valuable suggestions as well as his warmly appreciated support. His *Study Guide* contains learning objectives, chapter summaries, chapter outlines, review questions, extensive multiple-choice exercises, self-check lists of important concepts and events, and a variety of study aids and suggestions. The fifth edition also retains the study-review exercises on the interpretation of visual sources and major political ideas as well as suggested issues for discussion and essay, chronology reviews, and sections on studying effectively. To enable both students and instructors to use the *Study Guide* with the greatest possible flexibility, the guide is available in two volumes, with considerable overlapping of chapters. Instructors and students who use only Volumes A and B of the textbook have all the pertinent study materials in a single volume, *Study Guide,* Volume I (Chapters 1–23). Those who use only Volumes B and C of the textbook also have all the necessary materials in one volume, *Study Guide,* Volume II (Chapters 13–36).

The *Instructor's Resource Manual,* prepared by John Reisbord of Vassar College, contains instructional objectives, annotated chapter outlines, suggestions for lectures and discussion, paper and class activity topics, primary-source exercises, map activities, and lists of audio-visual resources. The accompanying *Test Items,* by Professor Charles Crouch of Georgia Southern University, offer identification, multiple-choice, map, and essay questions for a total of approximately two thousand test items. These test items are available to adopters in a computerized version, with editing capabilities.

In addition, a set of full-color *Map Transparencies* of all the maps in the textbook is available on adoption.

Acknowledgments

It is a pleasure to thank the many instructors who have read and critiqued the manuscript through its development.

Cynthia L. Brantley
University of California at Davis

Hugh R. Clark
Ursinus College

Linda T. Darling
University of Arizona

Larry Davis
Salem State College

Lane R. Earns
University of Wisconsin—Oshkosh

William Wayne Farris
University of Tennessee at Knoxville

James T. Gillam
Spelman College

Steve Gosch
University of Wisconsin—Eau Claire

Roland L. Guyotte
University of Minnesota at Morris

Craig Hendricks
Long Beach City College

Rebecca Horn
University of Utah

Joseph E. Inikori
University of Rochester

Gary P. Leupp
Tufts University

Andrea McElderry
University of Louisville

Dane Morrison
Salem State College

Barry T. Ryan
Point Loma Nazarene College

Mark W. Thurner
University of Florida

Sara W. Tucker
Washburn University

It is also a pleasure to thank our many editors at Houghton Mifflin for their efforts over many years. To Christina Horn, who guided production in the ever-more intensive email age, and to Dale Anderson, our development editor, we express our admiration and special appreciation. And we thank Carole Frohlich for her contributions in photo research and selection.

Many of our colleagues at the University of Illinois and at Georgetown University continued to provide information and stimulation, often without even knowing it. We thank them for it. John McKay wishes to thank and acknowledge Professor Charles Crouch of Georgia Southern University for his valuable contribution to the revision of Chapters 17–19, 23–26, and 29–30 in this edition. He also happily acknowledges the fine research assistance provided by Bryan Ganaway and Camille Monahan and thanks them for it. Finally, he also expresses his deep appreciation to Jo Ann McKay for her sharp-eyed editorial support and unfailing encouragement.

Each of us has benefited from the criticism of his or her coauthors, although each of us assumes responsibility for what he or she has written. John Buckler has written Chapters 1–2 and 5–6; Patricia Buckley Ebrey has contributed Chapters 3, 4, 7, and 11; Bennett Hill has continued the narrative in Chapters 8–10, 12–16, 20–22, and 28; and John McKay has written Chapters 17–19, 23–27, and 29–36. Finally, we continue to welcome the many comments and suggestions that have come from our readers, for they have helped us greatly in this ongoing endeavor.

J. P. M.   B. D. H.   J. B.   P. B. E.

13 Creativity and Crisis in the Central and Later Middle Ages

Dante's Inferno: frontispiece from an early manuscript of the *Divine Comedy.* Dante, wearing a red robe, is guided by Virgil, in blue, through the agonies of hell. *(Bibliothèque Nationale, Paris)*

The central Middle Ages witnessed some of the most remarkable achievements in the history of the Western world. Europeans displayed tremendous creativity in many facets of culture. The university, a unique Western contribution to civilization, came into being. The Gothic cathedral manifested medieval people's deep Christian faith, their sense of community, and their appreciation of the worlds of nature, humanity, and God.

In the medieval world, the nobility fought, the clergy prayed, and the peasantry worked to produce the food on which all depended. The lives of the vast majority of ordinary people continued to be conditioned by their local geography, climate, religion, and parish. For the peasantry, considerable social mobility existed in the central Middle Ages. Then, between 1300 and 1450, Europeans experienced a series of frightful shocks: economic dislocation, plague, war, and social upheaval. The last book of the New Testament—the Book of Revelation, dealing with visions of the end of the world, disease, war, famine, and death—inspired thousands of sermons and religious tracts. Death and preoccupation with death make the fourteenth century one of the most wrenching periods of Western civilization.

The progression from the vitality and creativity of the central Middle Ages to the crises of the later Middle Ages brings to mind a number of questions:

- How did the universities, the Gothic cathedrals, and troubadour poetry evolve, and what do they reveal about medieval ideals and society?
- How did people actually live, and what were their major preoccupations and lifestyles?
- What were the social and psychological effects of economic difficulties, disease, and war in the later Middle Ages?
- What impact did schism in the Christian church have on the lives of ordinary people?
- What political and social factors were reflected in the development of national literatures and in the expansion of literacy?

These are among the questions this chapter will explore.

 ## MEDIEVAL UNIVERSITIES

Just as the first strong secular states emerged in the thirteenth century, so did the first universities. This was no coincidence. The new bureaucratic states and the church needed educated administrators, and universities were a response to this need.

Since the time of the Carolingian Empire, monasteries and cathedral schools had offered the only formal instruction available. Monasteries were geared to religious concerns. They wished to maintain an atmosphere of seclusion and silence and were unwilling to accept large numbers of noisy lay students. In contrast, schools attached to cathedrals and run by the bishop and his clergy were frequently situated in bustling cities, and in the eleventh century in Bologna and other Italian cities wealthy businessmen established municipal schools. Inhabited by peoples of many backgrounds and "nationalities," cities stimulated the growth and exchange of ideas. In the course of the twelfth century, cathedral schools in France and municipal schools in Italy developed into universities.

The growth of the University of Bologna coincided with a revival of interest in Roman law. The study of Roman law as embodied in Justinian's *Code* had never completely died out in the West, but this sudden burst of interest seems to have been inspired by Irnerius (d. 1125), a great teacher at Bologna. His fame attracted students from all over Europe. Irnerius not only explained the Roman law of Justinian's *Code* but applied it to difficult practical situations. An important school of civil law was founded at Montpellier in France, but Bologna remained the greatest law school throughout the Middle Ages.

At Salerno, interest in medicine had persisted for centuries. Greek and Muslim physicians there had studied the use of herbs as cures and experimented with surgery. The twelfth century ushered in a new interest in Greek medical texts and in the work of Arab and Greek doctors. Students of medicine poured into Salerno and soon attracted royal attention. In 1140, when King Roger II (r. 1130–1154) of Sicily took the practice of medicine under royal control, his ordinance stated: "Who, from now on, wishes to practice medicine, has to present himself before our officials and examiners, in order to pass their judgment. . . . In this way we are taking care that our subjects are not endangered by the inexperience of the physicians."[1]

In the first decades of the twelfth century, students converged on Paris. They crowded into the cathedral school of Notre Dame and spilled over into the area later called the Latin Quarter—whose name probably reflects the Italian origin of many of the students. The cathedral school's international reputation had already drawn to Paris scholars from all over Europe. One of the most famous of them was Peter Abélard.

The son of a minor Breton knight, Peter Abélard (1079–1142) studied in Paris, quickly absorbed a large amount of material, and set himself up as a teacher. Fascinated by logic, which he believed could be used to solve most problems, Abélard used a method of systematic doubting in his writing and teaching. As he put it, "By doubting we come to questioning, and by questioning we perceive the truth." Other scholars merely asserted theological principles; Abélard discussed and analyzed them.

The influx of students eager for learning and the presence of dedicated and imaginative teachers created the atmosphere in which universities grew. In northern Europe—at Paris and later at Oxford and Cambridge in England—associations or guilds of professors organized universities. They established the curriculum, set the length of time for study, and determined the form and content of examinations. University faculties grouped themselves according to academic disciplines, or schools—law, medicine, arts, and theology. The professors, known as "schoolmen" or "Scholastics," developed a method of thinking, reasoning, and writing in which questions were raised and authorities cited on both sides of a question. The goal of the Scholastic method was to arrive at definitive answers and to provide a rational explanation for what was believed on faith.

The Scholastic approach rested on the recovery of classical philosophical texts and on ancient Greek and Arabic texts that had entered Europe in the early twelfth century. Thirteenth-century philosophers relied on Latin translations of these texts, especially translations of Aristotle. The Scholastics reinterpreted Aristotelian texts in a Christian sense.

In exploration of the natural world, Aristotle's axioms were not precisely followed. Medieval scientists argued from authority, such as the Bible, Justinian's *Code,* or ancient scientific treatises, rather than from direct observation and experimentation, as modern scientists do. Thus the conclusions of medieval scientists were often wrong. Nevertheless, natural science gradually emerged as a discipline distinct from philosophy.

Thirteenth-century Scholastics devoted an enormous amount of time to collecting and organizing knowledge on all topics. These collections were published as *summa,* or reference books. There were summa on law, philosophy, vegetation, animal life, and theology. Saint Thomas Aquinas (1225–1274), a professor at Paris, produced the most famous collection, the *Summa Theo-*

logica, which deals with a vast number of theological questions.

Aquinas drew an important distinction between faith and reason. He maintained that, although reason can demonstrate many basic Christian principles such as the existence of God, other fundamental teachings such as the Trinity and original sin cannot be proved by logic. That reason cannot establish them does not, however, mean they are contrary to reason. Rather, people understand such doctrines through revelation embodied in Scripture. Scripture cannot contradict reason, nor reason Scripture:

The light of faith that is freely infused into us does not destroy the light of natural knowledge [reason] implanted in us naturally. . . . Indeed, were that the case, one or the other would have to be false, and, since both are given to us by God, God would have to be the author of untruth, which is impossible.[2]

Thomas Aquinas and all medieval intellectuals held that the end of both faith and reason was the knowledge of, and union with, God. His work later became the fundamental text of Roman Catholic doctrine.

At all universities, the standard method of teaching was the *lecture*—that is, a reading. The professor read a passage from the Bible, Justinian's *Code,* or one of Aristotle's treatises. He then explained and interpreted the passage; his interpretation was called a *gloss.* Students wrote down everything. Because books had to be copied by hand, they were extremely expensive, and few students could afford them. Examinations were given after three, four, or five years of study, when the student applied for a degree. The professors determined the amount of material students had to know for each degree, and students frequently insisted that the professors specify precisely what that material was. Examinations were oral and very difficult. If the candidate passed, he was awarded the first, or bachelor's, degree. Further study, about as long, arduous, and expensive as it is today, enabled the graduate to try for the master's and doctor's degrees. Degrees were technically licenses to teach. Most students, however, did not become teachers. They staffed the expanding royal and papal administrations.

FROM ROMANESQUE GLOOM TO "UNINTERRUPTED LIGHT"

Between 1180 and 1270 in France alone, eighty cathedrals, about five hundred abbey churches, and tens of thousands of parish churches were constructed. This construction represents a remarkable investment for a country of scarcely 18 million people. More stone was quarried for churches in medieval France than had been mined in ancient Egypt, where the Great Pyramid alone consumed 40.5 million cubic feet of stone. All these churches displayed a new architectual style. Fifteenth-century critics called the new style Gothic because they mistakenly believed the fifth-century Goths had invented it. It actually developed partly in reaction to the earlier Romanesque style, which resembled ancient Roman architecture. Cathedrals, abbeys, and village churches testify to the deep religious faith and piety of medieval people.

In the ninth and tenth centuries, the Vikings and Magyars had burned hundreds of wooden churches. In the eleventh century, the abbots wanted to rebuild in a more permanent fashion, and after the year 1000 church building increased on a wide scale. Because fireproofing was essential, ceilings had to be made of stone. Therefore, builders replaced wooden roofs with arched stone ceilings called vaults. The stone ceilings were heavy; only thick walls would support them. Because the walls were so thick, the windows were small, allowing little light into the interior of the church. In northern Europe, twin bell towers often crowned these Romanesque churches, giving them a powerful, fortresslike appearance. Romanesque churches reflect the quasi-military, aristocratic, and pre-urban society that built them.

The inspiration for the Gothic style originated in the brain of one monk, Suger, abbot of Saint-Denis (1122–1151). When Suger became abbot, he decided to reconstruct the old Carolingian abbey church at Saint-Denis. Work began in 1137. On June 11, 1144, King Louis VII and a large crowd of bishops, dignitaries, and common people witnessed the solemn consecration of the first Gothic church in France.

The basic features of Gothic architecture—the pointed arch, the ribbed vault, and the flying buttress—allowed unprecedented interior lightness. Since the ceiling of a Gothic church weighed less than that of a Romanesque church, the walls could be thinner. Stained-glass windows were cut into the stone, so that the interior, Suger exulted, "would shine with the wonderful and uninterrupted light of most sacred windows, pervading the interior beauty."[3]

Begun in the Île-de-France, Gothic architecture spread throughout France with the expansion of royal power. French architects were soon invited to design and supervise the construction of churches in other parts of Europe, and the new style traveled rapidly.

The construction of a Gothic cathedral represented a gigantic investment of time, money, and corporate ef-

Interior of La Sainte-Chapelle, Paris   The central features of the Gothic style—the pointed arch, ribbed vaulting, and flying buttress—made possible the construction of churches higher than ever before and the use of stained glass to replace stone walls. King Louis IX built this church to house the crown of thorns and other relics that he brought back from the Crusades. The result is a building of breathtaking beauty, a jeweled reliquary. *(Art Resource, NY)*

fort. The bishop and the clergy of the cathedral made the decision to build, but they depended on the support of all social classes. Bishops raised revenue from kings, the nobility, the clergy, and those with the greatest amount of ready cash—the commercial classes.

Money was not the only need. A great number of craftsmen had to be assembled: quarrymen, sculptors, stonecutters, masons, mortarmakers, carpenters, blacksmiths, glassmakers, roofers. Unskilled laborers had to be recruited for the heavy work. The construction of a large cathedral was rarely completed in one lifetime; many cathedrals were never finished at all. Because generation after generation added to the building, many Gothic churches show the architectural influences of two or even three centuries.

Cathedrals served secular as well as religious purposes. The sanctuary containing the altar and the bishop's chair belonged to the clergy, but the rest of the church belonged to the people. In addition to marriages, baptisms, and funerals, there were scores of feast days on which the entire town gathered in the cathedral for festivities. Local guilds met in the cathedrals to arrange business deals and to plan recreational events and the support of disabled members. Magistrates and municipal officials held political meetings there. Pilgrims slept there, lovers courted there, and traveling actors staged plays there.

First and foremost, however, the cathedral was intended to teach the people the doctrines of Christian faith through visual images. Architecture became the servant of theology. The west front of the cathedral faced the setting sun, and its wall was usually devoted to the scenes of the Last Judgment. The north side, which received the least sunlight, displayed events from the Old Testament. The south side, washed in warm sunshine for much of the day, depicted scenes from the New Testament. This symbolism implied that the Jewish people of the Old Testament lived in darkness and that the Gospel brought by Christ illuminated the world. Every piece of sculpture, furniture, and stained glass had some religious or social significance.

Stained glass beautifully reflects the creative energy of the central Middle Ages. It is both an integral part of Gothic architecture and a distinct form of painting. The glassmaker "painted" the picture with small fragments of glass held together with strips of lead. As Gothic churches became more skeletal and had more windows, stained glass replaced manuscript illumination as the leading kind of painting. Thousands of scenes in the cathedral celebrate nature, country life, and the activities of ordinary people. All members of medieval society had a place in the City of God, which the Gothic cathedral represented.

TROUBADOUR POETRY

In the twelfth and thirteenth centuries, a remarkable literary culture blossomed in southern France. The word *troubadour* comes from the Provençal word *trobar,* which in turn derives from the Arabic *taraba,* meaning "to sing" or "to sing poetry." A troubadour was a poet of Provence who wrote lyric verse in his or her native language and sang it at one of the noble courts. Troubadour songs had a variety of themes. Men sang about "courtly love," the pure love a knight felt for his lady, whom he sought to win by military prowess and pa-

Fifteenth-Century Flemish Tapestry
The weavers of Tournai (in present-day Belgium) spent twenty-five years (1450–1475) producing this magnificent tapestry, which is based on the Old Testament story of Jehu, Jezebel, and the sons of Ahab (2 Kings 9–10). *(Isabella Stewart Gardner Museum, Boston)*

tience; about the love a knight felt for the wife of his feudal lord; or about carnal desires seeking satisfaction. Women troubadours *(trobairitz)* focused on their emotions, their intimate feelings, or their experiences with men. Some poems exalted the married state, and others idealized adulterous relationships; some were earthy and bawdy, and others advised young girls to remain chaste in preparation for marriage. The married Countess Beatrice of Dia (1150–1200?) expresses the hurt she felt after being jilted by a young knight:

Lovely lover, gracious, kind,
When will I overcome your fight?
O if I could lie with you one night!
Feel those loving lips on mine!
    Listen, one thing sets me afire:
Here in my husband's place I want you,
If you'll just keep your promise true:
    Give me everything I desire.[4]

Because of its varied and contradictory themes, courtly love has been one of the most hotly debated topics in all medieval studies. Troubadours certainly felt Hispano-Arabic influences. In the eleventh century, Christians of southern France were in intimate contact with the Arabized world of Andalusia, where reverence for the lady in a "courtly" tradition had long existed. Troubadour poetry represents another facet of the strong Muslim influence on European culture and life.[5]

The romantic motifs of the troubadours also influenced the northern French *trouvères,* who wrote adventure-romances in the form of epic poems. At the court of his patron Marie of Champagne, Chrétien de Troyes (ca 1135–1183) used the legends of the fifth-century British king Arthur to discuss contemporary chivalric ideals and their moral implications. Such poems as *The Romance of Tristan and Isolde* reveal Chrétien as the founding father of the Western romantic genre. The theme of these romances centers on the knight-errant, who seeks adventures and who, when faced with crises usually precipitated by love, acquires new values and grows in wisdom.

The songs of the troubadours and trouvères were widely imitated in Italy, England, and Germany, and they spurred the development of vernacular languages (see pages 403–404). Most of the troubadours and trouvères came from and wrote for the aristocratic classes, and their poetry suggests the interests and values of noble culture in the central Middle Ages.

LIFE IN CHRISTIAN EUROPE IN THE CENTRAL MIDDLE AGES

In the late ninth century, medieval intellectuals described Christian society as composed of those who pray (the monks), those who fight (the nobles), and those who work (the peasants). According to this image of social structure, function determined social classification.[6] Reality, however, was somewhat different. In the eleventh and twelfth centuries, most clerics and monks descended from the noble class and retained aristocratic attitudes and values, and the lay brothers who did most of the agricultural labor on monastic estates came from the peasant classes. The division of society into fighters, monks, and peasants also presents too static a view of a world in which there was considerable social mobility. Moreover, such a social scheme does not take into consideration townspeople and the emerging commercial classes. That omission, however, is easy to understand. Traders and other city dwellers were not typical members of medieval society. Medieval people were usually contemptuous (at least officially) of profitmaking activities, and even after the appearance of urban commercial groups, the ideological view of medieval Christian society remained the one formulated in the ninth century: the three-part division among peasants, nobles, and monks.

Those Who Work

According to one modern scholar, "Peasants were rural dwellers who possess (if they do not own) the means of agricultural production."[7] Some peasants worked continuously on the land. Others supplemented their ordinary work as brewers, carpenters, tailors, or housemaids with wage labor in the field. In either case, all peasants supported lords, clergy, townspeople, and themselves. The men and women who worked the land in the twelfth and thirteenth centuries made up the overwhelming majority of the population, probably more than 90 percent. Yet it is difficult to form a coherent picture of them. The records that serve as historical sources were written by and for the aristocratic classes.

It is important to remember that peasants' conditions varied widely across Europe and that geography and climate as much as human initiative and local custom determined the peculiar quality of rural life.[8] The problems that faced the farmer in Yorkshire, England, where the soil was rocky and the weather rainy, were very different from those of the Italian peasant in the sun-drenched Po Valley.

The Three Classes   Medieval people believed that their society was divided among clerics, warriors, and workers, here represented by a monk, a knight, and a peasant. The new commercial class had no recognized place in the agrarian military world. *(The British Library)*

Another obstacle to the creation of a coherent picture of the peasants has been historians' tendency to group all peasants into one social class. Although medieval theologians lumped everyone who worked the land into the "those who work" category, there were many kinds of peasants—ranging from complete slaves to free and very rich farmers. The status of the peasantry fluctuated widely all across Europe. The period from 1050 to 1250 was one of considerable social mobility.

Slaves were found in western Europe in the central Middle Ages, but in steadily declining numbers. That the word *slave* derives from *Slav* attests to the widespread trade in men and women from the Slavic areas. Legal language differed considerably from place to place, and the distinction between slave and serf was not always clear. Both lacked freedom—the power to do as one wished—and both were subject to the arbitrary will of one person, the lord. A serf, however, could not be bought and sold like an animal or an inanimate object, as the slave could.

The serf was required to perform labor services on the lord's land. The number of workdays varied, but it was usually three days a week except in the planting or harvest seasons, when it increased. Serfs frequently had to pay arbitrary levies, as for marriage or inheritance (see page 339). The precise amounts of tax paid to the lord depended on local custom and tradition. A free person had to do none of these things. For his or her landholding, rent had to be paid to the lord, and that was often the sole obligation. A free person could move and live as he or she wished.

Serfs were tied to the land, and serfdom was a hereditary condition. A person born a serf was likely to die a serf, though many did secure their freedom. About 1187 Glanvill, an official of King Henry II and an expert on English law, described how *villeins* (literally, "inhabitants of small villages")—as English serfs were called—could be made free:

No person of villein status can seek his freedom with his own money, . . . because all the chattels of a villein are deemed to be the property of his lord. If, however, a third party provides the money and buys the villein in order to free him, then he can maintain himself for ever in a state of freedom as against his lord who sold him. . . . If any villein stays peaceably for a year and a day in a privileged town and is admitted as a citizen into their commune, that is to say, their gild, he is thereby freed from villeinage.[9]

Thus, with the advent of a money economy, serfs could save money and, through a third-person intermediary, buy their freedom. (See the feature "Individuals in Society: Jean Mouflet of Sens.")

The economic revival that began in the eleventh century (see pages 359–361) advanced the cause of individual liberty. Hundreds of new towns arose in Ireland, in eastern Europe, and in reconquest Spain; their settlers often came from long distances. Some colonial towns were the offspring of colonial traders. For example, Venetian and Genoese merchants founded in the Crimean region trading posts that served as entrepôts on the routes to China. The thirteenth century witnessed enormous immigration to many parts of Europe that previously had been sparsely settled. Immigration and colonization provided the opportunity for freedom and social mobility.[10]

Another opportunity for increased personal freedom, or at least for a reduction in traditional manorial obligations and dues, was provided by the reclamation of waste- and forestland in the eleventh and twelfth centuries. Marshes and fens were drained and slowly made arable. This type of agricultural advancement frequently improved the peasants' social and legal condition. A serf could clear a patch of fen or forestland, make it productive, and, through prudent saving, buy more land and eventually purchase freedom. He secured personal liberty and owed his overlord only small payments.

In the central Middle Ages, most European peasants, free and unfree, lived on a *manor,* the estate of a lord. The manor was the basic unit of medieval rural organization and the center of rural life. All other generalizations about manors and manorial life have to be limited by variations in the quality of the soil, local climatic conditions, and methods of cultivation. Manors varied from several thousand acres to as little as 120 acres. Recent archaeological evidence suggests that a manor might include several villages, one village whose produce was divided among several lords, or an isolated homestead.

The arable land of the manor was divided into two sections. The *demesne,* or home farm, was cultivated by the peasants for the lord. The other, usually larger section was held by the peasantry. All the arable land, both the lord's and the peasants', was divided into strips, and the strips belonging to any given individual were scattered throughout the manor. All peasants cooperated in the cultivation of the land, working it as a group. All shared in any disaster as well as in any large harvest.

A manor usually held pasture- or meadowland for the grazing of cattle, sheep, and sometimes goats. Often the manor had some forestland as well. Forests were the source of wood for building and fuel, resin for lighting, ash for candles, and ash and lime for fertilizers and all sorts of sterilizing products. The forests were used for feeding pigs, cattle, and domestic animals on nuts, roots, and wild berries.

The fundamental objective of all medieval agriculture was the production of an adequate food supply. Using the method that historians have called the *open-field system,* peasants divided the arable land of a manor into two or three fields without hedges or fences to mark the individual holdings of the lord, serfs, and freemen. Beginning in the eleventh century in parts of France, England, and Germany, peasants divided all the arable land into three large fields. In any one year, two of the fields were cultivated and one lay fallow. One part of the land was sown with winter cereals such as rye and wheat, the other with spring crops such as peas, beans, and barley. Each year the crop was rotated. Local needs, the fertility of the soil, and dietary customs determined what was planted and the method of crop rotation.

In the early twelfth century, the production of iron increased greatly. In the thirteenth century, the wooden plow continued to be the basic instrument of agricultural production, but its edge was strengthened with iron. Only after the start of the fourteenth century, when lists of manorial equipment began to be kept, is there evidence of pitchforks, spades, axes, and harrows.

The plow and the harrow (a cultivating instrument with heavy teeth that breaks up and smoothes the soil) were increasingly drawn by horses. The development of the padded horse collar, resting on the horse's shoulders and attached to the load by shafts, led to an agricultural revolution. The horse collar let the animal put its entire weight into the task of pulling. In the twelfth century, the use of horses, rather than oxen, spread because horses' greater strength brought greater efficiency to farming. Horses, however, were an enormous investment, perhaps comparable to a modern tractor. They had to be shod (another indication of increased iron production), and the oats they ate were costly. Although horses represent a crucial element in the

Late Medieval Wheelless Plow   This plow has a sharp-pointed colter, which cut the earth while the attached mold-board lifted, turned, and pulverized the soil. As the man steers the plow, his wife prods the oxen. The caption reads, "God speed the plow, and send us corn (wheat) enough." *(Trinity College Library, Cambridge)*

improvement of husbandry, students of medieval agriculture are not sure whether the greater use of horses increased crop yields.

The thirteenth century witnessed a tremendous spurt in the use of horses to haul carts to market. Large and small farmers increasingly relied on horses to pull wagons because they could travel much faster than oxen. Consequently, goods reached a market faster, and the number of markets within an area to which the peasant had access increased. The opportunities and temptations for consumer spending on nonagricultural goods multiplied.[11]

Agricultural yields varied widely from place to place and from year to year. By twentieth-century standards, they were very low. Inadequate soil preparation, poor seed selection, lack of manure—all made low yields virtually inevitable. And, like farmers of all times and places, medieval peasants were at the mercy of the weather. Yet there was striking improvement over time. Researchers have tentatively concluded that between the ninth and early thirteenth centuries, yields of cereals approximately doubled, and on the best-managed estates farmers harvested five bushels of grain for every bushel of seed planted. A modern Illinois farmer ex-

pects to get 40 bushels of soybeans, 150 bushels of corn, and 50 bushels of wheat for every bushel of seed planted. Of course, modern costs of production in labor, seed, and fertilizer are quite high, but this yield is at least ten times that of the farmer's medieval ancestor. Some manors may have achieved a yield of 12 or even 15 to 1, but the *average* manor probably got a yield of only 5 to 1 in the thirteenth century.[12]

Life on the Manor   For most people in medieval Europe, life meant country life. A person's horizons were not likely to extend beyond the manor on which he or she was born. True, peasants who colonized sparsely settled regions such as eastern Germany must have traveled long distances. But most people rarely traveled more than twenty-five miles beyond their villages. Their world was small, narrow, and provincial: limited by the boundaries of the province. This way of life did not have entirely unfortunate results. A farmer had a strong sense of family and the certainty of its support and help in times of trouble. People knew what their life's work would be—the same as their mother's or father's. They had a sense of place, and pride in that place was re-

Individuals in Society

Jean Mouflet of Sens

The customary form of manumission, *not* the manner in which Jean Mouflet gained his freedom. *(British Library)*

Throughout most of Western history, the vast majority of people left little behind that identifies them as individuals. Baptismal, marriage, and death records; wills; grants for memorial masses; and, after the eighteenth century, brief census information collected by governments—these forms of evidence provide exciting information about groups of people but little about individuals. Before the nineteenth century, most people were illiterate; the relative few who could write, such as business people, used such literary skills as they had in matters connected with their work. The historian, therefore, has great difficulty reconstructing the life of an "ordinary" person. An exception occurs when a person committed a crime in a society that kept judicial records or when he or she made a legal agreement that was preserved. Such is the case of Jean Mouflet of Sens.[1]

We know little about him except what is revealed in a document granting what was probably the central desire of his life—his personal freedom. His ancestors had been serfs on the lands of the abbey of Saint-Pierre-le-Vif in the Sénonais region of France. There a serf was subject to legal disabilities that debased his dignity and implied inferior status. Work required on the lord's land bred resentment, because work was simultaneously needed on the rustic's own land. At death a peasant gave the lord a token, or not so token, gift—his best beast. Marriage presented another disability, first because one partner had to change dwelling and to do so had to gain the lord's permission; second because it raised the question of children: whose dependents did they become? Special "gifts" to the lord "encouraged" him to resolve these issues. Again, an unfree person, even if he or she possessed the expected dowry, could not become a monk or nun or enter holy orders without the lord's permission, because the lord stood to lose labor services. Finally, residence in a town for a year and a day did not always ensure freedom; years after the person settled there, the lord could claim him or her as a dependent.

In 1249 Jean Mouflet made an agreement with the abbot: in return for an annual payment, the monastery would recognize Jean as a "citizen of Sens." With a stroke of his quill, the abbot manumitted Jean and his heirs, ending centuries of servile obligations.

The agreement describes Jean as a leather merchant. Other evidence reveals that he had a large leather shop in the leather goods section of town[2] that he leased for the very high rent of fifty shillings a year. If not "rich," Jean was certainly well-to-do. Circumstantial evidence suggests that Jean's father had originally left the land to become a leatherworker and taught his son the trade. The agreement was witnessed by Jean's wife, Douce, daughter of a wealthy and prominent citizen of Sens, Félis Charpentier. To have been a suitable candidate for Douce, Jean would have to have been extremely industrious, very lucky, and accepted as a "rising young man" by the grudging burghers of the town. Such a giant step upward in one generation seems unlikely.

In addition to viticulture (the cultivation of grapes), the Sénonais was well suited for cereal production and for animal grazing. Jean undoubtedly bought hides from local herders and manufactured boots and shoes; saddles, bridles, and reins for horses; and belts and purses. He may also have made wineskins for local vintners or for those of Champagne. It is also fair to assume that the wealthy cathedral clergy, the townspeople, and, if his goods were of sufficiently high quality, the merchants of the nearby fairs of Champagne were his customers.

By private agreements with lords, servile peasants gained the most basic of human rights—freedom.

Questions for Analysis

1. What is human freedom?
2. How did trade and commerce contribute to the development of individual liberty?

1. This essay rests on the fine study of W. C. Jordan, *From Servitude to Freedom: Manumission in the Sénonais in the Thirteenth Century* (Philadelphia: University of Pennsylvania Press, 1986).
2. As in all medieval towns, merchants in particular trades—butchers, bakers, leatherworkers—had shops in one area. In 1990 Sens was still a major French leather-tanning center.

flected in adornment of the village church. Religion and the village gave people a sure sense of identity and with it psychological peace. Modern people—urban, isolated, industrialized, rootless, and thoroughly secularized—have lost many of these reinforcements.

But, even aside from the unending physical labor, life on the manor was dull. Medieval men and women must have had a crushing sense of frustration. Often they sought escape in heavy drinking. English judicial records of the thirteenth century reveal a surprisingly large number of "accidental" deaths. Strong, robust, commonsensical farmers do not ordinarily fall on their knives and stab themselves, or slip out of boats and drown, or get lost in the woods on a winter's night. They were probably drunk. Many of these accidents occurred, as the court records say, "coming from an ale." Brawls and violent fights were frequent at taverns.

Scholars have recently spent much energy investigating the structure of medieval peasant households. Because little concrete evidence survives, conclusions are very tentative. It appears, however, that a peasant household consisted of a simple nuclear family: a married couple alone, a couple of children, or a widow or widower with children. Peasant households were *not* extended families containing grandparents or married sons and daughters and their children. Before the first appearance of the Black Death (see pages 390–392), perhaps 94 percent of peasant farmers married, and both bride and groom were in their early twenties. The typical household numbered about five people—the parents and three children.[13]

Women played a significant role in the agricultural life of medieval Europe. Historians often overlook this obvious fact. Women worked with men in wheat and grain cultivation, in the vineyards, and in the harvest and preparation of crops needed by the textile industry—flax and plants used for dyeing cloth, such as madder (which produces shades of red) and woad (which yields blue dye). Especially at harvest time, women shared with their fathers and husbands the backbreaking labor in the fields, work that was especially difficult for them because of weaker muscular development and frequent pregnancies. Lords of great estates commonly hired female day laborers to shear sheep, pick hops (used in the manufacture of beer and ale), tend gardens, and do household chores such as cleaning, laundry, and baking. Servant girls in the country considered their hired status as temporary, until they married. Thrifty farm wives contributed to the family income by selling for cash the produce of their gardens or kitchens: butter, cheese, eggs, fruit, soap, mustard, cucumbers. In a

year of crisis, careful management was often all that separated a household from starvation. And starvation was a very real danger to the peasantry down to the eighteenth century.

Women managed the house. The size and quality of peasants' houses varied according to their relative prosperity and usually depended on the amount of land held. The poorest peasants lived in windowless cottages built of wood and clay or wattle and thatched with straw. These cottages consisted of one large room that served as the kitchen and living quarters for all. Everyone slept there. The house had an earthen floor and a fireplace. The lack of windows meant that the room was very sooty. A trestle table, several stools, one or two beds, and a chest for storing clothes constituted the furniture. A shed attached to the house provided storage for tools and shelter for animals. Prosperous peasants added rooms and furniture as they could be afforded, and some wealthy peasants in the early fourteenth century had two-story houses with separate bedrooms for parents and children.

Women dominated in the production of ale for the community market. They had to know how to mix the correct proportions of barley, water, yeast, and hops in twelve-gallon vats of hot liquid. Brewing was hard and dangerous work. Records of the English coroners' courts reveal that 5 percent of women who died lost their lives in brewing accidents, falling into the vats of boiling liquid.[14] Ale was the universal drink of the common people in northern Europe. By modern American standards, the rate of consumption was heroic. Each monk of Abingdon Abbey in twelfth-century England was allotted three gallons a day, and a man working in the fields for ten hours probably drank much more.[15]

The mainstay of the diet for peasants everywhere—and for all other classes—was bread. It was a hard, black substance made of barley, millet, and oats, rarely of expensive wheat flour. The housewife usually baked the household supply once a week. If sheep, cows, or goats were raised, she also made cheese.

The diet of those living in an area with access to a river, lake, or stream was supplemented with fish, which could be preserved by salting. In many places, there were severe laws against hunting and trapping in the forests. Deer, wild boars, and other game were strictly reserved for the king and nobility. These laws were flagrantly violated, however, and stolen rabbits and wild game often found their way to the peasants' tables.

Except for the rare chicken or illegally caught wild game, meat appeared on the table only on the great feast days of the Christian year: Christmas, Easter, and Pentecost. Then the meat was likely to be pork from the pig slaughtered in the fall and salted for the rest of the year. Some scholars believe that by the mid-thirteenth century, there was a great increase in the consumption of meat generally. If so, this improvement in diet is further evidence of an improved standard of living.

Once children were able to walk, they helped their parents in the hundreds of chores that had to be done. Small children were set to collecting eggs, if the family had chickens, or gathering twigs and sticks for firewood. As they grew older, children had more responsible tasks, such as weeding the family vegetable garden, shearing the sheep, helping with the planting or harvesting, and assisting their mothers in the endless tasks of baking, cooking, and preserving. Because of poor diet, terrible sanitation, and lack of medical care, the death rate among children was phenomenally high.

Health Care   What medical attention was available to the sick person in western Europe between 1050 and 1300? Scholars are only beginning to explore this question, and there are many aspects of public health that we know little about. The steady rise in population in these centuries is usually attributed to the beginnings of political stability, the reduction of violence, and the increases in cultivated land and food supply. It may also be ascribed partly to better health care. Survival to adulthood probably meant a tough people. A recent study of skeletal remains in the village of Brandes in Burgundy showed that peasants enjoyed very good health: they were well built, they had excellent teeth, and their bones revealed no signs of chronic disease. This evidence comes from only one village, but preliminary research confirms the impression that is given by romantic literature: in the prime of life, the average person had an innocent, raw vitality that enabled him or her to eat, drink, and make love with great gusto.[16]

Childhood diseases, poor hygiene, tooth decay, wounds received in fighting, and the myriad ailments and afflictions for which even modern medical science has no cure—from cancer to the common cold—must have caused considerable suffering. What care existed for the sick?

As in all ages and all continents, in Asia and Africa as well as in Europe, the sick depended on folk medicine and on the private nursing care of relatives and friends. For public health, English sources provide the largest evidence to date. In the British Isles, the twelfth century witnessed a momentous breakthrough in the establishment of institutional care in hospitals. In addition to the infirmaries run by monks and nuns, there were at least 113 hospitals in England with possibly as many as 3,494 beds. Medieval hospitals were built by the royal family, the clergy, barons, and ordinary people to alleviate the suffering of the sick, not just to house them. Hospitals attracted considerable popular support, and in their charitable contributions women played an especially strong role in the endowment of hospitals.[17]

As in the developed modern world, persons living in or near a town or city had a better chance of receiving some form of professional attention than did those in remote rural areas. English documents label at least ninety practitioners as *medicus,* meaning physician, surgeon, or medical man, but that is a pitifully small number in a population of perhaps 2 million. With so few doctors, only the largest cities—such as London, York, Winchester, and Canterbury, which all catered to pilgrims and travelers—had resident physicians. At other hospitals, physician consultants were brought in as the occasion required. Most people, of course, did not live in or near large towns. They relied for assistance on the chance presence of a local monk or nun with herb and pharmaceutical knowledge, a local person skilled in setting broken bones, or the wise village person experienced in treating diseases.

Since public morality and ancient tradition forbade the examination of female patients by men, women could practice obstetrics and gynecology. But although women played active roles as healers and in the general care of the sick, male doctors jealously guarded their status and admitted very few women to university medical schools when they were founded. "Francesca Romano, who was licensed as a surgeon in 1321 by Duke Carl of Calabria, is the exception that proves the rule."[18] The medical faculty at the University of Paris in the fourteenth century penalized women who practiced medicine because they lacked a degree—which they were not allowed to get.

Popular Religion   Apart from the land, the weather, and the peculiar conditions that existed on each manor, the Christian religion had the greatest impact on the daily lives of ordinary people in the central Middle Ages. Religious practices varied widely from country to country and even from province to province. But nowhere was religion a one-hour-on-Sunday or High Holy Days affair. Christian practices and attitudes permeated virtually all aspects of everyday life.

As the Germanic and Celtic peoples were Christianized, their new religion became a fusion of Jewish, pagan, Roman, and Christian practices. In the central Middle Ages, all people shared as a natural and public duty in the religious life of the community.

The village church was the center of community life—social, political, and economic as well as religious. Most of the important events in a person's life took place in or around the church. A person was baptized there, within hours of birth. Men and women confessed their sins to the village priest there and received, usually at Easter and Christmas, the sacrament of the Eucharist. In front of the church, the bishop reached down from his horse and confirmed a person as a Christian by placing his hands over the candidate's head and making the sign of the cross on the forehead. Young people courted in the churchyard and, so the sermons of the priests complained, made love in the church cemetery. Priests urged couples to marry publicly in the church, but many married privately, without witnesses (see page 399).

In the church, women and men could pray to the Virgin and the local saints. The saints had once lived on earth and thus, people believed, understood human problems. They could be helpful intercessors with Christ or with God the Father. They could perform miracles. The saint became the special property of the locality where his or her relics rested. Thus to secure the saint's support and to guarantee the region's prosperity, a busy traffic in relics developed—bones, articles of clothing, the saint's tears or saliva, even dust from the saint's tomb. The understanding that existed between the saint and the peasants rested on the customary medieval relationship of mutual fidelity and aid: peasants would offer the saint prayers, loyalty, and gifts to the shrine or church in return for the saint's healing and support. When saints failed to receive the attention they felt they deserved, they sometimes took offense and were vindictive. An English knight whose broken arm was healed by Saint James forgot to thank the saint at his shrine at Reading, whereupon the saint punished the knight by breaking his other arm.

Popular religion consisted largely of rituals heavy with symbolism. Before slicing a loaf of bread, the good wife tapped the sign of the cross on the loaf with her knife. Before the planting, the village priest customarily went out and sprinkled the fields with water, symbolizing refreshment and life. Shortly after a woman had successfully delivered a child, she was "churched." Churching was a ceremony of thanksgiving based on the Jewish rite of purification. When a child was baptized, a few grains of salt were dropped on its tongue. Salt had been the symbol of purity, strength, and incorruptibility for the ancient Hebrews, and the Romans had used it in their sacrifices. It was used in Christian baptism to drive away demons and to strengthen the infant in its new faith.

The entire calendar was designed with reference to Christmas, Easter, and Pentecost. Saints' days were legion. Everyone participated in village processions. The colored vestments the priests wore at Mass gave the villagers a sense of the changing seasons of the church's liturgical year. The signs and symbols of Christianity were visible everywhere.

What did people actually *believe*? It is difficult to say, partly because medieval peasants left few written records of their thoughts, partly because in any age there is often a great disparity between what people profess to believe and their conduct or the ways they act on their beliefs. Peasants accepted what family custom and the clergy taught them. Recent research has shown that in the central Middle Ages a new religious understanding emerged. "Whereas early Christianity looked to holy men and women and early medieval society turned to saints to effect the connection between God and humankind through prayers of intercession," in the twelfth century a sacramental system developed. The seven sacraments—Baptism, Penance, Eucharist, Confirmation, Marriage, Holy Orders, Extreme Unction—brought grace, the divine assistance or help needed to lead a good Christian life and to merit salvation. At the center of the sacramental system stood the Eucharist, the small piece of bread that through the words of priestly consecration at the Mass, became the living body of Christ and, when worthily consumed, became a channel of Christ's grace. The ritual of consecration, repeated at every altar of Christendom, became a unifying symbol in a complex world.[19]

The Mass was in Latin, but the priest delivered sermons on the Gospel in the vernacular—or he was supposed to. An almost universal criticism of the parish clergy in the twelfth and thirteenth centuries was that they were incapable of explaining basic Christian teaching to their parishioners. The only parish priest to be canonized in the entire Middle Ages, the Breton lawyer and priest Saint Yves (d. 1303), had resigned a position as a diocesan judge to serve rural parishioners. At the trial for his canonization, laypeople stressed not only that he led a simple and frugal life but also that he put his forensic skills to the service of preaching the Christian gospels. Saint Yves is the great exception that proves the rule that the medieval parish clergy were generally incapable of preaching in a rural milieu. Parish priests celebrated the liturgy and administered the sacraments, but they had other shortcomings. A thirteenth-century Alsatian chronicler said that the peasants of the region did not complain that their pastors lived in concubinage, because that made them less fearful for the virtue of their daughters.[20]

Christians had long had special reverence and affection for the Virgin Mary as the Mother of Christ. In the eleventh century, theologians began to emphasize the depiction of Mary at the crucifixion in the Gospel of John (19:25–27):

But standing by the cross of Jesus were his mother, and his mother's sister, Mary the wife of Clopas, and Mary Magdalene. When Jesus saw his mother and the disciple whom he loved standing near, he said to his mother, "Woman, behold, your son!" Then he said to the disciple, "Behold, your mother!"

Medieval scholars interpreted this passage as expressing Christ's compassionate concern for all humanity and Mary's spiritual motherhood of all Christians. The huge outpouring of popular devotions to Mary concentrated on her role as Queen of Heaven and, because of her special relationship to Christ, as all-powerful intercessor with him. Masses on Saturdays specially commemorated her, sermons focused on her unique influence with Christ, and hymns and prayers to her multiplied.

Those Who Fight

The nobility, though a small fraction of the total population, strongly influenced all aspects of medieval culture—political, economic, religious, educational, and artistic. For that reason, European society in the twelfth and thirteenth centuries may be termed aristocratic.

Members of the nobility enjoyed a special legal status. A nobleman was free personally and in his possessions. He was limited only by his military obligation to king, duke, or prince. As the result of his liberty, he had certain rights and responsibilities. He raised troops and commanded them in the field. He held courts that dispensed a sort of justice. Sometimes he coined money for use within his territories. As lord of the people who settled on his lands, he made political decisions affecting them, resolved disputes among them, and protected them in time of attack. The liberty and privileges of the noble were inheritable, perpetuated by blood and not by wealth alone.

The nobleman was a professional fighter. His social function, as churchmen described it, was to protect the weak, the poor, and the churches by arms. He possessed a horse and a sword. These, and the leisure time in which to learn how to use them in combat, were the visible signs of his nobility. He was encouraged to display chivalric virtues—courtesy, loyalty to his commander, and generosity. All nobles were knights, but not all knights were noble.[21]

Infancy, Childhood, and Youth   The rate of infant mortality (the number of babies who died before their first birthday) in the central Middle Ages must have been staggering. The limited information indicates that midwives surely contributed to the death rates of both newborns and mothers. Natural causes—disease and poor or insufficient food—also resulted in many deaths. Infanticide, however, which was common in the ancient world, seems to have declined in the central Middle Ages. Ecclesiastical pressure worked steadily against it. Infanticide in medieval Europe is another indication of the slow and very imperfect Christianization of European peoples.

The abandonment of infant children seems to have been the most favored form of family limitation, widely practiced throughout the entire Middle Ages. Abandonment was "the voluntary relinquishing of control over children by their natal parents or guardians, whether by leaving them somewhere, selling them, or legally consigning authority to some other person or institution."[22] Poverty or local natural disaster led some parents to abandon their children because they could not support them. Thus Saint Patrick wrote that, in times of famine, fathers would sell their sons and daughters so that the children could be fed. Parents sometimes gave children away because they were illegitimate or the result of incestuous unions.

Sometimes parents believed that someone of greater means or status might find the child and bring it up in better circumstances than the natal parents could provide. Disappointment in the sex of the child or its physical weakness or deformity might also lead parents to abandon it. Finally, some parents were indifferent—they "simply could not be bothered" with the responsibilities of parenthood.[23]

The Christian Middle Ages witnessed a significant development in the disposal of superfluous children: they were given to monasteries as *oblates,* or "offerings." By the seventh century, church councils and civil codes had defined the practice: "Parents of any social status could donate a child, of either sex, at least up to

Monastic Entrance   In a world that had few career opportunities for "superfluous children," monasteries served a valuable social function. Because a dowry was expected, monastic life was generally limited to the children of the affluent. Advising his son to be obedient, a father, with a bag of coins in his left hand, hands his son over to the abbot. The boy does not look very enthusiastic. *(Bibliothèque Municipale de Troyes)*

the age of ten." Contemporaries considered oblation a religious act, for the child was offered to God often in recompense for parental sin. But oblation also served social and economic functions. The monastery nurtured and educated the child in a familial atmosphere, and it provided career opportunities for the mature monk or nun despite his or her humble origins.[24] In the twelfth and thirteenth centuries, the incidence of noble parents giving their younger sons and daughters to religious houses increased dramatically; nobles wanted to preserve the estate intact for the eldest son. The abandonment of children was a socially acceptable institution. Ecclesiastical and civil authorities never legislated against it.[25]

For children of aristocratic birth, the years from infancy to around the age of seven or eight were primarily years of play. Infants had their rattles, as the twelfth-century monk Guibert of Nogent reports, and young children their special toys. Guibert of Nogent

speaks in several places in his autobiography of "the tender years of childhood"—the years from six to twelve. Describing the severity of the tutor whom his mother assigned to him, Guibert writes:

While others of my age wandered everywhere at will and were unchecked in the indulgence of such inclinations as were natural at their age, I, hedged in with constant restraints and dressed in my clerical garb, would sit and look at the troops of players like a beast awaiting sacrifice. Even on Sundays and saints' days I had to submit to the severity of school exercises.[26]

Guibert's mother had intended him for the church. At about the age of seven, a boy of the noble class who was not intended for the church was placed in the household of one of his father's friends or relatives. There he became a servant to the lord and received his formal training in arms. He was expected to serve the lord at the table, to assist him as a private valet when called on to do so, and, as he gained experience, to care for the lord's horses and equipment. The boy might have a great deal of work to do, depending on the size of the household and the personality of the lord. The work that children did, medieval people believed, gave them experience and preparation for later life.

Training was in the arts of war. The boy learned to ride and to manage a horse. He had to acquire skill in wielding a sword, which sometimes weighed as much as twenty-five pounds. He had to be able to hurl a lance, shoot with a bow and arrow, and care for armor and other equipment. Increasingly, in the eleventh and twelfth centuries, noble youths learned to read and write some Latin. Still, on thousands of charters from that period, nobles signed with a cross (+) or some other mark. Literacy for the nobility became more common in the thirteenth century. Formal training was concluded around the age of twenty-one with the ceremony of knighthood. The custom of knighting, though never universal, seems to have been widespread in France and England but not in Germany. Once knighted, a young man was supposed to be courteous, generous, and, if possible, handsome and rich. Above all, he was to be loyal to his lord and brave in battle. In a society lacking strong institutions of government, loyalty was the cement that held aristocratic society together. The greatest crime was called a *felony,* which meant treachery to one's lord.

Parents often wanted to settle daughters' futures as soon as possible. Men tended to prefer young brides. A woman in her late twenties or thirties had relatively few years in which to produce children; thus aristocratic girls in the central Middle Ages were married at around the age of sixteen.

The future of many young women was not enviable. For a girl of sixteen, marriage to a man in his thirties was not the most attractive prospect, and marriage to a widower in his forties and fifties was even less so. If there were a large number of marriageable young girls in a particular locality, their "market value" was reduced. In the early Middle Ages, it had been the custom for the groom to present a dowry to the bride and her family, but by the late twelfth century the process was reversed. Thereafter, the size of the marriage portions that brides and their families offered to prospective husbands rose higher and higher.

What was a young woman unhappily married to a much older man to do? The literature of courtly love is filled with stories of young bachelors in love with young married women. How hopeless their love was is not known. The cuckolded husband is a stock figure in mas-

terpieces such as *The Romance of Tristan and Isolde* and Chaucer's *The Merchant's Tale.*

Power and Responsibility The responsibilities of a noble in the central Middle Ages depended on the size and extent of his estates, the number of his dependents, and his position in his territory relative to others of his class and to the king. As a vassal a noble was required to fight for his lord or for the king when called on to do so. By the mid-twelfth century, this service was limited in most parts of western Europe to forty days a year. The noble was obliged to attend his lord's court on important occasions when the lord wanted to put on great displays, such as at Easter, Pentecost, and Christmas. When the lord knighted his eldest son or married off his eldest daughter, he called his vassals to his court. They were expected to attend and to present a contribution known as a "gracious aid."

Until the late thirteenth century, when royal authority intervened, a noble in France or England had great power over the knights and peasants on his estates. He maintained order among them and dispensed justice to them. The quality of justice varied widely: some lords were vicious tyrants who exploited and persecuted their peasants; others were reasonable and evenhanded. In any case, the quality of life on the manor and its productivity were related in no small way to the temperament and decency of the lord—and his lady.

Women played a large and important role in the functioning of the estate. They were responsible for the practical management of the household's "inner economy"—cooking, brewing, spinning, weaving, caring for yard animals. The lifestyle of the medieval warrior-nobles required constant travel, both for purposes of war and for the supervision of distant properties. Frequent pregnancies and the reluctance to expose women to hostile conditions kept the lady at home and therefore able to assume supervision of the family's fixed properties. When the lord was away for long periods—on crusade, for instance, the lord could be gone from two to five years, if he returned at all—his wife often became the sole manager of the family properties. Between 1060 and 1080, the lady Hersendis was the sole manager of her family's properties in northern France while her husband was on crusade in the Holy Land.

Nor were women's activities confined to managing households and estates in their husbands' absence. Medieval warfare was largely a matter of brief skirmishes, and few men were killed in any single encounter. But altogether the number slain ran high, and there were many widows. Aristocratic widows frequently controlled

Women Defending Castle As in virtually every other kind of activity, women shared with men the difficulties and dangers of defending castles. Armed with rocks, bows, and arrows, even a finger poked through the chain-mail helmet into the eye of a knight scaling the walls on a ladder, these noble ladies try to fight off attackers. (*Bibliothèque royale Albert 1ᵉʳ, Brussels*)

family properties and fortunes and exercised great authority. Although the evidence is scattered and sketchy, there are indications that women performed many of the functions of men. In Spain, France, and Germany they bought, sold, and otherwise transferred property. Gertrude, labeled "Saxony's almighty widow" by the chronicler Ekkehard of Aura, took a leading role in conspiracies against the emperor Henry V.

Those Who Pray

Monasticism represented some of the finest aspirations of medieval civilization. The monasteries were devoted to prayer, and their standards of Christian behavior influenced the entire church. The monasteries produced the educated elite that was continually drawn into the administrative service of kings and great lords. Monks kept alive the remains of classical culture and experimented with new styles of architecture and art. They in-

troduced new techniques of estate management and land reclamation. Although relatively few in number in the central Middle Ages, the monks played a significant role in medieval society.

Toward the end of his *Ecclesiastical History of England and Normandy,* when he was well into his sixties, Orderic Vitalis, a monk of the Norman abbey of Saint Evroul, interrupted his narrative to explain movingly how he happened to become a monk:

And so, O glorious God, you didst inspire my father Odeleric to renounce me utterly and . . . weeping, he gave me, a weeping child, into the care of the monk Reginald, and sent me away into exile for love of thee, and never saw me again. . . . [H]e promised me for his part that if I became a monk I should taste of the joys of Heaven. . . . And so, a boy of ten, I crossed the English channel and came into Normandy as an exile, unknown to all, knowing no one.[27]

Orderic Vitalis (ca 1075–ca 1140) was representative of the monks of the central Middle Ages in that although he had no doubt that God wanted him to be a monk, the decision was actually made by his parents. Orderic was the third son of a knight who held lands in western England. Concern for the provision of his two older sons probably led the knight to give his youngest boy to the monastery.

Medieval monasteries were religious institutions whose organization and structure fulfilled the social needs of the feudal nobility. The monasteries provided noble children with both an honorable and aristocratic life and opportunities for ecclesiastical careers.[28] As medieval society changed economically, and as European society ever so slowly developed middle-class traits, the monasteries almost inevitably drew their manpower, when they were able, from the middle classes. Until that time, they were preserves of the aristocratic nobility.

Through the Middle Ages, social class also defined the kinds of religious life open to women. Kings and nobles usually established convents for their daughters, sisters, aunts, or aging mothers. Entrance was restricted to women of the founder's class. Since a wellborn lady could not honorably be apprenticed to a tradesperson or do any kind of manual labor, the sole alternative to life at home was the religious life.

The founder's endowment and support influenced the later social, economic, and political status of the convent. A few convents received large endowments and could accept many women. Amesbury Priory in Wiltshire, England, for example, received handsome endowments from King Henry II and his successors. In 1256 Amesbury supported a prioress and 76 nuns, 7 priests, and 16 lay brothers. The convent raised £100 in annual rents and £40 from the wool clip—very large sums at the time. By 1317 Amesbury had 177 nuns.[29] Most houses of women, however, possessed limited resources and remained small in numbers.

The office of abbess or prioress, the house's superior, customarily went to a nun of considerable social standing. Since an abbess or a prioress had responsibility for governing her community and for representing it in any business with the outside world, she was a woman of local, sometimes national, power and importance. Although the level of intellectual life in the women's houses varied widely, the career of Hildegard of Bingen suggests the activities of some nuns in the central Middle Ages. The tenth child of a lesser noble family, Hildegard (1098–1179) was given when eight years old as an oblate to an abbey in the Rhineland, where she learned Latin and received a good education. In 1147 Hildegard founded the convent of Rupertsberg near Bingen. There she produced a body of writings including the *Scivias* (Know the Ways), a record of her mystical visions that incorporates vast theological learning; the *Physica* (On the Physical Elements), a classification of the natural elements, such as plants, animals, metals, and the movements of the heavenly bodies; a mystery play; and a medical work that led a distinguished twentieth-century historian of science to describe Hildegard as "one of the most original writers of the Latin West in the twelfth century." At the same time, she carried on a vast correspondence with scholars, prelates, and ordinary people and had such a reputation for wisdom that a recent writer has called her "the Dear Abby of the twelfth century to whom everyone came or wrote for advice or comfort."[30] An exceptionally gifted person, Hildegard represents the Benedictine ideal of great learning combined with a devoted monastic life. Like intellectual monks, however, intellectual nuns were not typical of the era.

In medieval Europe, the monasteries of men greatly outnumbered those of women. The pattern of life within individual monasteries varied widely from house to house and from region to region. One central activity, however—the work of God—was performed everywhere. Daily life centered on the liturgy.

Seven times a day and once during the night, the monks went to choir to chant the psalms and other prayers prescribed by Saint Benedict. Prayers were offered for peace, rain, good harvests, the civil authorities, the monks' families, and their benefactors. Monastic patrons in turn lavished gifts on the monasteries, which often became very wealthy. Through their prayers, the monks performed a valuable service for the rest of society.

Synagogue   Hildegard of Bingen, the first major German mystic, developed a rich theology on the basis of visions she received. Here Synagogue is portrayed as a tall woman commanded by God to prepare humanity for the coming of Christ. In her arms, Moses holds up the stone tablets of the commandments; in her lap are the patriarchs and prophets who foretold the birth of Christ. The headband symbolizes the Virgin Mary: because Mary gave the world the savior, Hildegard makes Synagogue the Mother of the Incarnation. *(Rheinische Bildarchiv)*

Prayer justified the monks' spending a large percentage of their income on splendid objects to enhance the liturgy; monks praised God, they believed, not only in prayer but also in everything connected with prayer. They sought to accumulate priestly vestments of the finest silks, velvets, and embroideries, as well as sacred vessels of embossed silver and gold and ornamented and bejeweled Gospel books. Every monastery tried to acquire the relics of its patron saint, which necessitated the production of a beautiful reliquary to house the relics. The liturgy, then, inspired a great deal of art, and the monasteries became the crucibles of art in Western Christendom.

The monks fulfilled their social responsibility by praying. It was generally agreed that they could best carry out this duty if they were not distracted by worldly needs. Thus great and lesser lords gave the monasteries lands that would supply the community with necessities.

The usual method of economic organization was the manor. Many monastic manors were small enough and close enough to the abbey to be supervised directly by the abbot. But if a monastery held and farmed vast estates, the properties were divided into administrative units under the supervision of one of the monks of the house.

Some monasteries lent their surplus revenues to the local nobility and peasantry. In the twelfth century the abbey of Savigny in Normandy, for example, acted as a banking house, providing loans at interest to many noble families of Normandy and Brittany. Although church law opposed usury—lending at interest—one reliable scholar has recently written that "it was clerics and ecclesiastical institutions (monasteries and nunneries) that constituted the main providers of credit."[31]

Whatever work particular monks did and whatever economic activities individual monasteries were involved in, monks also performed social services and exerted an influence for the good. In addition to running schools and "hospitals," monasteries like Saint Albans,

Bee Keeping at Monte Cassino   Because of the scarcity and expense of sugar, honey was the usual sweetener for pastries and liquids throughout the Middle Ages. This illustrator had never actually seen the process: without veils, nets, and gloves, the bee keepers would be badly stung. *(Biblioteca Apostolica Vaticana)*

situated north of London on a busy thoroughfare, served as hotels and resting places for travelers. In short, monasteries performed a variety of social services in an age when there was no "state" and no conception of social welfare as a public responsibility.

 CRISES OF THE LATER MIDDLE AGES

In the later years of the thirteenth century, Europeans seemed to run out of steam. The crusading movement gradually fizzled out. Few new cathedrals were constructed, and if a cathedral had not been completed by 1300, the chances were high that it never would be. The strong rulers of England and France, building on the foundations of their predecessors, increased their authority and gained the loyalty of all their subjects. The vigor of those kings, however, did not pass to their immediate descendants. Meanwhile, the church, which for two centuries had guided Christian society, began to face grave difficulties. A violent dispute between the papacy and the kings of England and France badly damaged the prestige of the pope. But religious struggle was only one of the crises that would face European society in the fourteenth century.

A Challenge to Religious Authority

In 1294 King Edward I of England and Philip the Fair of France declared war on each other. To finance this war, both kings laid taxes on the clergy. Kings had been taxing the church for decades. Pope Boniface VIII (r. 1294–1303), arguing from precedent, insisted that kings gain papal consent for taxation of the clergy and forbade churchmen to pay the taxes. But Edward and Philip refused to accept this decree, partly because it hurt royal finances and partly because the papal order threatened royal authority within their countries. Edward immediately denied the clergy the protection of the law, an action that meant its members could be attacked with impunity. Philip halted the shipment of all ecclesiastical revenue to Rome. Boniface had to back down.

Philip the Fair and his ministers continued their attack on all powers in France outside royal authority. Philip arrested a French bishop. When Boniface protested, Philip replied with the trumped-up charge that the pope was a heretic. The papacy and the French monarchy waged a bitter war of propaganda. Finally, in 1302, in a letter titled *Unam Sanctam* (because its opening sentence spoke of one holy Catholic church), Boni-

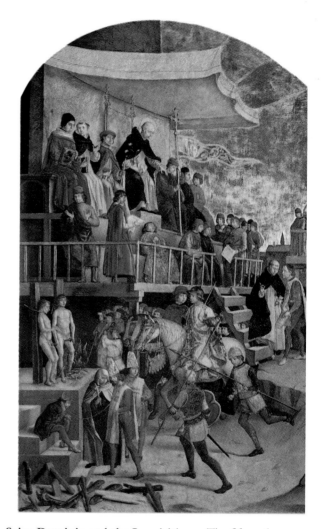

Saint Dominic and the Inquisition The fifteenth-century court painter to the Spanish rulers Ferdinand and Isabella, Pedro Berruguete here portrays an event from the life of Saint Dominic: Dominic presides at the trial of Count Raymond of Toulouse, who had supported the Albigensian heretics. Raymond, helmeted and on horseback, repented and was pardoned; his companions, who would not repent, were burned. Smoke from the fire has put one of the judges to sleep, and other officials, impervious to the human tragedy, chat among themselves. *(Museo del Prado, Madrid)*

face insisted that all Christians, including kings, are subject to the pope. Philip's university-trained advisers, with an argument drawn from Roman law, maintained that the king of France was completely sovereign in his kingdom and responsible to God alone. French mercenary troops went to Italy and arrested the aged pope. Although Boniface was soon freed, he died shortly afterward.

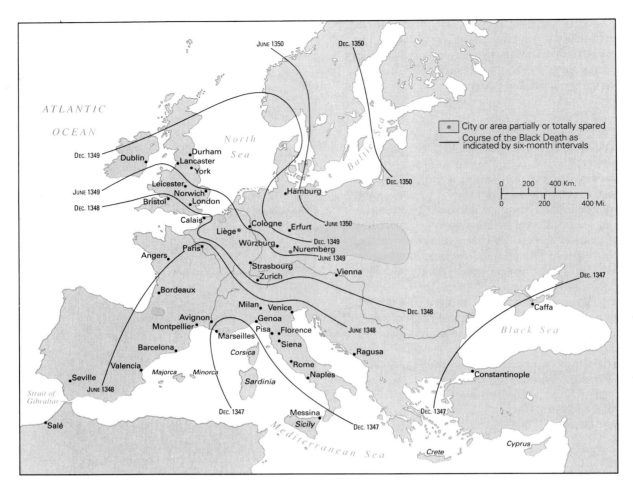

MAP 13.1 The Course of the Black Death in Fourteenth-Century Europe Note the routes that the bubonic plague took across Europe. How do you account for the fact that several regions were spared the "dreadful death"?

The Black Death

Economic difficulties originating in the later thirteenth century were fully manifest by the start of the four-teenth. In the first decade, the countries of northern Europe experienced considerable price inflation. The costs of grain, livestock, and dairy products rose sharply. Severe weather, which historical geographers label "the Little Ice Age," made a serious situation frightful. An unusual number of storms brought torrential rains, ru-ining the wheat, oat, and hay crops on which people and animals almost everywhere depended. Population had steadily increased in the twelfth and thirteenth cen-turies. The amount of food yielded, however, did not match the level of population growth. Bad weather had disastrous results. Poor harvests—one in four was likely

to be poor—led to scarcity and starvation. Almost all of northern Europe suffered a terrible famine in the years 1315 to 1317. Then in 1318 disease hit cattle and sheep, drastically reducing the herds and flocks. An-other bad harvest in 1321 brought famine, starvation, and death. Famine had dire social consequences: rustics were forced to sell or mortgage their lands for money to buy food; the number of vagabonds, or homeless peo-ple, greatly increased, as did petty crime; and the dis-possessed and starving focused their bitterness on land speculators and Jews. An undernourished population was ripe for the Grim Reaper, who appeared in 1348 in the form of the Black Death (Map 13.1).[32]

In October 1347, Genoese ships traveling from the Crimea in southern Russia brought the bubonic plague to Messina, from which it spread across Sicily and up into Italy. By late spring of 1348, southern Germany was attacked. Frightened French authorities chased a galley bearing the disease from the port of Marseilles, but not before plague had infected the city. In June 1348 two ships entered the Bristol Channel and introduced it into England. All Europe felt the scourge of this horrible disease.

The bacillus that causes the plague, *Pasteurella pestis,* likes to live in the bloodstream of an animal or, ideally, in the stomach of a flea. The flea in turn resides in the hair of a rodent, often the hardy, nimble, and vagabond black rat. In the fourteenth century, the host black rat traveled by ship, where it could feast for months on a cargo of grain or live snugly among bales of cloth. Fleas bearing the bacillus also had no trouble nesting in sad-dlebags.[33] Comfortable, well-fed, and having greatly multiplied, the black rats ended their ocean voyage and descended on the great cities of Europe.

The plague took two forms—bubonic and pneumonic. The rat was the transmitter of the bubonic form of the disease. The pneumonic form was communicated directly from one person to another.

Urban conditions were ideal for the spread of disease. Narrow streets filled with mud, refuse, and human excrement were as much cesspools as thoroughfares. Dead animals and sore-covered beggars greeted the traveler. Houses whose upper stories projected over the lower ones eliminated light and air. And extreme overcrowding was commonplace. When all members of an aristocratic family lived and slept in one room, it should

Procession of Saint Gregory   According to the *Golden Legend,* a thirteenth-century collection of saints' lives, the bubonic plague ravaged Rome when Gregory I was elected pope (590–604). He immediately ordered special prayers and processions around the city. Here, as people circle the walls, new victims fall. The architecture, the cardinals, and the friars all indicate that this painting dates from the fourteenth, not the sixth, century. *(Musée Condé, Chantilly/Art Resource, NY)*

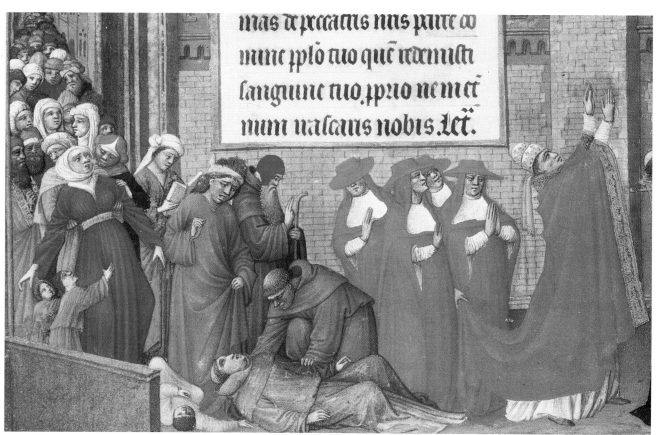

not be surprising that six or eight persons in a middle-class or poor household slept in one bed—if they had one.

Standards of personal hygiene remained frightfully low. Fleas and body lice were universal afflictions: one more bite did not cause much alarm. But if that nibble came from a bacillus-bearing flea, an entire household or area was doomed.

The symptoms of the bubonic plague started with a growth the size of a nut or an apple in the armpit, in the groin, or on the neck. This was the boil, or *buba,* that gave the disease its name and caused agonizing pain. If the buba was lanced and the pus thoroughly drained, the victim had a chance of recovery. The secondary stage was the appearance of black spots or blotches caused by bleeding under the skin. Finally, the victim began to cough violently and spit blood. This stage, indicating the presence of thousands of bacilli in the bloodstream, signaled the end, and death followed in two or three days. Rather than evoking compassion for the victim, a French scientist has written, everything about the bubonic plague provoked horror and disgust: "All the matter which exuded from their bodies let off an unbearable stench; sweat, excrement, spittle, breath, so fetid as to be overpowering; urine turbid, thick, black or red."[34]

Physicians could sometimes ease the pain but had no cure. Most people—lay, scholarly, and medical—believed that the Black Death was caused by some "vicious property in the air" that carried the disease from place to place. When ignorance was joined to fear and ancient bigotry, savage cruelty sometimes resulted. Many people believed that the Jews had poisoned the wells of Christian communities and thereby infected the drinking water. This charge led to the murder of thousands of Jews across Europe. According to one chronicler, sixteen thousand were killed at the imperial city of Strasbourg alone in 1349. That sixteen thousand is probably a typically medieval numerical exaggeration does not lessen the horror of the massacre.

The Italian writer Giovanni Boccaccio (1313–1375), describing the course of the disease in Florence in the preface to his book of tales, *The Decameron,* pinpointed the cause of the spread:

Moreover, the virulence of the pest was the greater by reason that intercourse was apt to convey it from the sick to the whole, just as fire devours things dry or greasy when they are brought close to it. Nay, the evil went yet further, for not merely by speech or association with the sick was the malady communicated to the healthy with consequent peril of common death, but any that touched the clothes of the sick or aught else that had been touched or used by them, seemed thereby to contract the disease.[35]

Because population figures for the period before the arrival of the plague do not exist for most countries and cities, only educated guesses can be made about mortality rates. Of a total English population of perhaps 4.2 million, probably 1.4 million died of the Black Death in its several visits.[36] Densely populated Italian cities endured incredible losses. Florence lost between one-half and two-thirds of its 1347 population of 85,000 when the plague visited in 1348. The disease recurred intermittently in the 1360s and 1370s and reappeared many times down to 1700. Population losses in Bohemia and Poland seem to have been much less. Historians of medicine have recently postulated that people with blood type O are immune to the bubonic disease; since this blood type predominated in Hungary, that region would have been slightly affected. No estimates of population losses have ever been attempted for Russia and the Balkans.

Economic historians and demographers sharply dispute the impact of the plague on the economy in the late fourteenth century. The traditional view that the plague had a disastrous effect has been greatly modified. In England it appears that by about 1375, most landlords enjoyed revenues near those of the pre-plague years. By the early fifteenth century, seigneurial prosperity reached a medieval peak. Why? The answer appears to lie in the fact that England and many parts of Europe suffered from overpopulation in the early fourteenth century. Population losses caused by the Black Death "led to increased productivity by restoring a more efficient balance between labour, land, and capital."[37] Population decline meant a sharp increase in per capita wealth. Increased demand for labor meant greater mobility among peasant and working classes. Wages rose, providing better distribution of income. The shortage of labor and steady requests for higher wages put landlords on the defensive. Some places, such as Florence, experienced economic prosperity as a long-term consequence of the plague.

Even more significant than the social effects were the psychological consequences. The knowledge that the disease meant almost certain death provoked the most profound pessimism. Imagine an entire society in the grip of the belief that it was at the mercy of a frightful affliction about which nothing could be done, a disgusting disease from which family and friends would flee, leaving one to die alone and in agony. It is not surprising that some sought release in orgies and gross sensuality, while others turned to the severest forms of asceticism and frenzied religious fervor. Groups of *flagellants,* men and women who whipped and scourged themselves as penance for their and society's sins, believed that the Black Death was God's punishment for humanity's wickedness.

The literature and art of the fourteenth century reveal a terribly morbid concern with death. One highly popular artistic motif, the Dance of Death, depicted a dancing skeleton leading away a living person. No wonder survivors experienced a sort of shell shock and a terrible crisis of faith. Lack of confidence in the leaders of society, lack of hope for the future, defeatism, and malaise wreaked enormous anguish and contributed to the decline of the Middle Ages. A long international war added further misery to the frightful disasters of the plague.

The Hundred Years' War (ca 1337–1453)

Another phase of the centuries-old struggle between the English and French monarchies, the Hundred Years' War was fought intermittently from 1337 to 1453. Its causes were both distant and immediate. The English claimed Aquitaine as an ancient feudal inheritance. In 1329 England's King Edward III (r. 1327–1377) paid homage to Philip VI (r. 1328–1350) for Aquitaine. French policy, however, was strongly expansionist, and in 1337 Philip, determined to exercise full jurisdiction there, confiscated the duchy. This action was the immediate cause of the war. Edward III maintained that the only way he could exercise his rightful sovereignty over Aquitaine was by assuming the title of king of France.[38] As the grandson and eldest surviving male descendant of Philip the Fair, he believed he could rightfully make this claim.

For centuries, economic factors involving the wool trade and the control of Flemish towns had served as justifications for war between France and England. The wool trade between England and Flanders was the cornerstone of both countries' economies; they were closely interdependent. Flanders was a fief of the French crown, and the Flemish aristocracy was highly sympathetic to the monarchy in Paris. But the wealth of Flemish merchants and cloth manufacturers depended on English wool, and Flemish burghers strongly supported the claims of Edward III.

The governments of both England and France manipulated public opinion to support the war. Kings in both countries instructed the clergy to deliver sermons filled with patriotic sentiment. The royal courts sensationalized the wickedness of the other side and stressed the great fortunes to be made from the war.

The Hundred Years' War was popular because it presented unusual opportunities for wealth and advancement. Poor knights and knights who were unemployed were promised regular wages. Criminals who enlisted were granted pardons. Great nobles expected to be rewarded with estates. Royal exhortations to the troops before battles repeatedly stressed that, if victorious, the men might keep whatever they seized. The French chronicler Jean Froissart wrote that, at the time of Edward III's expedition of 1359, men of all ranks flocked to the English king's banner. Some came to acquire honor, but many came in order "to loot and pillage the fair and plenteous land of France."[39]

The period of the Hundred Years' War witnessed the final flowering of the aristocratic code of medieval chivalry. Indeed, the enthusiastic participation of the nobility in both France and England was in response primarily to the opportunity the war provided to display chivalric behavior. War was considered an ennobling experience: there was something elevating, manly, fine, and beautiful about it. Describing the French army before the Battle of Poitiers (1356), a contemporary said:

Then you might see banners and pennons unfurled to the wind, whereon fine gold and azure shone, purple, gules and ermine. Trumpets, horns and clarions—you might hear sounding through the camp; the Dauphin's [title borne by the eldest son of the king of France] great battle made the earth ring.[40]

The chivalric code applied only to the aristocratic military elite. When English knights fought French ones, they were social equals fighting according to a mutually accepted code of behavior. The infantry troops were looked on as inferior beings. When a peasant force at Longueil destroyed a contingent of English knights, their comrades mourned them because "it was too much that so many good fighters had been killed by mere peasants."[41]

The war was fought almost entirely in France and the Low Countries (Map 13.2). It consisted mainly of a series of random sieges and cavalry raids. During the war's early stages, England was highly successful. At Crécy in northern France in 1346, English longbowmen scored a great victory over French knights and crossbowmen. Although the fire of the longbow was not very accurate, it allowed for rapid reloading, and English archers could send off three arrows to the

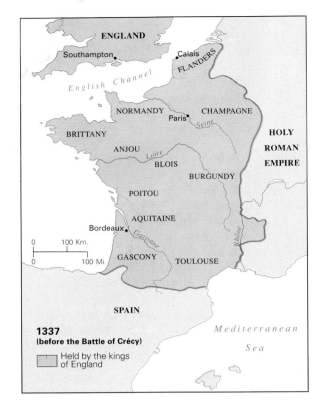

ENGLAND

Southampton

Calais
FLANDERS

English Channel

NORMANDY   CHAMPAGNE
Paris
Seine

BRITTANY

ANJOU   *Loire*

BLOIS   BURGUNDY

HOLY
ROMAN
EMPIRE

POITOU

AQUITAINE

Bordeaux   *Garonne*

GASCONY   TOULOUSE   *Rhône*

SPAIN

0   100 Km.
0   100 Mi.

*Mediterranean
Sea*

1337
(before the Battle of Crécy)

Held by the kings
of England

ENGLAND

Calais
FLANDERS
✕ Crécy
1346
Rouen

English Channel

NORMANDY   CHAMPAGNE
Paris
Seine

BRITTANY

ANJOU   *Loire*

BLOIS

HOLY
ROMAN
EMPIRE

Poitiers
1356 ✕
POITOU   BURGUNDY

AQUITAINE

Bordeaux   *Garonne*

GASCONY   TOULOUSE   *Rhône*

SPAIN

0   100 Km.
0   100 Mi.

*Mediterranean
Sea*

1360
(after the Battle of Poitiers)

Held by the kings
of England
✕   Major battles

ENGLAND

Calais
FLANDERS
✕
Agincourt
1415
Rouen   Reims

English Channel

NORMANDY   CHAMPAGNE
Paris   Domrémy
Seine

BRITTANY

Orléans

ANJOU   *Loire*

BLOIS

HOLY
ROMAN
EMPIRE

BURGUNDY

POITOU

AQUITAINE

Bordeaux   *Garonne*   *Rhône*

GASCONY   TOULOUSE

0   100 Km.
0   100 Mi.

SPAIN

*Mediterranean
Sea*

ca 1429
(after the siege of Orléans)

Held by the kings
of England
✕   Major battle

ENGLAND

Calais
FLANDERS

English Channel

NORMANDY   CHAMPAGNE
Paris
Seine

BRITTANY

ANJOU   *Loire*

BLOIS
BURGUNDY

HOLY
ROMAN
EMPIRE

POITOU

AQUITAINE

Bordeaux   *Garonne*   *Rhône*

GASCONY   TOULOUSE

0   100 Km.
0   100 Mi.

SPAIN

*Mediterranean
Sea*

1453
(end of war)

Held by the kings
of England

The Battle of Crécy, 1346
Pitched battles were unusual in the Hundred Years' War. At Crécy, the English (on the right with lions on their royal standard) scored a spectacular victory. The longbow proved a more effective weapon than the French crossbow, but characteristically the artist concentrated on the aristocratic knights. *(Bibliothèque Nationale, Paris)*

French crossbowmen's one. The result was a blinding shower of arrows that unhorsed the French knights and caused mass confusion. The firing of cannon—probably the first use of artillery in the West—created further panic. Thereupon the English horsemen charged and butchered the French.

Ten years later, Edward the Black Prince, using the same tactics as at Crécy, smashed the French at Poitiers, captured the French king, and held him for ransom. Again, at Agincourt near Arras in 1415, the chivalric English soldier-king Henry V (r. 1413–1422) gained the field over vastly superior numbers. By 1419 the English had advanced to the walls of Paris. But the French cause was not lost. Though England scored the initial victories, France won the war.

MAP 13.2 English Holdings in France During the Hundred Years' War   The year 1429 marked the greatest extent of English holdings in France. Why was it unlikely that England could have held these territories permanently?

The ultimate French success rests heavily on the actions of an obscure French peasant girl, Joan of Arc, whose vision and work revived French fortunes and led to victory. Born in 1412 to well-to-do peasants in the village of Domrémy in Champagne, Joan of Arc grew up in a pious household. During adolescence she began to hear voices, which she later said belonged to Saint Michael, Saint Catherine, and Saint Margaret. In 1428 these voices spoke to her with great urgency, telling her that the dauphin (the uncrowned King Charles VII) had to be crowned and the English expelled from France. Joan went to the French court, persuaded the king to reject the rumor that he was illegitimate, and secured his support for her relief of the besieged city of Orléans (see Map 13.2).

Joan arrived before Orléans on April 28, 1429. Seventeen years old, she knew little of warfare and believed that if she could keep the French troops from swearing and frequenting brothels, victory would be theirs. On May 8 the English, weakened by disease and lack of supplies, withdrew from Orléans. Ten days later,

Charles VII was crowned king at Reims. These two events marked the turning point in the war.

In 1430 England's allies, the Burgundians, captured Joan and sold her to the English. When the English handed her over to the ecclesiastical authorities for trial, the French court did not intervene. The English wanted Joan eliminated for obvious political reasons, but sorcery (witchcraft) was the charge at her trial. Witch persecution was increasing in the fifteenth century, and Joan's wearing of men's clothes appeared not only aberrant but indicative of contact with the Devil. In 1431 the court condemned her as a heretic. Her claim of direct inspiration from God, thereby denying the authority of church officials, constituted heresy. She was burned at the stake in the marketplace at Rouen. A new trial in 1456 rehabilitated her name. In 1920 she was canonized and declared a holy maiden, and today she is revered as the second patron saint of France.

The relief of Orléans stimulated French pride and rallied French resources. As the war dragged on, loss of life mounted, and money appeared to be flowing into a bottomless pit, demands for an end increased in England. The clergy and intellectuals pressed for peace. Parliamentary opposition to additional war grants stiffened. Slowly the French reconquered Normandy and finally ejected the English from Aquitaine. At the war's end in 1453, only the town of Calais remained in English hands (see Map 13.2).

For both France and England, the war proved a disaster. In France the English had slaughtered thousands of soldiers and civilians. In the years after the sweep of the Black Death, this additional killing meant a grave loss of population. The English had laid waste to hundreds of thousands of acres of rich farmland, leaving the rural economy of many parts of France a shambles. The war had disrupted trade and the great fairs, resulting in the drastic reduction of French participation in international commerce. Defeat in battle and heavy taxation contributed to widespread dissatisfaction and aggravated peasant grievances.

The long war had a profound impact on the political and cultural lives of the two countries. Most notably, it stimulated the development of the English Parliament. Between 1250 and 1450, representative assemblies from several classes of society flourished in many European countries. In the English Parliament, French Estates, German diets, and Spanish cortes, deliberative practices developed that laid the foundations for the representative institutions of modern liberal-democratic nations. Representative assemblies declined in most countries after the fifteenth century, but the English Parliament

endured. Edward III's constant need for money to pay for the war compelled him to summon not only the great barons and bishops but knights of the shires and burgesses from the towns as well. Between the outbreak of the war in 1337 and the king's death in 1377, parliamentary assemblies met twenty-seven times. Parliament met in thirty-seven of the fifty years of Edward's reign.[42]

In England theoretical consent to taxation and legislation was given in one assembly for the entire country. France had no such single assembly; instead, there were many regional or provincial assemblies. Why did a national representative assembly fail to develop in France? The initiative for convening assemblies rested with the king, who needed revenue almost as much as the English ruler.

No one in France wanted a national assembly. Linguistic, geographical, economic, legal, and political differences were very strong. People tended to think of themselves as Breton, Norman, Burgundian, or whatever, rather than French. Through much of the fourteenth and early fifteenth centuries, weak monarchs lacked the power to call a national assembly. Provincial assemblies, highly jealous of their independence, did not want a national assembly. The costs of sending delegates to it would be high, and the result was likely to be increased taxation. Finally, the Hundred Years' War itself hindered the growth of a representative body of government.

In both countries, however, the war did promote *nationalism*—the feeling of unity and identity that binds together a people who speak the same language, have a common ancestry and customs, and live in the same area. In the fourteenth century, nationalism largely took the form of hostility toward foreigners. Both Philip VI and Edward III drummed up support for the war by portraying the enemy as an alien, evil people.

After victories, each country experienced a surge of pride in its military strength. Just as English patriotism ran strong after Crécy and Poitiers, so French national confidence rose after Orléans. French national feeling demanded the expulsion of the enemy not merely from Normandy and Aquitaine but from French soil. Perhaps no one expressed this national consciousness better than Joan of Arc, when she exulted that the enemy had been "driven out of *France.*"

Religious Crisis

In times of crisis or disaster, people of all faiths have sought the consolation of religion. In the fourteenth century, however, the official Christian church offered very little solace. In fact, the leaders of the church added to the sorrow and misery of the times.

From 1309 to 1376, the popes lived in the city of Avignon in southeastern France. In order to control the church and its policies, Philip the Fair of France pressured Pope Clement V to settle in Avignon. Critically ill with cancer, Clement lacked the will to resist Philip. This period in church history is often called the Babylonian Captivity (referring to the seventy years the ancient Hebrews were held captive in Mesopotamian Babylon).

The Babylonian Captivity badly damaged papal prestige. The Avignon papacy reformed its financial administration and centralized its government. But the seven popes at Avignon concentrated on bureaucratic matters to the exclusion of spiritual objectives. In 1377 Pope Gregory XI (r. 1370–1378) brought the papal court back to Rome. Unfortunately, he died shortly after the return. At Gregory's death, Roman citizens demanded an Italian pope who would remain in Rome.

Urban VI (r. 1378–1389), Gregory's successor, had excellent intentions for church reform. He wanted to abolish simony, pluralism (holding several church offices at the same time), absenteeism, clerical extravagance, and ostentation, but he went about the work of reform in a tactless, arrogant, and bullheaded manner. He delivered blistering attacks on cardinals and threatened to excommunicate some of them. Advised that such excommunications would not be lawful unless the guilty had been warned three times, he shouted, "I can do anything, if it be my will and judgment."[43] Urban's quick temper and irrational behavior have led scholars to question his sanity. His actions brought disaster.

The cardinals slipped away from Rome, met at Anagni, and declared Urban's election invalid because it had come about under threats from the Roman mob. The cardinals then proceeded to elect Cardinal Robert of Geneva, the cousin of King Charles V of France, as pope. Cardinal Robert took the name Clement VII (r. 1378–1394) and set himself up at Avignon in opposition to the legally elected Urban. So began the Great Schism, which divided Western Christendom until 1417.

The powers of Europe aligned themselves with Urban or Clement along strictly political lines. France recognized the Frenchman, Clement; England, France's historic enemy, recognized Urban. The scandal provoked horror and vigorous cries for reform. The common people—hard-pressed by inflation, wars, and plague—were thoroughly confused about which pope was legitimate. The schism weakened the religious faith

of many Christians and gave rise to instability and religious excesses. At a time when ordinary Christians needed the consolation of religion and confidence in religious leaders, church officials were fighting among themselves for power.

The English scholar and theologian John Wyclif (1329–1384) wrote that papal claims of temporal power had no foundation in the Scriptures and that the Scriptures alone should be the standard of Christian belief and practice. He urged the abolition of such practices as the veneration of saints, pilgrimages, pluralism, and absenteeism. Sincere Christians, Wyclif said, should read the Bible for themselves. Wyclif's views had broad social and economic significance. He urged that the church be stripped of its property. His idea that every Christian free of mortal sin possessed lordship was seized on by peasants in England during a revolt in 1381 and used to justify their goals.

Although Wyclif's ideas were vigorously condemned by ecclesiastical authorities, they were widely disseminated by humble clerics and enjoyed great popularity in the early fifteenth century. The teachings of Wyclif's followers, called Lollards, allowed women to preach and to consecrate the Eucharist. Women, some well educated, played a significant role in the movement. After Anne, sister of Wenceslaus, king of Germany and Bohemia, married Richard II of England, members of Queen Anne's household carried Lollard principles back to Bohemia, where they were read by Jan Hus, rector of the University of Prague.

In response to continued calls throughout Europe for a council, the two colleges of cardinals—one at Rome, the other at Avignon—summoned a council at Pisa in 1409. A distinguished gathering of prelates and theologians deposed both popes and selected another. Neither the Avignon pope nor the Roman pope would resign, however, and the appalling result was the creation of a threefold schism.

Finally, because of the pressure of the German emperor Sigismund, a great council met at the imperial city of Constance (1414–1418). It had three objectives: to end the schism, to reform the church "in head and members" (from top to bottom), and to wipe out heresy. The council condemned Jan Hus as a Wycliffite, and he was burned at the stake. The council eventually deposed the three schismatic popes and elected a new leader, the Roman cardinal Colonna, who took the name Martin V (1417–1431).

Martin proceeded to dissolve the council. Nothing was done about reform. The schism was over, and though councils subsequently met at Basel and at Ferrara-Florence, in 1450 the papacy held a jubilee, celebrating its triumph over the conciliar movement. In the later fifteenth century, the papacy concentrated on Italian problems to the exclusion of universal Christian interests. The schism and the conciliar movement, however, had exposed the crying need for ecclesiastical reform, thus laying the foundations for the great reform efforts of the sixteenth century.

MARRIAGE AND THE PARISH IN THE LATER MIDDLE AGES

Marriage and the local parish church continued to be the center of the lives of most people. Scholars long believed that because peasants were illiterate and left very few statements about their marriages, generalizations could not be made about them. Research in manorial, ecclesiastical, and coroners' records, however, has uncovered fascinating material. Evidence abounds of teenage flirtations, and many young people had sexual contacts—some leading to conception. Premarital pregnancy may have been deliberate: because children were economically important, the couple wanted to be sure of fertility before entering marriage.

"Whether rich or poor, male or female, the most important rite de passage for peasant youth was marriage."[44] The evidence overwhelmingly shows, above all where land or other property accompanied the union, that parents took the lead in arranging their children's marriages. Parents might have to depend on a son- or daughter-in-law for care in old age. Marriage determined the life partner, the economic circumstances in which the couple would live, and the son-in-law who might take on the family land. Most marriages were between men and women of the same village; where the name and residence of a husband are known, perhaps 41 percent were outsiders. Once the prospective bride or groom had been decided on, parents paid the *merchet* (fine to the lord for a woman's marriage—since he stood to lose a worker) and gave the couple a cash settlement as a financial start. The couple then proceeded to the church door. There they made the vows, rings were blessed and exchanged, and the ceremony was concluded with some kind of festivity.[45]

The general pattern in late medieval Europe was marriage between men in their middle or late twenties and women under twenty.[46] Poor peasants and wage laborers, both men and women, did not marry until their mid- or late twenties. In the later Middle Ages, as earlier—indeed, until the nineteenth century—economic factors rather than romantic love or physical attraction determined whom and when a person married. The young agricultural laborer on the manor had to wait until he had sufficient land. Thus most men had to wait until their fathers died or yielded the holding. The late age of marriage affected the number of children a couple had. The journeyman craftsman in the urban guild faced the same material difficulties. Prudent young men selected (or their parents selected for them) girls who would bring the most land or money to the union.

With marriage for men postponed, was there any socially accepted sexual outlet? Other parts of the world provide interesting parallels. In traditional China, women were expected to conform to the Confucian ideal of chastity before, and monogamy after, marriage. Men were not; prostitutes were widely available. Pre-Columbian American societies and early African ones placed no severe taboos on either gender for premarital sexual activity. In Europe, municipal authorities in many towns set up legal houses of prostitution or red-light districts either outside the city walls or away from respectable neighborhoods. For example, authorities in Montpellier set aside Hot Street for prostitution, required public women to live there, and forbade anyone to molest them. Prostitution thus passed from being a private concern to being a social matter requiring public supervision.[47] Publicly owned brothels were more easily policed and supervised than privately run ones.

Prostitution was an urban phenomenon because only populous towns had large numbers of unmarried young men, communities of transient merchants, and a culture accustomed to a cash exchange. Although the risk of disease limited the number of years a woman could practice this profession, many women prospered. Some acquired sizable incomes. In 1361 Françoise of Florence, a prostitute working in a brothel in Marseilles, made a will in which she left legacies to various charities and left a large sum as a dowry for a poor girl to marry. Legalized prostitution suggests that public officials believed the prostitute could make a positive contribution to society; it does not mean the prostitute was respected. Rather, she was scorned and distrusted. Legalized brothels also reflect a greater tolerance for male than for female sexuality.[48]

Once a couple married, the union ended only with the death of one partner. Deep emotional bonds knit members of medieval families. Most parents delighted in their children, and the church encouraged a cult of paternal care. Divorce did not exist. The church held that a marriage validly entered into, with mutual oral consent or promise of two parties, could not be dissolved. Annulments were granted in extraordinary circumstances, such as male impotence, on the grounds that a lawful marriage had never existed.[49]

Theologians of the day urged that the couple's union be celebrated and witnessed in a church ceremony and blessed by a priest. A great number of couples, however, treated marriage as a private act. They made the promise and spoke the words of marriage to each other without witnesses and then proceeded to enjoy the sexual pleasures of marriage. This practice led to a great number of disputes, because one or the other of the two parties could later deny having made a marriage agreement. The records of the ecclesiastical courts reveal evidence of marriages contracted in a garden, in a blacksmith's shop, at a tavern, and, predictably, in a bed.

Marriage and collective work on the land remained the focus of life for the European peasantry in the thirteenth century. Craft guilds, however, provided the small minority of men and women living in towns and cities with the psychological satisfaction of involvement in the manufacture of a superior product. The guild member also had economic security. The guilds looked after the sick, the poor, the widowed, and the orphaned. Masters and employees worked side by side.

In the fourteenth century, those ideal conditions began to change. The fundamental objective of the craft guild was to maintain a monopoly on its product, and to do so recruitment and promotion were carefully restricted. Some guilds required a high entrance fee for apprentices; others admitted only relatives of members. Restrictions limited the number of apprentices and journeymen to match the anticipated openings for masters. Women experienced the same exclusion. A careful study of the records of forty-two craft guilds in Cologne, for example, shows that in the fifteenth century all but six became virtual male preserves.[50] The decreasing number of openings created serious frustrations. Strikes and riots occurred in the Flemish towns, in France, and in England.

The recreation of all classes reflected the fact that late medieval society was organized for war and that violence was common. The aristocracy engaged in tournaments or jousts; archery and wrestling had great popularity among ordinary people. Everyone enjoyed the cruel sports of bullbaiting and bearbaiting. The hangings and mutilations of criminals were exciting and well-attended events, with all the festivity of a university town before a Saturday football game. Chroniclers exulted in describing executions, murders, and massacres.

Shepherds Dancing   As in all ages, young people (and some not so young) enjoyed dancing, and the marriage or baptismal feast or harvest celebration provided an opportunity, perhaps accompanied by singing or the music of someone talented on the harmonica or bagpipe (lower right). *(Bibliothèque Nationale, Paris)*

Here a monk gleefully describes the gory execution of William Wallace in 1305:

Wilielmus Waleis, a robber given to sacrilege, arson and homicide . . . was condemned to most cruel but justly deserved death. He was drawn through the streets of London at the tails of horses, until he reached a gallows of unusual height, there he was suspended by a halter; but taken down while yet alive, he was mutilated, his bowels torn out and burned in a fire, his head then cut off, his body divided into four, and his quarters transmitted to four principal parts of Scotland.[51]

Violence was as English as roast beef and plum pudding, as French as bread, cheese, and *potage.*

PEASANT REVOLTS

In the fourteenth century, economic and political difficulties, disease, and war profoundly affected the lives of European peoples. Decades of slaughter and destruction, punctuated by the decimating visits of the Black Death, made a grave economic situation virtually disastrous. In many parts of France and the Low Countries, fields lay in ruin or untilled for lack of labor power. In England, as taxes increased, criticisms of government policy and mismanagement multiplied.

Peasant revolts occurred often in the Middle Ages. Early in the thirteenth century, the French preacher Jacques de Vitry asked rhetorically, "How many serfs have killed their lords or burnt their castles?"[52] And in the fourteenth and fifteenth centuries, social and economic conditions caused a great increase in peasant uprisings.

In 1358, when French taxation for the Hundred Years' War fell heavily on the poor, the frustrations of the French peasantry exploded in a massive uprising called the *Jacquerie,* after a supposedly happy agricultural laborer, Jacques Bonhomme (Good Fellow). Two years earlier, the English had captured the French king John and many nobles and held them for ransom. The peasants resented paying for their lords' release. Recently hit by plague, experiencing famine in some areas, and harassed by "fur-collar criminals," peasants erupted in anger and frustration in Picardy, Champagne, and the area around Paris. Crowds swept through the countryside, slashing the throats of nobles, burning their castles, raping their wives and daughters, and killing or maiming their horses and cattle. Artisans, small merchants, and parish priests joined the peasants. Urban and rural groups committed terrible destruction, and for several weeks the nobles were on the defensive. Then the upper class united to repress the revolt with merciless ferocity. Thousands of the "Jacques," innocent as well as guilty, were cut down.

The Peasants' Revolt in England in 1381, involving perhaps a hundred thousand people, was probably the largest single uprising of the entire Middle Ages. The causes of the rebellion were complex and varied from place to place. In general, though, the thirteenth century had witnessed the steady commutation of labor services for cash rents, and the Black Death had drastically cut the labor supply. As a result, peasants demanded higher wages and fewer manorial obligations. Thirty years earlier, the parliamentary Statute of Laborers of 1351 had declared:

Whereas to curb the malice of servants who after the pestilence were idle and unwilling to serve without securing excessive wages, it was recently ordained . . . that such servants, both men and women, shall be bound to serve in return for salaries and wages that were customary . . . five or six years earlier.[53]

This attempt by landlords to freeze wages and social mobility could not be enforced. As a matter of fact, the condition of the English peasantry steadily improved in the course of the fourteenth century. Why then was the outburst in 1381 so serious? It was provoked by a crisis of rising expectations.

The relative prosperity of the laboring classes led to demands that the upper classes were unwilling to grant. Unable to climb higher, the peasants found release for their economic frustrations in revolt. But economic grievances combined with other factors. The south of England, where the revolt broke out, had been subjected to frequent and destructive French raids. The English government did little to protect the south, and villages grew increasingly scared and insecure. Moreover, decades of aristocratic violence, much of it perpetrated against the weak peasantry, had bred hostility and bitterness. In France frustration over the lack of permanent victory increased. In England the social and religious agitation of the popular preacher John Ball fanned the embers of discontent. Sayings such as Ball's famous couplet "When Adam delved and Eve span; Who was then the gentleman?" reflect real revolutionary sentiment.

The straw that broke the camel's back in England was the reimposition of a head tax on all adult males. Beginning with assaults on the tax collectors, the uprising in England followed much the same course as had the Jacquerie in France. Castles and manors were sacked; manorial records were destroyed. Many nobles, including the archbishop of Canterbury, who had ordered the collection of the tax, were murdered. Urban discontent merged with rural violence. Apprentices and journeymen, frustrated because the highest positions in the guilds were closed to them, rioted.

The boy-king Richard II (r. 1377–1399) met the leaders of the revolt, agreed to charters ensuring the peasants' freedom, tricked them with false promises, and then proceeded to crush the uprising with terrible ferocity. Although the nobility tried to restore ancient duties of serfdom, virtually a century of freedom had elapsed, and the commutation of manorial services continued. Rural serfdom had disappeared in England by 1550.

John Ball   A priest of Kent, Ball often preached his radical egalitarianism out-of-doors after Mass: "Matters goeth not well . . . in England nor shall (they) till everything be common and . . . there be no villains (serfs) nor gentlemen. . . . What have we deserved, or why should we be kept thus in servage (servitude)?" All contemporary writers blamed Ball for fomenting the rebellion of 1381. But the evidence of peasant demands shows that they were limited and local: hunting rights in the woods, freedom from miscellaneous payments, exemption from special work on the lord's bridges or parks. *(Private collection)*

Conditions in England and France were not unique. In Florence in 1378, the *ciompi,* or poor propertyless workers, revolted. Serious social trouble occurred in Lübeck, Brunswick, and other German cities. In Spain in 1391, massive uprisings in Seville and Barcelona took the form of vicious attacks on Jewish communities. Rebellions and uprisings everywhere reveal deep peasant and working-class frustration and the general socioeconomic crisis of the time.

RACE AND ETHNICITY ON THE FRONTIERS

In the twelfth and thirteenth centuries, many people migrated from one part of Europe to another: the English into Scotland and Ireland; Germans, French, and Flemings into Poland, Bohemia, and Hungary; the French into Spain. In the fourteenth century, many Germans moved into eastern Europe, fleeing the Black Death. The colonization of frontier regions meant that peoples of different ethnic or racial backgrounds lived side by side. Race relations became a basic factor in the lives of peoples living in those frontier areas.

Racial categories rest on socially constructed beliefs and customs, not on any biological or anthropological classification. When late medieval chroniclers used the language of race—words such as *gens* (race or clan) and *natio* (species, stock, or kind)—they meant cultural differences. Medieval scholars held that peoples differed according to descent, language, customs, and laws. Descent or blood, basic to the color racism of the United States, played an insignificant part in medieval ideas about race and ethnicity. Rather, the chief marks of an ethnic group were language (which could be learned), customs (for example, dietary practices, dance, marriage and death rituals, clothing, and hairstyles, all of which could be adopted), and laws (which could be changed or modified). What role did race and ethnicity play in relations between native peoples and settlers in the later Middle Ages?

In the early periods of conquest and colonization, and in all frontier regions, a legal dualism existed: native peoples remained subject to their traditional laws; newcomers brought and were subject to the laws of the countries from which they came. On the Prussian and Polish frontier, for example, the law was that "men who come there . . . should be judged on account of any crime or contract engaged in there according to Polish custom if they are Poles and according to German custom if they are Germans."[54] The same dualism operated in Spain with respect to Muslims and Christians. Subject peoples experienced some disabilities, but the broad trend was toward a legal pluralism.

The great exception to this pattern was Ireland, where the English practiced an extreme form of racial discrimination toward the native Irish. The English distinguished between the free and the unfree, and the entire Irish population, simply by the fact of Irish birth, was unfree. A legal structure modeled on that of England, with county courts, itinerant justices, and the common law (see pages 355–357), was set up. But the Irish had no access to the common-law courts. In civil (property) disputes, an English defendant need not respond to his Irish plaintiff; no Irish person could make a will; and an Irish widow could not claim her dower rights (enjoyment of part of the estate during her lifetime). In criminal procedures, the murder of an Irishman was not considered a felony. In 1317–1318, Irish princes sent a Remonstrance to the pope complaining that "any non-Irishman is allowed to bring legal action against an Irishman, but an Irishman . . . except any prelate (bishop or abbot) is barred from every action by that fact alone." An English defendant in the criminal matter would claim "that he is not held to answer . . . since he [the plaintiff] is Irish and not of free blood."[55] This emphasis on blood descent naturally provoked bitterness, but only in the Tudor period (see Chapter 15) was the English common law opened to the subject Irish population.

The later Middle Ages witnessed a movement away from legal pluralism or dualism and toward a legal homogeneity and an emphasis on blood descent. Competition for ecclesiastical offices and the cultural divisions between town and country people became arenas for ethnic tension and racial conflict. Since bishoprics and abbacies carried religious authority, spiritual charisma, and often rights of appointment to subordinate positions, they were natural objects of ambition. When prelates of a language or "nationality" different from that of the local people gained church positions, the latter felt a loss of influence. Bishops were supposed to be pastors. Their pastoral work involved preaching, teaching, and comforting, duties that could be performed effectively only when the bishop (or priest) could communicate with the people. Ideally in a pluralistic society, he should be bilingual; often he was not.

In the late thirteenth century, as waves of Germans migrated into Danzig on the Baltic, into Silesia, and into the Polish countryside and towns, they encountered Jakub Swinka, archbishop of Gniezno (1283–

1314), whose jurisdiction included these areas of settlement. The bishop hated Germans and referred to them as "dog heads." His German contemporary, Bishop John of Cracow, detested the Poles, wanted to expel all Polish people, and refused to appoint Poles to any church office. In Ireland, English colonists and the native Irish competed for ecclesiastical offices until 1217, when the English government in London decreed:

Since the election of Irishmen in our land of Ireland has often disturbed the peace of that land, we command you . . . that henceforth you allow no Irishman to be elected . . . or preferred in any cathedral . . . (and) you should seek by all means to procure election and promotion to vacant bishoprics of . . . honest Englishmen.[56]

Although criticized by the pope and not totally enforceable, this law remained in effect in many dioceses for centuries.

Likewise, the arrival of Cistercians and mendicants (Franciscans and Dominicans) from France and Germany in Baltic and Slavic lands provoked racial and "national" hostilities. In the fourteenth and fifteenth centuries, in contrast to earlier centuries, racial or ethnic prejudices became conspicuous. Slavic prelates and princes saw the German mendicants as "instruments of cultural colonization," and Slavs were strongly discouraged from becoming members. In 1333, when John of Drazic, bishop of Prague, founded a friary at Roudnice (Raudnitz), he specified that "we shall admit no one to this convent or monastery of any nation except a Bohemian [Czech], born of two Czech-speaking parents."[57]

Everywhere in Europe, towns recruited people from the countryside (see pages 359–361). In frontier regions, townspeople were usually long-distance immigrants and, in eastern Europe, Ireland, and Scotland, ethnically different from the surrounding rural population. In eastern Europe, German was the language of the towns; in Ireland, French, the tongue of noble Norman or English settlers, predominated. In fourteenth-century Prague, between 63 percent and 80 percent of new burgesses bore identifiable German names, as did almost all city council members. Towns in eastern Europe "had the character of German islands in Slav, Baltic, Estonian, or Magyar seas."[58] Although native peoples commonly held humbler positions, both immigrant and native townspeople prospered during the expanding economy of the thirteenth century. When economic recession hit during the fourteenth century, ethnic tensions multiplied.

Just as the social and legal status of the Jews in western Europe worsened in the wake of the great famine and the Black Death (see pages 358 and 392), on the frontiers of Latin Europe discrimination, ghettoization, and racism—now based on blood descent—characterized the attitudes of colonists toward native peoples. But the latter also could express racial savagery. Regulations drawn up by various guilds were explicitly racist, with protectionist bars for some groups and exclusionist laws for others. One set of laws applicable to parts of eastern Europe required that applicants for guild membership be of German descent and sometimes prove it. Cobblers in fourteenth-century Beeskow, a town close to the large Slavic population of Lausitz in Silesia, required that "an apprentice who comes to learn his craft should be brought before the master and guild members. . . . We forbid the sons of barbers, linen workers, shepherds, Slavs." The bakers of the same town decreed:

Whoever wishes to be a member must bring proof to the councillors and guildsmen that he is born of legitimate, upright, German folk. . . . No one of Wendish (Slavic) race may be in the guild. In Limerick and Dublin in Ireland, guild masters agreed to accept "noo apprentice but that he be of English berthe."[59]

Intermarriage was forbidden in many places, such as Riga on the Baltic (now the capital of Latvia), where legislation for the bakers guild stipulated that "whoever wishes to have the privilege of membership in our company shall not take as a wife any woman who is ill-famed . . . or non-German; if he does marry such a woman, he must leave the company and office." Likewise, eligibility for public office depended on racial purity, as at the German burgher settlement of Pest in Hungary, where a town judge had to have four German grandparents. The most extensive attempt to prevent intermarriage and protect racial purity is embodied in Ireland's Statute of Kilkenny (1366), which states that

there were to be no marriages between those of immigrant and native stock; that the English inhabitants of Ireland must employ the English language and bear English names; that they must ride in the English way (i.e., with saddles) and have English apparel; that no Irishmen were

to be granted ecclesiastical benefices or admitted to monasteries in the English parts of Ireland; and that the Irish game of hurling and the maintenance of Irish minstrels were forbidden to English settlers.[60]

Rulers of the Christian kingdoms of Spain drew up comparable legislation discriminating against the Mudéjars.

All these laws had an economic basis: to protect the financial interests of the privileged German, English, or Spanish colonial minorities. The laws also reflect a racism that not only pervaded the lives of frontier peoples at the end of the Middle Ages but also sowed the seeds of difficulties still unresolved at the end of the twentieth century.

 ## VERNACULAR LITERATURE

Few developments expressed the growth of national consciousness more vividly than the emergence of national literatures. Across Europe people spoke the language and dialect of their particular locality and class. In England, for example, the common people spoke regional English dialects, while the upper classes conversed in French. Official documents and works of literature were written in Latin or French. Beginning in the fourteenth century, however, national languages—the vernacular—came into widespread use not only in verbal communication but in literature as well. Three masterpieces of European culture, Dante's *Divine Comedy* (1310–1320), Chaucer's *Canterbury Tales* (1387–1400), and Christine de Pisan's *City of Ladies* (1404), brilliantly manifest this new national pride.

Dante Alighieri (1265–1321) descended from an aristocratic family in Florence, where he held several positions in the city government. Dante called his work a "comedy" because he wrote it in Italian and in a different style from the "tragic" Latin; a later generation added the adjective *divine,* referring both to its sacred subject and to Dante's artistry. The *Divine Comedy* is an allegorical trilogy of one hundred cantos (verses) whose three equal parts (1 + 33 + 33 + 33) each describe one of the realms of the next world: Hell, Purgatory, and Paradise. Dante recounts his imaginary journey through these regions toward God. The Roman poet Virgil, representing reason, leads Dante through Hell, where he observes the torments of the damned and denounces the disorders of his own time, especially ecclesiastical ambition and corruption. Passing up into Purgatory, Virgil shows the poet how souls are purified of their disordered inclinations. From Purgatory, Beatrice, a woman Dante once loved and the symbol of divine revelation in the poem, leads him to Paradise. In Paradise, home of the angels and saints, Saint Bernard—representing mystic contemplation—leads Dante to the Virgin Mary. Through her intercession, he at last attains a vision of God.

The *Divine Comedy* portrays contemporary and historical figures, comments on secular and ecclesiastical affairs, and draws on Scholastic philosophy. Within the framework of a symbolic pilgrimage to the City of God, the *Divine Comedy* embodies the psychological tensions of the age. A profoundly Christian poem, it also contains bitter criticism of some church authorities. In its symmetrical structure and use of figures from the ancient world, such as Virgil, the poem perpetuates the classical tradition. But as the first major work of literature in the Italian vernacular, it is distinctly modern.

Geoffrey Chaucer (1340–1400), the son of a London wine merchant, was an official in the administrations of the English kings Edward III and Richard II and wrote poetry as an avocation. Chaucer's *Canterbury Tales* is a collection of stories in lengthy, rhymed narrative. On a pilgrimage to the shrine of Saint Thomas Becket at Canterbury (see page 357), thirty people of various social backgrounds each tell a tale. The Prologue sets the scene and describes the pilgrims, whose characters are further revealed in the story each one tells. For example, the gentle Christian Knight relates a chivalric romance; the gross Miller tells a vulgar story about a deceived husband; the earthy Wife of Bath, who has buried five husbands, sketches a fable about the selection of a spouse. In depicting the interests and behavior of all types of people, Chaucer presents a rich panorama of English social life in the fourteenth century. Like the *Divine Comedy*, *Canterbury Tales* reflects the cultural tensions of the times. Ostensibly Christian, many of the pilgrims are also materialistic, sensual, and worldly, suggesting the ambivalence of the broader so-

Schoolmaster and His Wife Teaching   Ambrosius Holbein, elder brother of the more famous Hans Holbein, produced this signboard for the Swiss educator Myconius; it is an excellent example of what we would call commercial art—art used to advertise, in this case Myconius's profession. The German script above promised that all who enrolled would learn to read and write. By modern standards the classroom seems bleak: the windows have glass panes but they don't admit much light, and the schoolmaster is prepared to use the sticks if the boy makes a mistake. *(Öffentliche Kunstsammlung Basel/Martin Bühler, photographer)*

ciety's concern for the next world and frank enjoyment of this one.

Perhaps the most versatile and prolific French writer of the later Middle Ages was Christine de Pisan (1363?–1434?). The daughter of a professor of astrology, Christine had acquired a broad knowledge of Greek, Latin, French, and Italian literature. The deaths of her father and husband left her with three small children and her mother to support, and she resolved to earn her living with her pen. In addition to poems and books on love, religion, and morality, Christine produced major historical works and many letters. *The City of Ladies* (1404) lists the great women of history and their contributions to society, and *The Book of Three Virtues* provides prudent and practical advice on household management for women of all social classes and at all stages of life. Christine de Pisan's wisdom and wit are illustrated in her autobiographical *Avison-Christine.* She records that a man told her that an educated woman is unattractive because there are so few, to which she responded that an ignorant man was even less attractive because there are so many. (See the feature "Listening to the Past: Christine de Pisan" on pages 410–411.)

In the fourteenth century, a vernacular literature also emerged in eastern Europe, often as a reaction to other cultures. In Bohemia, for example, the immigration of large numbers of Germans elicited increasing Czech self-consciousness, leading to an interest among the Czechs in their own language. Translations of knightly sagas from German into Czech multiplied. So did translations of religious writings—Psalters, prayers, a life of Christ—from Latin to Czech. Vernacular literature in eastern Europe especially represents an ethnic and patriotic response to foreigners.

From the fifth through the thirteenth century, the overwhelming majority of people who could read and write were priests, monks, and nuns. Beginning in the fourteenth century, a variety of evidence attests to the increasing literacy of laypeople. In England, as one scholar has shown, the number of schools in the diocese of York quadrupled between 1350 and 1500. Information from the Flemish and German towns is similar: children were sent to schools and received the fundamentals of reading, writing, and arithmetic. The penetration of laymen into the higher positions of government administration, long the preserve of clerics, indicates the rising lay literacy.

The spread of literacy represents a response to the needs of an increasingly complex society. Trade, commerce, and expanding government bureaucracies required more and more literate people. Late medieval culture remained an oral culture in which most people received information by word of mouth. But by the mid-fifteenth century, even before the printing press was turning out large quantities of reading materials, the evolution toward a literary culture was already perceptible.[61]

SUMMARY

Universities—institutions of higher learning unique to the West—emerged from cathedral and municipal schools and provided trained officials for the new government bureaucracies. The soaring Gothic cathedrals that medieval towns erected demonstrated civic pride, deep religious faith, and economic vitality.

The performance of agricultural services and the payment of rents preoccupied peasants throughout the Middle Ages. Though peasants led hard lives, the reclamation of waste- and forestlands, migration to frontier territory, or flight to a town offered a means of social mobility. The Christian faith, though perhaps not understood at an intellectual level, provided emotional and spiritual solace.

By 1100 the nobility possessed a strong class consciousness. Aristocratic values and attitudes shaded all aspects of medieval culture. Trained for war, nobles often devoted considerable time to fighting, and intergenerational squabbles were common. Yet a noble might shoulder heavy judicial, political, and economic responsibilities, depending on the size of his estates.

The monks and nuns exercised a profound influence on matters of the spirit. In their prayers, monks and nuns battled for the Lord, just as the chivalrous knights clashed on the battlefield. In their chants and rich ceremonials, in their architecture and literary productions, and in the examples of many monks' lives, the monasteries inspired Christian peoples to an incalculable degree. As the crucibles of sacred art, the monasteries became the cultural centers of Christian Europe.

Late medieval preachers likened the crises of their times to the Four Horsemen of the Apocalypse in the Book of Revelation, who brought famine, war, disease, and death. The crises of the fourteenth and fifteenth centuries were acids that burned deeply into the fabric of traditional medieval European society. Bad weather—beyond human control—brought poor harvests, which contributed to the international economic depression. Disease fostered widespread depression and dissatisfaction. Population losses caused by the Black Death and the Hundred Years' War encouraged the working classes to try to profit from the labor shortage by selling their services for a higher price. When peasant frustrations exploded in uprisings, the frightened nobility and upper middle class joined to crush the revolts. But events had heightened social consciousness among the poor.

The migration of peoples from the European heartland to the frontier regions of Iberia, Ireland, the Baltic, and eastern Europe led to ethnic friction between native peoples and new settlers. Economic difficulties heightened ethnic consciousness and spawned a vicious racism.

The increasing number of schools leading to the growth of lay literacy represents a positive achievement of the later Middle Ages. So also does the development of national literatures. The first sign of a literary culture appeared.

Religion held society together. European culture was a Christian culture. But the Great Schism weakened the prestige of the church and people's faith in papal authority. The conciliar movement, by denying the church's universal sovereignty, strengthened the claims of secular governments to jurisdiction over all their peoples. The later Middle Ages witnessed a steady shift of loyalty away from the church and toward the emerging national states.

NOTES

1. Quoted in H. E. Sigerist, *Civilization and Disease* (Chicago: University of Chicago Press, 1943), p. 102.

2. Quoted in J. H. Mundy, *Europe in the High Middle Ages, 1150–1309* (New York: Basic Books, 1973), pp. 474–475.

3. E. Panofsky, trans. and ed., *Abbot Suger on the Abbey Church of St.-Denis and Its Art Treasures* (Princeton, N.J.: Princeton University Press, 1946), p. 101.

4. Quoted in J. J. Wilhelm, ed., *Lyrics of the Middle Ages: An Anthology* (New York: Garland Publishers, 1993), pp. 94–95.

5. I have leaned on the very persuasive interpretation of M. R. Menocal, *The Arabic Role in Medieval Literary History* (Philadelphia: University of Pennsylvania Press, 1990), pp. ix–xv, 27–33.

6. G. Duby, *The Chivalrous Society,* trans. C. Postan (Berkeley: University of California Press, 1977), pp. 90–93.

7. B. A. Hanawalt, *The Ties That Bound: Peasant Families in Medieval England* (New York: Oxford University Press, 1986), p. 5.

8. E. Power, "Peasant Life and Rural Conditions," in J. R. Tanner et al., *The Cambridge Medieval History,* vol. 7 (Cambridge: Cambridge University Press, 1958), p. 716.

9. Glanvill, "De Legibus Angliae," bk. 5, chap. 5, in *Social Life in Britain from the Conquest to the Reformation,* ed. G. G. Coulton (London: Cambridge University Press, 1956), pp. 338–339.

10. See R. Bartlett, "Colonial Towns and Colonial Traders," in *The Making of Europe: Conquest, Colonization and Cultural Change, 950–1350* (Princeton, N.J.: Princeton University Press, 1993), pp. 167–196.

11. See John L. Langdon, *Horses, Oxen, and Technological Innovation: The Use of Draught Animals in English Farming, 1066–1500* (New York: Cambridge University Press, 1986), esp. pp. 254–270.

12. G. Duby, *The Early Growth of the European Economy: Warriors and Peasants from the Seventh to the Twelfth Century* (Ithaca, N.Y.: Cornell University Press, 1978), pp. 213–219.

13. See Hanawalt, *The Ties That Bound,* pp. 90–100.

14. Ibid., p. 149.

15. On this quantity and medieval measurements, see D. Knowles, "The Measures of Monastic Beverages," in *The Monastic Order in England* (Cambridge: Cambridge University Press, 1962), p. 717.

16. G. Duby, ed., *A History of Private Life.* Vol. 2: *Revelations of the Middle Ages* (Cambridge, Mass.: Harvard University Press, 1988), p. 585.

17. E. J. Kealey, *Medieval Medicus: A Social History of Anglo-Norman Medicine* (Baltimore: Johns Hopkins University Press, 1981), p. 102.

18. C. Klapisch-Zuber, ed., *A History of Women.* Vol. 2: *Silences of the Middle Ages* (Cambridge, Mass.: Harvard University Press, 1992), p. 299.

19. See M. Rubin, *Corpus Christi: The Eucharist in Late Medieval Culture* (New York: Cambridge University Press, 1992), p. 13 et seq.

20. A. Vauchez, *The Laity in the Middle Ages: Religious Beliefs and Devotional Practices,* ed. D. E. Bornstein, trans. M. J. Schneider (Notre Dame, Ind.: University of Notre Dame Press, 1993), pp. 99–102.

21. Duby, *The Chivalrous Society,* p. 98.

22. J. Boswell, *The Kindness of Strangers: The Abandonment of Children in Western Europe from Late Antiquity to the Renaissance* (New York: Pantheon Books, 1989), p. 24. This section relies heavily on this important work.

23. Ibid., pp. 428–429.

24. Ibid., pp. 238–239.

25. Ibid., pp. 297, 299, and the Conclusion.

26. J. F. Benton, ed. and trans., *Self and Society in Medieval France: The Memoirs of Abbot Guibert of Nogent* (New York: Harper & Row, 1970), p. 46.

27. M. Chibnall, ed. and trans., *The Ecclesiastical History of Orderic Vitalis* (Oxford: Oxford University Press, 1972), 2.xiii.

28. R. W. Southern, *Western Society and the Church in the Middle Ages* (Baltimore: Penguin Books, 1970), pp. 224–230, esp. p. 228.

29. See M. W. Labarge, *A Small Sound of the Trumpet: Women in Medieval Life* (Boston: Beacon Press, 1986), pp. 104–105.

30. J. M. Ferrante, "The Education of Women in the Middle Ages in Theory, Fact, and Fantasy," in *Beyond Their Sex: Learned Women of the European Past,* ed. P. H. Labalme (New York: New York University Press, 1980), pp. 22–24.

31. W. C. Jordan, *Women and Credit in Pre-Industrial and Developing Societies* (Philadelphia: University of Pennsylvania Press, 1993), p. 61.

32. See W. C. Jordan, *The Great Famine: Northern Europe in the Early Fourteenth Century* (Princeton, N.J.: Princeton University Press, 1996), pp. 97–102.

33. W. H. McNeill, *Plagues and Peoples* (New York: Doubleday, 1976), pp. 151–168.

34. Quoted in P. Ziegler, *The Black Death* (Harmondsworth, Eng.: Pelican Books, 1969), p. 20.

35. J. M. Rigg, trans., *The Decameron of Giovanni Boccaccio* (London: J. M. Dent & Sons, 1903), p. 6.

36. Ziegler, *The Black Death,* pp. 232–239.

37. J. Hatcher, *Plague, Population and the English Economy, 1348–1530* (London: Macmillan Education, 1986), p. 33.

38. See G. P. Cuttino, "Historical Revision: The Causes of the Hundred Years' War," *Speculum* 31 (July 1956): 463–472.

39. J. Barnie, *War in Medieval English Society: Social Values and the Hundred Years' War* (Ithaca, N.Y.: Cornell University Press, 1974), p. 34.

40. Quoted ibid., p. 73.

41. Ibid., pp. 72–73.

42. See G. O. Sayles, *The King's Parliament of England* (New York: W. W. Norton, 1974), app., pp. 137–141.

43. Quoted in J. H. Smith, *The Great Schism 1378: The Disintegration of the Medieval Papacy* (New York: Weybright & Talley, 1970), p. 141.

44. Hanawalt, *The Ties That Bound,* p. 197. This section leans heavily on Hanawalt's important work.

45. Ibid., pp. 194–204.

46. See D. Herlihy, *Medieval Households* (Cambridge, Mass.: Harvard University Press, 1985), pp. 103–111.

47. L. L. Otis, *Prostitution in Medieval Society: The History of an Urban Institution in Languedoc* (Chicago: University of Chicago Press, 1987), p. 2.

48. Ibid., pp. 118–130.

49. See R. H. Helmholz, *Marriage Litigation in Medieval England* (Cambridge: Cambridge University Press, 1974), pp. 28–29 and passim.

50. See M. C. Howell, *Women, Production, and Patriarchy in Late Medieval Cities* (Chicago: University of Chicago Press, 1986), pp. 134–135.

51. A. F. Scott, ed., *Everyone a Witness: The Plantagenet Age* (New York: Thomas Y. Crowell, 1976), p. 263.

52. Quoted in M. Bloch, *French Rural History,* trans. J. Sondeimer (Berkeley: University of California Press, 1966), p. 169.

53. C. Stephenson and G. F. Marcham, eds., *Sources of English Constitutional History,* rev. ed. (New York: Harper & Row, 1972), p. 225.

54. Quoted in R. Bartlett, *The Making of Europe: Conquest, Colonization and Cultural Change, 950–1350* (Princeton, N.J.: Princeton University Press, 1993), p. 205.

55. Quoted ibid., p. 215.

56. Quoted ibid., p. 224.

57. Quoted ibid., p. 228.

58. Ibid., p. 233.

59. Ibid., p. 238.

60. Quoted ibid., p. 239.

61. See M. Keen, *English Society in the Later Middle Ages, 1348–1500* (New York: Penguin Books, 1990), pp. 219–239.

SUGGESTED READING

For the new currents of thought in the central Middle Ages, see M. T. Clanchy, *Abelard: A Medieval Life* (1997), which incorporates the most recent international research, and C. H. Haskins, *The Renaissance of the Twelfth Century* (1971), a classic. For the development of literacy among laypeople and the formation of a literate mentality, the advanced student should see M. T. Clanchy, *From Memory to Written Record: England, 1066–1307,* 2d ed. (1992). Written by outstanding scholars in a variety of fields, R. L. Benson and G. Constable with C. D. Lanham, eds., *Renaissance and Renewal in the Twelfth Century* (1982), contains an invaluable collection of articles.

On the medieval universities, H. De Ridder-Symoens, ed., *A History of the University in Europe.* Vol. 1: *Universities in the Middle Ages* (1991), offers good interpretations by leading scholars. For the beginnings of Scholasticism and humanism, see the essential R. W. Southern, *Scholastic Humanism and the Unification of Western Europe,* vol. 1 (1994).

F. and J. Gies, *Cathedral, Forge, and Waterwheel* (1993), provides an illustrated survey of medieval technological achievements. The following studies are valuable for the evolution and development of the Gothic style: J. Harvey, *The Master Builders* (1971); P. Frankl, *The Gothic* (1960); and J. Bony, *French Gothic Architecture of the Twelfth and Thirteenth Centuries* (1983). C. A. Bruzelius, *The Thirteenth-Century Church at St. Denis* (1985), traces later reconstruction of the church. J. Gimpel, *The Medieval Machine: The Industrial Revolution of the Middle Ages* (1977), discusses the mechanical and scientific problems involved in early industrialization and shows how construction affected the medieval environment.

On troubadour poetry, see, in addition to the title by Wilhelm cited in the Notes, M. Bogin, *The Women Troubadours* (1980).

The following works are helpful for an understanding of medieval heresy: M. Lambert, *Medieval Heresy: Popular Movements from the Gregorian Reform to the Reformation,* rev. ed. (1992); E. Peters, *Heresy and Authority in Medieval Europe* (1980), *Inquisition* (1989), and *Torture* (1985); and R. Kieckhefer, *Magic in the Middle Ages* (1990).

The conflict between Pope Boniface VIII and the kings of France and England is well treated in J. R. Strayer, *The Reign of Philip the Fair* (1980), and M. Prestwich, *Edward I* (1988), both sound and important biographies.

Students seeking further elaboration of the material on social history will find the titles by Boswell, Duby, Hanawalt, Langdon, and Vauchez cited in the Notes especially valuable. For a broad treatment of frontier regions, see R. Bartlett, *The Making of Europe: Conquest, Colonization and Cultural Change, 950–1350* (1993).

The student interested in aspects of medieval slavery, serfdom, or the peasantry should see P. Bonnassie, *From Slavery to Feudalism* (1991); P. Freedman, *The Origins of Peasant Servitude in Medieval Catalonia* (1991); and the highly important work of W. C. Jordan, *From Servitude to Freedom: Manumission in the Sénonais in the Thirteenth Century* (1986).

On the religion of the people, in addition to the work by Vauchez cited in the Notes, two studies are recommended: R. and C. Brooke, *Popular Religion in the Middle Ages* (1984), a readable synthesis; and T. J. Heffernan, *Sacred Biography: Saints and Their Biographers in the Middle Ages* (1992), a study of the goals, assumptions, and audiences of saints' lives.

For the origins and status of the nobility in the central Middle Ages, students are strongly urged to see the studies by Duby cited in the Notes. Social mobility among both aristocracy and peasantry is discussed in T. Evergates, *Feudal Society in the Bailliage of Troyes Under the Counts of Champagne, 1152–1284* (1976).

On the monks, see the titles listed in the Suggested Reading for Chapter 7. B. D. Hill's articles "Benedictines" and "Cistercian Order," in J. R. Strayer, ed., *Dictionary of the Middle Ages,* vols. 2 and 3 (1982 and 1983), are broad surveys of the premier monastic orders with useful bibliographies. B. Harvey, *Living and Dying in England: The Monastic Experience, 1100–1540* (1993), has valuable material on monastic diet, clothing, routine, sickness, and death. L. J. Lekai, *The Cistercians: Ideals and Reality* (1977), synthesizes research on the white monks and carries their story down to the twentieth century. For a sound study of a uniquely English monastic order, see B.

Golding, *Gilbert of Sempringham and the Gilbertine Order, c. 1130–1300* (1995). J. Burton, *Monastic and Religious Orders in Britain, 1000–1300* (1995), treats many often neglected issues. B. P. McGuire, *Friendship and Community: The Monastic Experience, 350–1250* (1988), explores monastic friendships within the context of religious communities. Both W. Braunfels, *Monasteries of Western Europe: The Architecture of the Orders* (1972), and C. Brooke, *The Monastic World* (1974), have splendid illustrations and good bibliographies. The best study of medieval English Cistercian architecture is P. Fergusson, *Architecture of Solitude: Cistercian Abbeys in Twelfth Century England* (1984).

For women and children, in addition to the titles by Labarge and Boswell cited in the Notes, see B. Hanawalt, *Growing Up in Medieval London: The Experience of Childhood in History* (1993), which has exciting material on class and gender, apprenticeship, and the culture of matrimony; and C. Brooke, *The Medieval Idea of Marriage* (1991), which answers his question, "What is marriage and what sets it apart from other human relationships?" J. M. Bennett, *Women in the Medieval English Countryside* (1987), is an important and pioneering study of women in rural, preindustrial society. Also useful are A. Macfarlane, *Marriage and Love in England, 1300–1840* (1987), and B. Hanawalt, ed., *Women and Work in Preindustrial Europe* (1986), which describes the activities of women as alewives, midwives, businesswomen, nurses, and servants.

For further treatment of nuns, see J. K. McNamara, *Sisters in Arms* (1996), a broad survey tracing the lives of religious women, from the mothers of the Egyptian desert to the twentieth century; B. Newman, *Sister of Wisdom: St. Hildegard's Theology of the Feminine* (1987), a learned and lucidly written study; S. Elkins, *Holy Women in Twelfth-Century England* (1985); C. Bynum, *Jesus as Mother: Studies in the Spirituality of the High Middle Ages* (1984), which contains valuable articles on facets of women's religious history and an excellent contrast of the differing spirituality of monks and nuns; and C. Bynum, *Holy Feast and Holy Fast* (1987), which treats the significance of food for nuns and others in medieval society. For health and medical care, B. Rowland, *Medieval Woman's Guide to Health* (1981), makes very interesting reading.

The best starting point for study of the great epidemic that swept the European continent is D. Herlihy, *The Black Death and the Transformation of the West* (1997), a fine treatment of the causes and cultural consequences of the disease. For the social implications of the Black Death, see L. Poos, *A Rural Society After the Black Death: Essex, 1350–1525* (1991); G. Huppert, *After the Black Death: A Social History of Early Modern Europe* (1986); and W. H. McNeill, *Plagues and Peoples* (1976). For the economic effects of the plague, see J. Hatcher, *Plague, Population, and the English Economy, ca. 1300–1450* (1977). The older study of P. Ziegler, *The Black Death* (1969), remains important.

For the background and early part of the long military conflicts of the fourteenth and fifteenth centuries, see the provocative M. M. Vale, *The Origins of the Hundred Years War: The Angevin Legacy, 1250–1340* (1996). See also C. Allmand, *The Hundred Years War: England and France at War, ca 1300–1450* (1988). The broad survey of J. Keegan, *A History of Warfare* (1993), contains a useful summary of significant changes in military technology during the war. J. Keegan, *The Face of Battle* (1977), Chap. 2, "Agincourt," describes what war meant to the ordinary soldier. For strategy, tactics, armaments, and costumes of war, see H. W. Koch, *Medieval Warfare* (1978), a beautifully illustrated book.

T. F. Glick, *From Muslim Fortress to Christian Castle: Social and Cultural Change in Medieval Spain* (1995), explores the reorganization of Spanish society after the reconquest, bringing considerable cultural change. P. C. Maddern, *Violence and Social Order: East Anglia, 1422–1442* (1991), deals with social disorder in eastern England. I. M. W. Harvey, *Jack Cade's Rebellion of 1450* (1991), is an important work in local history. Students are especially encouraged to consult the brilliant work of E. L. Ladurie, *The Peasants of Languedoc,* trans. J. Day (1976). J. C. Holt, *Robin Hood* (1982), is a soundly researched and highly readable study of the famous outlaw.

D. Herlihy, *Women, Family and Society in Medieval Europe: Historical Essays, 1978–1991* (1995), contains several valuable articles dealing with the later Middle Ages, while the exciting study by B. Gottlieb, *The Family in the Western World from the Black Death to the Industrial Age* (1993), explores the family's political, emotional, and cultural roles. For prostitution, see, in addition to the title by Otis cited in the Notes, J. Rossiaud, *Medieval Prostitution* (1995), a very good treatment of prostitution's social and cultural significance.

For women's economic status in the late medieval period, see the titles by Howell and Hanawalt cited in the Notes. J. S. Bennett, *Ale, Beer, and Brewsters in England: Women's Work in a Changing World, 1300–1600* (1996), uses the experience of women in the brewing industry to stress the persistence of patriarchal attitudes. P. J. P. Goldberg, *Women, Work, and Life Cycle in a Medieval Economy: Women in York and Yorkshire, c 1300–1520* (1992), explores the relationship between economic opportunity and marriage.

The poetry of Dante, Chaucer, and Villon may be read in the following editions: D. Sayers, trans., *Dante: The Divine Comedy,* 3 vols. (1963); N. Coghill, trans., *Chaucer's Canterbury Tales* (1977); P. Dale, trans., *The Poems of Villon* (1973). The social setting of *Canterbury Tales* is brilliantly evoked in D. W. Robertson, Jr., *Chaucer's London* (1968). Students interested in further study of Christine de Pisan should consult A. J. Kennedy, *Christine de Pisan: A Bibliographical Guide* (1984), and C. C. Willard, *Christine de Pisan: Her Life and Works* (1984).

For religion and lay piety, A. D. Brown, *Popular Piety in Late Medieval England: The Diocese of Salisbury, 1250–1550* (1995), is a good case study showing the importance of guilds, charity, and heresy and how they affected parish life. F. Oakley, *The Western Church in the Later Middle Ages* (1979), is an excellent broad survey, while R. N. Swanson, *Church and Society in Late Medieval England* (1989), provides a good synthesis of English conditions. S. Ozment, *The Age of Reform, 1250–1550* (1980), discusses the Great Schism and the conciliar movement in the intellectual context of the ecclesiopolitical tradition of the Middle Ages. The important achievement of A. Vauchez, *The Laity in the Middle Ages: Religious Beliefs and Devotional Practices,* ed. D. E. Bornstein and trans. M. J. Schneider (1993), explores many aspects of popular piety and contains considerable material on women.

Christine de Pisan (1363?–1434?)

The passage below is taken from The Book of the City of Ladies, *one of the many writings of Christine de Pisan. Christine was a highly educated woman who wrote prolifically in French, her native tongue. Her patron was the queen of France. Christine wrote amid the chaos of the Hundred Years' War about a wide range of topics. The excerpt below is not reflective of all French women. Rather, it focuses on the behavior of courtly women only. And it expresses Christine's and her patron's views about women's role in the creation and stabilization of an elite court culture during a time of political and social upheaval.*

Just as the good shepherd takes care that his lambs are maintained in health, and if any of them becomes mangy, separates it from the flock for fear that it may infect the others, so the princess will take upon herself the responsibility for the care of her women servants and companions, who she will ensure are all good and chaste, for she will not want to have any other sort of person around her. Since it is the established custom that knights and squires and all men (especially certain men) who associate with women have a habit of pleading for love tokens from them and trying to seduce them, the wise princess will so enforce her regulations that there will be no visitor to her court so fool-hardy as to dare to whisper privately with any of her women or give the appearance of seduction. If he does it or if he is noticed giving any sign of it, immediately she should take such an attitude towards him that he will not dare to importune them any more. The lady who is chaste will want all her women to be so too, on pain of being banished from her company.

She will want them to amuse themselves with decent games, such that men cannot mock, as they do the games of some women, though at the time the men laugh and join in. The women should restrain themselves with seemly conduct among knights and squires and all men. They should speak demurely and sweetly and, whether in dances or other amusements, divert and enjoy themselves decorously and without wantonness. They must not be frolicsome, forward, or boisterous in speech, expression, bearing or laughter. They must not go about with their heads raised like wild deer. This kind of behaviour would be very unseemly and greatly derisory in a woman of the court, in whom there should be more modesty, good manners and courteous behaviour than in any others, for where there is most honour there ought to be the most perfect manners and behaviour. Women of the court in any country would be deceiving themselves very much if they imagined that it was more appropriate for them to be frolicsome and saucy than for other women. For this reason we hope that in time to come our doctrine in this book may be carried into many kingdoms, so that it may be valuable in all places where there might be any shortcoming.

We say generally to all women of all countries that it is the duty of every lady and maiden of the court, whether she be young or old, to be more prudent, more decorous, and better schooled in all things than other women. The ladies of the court ought to be models of all good things and all honour to other women, and if they do otherwise they will do no honour to their mistress nor to themselves. In addition, so that everything may be consistent in modesty, the wise princess will wish that the clothing and the ornaments of her women, though they be appropriately beautiful and rich, be of a modest fashion, well fitting and seemly, neat and properly cared for. There should be no deviation from this modesty nor any immodesty in the matter of plunging necklines or other excesses.

In all things the wise princess will keep her women in order just as the good and prudent abbess does her convent, so that bad reports about it may not circulate in the town, in distant regions or anywhere else. This princess will be so feared and respected because of the wise management that she will be seen to practise that no man or woman will be so foolhardy as to disobey her commands in any respect or to question her will, for there is no doubt that a lady is more feared and respected and held in greater reverence when she is seen to be wise and chaste and of firm behaviour. But there is nothing wrong or inconsistent in her being kind and gentle, for the mere look of the wise lady and her subdued reception is enough of a sign to correct those men and women who err and to inspire them with fear.

Questions for Analysis

1. How did Christine think courtly women should behave around men?

2. How did women fit into the larger picture of court culture? What was their role at court?

Source: Christine de Pisan, "The Book of the City of Ladies," in *Treasures of the City of Ladies,* trans. Sarah Lawson (Penguin, 1985), pp. 74–76.

Christine de Pisan, shown here producing her *Collected Works,* was devoted to scholarship. *(British Library)*

14 Civilizations of the Americas, ca 400–1500

Gold mask assemblage, at least 1,300 years old. Excavated from an ancient Peruvian tomb in the town of Sipán. *(Sipán Archaeological Project. Photo: Y. Yoshii)*

Between approximately 300 B.C. and A.D. 1500, sophisticated civilizations developed in the Western Hemisphere. But unlike most other societies in the world, which felt the influences of other cultures—sub-Saharan Africa, for example, experienced the impact of Muslims, Asians, and Europeans—American societies grew in almost total isolation from other peoples. Then, in 1501–1502, the Florentine explorer Amerigo Vespucci (1451–1512) sailed down the eastern coast of South America to Brazil. Convinced that he had found a new world, Vespucci published an account of his voyage. Shortly thereafter the German geographer Martin Waldseemüller proposed that this new world be called "America" to preserve Vespucci's memory. Initially applied only to South America, by the end of the sixteenth century the term *America* was used for both continents in the Western Hemisphere.

Our use of the word *Indian* for the indigenous peoples of the Americas stems from early European explorers' geographical misconceptions of where they were—they believed they were near the East Indies (see page 506). South America contained a great diversity of peoples, cultures, and linguistic groups. Modern scholars estimate that around 1500 there were 350 tribal groups, 15 distinct cultural centers, and 150 linguistic stocks. Historians and anthropologists have tended to focus attention on the Maya, Incas, and Aztecs, but the inhabitants of those three empires represent a minority of the total indigenous population; they lived in geographical regions that covered a small percentage of Mesoamerica and South America. Other native peoples included the Aymaras, Caribs, Chibchas, Chichimecas, Ge, Guaranis, Mapuches, Otonis, Pueblos, Quibayas, Tupis, and Zapotecs (Map 14.1). These peoples shared no unified sense of themselves as "Indians." None of their languages had the word *Indian*. Nor was there any tendency among these peoples to unite in a common resistance to the foreign invaders.[1] Rather, when confronting Europeans, each group or polity sought the most advantageous situation for itself alone. Of course, the idea of "discovery" meant nothing to them. Because much more is known about the Aztecs, Maya, and Incas than about other native peoples, the focus of this chapter is on them. The central feature of early American societies, however, is their great indigenous and cultural diversity.

- What is the geography of the Americas, and how did it shape the lives of the native peoples?

- What patterns of social and political organization did the Maya, Aztecs, and Incas display?
- What were the significant cultural achievements of the Maya, Aztecs, and Incas?

This chapter will consider these questions.

THE GEOGRAPHY AND PEOPLES OF THE AMERICAS

The distance from the Bering Strait, which separates Asia from North America, to the southern tip of South America is about eleven thousand miles. A mountain range extends all the way from Alaska to the tip of South America, crossing Central America from northwest to southeast and making for rugged country along virtually the entire western coast of both continents.

Scholars use the term *Mesoamerica* to designate the area of present-day Mexico and Central America. Mexico is dominated by high plateaus bounded by coastal plains. Geographers have labeled the plateau regions "cold lands," the valleys between the plateaus "temperate lands," and the Gulf and Pacific coastal regions "hot lands." The Caribbean coast of Central America—modern Belize, Guatemala, Honduras, Nicaragua, El Salvador, Costa Rica, and Panama—is characterized by thick jungle lowlands, heavy rainfall, and torrid heat; it is an area generally unhealthy for humans. Central America's western uplands, with their more temperate climate and good agricultural land, support the densest population in the region.

Like Africa, South America is a continent of extremely varied terrain (see Map 14.4). The entire western coast is edged by the Andes, the highest mountain range in the Western Hemisphere. On the east coast, another mountain range—the Brazilian Highlands—accounts for one-fourth of the area of modern-day Brazil. Three-fourths of South America—almost the entire interior of the continent—is lowland plains. The Amazon River, at 4,000 miles the second-longest river in the world, bisects the north-central part of the continent, draining 2.7 million square miles of land. Tropical lowland rain forests with dense growth and annual rainfall in excess of 80 inches extend from the Amazon and Orinoco River basins northward all the way to southern Mexico.

Most scholars believe that people began crossing the Bering Strait from Russian Siberia between fifty

MAP 14.1 The Peoples of South America   The major indigenous peoples of South America represented a great variety of languages and cultures. (*Source: Adapted from* The Times Atlas of World History, *3d ed. © Times Books. Reproduced by permission of HarperCollins Publishers Ltd.*)

thousand and twenty thousand years ago, when the strait was narrower than it is today. Skeletal finds indicate that these immigrants belonged to several ethnic groups now known collectively as American Indians, or Amerindians. Amerindians were nomadic peoples who lived by hunting small animals, fishing, and gathering wild fruits. As soon as an area had been exploited and a group had grown too large for the land to support, some families broke off from the group and moved on, usually southward. Gradually the newcomers spread throughout the Americas, losing contact with one another.

By the late fifteenth century, three kinds of Amerindian societies had emerged. First, largely nomadic groups depended on hunting, fishing, and gathering for subsistence; they had changed little from their ancestors who had crossed the Bering Strait thousands of years before. A second group of Amerindians, whom historians label sedentary or semi-sedentary, relied primarily on the domestication of plants for food; they led a settled or semi-settled farming life. A third group lived in large, sometimes densely populated settlements supported by agricultural surpluses; specialization of labor, large-scale construction projects, and different social classes characterized this group. These complex cultures existed only in Mesoamerica and western South America. In 1492 the polities of the Anáhuacs (Aztecs), Maya, and Tahuantinsuyas (Incas) were perhaps the best representatives of the third group.[2]

Amerindians in central Mexico built *chinampas,* floating gardens. They dredged soil from the bottom of a lake or pond, placed the soil on mats of woven twigs, and then planted crops in the soil. Chinampas were enormously productive, yielding up to three harvests a year. So extensive was this method of agriculture that central Mexico became known as the chinampas region. In Peru, meanwhile, people terraced the slopes of the Andes with stone retaining walls to keep the hillsides from sliding. Both chinampas and terraced slopes required the large labor force that became available with stable settlement.

Agricultural advancement had definitive social and political consequences. Careful cultivation of the land brought a reliable and steady food supply, which contributed to a relatively high fertility rate and in turn to a population boom. Because corn and potatoes require much less labor than does grain, Amerindian civilizations had a large pool of people who were not involved in agriculture and thus were available to construct religious and political buildings and serve in standing armies.[3]

 ## MESOAMERICAN CIVILIZATIONS FROM THE OLMECS TO THE TOLTECS

Several American civilizations arose between roughly 1500 B.C. and A.D. 900: the civilizations of the Olmecs, the Maya, Teotihuacán, and the Toltecs. Archaeological investigations of these civilizations are under way, and more questions than answers about them remain, but scholars generally accept a few basic conclusions about them.

Scholars believe that the Olmec civilization is the oldest of the early advanced Amerindian civilizations. Olmec culture, based on agriculture, spread over regions in central Mexico that lie thousands of miles apart. The Olmec practice of building scattered ceremonial centers found its highest cultural expression in the civilization of the Maya. The Maya occupied the area of present-day Yucatán, the highland crescent of eastern Chiapas in Mexico, and much of Guatemala and western Honduras. In the central plateau of Mexico, an "empire" centered at Teotihuacán arose. Scholars hotly debate whether the Teotihuacán territory constituted an empire, but they agree that Teotihuacán society was heavily stratified and that it exercised military, religious, and political power over a wide area. The Toltecs, whose culture adopted many features of the Teotihuacán and Olmec civilizations, were the last advanced Amerindian civilization before the rise of the Aztecs.

The Olmecs

The word *Olmec* comes from an Aztec term for the peoples living in southern Veracruz and western Tabasco, Mexico, between about 1500 and 300 B.C. They did not call themselves Olmecs or consider themselves a unified group, but their culture penetrated and influenced all parts of Mesoamerica. All later Mesoamerican cultures derived from the Olmecs. Modern knowledge of the Olmecs rests entirely on archaeological evidence—pyramids, jade objects, axes, figurines, and stone monuments.

The Olmecs cultivated maize, squash, beans, and other plants and supplemented that diet with wild game and fish. Originally they lived in egalitarian societies that had no distinctions based on status or wealth. After 1500 B.C., more complex, hierarchical societies evolved. Anthropologists call these societies chieftains. Most peoples continued to live in small hamlets, villages, and towns along the rivers of the region, while the leaders of the societies resided in the large cities to-day known as San Lorenzo, La Venta, Tres Zapotes, and Laguna de los Cerros. These cities contained palaces (large private houses) for the elite, large plazas, temples (ritual centers), ball courts, water reservoirs, and carved stone drains for the disposal of wastes. The Olmecs developed a sophisticated system of symbols, as shown in their art; this system clearly influenced the Maya (see page 419). They invented monumental stone sculptures (see below), a characteristic of every subsequent Mesoamerican civilization. In starting a tradition

of ruler portraits in stone, the Olmecs also laid the foundations for a practice adopted by the Maya and other peoples. They had sacred ceremonial sites where they sometimes practiced human sacrifice. They erected special courts on which men played a game with a hard rubber ball that was both religious ritual and sport. Finally, the Olmecs engaged in long-distance trade, exchanging rubber, cacao (from which chocolate is made), pottery, figurines, jaguar pelts, and the services of painters and sculptors for obsidian (a hard, black volcanic glass from which paddle-shaped weapons were

Colossal Head Monument from San Lorenzo   Measuring nine feet, four inches in height, and over ten tons in weight, this basalt head is a superb example of Olmec sculpture intended as architecture. The facial features have led some scholars to suggest African influences, but that hypothesis has not been proven. *(Nathaniel Tarn/Photo Researchers, Inc.)*

made), basalt, iron ore, shells, and various perishable goods. Commercial networks extended as far away as central and western Mexico and the Pacific coast.[4]

Around 900 B.C. San Lorenzo, the center of early Olmec culture, was destroyed, probably by migrating peoples from the north, and power passed to La Venta in Tabasco. Archaeological excavation at La Venta has uncovered a huge volcano-shaped pyramid. Standing 110 feet high at an inaccessible site on an island in the Tonala River, the so-called Great Pyramid was the center of the Olmec religion. The upward thrust of this monument, like that of the cathedrals of medieval Europe, may have represented the human effort to get closer to the gods. Built of huge stone slabs, the Great Pyramid required, scholars estimated, some 800,000 man-hours of labor. It testifies to the region's bumper harvests, which were able to support a labor force large enough to build such a monument. Around 300 B.C. La Venta fell, and Tres Zapotes, 100 miles to the northwest, became the leading Olmec site.

Olmec ceremonialism, magnificent sculpture, skillful stonework, social organization, and writing were important cultural advances that paved the way for the developments of the Classic period (A.D. 300–900), the golden age of Mesoamerican civilization. Just as the ancient Sumerians laid the foundations for later Mesopotamian cultures (see Chapter 1), so the Olmecs heavily influenced subsequent Mesoamerican societies.

MAP 14.2 The Maya World, A.D. 300–900   Archaeologists have discovered the ruins of dozens of Maya city-states. Only the largest of them are shown here. Called the "Greeks of the New World," the Maya perfected the only written language in the Western Hemisphere, developed a sophisticated political system and a flourishing trade network, and created elegant art.

The Maya of Central America

In the Classic period, the Maya attained a level of intellectual and artistic achievement equaled by no other Amerindian people and by few peoples anywhere. The Maya developed a sophisticated system of writing, perhaps derived partly from the Olmecs. They invented a calendar more accurate than the European Gregorian calendar. And they made advances in mathematics that Europeans did not match for several centuries.

Who were the Maya, and where did they come from? What was the basis of their culture? What is the significance of their intellectual and artistic achievement? The word *Maya* seems to derive from *Zamna,* the name of a Maya god. Linguistic evidence leads scholars to believe that the first Maya were a small North American Indian group that emigrated from southern Oregon and northern California to the western highlands of Guatemala. Between the third and second millennia B.C., various groups, including the Cholans and Tzeltalans, broke away from the parent group and moved north and east into the Yucatán peninsula. The Cholan-speaking

Maya, who occupied the area during the time of great cultural achievement, apparently created the culture.

Maya culture rested on agriculture. The staple crop in Mesoamerica was maize (corn). In 1972 a geographer and an aerial photographer studying the Campeche region of the Yucatán peninsula (Map 14.2) proved that the Maya practiced intensive agriculture in raised, narrow rectangular plots that they built above the low-lying, seasonally flooded land bordering rivers. Because of poor soil caused by heavy tropical rainfall and the fierce sun, farmers may also have relied on *milpa* for growing maize. Using this method, farmers cut down the trees in a patch of forest and set the wood and brush afire. They then used a stick to poke holes through the ash and planted maize seeds in the holes. A milpa (the word refers to both the area and the method) produced for only two years, after which it had to lie fallow for between four and seven years. Throughout the Yucatán peninsula, the method of burning and planting in the fertile ashes, known as *swidden agriculture,* remains the typical farming practice today.

In addition to maize, the Maya grew beans, squash, chili peppers, some root crops, and fruit trees. Turkeys were domesticated, but barkless dogs that were fattened on corn seem to have been the main source of protein. In the Yucatán, men trapped fish along the shores. The discovery of rich Maya textiles all over Mesoamerica indicates that cotton was widely exported.

The raised-field and milpa systems of intensive agriculture yielded food sufficient to support large population centers. The entire Maya region could have had as many as 14 million inhabitants. At Uxmal, Uaxactún, Copán, Piedras Negras, Tikal, Palenque, and Chichén Itzá (see Map 14.2), archaeologists have uncovered the palaces of nobles, elaborate pyramids where nobles were buried, engraved *steles* (stone-slab monuments), masonry temples, altars, sophisticated polychrome pottery, and courts for games played with a rubber ball. The largest site, Tikal, may have had forty thousand people. Since these centers lacked industrial activities,

scholars avoid calling them cities. Rather they were religious and ceremonial centers.

Public fairs accompanying important religious festivals in population centers seem to have been the major Maya economic institutions. Jade, obsidian, beads of red spiny oyster shell, lengths of cloth, and cacao (chocolate) beans—all in high demand in the Mesoamerican world—served as the medium of exchange. The extensive trade among Maya communities, plus a common language, promoted the union of the peoples of the region and gave them a common sense of identity. Merchants trading beyond Maya regions, such as with the Mije-speaking peoples of the Pacific coast, the post-Olmec people of the Gulf coast, the Zapotecs of the Valley of Oaxaca, and the Teotihuacanos of the central valley of Mexico, were considered state ambassadors bearing "gifts" to royal neighbors, who reciprocated with their own "gifts." Since this long-distance trade played an important part in international

Cylindrical Vessel Because the Maya suffered a high death rate from warfare, sacrificial ritual, and natural causes, the subject of death preoccupied them. Many art objects depict death as a journey into Xibalba, the Maya hell, and to rebirth for the Maya in children and grandchildren who replace them. Here three Xibalbans receive a sacrificial head on a drum. The scrawny torso of one has the look of starvation, and the excrement implies a revolting smell. The next figure, with a skeletal head, insect wings, and a distended stomach, suggests a parasitic disease. A common if nauseating scene. (© *Justin Kerr 1985. Courtesy Houston Art Museum*)

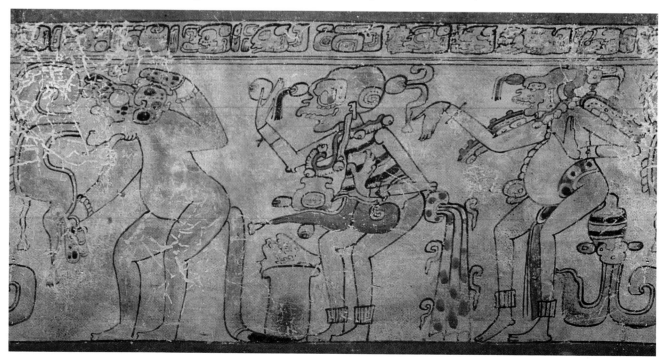

relations, the merchants conducting it were high nobles or even members of the royal family.

Lacking iron tools until a few centuries before the Spanish conquest and beasts of burden until after the conquest, how were goods transported to distant regions? The extensive networks of rivers and swamps were the main arteries of transportation; over them large canoes carved out of hardwood trees carried cargoes of cloth and maize. Wide roads also linked Maya centers; on the roads merchants and lords were borne in litters, goods and produce on human backs. Trade produced considerable wealth that seems to have been concentrated in a noble class, for the Maya had no distinctly mercantile class. They did have a sharply defined hierarchical society. A hereditary elite owned private land, defended society, carried on commercial activities, exercised political power, and directed religious rituals. The intellectual class also belonged to the ruling nobility. The rest of the people were free workers, serfs, and slaves.

The Maya developed a system of hieroglyphic writing with 850 characters and used it to record chronology, religion, and astronomy in books made of bark paper and deerskin. The recent deciphering of this writing has demonstrated that inscriptions on steles are actually historical documents recording the births, accessions, marriages, wars, and deaths of Maya kings. An understanding of the civilization's dynastic history allows

Palace Doorway Lintel at Yaxchilan, Mexico Lady Xoc, principal wife of King Shield-Jaguar, who holds a torch over her, pulls a thorn-lined rope through her tongue to sanctify with her blood the birth of a younger wife's child—reflecting the importance of blood sacrifice in Maya culture. The elaborate headdresses and clothes of the couple show their royal status. (© *Justin Kerr 1985*)

scholars to interpret more accurately Maya pictorial imagery and to detect patterns in Maya art. They are finding that the imagery explicitly portrays the text in pictorial scenes and on stelar carvings.[5]

In the sixteenth century, Spanish friars taught Maya students to write their language in the Roman script so that the friars could understand Maya culture. Maya deities and sacrificial customs, however, provoked Spanish outrage. To hasten Maya conversion to Christianity, the priests tried to extirpate all native religion by destroying Maya sculpture and books. Only one Maya hieroglyphic book survived: the *Popul Vuh,* or Book of Council, which was written in European script by a young Quiché noble. Scholars call this document the Maya "Bible," meaning that like the Judeo-Christian Scriptures, the *Popul Vuh* gives the Maya view of the creation of the world, concepts of good and evil, and the entire nature and purpose of the living experience.

A method of measuring and recording time to arrange and commemorate events in the life of a society and to plan the agricultural and ceremonial year is a basic feature of all advanced societies. From careful observation of the earth's movements around the sun, the Maya invented a calendar of eighteen 20-day months and one 5-day month, for a total of 365 days. Using a system of bars (— = 5) and dots (○ = 1), the Maya devised a form of mathematics based on the vigesimal (20) rather than the decimal (10) system. They proved themselves masters of abstract knowledge—notably in astronomy, mathematics, calendric development, and the recording of history.

Maya civilization lasted about a thousand years, reaching its peak between approximately A.D. 600 and 900, the period when the Tang Dynasty was flourishing in China, Islam was spreading in the Middle East, and Carolingian rulers were extending their sway in Europe. Between the eighth and tenth centuries, the Maya abandoned their cultural and ceremonial centers, and Maya civilization collapsed. Archaeologists and historians attribute the collapse to some combination of foreign invasions led by peoples attracted to the wealth of the great Maya centers, domestic revolts of subject peoples, disease, overpopulation resulting from crop failures, and the acquisition of so much territory by expansionist kings that rulers could not govern effectively.

In 1527 the Spaniards faced a formidable task when they attempted to conquer the Yucatán. The Maya polity did not involve a single unified political entity, as the Aztecs and Incas did; instead the Maya had several states. The Spaniards had great trouble imposing a cen-

tralized government on a divided people using guerrilla and hit-and-run tactics. Although the Spaniards established some degree of control in 1545, only in 1697 did the last independent Maya group fall to the Europeans.

Teotihuacán and Toltec Civilizations

During the Classic period, the Teotihuacán Valley in central Mexico witnessed the flowering of a remarkable civilization built by a new people from regions east and south of the Valley of Mexico. The city of Teotihuacán had a population of over 200,000—larger than any European city at the time. The inhabitants were stratified into distinct social classes. The rich and powerful resided in a special precinct, in houses of palatial splendor. Ordinary working people, tradespeople, artisans, and obsidian craftsmen lived in apartment compounds, or *barrios,* on the edge of the city. The inhabitants of the barrios seem to have been very poor and related by kinship ties and perhaps by shared common ritual interests. Agricultural laborers lived outside the city. Teotihuacán was a great commercial center, the entrepôt for trade and culture for all of Mesoamerica. It was also the ceremonial center of an entire society, a capital filled with artworks, a mecca that attracted thousands of pilgrims a year.

In the center of the city stood the Pyramids of the Sun and the Moon. The Pyramid of the Sun is built of sun-dried bricks and faced with stone. Each of its sides is seven hundred feet long and two hundred feet high. The smaller Pyramid of the Moon is similar in construction. In lesser temples, natives and outlanders worshiped the rain-god and the feathered serpent later called Quetzalcoatl. These gods were associated with the production of corn, the staple of the people's diet.

Although Teotihuacán dominated Mesoamerican civilization during the Classic period, other centers also flourished. In the isolated valley of Oaxaca at modern-day Monte Albán (see Map 14.3), for example, Zapotecan-speaking peoples established a great religious center whose temples and elaborately decorated tombs testify to the wealth of the nobility. The art—and probably the entire culture—of Monte Albán and other centers derived from Teotihuacán.

As had happened to San Lorenzo and La Venta, Teotihuacán collapsed before invaders. Around A.D. 700 less-developed peoples from the southwest burned Teotihuacán; Monte Albán fell shortly afterward. By 900 the golden age of Mesoamerica had ended. There followed an interregnum known as the "Time of Troubles" (ca 800–1000), characterized by disorder and ex-

Individuals in Society

Quetzalcoatl

Quetzalcoatl, or Precious Feather Snake. (© Musée de l'Homme)

Legends are popular beliefs about someone or something that are handed down from the past. They often lack a basis in historical—that is, verifiable—evidence, but they are generally believed to embody the ideals of a people or society. When legends become involved in religious faith, they acquire an established quality and become part of a people's core beliefs. Faith has been defined as "the confident assurance of what we hope for, and conviction of what we do not see" (Hebrews 11:1). How can we be confident of hopes and dreams, certain of what we do not see? Religious faith always presents a paradox, and belief systems have played a powerful part in historical events, as the Mexica god Quetzalcoatl illustrates.

Quetzalcoatl (pronounced kat-sal-koat-al), meaning "feathered serpent," was an important figure in Aztec culture. Students of the history of religions trace his origins either to an ancient deity of the Toltecs or to a historical Toltec ruler credited with the discovery of the cereal maize. He is believed to have been a great supporter of the arts, sciences, and the calendar; he was also associated with peace. We do not know whether the historical ruler took his name from the god or, as a successful king, he was revered and deified. Considered the god of civilization, Quetzalcoatl represented to the Mexica the forces of good and light. He was pitted against the Toltecs' original tribal god, Tezcatlipoca, who stood for evil, darkness, and war. When the Aztecs absorbed Toltec culture, they adopted Quetzalcoatl and linked him with the worship of Huitzilopochtli, their war-god.

We may plausibly assume that the Toltec king Toliptzin (see page 422) took the name Quetzalcoatl. According to the "Song of Quetzalcoatl," a long Aztec glorification of Toliptzin,

He was very rich and had everything necessary to eat and drink, and the corn under his reign was in abundance. . . . And more than that the said Quetzalcoatl had all the wealth of the world, gold and silver and green stones, jade and other precious things.[1]

Whatever reality lies behind this legend, it became a cornerstone of Aztec tradition; it also played a profound role in Mexica history. Later Aztec legends describe a powerful struggle between Tezcatlipoca, who required human sacrifices, and Quetzalcoatl.

Tezcatlipoca won this battle, and the priest-king Toliptzin-Quetzalcoatl was driven into exile. As he departed, he promised to return and regain his kingdom. By a remarkable coincidence, Quetzalcoatl promised to return in 1519, the year the Spanish explorer Hernando Cortés landed in Mexico. Cortés learned the legend and exploited it for his own purposes. Native and Spanish accounts tell us that Montezuma identified Cortés with the god Quetzalcoatl. Cortés took it as his right that Montezuma should house him in the imperial palace close to the shrine of the Aztec gods (and near the imperial treasury). When, on a tour of the city, Montezuma led Cortés up the many steps of the sacred temple, the emperor stopped and said to Cortés that he must be tired with all those steps. No, Cortés replied, "we" are never tired (as all mortals, but not gods, become). When Montezuma told Cortés that he would share all that he possessed with the Spaniards and that they "must truly be the men whom his ancestors had long ago prophesized, saying that they would come from the direction of the sunrise to rule over these lands," Cortés replied that "he did indeed come from the direction of the sunrise" and that he brought the message of the one true God, Jesus Christ. The conquistador knew that Montezuma would interpret his words as meaning that he was Quetzalcoatl.

Questions for Analysis

1. Assess the role of Quetzalcoatl in the fall of the Aztec Empire.

2. What is reality—what we believe or what can be scientifically demonstrated?

1. Quoted in I. Bernal, *Mexico Before Cortez: Art, History, and Legend,* rev. ed., trans. W. Barnstone (New York: Anchor Books, 1975), p. 68.

Sources: Bernal Díaz, *The Conquest of New Spain,* trans. J. M. Cohen (New York: Penguin Books, 1978); T. Todorov, *The Conquest of America,* trans. R. Howard (New York: Harper & Row, 1984).

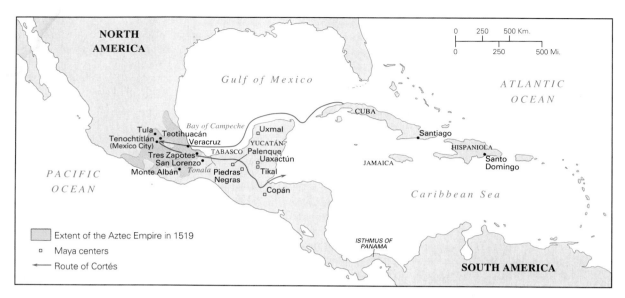

MAP 14.3 The Aztec Empire, 1519   The Aztecs controlled much of central Mexico. The Maya survived in the Yucatán peninsula and some of present-day Guatemala. Notice the number of cities.

treme militarism. Whereas nature gods and their priests seem to have governed the great cities of the earlier period, militant gods and warriors dominated the petty states that now arose. Among these states, the most powerful heir to Teotihuacán was the Toltec confederation, a weak union of strong states. The Toltecs admired the culture of their predecessors and sought to absorb and preserve it. Through intermarriage, they assimilated with the Teotihuacán people. In fact, every new Mesoamerican confederation became the cultural successor of earlier confederations.

Under Toliptzin (ca 980–1000), the Toltecs extended their hegemony over most of central Mexico. Toliptzin established his capital at Tula. Its splendor and power became legendary during his reign. (See the feature "Individuals in Society: Quetzalcoatl.")

After the reign of Toliptzin, troubles beset the Toltec state. Drought led to crop failure. Northern peoples, the Chichimecas, attacked the borders in waves. Weak, incompetent rulers could not quell domestic uprisings. When the last Toltec king committed suicide in 1174, the Toltec state collapsed. In 1224 the Chichimecas captured Tula.

The last of the Chichimecas to arrive in central Mexico were the Aztecs. As before, the vanquished strongly influenced the victors: the Aztecs absorbed the cultural achievements of the Toltecs. The Aztecs—building on Olmec, Maya, Teotihuacán, and Toltec antecedents—created the last unifying civilization in Mexico before the arrival of the Europeans.

 ## AZTEC SOCIETY: RELIGION AND WAR

Although the terms *Aztec* and *Mexica* are used interchangeably here, *Mexica* is actually the more accurate word because it is a pre-Columbian term designating the dominant ethnic people of the island capital of Tenochtitlán-Tlalelolco. Aztec derives from *Aztlan,* the legendary homeland of the Mexica people before their migration into the Valley of Mexico, is *not* a pre-Columbian word, and was popularized by nineteenth-century historians.[6]

The Aztecs who appeared in the Valley of Mexico spoke the same Nahuatl language as the Toltecs but otherwise had nothing in common with them. Poor, unwelcome, looked on as foreign barbarians, the Aztecs had to settle on a few swampy islands in Lake Texcoco. From these unpromising beginnings, they rapidly assimilated the culture of the Toltecs and in 1428 embarked on a policy of territorial expansion. By the time Cortés arrived in 1519, the Aztec confederation encompassed all of central Mexico from the Gulf of Mexico to the Pacific as far south as Guatemala (Map 14.3).

Thirty-eight subordinate provinces paid tribute to the Aztec king.

The growth of a strong mercantile class led to an influx of tropical wares and luxury goods: cotton, feathers, cocoa, skins, turquoise jewelry, and gold. The upper classes enjoyed an elegant and extravagant lifestyle; the court of Emperor Montezuma II (r. 1502–1520) was more magnificent than anything in western Europe. How, in less than two hundred years, had the Mexicans (from the Aztec word *mizquitl,* meaning "desolate land," or from *Mixitli,* the Aztec god of war) grown from an insignificant tribe of wandering nomads to a people of vast power and fabulous wealth?

The Aztecs' pictorial records attribute their success to the power of their war-god Huitzilopochtli and to their own drive and willpower. Will and determination they unquestionably had, but there is another explanation for their success: the Aztec state was geared for war. In the course of the fifteenth century, the tribesmen who had arrived in the Valley of Mexico in about 1325 transformed themselves into professional soldiers. Military campaigns continued; warriors were constantly subduing new states and crushing rebellions. A strong standing army was the backbone of the Aztec state, and war became the central feature of Mexica culture.

Warfare was a formal stylized ritual conducted according to rules whose goal was the capture, not the execution, of the enemy. Warriors hurled projectiles into their massed foes, intending to demoralize, not to kill. Then a crippling blow with his obsidian "sword" to a foe's knees or to one of the muscles in the back of the thigh enabled the Aztec warrior to bring him to the ground. Once subdued, men with ropes tied the captive and took him to the rear of the battlefield.[7]

Religion and Culture

In Mexica society, religion was the dynamic factor that transformed other aspects of the culture: economic security, social mobility, education, and especially war. War was an article of religious faith. The state religion of the Aztecs initially gave them powerful advantages over other groups in central Mexico; it inspired them to conquer vast territories in a remarkably short time.[8] But that religion also created economic and political stresses that could not easily be resolved and that ultimately contributed heavily to the society's collapse.

Chief among the Aztecs' many gods was Huitzilopochtli, who symbolized the sun blazing at high noon. The sun, the source of all life, had to be kept moving in its orbit if darkness was not to overtake the world. To keep it moving, Aztecs believed, the sun had

to be fed frequently precious fluids—that is, human blood. Human sacrifice was a sacred duty, essential for the preservation and prosperity of humankind. Black-robed priests carried out the ritual:

The victim was stretched out on his back on a slightly convex stone with his arms and legs held by four priests, while a fifth ripped him open with a flint knife and tore out his heart. The sacrifice also often took place in a manner which the Spanish described as gladiatorio: the captive was tied to a huge disk of stone . . . by a rope that left him free to move; he was armed with wooden weapons, and he had to fight several normally-armed Aztec warriors in turn. If, by an extraordinary chance, he did not succumb to their attacks, he was spared; but nearly always the "gladiator" fell, gravely wounded, and a few moments later he died on the stone, with his body opened by the black-robed, long-haired priests.[9]

Mass sacrifice was also practiced:

Mass sacrifices involving hundreds and thousands of victims could be carried out to commemorate special events. The Spanish chroniclers were told, for example, that at the dedication in 1487 of the great pyramid of Tenochtitlán, four lines of prisoners of war stretching for two miles each were sacrificed by a team of executioners who worked night and day for four days. Allotting two minutes for sacrifice, the demographer and historian Sherbourne Cook estimated that the number of victims associated with that single event was 14,100. The scale of these rituals could be dismissed as exaggerations were it not for the encounters of Spanish explorers with . . . rows of human skulls in the plazas of the Aztec cities. . . . In the plaza of Xocotlan "there were . . . more than one hundred thousand of them."[10]

The Mexica did not invent human sacrifice; it seems to have been practiced by many Mesoamerican peoples. The Maya, for example, dedicated their temples with the blood of freshly executed victims. Anthropologists have proposed several explanations—none of them completely satisfactory—for the Aztecs' practice of human sacrifice and the cannibalism that often accompanied it. Some suggest that human sacrifice served to regulate population growth. Yet ritual slaughter had been practiced by earlier peoples—the Olmecs, the Maya, the dwellers of Teotihuacán, and the Toltecs—in all likelihood before population density had reached the point of threatening the food supply. Moreover, since almost all the victims were men—warriors captured in battle—population growth could still have exceeded the death rate. Executing women of childbearing age would have had more of an effect on population growth.

The Goddess Tlazolteotl The Aztecs believed that Tlazolteotl (sometimes called "Mother of the Gods") consumed the sins of humankind by eating refuse. As the goddess of childbirth, Tlazolteotl was extensively worshiped. Notice the squatting position for childbirth, then common all over the world. *(Dumbarton Oaks Research Library and Collections, Washington, D.C.)*

the Aztec rulers crushed dissent with terror. The Aztecs controlled a large confederation of city-states by sacrificing prisoners seized in battle; by taking hostages from among defeated peoples as ransom against future revolt; and by demanding from subject states an annual tribute of people to be sacrificed to Huitzilopochtli. Unsuccessful generals, corrupt judges, and careless public officials, even people who accidentally entered forbidden precincts of the royal palaces, were routinely sacrificed. When the supply of such victims ran out, slaves, plebeians, and even infants torn from their mothers suffered ritual execution. The emperor Montezuma II, who celebrated his coronation with the sacrifice of fifty-one hundred people, could be said to have ruled by holocaust. Trumpets blasted and drums beat all day long announcing the sacrifice of yet another victim. Blood poured down the steps of the pyramids. Death and fear stalked everywhere.

How can we at the end of one century and the start of another understand such a terrifying and nightmarish daily ritual? How did "ordinary" Nahuatl-speaking people perceive this customary scene five hundred years ago? First, we have to remember that in the middle of our own century, as millions of human beings were marched to their deaths, most of the world said nothing (or very little) and went about their daily tasks. Likewise, through the 1990s, in the former Yugoslavia and in Africa, as "ethnic cleansing" and genocide took the lives of tens or hundreds of thousands, most world governments said or did nothing. The world watched. Five hundred years ago, as priests performed the actual sacrifices, "the average person" watched. All persons were involved in or complicit in the sacrifices by various means: by the pleasure and satisfaction a household took when one of its warriors brought back a victim for sacrifice; by members of the *calpullis,* the basic civic or local unit, taking their turns in duties at the sacrificial temples; by these groups presenting a sacrificial victim to a temple (much as European medieval guilds donated windows to the local church or cathedral); by the care in feeding, clothing, parading to the temples, and, if necessary, drugging victims for their sacrifice; and by the popular celebrations at mass executions. The Nahuatl-speaking people accepted the ritual sacrifices because the victims, whether captives from hostile tribes or social outcasts from within, represented outsiders, foreigners, "the other."[12]

The Mexica state religion required constant warfare for two basic reasons. One was to meet the gods' needs for human sacrifice; the other was to acquire warriors for the next phase of imperial expansion. "The sacred campaigns of Huitzilopochtli were synchronized with the

According to a second hypothesis, the ordinary people were given victims' bodies as a source of protein.[11] These people lived on a diet of corn, beans, squash, tomatoes, and peppers. Wildlife was scarce, and dog meat, chicken, turkey, and fish were virtually restricted to the upper classes. The testimony of modern nutritionists that beans supply ample protein, and the evidence that, in an area teeming with wild game, the Huron Indians of North America ritually executed captives and feasted on their stewed bodies, weaken the validity of this theory.

A third, more plausible, theory holds that ritual human sacrifice was an instrument of state terrorism—that political and economic needs of the Mexica nation as a whole."[13] Nobles, warriors, and commoners who secured captives on the battlefield shared in the booty, lands, and emperor's rich rewards of gold and silver jewelry, feathered costumes, and other articles of distinctive dress—depending on the number of captives they won. Nobles could grow wealthier, and ordinary soldiers could be promoted to the nobility. Social status, especially in the early period of Aztec expansion, depended on military performance. Warfare, therefore, offered the powerful incentive of upward social mobility. Moreover, defeated peoples had to pay tribute in foodstuffs to support rulers, nobles, warriors, and the imperial bureaucracy. The vanquished supplied laborers for agriculture, the economic basis of Mexica society. Likewise, conquered peoples had to produce workers for the construction and maintenance of the entire Aztec infrastructure—roads, dike systems, aqueducts, causeways, and the royal palaces. Finally, merchants also benefited, for war opened new markets for traders' goods in subject territories.

When the Spaniards under Hernando Cortés (1485–1547) arrived in central Mexico in 1519, the sacred cult of Huitzilopochtli had created a combination of interrelated problems for the emperor Montezuma II. The thirty-eight provinces of the empire, never really assimilated into the Mexica state and usually governed by members of the defeated dynasty, seethed with rebellion. Population increases at the capital, Tenochtitlán, had forced the emperor to lay increasingly heavier tribute on conquered provinces, which in turn murdered the tribute collectors. Invasion and reconquest followed. "The provinces were being crushed beneath a cycle of imperial oppression: increases in tribute, revolt, reconquest, retribution, higher tribute, resentment, and repeated revolt."[14] By causing death in battle and by sacrifice of thousands of food producers, Mexica religion destroyed the very economic basis of the empire.

Faced with grave crisis, Montezuma attempted to solve the problem by freezing social positions. He purged the court of many officials, drastically modified the dress and behavior of the merchant class, and severely limited the honors given to low-born warriors and all but the highest nobility. These reforms provoked great resentment, reduced incentive, and virtually ended social mobility. Scholars have traditionally portrayed Montezuma as weak-willed and indecisive when faced with the Spaniards. But recent research has shown that he was a very determined, even autocratic, ruler. Terrible domestic problems whose roots lay in a religious cult requiring appalling human slaughter offer the fundamental explanation for the Mexica collapse.[15]

Coronation Stone of Montezuma   Originally located within the ritual center at Tenochtitlán, this quadrangular stone, carved with hieroglyphics in the Nahual language of the Aztecs, commemorates the start of Montezuma's reign, July 15, 1503, the date of his coronation. The sculpture associates his rule with the cycle of birth, death, and renewal. (*Art Institute of Chicago, Major Acquisitions Centennial Endowment*)

The Life of the People

A wealth of information has survived about fifteenth- and sixteenth-century Mexico. The Aztecs were deeply interested in their own past, and in their pictographic script they wrote many books recounting their history, geography, and religious practices. They loved making speeches, and every public or social occasion gave rise to lengthy orations, which scribes copied down. The Aztecs also preserved records of their legal disputes, which alone amounted to vast files. The Spanish conquerors subsequently destroyed much of this material. But enough documents remain to construct a picture of the Mexica people at the time of the Spanish intrusion.

No sharp social distinctions existed among the Aztecs during their early migrations. All were equally poor. The head of a family was both provider and warrior, and a sort of tribal democracy prevailed in which all adult males participated in important decision making. By the early sixteenth century, however, Aztec society had changed. A stratified social structure had come into being, and the warrior aristocracy exercised great authority.

Scholars do not yet understand precisely how this change evolved. According to Aztec legend, the Mexica admired the Toltecs and chose their first king, Acamapichti, from among them. The many children he fathered with Mexica women formed the nucleus of the noble class. At the time of the Spanish intrusion into Mexico, men who had distinguished themselves in war occupied the highest military and social positions in the state. Generals, judges, and governors of provinces were appointed by the emperor from among his servants who had earned reputations as war heroes. These great lords, or *tecuhtli,* dressed luxuriously and lived in palaces. The provincial governors exercised full political, judicial, and military authority on the emperor's behalf. In their territories they maintained order, settled disputes, and judged legal cases; oversaw the cultivation of land; and made sure that tribute—in food or gold—was paid. The governors also led troops in wartime. These functions resembled those of feudal lords in western Europe during the Middle Ages (see pages 385–386). Just as only nobles in France and England could wear fur and carry a sword, just as gold jewelry and elaborate hairstyles for women distinguished royal and noble classes in African kingdoms, so in Mexica societies only the tecuhtli could wear jewelry and embroidered cloaks.

Beneath the great nobility of soldiers and imperial officials was the class of warriors. Theoretically every freeman could be a warrior, and parents dedicated their male children to war, burying a male child's umbilical cord with some arrows and a shield on the day of his birth. In actuality the sons of nobles enjoyed advantages deriving from their fathers' position and influence in the state. At the age of six, boys entered a school that trained them for war. Future warriors were taught to fight with a *macana,* a paddle-shaped wooden club edged with bits of obsidian (a volcanic rock similar to granite but as sharp as glass). This weapon could be brutally effective: during the Spanish invasion, Aztec warriors armed with macanas slashed off horses' heads

Aztec Youth   As shown in this codex, Aztec society had basic learning requirements for each age (indicated by dots) of childhood and youth. In the upper panel, boys of age thirteen gather firewood and collect reeds and herbs in a boat, while girls learn to make tortillas on a terra-cotta grill. At fourteen (lower panel), boys learn to fish from a boat, and girls are taught to weave. *(The Bodleian Library, Oxford. MS Arch. Selden. A.1, fol. 60r)*

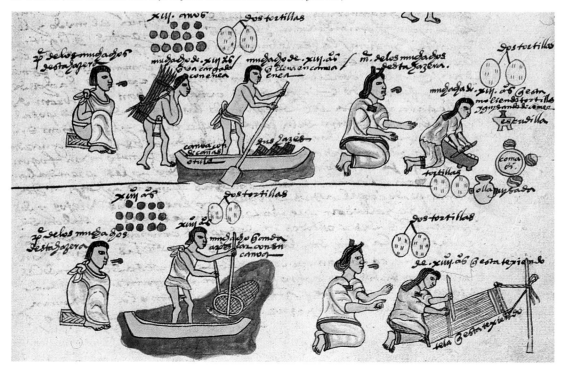

with one blow. Youths were also trained in the use of spears, bows and arrows, and lances fitted with obsidian points. They learned to live on little food and sleep and to accept pain without complaint. At about age eighteen, a warrior fought his first campaign. If he captured a prisoner for ritual sacrifice, he acquired the title *iyac,* or warrior. If in later campaigns he succeeded in killing or capturing four of the enemy, he became a *tequiua*—one who shared in the booty and thus was a member of the nobility. Warriors enjoyed a privileged position in Mexica society because they provided the state with the victims necessary for its survival. If a young man failed in several campaigns to capture the required four prisoners, he joined the *maceualtin,* the plebeian or working class.

The maceualtin were the ordinary citizens—the backbone of Aztec society and the vast majority of the population. The word *maceualti* means "worker" and implied boorish speech and vulgar behavior. Members of this class performed all sorts of agricultural, military, and domestic services and carried heavy public burdens not required of noble warriors. Government officials assigned the maceualtin work on the temples, roads, and bridges. Army officers called them up for military duty, but Mexica considered this an honor and a religious rite, not a burden. Unlike nobles, priests, orphans, and slaves, maceualtin paid taxes. Maceualtin in the capital, however, possessed certain rights: they held their plots of land for life, and they received a small share of the tribute paid by the provinces to the emperor.

Beneath the maceualtin were the *tlalmaitl,* the landless workers or serfs. Some social historians speculate that this class originated during the "Time of Troubles," a period of migrations and upheavals in which weak and defenseless people placed themselves under the protection of strong warriors (see page 420). The tlalmaitl provided agricultural labor at times of planting and harvesting, paid rents in kind, and were bound to the soil—they could not move off the land. The tlalmaitl resembled in many ways the serfs of western Europe, but unlike serfs they performed military service when called on to do so. They enjoyed some rights as citizens and generally were accorded more respect than slaves.

Slaves were the lowest social class. Like Asian, European, and African slaves, most were prisoners captured in war or kidnapped from enemy tribes. But Aztecs who stole from a temple or private house or plotted against the emperor could also be enslaved, and people in serious debt sometimes voluntarily sold themselves into slavery. Female slaves often became their masters' con-cubines. Mexica slaves, however, differed fundamentally from European ones: "Tlatlocotin slaves could possess goods, save money, buy land and houses and even slaves for their own service."[16] Slaves could purchase their freedom. If a male slave married a free woman, their offspring were free, and a slave who escaped and managed to enter the emperor's palace was automatically free. Most slaves eventually gained their freedom. Mexica slavery, therefore, had some humane qualities and resembled slavery in Islamic societies (see pages 259–261).

Women of all social classes played important roles in Mexica society, but those roles were restricted entirely to the domestic sphere. As the little hands of the newborn male child were closed around a tiny bow and arrow indicating his warrior destiny, so the infant female's hands were wrapped around miniature weaving instruments and a small broom: weaving was a sacred and exclusively female art; the broom signaled a female's responsibility for the household shrines and for keeping the household swept and free of contamination. Almost all of the Mexica people married, a man at about twenty when he had secured one or two captives, a woman a couple years earlier. As in pre-modern Asian and European societies, parents selected their children's spouses, using neighborhood women as go-betweens. Save for the few women vowed to the service of the temple, marriage and the household were a woman's fate; marriage represented social maturity for both sexes. Pregnancy became the occasion for family and neighborhood feasts, and a successful birth launched celebrations lasting from ten to twenty days. The rich foods available, such as frogs stewed with green chilies or gophers with sauce, as well as the many varieties of tamales, suggest that women had a sophisticated knowledge of food preparation. Women also had the care of small children.

Women took no part in public affairs—with a few notable exceptions. As the bearing of children was both a social duty and a sacred act, midwives enjoyed great respect. The number of midwives at a confinement indicated rank: a noblewoman often had two or three midwives. As in the medieval European West, in a very difficult birth midwives sacrificed the life of the child for that of the mother. Mexica society also awarded high status and authority to female physicians and herbalists. They treated men as well as women, setting broken bones and prescribing herbal remedies for a variety of ailments. The sources, though limited, imply that a few women skilled at market trading achieved economic independence. The woman weaver capable of executing complicated designs also had the community's esteem.

Prostitutes in the state brothels, not local Mexica but tribute girls from the provinces given to successful warriors as part of their rewards, probably did not enjoy esteem.[17]

Alongside the secular social classes stood the temple priests. Huitzilopochtli and each of the numerous lesser gods had many priests to oversee the upkeep of the temple, assist at religious ceremonies, and perform ritual sacrifices. The priests also did a brisk business in foretelling the future from signs and omens. Aztecs consulted priests on the selection of wives and husbands, on the future careers of newborn babies, and before leaving on journeys or for war. Temples possessed enormous wealth in gold and silver ceremonial vessels, statues, buildings, and land. Fifteen provincial villages had to provide food for the temple at Texcoco and wood for its eternal fires. The priests who had custody of all this property did not marry and were expected to live moral and upright lives. From the temple revenues and resources, the priests supported schools, aided the poor, and maintained hospitals. The chief priests had the ear of the emperor and often exercised great power and influence.

At the peak of the social pyramid stood the emperor. The various Aztec historians contradict one another about the origin of the imperial dynasty, but modern scholars tend to accept the verdict of one sixteenth-century authority that the "custom has always been preserved among the Mexicans (that) the sons of kings have not ruled by right of inheritance, but by election."[18] A small oligarchy of the chief priests, warriors, and state officials made the selection. If none of the sons proved satisfactory, a brother or nephew of the emperor was chosen, but election was always restricted to the royal family.

The Aztec emperor was expected to be a great warrior. He led Mexica and allied armies into battle. All his other duties pertained to the welfare of his people. It was up to the emperor to see that justice was done—he was the final court of appeal. He also held ultimate responsibility for ensuring an adequate food supply. The emperor Montezuma I (r. 1440–1467) distributed twenty thousand loads of stockpiled grain when a flood hit Tenochtitlán. The records show that the Aztec emperors took their public duties seriously.

Gender, Culture, and Power

In 1519 the council of the newly established port city of Veracruz on the Gulf of Mexico wrote to the emperor Charles V, "In addition to . . . children and men and women being killed and offered in sacrifices, we have learned and have been informed that they (the native peoples of Mexico) are doubtless all sodomites and engage in that abominable sin."[19] The sin the councilors referred to was sexual relations—usually anal, sometimes oral—between males. The councilors wanted imperial and papal permission to punish "evil and rebellious natives."

From the earliest Spanish encounters with native Americans, Europeans observed and were shocked by the natives' homosexual practices. What appalled the Spaniards were the *berdaches,* biological males dressed as women who performed the domestic tasks of women—cooking, cleaning, housekeeping, weaving, and embroidering—and who took the passive position in anal intercourse. Berdaches were not trained in military skills and did not go to war. According to information an Aztec elder provided the Franciscan missionary-ethnographer Bernardino de Sahagún, evidence that has been confirmed by many other sources, parents chose the gender roles of their male children. Why did parents cross-gender boys? (Girls were not cross-gendered.) When a mother had produced four or five consecutive sons, the next son was dressed in women's clothes and taught to act like a woman. Customarily, men (and boys) did not do women's work. Once made a transvestite, however, a male child played the female role for the rest of his life and never again assumed the dress or conduct of a male. Tribal customs and laws throughout the Americas fully sanctioned this practice.

At about the onset of puberty, the berdache began to serve the sexual needs of the young men of the community. He always held the passive (or receiving) position in sex. Fathers encouraged sons to seek the sexual solace of berdaches to prevent the rape of pubescent females in the group, to control the sexual activities of their sons before a heterosexual marriage was arranged, and to display possessions in polygynous societies where the rich and well-to-do had several wives or concubines. In the Mexica world *caciques* (chieftains or powerful lords), and in the Inca world (see pages 437–438) *oregones* (nobles), used berdaches for their personal pleasure or established them in brothels as prostitutes. In exchange for some service or price, the caciques and oregones supplied the berdaches to their friends and men of their class. The possession of large numbers of women or berdaches enhanced a lord's status and prestige. Berdaches, moreover, were stronger than women and could carry heftier burdens and perform heavier work.

George Catlin: Dance to the Berdache   Determined to study and paint the Indians, Catlin (1796–1872) lived among the Sioux in the Dakota Territory from 1832 to 1836. His paintings not only do not romanticize the Indians but also portray them as individuals and display none of the racist contempt typical of his time. The social role of the berdache shocked him, however, as it had sixteenth-century Spaniards. Observing the dance and sexual activities, Catlin commented that the berdache "is driven to the most servile and degrading duties. . . . This is one of the most disgusting customs I have ever seen in Indian country." The warriors seem to mock the berdache; why, since they have used him sexually? *(National Museum of American Art, Washington, D.C./Art Resource, NY)*

In addition to the peoples of Mexico, Central America, and the Andes, evidence of berdaches survives among many native American people of North America, including the Timucua tribe of what is now northern Florida, the Mohicans of New York and Connecticut, the Tulelos of Virginia, and the tribes of the Iroquois Confederacy of upper New York State.

How are we to interpret this phenomenon of socially institutionalized homosexuality among American indigenous peoples? The sources pose a major difficulty. Most information comes to us filtered through sixteenth- and seventeenth-century Iberian and French mentalities. That information, therefore, carries Christian moral and theological values. It also bears Spanish and French political, social, and cultural values. The conquistadors used charges of sodomy as a weapon with which to justify the forcible conquest of New World peoples. Europeans described the native peoples as "barbaric," and they came to Mexico, the Caribbean, and South America, they claimed, "to bring civiliza-

tion" and "to extirpate the evil of sodomitical behavior." Europeans knew of homosexual activity in their own societies (see pages 358–359), but they had never seen the permanent transvestism of the berdaches. Such American practices demonstrated to Europeans the peoples' "barbarism."

At the same time, the Nahuatl-speaking peoples of central and southern Mexico, the Incas of Peru, and the native Americans of North America did not have twentieth-century Western concepts of homosexuals and homosexuality. The Indians did not consider homosexual relations as sin or vice. They made no laws against it. Rather, chieftains used berdaches as instruments of pleasure and symbols of power. From a late-twentieth-century perspective, was the feminization of small boys a form of child abuse? Does an affirmative answer to that question indicate a failure in repect for other cultures?[20] Study of the Indian berdache is in an early stage, and perhaps only further scholarly research can resolve these issues.

The Cities of the Aztecs

When the Spanish entered Tenochtitlán (which they called Mexico City) in November 1519, they could not believe their eyes. According to Bernal Díaz, one of Cortés's companions,

when we saw all those cities and villages built in the water, and other great towns on dry land, and that straight and level causeway leading to Mexico, we were astounded. These great towns and cues (temples) and buildings rising from the water, all made of stone, seemed like an enchanted vision. . . . Indeed, some of our soldiers asked whether it was not all a dream.[21]

Tenochtitlán had about 60,000 households. The upper class practiced polygamy and had many children, and many households included servants and slaves. The total population probably numbered around 250,000. At the time, no European city and few Asian ones could boast a population even half that size. The total Aztec Empire has been estimated at around 5 million inhabitants.

Originally built on salt marshes, Tenochtitlán was approached by four great highways that connected it with the mainland. Bridges stood at intervals (comparable to modern Paris). Stone and adobe walls surrounded the city itself, making it (somewhat like medieval Constantinople; see page 233) highly defensible and capable of resisting a prolonged siege. Wide, straight streets and canals crisscrossed the city. Boats and canoes plied the canals. Lining the roads and canals stood thousands of rectangular one-story houses of mortar faced with stucco. Although space was limited, many small gardens and parks were alive with the colors and scents of flowers. The Mexica loved flowers and used them in ritual ceremonies.

A large aqueduct whose sophisticated engineering astounded Cortés carried pure water from distant springs and supplied fountains in the parks. Streets and canals opened onto public squares and marketplaces. Tradespeople offered every kind of merchandise. Butchers hawked turkeys, ducks, chickens, rabbits, and deer; grocers sold kidney beans, squash, avocados, corn, and all kinds of peppers. Artisans sold intricately designed

Tenochtitlán   The great Mexican archaeologist Ignacio Marquina reconstructed the central plaza of the Aztec capital as it looked in 1519. The huge temple of the god of war dominates the area; royal palaces are on each side. On the right stands the rack with tens of thousands of human skulls; in the center is the platform where captives met sacrificial death. *(Library of Congress)*

THE AMERICAS, CA 400–1500

ca 20,000 B.C.	Migration across the Bering Strait to the Americas
ca 1500 B.C.– A.D. 300	Rise of Olmec culture
ca A.D. 400–600	Height of Teotihuacán civilization
ca 600–900	Peak of Maya civilization
ca 800–1000	"Time of Troubles" in Mesoamerica
ca 980–1000	Toltec hegemony
ca 1000	Beginning of Inca expansion
ca 1325	Arrival of the Aztecs in the Valley of Mexico
mid-15th century	Height of Aztec culture
1438–1525	Great Age of Inca imperialism
1519	Arrival of the Spanish in central Mexico
1521	Collapse of the Aztecs
1532	Spanish execution of the Inca king and decline of the Inca Empire

gold, silver, and feathered jewelry. Seamstresses offered sandals, loincloths and cloaks for men, and blouses and long skirts for women—the clothing customarily worn by ordinary people—and embroidered robes and cloaks for the rich. Slaves for domestic service, wood for building, herbs for seasoning and medicine, honey and sweets, knives, jars, smoking tobacco, even human excrement used to cure animal skins—all these wares made a dazzling spectacle.

At one side of the central square of Tenochtitlán stood the great temple of Huitzilopochtli. Built as a pyramid and approached by three flights of 120 steps each, the temple was about 100 feet high and dominated the city's skyline. According to Cortés, it was "so large that within the precincts, which are surrounded by a very high wall, a town of some five hundred inhabitants could easily be built. All round inside this wall there are very elegant quarters with very large rooms and corridors where their priests live."[22]

Travelers, perhaps inevitably, compare what they see abroad with what is familiar to them at home. Tenochti-

tlán thoroughly astounded Cortés, and in his letter to the emperor Charles V, he describes the city in comparison to his homeland: "the market square," where 60,000 people a day came to buy and sell, "was twice as big as Salamanca"; the beautifully constructed "towers," as the Spaniards called the pyramids, rose higher "than the cathedral at Seville"; Montezuma's palace was "so marvelous that it seems to me to be impossible to describe its excellence and grandeur[;] . . . in Spain there is nothing to compare with it." Accustomed to the squalor and filth of Spanish cities, the cleanliness of Tenochtitlán dumbfounded the Spaniards, as did all the evidence of its ordered and elegant planning.[23]

Describing the Aztec way of life for the emperor, Cortés concluded, "Considering that they are barbarous and so far from the knowledge of God and cut off from all civilized nations, it is truly remarkable to see what they have achieved in all things."[24] Certainly Cortés's views reflect his own culture and outlook, but it is undeniable that Mexica culture was remarkable.

MAP 14.4 The Inca Empire, 1463–1532   South America, which extends 4,750 miles in length and 3,300 miles from east to west at its widest point, contains every climatic zone and probably the richest variety of vegetation on earth. Roads built by the Incas linked most of the Andean region.

 THE INCAS OF PERU

In the late 1980s, archaeologists working in the river valleys on the west coast of present-day Peru uncovered stunning evidence of complex societies that flourished between five thousand and three thousand years ago—roughly the same period as the great pyramids of Egypt. In spite of the altitude and dryness of the semi-desert region, scores of settlements existed (Map 14.4). Perhaps the most spectacular was the one at Pampa de las Llamas-Moxeke in the Casma Valley. Stepped pyramids and U-shaped buildings, some more than ten stories high, dominated these settlements. Were these structures warehouses for storing food or cultic temples? Were these settlements connected in some sort of political association? Was there sufficient commercial activity to justify calling them cities? Why did these

peoples, who lived on a diet of fish, sweet potatoes, beans, and peanuts, suddenly abandon their settlements and move into the Andean highlands? Scholars have only begun to process these vast remains, but radiocarbon dating has already demonstrated that the settlements are older than the Maya and Aztec structures.[25]

Another archaeological discovery is providing scholars with rich information about pre-Columbian society. For some time, the villagers of Sipán in northern Peru supplemented their meager incomes by plundering ancient cemeteries and pyramids. One night in 1987, while digging deep in a pyramid, they broke into one of the richest funerary chambers ever located, and they filled their sacks with ceramic, gold, and silver objects. A dispute about the distribution of the loot led one dissatisfied thief to go to the police. When archaeologists from Lima and the United States arrived, they ranked the discoveries at Sipán with those at Tutankhamen's tomb in Egypt and the terra-cotta statues of the Qin Dynasty warriors near Xian, China.

The treasures from the royal tombs at Sipán derive from the Moche civilization, which flourished along a 250-mile stretch of Peru's northern coast between A.D. 100 and 800. Rivers that flowed out of the Andes into the valleys allowed the Moche people to develop complex irrigation systems for agricultural development. Each Moche valley contained a large ceremonial center with palaces and pyramids surrounded by settlements of up to ten thousand people. The dazzling gold and silver artifacts, elaborate headdresses, and ceramic vessels display a remarkable skill in metalwork. Much of later Inca technology seems clearly based on the work of the Moche.[26]

Like the Aztecs, the Incas were "a small militaristic group that came to power late, conquered surrounding groups, and established one of the most extraordinary empires in the world."[27] Gradually, Inca culture spread throughout Peru. Modern knowledge of the Incas is concentrated in the last century before Spanish intrusion (1438–1532); today's scholars know far less about earlier developments.

In the center of Peru rise the cold highlands of the Andes. Six valleys of fertile and wooded land at altitudes ranging from eight thousand to eleven thousand feet punctuate highland Peru. The largest of these valleys are the Huaylas, Cuzco, and Titicaca. It was there that Inca civilization developed and flourished.

Archaeologists still do not understand how people of the Andean region acquired a knowledge of agriculture. Around 2500 B.C. they were relying on fish and mussels for food. Early agriculture seems to have involved cultivating cotton for ordinary clothing, ceremonial dress, and fishnets. Beautifully dyed cotton textiles, swatches of which have been found in ancient gravesites, may also have served as articles for trade.

Andean geography—with towering mountains, isolated valleys, and little arable land—posed an almost insurmountable barrier to agriculture. What land there was had to be irrigated, and human beings needed warm clothing to work in the cold climate. They also required a diet that included some meat and fat. Coca (the dried leaves of a plant native to the Andes and from which cocaine is derived), chewed in moderation as a dietary supplement, enhanced their stamina and their ability to withstand the cold.

Around 200 B.C. the Andean peoples displayed an enormous burst of creative energy. High-altitude valleys were connected to mountain life and vegetation to form a single interdependent agricultural system called "vertical archipelagoes," capable of supporting large communities. Such vertical archipelagoes often extended more than thirty-seven miles from top to bottom.[28] These terraces were shored up with earthen walls to retain moisture. With only a foot plow, bronze hoe, and guano (the dried excrement of sea birds) as fertilizer, the Amerindians of Peru produced bumper crops of white potatoes. By sheer will and muscle power, a topography of separation and scarcity was transformed into a land yielding plenty.

Potatoes ordinarily cannot be stored for long periods, but Andean peoples developed a product called *chuñu,* freeze-dried potatoes made by subjecting potatoes alternately to nightly frosts and daily sun. Chuñu will keep unspoiled for several years. The construction of irrigation channels also facilitated the cultivation of corn. Potatoes and corn required far less labor and time than did the cultivation of wheat in Europe or rice in China.

By the fifteenth century, enough corn, beans, chili peppers, squash, tomatoes, sweet potatoes, peanuts, avocados, and white potatoes were harvested to feed not only the farmers themselves but also massive armies and administrative bureaucracies and thousands of industrial workers. Wild animals had become almost extinct in the region and were the exclusive preserve of the nobility. Common people rarely ate any meat other than guinea pigs, which most families raised. Chicha, a beer fermented from corn, was the staple drink.

Inca Imperialism

Who were the Incas? *Inca* was originally the name of the governing family of an Amerindian group that settled in the basin of Cuzco (see Map 14.4). From that family, the name was gradually extended to all peoples living in the

Portrait Vessel of a Ruler   Artisans of the Moche culture on the northern coast of Peru produced objects representing many aspects of their world, including this flat-bottomed stirrup-spout jar with a ruler's face. The commanding expression conveys a strong sense of power, as does the elaborate headdress with the geometric designs of Moche textiles worn only by elite persons. (*Art Institute of Chicago. Kate S. Buckingham Endowment, 1955.2338*)

Andes valleys. The Incas themselves used the word to identify their ruler or emperor. Here the term is used for both the ruler and the people.

As with the Aztecs, so with the Incas: religious ideology was the force that transformed the culture. Religious concepts created pressure for imperialist expansion—with fatal consequences.

The Incas believed their ruler descended from the sun-god and that the health and prosperity of the state

Machu Picchu The citadel of Machu Picchu, surrounded by mountains in the clouds, clings to a spectacular crag in upland Peru. It was discovered in 1911 by the young American explorer Hiram Bingham. Its origin and the reason for its abandonment remain unknown. *(Photo Researchers, Inc.)*

depended on him. Dead rulers were thought to link the people to the sun-god. When the ruler died, his corpse was preserved as a mummy in elaborate clothing and housed in a sacred and magnificent chamber. The mummy was brought in procession to all important state ceremonies, his advice was sought in times of crisis, and hundreds of human beings were sacrificed to him. In ordinary times, the dead ruler was carried to visit his friends, and his heirs and relatives came to dine with him. Some scholars call this behavior the "cult of the royal mummies" because it was a kind of ancestor worship.

The mummies were not only the holiest objects in the Inca world but also a powerful dynamic force in Inca society. According to the principle of the "split inheritance," when an Inca ruler died, the imperial office, insignia, and rights and duties of the monarchy passed to the new king. The dead ruler, however, retained full and complete ownership of all his estates and properties. His royal descendants as a group managed his lands and sources of income for him and used the revenues to care for his mummy and to maintain his cult. Thus a new ruler came to the throne land- or property-poor. In order to live in the royal style, strengthen his administration, and reward his supporters, he had to win his own possessions by means of war and imperial expansion.[29]

Around A.D. 1000 the Incas were one of many small groups fighting among themselves for land and water. As they began to conquer their neighbors, a body of religious lore came into being that ascribed divine origin to their earliest king, Manco Capac (ca 1200), and

Chimu Brocaded Cloth, ca 1000–1400   In about 1200, Chimu people succeeded the Moche on the northern coast of Peru. They were urban dwellers with a complex social system and a powerful military. Like the Inca who absorbed the Chimu in about 1450, the Chimu believed that their ancestors were of divine descent and that when a king died, his mummy retained considerable property rights. This piece of cloth celebrates a deified ruler. *(Cotton and wool, 160 × 250 cm. The Art Museum, Princeton University. Museum purchase, gift of Herbert L. Lucas, Jr., Class of 1950, and Mrs. Lucas. Photo: Courtesy The Merrin Gallery)*

promised warriors the gods' favor and protection. Strong historical evidence, however, dates only from the reign of Pachacuti Inca (1438–1471), who launched the imperialist phase of Inca civilization. (See the feature "Listening to the Past: The Death of Inca Yupanque [Pachacuti Inca] in 1471" on pages 440–441.)

If the cult of ancestor or mummy worship satisfied some Inca social needs, in time it also created serious problems. The desire for conquest provided incentives for courageous (or ambitious) nobles: those who were victorious in battle and gained new territories for the state could expect lands, additional wives, servants, herds of llamas, gold, silver, fine clothes, and other symbols of high status. And even common soldiers who distinguished themselves in battle could be rewarded with booty and raised to noble status. The imperial interests of the emperor paralleled those of other social groups. Thus, under Pachacuti Inca and his successors, Topa

Inca (1471–1493) and Huayna Capac (1493–1525), Inca domination was gradually extended by warfare to the frontier of present-day Ecuador and Colombia in the north and to the Maule River in present-day Chile in the south (see Map 14.4), an area of about 350,000 square miles. Eighty provinces, scores of ethnic groups, and 16 million people came under Inca control. A remarkable system of roads held the empire together.

Before Inca civilization, each group that entered the Andes valleys had its own distinct language. These languages were not written and have become extinct. Scholars will probably never understand the linguistic condition of Peru before the fifteenth century when Pachacuti made Quechua (pronounced "keshwa") the official language of his people and administration. Conquered peoples were forced to adopt the language, and Quechua spread the Inca way of life throughout the Andes. Though not written until the Spanish in Peru adopted it as a second official language, Quechua had replaced local languages by the seventeenth and eighteenth centuries and is still spoken by most Peruvians today.

Both the Aztecs and the Incas ruled very ethnically diverse peoples. Whereas the Aztecs tended to control their subject peoples through terror, the Incas governed by means of imperial unification. They imposed not only their language but also their entire panoply of gods: the sun-god, divine ancestor of the royal family; his wife the moon-god; and the thunder-god, who brought life-giving rain. Magnificent temples scattered throughout the expanding empire housed idols of these gods and the state-appointed priests who attended them. Priests led prayers and elaborate rituals, and on such occasions as a terrible natural disaster or a great military victory, they sacrificed human beings to the gods. Subject peoples were required to worship the state gods. Imperial unification was also achieved through the forced participation of local chieftains in the central bureaucracy and through a policy of colonization called *mitima*. To prevent rebellion in newly conquered territories, Pachacuti transferred all their inhabitants to other parts of the empire, replacing them with workers who had lived longer under Inca rule and whose independent spirit had been broken.[30] An excellent system of roads—averaging three feet in width, some paved and others not—facilitated the transportation of armies and the rapid communication of royal orders by runners. The roads followed straight lines wherever possible but also crossed pontoon bridges and tunneled through hills. This great feat of Inca engineering bears striking comparison with ancient Roman roads, which also linked an empire.

Rapid Inca expansion, however, produced stresses. Although the pressure for growth remained unabated, in the reign of Topa Inca open lands began to be scarce. Topa Inca had some success in attacks on the eastern slopes of the Andes, but his attempts to penetrate the tropical Amazon forest east of the Andes led to repeated military disasters. The Incas waged wars with highly trained armies drawn up in massed formation and fought pitched battles on level ground, often engaging in hand-to-hand combat, or they launched formal assaults on fortresses. But in dense jungles, the troops could not maneuver or maintain order against enemies using guerrilla tactics and sniping at them with deadly blowguns. Another source of stress was discontent among subject peoples in conquered territories. Many revolted. It took Huayna Capac several years to put down a revolt in Ecuador. Even the system of roads and trained runners eventually caused administrative problems. The average runner could cover about 50

leagues, or 175 miles, per day—a remarkable feat of physical endurance, especially at high altitude—but the larger the empire became, the greater the distances to be covered. The roundtrip from the capital at Cuzco to Quito in Ecuador, for example, took from ten to twelve days, so that an emperor might have to base urgent decisions on incomplete or out-of-date information. The empire was overextended. "In short, the cult of the royal mummies helped to drive the Inca expansion, but it also linked economic stress, administrative problems, and political instabilities in a cyclical relationship."[31]

In 1525 the Inca Huayna Capac died of plague while campaigning in Ecuador. Between that date and the arrival of the Spanish conquistador Francisco Pizarro in 1532, the Inca throne was bitterly contested by two of Huayna's sons, the half brothers Huascar and Atauhualpa. Inca law called for a dying emperor to assign the throne to his most competent son by his principal wife, who had to be the ruler's full sister. Huascar, unlike Atauhualpa, was the result of such an incestuous union and thus had a legitimate claim to the throne. Atauhualpa, who had fought with Huayna Capac in his last campaign, tried to convince Huascar that their father had divided the kingdom and had given him (Atauhualpa) the northern part. Huascar bitterly rejected his half brother's claim.

When Huascar came to the throne, the problems facing the Inca Empire had become critical: the dead rulers controlled too much of Peru's land and resources. Huascar proposed a radical solution: "Annoyed one day with these dead (his ancestors), [he] said that he ought to order them all buried and take from them all that they had, and that there should not be dead men but living ones, because (the dead) had all that was best in the country."[32]

Although Atauhualpa had the grave liability of being born of a nonincestuous union, to the great nobility responsible for the cult of the royal mummies, Huascar's proposal represented a far graver threat to the established order: Huascar intended to insult the mummies who linked the Inca people to the gods, and if his proposals were enacted, the anger of the mummies would ensure a disastrous future. (The nobility did not say the obvious—that if Huascar buried the dead and took their vast properties, the nobles would be deprived of wealth and power.) Not surprisingly, the nobles threw their support behind Atauhualpa.

In the civil war that began in 1532, Atauhualpa's veteran warriors easily defeated Huascar's green recruits. On his way to his coronation at Cuzco, Atauhualpa encountered Pizarro and 168 Spaniards who had recently entered the kingdom. The Spaniards quickly became the real victors in the Inca kingdom (see pages 506–509). The cult of the royal mummies had brought, or at least contributed heavily to, the Inca collapse.

Inca Society

The *ayllu,* or clan, served as the fundamental social unit of Inca society; theoretically, all members of the ayllu descended from a common male ancestor. All members of the ayllu owed allegiance to the *curacas,* or headman, who conducted relations with outsiders. The ayllu held specific lands, granted it by hamlet or provincial authorities on a long-term basis, and individual families tended to work the same plots for generations. Cooperation in the cultivation of the land and intermarriage among members of the ayllu wove people there into a tight web of connections.

In return for the land, all men had to perform public duties and pay tribute to the authorities. Their duties included building and maintaining palaces, temples, roads, and irrigation systems. Tribute consisted of potatoes, corn, and other vegetables paid to the hamlet head, who in turn paid them to the provincial governor. A draft rotary system called *mita* (turn) determined when men of a particular hamlet performed public works; this responsibility rotated from ward to ward (divisions of the hamlet).

As the Inca Empire expanded, this pattern of social and labor organization was imposed on other, newly conquered indigenous peoples. Regional states had a distinct ethnic identity, and by the time of the Spanish intrusion, the Incas had well-established mechanisms for public labor drafts and tribute collection. Discontent among subject peoples, however, helps to explain the quick fragmentation of imperial authority and the relative swiftness of the Spanish conquest. After the conquest, the Spaniards adopted and utilized the indigenous organization as the basis for Spanish civil and ecclesiastical administration, just as the imperial Incas (and, in Mesoamerica, the Aztecs) had done.[33]

In the fifteenth century, Pachacuti Inca and Topa Inca superimposed imperial institutions on those of kinship. They ordered allegiance to be paid to the ruler at Cuzco rather than to the curacas. They drafted local men for distant wars and relocated the entire populations of certain regions through the mitima system. Entirely new ayllus were formed, based on residence rather than kinship.

The emperors sometimes gave newly acquired lands to victorious generals, distinguished civil servants, and favorite nobles. These lords subsequently exercised authority previously held by the native curacas. Whether

Mochica Earring   Elites of the Moche period (ca 100 B.C.–A.D. 500) on the northern coast of Peru commissioned vast quantities of jewelry. This gold and turquoise earring depicts a warrior-priest wearing an owlhead necklace, holding a removable war club (right hand) and shield (left hand), and flanked by attendants. Peanuts had recently been domesticated in the area, and the peanut beading around the edge suggests the leader's power over natural fertility in an agriculturally marginal region. The reverse side is of silver. *(UCLA, Fowler Museum of Cultural History. Photo: Susan Epstein)*

long-time residents or new colonists, common people had the status of peasant farmers, which entailed heavy agricultural or other obligations. Just as in medieval Europe peasants worked several days each week on their lord's lands, so the Inca people had to work on state lands (that is, the emperor's lands) or on lands assigned to the temple. Peasants also labored on roads and bridges; terraced and irrigated new arable land; served on construction crews for royal palaces, temples, and public buildings such as fortresses; acted as runners on the post roads; and excavated in the imperial gold, silver, and copper mines. The imperial government annually determined the number of laborers needed for these various undertakings, and each district had to supply an assigned quota. The government also made an ayllu responsible for the state-owned granaries and for the production of cloth for army uniforms.

The state required everyone to marry and even decided when and sometimes whom a person should marry. Men married around the age of twenty, women a little younger. A young man who wanted a certain girl hung around her father's house and shared in the work. The Incas did not especially prize virginity; premarital sex was common. The marriage ceremony consisted of the joining of hands and the exchange of a pair of sandals. This ritual was followed by a large wedding feast, at which the state presented the bride and groom with two complete sets of clothing, one for everyday wear and one for festive occasions. If a man or woman did not find a satisfactory mate, the provincial governor selected one for him or her. Travel was forbidden, so couples necessarily came from the same region. Like most warring societies with high male death rates, the Incas practiced polygamy, though the cost of supporting many wives restricted it largely to the upper classes.

The Incas relied heavily on local authorities and cultural norms for day-to-day matters, and local officials made the final decisions on routine issues. In some ways, however, the common people were denied choice and initiative and led regimented lives. The Incas did, however, take care of the poor and aged who could not look after themselves, distributed grain in times of shortage and famine, and supplied assistance in natural disasters. Scholars have debated whether Inca society was socialistic, totalitarian, or a forerunner of the welfare state; it may be merely a matter of definition. Although the Inca economy was strictly regulated, there certainly was not an equal distribution of wealth. Everything above and beyond the masses' basic needs went to the emperor and the nobility.

The backbreaking labor of ordinary people in the fields and mines made possible the luxurious lifestyle of the great Inca nobility. The nobles—called *oregones*, or "Big Ears," by the Spanish because they pierced their ears and distended the lobes with heavy jewelry—were the ruling Inca's kinsmen. Lesser nobles included the curacas, royal household servants, public officials, and entertainers. As the empire expanded in the fifteenth century, there arose a noble class of warriors, governors, and local officials, whose support the ruling Inca secured with gifts of land, precious metals, and llamas and alpacas (llamas were used as beasts of burden; alpacas were raised for their long fine wool). The nobility was exempt from agricultural work and from other kinds of public service.

SUMMARY

Several strong Amerindian civilizations flourished in the Western Hemisphere in the years between 300 B.C. and A.D. 1500. The Maya are justly renowned for their art and their accomplishments in abstract thought, especially mathematics. The Aztecs built a unified culture

based heavily on the Toltec heritage and distinguished by achievements in engineering, sculpture, and architecture. The Incas revealed a genius for organization, and their state was virtually unique in its time for assuming responsibility for all its people. In both the Mexica and the Inca societies, religious ideology shaped other facets of the culture. The Mexica cult of war and human sacrifice and the Inca cult of the royal mummies posed serious dilemmas and contributed to the weakening of those societies.

Inca culture did not die with the Spaniard Pizarro's strangulation of Atauhualpa (see page 509). In May 1536 his successor, Inca Mancu Yupanque, led a massive revolt against the Spanish and then led his people to Machu Picchu deep in the Valcahamba range of the Andes. Inca military resistance to Spanish domination continued throughout the sixteenth to eighteenth centuries. In 1780 Jose Gabriel Kunturkanki, a highly educated businessman and landowner, proclaimed himself Inca Tupac Amaru II and launched a native independence movement that the Spanish put down with the greatest difficulty.

NOTES

1. See J. Lockhart and S. B. Schwartz, *Early Latin America: A History of Colonial Spanish America and Brazil,* (Cambridge: Cambridge University Press, 1983), pp. 31–33; M. A. Burkholder and L. Johnson, *Colonial Latin America* (New York: Oxford University Press, 1998), pp. 1–5.
2. Lockhart and Schwartz, *Early Latin America,* pp. 33–49.
3. F. Braudel, *The Structures of Everyday Life: Civilization and Capitalism, 15th–18th Century,* vol. 1, trans. S. Reynolds (New York: Harper & Row, 1981), pp. 160–161.
4. R. A. Diehl and M. A. Coe, "Olmec Archeology," in *The Olmec World: Ritual and Rulership* (Princeton, N.J.: Princeton University Press, 1996), pp. 11–25.
5. L. Schele and M. E. Miller, *The Blood of Kings: Dynasty and Ritual in Maya Art* (New York: Braziller, 1986), pp. 14–15, passim.
6. G. W. Conrad and A. A. Demarest, *Religion and Empire: The Dynamics of Aztec and Inca Expansionism* (New York: Cambridge University Press, 1993), p. 71.
7. I. Clendinnen, *Aztecs: An Interpretation* (New York: Cambridge University Press, 1992), pp. 115–117.
8. J. Soustelle, *Daily Life of the Aztecs on the Eve of the Spanish Conquest,* trans. P. O'Brian (Stanford, Calif.: Stanford University Press, 1970), p. 97.
9. M. Harris, *Cannibals and Kings* (New York: Random House, 1977), pp. 99–110; the quotation is from p. 106.
10. Ibid., pp. 109–110.
11. R. Padden, *The Hummingbird and the Hawk* (Columbus: Ohio State University Press, 1967), pp. 76–99.

12. Clendinnen, *Aztecs,* pp. 88–110.
13. Conrad and Demarest, *Religion and Empire,* p. 49.
14. Ibid., p. 57.
15. Ibid., pp. 66–70.
16. Soustelle, *Daily Life of the Aztecs,* p. 74.
17. Clendinnen, *Aztecs,* pp. 153–173.
18. Quoted in Soustelle, *Daily Life of the Aztecs,* p. 89.
19. Quoted in R. Trexler, *Sex and Conquest: Gendered Violence, Political Order, and the European Conquest of the Americas* (Ithaca, N.Y.: Cornell University Press, 1995), p. 1. This section leans on Trexler's important and provocative study.
20. Ibid., Chaps. 1, 4, 5, and passim.
21. B. Díaz, *The Conquest of New Spain,* trans. J. M. Cohen (New York: Penguin Books, 1978), p. 214.
22. Quoted in J. H. Perry, *The Discovery of South America* (New York: Taplinger, 1979), pp. 161–163.
23. Quoted in Clendinnen, *Aztecs,* pp. 16–17.
24. Quoted in Perry, *The Discovery of South America,* p. 163.
25. William K. Stevens, "Andean Culture Found to Be as Old as the Great Pyramids," *New York Times,* October 3, 1989, p. C1.
26. John Noble Wilford, "Lost Civilization Yields Its Riches as Thieves Fall Out," *New York Times,* July 29, 1994, pp. C1, C28.
27. J. A. Mason, *The Ancient Civilizations of Peru* (New York: Penguin Books, 1978), p. 108.
28. W. Sullivan, *The Secret of the Incas: Myth, Astronomy, and the War Against Time* (New York: Crown Publishers, 1996), pp. 22–24.
29. Conrad and Demarest, *Religion and Empire,* pp. 91–94.
30. Mason, *The Ancient Civilization of Peru,* p. 123.
31. Ibid., p. 132.
32. Ibid., p. 136.
33. Lockhart and Schwartz, *Early Latin America,* pp. 37–48.

SUGGESTED READING

The titles by Clendinnen, Diehl and Coe, Conrad and Demarest, Lockhart and Schwartz, Schele and Miller, Sullivan, and Trexler cited in the Notes represent some of the most exciting research on pre-Columbian Mesoamerican and Andean societies. For the Maya, students should also see D. Freidel, *A Forest of Kings: The Untold Story of the Ancient Maya* (1990), a splendidly illustrated work providing expert treatment of many facets of the Maya world; R. Wright, *Time Among the Mayas* (1989), which gives a highly readable account of Maya agricultural and religious calendars; M. D. Coe, *The Maya,* 4th ed. (1987), a sound and well-illustrated survey; the same scholar's *Breaking the Maya Code* (1992); and R. J. Sharer, *Daily Life in Maya Civilization* (1996).

For the gradually expanding literature on the Aztecs, see J. Lockhart, *The Nahuas After the Conquest: A Social and Cultural History of the Indians of Central America, Sixteenth Through Eighteenth Centuries* (1992), and the same author's edition and translation of *We People Here: Nahuatl Accounts of the Conquest of Mexico* (1993). R. F. Townsend, *The Aztecs* (1992), discusses the various classes of Mexica society, as well as expansion, education, and religious ritual in a clearly illustrated study. M. León-Portilla, *The Aztec Image of Self and Society: An Introduction to Nahua Culture* (1992), is perhaps the best appreciation of Aztec religious ritual and symbolism. For warfare, R. Hassig, *Aztec Warfare: Imperial Expansion and Political Control* (1988), is probably the standard work.

J. de Batanzos, *Narrative of the Incas,* trans. and ed. R. Hamilton and D. Buchanan (1996), is an invaluable source for the Incas; it was written by a Spaniard married to an Inca princess, offers fascinating information about Inca customs, and reflects a female oral tradition. W. Sullivan, *The Secret of the Incas: Myth, Astronomy, and the War Against Time* (1996), explains the role of myth and astronomy in the rise and fall of the Inca Empire. For a fine survey of the best literature on preconquest Andean civilization, see B. Larson, "Andean Communities, Political Cultures, and Markets: The Changing Contours of a Field," in *Ethnicity, Markets, and Migration in the Andes: At the Crossroads of History and Anthropology,* ed. B. Larson and O. Harris (1995).

Students wanting to explore aspects of the entire hemisphere before the arrival of Columbus might begin with J. E. Kicza, "The People and Civilizations of the Americas Before Contact," in *Essays in Global and Comparative History,* ed. M. Adas (1998); J. E. Kicza, "Introduction," in *The Indian in Latin American History: Resistance, Resilience, and Acculturation* (1993); B. Fagan, *Kingdoms of Gold, Kingdoms of Jade* (1991), a fine work in comparative anthropology; and *America in 1492,* ed. A. M. Josephy (1992), an interesting collection of essays, many written by leading scholars. For the impact of the Spanish on Mesoamerican peoples, see I. Clendinnen, *Ambivalent Conquests: Maya and Spanish in Yucatan, 1517–1570* (1987), a profoundly sensitive, learned, and important study; R. Wright, *Stolen Continents: The Americas Through Indian Eyes Since 1492* (1992), which emphasizes the persistence and survival of native American cultures and peoples; and *In the Wake of Contact: Biological Responses to Conquest,* ed. C. S. Larsen and G. Milner (1994), a useful collection of articles dealing with many parts of the world.

The following older studies may also prove helpful for particular topics: S. Masuda, I. Shimada, and C. Morris, eds., *Andean Ecology and Civilization* (1985), and E. R. Wolfe, ed., *The Valley of Mexico: Studies in Pre-Hispanic Ecology and Society* (1976), are important for environmental research; L. Baudin, *A Socialist Empire: The Incas of Peru* (1961), gives a provocative interpretation of the Incas; V. W. Van Hagen, *Realm of the Incas* (1961), offers a popular account; F. Katz, *The Ancient American Civilisations* (1972), is a standard anthropological work that surveys all the major Mesoamerican cultures; and T. Todorov, *The Conquest of America,* trans. R. Howard (1984), is an important but difficult study of cross-cultural perceptions.

The Death of Inca Yupanque (Pachacuti Inca) in 1471

In 1551 the Spaniard Juan de Betanzos began to write Narrative of the Incas. *Although Betanzos had only the Spanish equivalent of a grade school education when he arrived in Peru, and although he lacked dictionaries and grammar books, he had two powerful assets. First, he learned Quechua and earned a reputation for being the best interpreter and translator in postconquest Peru. Second, Betanzos had married Angelina Yupanque, an Inca princess (her Inca name was Cuxirimay Ocllo) who was the widow of Atauhualpa and who also had been Pizarro's mistress. Through her, Betanzos gained immediate and firsthand access to the Inca oral tradition. When he finished his book six years later, modern scholars believe he had produced "the most authentic chronicle that we have."*

Narrative of the Incas *provides a mine of information about Inca customs and social history. There is so much description of marriage, childbirth, weaning, coming-of-age ceremonies, and death that the work shows a strong female experience, undoubtedly the influence of Betanzos's wife. Here is his account of the death of Inca Yupanque (Pachacuti Inca) in 1471.*

Since there were instructions for the idolatries and activities that you have heard about, Inca Yupanque ordered that immediately after he died these activities and sacrifices should be done. In addition, as soon as this was done, word should be sent to all the land, and from all the provinces and towns they should bring again all that was necessary for the service of the new lord, including gold, silver, livestock, clothing, and the rest of the things needed to replenish all the storehouses that, because of his death, had been emptied for the sacrifices and things he ordered to be done, and it should be so abundant because he realized that the state of the one who was thus Inca was growing greater.

While Inca Yupanque was talking and ordering what was to be done after he died, he raised his voice in a song that is still sung today in his memory by those of his generation. This song went as follows: "Since I bloomed like the flower of the garden, up to now I have given order and justice in this life and world as long as my strength lasted. Now I have turned into earth." Saying these words of his song, Inca Yupanque Pachacuti expired, leaving in all the land justice and order, as already stated. And his people were well supplied with idols, idolatries, and activities. After he was dead, he was taken to a town named Patallacta, where he had ordered some houses built in which his body was to be entombed. He was buried by putting his body in the earth in a large new clay urn, with him very well dressed. Inca Yupanque ordered that a golden image made to resemble him be placed on top of his tomb. And it was to be worshiped in place of him by the people who went there. Soon it was placed there. He ordered that a statue be made of his fingernails and hair that had been cut in his lifetime. It was made in that town where his body was kept. They very ceremoniously brought this statue on a litter to the city of Cuzco for the fiestas in the city. This statue was placed in the houses of Topa Inca Yupanque. When there were fiestas in the city, they brought it out for them with the rest of the statues. What is more laughable about this lord Inca Yupanque is that, when he wanted to make some idol, he entered the house of the Sun and acted as though the Sun spoke to him, and he himself answered the Sun to make his people believe that the Sun ordered him to make those idols and *guacas*[1] and so that they would worship them as such.

When the statue was in the city, Topa Inca Yupanque ordered those of his own lineage to bring this statue out for the feasts that were held in Cuzco. When they brought it out like this, they sang about the things that the Inca did in his life, both in the wars and in his city. Thus they served and revered him, changing its garments as he used to do, and serving it as he was served when he was alive. All of which was done thus.

This statue, along with the gold image that was on top of his tomb, was taken by Manco Inca from the city when he revolted. On the advice that Doña Angelina Yupanque gave to the Marquis Don Francisco Pizarro, he got it and the rest of the wealth with it. Only the body is in Patallacta at this time, and judging by it, in his lifetime he seems to have been a tall man. They say that he died at the age of one hundred twenty years. After his father's death, Topa Inca Yupanque ordered that none of the descendants of his father, Inca Yupanque, were to settle the area beyond the rivers of Cuzco. From that time until today the descendants of Inca Yupanque were called *Capacaillo Ynga Yupangue haguaynin,* which means "lineage of kings," "descendants and grandchildren of Inca Yupanque." These are the most highly regarded of all the lineages of Cuzco. These are the ones who were ordered to wear two feathers on their heads.

As time passed, this generation of *orejones* [*oregones*][2] multiplied. There were and are today many who became heads of families and renowned as firstborn. Because they married women who were not of their lineage, they took a variety of family names. Seeing this, those of Inca Yupanque ordered that those who had mixed with other people's blood should take new family names and extra names so that those of his lineage could clearly be called *Capacaillo* and descendants of Inca Yupanque. When the Spaniards came, all of this diminished, to the point where they all say they are from that lineage.

1. Any object, place, or person worshiped as a deity.
2. Nobles.

Questions for Analysis

1. How does this account of the Inca's death and burial relate to the "cult of the royal mummies" described on page 434?

2. Does Juan de Betanzos show any sign of disapproval, contempt, or "cultural limitation" for Inca funeral practices?

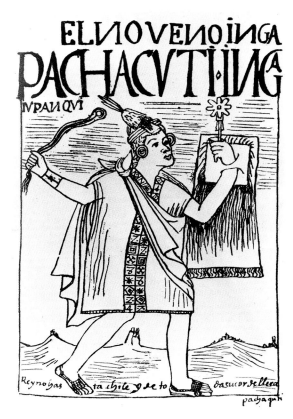

Revered as a great conqueror and lawgiver, Pachacuti Inca here wears the sacred fringed headband symbolizing his royal authority, and the large earrings of the oregones, the nobility. (*Pachacuti Inca, from* Nueva Coronica & Buen Gobierno, *by Guaman Poma de Ayala. Courtesy, Institut d'Ethnologie, Paris. © Musée de l'Homme*)

Source: Narrative of the Incas by Juan de Betanzos, trans. and ed. R. Hamilton and D. Buchanan from the Palma de Mallorca manuscript (Austin: University of Texas Press, 1996), pp. 138–139. Copyright © 1996. By permission of the University of Texas Press.

15
Europe in the Renaissance and Reformation

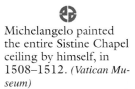

Michelangelo painted
the entire Sistine Chapel
ceiling by himself, in
1508–1512. *(Vatican Mu-
seum)*

While the Four Horsemen of the Apocalypse were carrying war, plague, famine, and death across the continent of Europe, a new culture was emerging in southern Europe. The fourteenth century witnessed the beginnings of remarkable changes in many aspects of Italian society. In the fifteenth century, these phenomena spread beyond Italy and gradually influenced society in northern Europe. These cultural changes have collectively been labeled the Renaissance.

The idea of reform is as old as Christianity itself: the need for reform of the individual Christian and of the institutional church is central to the Christian faith. The Christian humanists of the late fifteenth and early sixteenth centuries called for reform of the church on the pattern of the early church, primarily through educational and social change. These cries for reformation were not new. Men and women of every period believed the early Christian church represented a golden age. What was new were the criticisms of educated laypeople whose religious needs were not being met. In the sixteenth century, demands for religious reform became so strong that they became enmeshed with social, political, and economic factors.

- What does the term *Renaissance* mean?
- How did the Renaissance manifest itself in politics, government, art, and social organization?
- Why did the theological ideas of Martin Luther trigger political, social, and economic reactions?
- What response did the Catholic church make to the movements for reform?

This chapter will explore these questions.

ECONOMIC AND POLITICAL ORIGINS OF THE ITALIAN RENAISSANCE

The period extending roughly from 1050 to 1300 witnessed phenomenal commercial and financial development, the growing political power of self-governing cities in northern Italy, and great population expansion. The period from the late thirteenth to the late sixteenth century was characterized by an amazing flowering of artistic energies.[1] Scholars commonly use the term *Renaissance* to describe the cultural achievements of the fourteenth through sixteenth centuries. Those achievements rested on the economic and political developments of earlier centuries.

A Bank Scene, Florence   Originally a "bank" was just a counter; if covered with a carpet like this Ottoman geometric rug with a kufic border, it became a bank of distinction. Moneychangers who sat behind the counter became "bankers," exchanging different currencies and holding deposits for merchants and business people. *(Prato, San Francesco/Scala/Art Resource, NY)*

In the great commercial revival of the eleventh century, northern Italian cities led the way. By the middle of the twelfth century, Venice, supported by a huge merchant marine, had grown enormously rich from overseas trade. It profited tremendously from the diversion of the Fourth Crusade to Constantinople (see page 350). Genoa and Milan enjoyed the benefits of a large volume of trade with the Middle East and northern Europe. These cities fully exploited their geographical positions as natural crossroads for mercantile exchange between East and West.

Florence too possessed enormous wealth despite geographical constraints. It was an inland city without easy access to water transportation. But toward the end of the thirteenth century, Florentine merchants and bankers acquired control of papal banking. From their position as tax collectors for the papacy, Florentine mercantile families began to dominate European banking on both sides of the Alps. The profits from loans, investments, and money exchanges that poured back to Florence were pumped into urban industries, such as the Florentine wool industry, which was the major factor in the city's financial expansion and population increase.

In the course of the twelfth century, Milan, Florence, Genoa, Siena, and Pisa fought for and won political and economic independence from surrounding feudal nobles. The nobles, attracted by the opportunities for long-distance and maritime trade, the rising value of urban real estate, the new public offices available in the expanding cities, and the chances for advantageous marriages into rich commercial families, frequently settled within the cities. Marriage vows often sealed business contracts between the rural nobility and the mercantile aristocracy. This merger of the northern Italian feudal nobility and the commercial aristocracy brought into being a new social class—an urban nobility.

This new class made citizenship and political participation in the city-states dependent on a property qualification, years of residence within the city, and social connections. Only a tiny percentage of the male population possessed these qualifications. A new group, called the *pòpolo*, disenfranchised and heavily taxed, bitterly resented its exclusion from power. Throughout most of the thirteenth century, in city after city, the pòpolo used armed force and violence to take over the city governments. Members of the pòpolo could not establish civil order within their cities, however. Consequently, these movements for republican government—government in which political power theoretically resides in the people and is exercised by their chosen representatives—failed. By the year 1300, *signori* (despots, or one-man rulers) or *oligarchies* (the rule of merchant aristocracies) had triumphed everywhere.[2]

Thus in 1422 Venice had a population of 84,000, but 200 men held all the power; Florence had about 40,000 people, but 600 men ruled. Oligarchic regimes maintained only a façade of republican government. Nostalgia for the Roman form of government, combined with calculating shrewdness, prompted the leaders of Venice, Milan, and Florence to use the old forms.

In the fifteenth century, political power and elite culture centered at the princely courts of despots and oligarchs. "A court was the space and personnel around a prince as he made laws, received ambassadors, made appointments, took his meals, and proceeded through the streets."[3] The princely court afforded the despot or oligarchs the opportunity to display and assert their wealth and power. They flaunted their patronage of learning and the arts by munificent gifts to writers, philosophers, and artists, and they promoted occasions for magnificent pageantry and elaborate ritual—all designed to assert their wealth and power. The rulers of the city-states governed as monarchs. They crushed urban revolts, levied taxes, and killed their enemies. And they used massive building programs to employ, and the arts to overawe, the masses.

In the fifteenth century, five powers dominated the Italian peninsula: Venice, Milan, Florence, the Papal States, and the kingdom of Naples. Venice had a sophisticated constitution and was a republic in name, but an oligarchy of merchant-aristocrats actually ran the city. Milan was also called a republic, but despots of the Sforza family ruled harshly and dominated the smaller cities of the north. Likewise in Florence the form of government was republican, but between 1434 and 1494 power in Florence was held by the great Medici banking family. Though not public officers, Cosimo de' Medici (1434–1464) and Lorenzo de' Medici (1469–1492) ruled from behind the scenes. Central Italy consisted mainly of the Papal States, which during the Babylonian Captivity (see page 397) had come under the sway of important Roman families. Pope Alexander VI (r. 1492–1503), aided militarily and politically by his son Cesare Borgia, reasserted papal authority in the papal lands. Cesare Borgia, the inspiration for Machiavelli's *The Prince* (see page 453), began the work of uniting the peninsula by ruthlessly conquering and exacting total obedience from the principalities making up the Papal States. South of the Papal States, the kingdom of Naples had long been disputed by the Aragonese and by the French. In 1435 it passed to Aragon.

The five major Italian city-states competed furiously among themselves for territory. They used diplomacy, spies, paid informers, and any other means to advance their ambitions. While the states of northern Europe were moving toward centralization and consolidation, the world of Italian politics resembled a jungle where the powerful dominated the weak.

In one significant respect, however, the Italian city-states anticipated future relations among competing European states after 1500. Whenever one Italian state appeared to gain a dominant position on the peninsula, the other states joined forces to establish a *balance of power* against the major threat. In forming these shifting alliances, Renaissance Italians invented the machinery of modern diplomacy: permanent embassies with resident ambassadors in capitals where political relations and commercial ties needed continual monitoring. The resident ambassador is one of the great achievements of the Italian Renaissance.

At the end of the fifteenth century, Venice, Florence, Milan, and the Papal States possessed great wealth and represented high cultural achievement. However, their imperialistic ambitions at one another's expense, and their resulting inability to form a common alliance against potential foreign enemies, made Italy an inviting target for invasion. When Florence and Naples entered into an agreement to acquire Milanese territories, Milan called on France for support.

The invasion of Italy in 1494 by the French king Charles VIII (r. 1483–1498) inaugurated a new period in Italian and European power politics. Italy became the focus of international ambitions and the battleground of foreign armies. Charles swept the peninsula with little opposition.

In the sixteenth century, the political and social life of Italy was upset by the relentless competition for dominance between France and the Holy Roman Empire. The Italian cities suffered severely from the continual warfare, especially in the frightful sack of Rome in 1527 by imperial forces under Charles V. Thus the failure of the Italian city-states to form a common alliance against foreign enemies led to the continuation of the centuries-old subjection of the Italian peninsula by outside invaders.

✣ INTELLECTUAL HALLMARKS OF THE RENAISSANCE

Some Italians in the fourteenth and fifteenth centuries believed that they were living in a new era. Poet and humanist Francesco Petrarch (1304–1374), for example, thought that the Germanic invasions had caused a sharp cultural break with the glories of Rome and had ushered in what he called the "Dark Ages." In the opinion of Petrarch and many of his contemporaries, the thousand-year period between the fourth and the fourteenth centuries constituted a barbarian, or Gothic, or "middle" age (hence historians' use of the expression "Middle Ages"). The sculptors, painters, and writers of the Renaissance spoke contemptuously of their medieval predecessors and identified themselves with the thinkers and artists of Greco-Roman civilization. Petrarch believed he was witnessing a new golden age of intellectual achievement—a rebirth, or, to use the French word that came into English, a *renaissance*.

The division of historical time into periods is often arbitrary and done by historians for their own conve-

nience. In terms of the way most people lived and thought, no sharp division existed between the Middle Ages and the Renaissance. The guild and the parish, for example, continued to provide strong support for the individual and to exercise great social influence. Renaissance intellectuals, however, developed a new sense of historical distance, and some important poets, writers, and artists believed they were living in a new age.

The Renaissance also manifested itself in new attitudes toward individuals, learning, and the world at large. There was a renewal of belief in the importance of the individual, a rebirth of interest in the Latin classics and in antique lifestyles, and a restoration of interest in the material world.

Individualism

Though the Middle Ages had seen the appearance of remarkable individuals, recognition of such persons was limited. Christian humility discouraged self-absorption. In the fourteenth and fifteenth centuries, however, a large literature presenting a distinctly Renaissance individualism emerged.

Many distinctive individuals gloried in their uniqueness. Italians of unusual abilities were self-consciously aware of their singularity and unafraid to be different from their neighbors; they had enormous confidence in their ability to achieve great things. Leon Battista Alberti (1404–1474), a writer, architect, and mathematician, remarked, "Men can do all things if they will."[4] The Florentine goldsmith and sculptor Benvenuto Cellini (1500–1574) prefaced his *Autobiography* with a sonnet that declares:

My cruel fate hath warr'd with me in vain:
Life, glory, worth, and all unmeasur'd skill,
Beauty and grace, themselves in me fulfill
That many I surpass, and to the best attain.[5]

Certain of his genius, Cellini wrote so that the whole world might appreciate it.

Individualism stressed personality, uniqueness, and the full development of capabilities and talents. Artist, athlete, painter, scholar, sculptor, whatever—a person's abilities should be stretched until fully realized.

Humanism

In the cities of Italy, especially Rome, civic leaders and the wealthy populace showed great archaeological zeal for the recovery of manuscripts, statues, and monuments. The Vatican Library, planned in the fifteenth century to house the nine thousand manuscripts collected by Pope Nicholas V (r. 1447–1455), remains one of the richest repositories of ancient and medieval documents. Patrician Italians consciously copied the lifestyle of the ancients and tried to trace their genealogies back to ancient Rome.

The revival of interest in antiquity was also apparent in the serious study of the Latin classics. This feature of the Renaissance became known as the "new learning," or simply "humanism," the term used by the Florentine rhetorician and historian Leonardo Bruni (1370–1444). The words *humanism* and *humanist* derived from the Latin *humanitas,* which Cicero used to refer to the literary culture needed by anyone who wanted to be considered educated and civilized. Humanism focused on human beings—their achievements, interests, and capabilities. Although churchmen supported the new learning, by the later fifteenth century Italian humanism was increasingly a lay phenomenon.

Appreciation of the literary culture of the Romans had never died in the West. Bede (see page 335), for example, had studied and imitated the writings of the ancients. But medieval writers had accepted pagan and classical authors uncritically. Renaissance humanists, in contrast, were skeptical of their authority, conscious of the historical distance separating themselves from the ancients, and fully aware that classical writers often disagreed among themselves. Medieval writers looked to the classics to reveal God. Renaissance humanists studied the classics to understand human nature, though from a strongly Christian perspective. For example, in a remarkable essay, *On the Dignity of Man,* the Florentine writer Pico della Mirandola (1463–1494) stressed that man possesses great dignity because he was made in the image of God before the Fall and as Christ after the Resurrection. According to Pico, man's place in the universe is somewhere between the beasts and the angels, but, because of the divine image planted in him, there are no limits to what man can accomplish.

The leading humanists of the early Renaissance were rhetoricians, seeking effective and eloquent communication, both oral and written. They loved the language of the classics and scorned the corrupt, "barbaric" Latin of the medieval schoolmen.

Secular Spirit

Secularism is a basic concern with the material world instead of with eternal and spiritual matters. A secular way of thinking tends to find the ultimate explanation of everything and the final end of human beings within

the limits of what the senses can discover. Medieval business people ruthlessly pursued profits, while medieval monks fought fiercely over property. But medieval society was religious, not secular: the dominant ideals focused on the otherworldly, on life after death. Renaissance people often held strong and deep spiritual beliefs. But Renaissance society was secular: attention was concentrated on the here and now, often on the acquisition of material things. The fourteenth and fifteenth centuries witnessed the slow but steady growth of secularism in Italy.

The economic changes and rising prosperity of the Italian cities in the thirteenth century worked a fundamental change in social and intellectual attitudes and values. Worries about shifting rates of interest, shipping routes, personnel costs, and employee relations did not leave much time for thoughts about penance and purgatory. Wealth made possible greater material pleasures, a more comfortable life, the leisure time to appreciate and patronize the arts. Money could buy many sensual gratifications, and the rich, social-climbing bankers and merchants of the Italian cities came to see life more as an opportunity to be enjoyed than as a painful pilgrimage to the City of God.

In *On Pleasure,* the humanist Lorenzo Valla (1406–1457) defends the pleasures of the senses as the highest good. Scholars praise Valla as a father of modern historical criticism. His study *On the False Donation of Constantine* (1444) demonstrates by careful textual examination that an anonymous eighth-century document supposedly giving the papacy jurisdiction over vast territories in western Europe was a forgery. The proof that the Donation was a forgery weakened papal claims to temporal authority. Lorenzo Valla's work exemplifies the application of critical scholarship to old and almost-sacred writings, as well as the new secular spirit of the Renaissance.

Renaissance writers justified the accumulation and enjoyment of wealth with references to ancient authors, and church leaders did little to combat the new secular spirit. Renaissance popes beautified the city of Rome, patronized artists and men of letters, and expended enormous enthusiasm and huge sums of money. Pope Julius II (r. 1503–1513) tore down the old Saint Peter's Basilica and began work on the present structure in 1506. Michelangelo's dome for Saint Peter's is still considered his greatest work.

Although papal interests fostered the new worldly attitude, the broad mass of the people and the intellectuals and leaders of society remained faithful to the Christian church. Few questioned the basic tenets of the Christian religion. The thousands of pious paintings, sculptures, processions, and pilgrimages of the Renaissance period prove that strong religious feeling persisted.

Art and the Artist

No feature of the Renaissance evokes greater admiration than its artistic masterpieces. The 1400s (called *quattrocento* in Italian) and 1500s *(cinquecento)* bore witness to a dazzling creativity in painting, architecture, and sculpture. In all the arts, the city of Florence first led the way. In the period art historians describe as the High Renaissance (1500–1527), Rome took the lead. The main characteristics of High Renaissance art—classical balance, harmony, and restraint—are revealed in the masterpieces of Leonardo da Vinci (1452–1519), Raphael (1483–1520), and Michelangelo (1475–1564), all of whom worked in Rome.

In early Renaissance Italy, art manifested corporate power. Powerful urban groups such as guilds and reli-gious confraternities commissioned works of art. The Florentine cloth merchants, for example, delegated Filippo Brunelleschi (1377–1446) to build the magnificent dome on the cathedral of Florence and selected Lorenzo Ghiberti (1378–1455) to design the bronze doors of the Baptistry. These works were signs of the merchants' dominant influence in the community. The subject matter of art through the early fifteenth century, as in the Middle Ages, remained overwhelmingly religious.

Increasingly in the later quattrocento, individuals and oligarchs, rather than corporate groups, sponsored works of art. Merchants, bankers, popes, and princes supported the arts as a means of glorifying themselves, their families, and their power. Vast sums were spent on family chapels, frescoes, religious panels, and tombs.

As the fifteenth century advanced, the subject matter of art became steadily more secular. Religious topics, such as the Annunciation of the Virgin, remained popular among both patrons and artists, but classical themes and motifs, such as the lives and loves of pagan gods and goddesses, figured increasingly in painting

Gentile Bellini: Procession in the Piazza San Marco   Gentile's masterpiece celebrates Venice's annual festival on the Feast of Saint Mark (April 25). In the center of the piazza, a vast section of a cosmopolitan society appears: patricians and ordinary citizens, German merchants, priests, Greeks in black hats, Turks, a black man. The picture shows the artist's superb understanding of perspective, eye for detail (women witness the scene from the arched openings), insight into individual personalities (contemporaries could have identified many persons), and rich appreciation of color. Under the red canopy is a golden monstrance holding a relic of the True Cross. A fine example of Renaissance narrative painting. *(Scala/Art Resource, NY)*

Andrea Mantegna: Adoration of the Magi (ca 1495–1505) Applying his study of ancient Roman relief sculpture, and elaborating on a famous Scriptural text (Matthew 2:1),
Mantegna painted for the private devotion of the Gonzaga family of Mantua this scene of the
Three Kings coming to recognize the divinity of Christ. The Three Kings represent the entire
world—that is, the three continents known to medieval Europeans: Europe, Asia, and Africa.
They also symbolize the three stages of life: youth, maturity, and old age. Here Melchior, the
oldest, his large cranium symbolizing wisdom, personifies Europe. He offers gold in a Chinese porcelain cup from the Ming Dynasty. Balthazar, with an olive complexion and dark
beard, stands for Asia and maturity. He presents frankincense in a stunning vessel of Turkish
tombac ware. Caspar, representing Africa and youth, gives myrrh in an urn of striped marble.
The child responds with a blessing. The black background brings out the rich colors. (*The J.
Paul Getty Museum, Los Angeles. Mantegna, Andrea,* Adoration of the Magi, *ca 1495–1505, distemper
on linen, 54.6 × 70.7 cm [85.PA.417]*)

and sculpture. The individual portrait emerged as a distinct artistic genre. Rather than reflecting a spiritual
ideal, as medieval painting and sculpture tended to do,
Renaissance portraits mirrored reality.

The Florentine painter Giotto (1276–1337) led the
way in the use of realism; his treatment of the human
body and face replaced the formal stiffness and arti-
ficiality that had for so long characterized the representation of the human body. The sculptor Donatello's
(1386–1466) many statues express an appreciation of
the incredible variety of human nature. He revived the
classical figure with its balance and self-awareness. The
short-lived Florentine Masaccio (1401–1428), sometimes called the father of modern painting, inspired a

new style characterized by great realism, narrative
power, and effective use of light and dark.

As important as realism was the new "international
style," so called because of the wandering careers of influential artists, the close communications and rivalry of
princely courts, and the increased trade in works of art.
Rich color, decorative detail, curvilinear rhythms, and
swaying forms characterized the international style. As
the term *international* implies, this style was European,
not merely Italian.

The growing secular influences on art are reflected in
the improved social status of the artist in the Renaissance. The lower-middle-class medieval master mason
had been viewed in the same light as a mechanic. The

artist in the Renaissance was considered a free intellectual worker. Artists did not produce unsolicited pictures or statues for the general public; that could mean loss of status. They usually worked on commission from a powerful prince. The artist's reputation depended on the support of powerful patrons, and through them some artists and architects achieved not only economic security but great wealth. All aspiring artists received a practical (not theoretical) education in a recognized master's workshop. (See the feature "Individuals in Society: Gentile Bellini.")

Renaissance society respected and rewarded the distinguished artist. At a time when a person could live in a princely fashion on 300 ducats a year, Leonardo da Vinci was making 2,000 ducats annually. Michelangelo was paid 3,000 ducats for painting the ceiling of the Sistine Chapel.

The Renaissance witnessed the birth of the concept of the artist as genius. In the Middle Ages, people believed that only God created, albeit through individuals; the medieval conception recognized no particular value in artistic originality. Boastful Renaissance artists and humanists came to think that a work of art was the deliberate creation of a unique personality, of an individual who transcended traditions, rules, and theories. A genius had a peculiar gift, which ordinary laws should not inhibit. Cosimo de' Medici described a painter, because of his genius, as "divine," implying that the artist shared in the powers of God. Others applied the word *divine* to Michelangelo.

But the student must remember that Italian Renaissance culture was that of a small mercantile elite, a business patriciate with aristocratic pretensions. Renaissance culture did not directly affect the broad middle classes, let alone the vast urban proletariat. Renaissance humanists were a smaller and narrower group than the medieval clergy had ever been. In the Middle Ages, high churchmen had commissioned the construction of the Gothic cathedrals, but, once finished, the buildings were for all to enjoy. Nothing comparable was built in the Renaissance. A small, highly educated group of literary humanists and artists created the culture of and for an exclusive elite. They cared little for ordinary people.[6]

The Renaissance in the North

In the last quarter of the fifteenth century, Italian Renaissance thought and ideals penetrated northern Europe. Students from the Low Countries, France, Germany, and England flocked to Italy, imbibed the "new learning," and carried it back to their countries. However, cultural traditions of northern Europe

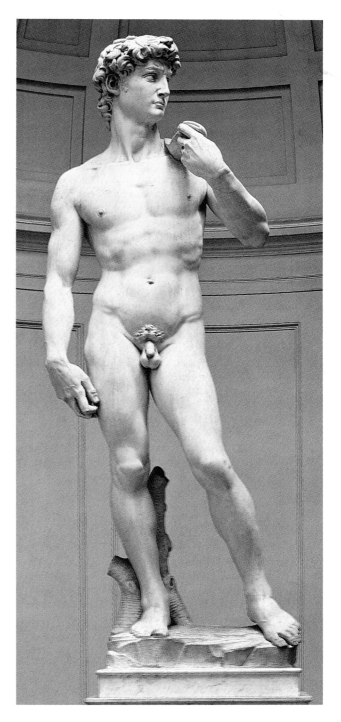

Michelangelo: David   In 1501 the new republican government of Florence commissioned the twenty-six-year-old Michelangelo to carve David as a symbol of civic independence and resistance to oligarchical tyranny. Tensed in anticipation of action but certain of victory over his unseen enemy Goliath (1 Samuel 17), this male nude represents the ideal of youthful physical perfection. *(Scala/Art Resource, NY)*

Gentile Bellini (ca 1431–1507)

Bellini's *Turkish Scribe*. We have no likeness of Bellini himself. *(Isabella Stewart Gardner Museum, Boston)*

In 1474 the Venetian Senate, the city's governing body, voted to accept the offer of "Maistro Gentile Bellini, eminent painter and excellent master," to restore the paintings in the Great Council Hall, "which is one of the principal ornaments of our city."[1] The son, brother, and brother-in-law of distinguished artists, named for Gentile da Fabriano (ca 1370–1427), the exponent of the international Gothic style, Gentile Bellini was formed in a rich artistic milieu. His father, Jacopo, taught his sons the elements of design; father and sons worked together in the family workshop. By 1469 Gentile's reputation was so strong that the Holy Roman emperor Frederick III on a visit to Venice rewarded him with the title palatine knight, possibly for a portrait of Frederick. The sixteenth-century biographer Giorgio Vasari combined Jacopo and his sons Giovanni and Gentile in one sketch of their lives and works, but Gentile stands out from them as a narrative painter, a representative of civil humanism, and a diplomat to Constantinople.

Venetian commercial ties with Constantinople stretching back to the eleventh century and vastly expanded by the Fourth Crusade (see page 350) were jeopardized by the Ottoman conquest of Constantinople. An agreement signed at Venice in 1479 provided the opportunity for the sultan's ambassador to see Gentile Bellini's paintings in the Great Council Hall. Four months later, "a Jewish orator[2] from the Lord Turk arrived with letters. He wished the Senate to send him a good painter. . . . The Senate responded . . . and sent Gentile Bellini."[3] He went both as an artist and as a sort of "extraordinary ambassador," or informant, charged with reporting conditions in the Ottoman capital.

Bellini spent about a year in Constantinople. He did a splendid portrait on canvas of Mehmet II, another portrait in bronze, various genre paintings of the city, and *cosi di lussuria,* usually translated as "erotic pictures" but recently described as scenes of festive occasions at the Ottoman court. The sultan was so pleased that he made him a Golden Knight of the Ottoman Empire and showered him with gifts, including a heavy gold chain. He was welcomed home with fanfare, but the contents of his political report have not survived.

Perhaps the most famous of Bellini's extant paintings is the *Procession in the Piazza San Marco* (shown on page 447), executed between 1494 and 1505 for a local confraternity. Confraternities provided social and financial support for their members. Venetian confraternities, in contrast to those in other Italian cities, also performed a civic function: they used artworks and festive occasions to glorify the Republic of Saint Mark. In a long procession, members of the confraternity hold center stage. To the left, other confraternities have completed marching and wait in formal ranks. To the right, officials and dignitaries bring up the rear of the procession. Dominating the scene is the great basilica of Saint Mark, the republic's political and religious center, with its Byzantine architectural style.

Someone once wrote, "There are more valid facts and details in works of art than there are in history books." This reflects a mistaken notion of what history is all about. Art is a history book. Gentile Bellini has left us a richly appealing slice of Renaissance life.

Questions for Analysis

1. How did Gentile Bellini follow the pattern of other humanists, such as Petrarch and Machiavelli?
2. What does the *Procession in the Piazza San Marco* tell us about Venetian society?

1. Quoted in Patricia Fortini Brown, *Venetian Narrative Painting in the Age of Carpaccio* (New Haven, Conn.: Yale University Press, 1989), p. 51.
2. Just as Jews sometimes served in the papal bureaucracy, so they served in Muslim governments. Because Muslims found Europeans hostile, they often employed Jews on commercial and diplomatic missions.
3. Quoted in Brown, *Venetian Narrative Painting,* p. 54.

tended to remain more distinctly Christian, or at least pietistic, than those of Italy. What fundamentally distinguished Italian humanists from northern ones is that the latter had a program for broad social reform based on Christian ideals.

Christian humanists in northern Europe were interested in the development of an ethical way of life. To achieve it, they believed, the best elements of classical and Christian cultures should be combined. For example, the classical ideals of calmness, stoical patience, and broad-mindedness should be joined in human conduct with the Christian virtues of love, faith, and hope. Christian humanists had a profound faith in the power of human intellect to bring about moral and institutional reform. They believed that human nature had been corrupted by sin but nevertheless was fundamentally good and capable of improvement through education, which would lead to piety and an ethical way of life.

The Englishman Thomas More (1478–1535) towers above other figures in sixteenth-century English social and intellectual history. More, who practiced law, entered government service during the reign of Henry VIII and was sent as ambassador to Flanders. There More found the time to write *Utopia* (1516), which presents a revolutionary view of society.

Utopia, which literally means "nowhere," describes an ideal socialistic community on an island somewhere off the mainland of the New World. All its children receive a good education, and since the goal of all education is to develop rational faculties, adults divide their days equally between manual labor or business pursuits and various intellectual activities. The profits from business and property are held strictly in common, so there is absolute social equality. The Utopians use gold and silver both to make chamber pots and to prevent wars by buying off their enemies. By this casual use of precious metals, More meant to suggest that the basic problems in society are caused by greed. Utopian law exalts mercy above justice. Citizens of Utopia lead a nearly perfect existence because they live by reason. More punned on the word *Utopia,* which he termed "a good place. A good place which is no place."

More's ideas were profoundly original in the sixteenth century. The long-prevailing view was that vice and violence exist because women and men are basically corrupt. But More maintained that acquisitiveness and private property promote all sorts of vices and civil disorders and that because society protects private property, *society's* flawed institutions are responsible for corruption and war. Today people take this view so much for granted that it is difficult to appreciate how radical it was in the sixteenth century. According to More, the key to improvement and reform of the individual is reform of the social institutions that mold the individual.

Better known by contemporaries than Thomas More was the Dutch humanist Desiderius Erasmus of Rotterdam (1466?–1536), whose lifework became the application of the best humanistic learning to the study and explanation of the Bible.

Erasmus's long list of publications includes *The Education of a Christian Prince* (1504), which combines idealistic and practical suggestions for the formation of a ruler's character; *The Praise of Folly* (1509), a satire on worldly wisdom and a plea for the simple and spontaneous Christian faith of children; and, most important of all, a critical edition of the Greek New Testament (1516). In the preface to the New Testament, Erasmus explains the purpose of his great work:

For I utterly dissent from those who are unwilling that the sacred Scriptures should be read by the unlearned translated into their vulgar tongue, as though Christ had taught such subtleties that they can scarcely be understood even by a few theologians. . . . Christ wished his mysteries to be published as openly as possible.[7]

Two fundamental themes run through all of Erasmus's scholarly work. First, education—study of the Bible and the classics—is the means to reform, the key to moral and intellectual improvement. Second, the essence of Erasmus's thought is, in his own phrase, "the philosophy of Christ." By this Erasmus meant that Christianity is an inner attitude of the heart or spirit. Christianity is not formalism, special ceremonies, or law; Christianity is Christ—his life and what he said and did, not what theologians have written about him.

The distinctly religious orientation of the literary works of the Renaissance in the north also characterized northern art and architecture. Some Flemish painters, notably Rogier van der Weyden (1399/1400–1464) and Jan van Eyck (1366–1441), were considered the artistic equals of Italian painters, were much admired in Italy, and worked a generation before Leonardo and Michelangelo. One of the earliest artists successfully to use oil-based paints, van Eyck, in paintings such as *Ghent Altarpiece* and the portrait *Giovanni Arnolfini and His Bride,* shows the Flemish love for detail; the effect is great realism and remarkable attention to human personality.

A quasi-spiritual aura infuses architectural monuments in the north. The city halls of wealthy Flemish towns such as Bruges, Brussels, Louvain, and Ghent

Gerard David: Triptych with the Nativity A triptych is a painting with three panels, the side panels hinged to fold over the central one. In the central panel here, angels descend and shepherds peer through the broken wall as Joseph and Mary adore the child. An ox, metaphor for strength, patience, and docility, and an ass, symbolizing humility and long-suffering, guard the scene. At left a bishop holds a staff, and the donor (who commissioned the painting) wears a fur-trimmed coat, showing his wealth. At right a deacon in dalmatic holds the Gospel book, as the donor's wife kneels. *(The Metropolitan Museum of Art, The Jules Bache Collection, 1949 [49.7.20a–c])*

strike the viewer more as shrines to house the bones of saints than as settings for the mundane decisions of politicians and business people. Northern architecture was little influenced by the classical revival so obvious in Renaissance Rome and Florence.

SOCIAL CHANGE DURING THE RENAISSANCE

The Renaissance changed many aspects of Italian and, subsequently, European society. The new developments brought about real breaks with the medieval past in education and political thought, through new printing technology, and in the experiences of women and blacks.

Education and Political Thought

Education and moral behavior were central preoccupations of the humanists. Humanists poured out treatises, often in the form of letters, on the structure and goals of education and the training of rulers. In one of the earliest systematic programs for the young, Peter Paul Vergerio (1370–1444) wrote Ubertinus, the ruler of Carrara:

For the education of children is a matter of more than private interest; it concerns the State, which indeed regards

the right training of the young as, in certain aspects, within its proper sphere. . . . Above all, respect for Divine ordinances is of the deepest importance; it should be inculcated from the earliest years. Reverence towards elders and parents is an obligation closely akin.

We call those studies liberal which are worthy of a free man; those studies by which we attain and practice virtue and wisdom.[8]

No book on education had broader influence than Baldassare Castiglione's *The Courtier* (1528). This treatise sought to train, discipline, and fashion the young man into the courtly ideal, the gentleman. According to Castiglione (1478–1529), the educated man of the upper class should have a broad background in many academic subjects, and his spiritual and physical, as well as intellectual, capabilities should be trained. The courtier should have easy familiarity with dance, music, and the arts. Castiglione envisioned a man who could compose a sonnet, wrestle, sing a song and accompany himself on an instrument, ride expertly, solve difficult mathematical problems, and above all speak and write eloquently. In the sixteenth and seventeenth centuries, the courtier envisioned by Castiglione became the model of the European gentleman.

No Renaissance book on any topic has been more widely read and studied in all the centuries since its publication in 1513 than the short political treatise *The Prince,* by Niccolò Machiavelli (1469–1527). The subject of *The Prince* is political power: how the ruler should gain, maintain, and increase it. A good humanist, Machiavelli explored the problems of human nature and concluded that human beings are selfish and out to advance their own interests. This pessimistic view of humanity led him to maintain that the prince may have to manipulate the people in any way he finds necessary:

For a man who, in all respects, will carry out only his professions of good, will be apt to be ruined amongst so many who are evil. A prince therefore who desires to maintain himself must learn to be not always good, but to be so or not as necessity may require.[9]

The prince should combine the cunning of a fox with the ferocity of a lion to achieve his goals. Pondering the question of whether it is better for a ruler to be loved or feared, Machiavelli wrote:

It will naturally be answered that it would be desirable to be both the one and the other; but as it is difficult to be both at the same time, it is much more safe to be feared than to be loved, when you have to choose between the two. For it may be said of men in general that they are ungrateful and fickle, dissemblers, avoiders of danger, and greedy of gain. So long as you shower benefits upon them, they are all yours.[10]

Medieval political theorists and theologians had stressed the way government *ought* to be. They had set high moral and Christian standards for the ruler's conduct. In their opinion, the test of good government is whether it provides justice, law, and order. Machiavelli maintained that the ruler should be concerned not with the way things ought to be but with the way things actually are. The sole test of whether a government is "good" is whether it is effective, whether the ruler increases his power. Machiavelli believed that political action cannot be restricted by moral considerations, but he did not advocate amoral behavior. On the basis of a simplistic interpretation of *The Prince,* the adjective *Machiavellian* entered the language as a synonym for devious, corrupt, and crafty politics in which the end justifies the means. Machiavelli's ultimate significance rests on two ideas: that one permanent social order reflecting God's will cannot be established and that politics has its own laws and ought to be considered a science.[11]

Movable Type and the Spread of Literacy

Sometime in the thirteenth century, paper money and playing cards from China reached the West. They were block-printed—that is, each word, phrase, or picture was carved on a separate wooden block to be inked and used for printing. This method of reproduction was extraordinarily expensive and slow. By the middle of the fifteenth century, Europeans had mastered paper manufacture, which also originated in China and was introduced by the Arabs to the West in the twelfth century. Then around 1455, probably through the combined efforts of three men—Johann Gutenberg, Johann Fust, and Peter Schöffer, all experimenting at Mainz—movable type came into being in the West. The mirror image of each letter (rather than entire words or phrases) was carved in relief on a small block. Individual letters, easily movable, were put together to form words in lines of type that made up a page. An infinite variety of texts could be printed by reusing and rearranging pieces of type.

The effects of the invention of movable-type printing were not obvious overnight. But within a half century of the publication of Gutenberg's Bible of 1456, printing from movable type brought about radical changes. It transformed both the private and the public lives of Europeans. Governments that "had employed the cumbersome methods of manuscripts to communicate with their subjects switched quickly to print to announce declarations of war, publish battle accounts, promulgate treaties or argue disputed points in pamphlet form. Theirs was an effort 'to win the psychological war.'" Printing made propaganda possible, emphasizing differences between opposing groups such as Crown and nobility, church and state. These differences laid the basis for the formation of distinct political parties.

Printing also stimulated the literacy of laypeople and eventually came to have a deep effect on their private lives. Although most of the earliest books and pamphlets dealt with religious subjects, students, housewives, businessmen, and upper- and middle-class people sought books on all subjects. Broadsides and flysheets allowed great public festivals, religious ceremonies, and political events to be experienced vicariously by the stay-at-home. Since books and other printed materials were read aloud to illiterate listeners, print bridged the gap between written and oral cultures.[12]

Women

During the Renaissance, the status of upper-class women declined. If women in the central Middle Ages are compared with those of fifteenth- and sixteenth-century Italy with respect to the kind of work they performed, their access to property and political power,

Sofonisba Anguissola: The Artist's Sister Minerva   A nobleman's daughter and one of the first Italian women to become a recognized artist, Sofonisba did portraits of her five sisters and of prominent people. The coiffure, elegant gown, necklaces, and rings depict aristocratic dress in the mid-sixteenth century. *(Milwaukee Art Museum)*

and their role in shaping the outlook of their society, it is clear that ladies in the Renaissance ruling classes generally had less power than comparable ladies in the feudal age.

In the cities of Renaissance Italy, well-to-do girls received an education similar to boys'. Young ladies learned their letters and studied the classics. Many read Greek as well as Latin, knew the poetry of Ovid and Virgil, and could speak one or two "modern" languages, such as French or Spanish. In this respect, Renaissance humanism represented a real educational advance for women. Some women, though a small minority among humanists, acquired great learning and fame. Some Italian women published books, and Sofonisba Anguissola (1530–1625) achieved international renown for her paintings.

Ordinary girls of the urban upper middle class received some training in painting, music, and dance, in addition to a classical education. What were they to do with this training? They were to be gracious, affable, charming—in short, decorative. Renaissance women were better educated than their medieval counterparts. But whereas education trained a young man to participate in the public affairs of the city, it prepared a woman for the social functions of the home. An educated lady was supposed to know how to attract artists and literati to her husband's court and how to grace her husband's household. An educated man was supposed to know how to rule and participate in public affairs.

With respect to love and sex, the Renaissance witnessed a downward shift in women's status. In contrast to the medieval tradition of relative sexual equality, Renaissance humanists laid the foundations for the bourgeois double standard. Men, and men alone, operated in the public sphere; women belonged in the home. Castiglione, the foremost spokesman of Renaissance love and manners, completely separated love from sexuality. For women, sex was restricted entirely to marriage. Ladies were bound to chastity, to the roles of wife and mother in a politically arranged marriage. Men, however, could pursue sensual indulgence outside marriage.[13]

Did the Renaissance have an impact on the lives of ordinary women? Women, of course, continued to perform economic functions in the expanding industries. Rural women assisted husbands and fathers in agricultural tasks. Urban women helped in the shops and were heavily involved in the Florentine textile industry, weaving cloth and reeling and winding silk. In the Venetian Arsenal, the state-controlled dock and ship construction area—the largest single industrial plant in Europe—women made sails. Widows frequently ran their husbands' businesses, and in Italy and France some became full members of guilds.

Blacks

The presence of black Africans in Renaissance Europe, sometimes in sizable numbers, illustrates cross-continental and cross-cultural contacts before the "Age of Discovery" and the huge migrations of blacks to the Americas, Asia, and Europe in the sixteenth through nineteenth centuries. Until the fifteenth century, the number of blacks living in western Europe was small. Then, in the fifteenth century, increasing numbers of black slaves began to enter Europe. Portuguese explorers imported perhaps a thousand a year and sold them at the markets of Seville, Barcelona, Marseilles, and Genoa. By the mid-sixteenth century, blacks, slave and free, constituted about 10 percent of the populations of the Portuguese cities of Lisbon and Évora; other cities had smaller percentages. In all, blacks made up roughly 3 percent of the Portuguese population. The Venetians specialized in the import of white slaves, but blacks were so greatly in demand at the Renaissance courts of northern Italy that the Venetians defied papal threats of excommunication to secure them.

What roles did blacks play in Renaissance society? What image did Europeans have of Africans? The medieval interest in curiosities, the exotic, and the marvelous continued into the Renaissance. Because of their rarity, black servants were highly prized and a symbol of wealth. In the late fifteenth century, Isabella, the wife of Gian Galazzo Sforza, took pride in the fact that she had ten black servants.

Adult black slaves filled a variety of positions. Many served as maids, valets, and domestic servants. The Venetians employed blacks—slave and free—as gondoliers and stevedores on the docks. In Portugal, they supplemented the labor force in virtually all occupations.[14] In Renaissance Spain and Italy, blacks performed as dancers, as actors and actresses in courtly dramas, and as musicians, sometimes making up full orchestras.[15] Slavery during the Renaissance foreshadowed the American, especially the later Brazilian, pattern.

Before the sixteenth-century "discoveries" of the non-European world, Europeans had little concrete knowledge of Africans and their cultures. Europeans knew little about them beyond biblical accounts, and their attitude toward Africans was ambivalent.[16] On the one hand, Europeans perceived Africa as a remote place, the home of strange people isolated by heresy and Islam from supposedly superior European civilization. They believed that contact with Christian Europeans could only "improve" black Africans. Theologians taught that God was light, and blackness, the opposite of light, was believed to represent the hostile forces of evil, sin, and the Devil. Thus in medieval and early Renaissance art, the Devil was commonly represented as a black man. On the other hand, blackness was also associated with certain positive qualities. It symbolized the emptiness of worldly goods and the humility of the monastic way of life. Black vestments and funeral trappings indicated grief, and Christ had said that those who mourn are blessed. In Renaissance society blacks—like women—also were signs of wealth; both were used for display.

Drummer   In the early sixteenth century, blacks—such as this drummer in the court of the Emperor Charles V—were highly visible in Portuguese, Spanish, and Italian societies. *(Photographs and Prints Division, Schomburg Center for Research in Black Culture, The New York Public Library, Astor, Lenox, and Tilden Foundations)*

POLITICS AND THE STATE IN THE RENAISSANCE (CA 1450–1521)

The central Middle Ages witnessed the beginnings of many of the basic institutions of the modern state. The linchpin for the development of states was strong monarchy, and during the period of the Hundred Years' War, no ruler in western Europe was able to provide effective leadership. The resurgent power of feudal nobilities weakened the centralizing work begun earlier.

Beginning in the fifteenth century, rulers utilized the aggressive methods implied by Renaissance political ideas to rebuild their governments. First in Italy (see page 444), then in France, England, and Spain, rulers began the work of reducing violence, curbing unruly nobles and troublesome elements, and establishing domestic order. The Holy Roman Empire of Germany, however, remained divided into scores of independent principalities.

The despots and oligarchs of the Italian city-states, together with Louis XI of France, Henry VII of

England, and Ferdinand of Aragon, were tough, cynical, calculating rulers. In their ruthless push for power and strong governments, they subordinated morality to hard results. They preferred to be secure and feared rather than loved. They could not have read Machiavelli's *The Prince,* but their actions were in harmony with its ideas.

Some historians have called Louis XI (r. 1461–1483), Henry VII (r. 1485–1509), and Ferdinand and Isabella in Spain (r. 1474–1516) "new monarchs" because they invested kingship with a strong sense of royal authority and national purpose. They stressed that the monarchy was the one institution that linked all classes and peoples within definite territorial boundaries. They insisted on the respect and loyalty of all subjects and ruthlessly suppressed opposition and rebellion, especially from the nobility. And they loved the business of kingship and worked hard at it.

In other respects, however, the methods of these rulers, which varied from country to country, were not so new. They reasserted long-standing ideas and practices of strong monarchs in the Middle Ages. To advance their authority, they seized on the maxim of the Justinian *Code*: "What pleases the prince has the force of law." Like medieval rulers, Renaissance rulers tended to rely on middle-class civil servants. Using tax revenues, medieval rulers had built armies to crush feudal anarchy. Renaissance townspeople with commercial and business interests wanted a reduction of violence, and usually they were willing to pay taxes in order to achieve it.

France

The Hundred Years' War left France badly divided, drastically depopulated, commercially ruined, and agriculturally weak. Nonetheless, the ruler whom Joan of Arc had seen crowned at Reims, Charles VII (r. 1422–1461), revived the monarchy and France. He seemed an unlikely person to do so. Frail, indecisive, and burdened with questions about his paternity (his father was deranged, his mother notoriously promiscuous), Charles VII nevertheless began France's long recovery.

Charles reorganized the royal council, giving increased influence to middle-class men, and strengthened royal finances through taxes such as the *gabelle* (on salt) and the *taille* (on land). By establishing regular companies of cavalry and archers—recruited, paid, and inspected by the state—Charles created the first permanent royal army. In 1438 he published the Pragmatic Sanction of Bourges, giving the French crown major control over the appointment of bishops and depriving the pope of French ecclesiastical revenues. The

Pragmatic Sanction affirmed the special rights of the French crown over the French church.

Charles's son Louis XI (r. 1461–1483), called the "Spider King" by his subjects because of his treacherous and cruel character, was very much a Renaissance prince. Facing the perpetual French problems of unification of the realm and reduction of feudal disorder, he saw money as the answer. Louis promoted new industries, such as silk weaving at Lyons and Tours, and entered into commercial treaties with other countries. The revenues raised through these economic activities and severe taxation were used to improve the army. With the army, Louis stopped aristocratic brigandage and slowly cut into urban independence. He was also able to gain territory that furthered his goal of expanding royal authority and unifying the kingdom. Some scholars have credited Louis XI with laying the foundations for later French royal absolutism.

England

English society suffered severely from the disorders of the fifteenth century. The aristocracy dominated the government and indulged in mischievous violence at the local level. Population, decimated by the Black Death, continued to decline. Then between 1455 and 1471, supporters of the ducal houses of York and Lancaster waged civil war, commonly called the Wars of the Roses because the symbol of the Yorkists was a white rose and that of the Lancastrians a red one. The chronic disorder hurt trade, agriculture, and domestic industry, and the authority of the monarchy sank lower than it had been in centuries.

The Yorkist Edward IV (r. 1461–1483) began reestablishing domestic tranquillity. He defeated the Lancastrian forces and after 1471 began to reconstruct the monarchy and consolidate royal power. Henry VII (r. 1485–1509) of the Welsh house of Tudor advanced the work of restoring royal prestige by crushing the power of the nobility and establishing order and law at the local level.

The Hundred Years' War had cost the nation dearly, and the money to finance it had been raised by Parliament, the arena where the nobility exerted its power. As long as the monarchy was dependent on the Lords and the Commons for revenue, the king had to call Parliament. Thus Edward IV, and subsequently the Tudors except for Henry VIII, conducted foreign policy by means of diplomacy and avoided expensive wars. Unlike the continental countries of Spain and France, England had no standing army or professional civil service bureaucracy. The Tudors relied on the support of unpaid local justices of the peace—influential landowners in the shires—to handle the work of local government. From the royal point of view, they were an inexpensive method of government. Thus for a time, the English monarchy did not depend on Parliament for money, and the Crown undercut that source of aristocratic influence.

The center of royal authority under Henry VII was the royal council, which governed at the national level. The royal council handled any business the king put before it—executive, legislative, judicial. It also dealt with real or potential aristocratic threats through a judicial offshoot, the Court of Star Chamber, so called because of the stars painted on the ceiling of the room in which it met. The court applied principles of Roman law, a system that exalted the power of the Crown as the embodiment of the state. The court's methods were sometimes terrifying: evidence and proceedings were secret, torture could be applied, and juries were not called. These procedures ran directly counter to English common-law precedents, but they effectively reduced aristocratic troublemaking.

The Tudors won the support of the influential upper middle class because the Crown linked government policy with the interests of that class. A commercial or agricultural upper class fears and dislikes few things more than disorder and violence. Grave, secretive, cautious, and always thrifty, Henry VII promoted peace and social order, and the gentry did not object to arbitrary methods, like those used by the Court of Star Chamber, because the government had ended the long period of anarchy. At the same time, both English exports of wool and the royal export tax on that wool steadily increased. When Henry VII died in 1509, he left a country at peace both domestically and internationally, a substantially augmented treasury, and the dignity and role of the royal majesty much enhanced.

Spain

The central theme in the history of medieval Spain's separate kingdoms was disunity and plurality. Different languages, laws, and religious communities made for a rich cultural diversity shaped by Hispanic, Roman, Visigothic, Muslim, and Jewish traditions.

By the middle of the fifteenth century, the centuries-long *reconquista*—the attempts of the northern Christian kingdoms to control the entire peninsula—was nearing completion. The kingdoms of Castile and Aragon dominated weaker kingdoms, and with the exception of Granada, the Iberian Peninsula had been won

for Christianity. The wedding in 1469 of the dynamic and aggressive Isabella, heiress of Castile, and the crafty and persistent Ferdinand, heir of Aragon, was the final major step in the unification and Christianization of Spain.

Ferdinand and Isabella pursued a common foreign policy. Under their rule Spain remained a loose confederation of separate states, but they determined to strengthen royal authority. In the towns, popular groups called *hermandades,* or brotherhoods, were given the authority to act both as local police forces and as judicial tribunals. The hermandades repressed violence with such savage punishments that by 1498 they could be disbanded. The decisive step that Ferdinand and Isabella took to curb aristocratic power was the restructuring of the royal council. The king and queen appointed to the council only people of middle-class background; they rigorously excluded aristocrats and great territorial magnates. The council and various government boards recruited men trained in Roman law.

In the extension of royal authority and the consolidation of the territories of Spain, the church was the linchpin. Through a diplomatic alliance with the Spanish pope Alexander VI, the Spanish monarchs secured the right to appoint bishops in Spain and in the Hispanic territories in America. This power enabled the "Most Catholic Kings of Spain," a title that the pope granted to Ferdinand and Isabella, to establish, in effect, a national church.[17] Revenues from ecclesiastical estates provided the means to raise an army to continue the reconquista. The victorious entry of Ferdinand and Isabella into Granada on January 6, 1492, signaled the conclusion of eight centuries of Spanish struggle against the Arabs in southern Spain. In 1512 Ferdinand conquered Navarre in the north.

Although the Muslims had been defeated, there still remained a sizable and, in the view of the Catholic sovereigns, potentially dangerous minority, the Jews. In the late fourteenth century, anti-Semitic riots and pogroms led many Spanish Jews to convert to Christianity; such people were called *conversos.*

By the middle of the fifteenth century, many conversos held high positions in Spanish society as financiers, physicians, merchants, tax collectors, and even officials of the church hierarchy. Numbering perhaps 200,000 in a total population of about 7.5 million, Jews exercised an influence quite disproportionate to their numbers. Aristocratic grandees who borrowed heavily from Jews resented their financial dependence, and churchmen questioned the sincerity of Jewish conversions. At first Isabella and Ferdinand continued the

 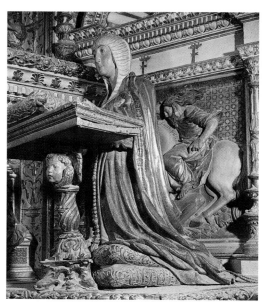

Felipe Bigarny: Ferdinand the Catholic and Isabella the Catholic All governments try to cultivate a popular image. For Ferdinand and Isabella, it was the appearance of piety. Contemporaries, such as the Burgundian sculptor Bigarny, portrayed them as paragons of Christian piety, as shown in these polychrome wooden statues. If Isabella's piety was perhaps more genuine, she used it—together with rich ceremony, elaborate dress, and a fierce determination—to assert royal authority. *(Capilla Real, Granada/Laurie Platt Winfrey, Inc.)*

policy of royal toleration—Ferdinand himself had inherited Jewish blood from his mother. But public hostility to Jews in the form of urban rioting prompted Ferdinand and Isabella in 1478 to secure Rome's permission to revive the Inquisition, a medieval judicial procedure for the punishment of heretics.

Although the Inquisition was a religious institution established to safeguard the Catholic faith, in Spain it was controlled by the Crown and served primarily as a political unifying force. Because the Spanish Inquisition commonly applied torture to extract confessions—first from lapsed conversos, then from Muslims, and later from Protestants—it gained a notorious reputation. Thus the word *inquisition,* meaning "any judicial inquiry conducted with ruthless severity," came into the English language.

In 1492 Isabella and Ferdinand took a further dire and drastic step against backsliding conversos. They issued an edict expelling all practicing Jews from Spain. Of the community of perhaps 200,000 Jews, 150,000 fled. (Efforts were made, through last-minute conversions, to retain good Jewish physicians.) Absolute religious orthodoxy and purity of blood (untainted by Jews or Muslims) became the theoretical foundation of the Spanish national state.

The diplomacy of the Catholic rulers of Spain achieved a success they never anticipated. Partly out of hatred for the French and partly to gain international recognition for their new dynasty, Ferdinand and Isabella in 1496 married their second daughter, Joanna, heiress to Castile, to the archduke Philip, heir through his mother to the Burgundian Netherlands and through his father to the Holy Roman Empire.

Germany and the Habsburg Dynasty

The marriage in 1477 of Maximilian I of the house of Habsburg and Mary of Burgundy was a decisive event in early modern European history. Burgundy consisted of two parts: the French duchy with its capital at Dijon, and the Burgundian Netherlands with its capital at Brussels. Through this union with the rich and powerful duchy of Burgundy, the Austrian house of Habsburg, the strongest ruling family in the empire, started to become an international power.

The Habsburg-Burgundian marriage angered the French, who considered Burgundy part of French territory. Within the empire, German principalities that resented Austria's pre-eminence began to see that they shared interests with France. The marriage of Maximilian and Mary inaugurated centuries of conflict between the Austrian house of Habsburg and the kings of France. Germany was to be the chief arena of the struggle.

The heir of Mary and Maximilian, Philip of Burgundy, married Joanna of Castile, daughter of Ferdinand and Isabella of Spain. Philip and Joanna's son Charles V (1500–1558) fell heir to a vast conglomeration of territories. Through a series of accidents and unexpected deaths, Charles inherited Spain from his mother, together with her possessions in the Americas and the Spanish dominions in Italy, Sicily, Sardinia, and Naples. From his father he inherited the Habsburg lands in Austria, southern Germany, the Low Countries, and Franche-Comté in east-central France.

Charles's inheritance was an incredibly diverse collection of states and peoples, each governed in a different manner and held together only by the person of the emperor (Map 15.1). Charles was convinced that it was his duty to maintain the political and religious unity of Western Christendom. In this respect, Charles V was the last medieval emperor.

Charles needed and in 1519 secured the imperial title from the electors. Forward-thinking Germans proposed government reforms, but Charles continued the Burgundian policy of his grandfather Maximilian. German revenues and German troops were subordinated to the needs of other parts of the empire, first Burgundy and then Spain. Habsburg international interests came before the need for reform in Germany.

THE CONDITION OF THE CHURCH (CA 1400–1517)

The papal conflict with the German emperor Frederick II in the thirteenth century, followed by the Babylonian Captivity and then the Great Schism (see pages 396–398), badly damaged the prestige of church leaders. In the fourteenth and fifteenth centuries, leaders of the conciliar movement reflected educated public opinion when they called for the reform of the church "in head and members" (see page 397). The humanists of Italy and the Christian humanists of northern Europe denounced corruption in the church. In *The Praise of Folly*, for example, Erasmus condemned the absurd superstitions of the parish clergy and the excessive rituals of the monks.

In the early sixteenth century, critics of the church concentrated their attacks on three disorders: clerical immorality, clerical ignorance, and clerical pluralism. There was little pressure for doctrinal change; the emphasis was on moral and administrative reform.

Since the fourth century, church law had required candidates for the priesthood to accept absolute celibacy. The requirement had always been difficult to enforce. Many priests, especially those ministering to country people, had concubines, and reports of neglect of the rule of celibacy were common. Immorality, of course, included more than sexual transgressions. Clerical drunkenness, gambling, and indulgence in fancy dress were frequent charges. There is no way of knowing how many priests were guilty of such behavior. But because such conduct was so much at odds with the church's rules and moral standards, it scandalized the educated faithful.

The bishops casually enforced regulations regarding the education of priests. As a result, standards for ordination were shockingly low. Parish priests throughout Europe were not as educated as the educated laity. Predictably, Christian humanists, with their concern for learning, condemned the ignorance or low educational level of the clergy. Many priests could barely read and write, and critics laughed at the illiterate priest mumbling Latin words to the Mass that he could not understand.

Pluralism and absenteeism constituted the third major abuse. Many clerics, especially higher ecclesiastics, held several *benefices,* or offices, simultaneously but seldom visited them, let alone performed the spiritual responsibilities those offices entailed. Instead, they collected revenues from each benefice and paid a poor priest a fraction of the income to fulfill the spiritual duties of a particular local church. The French king Louis XII's diplomat Antoine du Prat is perhaps the most notorious example of absenteeism. He was archbishop of Sens, but the first time he entered his cathedral was in his own funeral procession.

The Christian church, with its dioceses and abbeys, possessed a large proportion of the wealth of the countries of Europe. What better way for a ruler to reward government officials, who were usually clerics, than with bishoprics and other high church offices? Thus churchmen who served as royal councilors, diplomats, treasury officials, chancellors, viceroys, and judges were paid by the church for their services to the state.

In most countries except England, members of the nobility occupied the highest church positions. The spectacle of proud, aristocratic prelates living in magnificent splendor contrasted very unfavorably with the simple fishermen who were Christ's disciples. Nor did the popes of the period 1450 to 1550 set much of an example.

The court of the Spanish pope Rodrigo Borgia, Alexander VI (r. 1492–1503), who publicly acknowledged his mistress and children, reached new heights of

MAP 15.1 The European Empire of Charles V Charles V exercised theoretical jurisdiction over more territory than anyone since Charlemagne. This map does not show his Latin American possessions.

impropriety. Pope Julius II (r. 1503–1513) donned military armor and personally led papal troops against the French invaders of Italy in 1506. After him, Giovanni de' Medici, the son of Lorenzo de' Medici, carried on as Pope Leo X (r. 1513–1521) the Medicean tradition of being a great patron of the arts.

Calls for reform testify to the spiritual vitality of the church as well as to its problems. In the late fifteenth and early sixteenth centuries, both individuals and groups within the church were working actively for reform. In Spain, for example, Cardinal Francisco Jiménez (1436–1517) visited religious houses, encouraged the monks and friars to obey their rules and constitutions, and set high standards for the training of the diocesan clergy.

In Holland, beginning in the late fourteenth century, a group of pious laypeople called Brethren of the Common Life sought to make religion a personal, inner experience. They lived in stark simplicity while daily carrying out the Gospel teaching of feeding the hungry, clothing the naked, and visiting the sick. The Brethren also taught in local schools to prepare devout candidates for the priesthood and the monastic life. The spirituality of the Brethren of the Common Life found its finest expression in the classic *The Imitation of Christ* by Thomas à Kempis, which urges Christians to take Christ as their model and seek perfection in a simple way of life. In the mid-fifteenth century, the movement had houses in the Netherlands, in central Germany, and in the Rhineland; it was a true religious revival.[18]

The papacy also expressed concern for reform. Pope Julius II summoned an ecumenical, or universal, council, which met in the church of Saint John Lateran in Rome from 1512 to 1517. The bishops and theologians who attended the Lateran Council strove earnestly to reform the church. The council recommended higher standards for education of the clergy and instruction of the common people. The bishops placed the responsibility for eliminating bureaucratic corruption squarely on the papacy and suggested significant doctrinal reforms. But many obstacles stood in the way of ecclesiastical change. Nor did the actions of an obscure German friar immediately force the issue.

🌐 MARTIN LUTHER AND THE BIRTH OF PROTESTANTISM

As a result of a personal religious struggle, a German Augustinian friar, Martin Luther (1483–1546), launched the Protestant Reformation of the sixteenth century. Luther articulated the widespread desire for reform of the Christian church and the deep yearning for salvation that were typical of his time.

Martin Luther was born at Eisleben in Saxony, the second son of a copper miner who later became a mine owner. At considerable sacrifice, his father sent him to school and then to the University of Erfurt. Hans Luther intended his son to study law and have a legal career, which for centuries had been the steppingstone to public office and material success. Badly frightened during a thunderstorm, however, young Luther vowed to become a friar. Without consulting his father, he entered a monastery at Erfurt in 1505. Luther was ordained a priest in 1507 and after additional study earned a doctorate of theology. From 1512 until his death, he served as professor of Scripture at the new University of Wittenberg.

Martin Luther was exceedingly scrupulous in his monastic observances and was devoted to prayer, penance, and fasting. But the doubts and conflicts that trouble any sensitive young person who has just taken a grave step were especially intense in young Luther. He had terrible anxiety about sin, and he worried continually about his salvation. Luther intensified his monastic observances but still found no peace of mind.

Luther's wise and kindly confessor, John Staupitz, directed him to the study of Saint Paul's letters. Gradually, Luther arrived at a new understanding of the Pauline letters and of all Christian doctrine. He came to believe that salvation comes not through external observances and penance but through a simple faith in Christ. Faith is the means by which God sends humanity his grace, and faith is a free gift that cannot be earned.

Luther's Theology

An incident illustrative of the condition of the church in the early sixteenth century propelled Martin Luther onto the stage of history and brought about the Reformation in Germany. The University of Wittenberg lay within the archdiocese of Magdeburg. The archbishop of Magdeburg, Albert, held two other high ecclesiastical offices. To hold all three offices simultaneously—blatant pluralism—required papal dispensation. Archbishop Albert borrowed money from the Fuggers, a wealthy banking family of Augsburg, to pay Pope Leo X for the dispensation (the pope wanted the money to complete work on Saint Peter's Basilica). Leo X then authorized Archbishop Albert to sell indulgences in Germany to repay the Fuggers.

Lucas Cranach the Younger: Luther and the Wittenberg Reformers   The massive figure of Frederick, elector of Saxony, who protected and supported Luther, dominates this group portrait. Luther is on the far left, his associate Philipp Melanchthon in the front row on the right. Luther's face shows a quiet determination. *(The Toledo Museum of Art, Toledo, Ohio; Gift of Edward Drummond Libbey)*

Wittenberg was in the political jurisdiction of the elector Frederick of Saxony. When Frederick forbade the sale of indulgences within his duchy, the people of Wittenberg, including some of Professor Luther's students, streamed across the border from Saxony into Jütenborg in Thuringia to buy them.

What exactly was an *indulgence?* According to Catholic theology, individuals who sin alienate themselves from God and his love. In order to be reconciled to God, the sinner must confess his or her sins to a priest and do the penance that the priest assigns. The doctrine

of indulgence rested on three principles. First, God is merciful, but he is also just. Second, Christ and the saints, through their infinite virtue, established a "treasury of merits" on which the church, because of its special relationship with Christ and the saints, can draw. Third, the church has the authority to grant sinners the spiritual benefits of those merits. Originally, an indulgence was a remission of the temporal (priest-imposed) penalties for sin. Beginning in the twelfth century, the papacy and bishops had given Crusaders such indulgences. By the later Middle Ages, people widely believed that an indulgence secured total remission of penalties for sin—on earth or in purgatory—and ensured swift entry into Heaven.

Archbishop Albert hired the Dominican friar John Tetzel to sell the indulgences. Tetzel mounted an advertising blitz. One of his slogans—"As soon as coin in coffer rings, the soul from purgatory springs"—brought phenomenal success. Men and women bought indulgences not only for themselves but also for deceased parents, relatives, or friends.

Luther was severely troubled that ignorant people believed they had no further need for repentance once they had purchased an indulgence. Thus, according to historical tradition, in the academic fashion of the times, on the eve of All Saints' Day (October 31), 1517, he attached to the door of the church at Wittenberg Castle a list of ninety-five theses (or propositions) on indulgences. By this act, Luther intended only to start a theological discussion of the subject and to defend the theses publicly.

Luther's theses were soon translated from Latin into German, printed, and read throughout the empire. Immediately, broad theological issues were raised. When questioned, Luther rested his fundamental argument on the principle that there was no biblical basis for indulgences. But, replied Luther's opponents, to deny the legality of indulgences was to deny the authority of the pope who had authorized them. The issue was drawn: where did authority lie in the Christian church?

The papacy responded with a letter condemning some of Luther's propositions, ordering that his books be burned, and giving him two months to recant or be excommunicated. Luther retaliated by publicly burning the letter. By January 3, 1521, when the excommunication was supposed to become final, the controversy involved more than theological issues. The papal legate wrote, "All Germany is in revolution. Nine-tenths shout 'Luther' as their war cry; and the other tenth cares nothing about Luther, and cries 'Death to the court of Rome.' "[19]

In this highly charged atmosphere, the twenty-one-year-old emperor Charles V held his first diet at Worms and summoned Luther to appear before it. When ordered to recant, Luther replied in language that rang all over Europe:

Unless I am convinced by the evidence of Scripture or by plain reason—for I do not accept the authority of the Pope or the councils alone, since it is established that they have often erred and contradicted themselves—I am bound by the Scriptures I have cited and my conscience is captive to the Word of God. I cannot and will not recant anything, for it is neither safe nor right to go against conscience. God help me. Amen.[20]

The emperor declared Luther an outlaw of the empire and denied him legal protection. Duke Frederick of Saxony, however, protected him.

Between 1520 and 1530, Luther worked out the basic theological tenets that became the articles of faith for his new church and subsequently for all Protestant groups. At first the word *Protestant* meant "Lutheran," but with the appearance of many protesting sects, it became a general term applied to all non-Catholic Christians. Ernst Troeltsch, a German student of the sociology of religion, has defined *Protestantism* as a "modification of Catholicism, in which the Catholic formulation of questions was retained, while a different answer was given to them." Luther provided new answers to four old, basic theological issues.[21]

First, how is a person to be saved? Traditional Catholic teaching held that salvation was achieved by both faith and good works. Luther held that salvation comes by faith alone. Women and men are saved, said Luther, by the arbitrary decision of God, irrespective of good works or the sacraments. God, not people, initiates salvation.

Second, where does religious authority reside? Christian doctrine had long maintained that authority rests both in the Bible and in the traditional teaching of the church. Luther maintained that authority rests in the Word of God as revealed in the Bible alone and as interpreted by an individual's conscience. He urged that each person read and reflect on the Scriptures.

Third, what is the church? Medieval churchmen had tended to identify the church with the clergy. Luther reemphasized the Catholic teaching that the church consists of the entire community of Christian believers.

Finally, what is the highest form of Christian life? The medieval church had stressed the superiority of the monastic and religious life over the secular. Luther argued that all vocations, whether ecclesiastical or secular, have equal merit and that every person should serve God according to his or her individual calling. Protestantism, in sum, represented a reformulation of the Christian heritage.

The Social Impact of Luther's Beliefs

As early as 1521, Luther had a vast following. By the time of his death in 1546, people of all social classes had become Lutheran.

Two significant late medieval developments prepared the way for Luther's ideas. First, since the fifteenth century, city governments had expressed resentment at clerical exemption from taxes and from civic responsibilities such as defending the city. Second, critics of the late medieval church, especially informed and intelligent townspeople, had condemned the irregularity and poor quality of sermons. As a result, prosperous burghers in many towns had established preacherships. Preachers were men of superior education who were required to deliver about a hundred sermons a year. Luther's ideas attracted many preachers, and in many towns preachers became Protestant leaders. Preacherships also encouraged the Protestant form of worship, in which the sermon, not the Eucharist, is the central part of the service.[22]

In the countryside, the attraction of the German peasants to Lutheran beliefs was almost predictable. Luther himself came from a peasant background and admired the peasants' ceaseless toil. Peasants respected Luther's defiance of church authority. Moreover, they thrilled to the words Luther used in his treatise *On Christian Liberty* (1520): "A Christian man is the most free lord of all and subject to none." Taken out of context, these words easily stirred social unrest.

In the early sixteenth century, the economic condition of the peasantry varied from place to place but was generally worse than it had been in the fifteenth century and was deteriorating. The peasants believed their demands conformed to Scripture and cited Luther as a theologian who could prove that they did.

Luther wanted to prevent rebellion. At first he sided with the peasants and in his tract *An Admonition to Peace* blasted the nobles:

We have no one on earth to thank for this mischievous rebellion, except you lords and princes, especially you blind bishops and mad priests and monks. . . . In your government you do nothing but flay and rob your subjects in order that you may lead a life of splendor and pride, until the poor common folk can bear it no longer.[23]

But nothing justified the use of armed force, he warned: "The fact that rulers are unjust and wicked does not excuse tumult and rebellion; to punish wickedness does not belong to everybody, but to the worldly rulers who bear the sword."[24] As for biblical support for the peasants' demands, he maintained that Scripture had nothing to do with earthly justice or material gain.

Massive revolts first broke out near the Swiss frontier and then swept through Swabia, Thuringia, the Rhineland, and Saxony. The crowds' slogans came directly from Luther's writings. "God's righteousness" and the "Word of God" were invoked in the effort to secure social and economic justice. The peasants who expected Luther's support were soon disillusioned. He had written of the "freedom" of the Christian, but he had meant the freedom to obey the Word of God, for in sin men and women lose their freedom and break their relationship with God. To Luther, freedom meant independence from the authority of the Roman church; it did *not* mean opposition to legally established secular powers. Firmly convinced that rebellion hastened the end of civilized society, he wrote a tract *Against the Murderous, Thieving Hordes of the Peasants:* "Let everyone who can smite, slay, and stab [the peasants], secretly and openly, remembering that nothing can be more poisonous, hurtful or devilish than a rebel."[25] The nobility ferociously crushed the revolt. Historians estimate that over seventy-five thousand peasants were killed in 1525.

Luther took literally these words in Saint Paul's Letter to the Romans: "Let every soul be subject to the higher powers. For there is no power but of God: the powers that be are established by God. Whosoever resists the power, resists the ordinance of God: and they that resist shall receive to themselves damnation."[26] As it developed, Lutheran theology exalted the state, subordinated the church to the state, and everywhere championed "the powers that be." The revolt of 1525 strengthened the authority of lay rulers. Peasant economic conditions, however, moderately improved. For example, in many parts of Germany, enclosed fields, meadows, and forests were returned to common use.

Like the peasants, educated people and humanists were much attracted by Luther's words. He advocated a simpler, personal religion based on faith and the Scriptures, a return to the spirit of the early church, and the abolition of elaborate ceremonials—precisely the reforms the northern humanists had been calling for. Ulrich Zwingli (1484–1531), for example, a humanist from Zurich, was strongly influenced by Luther's bold stand. It stimulated Zwingli's reforms in the Swiss city of Zurich and later in Bern.

Luther's linguistic skill, together with his translation of the New Testament in 1523, led to the acceptance of his dialect of German as the standard version of German. His insistence that everyone should read and reflect on the Scriptures attracted the literate and thoughtful middle classes partly because he appealed to their intelligence. Moreover, the business classes, preoccupied with making money, envied the church's wealth, disapproved of the luxurious lifestyle of some churchmen, and resented tithes and ecclesiastical taxation. Luther's doctrines of salvation by faith and the priesthood of all believers not only raised the religious status of the commercial classes but protected their pocketbooks as well.

Hymns, psalms, and Luther's two *Catechisms* (1529)—compendiums of basic religious knowledge—also show the power of language in spreading the ideals of the Reformation. Lutheran hymns such as "A Mighty Fortress Is Our God" expressed deep feelings, were easily remembered, and imprinted on the mind central points of doctrine. Though originally intended for the instruction of pastors, Luther's *Catechisms* became powerful tools for the indoctrination of men and women of all ages, especially the young.[27]

What appeal did Luther's message have for women? Luther's argument that all vocations have equal merit in the sight of God gave dignity to those who performed ordinary, routine, domestic tasks. The abolition of monasticism in Protestant territories led to the exaltation of the home, which Luther and other reformers stressed as the special domain of the wife. Protestants established schools where girls, as well as boys, became literate in the catechism and the Bible. The reformers stressed marriage as the cure for clerical concupiscence. Protestantism thus proved attractive to the many women who had been priests' concubines and mistresses: they became legal and honorable wives.[28]

For his time, Luther held enlightened views on matters of sexuality and marriage. He wrote to a young man, "Dear lad, be not ashamed that you desire a girl, nor you my maid, the boy. Just let it lead you into matrimony and not into promiscuity, and it is no more cause for shame than eating and drinking."[29] He believed, that marriage was a woman's career. A happy marriage to the former nun Katharine von Bora mellowed him, and a student quoted him as saying, "Next to God's Word there is no more precious treasure than holy matrimony. God's highest gift on earth is a pious, cheerful, God-fearing, home-keeping wife, with whom you may live peacefully, to whom you may entrust your goods, and body and life."[30] Though Luther deeply loved his "dear Katie," he believed that women's principal concerns were children, the kitchen, and the church.

The Political Impact of Luther's Beliefs

In the sixteenth century, the practice of religion remained a public matter. Everyone participated in the religious life of the community, just as almost everyone shared in the local agricultural work. Whatever spiritual convictions individuals held in the privacy of their consciences, the emperor, king, prince, magistrate, or other civil authority determined the official form of public religious practice within his jurisdiction. Almost everyone believed that the presence of a faith different from that of the majority represented a political threat to the security of the state. Only a tiny minority, and certainly none of the princes, believed in religious liberty.

The religious storm launched by Martin Luther swept across Germany. Several elements in his religious reformation stirred patriotic feelings. Anti-Roman sentiment ran high. Humanists lent eloquent intellectual support. And Luther's translation of the New Testament into German evoked national pride.

For decades devout laypeople and churchmen had called on the German princes to reform the church. In 1520 Luther took up the cry in his *Appeal to the Christian Nobility of the German Nation.* Unless the princes destroyed papal power in Germany, Luther argued, reform was impossible. He urged the princes to confiscate ecclesiastical wealth and to abolish indulgences, dispensations, pardons, and clerical celibacy. He told them that it was their public duty to bring about the moral reform of the church. Luther based his argument in part on the papacy's financial exploitation of Germany: "How comes it that we Germans must put up with such robbery and such extortion of our property at the hands of the pope? Why do we Germans let them make such fools and apes of us?"[31] These words fell on welcome ears and itchy fingers. Luther's appeal to German patriotism gained him strong support, and national feeling influenced many princes otherwise confused by or indifferent to the complexities of the religious issues.

The church in Germany possessed great wealth. And unlike other countries, Germany had no strong central government to check the flow of gold to Rome. Rejection of Roman Catholicism and adoption of Protestantism would mean the legal confiscation of lush farmlands, rich monasteries, and wealthy shrines. Some German princes were sincerely attracted to Lutheranism, but many civil authorities realized that they had a great deal to gain by embracing the new faith. A steady stream of duchies, margraviates, free cities, and

bishoprics did so and secularized church property. Many princes used the religious issue to extend their financial and political independence. The results were unfortunate for the improvement of German government. The Protestant movement ultimately proved a political disaster for Germany.

Charles V must share blame with the German princes for the disintegration of imperial authority in the empire. He neither understood nor took an interest in the constitutional problems of Germany, and he lacked the material resources to oppose Protestantism effectively there. Throughout his reign, he was preoccupied with his Flemish, Spanish, Italian, and American territories. Moreover, the Turkish threat prevented him from acting effectively against the Protestants; Charles's brother Ferdinand needed Protestant support against the Turks who besieged Vienna in 1529.

Five times between 1521 and 1555, Charles V went to war with the Valois kings of France. The issue each time was the Habsburg lands acquired by the marriage of Maximilian and Mary of Burgundy. Much of the fighting occurred in Germany. The cornerstone of French foreign policy in the sixteenth and seventeenth centuries was the desire to keep the German states divided. Thus Europe witnessed the paradox of the Catholic king of France supporting the Lutheran princes in their challenge to his fellow Catholic, Charles V. The Habsburg-Valois Wars advanced the cause of Protestantism and promoted the political fragmentation of the German Empire.

Finally, in 1555, Charles agreed to the Peace of Augsburg, which officially recognized Lutheranism. Each prince was permitted to determine the religion of his territory. Most of northern and central Germany became Lutheran; the south remained Roman Catholic. There was no freedom of religion, however. Princes or town councils established state churches to which all subjects of the area had to belong. Dissidents, whether Lutheran or Catholic, had to convert or leave. The political difficulties Germany inherited from the Middle Ages had been compounded by the religious crisis of the sixteenth century.

 ## THE GROWTH OF THE PROTESTANT REFORMATION

By 1555 much of northern Europe had broken with the Roman Catholic church. All of Scandinavia, England (except during the reign of Mary Tudor), and Scotland, and large parts of Switzerland, Germany, and France, had rejected the religious authority of Rome and

John Calvin   The lean, ascetic face with the strong jaw reflects the iron will and determination of the organizer of Protestantism. The fur collar represents his training in law. *(Bibliothèque Nationale/Snark/Art Resource, NY)*

adopted new faiths. Because a common religious faith had been the one element uniting all of Europe for almost a thousand years, the fragmentation of belief led to profound changes in European life and society. The most significant new form of Protestantism was Calvinism, of which the Peace of Augsburg had made no mention at all.

Calvinism

In 1509, while Luther was studying for a doctorate at Wittenberg, John Calvin (1509–1564) was born in Noyon in northwestern France. Luther inadvertently launched the Protestant Reformation. Calvin, however, had the greater impact on future generations. In 1533 he experienced a religious crisis, as a result of which he converted to Protestantism. His theological writings profoundly influenced the social thought and attitudes

of Europeans and English-speaking peoples all over the world, especially in Canada and the United States.

Convinced that God selects certain people to do his work, Calvin believed that God had specifically called him to reform the church. Accordingly, he accepted an invitation to assist in the reformation of the city of Geneva. There, beginning in 1541, Calvin worked assiduously to establish a Christian society ruled by God through civil magistrates and reformed ministers. Geneva, "a city that was a Church," became the model of a Christian community for sixteenth-century Protestant reformers. (See the feature "Listening to the Past: Calvin's Vision for Christian Renewal" on pages 486–487.)

To understand Calvin's Geneva, it is necessary to understand Calvin's ideas. These he embodied in *The Institutes of the Christian Religion,* first published in 1536 and definitively issued in 1559. The cornerstone of Calvin's theology was his belief in the absolute sovereignty and omnipotence of God and the total weakness of humanity. Before the infinite power of God, he asserted, men and women are as insignificant as grains of sand.

Calvin did not ascribe free will to human beings, because that would detract from the sovereignty of God. Men and women cannot actively work to achieve salvation; rather, God in his infinite wisdom decided at the beginning of time who would be saved and who damned. This viewpoint constitutes the theological principle called *predestination:*

Predestination we call the eternal decree of God, by which he has determined in himself, what he would have become of every individual of mankind. . . . God has once for all determined, both whom he would admit to salvation, and whom he would condemn to destruction. We affirm that this counsel, as far as concerns the elect, is founded on his gratuitous mercy, totally irrespective of human merit. . . . How exceedingly presumptuous it is only to inquire into the causes of the Divine will.[32]

"This terrible decree," as even Calvin called it, did not lead to pessimism or fatalism. Rather, the Calvinist believed in the redemptive work of Christ and was confident that God had elected (saved) him or her. Predestination served as an energizing dynamic, forcing a person to undergo hardships in the constant struggle against evil.

Calvin aroused Genevans to a high standard of morality. Using his sermons and a program of religious education, God's laws and man's were enforced in Geneva.

The Genevan Consistory exercised a powerful civic role. This body consisted of twelve laymen, plus the

Company of Pastors, of which Calvin was the permanent moderator (presider). The duties of the Consistory were "to keep watch over every man's life [and] to admonish amiably those whom they see leading a disorderly life." Calvin emphasized that the Consistory's activities should be thorough and "its eyes may be everywhere," but corrections were only "medicine to turn sinners to the Lord."[33]

Although all municipal governments in early modern Europe regulated citizens' conduct, none did so with the severity of Geneva's Consistory under Calvin's leadership. Nor did it make any distinction between what we would consider crimes against society and simple un-Christian conduct. The Consistory investigated and punished absence from sermons, criticism of ministers, dancing, playing cards, family quarrels, and heavy drinking. The civil authorities handled serious crimes and heresy and, with the Consistory's approval, sometimes used torture to extract confessions. Between 1542 and 1546 alone, seventy-six persons were banished from Geneva and fifty-eight executed for heresy, adultery, blasphemy, and witchcraft.

To many sixteenth-century Europeans, Calvin's Geneva seemed "the most perfect school of Christ since the days of the Apostles." Religious refugees from France, England, Spain, Scotland, and Italy visited the city. Subsequently, the Reformed church of Calvin served as the model for the Presbyterian church in Scotland, the Huguenot church in France, and the Puritan churches in England and New England. The Calvinist provision for congregational participation and vernacular liturgy helped to satisfy women's desire to belong to and participate in a meaningful church organization. The Calvinist ethic of the "calling" dignified all work with a religious aspect: hard work, well done, was said to be pleasing to God. This doctrine encouraged an aggressive, vigorous activism. In the *Institutes* Calvin provided a systematic theology for Protestantism. The Reformed church of Calvin had a strong and well-organized machinery of government. These factors, together with the social and economic applications of Calvin's theology, made Calvinism the most dynamic force in sixteenth- and seventeenth-century Protestantism.

The Anabaptists

The name *Anabaptist* derives from a Greek word meaning "to baptize again." The Anabaptists, sometimes described as the left wing of the Reformation, believed that only adults could make a free choice about religious faith, baptism, and entry into the Christian community. Thus they considered the practice of baptizing infants and children preposterous and wanted to rebaptize believers who had been baptized as children. Anabaptists took the Gospel and, at first, Luther's teachings absolutely literally and favored a return to the kind of church that had existed among the earliest Christians—a voluntary association of believers who had experienced an inner light.

Anabaptists maintained that only a few people would receive the inner light. This position meant that the Christian community and the Christian state were not identical. In other words, Anabaptists believed in the separation of church and state and in religious tolerance. They almost never tried to force their values on others. In an age that believed in the necessity of state-established churches, Anabaptist views on religious liberty were thought to undermine that concept.

Each Anabaptist community or church was entirely independent; it selected its own ministers and ran its own affairs. Anabaptists admitted women to the ministry. They shared goods as the early Christians had done, refused all public offices, and would not serve in the armed forces. In fact, they laid great stress on pacifism.

Ideas such as absolute pacifism and the distinction between the Christian community and the state brought down on these unfortunate people fanatical hatred and bitter persecution. Zwingli, Luther, Calvin, and Catholics all saw—quite correctly—the separation of church and state as leading ultimately to the complete secularization of society. The Quakers with their gentle pacifism, the Baptists with their emphasis on an inner spiritual light, the Congregationalists with their democratic church organization, and, in 1787, the authors of the U.S. Constitution with their concern for the separation of church and state—all trace their origins in part to the Anabaptists of the sixteenth century.

The English Reformation

As on the continent of Europe, the Reformation in England had social and economic causes as well as religious ones. As elsewhere, too, Christian humanists had for decades been calling for the purification of the church. When the personal matter of the divorce of King Henry VIII (r. 1509–1547) became enmeshed with political issues, a complete break with Rome resulted.

Traditional Catholicism exerted an enormously strong, diverse, and vigorous hold over the imagination and loyalty of the people. The teachings of Christianity were graphically represented in the liturgy, constantly reiterated in sermons, enacted in plays, and carved and printed on walls, screens, and the windows of parish churches. A zealous clergy, increasingly better educated, engaged in a "massive catechetical enterprise." No substantial gulf existed between the religion of the clergy and educated elite and the broad mass of the English people.[34] The Reformation in England was an act of state, initiated by the king's emotional life.

In 1527, having fallen in love with Anne Boleyn, Henry wanted his marriage to Catherine of Aragon annulled. Catherine had failed to bear a boy child, and Henry claimed that only a male heir to the throne could prevent a disputed succession. He thus petitioned Pope Clement VII (r. 1523–1534) for an annulment. When Henry had married Catherine, he had secured a dispensation from Pope Julius II eliminating all legal technicalities about Catherine's previous union with Henry's late brother, Arthur. Henry now argued that Pope Julius's dispensation had contradicted the law of God—that a man may not marry his brother's widow. The English king's request reached Rome at the very time that Luther was widely publishing tracts condemning the papacy. If Clement had granted Henry's annulment and thereby admitted that Julius II had erred, Clement would have given support to the Lutheran assertion that popes substitute their own evil judgments for the law of God. This Clement could not do, so he delayed acting on Henry's request.[35]

Since Rome appeared to be thwarting Henry's matrimonial plans, he decided to remove the English church from papal jurisdiction. Henry used Parliament to legalize the Reformation in England. The Act in Restraint of Appeals (1533) declared the king to be the supreme sovereign in England and forbade judicial appeals to the papacy, thus establishing the Crown as the highest legal authority in the land. The Act for the Submission of the Clergy (1534) required churchmen to submit to the king and forbade the publication of ecclesiastical laws without royal permission. The Supremacy Act of 1534 declared the king the supreme head of the Church of England. In January 1533, Henry and Anne quietly married, but when she failed twice to produce a male heir, Henry had her beheaded.

Between 1535 and 1539, under the influence of his chief minister, Thomas Cromwell, Henry decided to dissolve the English monasteries because he wanted their wealth. The closing of the monasteries did not achieve a more equitable distribution of land and wealth. Rather, redistribution of land strengthened the upper classes and tied them to the Tudor dynasty.

Henry retained such traditional Catholic practices and doctrines as auricular confession, clerical celibacy, and *transubstantiation* (the doctrine that the bread and

wine of the Eucharist are transformed into the body and blood of Christ although their appearance does not change). But Protestant literature circulated, and Henry approved the selection of men of Protestant sympathies as tutors for his son.

Did the religious changes have broad popular support? Recent scholarship has emphasized that the English Reformation came from above. The surviving evidence does not allow us to gauge the degree of opposition to (or support for) Henry's break with Rome. Certainly, many laypeople wrote to the king, begging him to spare the monasteries. "Most laypeople acquiesced in the Reformation because they hardly knew what was going on, were understandably reluctant to jeopardise life or limb, a career or the family's good name."[36] But not all quietly acquiesced. In 1536 popular opposition in the north to the religious changes led to the Pilgrimage of Grace, a massive multiclass rebellion that proved the largest in English history. In 1546 serious rebellions in East Anglia and in the west, despite possessing economic and Protestant components, reflected considerable public opposition to the state-ordered religious changes.[37]

After Henry's death, the English church shifted left and right. In the short reign of Henry's sickly son Edward VI (r. 1547–1553), strongly Protestant ideas exerted a significant influence on the religious life of the country. Archbishop Thomas Cranmer simplified the liturgy, invited Protestant theologians to England, and prepared the first *Book of Common Prayer* (1549). In stately and dignified English, the *Book of Common Prayer* included, together with the Psalter, the order for all services of the Church of England.

The equally brief reign of Mary Tudor (r. 1553–1558) witnessed a sharp move back to Catholicism. The devoutly Catholic daughter of Catherine of Aragon and Henry, Mary rescinded the Reformation legislation of her father's reign and fully restored Roman Catholicism. Mary's marriage to her cousin Philip of Spain, son of the emperor Charles V, proved highly unpopular in England, and her persecution and execution of several hundred Protestants further alienated her subjects. Mary's death raised to the throne her sister Elizabeth (r. 1558–1603) and inaugurated the beginnings of religious stability.

Elizabeth had been raised a Protestant, but at the start of her reign sharp differences existed in England. Catholics wanted a Roman Catholic ruler, but a vocal number of returning exiles wanted all Catholic elements in the Church of England eliminated. Members of the latter group were called Puritans because they wanted to "purify" the church. Probably one of the

Allegorical Painting, ca 1548   Henry VIII on his deathbed points to his heir Edward, surrounded by Protestant worthies, as the wave of the future. The pope collapses and monks flee; through the window iconoclasts knock down statues, symbolizing error and superstition. Stressing Protestantism's focus on Scripture, the Bible is open to 1 Peter 1:24: "The word of the Lord endures forever." Because the new order lacked broad popular support, propagandistic paintings like this and the printing press had to be mobilized to sway public opinion. *(Reproduced by courtesy of the Trustees, National Portrait Gallery, London)*

shrewdest politicians in English history, Elizabeth chose a middle course between Catholic and Puritan extremes. She insisted on dignity in church services and political order in the land, and she avoided precise doctrinal definitions.

The parliamentary legislation of the early years of Elizabeth's reign—laws sometimes labeled the "Elizabethan Settlement"—required outward conformity to the Church of England and uniformity in all ceremonies. Everyone had to attend Church of England services; those who refused were fined. During Elizabeth's reign, the Anglican church (from the Latin *Ecclesia Anglicana*), as the Church of England was called, moved in a moderately Protestant direction. Services were conducted in English, monasteries were not re-established, and the clergy were allowed to marry. But the bishops remained as church officials, and apart from language, the services were quite traditional.

THE CATHOLIC REFORMATION AND THE COUNTER-REFORMATION

Between 1517 and 1547, the reformed versions of Christianity known as Protestantism made remarkable advances. All of England and Scandinavia, much of Scotland and Germany, and sizable parts of France and Switzerland adopted the creeds of Luther, Calvin, and other reformers. Still, the Roman Catholic church made a significant comeback. After about 1540, no new large areas of Europe, except for the Netherlands, accepted Protestant beliefs (Map 15.2).

Historians distinguish between two types of reform within the Catholic church in the sixteenth and seventeenth centuries. The Catholic Reformation began before 1517 and sought renewal basically through the stimulation of a new spiritual fervor. The Counter-Reformation started in the 1540s as a reaction to the rise and spread of Protestantism. The Counter-Reformation was a Catholic effort to convince or coerce dissidents or heretics to return to the church.

Why did the popes, spiritual leaders of the Western church, move so slowly? The answers lie in the personalities of the popes themselves, in their preoccupation with political affairs in Italy, and in the awesome difficulty of reforming so complicated a bureaucracy as the Roman curia. Clement VII, a true Medici, was far more interested in elegant tapestries and Michelangelo's painting of the Last Judgment than in theological disputes in barbaric Germany or far-off England.

The idea of reform was closely linked to the idea of a general council representing the entire church. Popes such as Clement VII, remembering fifteenth-century conciliar attempts to limit papal authority, resisted calls for a council, fearing loss of power, revenue, and prestige.

The Council of Trent

Pope Paul III (r. 1534–1549), a Roman aristocrat, humanist, and astrologer, seemed an unlikely person to undertake serious reform. Yet Paul III appointed as cardinals several learned and reform-minded men; established the Inquisition in the Papal States; and called a council, which finally met at Trent, an imperial city close to Italy (see Map 15.2).

The Council of Trent met intermittently from 1545 to 1563. It was called not only to reform the church but also to secure reconciliation with the Protestants. Lutherans and Calvinists were invited to participate, but also their insistence that the Scriptures be the sole basis for discussion made reconciliation impossible. International politics repeatedly cast a shadow over the theological debates. Charles V opposed discussions on any matter that might further alienate his Lutheran subjects. The French kings worked against any reconciliation of Roman Catholicism and Lutheranism, wanting the German states to remain divided.

Another problem was the persistence of the conciliar theory of church government. Some bishops wanted a concrete statement asserting the supremacy of a church council over the papacy. The bishops had a provincial and national outlook; only the papacy possessed an international religious perspective. The centralizing tenet was established that all acts of the council required papal approval.

In spite of the obstacles, the achievements of the Council of Trent are impressive. It dealt with both doctrinal and disciplinary matters. The council gave equal validity to the Scriptures and to tradition as sources of religious truth and authority. It reaffirmed the seven sacraments and the traditional Catholic teaching on transubstantiation, rejecting Lutheran and Calvinist positions.

The council tackled the problems arising from ancient abuses by strengthening ecclesiastical discipline. Decrees required bishops to reside in their own dioceses, suppressed pluralism and simony, and forbade the sale of indulgences. Clerics who kept concubines were to give them up. In a highly original canon, the council required every diocese to establish a seminary for the education and training of the clergy and insisted that preference for admission be given to sons of the poor. Seminary professors were to determine whether candidates for ordination had *vocations*—genuine callings as evidenced by purity of life, detachment from the broader secular culture, and a steady inclination toward the priesthood. This was a novel idea, since from the time of the early church, parents had determined their sons' (and daughters') religious careers. Also, great emphasis was laid on preaching and instructing the laity, especially the uneducated.

One decision had especially important social consequences for laypeople. Since the time of the Roman Empire, many couples had treated marriage as a completely personal matter, exchanged vows privately without witnesses, and thus formed clandestine (secret) unions. This widespread practice frequently led later to denials by one party that a marriage had taken place, to conflicts over property, and to disputes in the ecclesiastical courts that had jurisdiction over marriage. The decree *Tametsi* (1563) stipulated that for a marriage to be valid, consent (the essence of marriage) as expressed in the vows had to be given publicly before witnesses, one of whom had to be the parish priest. Trent thereby ended secret marriages in Catholic countries.

The Council of Trent did not bring about reform immediately. But the decrees laid a solid basis for the spiritual renewal of the church and for the enforcement of correction. For four centuries, the doctrinal and disciplinary legislation of Trent served as the basis for Roman Catholic faith, organization, and practice.

New Religious Orders and the Inquisition

The establishment of new religious orders within the church reveals a central feature of the Catholic Reformation. These new orders developed in response to the need to raise the moral and intellectual level of the clergy and people. Education was a major goal of them all.

The Ursuline order of nuns, founded by Angela Merici (1474–1540), attained enormous prestige for the education of women. Angela Merici worked for many years among the poor, sick, and uneducated around her native Brescia in northern Italy. In 1535 she established the Ursuline order to combat heresy through Christian education of young girls. The Ursulines sought to re-Christianize society by training future wives and mothers. Approved as a religious community by Paul III in 1544, the Ursulines rapidly grew and spread to France and the New World. Their schools in North America, stretching from Quebec to New Orleans, provided superior education for young women and inculcated the spiritual ideals of the Catholic Reformation.

The Society of Jesus, founded by Ignatius Loyola (1491–1556), a former Spanish soldier, played a powerful international role in resisting the spread of Protestantism, converting Asians and Latin American Indians to Catholicism, and spreading Christian education all over Europe. While recuperating from a severe battle wound to his legs, Loyola studied a life of Christ and other religious books and decided to give up his military career and become a soldier of Christ. His great classic, *Spiritual Exercises,* directed the individual imagination and will to the reform of life and a new spiritual piety.

Loyola was apparently a man of considerable personal magnetism. After study at the universities in Salamanca and Paris, he gathered a group of six companions and in 1540 secured papal approval of the new Society of Jesus, whose members were called Jesuits. The first Jesuits were recruited primarily from the wealthy merchant and professional classes. They saw the Reformation as a pastoral problem, its causes and cures related not to doctrinal issues but to people's spiritual condition. Reform of the church as Luther and Calvin understood the word *reform* played no role in the future the Jesuits planned for themselves. Their goal was "to help souls." Loyola also possessed a gift for leadership that consisted of spotting talent and of "the ability to see how at a given juncture change is more consistent with one's scope than staying the course."[38]

The Society of Jesus developed into a highly centralized, tightly knit organization. Candidates underwent a two-year novitiate, in contrast to the usual one-year probation required by older religious orders. Professed members vowed "special obedience to the sovereign pontiff regarding missions."[39] Thus, as stability—the promise to live one's life in the monastery—was what made a monk, so mobility—the commitment to go anywhere—was the defining characteristic of a Jesuit. Flexibility and the willingness to respond to the needs of time and circumstance formed the Jesuit tradition. In this respect, they were very modern, and they attracted many recruits.

The Society of Jesus achieved phenomenal success for the papacy and the reformed Catholic church. Jesuit schools adopted the modern humanist curricula and methods. They first concentrated on the children of the poor but soon were educating the sons of the nobility. As confessors and spiritual directors to kings, Jesuits exerted great political influence. Operating on the principle that the end sometimes justifies the means, they were not above spying. Indifferent to physical comfort and personal safety, they carried Christianity to India and Japan before 1550 and to Brazil, North America, and the Congo in the seventeenth century. Within Europe, the Jesuits brought southern Germany and much of eastern Europe back to Catholicism.

In 1542 Pope Paul III established the Sacred Congregation of the Holy Office with jurisdiction over the Roman Inquisition, a powerful instrument of the Counter-Reformation. A committee of six cardinals, the Roman Inquisition had judicial authority over all Catholics and the power to arrest, imprison, and execute. Under the fanatical Cardinal Caraffa, it vigorously attacked heresy. The Holy Office published the *Index of Prohibited Books,* a catalogue of forbidden reading. Within the Papal States, the Roman Inquisition effectively destroyed heresy (and some heretics). Outside the papal territories, its influence was slight. Governments had their own judicial systems for the suppression of treasonable activities, as religious heresy was then considered.[40]

 ## POLITICS, RELIGION, AND WAR

In 1559 France and Spain signed the Treaty of Cateau-Cambrésis, which ended the long conflict known as the Habsburg-Valois Wars. This event marks a watershed in early modern European history. Spain (the Habsburg side) was the victor. France, exhausted by the struggle, had to acknowledge Spanish dominance in Italy, where

472

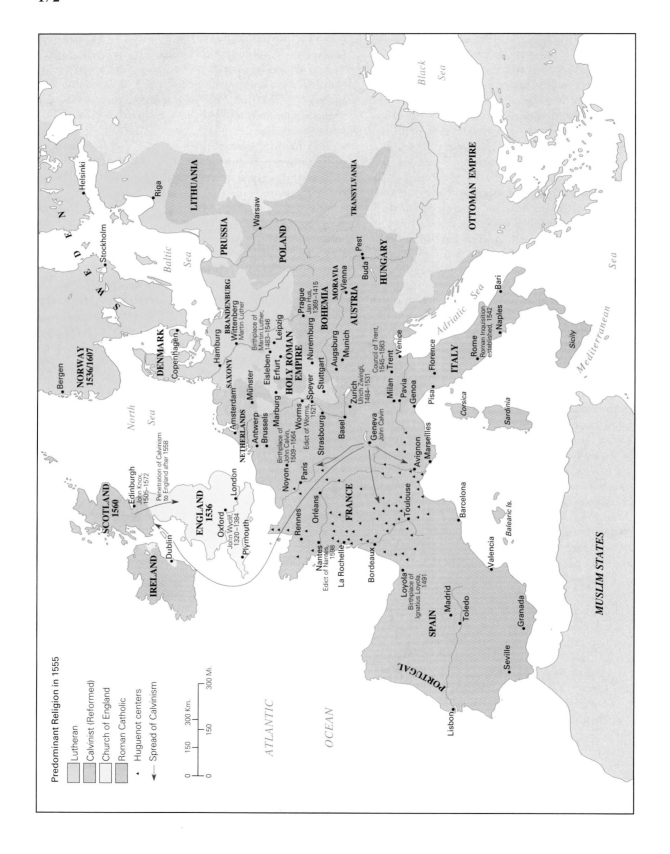

Predominant Religion in 1555

Lutheran

Calvinist (Reformed)

Church of England

Roman Catholic

▲ Huguenot centers

→ Spread of Calvinism

much of the war had been fought. Spanish governors ruled in Sicily, Naples, and Milan, and Spanish influence was strong in the Papal States and Tuscany. The Treaty of Cateau-Cambrésis ended an era of strictly dynastic wars and initiated a period of conflicts in which politics and religion played the dominant roles.

The wars of the late sixteenth century differed considerably from earlier wars. Sixteenth- and seventeenth-century armies were bigger than medieval ones; some forces numbered as many as fifty thousand men. Because large armies were expensive, governments had to reorganize their administrations to finance them. The use of gunpowder altered both the nature of warfare and popular attitudes toward it. Guns and cannon killed and wounded from a distance, indiscriminately. Writers scorned gunpowder as a coward's weapon that allowed a common soldier to kill a gentleman. Gunpowder weakened the notion, common during the Hundred Years' War (1337–1453), that warfare was an ennobling experience. Governments utilized propaganda, pulpits, and the printing press to arouse public opinion to support war.[41]

Late-sixteenth-century conflicts fundamentally tested the medieval ideal of a unified Christian society governed by one political ruler—the emperor—to whom all rulers were theoretically subordinate, and one church, to which all people belonged. The Protestant Reformation had killed this ideal, but few people recognized it as dead. Catholics continued to believe that Calvinists and Lutherans could be reconverted; Protestants persisted in thinking that the Roman church should be destroyed. Most people believed that a state could survive only if its members shared the same faith. The settlement finally achieved in 1648, known as the Peace of Westphalia, signaled the end of the medieval ideal.

The Origins of Difficulties in France (1515–1559)

In the first half of the sixteenth century, France continued the recovery begun during the reign of Louis XI (r. 1461–1483). The population losses caused by the plague and the disorders accompanying the Hundred Years' War had created such a labor shortage that serfdom virtually disappeared. Cash rents replaced feudal rents and servile obligations. This development clearly benefited the peasantry. Meanwhile, the declining buying power of money hurt the nobility. Domestic and foreign trade picked up; mercantile centers expanded.

The charming and cultivated Francis I (r. 1515–1547) and his athletic, emotional son Henry II (r. 1547–1559) governed through a small, efficient council. In 1539 Francis issued an ordinance that placed the whole of France under the jurisdiction of the royal law courts and made French the language of those courts. This act had a powerful centralizing impact. The *taille*, a tax on land, provided what strength the monarchy had and supported a strong standing army. Unfortunately, the tax base was too narrow to support France's extravagant promotion of the arts and ambitious foreign policy.

The Habsburg-Valois Wars, which had begun in 1522, cost more than the government could afford. In addition to the time-honored practices of increasing taxes and heavy borrowing, Francis I tried two new devices to raise revenue: the sale of public offices and a treaty with the papacy. The former proved to be only a temporary source of money. The offices sold tended to become hereditary within a family, and once a man bought an office, he and his heirs were tax-exempt. The sale of public offices thus created a tax-exempt class known as the "nobility of the robe."

The treaty with the papacy was the Concordat of Bologna (1516), in which Francis agreed to recognize the supremacy of the papacy over a universal council, thereby accepting a monarchical, rather than a conciliar, view of church government. In return, the French crown gained the right to appoint all French bishops and abbots. This understanding gave the monarchy a rich supplement of money and offices, as well as power over ecclesiastical organization that lasted until the Revolution of 1789. The Concordat of Bologna helps to explain why France did not later become Protestant: in effect, it established Catholicism as the state religion.

After the publication of Calvin's *Institutes of the Christian Religion* in 1536, sizable numbers of French people were attracted to the "reformed religion," as Calvinism was called. Because Calvin wrote in French rather than Latin, his ideas gained wide circulation. At first Calvinism drew converts from among reform-minded members of the Catholic clergy, the industrious middle classes, and artisan groups. Most Calvinists lived in Paris, Lyons, Meaux, Grenoble, and other major cities.

MAP 15.2 The Protestant and the Catholic Reformations   The Reformations shattered the religious unity of Western Christendom. What common cultural traits predominated in regions where a particular branch of the Christian faith was maintained or took root?

Primaticcio: Duchess of Etampes's Chamber In spite of the enormous financial burdens that continuous war placed on his resources, Francis I lavished money on architecture and the arts. To "modernize" the royal residence at Fontainebleau, he summoned the Italian architect and designer Francesco Primaticcio (1504/5–1570), who spent decades on the bedchamber of the king's mistress, Diana, ornamenting it with garlands, woodworking, mythological figures, fresco paintings, and, according to Vasari, the first stucco works in France. Primaticcio inaugurated what was called the School of Fontainebleau. *(Foto Marburg/Art Resource, NY)*

In spite of condemnation by the universities, government bans, and massive burnings at the stake, the numbers of Protestants in France grew steadily. When Henry II died in 1559, perhaps one-tenth of the population had become Calvinist.

Religious Riots and Civil War in France (1559–1589)

The three weak sons of Henry II could not provide adequate leadership, and the French nobility took advantage of this monarchical weakness. In the second half of the sixteenth century, between two-fifths and one-half of the nobility at one time or another became Calvinist, frequently adopting the "reformed religion" as a religious cloak for their independence from the monarchy. Armed clashes between Catholic royalist lords and Calvinist antimonarchical lords occurred in many parts of France.

Among the upper classes, the fundamental object of the struggle was power. At lower social levels, however, religious concerns were paramount. Working-class crowds composed of skilled craftsmen and the poor wreaked terrible violence on people and property. Both Calvinists and Catholics believed that the others' books, services, and ministers polluted the community. Preachers incited violence, and ceremonies like baptisms, marriages, and funerals triggered it.

In earlier centuries, attacks on great nobles and rich prelates had expressed economic grievances. In contrast, religious rioters of the sixteenth century believed that they could assume the power of public magistrates and rid the community of corruption. Municipal officials criticized the crowds' actions, but the participation of pastors and priests in these riots lent them some legitimacy.[42]

A savage Catholic attack on Calvinists in Paris on August 24, 1572 (Saint Bartholomew's Day), followed the usual pattern. The occasion was a religious ceremony— the marriage of the king's sister Margaret of Valois to the Protestant Henry of Navarre—that was intended to help reconcile Catholics and Huguenots, as French Calvinists were called. The night before the wedding, the leader of the Catholic aristocracy, Henry of Guise, had Gaspard de Coligny, leader of the Huguenot party, attacked. Rioting and slaughter followed. The Huguenot gentry in Paris was massacred, and religious violence spread to the provinces. Between August 25 and October 3, perhaps twelve thousand Huguenots perished at Meaux, Lyons, Orléans, and Paris.

The Saint Bartholomew's Day massacre led to the War of the Three Henrys, a civil conflict among factions led by the Protestant Henry of Navarre, by King Henry III (who succeeded the tubercular Charles IX), and by the Catholic Henry of Guise. The Guises wanted not only to destroy Calvinism but to replace Henry III with a member of the Guise family. France suffered fifteen more years of religious rioting and domestic anarchy. Agriculture in many areas was destroyed; commercial life declined severely; starvation and death haunted the land.

What ultimately saved France was a small group of moderates of both faiths called *politiques*. They believed that no religious creed was worth the incessant disorder and destruction and that only the restoration of a strong monarchy could reverse the trend toward collapse. The assassinations of Henry of Guise and King

Henry III paved the way for the accession of Henry of Navarre, a politique who ascended the throne as Henry IV (r. 1589–1610).

This glamorous prince, "who knew how to fight, to make love, and to drink," as a contemporary remarked, knew that the majority of the French were Roman Catholics. Declaring "Paris is worth a Mass," Henry knelt before the archbishop of Bourges and was received into the Roman Catholic church. Henry's willingness to sacrifice religious principles in the interest of a strong monarchy saved France. The Edict of Nantes, which Henry published in 1598, granted to Huguenots liberty of conscience and liberty of public worship in two hundred fortified towns, such as La Rochelle. The reign of Henry IV and the Edict of Nantes prepared the way for French absolutism in the seventeenth century (see pages 527–528) by helping to restore internal peace in France.

The Revolt of the Netherlands and the Spanish Armada

In the last quarter of the sixteenth century, the political stability of England, the international prestige of Spain, and the moral influence of the Roman papacy all became mixed up with a religious crisis in the Low Countries. By this time, the Netherlands was the pivot around which European money, diplomacy, and war revolved. What began as a movement for the reformation of the Catholic church developed into a struggle for Dutch independence from Spanish rule.

The Habsburg emperor Charles V (r. 1519–1556) had inherited the seventeen provinces that compose present-day Belgium and Holland. The French-speaking southern towns produced fine linens and woolens; the wealth of the Dutch-speaking northern cities rested on fishing, shipping, and international banking. In the cities of both regions of the Low Countries, trade and commerce had produced a vibrant cosmopolitan atmosphere.

In the Low Countries, as elsewhere, corruption in the Roman church and the critical spirit of the Renaissance provoked pressure for reform. But Charles's Flemish loyalty checked the spread of Lutheranism. Charles had been born in Ghent and raised in the Netherlands; he was Flemish in language and culture. He identified with the Flemish and they with him. In 1556, however, Charles V abdicated and divided his territories. His younger brother Ferdinand received Austria and the Holy Roman Empire and ruled as Ferdinand I (r. 1558–1564). His son Philip inherited Spain, the Low Countries, Milan and the kingdom of Sicily, and the Spanish possessions in America and ruled as Philip II (r. 1556–1598).

The spread of Calvinism in the Low Countries upset the apple cart. By the 1560s, there was a strong, militant minority of Calvinists to whom Calvinism appealed because of its intellectual seriousness, moral gravity, and approval of any form of labor well done. Many working-class people converted because Calvinist employers would hire only fellow Calvinists. Well organized and with the backing of rich merchants, Calvinists quickly gained a wide following and encouraged opposition to "illegal" civil authorities.

In August 1566, a year of very high grain prices, fanatical Calvinists, primarily of the poorest classes, embarked on a rampage of frightful destruction. As in France, Calvinist destruction in the Low Countries was incited by popular preaching, and attacks were aimed at religious images as symbols of false doctrines, not at people. The cathedral of Notre Dame at Antwerp—which stood as a monument to the commercial prosperity of Flanders, the piety of the business classes, and the artistic genius of centuries—was the first target. Crowds swept through the nave, attacking altars, paintings, books, ecclesiastical vestments, stained-glass windows, and sculptures. Before the havoc was over, thirty more churches had been sacked and irreplaceable libraries burned. From Antwerp the destruction spread to Brussels and Ghent and north to the provinces of Holland and Zeeland.

From Madrid Philip II sent twenty thousand Spanish troops led by the duke of Alva to pacify the Low Countries. Alva interpreted "pacification" to mean the ruthless extermination of religious and political dissidents. His repressive measures and heavy taxation triggered widespread revolt.

For ten years, between 1568 and 1578, civil war raged in the Netherlands between Catholics and Protestants and between the seventeen provinces and Spain. Spanish generals could not halt the fighting. In 1576 the seventeen provinces united under the leadership of Prince William of Orange, called "the Silent" because of his remarkable discretion. In 1578 Philip II sent his nephew Alexander Farnese, duke of Parma, with an army of German mercenaries to crush the revolt once and for all. Avoiding pitched battles, Farnese fought by patient sieges. One by one, the cities of the south fell, and finally Antwerp, the financial capital of northern Europe, also succumbed.

Antwerp marked the farthest extent of Spanish jurisdiction and ultimately the religious division of the

MAP 15.3 The Netherlands, 1578–1609   Though small in geographical size, the Netherlands held a strategic position in the religious struggles of the sixteenth century. Why?

Netherlands. The ten southern provinces, the Spanish Netherlands (the future Belgium), remained Catholic and under the control of the Spanish Habsburgs. The seven northern provinces were Protestant and, led by Holland, formed the Union of Utrecht and in 1581 declared their independence from Spain. Thus was born the United Provinces of the Netherlands (Map 15.3).

Geography and sociopolitical structure differentiated the two countries. The northern provinces were ribboned with sluices and canals and therefore were highly defensible. Several times the Dutch had broken the dikes and flooded the countryside to halt the advancing Farnese. In the southern provinces, the Ardennes mountains interrupt the otherwise flat terrain. In the north, the commercial aristocracy possessed the predominant power; in the south, the landed nobility had the greater influence.

Philip II and Alexander Farnese did not accept the division of the Low Countries, and the struggle continued after 1581. The Protestant United Provinces repeatedly asked the Protestant Queen Elizabeth of England for assistance, but she was reluctant to antagonize Philip II by supporting the Dutch.

Three developments forced Elizabeth's hand. First, the wars in the Low Countries—the chief market for English woolens—badly hurt the English economy. When wool was not exported, the Crown lost valuable customs revenues. Second, the murder of William the Silent in July 1584 eliminated not only a great Protestant leader but also the chief military check on the Farnese advance. Third, the collapse of Antwerp appeared to signal a Catholic sweep through the Netherlands. The next step, the English feared, would be a Spanish invasion of their island. For these reasons, Elizabeth pumped £250,000 and two thousand troops into the Protestant cause in the Low Countries between 1585 and 1587.

Philip of Spain considered himself the international defender of Catholicism and heir to the medieval imperial power. When Pope Sixtus V (r. 1585–1590) heard of the death of the Catholic Mary, Queen of Scots (which Elizabeth had ordered), he promised to pay Philip a million gold ducats the moment Spanish troops landed in England. In addition, Alexander Farnese had repeatedly warned that, to subdue the Dutch, he would have to conquer England and cut off the source of Dutch support.

In these circumstances, Philip prepared a vast fleet to sail from Lisbon to Flanders, fight off Elizabeth's navy if it attacked, rendezvous with Farnese, and escort his barges across the English Channel. The expedition's purpose was to transport the Flemish army for a cross-Channel assault. Philip expected to receive the support of English Catholics and anticipated a great victory for Spain.

On May 9, 1588, the 130 vessels of *la felicissima armada*—"the most fortunate fleet," as it was called in official documents—sailed from Lisbon harbor. An English fleet of about 150 ships—smaller, faster, and more maneuverable than the Spanish ships, and many having greater firepower—met the Spanish fleet in the Channel. A combination of storms and squalls, spoiled food and rank water aboard the Spanish ships, inadequate Spanish ammunition, and, to a lesser extent, English fire ships that caused the Spanish to scatter gave England the victory. Many Spanish ships sank on the journey home around Ireland; perhaps 65 managed to reach home ports.

The battle in the Channel had mixed consequences. Spain soon rebuilt its navy, and after 1588 the quality of the Spanish fleet improved. The war between England and Spain dragged on for years. But the defeat of the Spanish Armada did prevent Philip II from reimposing unity on western Europe by force. He did not conquer England, and Elizabeth continued her financial and military support of the Dutch. In the Netherlands, neither side gained significant territory. The borders of 1581 tended to become permanent. In 1609 Philip III of Spain (r. 1598–1621) agreed to a truce, in effect recognizing the independence of the United Provinces. In seventeenth-century Spain, the memory of the loss of the Armada contributed to a spirit of defeatism. In England the victory gave rise to a David and Goliath legend that enhanced English national sentiment.

The Thirty Years' War (1618–1648)

Meanwhile, the political-religious situation in central Europe deteriorated. An uneasy truce had prevailed in the Holy Roman Empire since the Peace of Augsburg of 1555 (see page 465). Later in the century, Catholics grew alarmed because Lutherans, in violation of the Peace of Augsburg, were steadily acquiring German bishoprics. And Protestants were not pleased by militant Jesuits' success in reconverting several Lutheran princes to Catholicism. The spread of Calvinism further confused the issue. Lutherans feared that Catholic and Calvinist gains would totally undermine the Augsburg principles. In an increasingly tense situation, Lutheran princes formed the Protestant Union (1608). Catholics retaliated with the Catholic League (1609). The Holy Roman Empire was divided into two armed camps.

Dynastic interests were also at stake. The Spanish Habsburgs strongly supported the goals of the Austrian Habsburgs: the unity of the empire under Habsburg rule and the preservation of Catholicism within the empire.

Violence erupted first in Bohemia (Map 15.4), where in 1617 Ferdinand of Styria, the new Catholic king of Bohemia, closed some Protestant churches. In retaliation, on May 23, 1618, Protestants hurled two of Ferdinand's officials from a castle window in Prague. They fell seventy feet but survived: Catholics claimed that angels had caught them; Protestants said the officials fell on a heap of soft horse manure. Called the "defenestration of Prague," this event marked the beginning of the Thirty Years' War (1618–1648).

Historians traditionally divide the war into four phases. The first, or Bohemian, phase (1618–1625) was characterized by civil war in Bohemia, as Bohemians fought for religious liberty and independence from Austrian Habsburg rule. In 1620 Ferdinand, newly elected Holy Roman emperor Ferdinand II (r. 1619–1637), totally defeated Protestant forces at the Battle of the White Mountain and followed up his victories by wiping out Protestantism in Bohemia.

The second, or Danish, phase of the war (1625–1629)—so called because of the participation of King Christian IV of Denmark (r. 1588–1648), the ineffective leader of the Protestant cause—witnessed additional Catholic victories. The year 1629 marked the peak of Habsburg power. The Jesuits persuaded Ferdinand to issue the Edict of Restitution. It specified that all Catholic properties lost to Protestantism since 1552 were to be restored and only Catholics and Lutherans (*not* Calvinists, Hussites, or other sects) were to be allowed to practice their faiths. Ferdinand appeared to be embarked on a policy to unify the empire. Protestants throughout Europe feared collapse of the balance of power in north-central Europe.

The third, or Swedish, phase of the war (1630–1635) began when Swedish king Gustavus Adolphus (1594–1632) intervened to support the Protestant cause within the empire. The participation of the Swedes in the Thirty Years' War proved decisive for the future of Protestantism and later German history. The Swedish victories ended the Habsburg ambition of uniting all the German states under imperial authority.

The death of Gustavus Adolphus, followed by the defeat of the Swedes at the Battle of Nördlingen in 1634, prompted the French to enter the war on the side of the Protestants. Thus began the French, or international, phase of the Thirty Years' War (1635–1648). For almost a century, French foreign policy had been based on opposition to the Habsburgs, because a weak Holy Roman Empire enhanced France's international stature. Now, in 1635, France declared war on Spain and again sent financial and military assistance to the Swedes and the German Protestant princes. The war dragged on; neither side had the resources to win a quick, decisive victory. French, Dutch, and Swedes, supported by Scots, Finns, and German mercenaries, burned, looted, and destroyed German agriculture and commerce.

Finally, in October 1648, peace was achieved. The treaties signed at Münster and Osnabrück—the Peace of Westphalia—mark a turning point in European political, religious, and social history. The treaties recognized the sovereign, independent authority of the German princes. With no central government, courts,

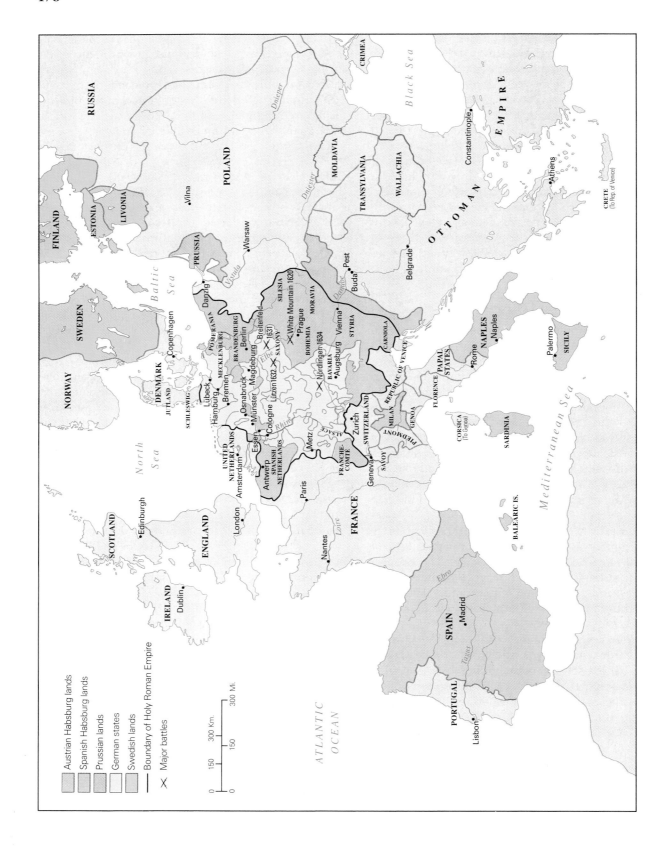

FINLAND

RUSSIA

SWEDEN

NORWAY

ESTONIA
LIVONIA

Vilna

POLAND

Baltic Sea

PRUSSIA

Warsaw

Vistula

Danzig

Dnieper

CRIMEA

Black Sea

MOLDAVIA

TRANSYLVANIA

WALLACHIA

Dniester

OTTOMAN EMPIRE

Constantinople

Athens

CRETE
(To Rep. of Venice)

SILESIA

White Mountain 1620

Pest
Buda

Danube

Belgrade

POMERANIA

MECKLENBURG

BRANDENBURG

Berlin

SAXONY

SILESIA

MORAVIA

BOHEMIA

Prague

Vienna

STYRIA

CARNIOLA

Breitenfeld
1631

DENMARK

Copenhagen

JUTLAND

SCHLESWIG

Lübeck

Hamburg

Bremen

Osnabrück

Münster

Magdeburg

Elbe

Lützen 1632

Cologne

Essen

Nördlingen 1634

BAVARIA

Augsburg

REPUBLIC OF VENICE

PAPAL STATES

Rome

NAPLES

Naples

Palermo

SICILY

NORTH Sea

UNITED NETHERLANDS

Amsterdam

SPANISH NETHERLANDS

Antwerp

Rhine

Metz

Paris

ALSACE

FRANCHE-COMTÉ

Zurich

SWITZERLAND

Geneva

SAVOY

PIEDMONT

MILAN

GENOA

FLORENCE

CORSICA
(To Genoa)

SARDINIA

BALEARIC IS.

Mediterranean Sea

SCOTLAND

Edinburgh

ENGLAND

London

IRELAND

Dublin

Nantes

Loire

FRANCE

Ebro

SPAIN

Madrid

Tagus

PORTUGAL

Lisbon

ATLANTIC OCEAN

Austrian Habsburg lands
Spanish Habsburg lands
Prussian lands
German states
Swedish lands
Boundary of Holy Roman Empire
✕ Major battles

0   150   300 Km.
0   150   300 M.

Soldiers Pillage a Farmhouse   Billeting troops on civilian populations caused untold hardships. In this late seventeenth-century Dutch illustration, brawling soldiers take over a peasant's home, eat his food, steal his possessions, and insult his family. Peasant retaliation sometimes proved swift and bloody. *(Rijksmuseum-Stichting Amsterdam)*

or means of controlling unruly rulers, the Holy Roman Empire as a real state was effectively destroyed.

The independence of the United Provinces of the Netherlands was acknowledged. The political divisions within the empire and the acquisition of the province of Alsace increased France's size and prestige, and the treaties allowed France to intervene at will in German affairs. Sweden achieved a powerful presence in northeastern Germany (see Map 15.4). The treaties also denied the papacy the right to participate in German religious affairs—a restriction symbolizing the reduced role of the church in European politics.

The Westphalian treaties stipulated that the Augsburg religious agreement of 1555 should stand permanently. The sole modification made Calvinism, along with Catholicism and Lutheranism, a legally permissible creed. In practice, the north German states remained Protestant, the south German states Catholic.

The Thirty Years' War settled little and was a disaster for the German economy and society—probably the most destructive event in German history before the twentieth century. Population losses were frightful. Perhaps one-third of the urban residents and two-fifths of the inhabitants of rural areas died.

In Germany the European-wide economic crisis caused primarily by the influx of silver from South America was badly aggravated by the war. Scholars still cannot estimate the value of losses in agriculture and in trade and commerce, which, compounded by the flood of Spanish silver, brought on severe inflation that was worse in Germany than anywhere else in Europe.

The population decline caused a rise in the value of labor. Owners of great estates had to pay more for

MAP 15.4 Europe in 1648   Which country emerged from the Thirty Years' War as the strongest European power? What dynastic house was that country's major rival in the early modern period?

agricultural workers. Farmers who needed only small amounts of capital to restore their lands started over again. Many small farmers, however, lacked the revenue to rework their holdings and became day laborers. Nobles and landlords were able to buy up many small holdings and amass great estates. In some parts of Germany, especially east of the Elbe River in areas like Mecklenburg and Pomerania, peasants' loss of land led to a new serfdom.[43] The Thirty Years' War contributed to the legal and economic decline of the largest segment of German society.

CHANGING ATTITUDES

The age of religious wars revealed extreme and violent contrasts. It was a deeply religious period in which men fought passionately for their beliefs; 70 percent of the books printed dealt with religious subjects. Yet the times saw the beginnings of religious skepticism. Europeans explored new continents, partly with the missionary aim of Christianizing the peoples they encountered. Yet the Spanish, Portuguese, Dutch, and English proceeded to dominate and enslave the Indians and blacks they encountered. While Europeans indulged in gross sensuality, the social status of women declined. The exploration of new continents reflects deep curiosity and broad intelligence. Yet Europeans believed in witches and burned thousands at the stake. Sexism, racism, and skepticism had all originated in ancient times. But late in the sixteenth century they began to take on their familiar modern forms.

The Status of Women

Did new ideas about women appear in this period? Theological and popular literature on marriage published in Reformation Europe helps to answer this question. Manuals emphasized the qualities expected of each partner. A husband was obliged to provide for the material welfare of his wife and children, to protect his family while remaining steady and self-controlled. He was to rule his household firmly but justly; he was not to behave like a tyrant—a guideline that counselors repeated frequently. A wife was to be mature, a good household manager, and subservient and faithful to her spouse. The husband also owed fidelity. Both Protestant and Catholic moralists rejected the double standard of sexual morality, considering it a threat to family unity. Counselors believed that marriage should be based on mutual respect and trust. Although they dis-

couraged impersonal unions arranged by parents, they did not think romantic attachments—based on physical attraction and love—a sound basis for an enduring relationship.

A woman might assist in her own or her husband's business and do charitable work. But moralists held that involvement in social or public activities was inappropriate because it distracted the wife from her primary responsibility: her household. If a woman suffered under her husband's yoke, writers explained, her submission, like the pain of childbearing, was a punishment inherited from Eve, penance for man's fall. Moreover, they said, a woman's lot was no worse than a man's: he had to earn the family's bread by the sweat of his brow.[44]

Catholics viewed marriage as a sacramental union; validly entered into, it could not be dissolved. Protestants stressed the contractual nature of marriage: each partner promised the other support, companionship, and the sharing of mutual property. Protestants recognized the right of both parties to divorce and remarry for various reasons, including adultery and irreparable breakdown.[45]

Society in the early modern period was patriarchal. Women neither lost their identity nor lacked meaningful work, but the all-pervasive assumption was that men ruled. Leading students of the Lutherans, Catholics, French Calvinists, and English Puritans tend to agree that there was no improvement in women's longstanding subordinate status.

Artists' drawings of plump, voluptuous women and massive, muscular men reveal the contemporary standards of physical beauty. It was a sensual age that gloried in the delights of the flesh. Some people, such as the humanist poet Pietro Aretino (1492–1556), found sexual satisfaction with people of either sex. Reformers and public officials simultaneously condemned and condoned sexual "sins."

Prostitution was common because desperate poverty forced women and young men into it. Since the later Middle Ages, licensed houses of prostitution had been common in urban centers. When in 1566 Pope Pius IV (r. 1559–1565) expelled all the prostitutes from Rome, so many people left and the city suffered such a loss of revenue that in less than a month the pope was forced to rescind the order. Scholars debated Saint Augustine's notion that prostitutes serve a useful social function by preventing worse sins. Civil authorities in both Catholic and Protestant countries licensed houses of public prostitution. These establishments were intended for the convenience of single men, and some Protestant cities, such as Geneva and Zurich, installed officials in the brothels with the express purpose of preventing married men from patronizing them.

Single women of the middle and working classes in the sixteenth and seventeenth centuries worked in many occupations and professions—as butchers, shop-keepers, nurses, goldsmiths, and midwives and in the weaving and printing industries. Most women who were married assisted in their husbands' businesses. What became of the thousands of women who left convents and nunneries during the Reformation? This question pertains primarily to women of the upper classes, who formed the dominant social group in the religious houses of late medieval Europe. Luther and the Protestant reformers believed that celibacy had no scriptural basis and that young girls were forced by their parents into convents and, once there, were bullied by men into staying. Therefore, reformers favored the suppression of women's religious houses and encouraged former nuns to marry. Marriage, the reformers maintained, not only gave women emotional and sexual satisfaction but also freed them from clerical domination, cultural deprivation, and sexual repression.[46] It appears that these women passed from clerical domination to subservience to husbands.

Some nuns in the Middle Ages probably did lack a genuine religious vocation, and some religious houses did witness financial mismanagement and moral laxness. Nevertheless, convents had provided women of the upper classes with an outlet for their literary, artistic, medical, or administrative talents if they could not or would not marry. When the convents were closed, marriage became virtually the only occupation available to upper-class Protestant women.

The great European witch scare reveals more about contemporary attitudes toward women. The period of the religious wars witnessed a startling increase in the phenomenon of witch-hunting, whose prior history was long but sporadic. "A witch," according to Chief Justice Edward Coke of England (1552–1634), "was a person who hath conference with the Devil to consult with him or to do some act." This definition by the highest legal authority in England demonstrates that educated people, as well as the ignorant, believed in witches. Witches were thought to mysteriously injure other people or animals—by causing a person to become blind or impotent, for instance, or by preventing a cow from giving milk.

Religious reformers' extreme notions of the Devil's powers and the insecurity created by the religious wars contributed to the growth of belief in witches. The idea developed that witches made pacts with the Devil in return for the power to work mischief on their enemies.

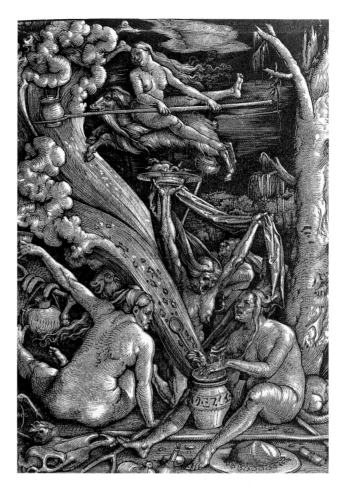

Hans Baldung Grien (1484/5–1545): Witches' Sabbat (1510) Trained by the great German graphic artist and painter Albrecht Dürer at Nuremberg, Baldung (as he was known) in this woodcut combines learned and stereotypical beliefs about witches: They traveled at night on broomsticks, met at *sabbats* (assemblies), feasted on infants (in dish held high), concocted strange potions, and possessed an aged and debauched sensuality. *(Germanisches Nationalmuseum Nürnberg)*

Since pacts with the Devil meant the renunciation of God, witchcraft was considered heresy, and persecution for it had actually begun in the later fourteenth century when it was so declared. Persecution reached its most virulent stage in the late sixteenth and seventeenth centuries.

Fear of witches took a terrible toll on innocent lives in several parts of Europe. In southwestern Germany, 3,229 witches were executed between 1561 and 1670, most by burning. The communities of the Swiss Confederation in central Europe tried 8,888 persons between 1470 and 1700 and executed 5,417 of them as witches. In all the centuries before 1500, witches in

England had been suspected of causing perhaps "three deaths, a broken leg, several destructive storms and some bewitched genitals." Yet between 1559 and 1736, almost 1,000 witches were executed in England.[47]

Some scholars maintain that charges of witchcraft were a means of accounting for inexplicable misfortunes. Some scholars think that in small communities, which typically insisted on strict social conformity, charges of witchcraft were a means of attacking and eliminating the nonconformist; witches, in other words, served the collective need for scapegoats. The evidence of witches' trials, some writers suggest, shows that women were not accused because they harmed or threatened their neighbors; rather, people believed such women worshiped the Devil, engaged in wild sexual activities with him, and ate infants. Other scholars argue the exact opposite: that people were tried and executed as witches because their neighbors feared their evil powers. According to still another theory, the unbridled sexuality attributed to witches was a figment of their accusers' imagination—a psychological projection by their accusers resulting from Christianity's repression of sexuality. Despite an abundance of hypotheses, scholars cannot fully understand the phenomenon. The most important capital crime for women in early modern times, witchcraft has considerable significance for the history and status of women.[48]

 ## LITERATURE, ART, AND MUSIC

The age of religious wars witnessed extraordinary intellectual and artistic ferment. This effervescence can be seen in prose, poetry, and drama, in art, and in music. In many ways, the literature, visual arts, music, and drama of the period mirrored the social and cultural conditions that gave rise to them.

Literature

Decades of religious fanaticism brought famine, civil anarchy, and death and led both Catholics and Protestants to doubt that any one faith contained absolute truth. The late sixteenth and seventeenth centuries witnessed the beginning of modern *skepticism,* a school of thought founded on doubt that total certainty or definitive knowledge is ever attainable. The skeptic is cautious and critical and suspends judgment. Perhaps the finest representative of early modern skepticism is the Frenchman Michel de Montaigne (1533–1592).

Montaigne developed a new literary genre, the essay—from the French word *essayer,* meaning "to test or try"—to express his thoughts and ideas. His *Essays* provide insight into the mind of a remarkably humane, tolerant, and civilized man. "On Cannibals" reflects the impact of overseas discoveries on Europeans' consciousness. Montaigne's tolerant mind rejected the notion that one culture is superior to another:

I long had a man in my house that lived ten or twelve years in the New World, discovered in these latter days, and in that part of it where Villegaignon landed [Brazil]. . . .

I find that there is nothing barbarous and savage in [that] nation, by anything that I can gather, excepting, that every one gives the title of barbarism to everything that is not in use in his own country.[49]

In his belief in the nobility of human beings in the state of nature, uncorrupted by organized society, and in his cosmopolitan attitude toward different civilizations, Montaigne anticipated many eighteenth-century thinkers.

The thought of Michel de Montaigne marks a sharp break with the past. Faith and religious certainty had characterized the intellectual attitudes of Western society for a millennium. Montaigne's rejection of any kind of dogmatism, his secularism, and his skepticism thus represent a basic change.

In addition to the development of the essay as a literary genre, the period fostered remarkable creativity in other branches of literature. England, especially in the latter part of Elizabeth's reign and in the first years of her successor, James I (r. 1603–1625), witnessed unparalleled brilliance. The immortal dramas of William Shakespeare (1564–1616) and the stately prose of the Authorized, or King James, Bible mark the Elizabethan and Jacobean periods as the golden age of English literature.

Shakespeare's genius lies in the originality of his characterizations, the diversity of his plots, his understanding of human psychology, and his unexcelled gift for language. Shakespeare was a Renaissance man in his deep appreciation for classical culture, individualism, and humanism. Such plays as *Julius Caesar, Pericles,* and *Antony and Cleopatra* deal with classical subjects and figures. Several of his comedies have Italian Renaissance settings. His nine history plays, including *Richard II, Richard III,* and *Henry IV,* enjoyed the greatest popularity among his contemporaries. Written during the decade after the defeat of the Spanish Armada, the history plays express English national consciousness.

Shakespeare's later plays, above all the tragedies *Hamlet, Othello,* and *Macbeth,* explore an enormous range of human problems and are open to an almost infinite variety of interpretations. The central figure in *Hamlet,* a play suffused with individuality, wrestles with moral problems connected with revenge and with man's relationship to life and death. The soliloquy in which Hamlet debates suicide is perhaps the most widely quoted passage in English literature:

To be, or not to be: that is the question:
Whether 'tis nobler in the mind to suffer
The slings and arrows of outrageous fortune,
Or to take arms against a sea of troubles,
And by opposing end them?

Hamlet's sad cry, "There is nothing either good or bad but thinking makes it so," expresses the anguish and uncertainty of modern man. *Hamlet* has always enjoyed great popularity, because in his many-faceted personality people have seen an aspect of themselves.

The other great masterpiece of the Jacobean period was the Authorized, or King James, Bible (1611). Based on the best scriptural research of the time and divided into chapters and verses, the Authorized Bible is actually a revision of earlier versions rather than an original work. Yet it provides a superb expression of the mature English vernacular in the early seventeenth century. Consider Psalm 37:

Fret not thy selfe because of evill doers, neither bee thou
*   envious against the workers of iniquitie.*
For they shall soone be cut downe like the grasse; and
*   wither as the greene herbe.*
Trust in the Lord, and do good, so shalt thou dwell in the
*   land, and verely thou shalt be fed.*
Delight thy selfe also in the Lord; and he shall give thee
*   the desires of thine heart.*

The Authorized Bible, so called because it was produced under royal sponsorship—it had no official ecclesiastical endorsement—represented the Anglican and Puritan desire to encourage laypeople to read the Scriptures. It quickly achieved great popularity and displaced all earlier versions. British settlers carried this Bible to the North American colonies, where it became known as the King James Bible. For centuries this version of the Bible has had a profound influence on the language and lives of English-speaking peoples.

Baroque Art and Music

Throughout European history, the cultural tastes of one age have often seemed quite unsatisfactory to the next. So it was with the baroque. The term *baroque* may

Velázquez: Juan de Pareja   This portrait (1650) of the Spanish painter Velázquez's one-time assistant, a black man of obvious intellectual and sensual power and himself a renowned religious painter, suggests the integration of some blacks in seventeenth-century society. The elegant lace collar attests to his middle-class status. *(The Metropolitan Museum of Art, Fletcher Fund, Rogers Fund, and Bequest of Miss Adelaide Milton de Groot (1876–1967), by exchange, supplemented by gifts from friends of the Museum, 1971. [1971.86]. Photograph © 1986 The Metropolitan Museum of Art)*

have come from a Portuguese word for an "odd-shaped, imperfect pearl." Late-eighteenth-century art critics used it as an expression of scorn for what they considered an overblown, unbalanced style. The hostility of these critics has long since passed, and modern specialists agree that the triumphs of the baroque mark one of the high points in the history of Western culture.

The early development of the baroque is complex. Most scholars stress the influence of Rome and the revitalized Catholic church of the later sixteenth century. The papacy and the Jesuits encouraged the growth of an intensely emotional, exuberant art. These patrons wanted artists to go beyond the Renaissance focus on pleasing a small, wealthy cultural elite. They wanted artists to appeal to the senses and thereby touch the souls and kindle the faith of ordinary churchgoers while proclaiming the power and confidence of the reformed Catholic church. In addition to this underlying religious emotionalism, the baroque drew its sense of drama, motion, and ceaseless striving from the Catholic Reformation. The interior of the famous Jesuit Church of Jesus in Rome—the Gesù—combined all these characteristics in its lavish, shimmering, wildly active decorations and frescoes.

Taking definite shape in Italy after 1600, the baroque style in the visual arts developed with exceptional vigor in Catholic countries—in Spain and Latin America, Austria, southern Germany, and Poland. Yet baroque art was more than just "Catholic art" in the seventeenth century and the first half of the eighteenth. True, neither Protestant England nor the Netherlands ever came fully under the spell of the baroque, but neither did Catholic France. And Protestants accounted for some of the finest examples of baroque style, especially in music. The baroque style spread partly because its tension and bombast spoke to an agitated age, which was experiencing great violence and controversy in politics and religion.

In painting, the baroque reached maturity early in the work of Peter Paul Rubens (1577–1640), the most outstanding and representative of baroque painters. Rubens developed a rich, sensuous, colorful style, characterized by animated figures, melodramatic contrasts, and monumental size.

In music, the baroque style reached its culmination almost a century later in the dynamic, soaring lines of the endlessly inventive Johann Sebastian Bach (1685–1750), one of the greatest composers of the Western world. Organist and choirmaster of several Lutheran churches across Germany, Bach was equally at home writing secular concertos and sublime religious cantatas. Bach's organ music, the greatest ever written, combines the baroque spirit of invention, tension, and emotion in an unforgettable striving toward the infinite. Unlike Rubens, Bach was not fully appreciated in his lifetime, but since the early nineteenth century his reputation has grown steadily.

SUMMARY

From about 1050 to 1300, a new economy emerged in Italy, based on Venetian and Genoese shipping and long-distance trade and on Florentine banking and cloth manufacture. The combination of these commercial activities and the struggle of urban communities for political independence from surrounding feudal lords led to the appearance of a new wealthy aristocratic class. With this foundation, Italy was the scene of a re-

markable intellectual and artistic flowering. Based on renewed interest in the Greco-Roman world, the Renaissance had a classicizing influence on many facets of culture. Despots or oligarchs ruled the city-states of fifteenth- and sixteenth-century Italy and manipulated Renaissance culture to enhance their personal power. Moving beyond Italy, the individualism, humanism, and secular spirit characteristic of the Italian Renaissance affected the culture of all Europe.

In northern Europe, city merchants and rural gentry allied with rising monarchies. Using taxes provided by business people, kings provided a greater degree of domestic peace and order, conditions essential for trade. In Spain, France, and England, rulers also emphasized royal dignity and authority. Except in the Holy Roman Empire, feudal monarchies gradually evolved in the direction of nation-states.

In the sixteenth and seventeenth centuries, religion and religious issues continued to play a major role in the lives of individuals, in rising national consciousness, and in the policies of governments. The break with Rome and the rise of Lutheran, Calvinist, Anglican, and other faiths destroyed European unity as an organic Christian society. Europeans used religious doctrine to explain what they did politically and economically. Religious ideology served as justification for the French nobles' opposition to the Crown, the Dutch struggle for independence from Spain, and the political fragmentation of Germany during and after the Thirty Years' War. The age of Reformation and religious wars marks a decisive watershed between the religious culture of the Middle Ages and the pluralism characteristic of modern times. Though a period of incredible literary and artistic achievement, the age of religious conflict also witnessed the beginnings of skepticism, sexism, and secularism in their modern forms.

NOTES

1. See L. Martines, *Power and Imagination: City-States in Renaissance Italy* (New York: Vintage Books, 1980), esp. pp. 332–333.
2. Ibid., pp. 22–61.
3. Ibid., pp. 221–237, esp. p. 221.
4. Quoted in J. Burckhardt, *The Civilization of the Renaissance in Italy* (London: Phaidon Books, 1951), p. 89.
5. *Memoirs of Benvenuto Cellini; A Florentine Artist; Written by Himself* (London: J. M. Dent & Sons, 1927), p. 2.
6. A. Hauser, *The Social History of Art,* vol. 2 (New York: Vintage Books, 1959), pp. 48–49.
7. Quoted in F. Seebohm, *The Oxford Reformers* (London: J. M. Dent & Sons, 1867), p. 256.

8. Quoted in W. H. Woodward, *Vittorino da Feltre and Other Humanist Educators* (Cambridge: Cambridge University Press, 1897), pp. 96–97.

9. C. E. Detmold, trans., *The Historical, Political and Diplomatic Writings of Niccolò Machiavelli* (Boston: J. R. Osgood, 1882), pp. 51–52.

10. Ibid., pp. 54–55.

11. See F. Gilbert, *Machiavelli and Guicciardini: Politics and History in Sixteenth Century Florence* (New York: W. W. Norton, 1984), pp. 197–200.

12. E. L. Eisenstein, *The Printing Press as an Agent of Change: Communications and Cultural Transformations in Early Modern Europe,* vol. 1 (New York: Cambridge University Press, 1979), p. 135; for an overall discussion, see pp. 126–159.

13. This account rests on J. Kelly-Gadol, "Did Women Have a Renaissance?" in *Becoming Visible: Women in European History,* ed. R. Bridenthal and C. Koonz (Boston: Houghton Mifflin, 1977), pp. 137–161, esp. p. 161.

14. See C. M. Saunders, *A Social History of Black Slaves and Freedmen in Portugal, 1441–1555* (New York: Cambridge University Press, 1982), pp. 59, 62–88, 176–179.

15. Ibid., pp. 190–194.

16. Ibid., pp. 255–258.

17. See J. H. Elliott, *Imperial Spain, 1469–1716* (New York: Mentor Books, 1963), esp. pp. 75, 97–108.

18. See R. R. Post, *The Modern Devotion: Confrontation with Reformation and Humanism* (Leiden: E. J. Brill, 1968), esp. pp. 237–238, 255, 323–348.

19. Quoted in O. Chadwick, *The Reformation* (Baltimore: Penguin Books, 1976), p. 55.

20. Quoted in E. H. Harbison, *The Age of Reformation* (Ithaca, N.Y.: Cornell University Press, 1963), p. 52.

21. This discussion is based heavily on Ibid., pp. 52–55.

22. See S. E. Ozment, *The Reformation in the Cities: The Appeal of Protestantism to Sixteenth-Century Germany and Switzerland* (New Haven, Conn.: Yale University Press, 1975), pp. 32–45.

23. S. E. Ozment, *The Age of Reform, 1250–1550: An Intellectual and Religious History of Late Medieval and Reformation Europe* (New Haven, Conn.: Yale University Press, 1980), p. 280.

24. Quoted ibid., p. 281.

25. Quoted ibid., p. 284.

26. Romans 13:1–2.

27. G. Strauss, *Luther's House of Learning: Indoctrination of the Young in the German Reformation* (Baltimore: Johns Hopkins University Press, 1978), esp. pp. 159–162, 231–233.

28. See R. H. Bainton, *Women of the Reformation in Germany and Italy* (Minneapolis: Augsburg, 1971), pp. 9–10; and Ozment, *The Reformation in the Cities,* pp. 53–54, 171–172.

29. Quoted in H. G. Haile, *Luther: An Experiment in Biography* (Garden City, N.Y.: Doubleday, 1980), p. 272.

30. Quoted in J. Atkinson, *Martin Luther and the Birth of Protestantism* (Baltimore: Penguin Books, 1968), pp. 247–248.

31. *Martin Luther: Three Treatises* (Philadelphia: Muhlenberg Press, 1947), pp. 28–31.

32. J. Allen, trans., *John Calvin: The Institutes of the Christian Religion* (Philadelphia: Westminster Press, 1930), bk. 3, chap. 21, paras. 5, 7.

33. E. W. Monter, *Calvin's Geneva* (New York: Wiley, 1967), p. 137.

34. E. Duffy, *The Stripping of the Altars: Traditional Religion in England, 1400–1580* (New Haven, Conn.: Yale University Press, 1992), pp. 2–6 and passim.

35. See R. Marius, *Thomas More: A Biography* (New York: Knopf, 1984), pp. 215–216.

36. J. J. Scarisbrick, *The Reformation and the English People* (Oxford: Basil Blackwell, 1984), pp. 81–84, esp. p. 81.

37. Ibid.

38. See J. W. O'Malley, *The First Jesuits* (Cambridge, Mass.: Harvard University Press, 1993), p. 376.

39. Ibid., p. 298.

40. See P. Grendler, *The Roman Inquisition and the Venetian Press, 1540–1605* (Princeton, N.J.: Princeton University Press, 1977).

41. See J. Hale, "War and Public Opinion in the Fifteenth and Sixteenth Centuries," *Past and Present* 22 (July 1962): 29.

42. See N. Z. Davis, "The Rites of Violence: Religious Riot in Sixteenth Century France," *Past and Present* 59 (May 1973): 51–91.

43. H. Kamen, "The Economic and Social Consequences of the Thirty Years' War," *Past and Present* 39 (April 1968): 44–61.

44. This passage is based heavily on S. E. Ozment, *When Fathers Ruled: Family Life in Reformation Europe* (Cambridge, Mass.: Harvard University Press, 1983), pp. 50–99.

45. Ibid., pp. 85–92.

46. Ibid., pp. 9–14.

47. N. Cohn, *Europe's Inner Demons: An Enquiry Inspired by the Great Witch-Hunt* (New York: Basic Books, 1975), pp. 253–254; K. Thomas, *Religion and the Decline of Magic* (New York: Charles Scribner's Sons, 1971), pp. 450–455.

48. See E. W. Monter, "The Pedestal and the Stake: Courtly Love and Witchcraft," in *Becoming Visible: Women in European History,* ed. R. Bridenthal and C. Koonz (Boston: Houghton Mifflin, 1977), pp. 132–135; and A. Fraser, *The Weaker Vessel* (New York: Random House, 1985), pp. 100–103.

49. C. Cotton, trans., *The Essays of Michel de Montaigne* (New York: A. L. Burt, 1893), pp. 207, 210.

(continued on page 488)

Calvin's Vision for Christian Renewal

John Calvin (1509–1564) was one of the many reformers who challenged the tradition and doctrine of the Christian church in the sixteenth century. As part of his reform efforts, Calvin established a community in Geneva, Switzerland. The members of his community were to live according to his social and moral ideas. The first excerpt below derives from his writings on this community and, in particular, on its posture toward its members who erred.

In the second excerpt, Calvin tries to clarify one version of his teachings for Geneva's youth. This piece concerns the Eucharist. Like other reformers, Calvin departed from Catholics on their interpretation of the Eucharist, for he rejected the notion of transubstantiation—that is, the idea that the bread and wine of the Last Supper become the body and blood of Christ during the church service.

Our Lord established excommunication as a means of correction and discipline, by which those who led a disordered life unworthy of a Christian, and who despised to mend their ways and return to the strait way after they had been admonished, should be expelled from the body of the church and cut off as rotten members until they come to themselves and acknowledge their fault. . . . We have an example given by St. Paul (1 Tim. i and 1 Cor. v), in a solemn warning that we should not keep company with one who is called a Christian but who is, none the less, a fornicator, covetous, an idolater, a railer, a drunkard, or an extortioner. So if there be in us any fear of God, this ordinance should be enforced in our Church.

To accomplish this we have determined to petition you [i.e., the town council] to establish and choose, according to your good pleasure, certain persons [namely, the elders] of upright life and good repute among all the faithful, likewise constant and not easy to corrupt, who shall be assigned and distributed in all parts of the town and have an eye on the life and conduct of every individual. If one of these see any obvious vice which is to be reprehended, he shall bring this to the attention of some one of the ministers, who shall admonish whoever it may be who is at fault and exhort him in a brotherly way to correct his ways. If it is apparent that such remonstrances do no good, he shall be warned that his obstinacy will be reported to the church. Then if he repents, there is in that alone excellent fruit of this form of discipline. If he will not listen to warnings, it shall be time for the minister, being informed by those who have the matter in charge, to declare publicly to the congregation the efforts which have been made to bring the sinner to amend, and how all has been in vain.

Should it appear that he proposes to persevere in his hardness of heart, it shall be time to excommunicate him; that is to say, that the offender shall be regarded as cast out from the companionship of Christians and left in the power of the devil for his temporal confusion, until he shall give good proofs of penitence and amendment. In sign of his casting out he shall be excluded from the communion, and the faithful shall be forbidden to hold familiar converse with him. Nevertheless he shall not omit to attend the sermons in order to receive instruction, so that it may be seen whether it shall please the Lord to turn his heart to the right way.

The offenses to be corrected in this manner are those named by St. Paul above, and others like them. When others than the said deputies—for example, neighbors or relatives—shall first have knowledge of such offenses, they may make the necessary remonstrances themselves. If they accomplish nothing, then they shall notify the deputies to do their duty.

This then is the manner in which it would seem expedient to us to introduce excommunication into our Church and maintain it in its full force; for beyond this form of correction the Church does not go. But should there be insolent persons, . . . who only laugh when they are excommunicated and do not mind living and dying in that condition of rejection, it shall be your affair to determine whether you should long suffer such contempt and mocking of God to pass unpunished. . . .

If those who agree with us in faith should be punished by excommunication for their offenses, how much more should the Church refuse to tolerate those who oppose us in religion? The remedy that we have thought of is to petition you to require all the inhabitants of your city to make a confession and give an account of their faith, so that you may know who agree with the gospel and who, on the contrary, would prefer the kingdom of the pope to the kingdom of Jesus Christ.

In the passage on the Eucharist that follows, Calvin adopts a different tone. He imagines a conversation between a minister and a child who responds to his minister's questions. But what follows not only illuminates Calvin's position on a key doctrinal issue; it also reveals his belief that social reform is an integral part of spiritual renewal. Here he goes beyond the prescription in the previous passage to teach children, who represent the future of the community, the fundamental principles of his religion.

Concerning the Lord's Supper.

The minister. Have we in the supper simply a signification of the things above mentioned, or are they given to us in reality?

The child. Since Jesus Christ is truth itself there can be no doubt that the promises he has made regarding the supper are accomplished, and that what is figured there is verified there also. Wherefore according as he promises and represents I have no doubt that he makes us partakers of his own substance, in order that he may unite us with him in one life.

The minister. But how may this be, when the body of Jesus Christ is in heaven, and we are on this earthly pilgrimage?

The child. It comes about through the incomprehensible power of his spirit, which may indeed unite things widely separated in space.

The minister. You do not understand then that the body is enclosed in the bread, or the blood in the cup?

The child. No. On the contrary, in order that the reality of the sacrament be achieved our hearts must be raised to heaven, where Jesus Christ dwells in the glory of the Father, whence we await him for our redemption; and we are not to seek him in these corruptible elements.

The minister. You understand then that there are two things in this sacrament: the natural bread and wine, which we see with the eye, touch with the hand and perceive with the taste; and Jesus Christ, through whom our souls are inwardly nourished?

The child. I do. In such a way moreover that we have there the very witness and so say a pledge of

In this Limoges enamel, Swiss reformer Pierre Viret (1511–1571) preaches before Calvin and others on the fourth petition of the Lord's Prayer, "Give us this day our daily bread." *(Louvre © Photo R.M.N.)*

the resurrection of our bodies; since they are made partakers in the symbol of life.

Questions for Analysis

1. What happened in Calvin's community if one of its members sinned?

2. Does it seem fair to you that the state—in this case, the leaders of Calvin's community—legislate morality?

3. How does this picture of community differ from that of Martin Luther? How does it differ from the community envisioned by the reformed Catholic church?

4. Why did Calvin consider the topic of the Eucharist so critical?

5. Do you think the passage on the Eucharist would have effectively persuaded young Protestants to espouse Calvin's position?

Sources: "John Calvin's Proposal to Geneva Town Council," in *Readings in European History,* ed. James Harvey Robinson (Boston: Ginn, 1904), 2:124–126; John Calvin, *The Genevan Catechism,* in *Translations and Reprints from the Original Sources of European History* (Philadelphia: University of Pennsylvania Press, 1898), 3/2:8–9.

SUGGESTED READING

There are exciting studies available on virtually all aspects of the Renaissance. The curious student might begin with M. Mallett, "Politics and Society in Italy, 1250–1600," a lucid sketch of political change in the various cities, and G. Holmes, "Renaissance Culture," a fine appreciation of the conflict of secular and religious values in art and literature. These articles appear in G. Holmes, ed., *The Oxford History of Italy* (1997). G. Chittolini, "Cities, 'City-States,' and Regional States in North-Central Italy," in *Cities and the Rise of States in Europe, A.D. 1000 to 1800,* eds. C. Tilly and W. P. Blockmans (1994), provides a good explanation of why Italy lagged in developing a national state, while P. Burke, *The Italian Renaissance: Culture and Society in Italy* (1986), offers an important sociological interpretation. P. Burke, *The Historical Anthropology of Early Modern Italy* (1987), contains many useful essays on Italian cultural history in a comparative European framework, while G. Holmes, ed., *Art and Politics in Renaissance Italy* (1993), treats the art of Florence and Rome against a political background. For the Renaissance court, see the splendid achievement of G. Lubkin, *A Renaissance Court: Milan Under Galeazzo Maria Sforza* (1994). The sophisticated intellectual biography by S. de Grazia, *Machiavelli in Hell* (1989), is based on Machiavelli's literary as well as political writing.

J. Huizinga, *The Waning of the Middle Ages: A Study of the Forms of Life, Thought, and Art in France and the Netherlands in the Dawn of the Renaissance* (1954) challenges the whole idea of the Renaissance. R. J. Knecht, *Renaissance Warrior and Patron: The Reign of Francis I* (1994), is the standard study of Francis. W. Blockmans and W. Prevenier, *The Burgundian Netherlands* (1986), is essential for the culture of Burgundy. The sophisticated study of J. D. Tracy, *Erasmus of the Low Countries* (1996), is probably the best recent work on the great northern humanist, while P. Ackroyd, *The Life of Thomas More* (1997), is a superb appreciation of the English lawyer, statesman, and saint.

For the status of women, see C. Klapisch-Zuper, ed., *A History of Women,* vol. 3 (1994); R. Chartier, ed., *A History of Private Life.* Vol. 3: *Passions of the Renaissance* (1990); and I. Maclean, *The Renaissance Notion of Women* (1980).

The following studies should be helpful to students interested in the political and religious history of Spain: N. Rubin, *Isabella of Castile: The First Renaissance Queen* (1991); P. Lis, *Isabel the Queen: Life and Times* (1992); J. S. Gerber, *The Jews of Spain: A History of the Sephardic Experience* (1992); H. Kamen, *Inquisition and Society in Spain in the Sixteenth and Seventeenth Centuries* (1985); P. F. Albaladejo, "Cities and the State in Spain," in *Cities and the Rise of States in Europe, A.D. 1000 to 1800,* eds. C. Tilly and W. P. Blockmans (1994); and B. Netanyahu, *The Origins of the Inquisition in Fifteenth Century Spain* (1995).

The best reference work on the Reformation is H. J. Hillerbrand, ed., *The Oxford Encyclopedia of the Reformation,* 4 vols. (New York: Oxford University Press, 1996). A. Pettegree, ed., *The Early Reformation in Europe* (1992),

explores the Reformation as an international movement and compares developments in different parts of Europe. L. W. Spitz, *The Protestant Reformation, 1517–1559* (1985), provides a comprehensive survey.

For Martin Luther, students should see Atkinson and Haile in the Notes; G. Brendler, *Martin Luther: Theology and Revolution* (1991), a response to the Marxist view of Luther as a tool of the aristocracy who sold out the peasantry; and H. Boehmer, *Martin Luther: Road to Reformation* (1960), a well-balanced work treating Luther's formative years.

The best study of John Calvin is W. J. Bouwsma, *John Calvin: A Sixteenth-Century Portrait* (1988), which puts Calvin within Renaissance culture. D. C. Steinmetz, *Calvin in Context* (1995), treats Calvin as an interpreter of the Bible. W. E. Monter, *Calvin's Geneva* (1967), shows the effect of his reforms on the social life of that city. For the left wing of the Reformation, see the profound, though difficult, work of G. H. Williams, *The Radical Reformers* (1962).

For various aspects of the social history of the period, see, in addition to Bainton and Ozment cited in the Notes, S. Ozment, *Magdalena and Balthasar* (1987), which reveals social life through the letters of a Nuremberg couple. For women, see M. E. Wiesner, *Women and Gender in Early Modern Europe* (1993); L. Roper, *The Holy Household: Women and Morals in Reformation Augsburg* (1991), an important study in local religious history as well as the history of gender; and M. Wiesner, *Women in the Sixteenth Century: A Bibliography* (1983), a useful reference tool. The best treatment of marriage and the family is S. Ozment, *When Fathers Ruled: Family Life in Reformation Europe* (1983).

The legal implications of Henry VIII's divorces have been well analyzed in J. J. Scarisbrick, *Henry VIII* (1968), an almost definitive biography. On the dissolution of the English monasteries, see D. Knowles, *The Religious Orders in England,* vol. 3 (1959), a fine example of historical prose.

The definitive study of the Council of Trent was written by H. Jedin, *A History of the Council of Trent,* 3 vols. (1957–1961). For the Jesuits, see W. W. Meissner, *Ignatius of Loyola: The Psychology of a Saint* (1993), and J. W. O'Malley, *The First Jesuits* (1993). These books refute many myths. Perhaps the best recent work on the Spanish Inquisition is W. Monter, *Frontiers of Heresy: The Spanish Inquisition from the Basque Lands to Sicily* (1990). For the impact of the Counter-Reformation on ordinary Spanish people, see H. Kamen, *The Phoenix and the Flame: Catalonia and the Counter Reformation* (New Haven, Conn.: Yale University Press, 1993).

For the religious wars, see M. P. Holt, *The French Wars of Religion, 1562–1629* (1995), and J. B. Collins, *The State in Early Modern France* (1995). For the two major monarchs of the age, see W. MacCaffrey, *Elizabeth I* (1993), and H. Kamen, *Philip of Spain* (1997), both excellent revisionist portraits of rulers at the center of international affairs.

For the Thirty Years' War, see R. G. Asch, *The Thirty Years' War: The Holy Roman Empire and Europe* (1997), is an important revisionist study. The titles by Cohn and Monter cited in the Notes are helpful for the study of witchcraft.

16 The Acceleration of Global Contact

Chinese vase of the Yuan (Mongol) period. With underglaze of cobalt blue—likely introduced from Mesopotamia and Persia. *(Museum of Fine Arts, Boston)*

Between about 1400 and 1700, almost all parts of the world for the first time came into contact with each other. The European search for Southeast Asian spices led to the accidental discovery of the Western Hemisphere. Within a short time, South and North America were joined in a worldwide economic web. The fundamental instrument of globalization was trade and commerce. Islam, originating in and expanding out of the Middle East, had always placed a high premium on mercantile activity (see pages 264–267). In early modern times, merchants and sailors sought new opportunities in East Africa and Southeast Asia. When artisans, scholars, teachers, soldiers, and mercenaries from Arabia and Anatolia followed, a Muslim diaspora resulted. Elite classes everywhere prized Chinese porcelains and silks, while wealthy members of the Celestial Kingdom, as China called itself, wanted ivory, black slaves from East Africa, and exotic goods and peacocks from India. African peoples wanted textiles from India and cowrie shells from the Maldive Islands. Europeans craved spices.

In the fifteenth to seventeenth centuries, the locus of all these desires and commercial exchanges was the Indian Ocean. Arab, Persian, Turkish, Indian, black African, Chinese, and European merchants and adventurers fought each other for the trade that brought great wealth. They also jostled with Muslim scholars, Buddhist teachers, and Christian missionaries, who competed for the religious adherence of the peoples of the Malay Archipelago, Sumatra, Java, Borneo, and the Philippine Islands. The ancient civilizations of Africa, the Americas, Asia, and Southeast Asia confronted each other, and those confrontations sometimes led to conquest, exploitation, and profound social change.

- What were the distinctive features of Southeast Asian cultures? Compare the status of women in Southeast Asia to that of women in other premodern cultures in Africa, East Asia, and Europe.
- What was the impact of Islam and Christianity on Southeast Asian peoples?
- Why and how did Europeans gain control of the major sea-lanes of the world and establish political and economic hegemony on distant continents?
- How did a few Spaniards, fighting far from home, overcome the powerful Aztec and Inca Empires in America?
- How and why did African slave labor become the dominant form of labor organization in America?

- What effect did overseas expansion have on Europe and on conquered societies?

This chapter will address these questions.

 ## THE WORLD OF THE INDIAN OCEAN

Extending over 28,350,000 square miles, measuring 4,000 miles wide at the equator, and covering 20 percent of the earth's total ocean area, the Indian Ocean is the globe's third-largest (after the Atlantic and Pacific) waterway. To the west, its arms reach into the Red and Arabian Seas, through the former up to the Mediterranean Sea, and through the latter into the Persian Gulf and southwestern Asia. To the north the Indian Ocean joins the Bay of Bengal, to the east the Pacific, to the south the west coast of Australia (Map 16.1). The Chinese called this vast region the Southern Ocean. Arabs, Indians, and Persians described it as "the lands below the winds," meaning the seasonal monsoons that carried ships across the ocean. Moderate and predictable, the monsoon winds blow from the west or south between April and August, from the northwest or northeast between December and March. Only in the eastern periphery, near the Philippine Islands, is there a dangerous typhoon belt—whirlwinds bringing tremendous rains and possible tornadoes.

High temperatures and abundant rainfall all year round contribute to a heavily forested environment. Throughout Southeast Asia, forests offer "an abundance and diversity of forms (of trees) . . . without parallel anywhere else in the world."[1] In earlier times, land set aside for cultivation represented only small pockets in a heavily forested region. The abundance of bamboo, teak, mahogany, and other woods close to the waterways made the area especially favorable for maritime activity. Household equipment usually included a small boat.

Peoples and Cultures

From at least the first millennium B.C., the peoples of Southeast Asia have been open to waterborne commerce. With trade came settlers from the Malay Peninsula (the southern extremity of the Asian continent), India, China, and East Africa, resulting in an enormous variety of languages, cultures, and religions. In spite of

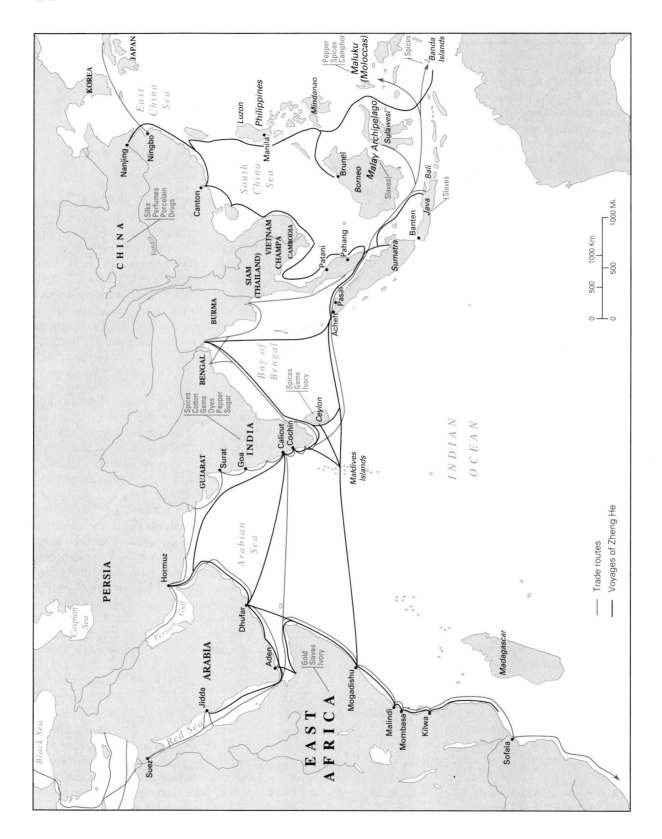

KOREA

JAPAN

East China Sea

Nanjing Ningbo

C H I N A

Silks
Perfumes
Porcelain
Drugs

Canton

Yangzi

Luzon

Philippines

Manila

South China Sea

Mindanao

Malay Archipelago

Sulawesi

Pepper
Spices
Camphor

*Maluku
(Moloccas)*

Spices

*Banda
Islands*

Brunei

Borneo

Slaves

Bali

Slaves

BURMA

VIETNAM
CHAMPA
CAMBODIA

SIAM
(THAILAND)

Patani

Pahang

Banten

Java

Sumatra

BENGAL

*Bay of
Bengal*

Acheh
Pasai

Spices
Cotton
Gems
Dyes
Pepper
Sugar

Spices
Gems
Ivory

INDIA

Calicut
Cochin

Ceylon

GUJARAT

Surat
Goa

I N D I A N   O C E A N

*Maldives
Islands*

PERSIA

*Caspian
Sea*

Hormuz

*Arabian
Sea*

Persian Gulf

Dhufar

ARABIA

Aden

Jidda

Gold
Slaves
Ivory

Mogadishu

Madagascar

*Black
Sea*

Suez

Red Sea

E A S T
A F R I C A

Malindi
Mombasa
Kilwa

Sofala

— Trade routes

— Voyages of Zheng He

1000 Mi.

1000 Km.

500

500

500

0

0

Agricultural Work in Southeast Asia   Using a water buffalo (a common draft animal in Southeast Asia), a man plows a rice field, while a woman husks rice in this Filipino scene from the early eighteenth century. Their house is on stilts as protection against floods. *(Bibliothèque Nationale, Paris)*

this diversity, certain sociocultural similarities connected the region.

First, by the fifteenth century, the peoples of what we call Indonesia, Malaysia, the Philippines, and the many islands in between all spoke a language of the Austronesian family. Southeast Asian languages have common elements, reflecting continuing interactions among the peoples speaking them. Second, a common environment, and adaptation to that environment, led to a diet based on rice, fish, palms, and palm wine. Rice is probably indigenous to the region, and from Luzon in the Philippines westward to Java, Sumatra, Siam

MAP 16.1 Indian Ocean Trade Routes   The faith of Islam took strong root on the east coast of Africa and in northern India, Sumatra, the Malay Archipelago, and the southern Philippines. In the sixteenth and seventeenth centuries Christianity competed with Islam for the adherence of peoples on all the Indian Ocean islands. *(Source: Some data from* The Times Atlas of World History*, 3d ed., page 146.)*

(Thailand), and Vietnam, rice, harvested by women, formed the staple of the diet. The seas provided many varieties of fish and crustaceans such as crabs and shrimp. A paste made from fish and spices garnished the rice. Everywhere fishing, called "the secondary industry" (after commerce), served as the chief male occupation, well ahead of agriculture. The fish were caught in large nets put out from several boats, or they were snared in stationary bamboo traps. Lacking grasslands, Southeast Asia has no pastoral tradition, no cattle or sheep, and thus meat and milk products from these animals played a small role in the diet. Animal protein came only from pigs, which were raised almost everywhere and were the center of feasting; from chickens; and in some places from water buffalo. Cucumbers, onions, and gourds supplemented the diet, and fruits—coconuts, bananas, mangoes, limes, and pineapples (after they were introduced from the Americas)—substituted for vegetables. Sugar cane, probably native to Southeast Asia, grew in profusion. It was chewed as a confectionery and used as a sweetener in desserts.[2]

In comparison to India, China, or even Europe (after the Black Death), Southeast Asia was very sparsely populated. People were concentrated in the port cities and in areas of intense rice cultivation. The seventeenth and eighteenth centuries witnessed slow but steady population growth, while the nineteenth century, under European colonial rule, witnessed very rapid expansion. Almost all Southeast Asian people married at a young age (about twenty). Marriage practices varied greatly from Indian, Chinese, and European ones, reflecting marked differences in the status of women.

The important role played by women in planting and harvesting rice gave them authority and economic power. Because of women's reproductive role, daughters had a high value. In contrast to India, China, the Middle East, and Europe, in Southeast Asia the more daughters a man had, the richer he was. At marriage the groom paid the bride (or sometimes her family) a sum of money, called bride wealth, which remained under her control. This practice was in sharp contrast to the Chinese, Indian, and European dowry, which was provided by the wife's family and came under the husband's control. Unlike the Chinese practice, married couples usually resided in the wife's village. Southeast Asian law codes stipulated that all property should be administered jointly, in contrast to the Chinese principle and Indian practice that wives had no say in the disposal of family property. All children, regardless of gender, inherited equally, and when Islam eventually took root in parts of the region, the rule that sons receive double the inheritance of daughters was never implemented.

Likewise, in sexual matters Southeast Asian custom stressed the satisfaction of the woman. Literature shows that women took an unusually active role in courtship and lovemaking and that they expected sexual and emotional satisfaction. Men sometimes underwent painful surgery, having small balls or bells inserted under the loose skin of the penis, to increase a woman's erotic pleasure, a practice that has no counterpart anywhere in the world. This practice also reveals the strong sociocultural position of women.

Although rulers commonly had multiple wives or concubines for status or diplomatic reasons, the vast majority of ordinary people were monogamous. In contrast to most parts of the world except Africa, Southeast Asian peoples regarded premarital sexual activity with indulgence, and no premium was placed on virginity at marriage. Once couples were married, however, their "fidelity and devotedness . . . appears to have surpassed

Woman Offering Betel   In Southeast Asia, betel served as *the* basic social lubricant. A combination of the betel nut, leaf, and lime, betel sweetened the breath and relaxed the mind; it was central to the rituals of lovemaking; and it was offered on all important social occasions, such as birth, marriage, and death. *(Rijksuniversiteit Leiden, LOr 8655)*

[that of] Europeans." Foreign observers seemed astonished at the affection married couples showed each other. Still, divorce was very easy if a pair proved incompatible; common property and children were divided. Divorce carried no social stigma, and either the woman or the man could initiate it. Even after Islam was introduced to the region, a woman's status and livelihood were not diminished by divorce. Such freedom and independence stands in marked contrast to practices elsewhere in the early modern world.[3]

Religious Revolutions

Diversity—by district, community, village, and even individual—characterized religious practice in Southeast Asia. The region had no written religious tradition (as do Judaism, Christianity, and Islam). Nor did any distinction exist between the religious and material spheres. Rather, people held that spiritual forces suffused the material world. They practiced a kind of animism, believing that spiritual powers inhabited natural objects. To survive and prosper, a person had to know how to please, appease, and manipulate those forces. To ensure human fertility, cure sickness, produce a good harvest, safeguard the living, and help the dead attain a contented afterlife, the individual propitiated the forces by providing the appropriate sacrificial offerings or feasts. For example, in the Philippines and eastern Indonesia, certain activities were forbidden during the period of mourning following death, but great feasting then followed. Exquisite clothing, pottery, and jewelry were buried with the corpse to ensure his or her status in the afterlife. In Borneo, Cambodia, Burma, and the Philippines, slaves were sometimes killed to serve their deceased owners. Death rituals, like life rituals, had enormous variation in Southeast Asia.

Throughout the first millennium A.D., Hindu and Buddhist cults; Confucianists; and Jewish, Christian, and Muslim traders and travelers carried their beliefs to Southeast Asia. Rulers tolerated them because they did not expect those beliefs to have much impact. Beginning in the late thirteenth century, Muslim merchants established sizable trading colonies in the ports of northern Sumatra, eastern Java, Champa, and the east coast of the Malay Peninsula (see Map 16.1). Once the ruler of Malacca, the largest port city in Indonesia, accepted Islam, Muslim businessmen controlled all business transactions there; the saying went that these transactions were "sealed with a handshake and a glance at heaven." Islamic success continued from 1400 to 1650. Rulers of the port states on the spice route to northern Java and the Moluccas (Maluku), and those on the trading route to Brunei in Borneo and Manila in the Philippines, adhered to the faith of Allah. Pilgrims and scholars arrived from Mecca, Egypt, and the entire North African Muslim world.

With the arrival of the Portuguese in 1498 (see page 500) and their capture of Malacca in 1511, fierce competition ensued between Muslims and Christians for the religious affiliation of Southeast Asian peoples. The middle years of the sixteenth century witnessed the galvanized energy of the Counter-Reformation in Europe (see pages 469–471) and the expansion of the Ottoman Empire through southwestern Asia and southeastern Europe (see pages 648–652). From Rome the first Jesuit, Saint Francis Xavier (1506–1552), reached Malacca in 1542. Likewise, Suleiman the Magnificent and his successors sent proselytizers. After the Spanish occupation of Manila in the Philippines in 1571, the Spanish crown, with the wealth of South America at its disposal, flooded Southeast Asia with missionaries. Unlike Southeast Asian animism, the two prophetic faiths, Islam and Christianity, insisted on an exclusive path to salvation: the renunciation of paganism and some outward sign of membership in the new faith.

What was the reaction of Southeast Asian peoples to these religions? How did adherents of the Middle Eastern religions spread their faiths? What impact did they have on peoples' lives in the sixteenth and seventeenth centuries? Southeast Asians saw Muslims and Christians as wealthy, powerful traders and warriors. Thus native peoples believed that the foreigners must possess some secret ability to manipulate the spirit world. A contemporary Spaniard wrote that Southeast Asians believed "that paradise and successful (business) enterprises are reserved for those who submit to the religion of the Moros (Muslims) of Brunei[;] . . . they are the richer people." Some Filipinos adopted the Muslim taboo regarding eating pork, believing that abstention was the key to material success. Southeast Asians also were impressed by Muslim and European ships, and especially by their firearms. The foreigners seemed to have a more ruthless view of war (perhaps because they had no place to retreat to) than the natives. As the Muslims and Christians fought for commercial superiority throughout the sixteenth century, the indigenous peoples watched closely, "partly for reasons of self-preservation, partly that they might adopt the spiritual and practical techniques of the winners."[4]

Christian priests and Muslim teachers rested their authority on the ability to read and explain the Bible and

Minaret at Kudus in Central Java More than one-third of all Muslims live east of India, in China or Southeast Asia. When Islam spread in the Malay Archipelago, Muslims adapted indigenous building styles to the needs of the mosque. Although most minarets were built of wood and bamboo, this red brick one has the form of the traditional Hindu temple and is similar to Balinese towers, where drums are sounded to summon people to prayer. (In Arabia before loudspeakers, the muezzin chanted the *adban,* or summons to prayer.) *(From George Michell, ed.,* Architecture of the Islamic World: Its History and Social Meaning *[London: Thames & Hudson, 1995])*

tic zeal for the destruction of pagan idols, statues, and temples that the Christians did. The Muslims did face a major obstacle, however: the indigenous peoples' attachment to pork, the main meat source and the central dish in all feasting. The extermination of pigs (signifying abandonment of pork) as well as male circumcision, an unavoidable requirement, implied conversion to Islam.

Acceptance of one of the prophetic religions varied with time and place. Recent scholars speak of the "adherence" of peoples in the sixteenth century to Islam, rather than their "conversion." The coastal port cities on major trade routes had "substantial" numbers of Muslims, and rulers of the port states of Sumatra, the Malay Peninsula, northern Java, and the Moluccas identified themselves as Muslims. Because of scanty evidence, we do not know how deeply Islam penetrated the rural hinterland. By 1700, however, most rural and urban people had abandoned pork and pagan practices, adopted Islamic dress, submitted to circumcision, and considered themselves part of the international Muslim community. In Java in 1700, the distinction between Javanese tradition and acceptable Muslim behavior remained perceptible. In the Philippines, Islam achieved some success, especially in the south. But Magellan's military conquest, the enormous enthusiasm of the Jesuit missionaries, and the vigorous support of the Spanish crown led to the Christianization of most of the islands. As elsewhere, whether individuals conformed to Muslim or Christian standards was another matter. The official acceptance of one of the two Scripture-based religions by more than half the people of Southeast Asia has had lasting importance.

the Qur'an. They quickly learned the locals' languages and translated their Scriptures into those languages. The instruction of rulers and the educated into either faith was by memorization of the catechism, or sacred texts; teaching the masses was oral—they were expected to learn the basic prayers and customs of the new faiths. The Muslims and Christians differed in one fundamental strategy: whereas the Christians relied on a celibate clergy that defined the new community through baptism, the Muslims often married locally and accepted Southeast Asian cultures much more readily than did Spanish priests. Since no Asian was ordained a priest or served as catechist before 1700, European and Iberian terms defined Christian boundaries in Southeast Asia. By contrast, the Muslims showed little of the iconoclas-

Trade and Commerce

Since Han and Roman times (see pages 185 and 171–173), seaborne trade between China (always the biggest market for Southeast Asian goods), India, the Middle East, and Europe had flowed across the Indian Ocean. From the seventh through the thirteenth centuries, the volume of this trade steadily increased. In the late fourteenth century, with the European and West Asian populations recovering from the Black Death, demand for Southeast Asian goods accelerated.

Other developments stimulated the market for Southeast Asian goods. The collapse of the Central Asian overland caravan route, the famous Silk Road, gave a boost to the traffic originating in the Indian Ocean and

Vessels off the Java Coast   This sixteenth-century Dutch engraving shows four types of vessels, clockwise from top: a Javanese trading sailboat; a Chinese junk—a flatbottomed ship with high poop (exposed partial deck) and battens (material to fasten down hatches in foul weather); a local fishing boat; and a Javanese junk. *(From Lodewycksk, 1598)*

flowing up the Red Sea to Damascus, Beirut, Cairo, and Alexandria. A Venetian treaty with the Mamluk rulers of Egypt (see page 363) led to fabulous wealth for the spice merchants of Cairo and Venice. Chinese expansion into Vietnam and Burma increased the population of the Celestial Kingdom and the demand for exotic goods. Above all, the seven voyages of the Chinese admiral Zheng He in 1405 launched for Southeast Asia "the age of commerce." (See the feature "Individuals in Society: Zheng He.")

In the fifteenth century, Malacca became the great commercial entrepôt on the Indian Ocean. To Malacca came Chinese porcelains, silks, and camphor (used in the manufacture of many medications, including those to reduce fevers); pepper, cloves, nutmeg, and raw materials such as sappanwood and sandalwood from the Moluccas; sugar from the Philippines; and Indian printed cotton and woven tapestries, copper weapons, incense, dyes, and opium (which already had a sizable market in China). Muslim merchants in other port cities, such as Patani on the Malay Peninsula, Pasai in Sumatra, and Demak in Java, shared in this trade. They also exchanged cowrie shells from the Maldive Islands. These shells were in enormous demand throughout Africa as symbols of wealth and status, as decoration, and as a medium of currency in African trade. These Muslim businessmen in Southeast Asia thus had dealings with their coreligionists in the East African ports of Mogadishu, Kilwa, and Sofala.

Merchants at Malacca stockpiled goods in fortified warehouses while waiting for the next monsoon. A river, spanned by a bridge, divided Malacca, with business people living on the north side and the court and aristocracy living on the south. Whereas the wealth of cities in Mughal India (see page 667) rested mainly on agriculture, that of Malacca and other Southeast Asian cities depended on commerce. In all of Asia, Malacca, with its many mosques and elegant homes, enjoyed the reputation of being a sophisticated city, full of "music, ballads, and poetry."[5]

Individuals in Society

Zheng He (1373?–1435)

In 1403 the Chinese emperor Yongle (r. 1403–1424) ordered his coastal provinces to build a vast fleet of ships, with construction centered at Longjiang near Nanjing; the inland provinces were to provide wood and float it down the Yangzi River. Thirty thousand shipwrights, carpenters, sailmakers, ropers, and caulkers worked in a frenzy. As work progressed, Yongle selected a commander for the fleet. Although the emperor feared he was too old (thirty-five) for so politically important an expedition, he chose Zheng He. The decision rested on Zheng He's unquestioned loyalty, strength of character, energy, ability, and eloquence. These qualities apparently were expected to compensate for Zheng He's lack of seamanship.

The southwestern province of Yunnan had a large Muslim population, and Zheng He was born into that group. When the then Prince Zhi Di defeated the Mongols in Yunnan, Zheng He's father was killed in the related disorder. The young boy was taken prisoner and, as was the custom, castrated. Raised in Zhi Di's household, he learned to read and write, studied Confucian writings, and accompanied the prince on all military expeditions. By age twenty, Zheng He was not the soft, effeminate stereotype of the eunuch; rather he was "seven feet tall and had a waist five feet in circumference. His cheeks and forehead were high . . . [and] he had glaring eyes . . . [and] a voice loud as a bell. . . . He was accustomed to battle." Zheng He must have made an imposing impression. A devout Muslim, he persuaded the emperor to place mosques under imperial protection after a period of persecution. On his travels, he prayed at mosques at Malacca and Hormuz. Unable to sire sons, he adopted a nephew. In Chinese history, he was the first eunuch to hold such an important command.

The first fleet, composed of 317 junks, 100 supply ships, water tankers, warships, transports for horses, and patrol boats, and carrying 28,000 sailors and soldiers, represents the largest naval force in world history before World War I. Because it bore tons of beautiful porcelains, elegant silks, lacquer ware, and exquisite artifacts to be exchanged for goods abroad, it was called the "treasure fleet." Zheng He may have been appointed commander because as a Muslim he could more easily negotiate with Muslim merchants on the Indian Ocean.

Zheng He: voyager to India, Persia, Arabia, and Africa. (*From Lo Mon-teng, The Western Sea Cruises of Eunuch San Pao, 1597*)

Between 1405 and 1433, Zheng He led seven voyages, which combined the emperor's diplomatic, political, geographical, and commercial goals. Yongle wanted to secure China's hegemony over tributary states and collect pledges of loyalty from them. To gain information on winds, tides, distant lands, and rare plants and animals, Zheng He sailed as far west as Egypt. Smallpox epidemics had recently hit China, and one purpose of his voyages was to gather pharmacological products; an Arab text on drugs and therapies was secured and translated into Chinese. He also brought back a giraffe and mahogany, a wood ideal for ships' rudders because of its hardness. Chinese emperors had long found Korean women especially attractive. In 1408 Zheng He delivered 300 virgins to the emperor. The next year, the emperor wanted more.

Just before his death, Zheng He recorded his accomplishments on stone tablets. The expeditions had unified "seas and continents . . . the countries beyond the horizon from the ends of the earth have all become subjects . . . and the distances and routes between distant lands may be calculated," implying that China had accumulated considerable geographical information. From around the Indian Ocean, official tribute flowed to the Ming court. A vast immigration of Chinese people to Southeast Asia, sometimes called the Chinese diaspora, followed the expeditions. Immigrants carried with them Chinese culture, including social customs, diet, and practical objects of Chinese technology—calendars, books, scales for weights and measures, and musical instruments. With legends collected about him and monuments erected to him, Zheng He became a great cult hero.

Questions for Analysis

1. What do the voyages of the treasure fleet tell us about China in the fifteenth century?
2. What was Zheng He's legacy?

Source: Louise Levathes, *When China Ruled the Seas: The Treasure Fleet of the Dragon Throne, 1405–1433* (New York: Oxford University Press, 1996).

EUROPEAN DISCOVERY, RECONNAISSANCE, AND EXPANSION

Historians of Europe have called the period from 1450 to 1650 the "Age of Discovery," "Age of Reconnaissance," and "Age of Expansion." All three labels are appropriate. "Age of Discovery" refers to the era's phenomenal advances in geographical knowledge and technology, often achieved through trial and error. In 1350 it took as long to sail from the eastern end of the Mediterranean to the western end as it had taken a thousand years earlier. Even in the fifteenth century, Europeans knew little more about the earth's surface than the Romans had known. Europeans' geographical knowledge was confined largely to the Mediterranean and southwestern Asia. They lacked the scientific and technological information the Chinese had, and they could not have launched the massive expeditions that China sent out under Zheng He (see page 498). By 1650, however, Europeans had made an extensive reconnaissance—or preliminary exploration—and had sketched fairly accurately the physical outline of the earth. Much of the geographical information they had gathered was tentative and not fully understood—hence the appropriateness of "Age of Reconnaissance."

The designation "Age of Expansion" refers to the migration of Europeans to other parts of the world. This colonization resulted in political control of much of South and North America; coastal regions of Africa, India, China, and Japan; and many Pacific islands. Political hegemony was accompanied by economic exploitation, religious domination, and the introduction of European patterns of social and intellectual life. The sixteenth-century expansion of European society launched a new age in world history. None of the three "Age" labels reflects the experiences of non-European peoples. Africans, Asians, and native Americans had known the geographies of their regions for centuries. They made no "discoveries" and, with the notable exception of the Chinese, undertook no reconnaissance.

Overseas Exploration and Conquest

Migration is a constant theme in the history of world societies. The outward expansion of Europe began with the Viking voyages across the Atlantic in the ninth and tenth centuries. Under Eric the Red and Leif Ericson, the Vikings discovered Greenland and the eastern coast of North America. They made permanent settlements in, and a legal imprint on, Iceland, Ireland, England, Normandy, and Sicily. The Crusades of the eleventh through thirteenth centuries were another phase in Europe's attempt to explore and exploit peoples on the periphery of the continent. But the lack of a strong territorial base, superior Muslim military strength, and sheer misrule combined to make the Crusader kingdoms short-lived. In the mid-fifteenth century, Europe seemed ill prepared for further international ventures. Europeans, however, saw Ottoman Turkish expansion as a grave threat.

Combining excellent military strategy with efficient administration of their conquered territories, the Turks had subdued most of Asia Minor and begun to settle on the western side of the Bosporus. The Muslim Ottoman Turks under Sultan Mohammed II (r. 1451–1481) captured Constantinople in 1453, pressed northwest into the Balkans, and by the early sixteenth century controlled the eastern Mediterranean. The Turkish menace badly frightened Europeans. In France in the fifteenth and sixteenth centuries, twice as many books were printed about the Turkish threat as about the American discoveries. Yet the fifteenth and sixteenth centuries witnessed a fantastic continuation, on a global scale, of European expansion.

Political centralization in Spain, France, and England helps to explain those countries' outward push. In the fifteenth century, Isabella and Ferdinand had consolidated their several kingdoms to achieve a more united Spain. The Catholic rulers revamped the Spanish bureaucracy and humbled dissident elements, notably the Muslims and the Jews. The Spanish monarchy was stronger than ever before and in a position to support foreign ventures; it could bear the costs and dangers of exploration. But Portugal, situated on the extreme southwestern edge of the European continent, got the start on the rest of Europe. Still insignificant as a European land power despite its recently secured frontiers, Portugal sought greatness in the unknown world overseas.

Portugal's taking of Ceuta, an Arab city in northern Morocco, in 1415 marked the beginning of European exploration and control of overseas territory (Map 16.2). The objectives of Portuguese policy included the historic Iberian crusade to Christianize Muslims and the search for gold, for an overseas route to the spice markets of India, and for the mythical Christian ruler of Ethiopia, Prester John.

In the early phases of Portuguese exploration, Prince Henry (1394–1460), called "the Navigator" because of the annual expeditions he sent down the western coast of Africa, played the leading role. In the fifteenth

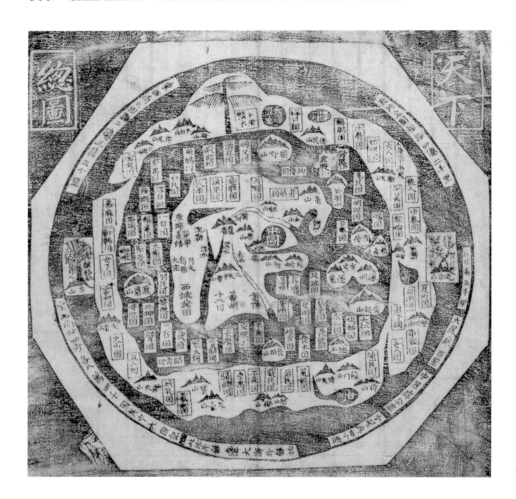

Kangnido Map (1684)
Diplomatic relations between
Korea and the Ming Chinese
court brought Korean scholars
in touch with Chinese
thought. This Korean map of
the world is probably based on
a Chinese model. *(From Lee
Chan, Hanguk ui ko chido/Yi
Chan cho [Old Maps of Korea],
1997. Reproduced with
permission)*

century, most of the gold that reached Europe came
from the Sudan in West Africa and from the Akan peoples living near the area of present-day Ghana. Muslim
caravans brought the gold from the African cities of Ni-
ani and Timbuktu and carried it north across the Sahara
to Mediterranean ports. Then the Portuguese muscled
in on this commerce in gold. Prince Henry's carefully
planned expeditions succeeded in reaching Guinea, and
under King John II (r. 1481–1495) the Portuguese established trading posts and forts on the Guinea coast
and penetrated into the continent all the way to Timbuktu (see Map 16.2). Portuguese ships transported
gold to Lisbon, and by 1500 Portugal controlled the
flow of gold to Europe. The golden century of Portuguese prosperity had begun.

The spices Europeans wanted, however, came from
South Asia and the Moluccas, not from African king-

doms. Thus the Portuguese pushed farther south down
the west coast of Africa. In 1487 Bartholomew Diaz
rounded the Cape of Good Hope at the southern tip,
but storms and a threatened mutiny forced him to turn
back. On a second expedition (1497–1499), the Portuguese mariner Vasco da Gama reached India and returned to Lisbon loaded with samples of Indian wares.
King Manuel (r. 1495–1521) promptly dispatched thirteen ships under the command of Pedro Alvares Cabral,
assisted by Diaz, to set up trading posts in India. On
April 22, 1500, the coast of Brazil in South America
was sighted and claimed for the crown of Portugal.
Cabral then proceeded south and east around the Cape
of Good Hope and reached India. Half of the fleet was
lost on the return voyage, but the six spice-laden vessels
that dropped anchor in Lisbon harbor in July 1501
more than paid for the entire expedition. Thereafter,

convoys were sent out every March. Lisbon became the entrance port for Asian goods into Europe.

Black pepper originally derived from the Malabar Coast of southwestern India between Goa and Cochin—"the pepper country" to medieval European and Middle Eastern travelers. In 1500 this region supplied the European demand for pepper. In the next sixty years, pepper production spread in India, as well as to the Malay Peninsula, Sumatra, and Java. Nutmeg and cloves, well known to the Chinese but extremely rare and expensive for Europeans before the sixteenth century, grew in the Moluccas. From the Southeast Asian perspective, rice, salt, pickled or dried fish, and metal ware represented the major items for trade; spices originally were minor. With the arrival of Europeans, however, spices brought the larger profits.

As we have seen (see pages 495–496), Muslims (of Middle Eastern, Indian, Southeast Asian, and Chinese ethnic backgrounds) had controlled the Indian Ocean trade for centuries. They did not surrender it willingly. With the Portuguese entry into the region in 1498, the brisk Muslim trade was drastically disrupted, as the Portuguese sank or plundered every Muslim spice ship they met. Between 1502 and 1520, no Moluccan spices reached Mediterranean ports via the Red Sea. Portuguese ships sailing around the Cape of Good Hope carried about one-fourth the goods the Muslims had transported through southwestern Asia. Then, in 1511, Alfonso de Albuquerque, whom the Portuguese crown had named governor of India (1509–1515), captured Malacca, the great Indian Ocean trading entrepôt. Thereafter Portuguese commercial wealth gradually increased; the Portuguese dominated the European market by delivering on average thirty tons of cloves and ten tons of nutmeg each year. The Middle Eastern route declined. Albuquerque's bombardment of Goa, Calicut, and Malacca laid the foundations for Portuguese imperialism in the sixteenth and seventeenth centuries—a strange way to bring Christianity to "those who were in darkness." As one scholar wrote about the opening of China to the West, "while Buddha came to China on white elephants, Christ was borne on cannon balls."[6]

In March 1493, between the voyages of Diaz and da Gama, Spanish ships entered Lisbon harbor bearing a triumphant Italian explorer in the service of the Spanish monarchy. Christopher Columbus (1451–1506), a Genoese mariner, had secured Spanish support for an expedition to the East. He sailed from Palos, Spain, to the Canary Islands and crossed the Atlantic to the Bahamas, landing in October 1492 on an island that he named San Salvador and believed to be the coast of India. (See the feature "Listening to the Past: Columbus Describes His First Voyage" on pages 524–525.)

Technological Stimuli to Exploration

Technological developments were the key to Europe's remarkable outreach. By 1350 cannon made of iron or bronze and able to fire iron or stone balls had been fully developed in western Europe. This artillery emitted frightening noises and great flashes of fire and could batter down fortresses and even city walls. Sultan Mohammed II's siege of Constantinople in 1453 provides a classic illustration of the effectiveness of cannon fire.

Constantinople had very strong walled fortifications. The sultan secured the services of a Western technician, who built fifty-six small cannon and a gigantic gun that could hurl stone balls weighing about eight hundred pounds. The gun had to be moved by several hundred oxen and could be loaded and fired only by about a hundred men working together. Reloading took two hours. This awkward but powerful weapon breached the walls of Constantinople before it cracked on the second day of the bombardment. Lesser cannon finished the job.

Although early cannon posed serious technical difficulties for land warfare, they could be used at sea. The mounting of cannon on ships and improved techniques of shipbuilding gave impetus to European expansion. Since ancient times, most seagoing vessels had been narrow, open boats called *galleys,* propelled largely by oarsmen: slaves or convicts who had been sentenced to the galleys manned the oars of the cargo ships and warships that sailed the Mediterranean (both types of ships carried soldiers for defense). Well suited to the calm and thoroughly explored waters of the Mediterranean, galleys could not withstand the rough winds and uncharted shoals of the Atlantic. The need for sturdier craft, as well as population losses caused by the Black Death, forced the development of a new style of ship that did not require soldiers for defense or a large crew of oarsmen.

In the course of the fifteenth century, the Portuguese developed the *caravel,* a small, light, three-masted sailing ship. Though somewhat slower than the galley, the caravel held more cargo and was highly maneuverable. When fitted with cannon, it could dominate larger vessels, such as the round ships commonly

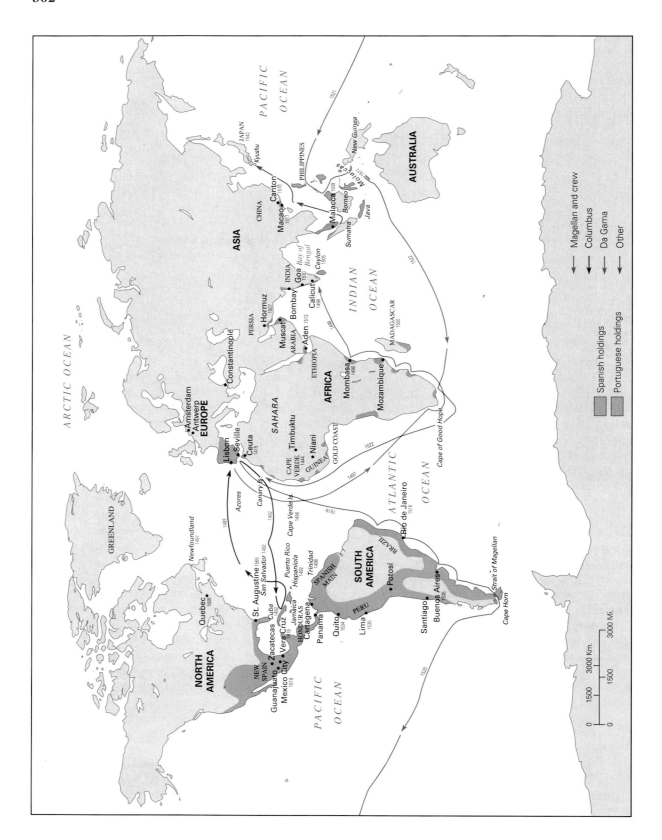

Nocturnal   An instrument for determining the hour of night at sea by finding the progress of certain stars around the polestar (center aperture). *(National Maritime Museum, London)*

used in commerce. The substitution of wind power for manpower, and artillery fire for soldiers, signaled a great technological advance and gave Europeans navigational and fighting ascendancy over the rest of the world.[7]

Other fifteenth-century developments in navigation helped make possible the conquest of the Atlantic. The magnetic compass enabled sailors to determine their direction and position at sea. The astrolabe, an instrument developed by Muslim navigators in the twelfth century and used to determine the altitude of the sun and other celestial bodies, permitted mariners to plot their latitude, or position north or south of the equator. Steadily improved maps and sea charts provided information about distances, sea depths, and geography.

MAP 16.2 European Exploration and Conquest, Fifteenth and Sixteenth Centuries   The European voyages of discovery marked another phase in the centuries-old migrations of peoples. Consider the major contemporary significance of each of the three voyages depicted on the map.

The Explorers' Motives

The expansion of Europe was not motivated by demographic pressures. The Black Death had caused serious population losses from which Europe had not recovered in 1500. Few Europeans immigrated to North or South America in the sixteenth century. Half of those who did sail to begin a new life in America died en route; half of those who reached what they regarded as the New World eventually returned to their homeland. Why, then, did explorers brave the Atlantic, Pacific, and Indian Oceans, risking their lives to discover new continents and spread European culture?

The reasons are varied and complex. People of the sixteenth century were still basically medieval: their attitudes and values were shaped by religion and expressed in religious terms. In the late fifteenth century, crusading fervor remained a basic part of the Portuguese and Spanish national ideals. The desire to Christianize Muslims and pagan peoples played a central role in European expansion. Queen Isabella of Spain, for example, showed a fanatical zeal for converting the Muslims to Christianity and concentrated her efforts on the Muslims in Granada. But after the abortive crusading

Pepper Harvest   To break the monotony of their bland diet, Europeans had a passion for pepper, which—along with cinnamon, cloves, nutmeg, and ginger—was the main object of the Asian trade. Since one kilo of pepper cost 2 grams of silver at the place of production in the East Indies and from 10 to 14 grams of silver in Alexandria, 14 to 18 grams in Venice, and 20 to 30 grams at the markets of northern Europe, we can appreciate the fifteenth-century expression "As dear as pepper." Here natives fill vats, and the dealer tastes a peppercorn for pungency. *(Bibliothèque Nationale, Paris)*

attempts of the thirteenth century, Isabella and other rulers realized full well that they lacked the material resources to mount the full-scale assault on Islam necessary for victory. Crusading impulses thus shifted from the Muslims to the pagan peoples of other continents.

Moreover, after the *reconquista*—the Christian reconquest of Muslim areas—enterprising young men of the Spanish upper classes found economic and political opportunities severely limited. As a study of the Castilian city Ciudad Real shows, the traditional aristocracy controlled the best agricultural land and monopolized urban administrative posts. Great merchants and a few nobles (surprisingly, since Spanish law forbade nobles' participation in commercial ventures) dominated the textile and leather-glove manufacturing industries. Thus many ambitious men immigrated to the Americas to seek their fortunes.[8]

Government sponsorship and encouragement of exploration also help to account for the results of the various voyages. Individual mariners and explorers could not afford the massive sums needed to explore mysterious oceans and to control remote continents. The strong financial support of Prince Henry the Navigator led to Portugal's success in the spice trade. Even the grudging and modest assistance of Isabella and Ferdinand eventually brought untold riches—and complicated problems—to Spain. The Dutch in the seventeenth century, through such government-sponsored trading companies as the Dutch East India Company, reaped enormous wealth, and although the Netherlands was a small country, it dominated the European economy in 1650.

Scholars have frequently described the European discoveries as a manifestation of Renaissance curiosity about the physical universe—the desire to know more about the geography and peoples of the world. There is truth to this explanation. Cosmography, natural history, and geography aroused enormous interest among educated people in the fifteenth and sixteenth centuries. Just as science fiction and speculation about life on other planets excite readers today, quasi-scientific literature about Africa, Asia, and the Americas captured the imaginations of Europeans. Oviedo's *General History of the Indies* (1547), a detailed eyewitness account of plants, animals, and peoples, was widely read.

Spices were another important incentive to voyages of discovery. Introduced into western Europe by the Crusaders in the twelfth century, nutmeg, mace, ginger, cinnamon, and pepper added flavor and variety to the monotonous diet of Europeans. Spices were also used in the preparation of medicinal drugs and incense for religious ceremonies. In the late thirteenth century, the Venetian Marco Polo (1254?–1324?), the greatest of medieval travelers, had visited the court of the Chinese emperor. His widely publicized account, *Travels,* stimulated the trade in spices between Asia and Italy. The Venetians came to hold a monopoly of trade in western Europe.

Spices were grown in India and China, shipped across the Indian Ocean to ports on the Persian Gulf, and then transported by Arabs across the Arabian Desert to Mediterranean ports. But the rise of the Ming Dynasty in China in the late fourteenth century resulted in the expulsion of foreigners. And the steady penetration of the Ottoman Turks into the eastern Mediterranean and of Muslims across North Africa forced Europeans to seek a new route to the Asian spice markets.

The basic reason for European exploration and expansion, however, was the quest for material profit. Mariners and explorers frankly admitted this. As Bartholomew Diaz put it, his motives were "to serve God and His Majesty, to give light to those who were in darkness and to grow rich as all men desire to do." When Vasco da Gama reached the port of Calicut, India, in 1498, a native asked what the Portuguese wanted. Da Gama replied, "Christians and spices."[9] The bluntest of the Spanish conquistadors, Hernando Cortés, announced as he prepared to conquer Mexico, "I have come to win gold, not to plow the fields like a peasant."[10]

A sixteenth-century diplomat, Ogier Gheselin de Busbecq, summed up explorers' paradoxical attitude: in expeditions to the Indies and the Antipodes, he said, "religion supplies the pretext and gold the motive."[11]

The Problem of Christopher Columbus

The year 1992, which marked the quincentenary of Columbus's first voyages to the Americas, spawned an enormous amount of discussion about the significance of his voyages. Journalists, scholars, amateurs, and polemicists debated Columbus's accomplishments and failures. Until the 1980s, most writers generally would have agreed with the Harvard historian Samuel Eliot Morison in his 1942 biography of Columbus:

The whole history of the Americas stems from the Four Voyages of Columbus; and as the Greek city-states looked back to the deathless gods as their founders, so today a score of independent nations and dominions unite in homage to Columbus, the stouthearted son of Genoa, who carried Christian civilization across the Ocean Sea.[12]

In 1942, we must remember, the Western Powers believed they were engaged in a life-and-death struggle to defend "Christian civilization" against the evil forces of fascism. As the five hundredth anniversary of his famous voyage approached, however, Columbus underwent severe criticism.

Critics charged that he enslaved and sometimes killed the Indians and was a cruel and ineffective governor of Spain's Caribbean colony. Moreover, they said, he did not discover a previously unknown continent: Africans and other Europeans had been to the Western Hemisphere before him. And not only did he not discover a "new" continent, he did not realize what he had found. In short, according to his harshest critics, he was a fool who didn't know what was going on around him. Some claim that he was the originator of European exploitation of the non-European world and destroyed the paradise that had been the New World.[13]

Because those judgments rest on social and ethical standards that did not exist in Columbus's world, responsible scholars consider them ahistorical. Instead, using the evidence of his *Journal* (sea log) and letters, let us ask three basic questions: (1) What kind of man was Columbus, and what forces or influences shaped him? (2) In sailing westward from Europe, what were his goals? (3) Did he achieve his goals, and what did he make of his discoveries?

The central feature in the character of Christopher Columbus is that he was a deeply religious man. He began the *Journal* of his voyage to the Americas, written as a letter to Ferdinand and Isabella of Spain, with this recollection:

On 2 January in the year 1492, when your Highnesses had concluded their war with the Moors who reigned in Europe, I saw your Highnesses' banners victoriously raised on the towers of the Alhambra, the citadel of the city, and the Moorish king come out of the city gates and kiss the hands of your Highnesses and the prince, My Lord. And later in that same month, on the grounds of information I had given your Highnesses concerning the lands of India . . . your Highnesses decided to send me, Christopher Columbus, to see these parts of India and the princes and peoples of those lands and consider the best means for their conversion.[14]

He had witnessed the Spanish reconquest of Granada and shared fully in the religious and nationalistic fervor surrounding that event. Just seven months separated Isabella and Ferdinand's entry into Granada on January 6 and Columbus's departure westward on August 3, 1492. In his mind, the two events were clearly linked. Long after Europeans knew something of Columbus's discoveries in the Caribbean, they considered the restoration of Muslim Granada to Christian hands as Ferdinand and Isabella's greatest achievements; for the conquest, in 1494 the Spanish pope Alexander VI (r. 1492–1503) rewarded them with the title of "Most Catholic Kings." Like the Spanish rulers and most Europeans of his age, Columbus understood Christianity as a missionary religion that should be carried to places and peoples where it did not exist. Although Columbus's character certainly included material and secular qualities, first and foremost, as he wrote in 1498, he believed he was a divine agent: "God made me the messenger of the new heaven and the new earth of which he spoke in the Apocalypse of St. John after having spoken of it through the mouth of the prophet Isaiah; and he showed me the post where to find it."[15]

A second and fundamental facet of Columbus the man is that he was very knowledgeable about the sea. He was familiar with fifteenth-century Portuguese navigational aids such as *portolans*—written descriptions of routes showing bays, coves, capes, ports, and the distances between these places—and the magnetic compass. He had spent years consulting geographers, mapmakers, and navigators. And, as he implies in his *Journal,* he had acquired not only theoretical but practical experience: "I have spent twenty-three years at sea and have not left it for any length of time worth mentioning, and I have seen everything from east to west [meaning he had been to England] and I have been to Guinea [North and West Africa]."[16] Some of Columbus's calculations, such as his measurement of the distance from Portugal to Japan as 2,760 miles (it is actually 12,000), proved inaccurate. But his successful thirty-three-day voyage to the Caribbean owed a great deal to his seamanship and his knowledge and skillful use of instruments.

What was the object of his first voyage? What did Columbus set out to do? He went through Marco Polo's *Travels* with a fine-toothed comb and, as his marginal comments in the book show, while he seemed most intrigued by the sexual practices of Asian peoples, he highlighted Polo's references to gold, silver, bulk sales, trade opportunities, and the seasonal times of monsoon-fleet sailings.[17] The name of his expedition,

"The Enterprise of the Indies," reveals his object. He wanted to find a direct ocean route to Asia, which would provide the opportunity for a greatly expanded trade, a trade in which the European economy, and especially Spain, would participate. Two scholars have written, "If Columbus had not sailed westward in search of Asia, someone else would have done so. The time was right for such a bold undertaking."[18] Someone else might have done so, but the fact remains that Columbus, displaying a characteristic Renaissance curiosity and restless drive, actually accepted the challenge.

How did Columbus interpret what he had found, and did he think he had achieved what he set out to do? His mind had been formed by the Bible and the geographical writings of classical authors, as were the minds of most educated people of his time. Thus, as people in every age have often done, Columbus ignored the evidence of his eyes; he described what he saw in the Caribbean as an idyllic paradise, a peaceful Garden of Eden. When accounts of his travels were published, Europeans' immediate fascination with this image of the New World meant that Columbus's propaganda created an instant myth. But when he sensed that he had not found the spice markets and bazaars of Asia, his goal changed from establishing trade with the (East) Indians and Chinese to establishing the kind of trade the Portuguese were then conducting with Africa and with Cape Verde and other islands in the Atlantic (see Map 16.2). That meant setting up some form of government in the Caribbean islands, even though Columbus had little interest in, or capacity for, governing. In 1496 he forcibly subjugated the island of Hispaniola, enslaved the Indians, and laid the basis for a system of land grants tied to the Indians' labor service. Borrowing practices and institutions from reconquest Spain and the Canary Islands, Columbus laid the foundation for Spanish imperial administration. In all of this, Columbus was very much a man of his times. He never understood, however, that the scale of his discoveries created problems of trade, settlers, relations with the Indians, and, above all, government bureaucracy.[19]

The Conquest of Aztec Mexico and Inca Peru

Technological development also helps to explain the Spanish conquest of Aztec Mexico and Inca Peru.

The strange end of the Aztec nation remains one of the most fascinating events in the annals of human societies. The Spanish adventurer Hernando Cortés (1485–1547) landed at Veracruz in February 1519. In No-

Mexica-Spaniard Encounter   The Mexica are armed with spears, the Spaniards with firearms and longbows. The colorful dress of the Mexica—indicating that war was a ceremonial rite for them—contrasts with the dull metallic gray of the Spaniards' armor. *(Institut Amatller d'Art Hispanic)*

vember he entered Tenochtitlán (Mexico City) and soon had the emperor Montezuma II (r. 1502–1520) in custody. In less than two years, Cortés destroyed the monarchy, gained complete control of the Mexica capital, and extended his jurisdiction over much of the Aztec Empire. Why did a strong people defending its own territory succumb so quickly to a handful of Spaniards fighting in dangerous and completely unfamiliar circumstances? How indeed, since Montezuma's scouts sent him detailed reports of the Spaniards' movements? The answers to these questions lie in the fact that at the time of the Spanish arrival, the Aztec and Inca Empires faced grave internal difficulties brought on by their religious ideologies; by the Spaniards' boldness, timing, and technology; and by Aztec and Inca psychology and attitudes toward war.

The Spaniards arrived in late summer, when the Aztecs were preoccupied with harvesting their crops and not thinking of war. From the Spaniards' perspective, their timing was ideal. A series of natural phenomena, signs, and portents seemed to augur disaster for the Aztecs. A comet was seen in daytime, a column of fire had appeared every midnight for a year, and two temples were suddenly destroyed, one by lightning unaccompanied by thunder. These and other apparently inexplicable events seemed to presage the return of the Aztec god Quetzalcoatl (see page 421) and had an unnerving effect on the Aztecs. They looked on the Europeans riding "wild beasts" as extraterrestrial forces coming to establish a new social order. Defeatism swept the nation and paralyzed its will.

The Aztec state religion, the sacred cult of Huitzilopochtli, necessitated constant warfare against neighboring peoples to secure captives for religious sacrifice and laborers for agricultural and infrastructural work. Lacking an effective method of governing subject peoples, the Aztecs controlled thirty-eight provinces in central Mexico through terror. When Cortés landed, the provinces were being crushed under a cycle of imperial oppression: increases in tribute provoked revolt, which led to reconquest, retribution, and demands for higher tribute, which in turn sparked greater resentment and fresh revolt. When the Spaniards appeared, the Totonacs greeted them as liberators, and other subject peoples joined them against the Aztecs. Even before the coming of the Spaniards, Montezuma's attempts to resolve the problem of constant warfare by freezing social positions—thereby ending the social mobility that war provided—aroused the resentment of his elite, mercantile, and lowborn classes. Montezuma faced terrible external and internal difficulties.[20]

Montezuma refrained from attacking the Spaniards as they advanced toward his capital and welcomed Cortés and his men into Tenochtitlán. Historians have often condemned the Aztec ruler for vacillation and weakness. But he relied on the advice of his state council, itself divided, and on the dubious loyalty of tributary communities. When Cortés—with incredible boldness—took Montezuma hostage, the emperor's influence over his people crumbled.

The major explanation for the collapse of the Aztec Empire to six hundred Spaniards lies in the Aztecs' notion of warfare and their level of technology. Forced to leave Tenochtitlán to settle a conflict elsewhere, Cortés placed his lieutenant, Alvarado, in charge. Alvarado's harsh rule drove the Aztecs to revolt, and they almost succeeded in destroying the Spanish garrison. When Cortés returned just in time, the Aztecs allowed his reinforcements to join Alvarado's besieged force. No threatened European or Asian state would have conceived of doing such a thing: dividing an enemy's army and destroying the separate parts was basic to their military tactics. But for the Aztecs, warfare was a ceremonial act in which "divide and conquer" had no place.

Having allowed the Spanish forces to reunite, the entire population of Tenochtitlán attacked the invaders. The Aztecs killed many Spaniards. In retaliation, the Spaniards executed Montezuma. The Spaniards escaped from the city and inflicted a crushing defeat on the Aztec army at Otumba near Lake Texcoco on July 7, 1520. The Spaniards won because "the simple Indian methods of mass warfare were of little avail against the manoeuvring of a well-drilled force."[21] Aztec weapons proved no match for the terrifyingly noisy and lethal Spanish cannon, muskets, crossbows, and steel swords. European technology decided the battle. Cortés began the systematic conquest of Mexico.

From 1493 to 1525, the Inca Huayna Capac ruled as a benevolent despot (the word *Inca* refers both to the ruler of the Amerindians who lived in the valleys of the Andes in present-day Peru and to the people themselves). His power was limited only by custom. His millions of subjects considered him a god, firm but just to his people, merciless to his enemies. Only a few of the Inca's closest relatives dared look at his divine face. No-

bles approached him on their knees, and the masses kissed the dirt as he rode by in his litter. The borders of his vast empire were well fortified and threatened by no foreign invaders. Grain was plentiful, and apart from an outbreak of smallpox in a distant province—introduced by the Spaniards—no natural disaster upset the general peace. An army of fifty thousand loyal troops stood at the Inca's disposal. Why did this powerful empire fall so easily to Francisco Pizarro and his band of 175 men armed with one small, ineffective cannon?

The Incas were totally isolated. They had no contact with other Amerindian cultures and knew nothing at all of Aztec civilization or its collapse to the Spaniards in 1521. Since about the year 1500, Inca scouts had reported "floating houses" on the seas, manned by white men with beards. Tradesmen told of strange large animals with feet of silver (as horseshoes appeared in the brilliant sunshine). Having observed a border skirmish between Indians and white men, intelligence sources advised Huayna Capac that the Europeans' swords were as harmless as women's weaving battens. A coastal chieftain had poured chicha, the native beer, down the barrel of a gun to appease the god of thunder. These incidents suggest that Inca culture provided no basis for understanding the Spaniards and the significance of their arrival. Moreover, even if the strange pale men planned war, there were very few of them, and the Incas believed that they could not be reinforced from the sea.[22]

At first the Incas did not think that the strangers intended trouble. They believed the old Inca legend that the creator-god Virocha—who had brought civilization to them, become displeased, and sailed away promising to return someday—had indeed returned. Belief in a legend prevented the Incas, like the Aztecs, from taking prompt action.

Religious ideology contributed to grave domestic crisis within the empire. When the ruler died, his corpse was preserved as a mummy. The mummy was both a holy object and a dynamic force in Inca society. It was housed in a sacred chamber and dressed in fine clothing. It was carried in procession to state ceremonies and was asked for advice in times of trouble. This cult of the royal mummies left a new Inca (ruler) with the title and insignia of his office but little else. Because each dead Inca retained possession of the estates and properties he had held in life, each new Inca lacked land. Thus, to strengthen his administration, secure the means to live in the royal style, and reward his supporters, a new Inca had to engage in warfare to acquire land.

In 1525 Huascar succeeded his father, Huayna Capac, as Inca and was crowned at Cuzco, the Incas' capital city, with the fringed headband symbolizing his imperial office. By this time, the dead rulers controlled most of Peru's land and resources. The nobility managed the estates of the dead Inca rulers. Needing land and other possessions, Huascar proposed burying the mummies of all the dead Incas and using the profits from their estates for the living.

According to Inca law, the successor of a dead Inca had to be a son by the ruler's principal wife, who had to be the ruler's full sister. Huascar was the result of such an incestuous union. His half brother Atauhualpa was not. Atauhualpa tried to persuade Huascar to split the kingdom with him, claiming that their father's dying wish was for both sons to rule. Huascar rejected this claim. The great nobles responsible for the cult of the royal mummies, however, were alarmed and outraged by Huascar's proposal to bury the mummies. Not only would Huascar be insulting the dead mummies and thus provoke their anger and retaliation, but the nobility would be deprived of the wealth and power they enjoyed as custodians of the cult. Willing to ignore the fact that Atauhualpa had not been born of an incestuous union, the nobles supported Atauhualpa's claim to rule. Civil war ensued, and Atauhualpa emerged victorious.[23] The five-year struggle may have exhausted him and damaged his judgment.

Francisco Pizarro (ca 1475–1541) landed on the northern coast of Peru on May 13, 1532, the very day Atauhualpa won the decisive battle against his brother. The Spaniard soon learned about the war and its outcome. As Pizarro advanced across the steep Andes toward Cuzco, Atauhualpa was proceeding to the capital for his coronation. Atauhualpa stopped at the provincial town of Cajamarca. He, like Montezuma in Mexico, was kept fully informed of the Spaniards' movements. His plan was to lure the Spaniards into a trap, seize their horses and ablest men for his army, and execute the rest. What had the Inca, surrounded by his thousands of troops, to fear? Atauhualpa thus accepted Pizarro's invitation to meet in the central plaza of Cajamarca with his bodyguards "unarmed so as not to give offense." He rode right into the Spaniard's trap. Pizarro knew that if he could capture that Inca, from whom all power devolved, he would have the "Kingdom of Gold" for which he had come to the New World.

The Inca's litter arrived in the ominously quiet town square. One cannon blast terrified the Indians. The Spaniards rushed out of hiding and slaughtered them. Atauhualpa's fringed headband was instantly torn from his head. He offered to purchase his freedom with a roomful of gold. Pizarro agreed to this ransom, and an appropriate document was drawn up and signed. But after the gold had been gathered from all parts of the empire to fill the room—its dimensions were seventeen by twenty-two by nine feet—the Spaniards trumped up charges against Atauhualpa and strangled him. The Inca Empire lay at Pizarro's feet.

 ## GLOBAL TRADE NETWORKS

By 1550 European overseas reconnaissance had led to the first global seaborne trade. Muslim expeditions had been across Asian and African land routes. The Europeans' discovery of the Americas and their exploration of the Pacific for the first time linked the entire world by intercontinental seaborne trade. That trade brought into being three successive commercial empires: the Portuguese, the Spanish, and the Dutch.

In the sixteenth century, naval power and shipborne artillery gave Portugal hegemony over the sea route to India. To Lisbon the Portuguese fleet brought spices, which the Portuguese paid for with textiles produced at Gujarat and Coromandel in India and with gold and ivory from East Africa (Map 16.3). From their fortified bases at Goa on the Arabian Sea and at Malacca on the Malay Peninsula, ships of Malabar teak carried goods to the Portuguese settlement at Macao in the South China Sea. From Macao, loaded with Chinese silks and porcelains, Portuguese ships sailed to the Japanese port of Nagasaki and to the Philippine port of Manila, where Chinese goods were exchanged for Spanish (that is, Latin American) silver. Throughout Asia, the Portuguese traded in slaves—black Africans, Chinese, and Japanese. The Portuguese exported to India horses from Mesopotamia and copper from Arabia; from India they exported hawks and peacocks for the Chinese and Japanese markets.

Across the Atlantic, Portuguese Brazil provided most of the sugar consumed in Europe in the sixteenth and early seventeenth centuries. African slave labor produced the sugar on the plantations of Brazil, and Portuguese merchants controlled both the slave trade between West Africa and Brazil (see pages 634–638) and the commerce in sugar between Brazil and Portugal. The Portuguese were the first worldwide traders, and Portuguese was the language of the Asian maritime trade.

Spanish possessions in the New World constituted basically a land empire, and in the sixteenth century the Spaniards devised a method of governing that

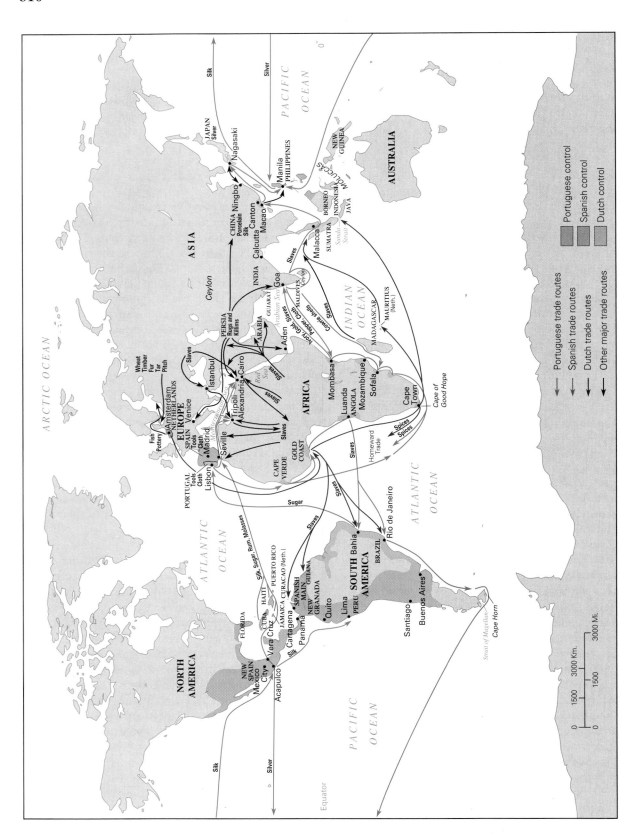

empire (see page 517). But across the Pacific, the Spaniards also built a seaborne empire, centered at Manila in the Philippines, which had been "discovered" by Ferdinand Magellan in 1521. Between 1564 and 1571, the Spanish navigator Miguel Lopez de Legazpi sailed from Mexico and through a swift and almost bloodless conquest took over the Philippine Islands. Legazpi founded Manila, which served as the transpacific bridge between Spanish America and the extreme Eastern trade.

Chinese silk, sold by the Portuguese in Manila for American silver, was transported to Acapulco in Mexico, from which it was carried overland to Veracruz for re-export to Spain. Because hostile Pacific winds prohibited direct passage from the Philippines to Peru, large shipments of silk also went south from Acapulco to Peru (see Map 16.3). Spanish merchants could never satisfy the European demand for silk, so huge amounts of bullion went from Acapulco to Manila. For example, in 1597, 12 million pesos of silver, almost the total value of the transatlantic trade, crossed the Pacific. After about 1640, the Spanish silk trade declined because it could not compete with Dutch imports.

Stimulated by a large demand for goods in Europe, India, China, and Japan, a worldwide commercial boom occurred from about 1570 to 1630. In Japan the gradual decline of violence, unification, and the development of marketing networks led to a leap in orders for foreign products: textiles from India, silks and porcelains from China, raw materials and spices from Southeast Asia. The Japanese navy expanded, and Japanese mines poured out vast quantities of silver that paid for those wares. Then, in 1635, maritime trade stopped when the Tokugawa Shogunate closed the islands to trade and forbade merchants to travel abroad under penalty of death (see page 702).

China, with a population increase, urban growth, and a rare period of government-approved foreign trade, also underwent international commercial expansion. China wanted raw materials, sugar, and spices from Southeast Asia; ivory and slaves from Africa; and cotton cloth from India. Merchants in Mughal India (see page 671) conducted a huge long-distance trade extending as far north as Poland and Russia. India also sought spices from the Moluccas, sugar from Vietnam and the Philippines, and rice and raw materials from Southeast Asia. In this early modern "age of commerce," Southeast Asia exchanged its pepper, spices, woods, resin, pearls, and sugar for textiles from India; silver from the Americas and Japan; and silk, ceramics, and manufactures from China. The Southeast Asian merchant marine also expanded. The European demand for Indian pepper, Southeast Asian nutmeg and cloves, and Chinese silks and porcelains was virtually insatiable. But Europeans offered nothing that Asian peoples wanted. Therefore, Europeans had to pay for their purchases with silver or gold—hence the steady flow of specie from Mexico and South America to Asia.

Throughout the world, many people profited: capitalists who advanced money for voyages, captains and crews of ships, and port officials. As spices moved westward or northward, as silks and porcelains moved southward and westward, and as cloth moved eastward and westward, these various goods grew more valuable in the boom of long-distance trade.[24]

In the latter half of the seventeenth century, the worldwide Dutch seaborne trade predominated. The Dutch Empire was built on spices. In 1599 a Dutch fleet returned to Amsterdam carrying 600,000 pounds of pepper and 250,000 pounds of cloves and nutmeg. Those who had invested in the expedition received a 100 percent profit. The voyage led to the establishment in 1602 of the Dutch East India Company, founded with the stated intention of capturing the spice trade from the Portuguese.

The Dutch fleet, sailing from the Cape of Good Hope and avoiding the Portuguese forts in India, steered directly for the Sunda Strait in Indonesia (see Map 16.3). The Dutch wanted direct access to and control of the Indonesian sources of spices. In return for assisting Indonesian princes in local squabbles and disputes with the Portuguese, the Dutch won broad commercial concessions. Through agreements, seizures, and outright war, they gained control of the western access to the Indonesian archipelago. Gradually, they acquired political domination over the archipelago itself. Exchanging European manufactured goods—armor, firearms, linens, and toys—the Dutch soon had a monopoly on the very lucrative spice trade.[25]

The seaborne empires profited from the geographical reconnaissance and technological developments of the sixteenth century. The empires of Portugal, Spain, and Holland had strong commercial ambitions. They also

MAP 16.3 Seaborne Trading Empires in the Sixteenth and Seventeenth Centuries By the mid-seventeenth century, trade linked all parts of the world, except for Australia. Notice that trade in slaves was not confined to the Atlantic but involved almost all parts of the world. In 1999, it was confined to Africa and the Indian Ocean.

paved the way for the eighteenth-century mercantilist empires of France and Great Britain.

THE CHINESE AND JAPANESE DISCOVERY OF THE WEST

The desire to Christianize pagan peoples was a major motive in Europeans' overseas expansion. The Indians of Central and South America, the Muslims and polytheistic peoples of the Pacific, and the Confucian, Buddhist, and Shinto peoples of China and Japan became objects of Christianizing efforts. In this missionary activity, the new Jesuit order was dominant and energetic.

In 1582 the Jesuit Matteo Ricci (1552–1610) settled at Macao on the mouth of the Canton River. Like the Christian monks who had converted the Germanic tribes of early medieval Europe, Ricci sought first to convert the emperor and elite groups and then, through gradual assimilation, to win the throngs of Chinese. He tried to present Christianity to the Chinese in Chinese terms. He understood the Chinese respect for learning and worked to win converts among the scholarly class. When Ricci was admitted to the Imperial City at Beijing (Peking), he addressed the emperor Wan-li:

Li Ma-tou [Ricci's name transliterated into Chinese], your Majesty's servant, comes from the Far West, addresses himself to Your Majesty with respect, in order to offer gifts from his country. Despite the distance, fame told me of the remarkable teaching and fine institutions with which the imperial court has endowed all its peoples. I desired to share these advantages and live out my life as one of Your Majesty's subjects, hoping in return to be of some small use.[26]

Ricci presented the emperor with two clocks, one of them decorated with dragons and eagles in the Chinese style. The emperor's growing fascination with clocks gave Ricci the opportunity to display other examples of Western technology. He instructed court scholars about astronomical equipment and the manufacture of cannon and drew for them a map of the world—with China at its center. These inventions greatly impressed the Chinese intelligentsia. Over a century later, a Jesuit wrote, "The Imperial Palace is stuffed with clocks, . . . watches, carillons, repeaters, organs, spheres, and astronomical clocks of all kinds—there are more than four thousand pieces from the best masters of Paris and London."[27] The Chinese first learned about Europe from the Jesuits.

But the Christians and the Chinese did not understand one another. Because the Jesuits served the imperial court as mathematicians, astronomers, and cartographers, the Chinese emperors allowed them to remain in Beijing. The Jesuits, however, were primarily interested in converting the Chinese to Christianity. The missionaries thought that by showing the pre-eminence of Western science, they were demonstrating the superiority of Western religion. This was a relationship that the Chinese did not acknowledge. They could not accept a religion that required total commitment and taught the existence of an absolute. Only a small number of the highly educated, convinced of a link between ancient Chinese tradition and Christianity, became Christians. Most Chinese were hostile to the Western faith. They accused Christians of corrupting Chinese morals because they forbade people to honor their ancestors—and corruption of morals translated into disturbing the public order. They also accused Christians of destroying Chinese sanctuaries, of revering a man (Christ) who had been executed as a public criminal, and of spying on behalf of the Japanese.

The "Rites Controversy," a dispute over ritual between the Jesuits and other Roman Catholic religious orders, sparked a crisis. The Jesuits supported the celebration of the Mass in Chinese and the performance of other ceremonies in terms understandable to the Chinese. The Franciscans and other missionaries felt that the Jesuits had sold out the essentials of the Christian faith in order to win converts.

One burning issue was whether Chinese reverence for ancestors was homage to the good that the dead had done during their lives or an act of worship. The Franciscans secured the support of Roman authorities who considered themselves experts on Chinese culture and decided against the Jesuits. In 1704 and again in 1742, Rome decreed that Roman ceremonial practice in Latin (not in Chinese) was to be the law for Chinese missions. (This decision continued to govern Roman Catholic missionary activity until the Second Vatican Council in 1962.) Papal letters also forbade Chinese Christians from participating in the rites of ancestor worship. The emperor in turn banned Christianity in China, and the missionaries were forced to flee.

The Christian West and the Chinese world learned a great deal from each other. The Jesuits probably were "responsible for the rebirth of Chinese mathematics in the seventeenth and eighteenth centuries," and Western contributions stimulated the Chinese development of other sciences.[28] From the Chinese, Europeans got the idea of building bridges suspended by chains. The first Western experiments in electrostatics and magnetism in the seventeenth century derived from Chinese models. Travel accounts about Chinese society and customs had a profound impact on Europeans, making them more sensitive to the beautiful diversity of peoples and manners.

Initial Japanese contacts with Europeans paralleled those of the Chinese. In 1542 Portuguese merchants arrived in Japan and quickly won large profits carrying goods between China and Japan. Dutch and English ships followed, also enjoying the rewards of the East Asian trade. The Portuguese merchants vigorously supported Christian missionary activity, and in 1547 the Jesuit missionary St. Francis Xavier landed at Kagoshima, preached widely, and in two years won many converts. From the beginning, however, the Japanese government feared that native converts might have conflicting political loyalties. Divided allegiance could encourage European invasion of the islands—the Japanese authorities had the example of the Philippines, where Spanish conquest followed missionary activity.

Convinced that European merchants and missionaries had contributed to the general civil disorder, which the regime was trying to eradicate, the Japanese government decided to expel the Spanish and Portuguese and to close Japan to all foreign influence. A decree of 1635 was directed at the commissioners of the port of Nagasaki, a center of Japanese Christianity:

If there is any place where the teachings of the padres (Catholic priests) is practiced, the two of you must order a thorough investigation. . . . If there are any Southern Barbarians (Westerners) who propagate the teachings of the padres, or otherwise commit crimes, they may be incarcerated in the prison.[29]

In 1639 an imperial memorandum decreed, "Hereafter entry by the Portuguese galeota [galleon or large oceangoing warship] is forbidden. If they insist on coming [to Japan], the ships must be destroyed and anyone aboard those ships must be beheaded."[30]

When tens of thousands of Japanese Christians made a stand on the peninsula of Shimabara, the Dutch lent the Japanese government cannon. The Protestant Dutch hated Catholicism, and as businessmen they hated the Portuguese, their great commercial rivals. Convinced that the Dutch had come only for trade and did not want to proselytize, the imperial government allowed them to remain. But Japanese authorities ordered them to remove their factory-station from Hirado on the western tip of Kyushu to the tiny island of Deshima, which covered just 2,100 square feet. The

government limited Dutch trade to one ship a year, watched the Dutch very closely, and required Dutch officials to pay an annual visit to the capital to renew their loyalty. The Japanese also compelled the Dutch merchants to perform servile acts that other Europeans considered humiliating.

Long after Christianity ceased to be a potential threat to the Japanese government, the fear of Christianity sustained a policy of banning Western books on science or religion. Until well into the eighteenth century, Japanese intellectuals were effectively cut off from Western developments. The Japanese opinion of Westerners was not high. What little the Japanese knew derived from the few Dutch businessmen at Deshima. Very few Japanese people ever saw Europeans. If they did, they considered them "a special variety of goblin that bore only a superficial resemblance to a normal human being." The widespread rumor was that when Dutchmen urinated, they raised one leg like dogs.[31]

 ## THE IMPACT OF CONTACT

In the sixteenth and seventeenth centuries, following Columbus's voyages, substantial numbers of Spaniards crossed the Atlantic for ports in the Caribbean, the Spanish Main, and present-day Argentina. Thousands of Portuguese sailed for Brazil. The ships on which they traveled were not as large as the so-called Indiamen going to the Indian Ocean; the latter had larger carrying capacities and were expected to return with tons of spices, pepper, sugar, and gold. Only half the migrants, merchants, missionaries, royal officials, soldiers, wives, concubines, and slaves reached American (or Indian Ocean) ports. Poor health, poor shipboard hygiene, climatic extremes, rancid food, and putrid water killed the other half.[32] Those who reached America, however, eventually had an enormous impact, not only there but also on the whole world.

The Columbian Exchange

Nearly thirty years ago, a historian asserted that "the most important changes brought on by the Columbian voyages were biological in nature."[33] His book explored on a global scale the biosocial consequences of 1492. The migration of peoples led to the exchange of flora and fauna, of animals and diseases. Settlers launched an agricultural revolution with worldwide implications.

Arrival of the Nanbanjin or "Southern Barbarians"   Between about 1590 and 1614, many Portuguese ships arrived at the port of Nagasaki with goods to satisfy the Japanese thirst for things Western. Screens created for the homes of rich Japanese merchants record the events. From the left, the captain arrives, shaded by a vast parasol carried by a black servant (or slave); black porters carry boxes of goods and cages of rare animals as gifts for Japanese merchants. They are received by tall, black-robed Jesuits, one wearing eyeglasses (which fascinated the Japanese) and a brown-robed Franciscan. From windows, doors, and fences, Japanese people peer out at the "southern barbarians," so called because of their terrible manners and lack of baths. In the upper background is the Jesuit residence. *(The Namban Bunka Kan, Osaka)*

When people travel to another country, they often want to eat the same foods with which they are familiar. They want to re-create the circumstances they know at home. What Iberian settlers considered essential— wheat for bread, grapes for wine, olive oil for both culinary and sacramental purposes—were not grown in America. So the migrants sought to turn the New World into the Old: they searched for climatic zones fa- vorable to those crops. Everywhere they settled, they raised wheat: in the highlands of Mexico, the Rio de la Plata, New Granada (in northern South America), and Chile. By 1535 Mexico was exporting wheat. Grapes did well in parts of Peru and Chile. It took the Spanish longer to discover areas where suitable soil and ade- quate rainfall would nourish olive trees, but by the 1560s the coastal valleys of Peru and Chile were dotted

Indians Harvesting Wheat Sixteenth-century Spaniards introduced wheat into Latin America, where it competed with the native corn and manioc. By the nineteenth century, wheat enjoyed great success in Argentina, Chile, Mexico, the Canadian prairies, the Middle West of the United States, South Africa, and northern China. A symbol of the Columbian Exchange and of European expansion. *(Institut d'Atmatller d'Art Hispanic)*

with olive groves. Columbus had brought sugar plants on his second voyage; Spaniards also introduced rice and bananas from the Canary Islands, and the Portuguese carried these items to Brazil. All plants and trees had to be brought from Europe, but not all plants arrived intentionally. In clumps of mud on shoes and the folds of textiles came immigrant grasses such as Kentucky bluegrass, daisies, and the common dandelion.

Apart from wild turkeys and game, native Americans had no animals for food; apart from alpacas and llamas, they had no animals for travel or to use as beasts of burden. (Human power had moved the huge stones needed to build the monumental Aztec temples.) On his second voyage in 1493, Columbus introduced horses, cattle, sheep, dogs, pigs, chickens, and goats. The multiplication of these animals proved spectacular. By the 1550s, when the Spaniards explored, they took herds of swine. The horse enabled the Spanish conquerors and the Indians to travel faster and farther and to transport heavy loads.

In return, the Spanish and Portuguese took back to Europe the main American cereal, maize (corn), from Mexico; white potatoes from Peru; and many varieties of beans, squash, pumpkins, avocados, and tomatoes (which Europeans distrusted, fearing that they were sexually stimulating). Maize was the great gift of the American Indians to all the peoples of the world as food for humans and livestock. Because maize grows in climates too dry for rice and too wet for wheat, gives a high yield per unit of land, and has a short growing season, it proved an especially important crop for Europeans. Initially they looked on the white potato with contempt, but they gradually recognized its nutritional value. Its cultivation slowly spread from west to east—to Ireland, England, and France in the seventeenth century; to Germany, Poland, Hungary, and Russia in the eighteenth. Ironically, the white potato reached New England from old England in 1718.

Africa and Asia also shared in the Columbian Exchange. Merchants took maize to West Africa before the mid-sixteenth century, and its cultivation spread rapidly to the Gold Coast, the Congo, Angola, and southern Africa. Perhaps more important than maize for Africans was the South American plant manioc, or cassava, which Americans know as the dessert tapioca. It grows in almost any kind of soil, is resistant to African pests, and yields bumper crops in Africa. In the island countries of the Indian Ocean such as Java, American Indian food products arrived with Europeans. By the seventeenth century, sweet potatoes, beans, and maize were all raised there; by 1800 maize was the most important crop after rice. The Chinese adopted American foods faster than any other Old World people: peanuts introduced by the Portuguese from Brazil, maize and manioc, and sweet and white potatoes, all of which flourished in China by 1550.

So far as limited evidence allows scholars to estimate, between the mid-seventeenth and early nineteenth centuries, every region of the world except Africa experienced considerable population growth. Whatever political, medical, or hygienic reasons there may have been for this growth in different parts of the globe, there can be no doubt that the spread of American agricultural products contributed heavily to demographic change. Around 1500 to 1800, Europe underwent a population explosion, solved partly by immigration to the Americas. The transfer of Old World animals enhanced the Americas' ability to feed their growing population.

The Columbian Exchange had a negative side. While Spaniards brought smallpox, measles, and other European diseases to the Americas (see below), the Indians gave the Spaniards the venereal disease syphilis. Sailors and settlers probably carried it back to Europe in 1493. Medical researchers trying to find the origins of the "pox" have examined bones of the dead; they have found no evidence of it before 1493 but have unequivocal proof of syphilitic damage after that date. Whatever its precise origins, this horrible disease raced across Europe, then spread into Asia.[34]

The Native American Holocaust

In the sixteenth century, perhaps 200,000 Spaniards immigrated to the New World. Soldiers demobilized from the Spanish and Italian campaigns, adventurers and drifters unable to find work in Spain—they did not intend to work in the New World. After assisting in the conquest of the Aztecs and the subjugation of the Incas, these drifters wanted to settle down and become a ruling class. In temperate grazing areas, they carved out vast estates and imported Spanish sheep, cattle, and horses for the kinds of ranching with which they were familiar. In the coastal tropics, unsuited for grazing, the Spanish erected huge sugar plantations. Columbus had introduced sugar into the West Indies; Cortés had introduced it into Mexico. Sugar was a great luxury in Europe, and demand for it was high. Around 1550 the discovery of silver at Zacatecas and Guanajuato in Mexico and Potosí in present-day Bolivia stimulated silver rushes. How were the cattle ranches, sugar plantations, and silver mines to be worked? Obviously, by the Indians.

The Spanish quickly established the *encomienda* system, whereby the Crown granted the conquerors the right to employ groups of Indians in a town or area as agricultural or mining laborers or as tribute payers. Theoretically, the Spanish were forbidden to enslave the Indian natives; in actuality, the encomiendas were a legalized form of slavery. The European demand for sugar, tobacco, and silver prompted the colonists to exploit the Indians mercilessly. Unaccustomed to forced labor, especially in the blistering heat of tropical cane fields or the dark, dank, and dangerous mines, Indians died like flies. Recently scholars have tried to reckon the death rate of the Amerindians in the sixteenth century. Some historians maintain that the Indian population of

Peru fell from 1.3 million in 1570 to 600,000 in 1620; central Mexico had 25.3 million Indians in 1519 and 1 million in 1605.[35] Some demographers dispute these figures, but all agree that the decline of the native Indian population in all of Spanish-occupied America amounted to a catastrophe greater in scale than any that has occurred even in the twentieth century.

What were the causes of this devastating slump in population? Students of the history of medicine have suggested the best explanation: disease. The major cause of widespread epidemics is migration, and those peoples isolated longest from other societies suffer most. Contact with disease builds up bodily resistance. At the beginning of the sixteenth century, Amerindians probably had the unfortunate distinction of longer isolation from the rest of humankind than any other people on earth. Crowded concentrations of laborers in the mining camps bred infection, which the miners carried to their home villages. With little or no resistance to diseases brought from the Old World, the inhabitants of the highlands of Mexico and Peru, especially, fell victim to smallpox. According to one expert, smallpox caused "in all likelihood the most severe single loss of aboriginal population that ever occurred."[36]

Although disease was the prime cause of the Indian holocaust, the Spaniards themselves contributed heavily to the Indians' death rate.[37] According to the Franciscan missionary Bartolomé de Las Casas (1474–1566), the Spanish maliciously murdered thousands:

This infinite multitude of people [the Indians] was . . . without fraud, without subtilty or malice . . . toward the Spaniards whom they serve, patient, meek and peaceful. . . .

To these quiet Lambs . . . came the Spaniards like most c(r)uel Tygres, Wolves and Lions, enrag'd with a sharp and tedious hunger; for these forty years past, minding nothing else but the slaughter of these unfortunate wretches, whom with divers kinds of torments neither seen nor heard of before, they have so cruelly and inhumanely butchered, that of three millions of people which Hispaniola it self did contain, there are left remaining alive scarce three hundred persons.[38]

Las Casas's remarks concentrate on the tropical lowlands, but the death rate in the highlands was also staggering.

The Christian missionaries who accompanied the conquistadors and settlers—Franciscans, Dominicans, and Jesuits—played an important role in converting the Indians to Christianity, teaching them European methods of agriculture, and inculcating loyalty to the Spanish crown. In terms of numbers of people baptized, missionaries enjoyed phenomenal success, though the depth of the Indians' understanding of Christianity remains debatable. Missionaries, especially Las Casas, asserted that the Indians had human rights, and through Las Casas's persistent pressure, the emperor Charles V in 1531 abolished the worst abuses of the encomienda system.

Some scholars offer a psychological explanation for the colossal death rate of the Indians, suggesting that they simply lost the will to survive because their gods appeared to have abandoned them to a world over which they had no control. Hopelessness, combined with abusive treatment and overwork, pushed many men to suicide, many women to abortion or infanticide.

Whatever its precise causes, the astronomically high death rate created a severe labor shortage in Spanish America. As early as 1511, King Ferdinand of Spain observed that the Indians seemed to be "very frail" and that "one black could do the work of four Indians."[39] Thus was born an absurd myth and the massive importation of black slaves from Africa (see pages 633–635).

South American conditions were not unique; the same patterns of epidemic disease struck the indigenous peoples of North America. Between 1539 and 1543, the Spanish explorer Hernando de Sota (ca 1500–1542), who had served under Pizarro in Peru, led an expedition from northern Florida to the Mississippi River in search of silver and gold. Everywhere the Spaniards went, they introduced germs that had a devastating effect on native societies. Historians estimate that between 1550 and 1700, the aboriginal peoples of the Southeast suffered an 80 percent population loss from disease. In the mid-seventeenth century in his book *Of Plymouth Plantation,* William Bradford (1590–1657), who had crossed the Atlantic on the *Mayflower* and become governor of Plymouth Colony in Massachusetts, expressed horror at the effects of smallpox and tuberculosis on the Indians of New England. Although Spanish and English immigrants to the Americas did not plan or intend these disasters, the term *holocaust* captures their magnitude.

Colonial Administration

Having seized the great Indian ceremonial centers in Mexico and Peru, the Spanish conquistadors proceeded to subdue the main areas of native American civilization in the New World. Columbus, Cortés, and Pizarro claimed the lands they had "discovered" for the Spanish crown. How were these lands to be governed?

According to the Spanish theory of absolutism, the Crown was entitled to exercise full authority over all imperial lands. In the sixteenth century, the Crown divided Spain's New World territories into four *viceroyalties,* or administrative divisions. New Spain, with its capital at Mexico City, consisted of Mexico, Central America, and present-day California, Arizona, New Mexico, and Texas. Peru, with its viceregal seat at Lima, originally consisted of all the lands in continental South America but later was reduced to the territory of modern Peru, Chile, Bolivia, and Ecuador. New Granada, with Bogotá as its administrative center, included present-day Venezuela, Colombia, Panama, and, after 1739, Ecuador. La Plata, with Buenos Aires as its capital, consisted of Argentina, Uruguay, and Paraguay. Within each territory a *viceroy,* or imperial governor, had broad military and civil authority as the Spanish sovereign's direct representative. The viceroy presided over the *audiencia,* twelve to fifteen judges who served as advisory council and as the highest judicial body.

From the early sixteenth century to the beginning of the nineteenth, the Spanish monarchy acted on the mercantilist principle that the colonies existed for the financial benefit of the mother country. The mining of gold and silver was always the most important industry in the colonies. The Crown claimed the *quinto,* one-fifth of all precious metals mined in the Americas. Gold and silver yielded the Spanish monarchy 25 percent of its total income. In return, Spain shipped manufactured goods to the New World and discouraged the development of native industries.

The Portuguese governed their colony of Brazil in a similar manner. After the union of the Portuguese and Spanish crowns in 1580, Spanish administrative forms were introduced. Local officials called *corregidores* held judicial and military powers. Mercantilist policies placed severe restrictions on Brazilian industries that might compete with those of Portugal. In the seventeenth century, the use of black slave labor made possible the cultivation of coffee, cotton, and sugar. In the eighteenth century, Brazil led the world in the production of sugar. The unique feature of colonial Brazil's culture and society was its thoroughgoing mixture of Indians, whites, and blacks.

Slavery and the Origins of American Racism

Americans commonly link the words *slavery* and *Africa.* It is true that from the early sixteenth to the late nineteenth century, Africa was the great source of slave labor for South and North America. From a global perspective, however, the Atlantic slave trade represents only one aspect of a worldwide phenomenon. The Indian Ocean has served as a major conduit for slaves

African Slave and Indian Woman A black slave approaches an Indian prostitute. Unable to explain what he wants, he points with his finger; she eagerly grasps for the coin. The Spanish caption above moralizes on the black man using stolen money—yet the Spaniards ruthlessly expropriated all South American mineral wealth. *(New York Public Library)*

down to the present. China and India imported slaves from East Africa, Madagascar, and Southeast Asia. Portuguese, Spanish, and Dutch merchants enslaved thousands of Malayan, Filipino, and Japanese people.[40] Muslims of the Ottoman and Safavid Empires (see Chapter 21) brought slaves from western and central Africa (as they had done for centuries) and from the Circassian region of what is today southern Russia. Slavery took different forms in different places according to perceived economic, social, and cultural needs, but everywhere slaves lacked the freedom to move about as they wished. Slavery remains pervasive in parts of Africa today. In December 1998, grade school children in Aurora, Colorado, saved their dimes, nickels, and pennies to purchase and free slave children in the Sudan. The $35,000 these American children raised will obtain the freedom of more than six hundred people (at about $50 per person) from chattel slavery.[41]

Except for the Aborigines of Australia, almost all peoples in the world have engaged in the enslavement of other human beings at some time in their histories. Since ancient times, victors in battle have enslaved conquered peoples. In the later Middle Ages, slavery was deeply entrenched in southern Italy, Sicily, Crete, and Mediterranean Spain. The bubonic plague, famines, and other epidemics created a severe shortage of agricultural and domestic workers throughout Europe, encouraging Italian merchants to buy slaves from the Balkans, Thrace, southern Russia, and central Anatolia for sale in the West. In 1364 the Florentine government allowed the unlimited importation of slaves as long as they were not Catholics. Between 1414 and 1423, at least ten thousand slaves were sold in Venice alone. The slave trade was a lucrative business enterprise in Italy during the Renaissance. Where profits were high, papal threats of excommunication failed to stop it. Genoese slave traders set up colonial stations in the Crimea and along the Black Sea, and according to an international authority on slavery, these outposts were "virtual laboratories" for the development of slave plantation agriculture in the New World.[42] This form of slavery had nothing to do with race; almost all of these slaves were white. How, then, did black African slavery enter the European picture and take root in the New World?

The capture of Constantinople by the Ottoman Turks in 1453 halted the flow of white slaves from the Black Sea region and the Balkans. Mediterranean Europe, cut off from its traditional source of slaves, had no alternative source for slave labor but sub-Saharan Africa. The centuries-old trans-Saharan trade in slaves was greatly stimulated by the existence of a ready market for slaves in the vineyards and sugar plantations of Sicily and Majorca. By the later fifteenth century, before the discovery of America, the Mediterranean had developed an "American" form of slavery.

Meanwhile, the Genoese and other Italians had colonized the Canary Islands in the western Atlantic. And sailors working for Portugal's Prince Henry the Navigator (see page 499) discovered the Madeira Islands and made settlements there. In this stage of European expansion, "the history of slavery became inextricably tied up with the history of sugar."[43] Population increases and monetary expansion in the fifteenth century led to an increasing demand for sugar even though it was an

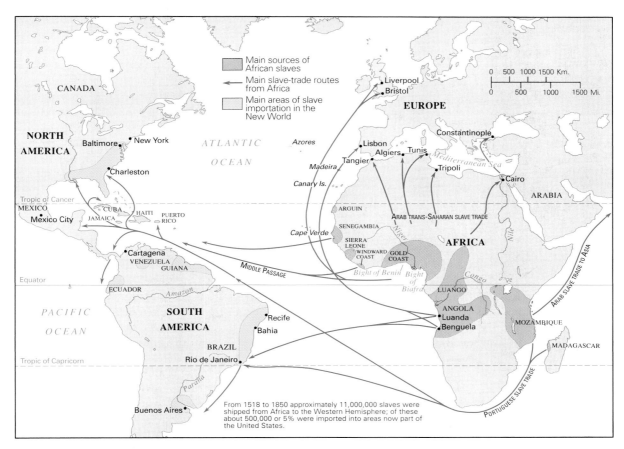

MAP 16.4 The African Slave Trade   Decades before the discovery of America, Greek, Russian, Bulgarian, Armenian, and then black slaves worked the plantation economies of southern Italy, Sicily, Portugal, and Mediterranean Spain—thereby serving as models for the American form of slavery.

expensive luxury that only the affluent could afford. Between 1490 and 1530, three hundred to two thousand black slaves arrived annually at the port of Lisbon (Map 16.4). From Lisbon, where African slaves performed most of the manual labor and constituted 10 percent of the city's population, slaves were transported to the sugar plantations of Madeira, the Azores, the Cape Verde Islands, and then Brazil. Sugar and those small Atlantic islands gave slavery in the Americas its distinctive shape. Columbus himself spent a decade in Madeira and took sugar plants on his voyages to "the Indies."

As European economic exploitation of the Americas proceeded, the major problem settlers faced was a shortage of labor. As early as 1495, the Spanish solved the problem by enslaving the native Indians. In the next two centuries, the Portuguese, Dutch, and English followed suit.

Unaccustomed to any form of forced labor, certainly not to panning for gold for more than twelve hours a day in the broiling sun, the Indians died "like fish in a bucket," one Spanish settler reported.[44] In 1515 the Spanish missionary Bartolomé de Las Casas (see page 516), who had seen the evils of Indian slavery, urged the future emperor Charles V to end Indian slavery in his American dominions. Las Casas recommended the importation of blacks from Africa, both because church law did not strictly forbid black slavery and because he thought blacks could better survive under South American conditions. Charles agreed, and in 1518 the African slave trade began. (When the blacks arrived, Las Casas immediately regretted his suggestion.) Columbus's introduction of sugar plants, moreover, stimulated the need for black slaves, and the experience and model of plantation slavery in Portugal and on the

Atlantic islands encouraged the establishment of a similar agricultural pattern in the New World.

Several European nations participated in the African slave trade. Portugal brought the first slaves to Brazil; by 1600, 4,000 were being imported annually. After its founding in 1621, the Dutch West India Company, with the full support of the government of the United Provinces, transported thousands of Africans to Brazil and the Caribbean. Only in the late seventeenth century, with the chartering of the Royal African Company, did the English get involved. Thereafter, large numbers of African blacks poured into the West Indies and North America. In 1790 there were 757,181 blacks in a total U.S. population of 3,929,625. When the first census was taken in Brazil in 1798, blacks numbered about 2 million in a total population of 3.25 million.

European settlers brought to the Americas the racial attitudes they had absorbed in Europe. Their beliefs and attitudes toward blacks derived from two basic sources: Christian theological speculation about the nature of God (light) and the Devil (black), and Muslim ideas. In the sixteenth and seventeenth centuries, the English, for example, were extremely curious about Africans' lives and customs, and slavers' accounts were extraordinarily popular. Travel literature depicted Africans as savages because of their eating habits, morals, clothing, and social customs; as barbarians because of their language and methods of war; and as heathens because they were not Christian. English people saw similarities between apes and Africans; thus the terms *bestial* and *beastly* were frequently applied to Africans. Africans were believed to possess a potent sexuality. One seventeenth-century observer considered Africans "very lustful and impudent, . . . their members' extraordinary greatness is a token of their lust." African women were considered sexually aggressive with a "temper hot and lascivious."[45]

"At the time when Columbus sailed to the New World, Islam was the largest world religion, and the only world religion that showed itself capable of expanding rapidly in areas as far apart and as different from each other as Senegal [in northwest Africa], Bosnia [in the Balkans], Java, and the Philippines."[46] Medieval Arabic literature emphasized blacks' physical repulsiveness, mental inferiority, and primitivism. In contrast to civilized peoples from the Mediterranean to China, some Muslim writers claimed, sub-Saharan blacks were the only peoples who had produced no sciences or stable states. The fourteenth-century Arab historian Ibn Khaldun (1332–1406) wrote that "the only people who accept slavery are the Negroes, owing to their low degree of humanity and their proximity to the animal stage." Though black kings, Khaldun alleged, sold their subjects without even a pretext of crime or war, the victims bore no resentment because they gave no thought to the future and had "by nature few cares and worries; dancing and rhythm are for them inborn."[47] It is easy to see how such absurd images developed into the classic stereotypes used to justify black slavery in South and North America in the seventeenth, eighteenth, and nineteenth centuries. Medieval Christians and Muslims had similar notions of blacks as inferior and primitive people ideally suited to enslavement. Perhaps centuries of commercial contacts between Muslim and Mediterranean peoples had familiarized the latter with Muslim racial attitudes. The racial beliefs that the Portuguese, Spanish, Dutch, and English brought to the New World, however, derive primarily from Christian theological speculation.

Europeans had no monopoly on ridiculous racist notions. The Chinese, for example, had used enslavement as a form of punishment since the Han Dynasty. Records from the tenth century show that the Chinese greatly prized slaves from Africa for their physical differences. A customs official noted in his private diary that "(in the West) there is an island in the sea (Madagascar?) in which there are many savages. Their bodies are as black as lacquer and they have frizzled hair. They are enticed by (offers of) food and then captured and sold as slaves to Arabic countries where they fetch a high price." In China Africans worked as gatekeepers at private estates and as divers to repair leaky boats (because they "swam without blinking their eyes"). They were forced to carry heavy loads and generally treated as beasts of burden. Wealthy people in the city of Guangzhou (Canton) "kept devil slaves," as the Chinese described them.[48]

The Economic Effects of Spain's Discoveries

The sixteenth century has often been called Spain's golden century. The influence of Spanish armies, Spanish Catholicism, and Spanish wealth was felt all over Europe. This greatness rested largely on the influx of precious metals from the Americas.

At an altitude of 15,000 feet, where nothing grew because of the cold, and after a two-and-a-half-month journey by pack animal from Lima, Peru, an incredible source of silver was discovered at Potosí (in present-day Bolivia) in 1545. The place had no population. By 1600, 160,000 people lived there, making it smaller than Nanjing or Delhi but about the size of London. In the second half of the sixteenth century, Potosí yielded perhaps 60 percent of all the silver mined in the world.

From Potosí and the mines at Zacatecas and Guanajuato in Mexico, huge quantities of precious metals poured forth.

To protect this treasure from French and English pirates, armed convoys transported it each year to Spain. Between 1503 and 1650, 16 million kilograms of silver and 185,000 kilograms of gold entered Seville's port. Spanish predominance, however, proved temporary.

In the sixteenth century, Spain experienced a steady population increase, creating a sharp rise in the demand for food and goods. Spanish colonies in the Americas also represented a demand for products. Since Spain had expelled some of the best farmers and businessmen—the Muslims and Jews—in the fifteenth century, the Spanish economy was suffering and could not meet the new demands. Prices rose. Because the cost of manufacturing cloth and other goods increased, Spanish products could not compete in the international market with cheaper products made elsewhere. The textile industry was badly hurt. Prices spiraled upward faster than the government could levy taxes to dampen the economy. (Higher taxes would have cut the public's buying power; with fewer goods sold, prices would have come down.)

Did the flood of silver bullion from America cause the inflation? Prices rose most steeply before 1565, but bullion imports reached their peak between 1580 and 1620. Thus there is no direct correlation between silver imports and the inflation rate. Did the substantial population growth accelerate the inflation rate? It may have done so. After 1600, when the population pressure declined, prices gradually stabilized. One fact is certain: the price revolution severely strained government budgets. Several times between 1557 and 1647, Spain's King Philip II and his successors repudiated the state debt, thereby undermining confidence in the government and leading the economy into a shambles.

As Philip II paid his armies and foreign debts with silver bullion, Spanish inflation was transmitted to the rest of Europe. Between 1560 and 1600, much of Europe experienced large price increases. Prices doubled and in some cases quadrupled. Spain suffered most severely, but all European countries were affected. People who lived on fixed incomes, such as the continental nobles, were badly hurt because their money bought less. Those who owed fixed sums of money, such as the middle class, prospered: in a time of rising prices, debts had less value each year. Food costs rose most sharply, and the poor fared worst of all.

And what of Asia? What economic impact did the Spanish and Portuguese discoveries have on Asian societies and on world trade? Some recent scholars argue that the key to understanding world trade in the sixteenth and early seventeenth centuries is not Europe, where hitherto most research has focused, but China. They also claim that the silver market explains the emergence of world trade. China was the main buyer of world silver—that is, China exchanged its silks and porcelains for silver. While the mines of South America and Mexico poured out silver, so too did Japanese mines, shipping to Manila and Macao perhaps two hundred tons a year. "When silver from Mexico and Japan entered the Ming empire in great quantity, the value of silver began to decline and inflation set in, for as the metal became more abundant its buying power diminished."[49] This inflationary trend affected the values of all commodities. Europeans were only the middlemen in the trade between Europe, the New World, and China.

China demanded silver for its products, and the value of silver was initially very high. As the heart of world trade was China, so the center of early modern trade was not Europe, but China. The silver market drove world trade, with the Americas and Japan being the mainstays on the supply side and China dominating the demand side.

Within China the overissue of paper money had by 1450 reduced the value of that medium of currency to virtually nothing. Gold was too valuable for ordinary transactions. So the Ming government shifted to a silver-based currency. American and Japanese silver had a profound impact on China. On the one hand, it contributed to the rise of a merchant class that converted to a silver zone. On the other hand, the Ming Dynasty, by allowing the payment of taxes in silver instead of the traditional rice, weakened its financial basis. As the purchasing power of silver declined in China, so did the value of silver taxes. This development led to a fiscal crisis that helped bring down the Ming Dynasty and lead to the rise of the Qing (see Chapter 22). From a global perspective, however, the economic impact of China on the West was far greater than any European influence on China or the rest of Asia.[50]

SUMMARY

From the late fifteenth through the early seventeenth centuries, Indian Ocean trade and commerce attracted the attention and pecuniary ambitions of countries in all parts of the world. Merchants and business people in China, Japan, India, and the Middle East fought for shares in that rich trade. The trade also drew the attention of Europeans, who, in their search for a direct route to "the Indies," inadvertently "discovered" the continents of the Western Hemisphere. Within a short time, South America was joined to a worldwide commercial network.

This Age of Reconnaissance and Age of Discovery had profound global consequences. In Southeast Asia, it stimulated the production of pepper and spices and led to the arrival of Christian missionaries and Muslim teachers, who competed for the adherence of native peoples. In China the lure of international trade encouraged the development of the porcelain and silk industries, as well as the immigration of thousands of Chinese people to Southeast Asia. In Japan the Indian Ocean trade in spices, silks, and Indian cotton prompted the greater exploitation of Japanese silver mines to yield the ore with which to pay for foreign goods. European intrusion into the Americas led to the forcible subjugation of native peoples for use in American silver and gold mines, along with the establishment of political and ecclesiastical administrations to govern the new territories. For mining and even more for agricultural purposes, Europeans introduced African slaves into the Americas, thereby intensifying the ancient African tradition of slave labor. The spread of American plants, especially maize and potatoes, improved the diets of Asian, African, and European peoples and contributed to an almost worldwide population boom beginning in the mid-seventeenth century. Europeans carried smallpox and other diseases to the Americas, causing a holocaust among native American peoples. Europeans returned home with syphilis, which rapidly spread across Europe and went with the thousands of migrants from Europe to Asia and Africa.

NOTES

1. A. Reid, *Southeast Asia in the Age of Commerce, 1450–1680*. Vol. 1: *The Land Under the Winds* (New Haven, Conn.: Yale University Press, 1988), p. 2.
2. Ibid., pp. 3–20.
3. Ibid., pp. 146–155.
4. A. Reid, *Southeast Asia in the Age of Commerce, 1450–1680*. Vol. 2: *Expansion and Crisis* (New Haven, Conn.: Yale University Press, 1993), pp. 133–192; the quotation is on p. 151.
5. Ibid., Chaps. 1 and 2, pp. 1–131.
6. Quoted in C. M. Cipolla, *Guns, Sails, and Empires: Technological Innovation and the Early Phases of European Expansion, 1400–1700* (New York: Minerva Press, 1965), pp. 115–116.
7. J. H. Parry, *The Age of Reconnaissance* (New York: Mentor Books, 1963), Chaps. 3 and 5.
8. C. R. Phillips, *Ciudad Real, 1500–1750: Growth, Crisis, and Readjustment in the Spanish Economy* (Cambridge, Mass.: Harvard University Press, 1979), pp. 103–104, 115.
9. Quoted in Cipolla, *Guns, Sails, and Empires,* p. 132.
10. Quoted in F. H. Littell, *The Macmillan Atlas History of Christianity* (New York: Macmillan, 1976), p. 75.
11. Quoted in Cipolla, *Guns, Sails, and Empires,* p. 133.
12. S. E. Morison, *Admiral of the Ocean Sea: A Life of Christopher Columbus* (Boston: Little, Brown, 1942), p. 339.
13. T. K. Rabb, "Columbus: Villain or Hero?" *Princeton Alumni Weekly,* October 14, 1992, pp. 12–17.
14. J. M. Cohen, ed. and trans., *The Four Voyages of Christopher Columbus* (New York: Penguin Books, 1969), p. 37.
15. Quoted in R. L. Kagan, "The Spain of Ferdinand and Isabella," in *Circa 1492: Art in the Age of Exploration,* ed. J. A. Levenson (Washington, D.C.: National Gallery of Art, 1991), p. 60.
16. Quoted in F. Maddison, "Tradition and Innovation: Columbus' First Voyage and Portuguese Navigation in the Fifteenth Century," in *Circa 1492: Art in the Age of Exploration,* ed. J. A. Levenson (Washington, D.C.: National Gallery of Art, 1991), p. 69.
17. J. D. Spence, *The Chan's Great Continent: China in Western Minds* (New York: W. W. Norton, 1998), pp. 17–18.
18. W. D. Phillips and C. R. Phillips, *The Worlds of Christopher Columbus* (Cambridge: Cambridge University Press, 1992), p. 273.
19. Ibid.
20. G. W. Conrad and A. A. Demarest, *Religion and Empire: The Dynamics of Aztec and Inca Expansionism* (New York: Cambridge University Press, 1993), pp. 67–69.
21. G. C. Vaillant, *Aztecs of Mexico* (New York: Penguin Books, 1979), p. 241. Chapter 15, on which this section leans, is fascinating.
22. V. W. Von Hagen, *Realm of the Incas* (New York: New American Library, 1961), pp. 204–207.
23. Conrad and Demarest, *Religion and Empire,* pp. 135–139.
24. Reid, *Southeast Asia,* vol. 2, pp. 10–26.
25. Parry, *The Age of Reconnaissance,* Chaps. 12, 14, and 15.
26. Quoted in S. Neill, *A History of Christian Missions* (New York: Penguin Books, 1977), p. 163.
27. Quoted in C. M. Cipolla, *Clocks and Culture: 1300–1700* (New York: W. W. Norton, 1978), p. 86.
28. J. Gernet, *A History of Chinese Civilization* (New York: Cambridge University Press, 1982), p. 458.
29. Quoted in A. J. Andrea and J. H. Overfield, *The Human Record,* vol. 1 (Boston: Houghton Mifflin, 1990), pp. 406–407.
30. Quoted ibid., p. 408.
31. D. Keene, *The Japanese Discovery of Europe,* rev. ed. (Stanford, Calif.: Stanford University Press, 1969), pp. 1–17; the quotation is on p. 16.
32. A. J. R. Russell-Wood, *The Portuguese Empire, 1415–1808: A World on the Move* (Baltimore: Johns Hopkins University Press, 1998), pp. 58–59.

33. A. W. Crosby, *The Columbian Exchange: Biological and Cultural Consequences of 1492* (Westport, Conn.: Greenwood, 1972), p. xiv.

34. Ibid., passim. This section rests on Crosby's fascinating book.

35. N. Sanchez-Albornoz, *The Population of Latin America: A History,* trans. W. A. R. Richardson (Berkeley: University of California Press, 1974), p. 41.

36. Quoted in Crosby, *The Columbian Exchange,* p. 39.

37. Ibid., pp. 35–59.

38. Quoted in C. Gibson, ed., *The Black Legend: Anti-Spanish Attitudes in the Old World and the New* (New York: Knopf, 1971), pp. 74–75.

39. Quoted in L. B. Rout, Jr., *The African Experience in Spanish America* (New York: Cambridge University Press, 1976), p. 23.

40. For slavery in the Spice Islands, see Reid, *Southeast Asia,* vol. 2, pp. 35, 86, 108.

41. M. Sink, "Schoolchildren Set Out to Liberate Slaves in the Sudan," *New York Times,* December 2, 1998, p. B14.

42. C. Verlinden, *The Beginnings of Modern Colonization,* trans. Y. Freccero (Ithaca, N.Y.: Cornell University Press, 1970), pp. 5–6, 80–97.

43. This section leans heavily on D. B. Davis, *Slavery and Human Progress* (New York: Oxford University Press, 1984), pp. 54–62.

44. Quoted in D. P. Mannix with M. Cowley, *Black Cargoes: A History of the Atlantic Slave Trade* (New York: Viking Press, 1968), p. 5.

45. Quoted ibid., p. 19.

46. P. Brown, "Understanding Islam," *New York Review of Books,* February 22, 1979, pp. 30–33.

47. Davis, *Slavery and Human Progress,* pp. 43–44.

48. L. Levathes, *When China Ruled the Seas: The Treasure Fleet of the Dragon Throne, 1405–1433* (New York: Oxford University Press, 1996), pp. 37–38.

49. Quoted in D. O. Flynn and A. Giráldez, "Born with a 'Silver Spoon': The Origin of World Trade in 1571," *Journal of World History* 6 (Fall 1985): 203.

50. Ibid., pp. 217–218.

SUGGESTED READING

Many of the titles listed in the Notes should prove helpful to students interested in exploring specific topics related to the acceleration of global contacts. Reid's two-volume work provides a broad, detailed, and fascinating study of many facets of Southeast Asian cultures and of the changes brought by Chinese and European intrusion. These books might be supplemented by K. McPherson, *The Indian Ocean: A History of People and the Sea* (1993), which stresses that regional history is the foundation of global history. Spence's work, cited in the Notes, treats Europeans' views of China from Marco Polo to the present. A useful anthology for all the Chinese emperors and their interests is A. Paludan, *Chronicle of the Chinese Emperors: The Reign-by-Reign Record of the Rulers of Imperial China* (1998), which has many illustrations and charts. Russell-Wood's book, cited in the Notes, describes the geographical, navigational, and human factors involved in the rise and decline of that empire. For the Spanish, Dutch, and English Empires, see the Suggested Reading for Chapters 15 and 17. Crosby's book, cited in the Notes, is now a standard and stimulating account of the biological implications of global contact. His *Measure of Reality: Quantification and Western Society, 1250–1600* (1997) shows how Europeans' shift from a qualitative to a quantitative method of perception helped them to become world leaders in business practices, navigation, and technology.

Perhaps the best starting point for the study of European society in the age of exploration is Parry's book, cited in the Notes, which treats the causes and consequences of the voyages of discovery. His splendidly illustrated *The Discovery of South America* (1979) examines Europeans' reactions to the maritime discoveries and treats the entire concept of new discoveries. For the earliest European reaction to the Japanese, see D. Massarella, *A World Elsewhere: Europe's Encounter with Japan in the Sixteenth and Seventeenth Centuries* (1990). The urbane studies of C. M. Cipolla present fascinating material on technological and sociological developments written in a lucid style. In addition to the titles cited in the Notes, see *Cristofano and the Plague: A Study in the History of Public Health in the Age of Galileo* (1973) and *Public Health and the Medical Profession in the Renaissance* (1976). Morison's work, cited in the Notes, is the standard biography of Columbus. The advanced student should consult F. Braudel, *Civilization and Capitalism, 15th–18th Century,* trans. S. Reynolds. Vol. 1: *The Structures of Everyday Life* (1981); vol. 2: *The Wheels of Commerce* (1982); and vol. 3: *The Perspective of the World* (1984). These three fat volumes combine vast erudition, a global perspective, and remarkable illustrations. For the political ideas that formed the background of the first Spanish overseas empire, see A. Pagden, *Spanish Imperialism and the Political Imagination* (1990).

The Suggested Reading for Chapters 20 and 28 offer many titles on racism and slavery. As background to these issues in North and South America, students should see J. L. Watson, ed., *Asian and African Systems of Slavery* (1980), a valuable collection of essays. Davis's *Slavery and Human Progress,* cited in the Notes, shows how slavery was viewed as a progressive force in the expansion of the Western world. For North American conditions, interested students should consult W. D. Jordan, *The White Man's Burden: Historical Origins of Racism in the United States* (1974), and the title by Mannix and Cowley listed in the Notes, a hideously fascinating account. For Caribbean and South American developments, see F. P. Bowser, *The African Slave in Colonial Peru* (1974); J. S. Handler and F. W. Lange, *Plantation Slavery in Barbados: An Archeological and Historical Investigation* (1978); and R. E. Conrad, *Children of God's Fire: A Documentary History of Black Slavery in Brazil* (1983).

LISTENING TO THE PAST

Columbus Describes His First Voyage

On his return voyage to Spain in January 1493, Christopher Columbus composed a letter intended for wide circulation and had copies of it sent ahead to Isabella and Ferdinand and others when the ship docked at Lisbon. Because the letter sums up Columbus's understanding of his achievements, it is considered the most important document of his first voyage. Remember that his knowledge of Asia rested heavily on Marco Polo's Travels, *published around 1298.*

Since I know that you will be pleased at the great success with which the Lord has crowned my voyage, I write to inform you how in thirty-three days I crossed from the Canary Islands to the Indies, with the fleet which our most illustrious sovereigns gave me. I found very many islands with large populations and took possession of them all for their Highnesses; this I did by proclamation and unfurled the royal standard. No opposition was offered.

I named the first island that I found "San Salvador," in honour of our Lord and Saviour who has granted me this miracle. . . . When I reached Cuba, I followed its north coast westwards, and found it so extensive that I thought this must be the mainland, the province of Cathay.[1] . . . From there I saw another island eighteen leagues eastwards which I then named "Hispaniola."[2] . . .

Hispaniola is a wonder. The mountains and hills, the plains and meadow lands are both fertile and beautiful. They are most suitable for planting crops and for raising cattle of all kinds, and there are good sites for building towns and villages. The harbours are incredibly fine and there are many great rivers with broad channels and the majority contain gold.[3] The trees, fruits and plants are very different from those of Cuba. In Hispaniola there are many spices and large mines of gold and other metals. . . .[4]

The inhabitants of this island, and all the rest that I discovered or heard of, go naked, as their mothers bore them, men and women alike. A few of the women, however, cover a single place with a leaf of a plant or piece of cotton which they weave for the purpose. They have no iron or steel or arms and are not capable of using them, not because they are not strong and well built but because they are amazingly timid. All the weapons they have are canes cut at seeding time, at the end of which they fix a sharpened stick, but they have not the courage to make use of these, for very often when I have sent two or three men to a village to have conversation with them a great number of them have come out. But as soon as they saw my men all fled immediately, a father not even waiting for his son. And this is not because we have harmed any of them; on the contrary, wherever I have gone and been able to have conversation with them, I have given them some of the various things I had, a cloth and other articles, and received nothing in exchange. But they have still remained incurably timid. True, when they have been reassured and lost their fear, they are so ingenuous and so liberal with all their possessions that no one who has not seen them would believe it. If one asks for anything they have they never say no. On the contrary, they offer a share to anyone with demonstrations of heartfelt affection, and they are immediately content with any small thing, valuable or valueless, that is given them. I forbade the men to give them bits of broken crockery, fragments of glass or tags of laces, though if they could get them they fancied them the finest jewels in the world.

I hoped to win them to the love and service of their Highnesses and of the whole Spanish nation and to persuade them to collect and give us of the things which they possessed in abundance and which we needed. They have no religion and are not idolaters; but all believe that power and goodness dwell in the sky and they are firmly convinced that I have come from the sky with these ships and people. In this belief they gave me a good reception everywhere, once they had overcome their fear; and this is not because they are stupid—far from it, they are men of great intelligence, for they navigate all those seas, and give a marvellously good account of everything—but because they have never before seen men clothed or ships like these. . . .

In all these islands the men are seemingly content with one woman, but their chief or king is allowed more than twenty. The women appear to work more than the men and I have not been able to find out if they have private property. As far as I could see whatever a man had was shared among all the rest and this particularly applies to food. . . . In another island, which I am told is larger than Hispaniola, the people have no hair. Here there is a vast quantity of gold, and from here and the other islands I bring Indians as evidence.

In conclusion, to speak only of the results of this very hasty voyage, their Highnesses can see that I will give them as much gold as they require, if they will render me some very slight assistance; also I will give them all the spices and cotton they want. . . . I will also bring them as much aloes as they ask and as many slaves, who will be taken from the idolaters. I believe also that I have found rhubarb and cinnamon and there will be countless other things in addition. . . .

So all Christendom will be delighted that our Redeemer has given victory to our most illustrious King and Queen and their renowned kingdoms, in this great matter. They should hold great celebrations and render solemn thanks to the Holy Trinity with many solemn prayers, for the great triumph which they will have, by the conversion of so many peoples to our holy faith and for the temporal benefits which will follow, for not only Spain, but all Christendom will receive encouragement and profit.

This is a brief account of the facts.
Written in the caravel off the Canary Islands.[5]

15 February 1493

At your orders
THE ADMIRAL

Questions for Analysis

1. How did Columbus explain the success of his voyage?

German woodcut depicting Columbus's landing on San Salvador. *(New York Public Library)*

2. What was Columbus's view of the native Americans he met?

3. Evaluate his statements that the Caribbean islands possessed gold, cotton, and spices.

4. Why did Columbus cling to the idea that he had reached Asia?

1. Cathay is the old name for China. In the logbook and later in this letter Columbus accepts the native story that Cuba is an island which they can circumnavigate in something more than twenty-one days, yet he insists here and later, during the second voyage, that it is in fact part of the Asiatic mainland.
2. Hispaniola is the second-largest island of the West Indies; Haiti occupies the western third of the island, the Dominican Republic the rest.
3. This did not prove to be true.
4. These statements are also inaccurate.
5. Actually, Columbus was off Santa Maria in the Azores.

Source: J. M. Cohen, ed. and trans., *The Four Voyages of Christopher Columbus* (New York: Penguin Classics, 1969), pp. 115–123. Copyright © J. M. Cohen, 1969. Reproduced by permission of Penguin Books, Ltd.

17

Absolutism and Constitutionalism in Europe, ca 1589–1725

The Queen's staircase is among the grandest of the surviving parts of Louis XIV's Versailles. *(© Photo R.M.N.— Mercator)*

The seventeenth century in Europe was an age of intense conflict and crisis. The crisis had many causes, but the era's almost continuous savage warfare was probably the most important factor. War drove governments to build enormous armies and levy ever higher taxes on an already hard-pressed, predominately peasant population. Deteriorating economic conditions also played a major role. Europe as a whole experienced an unusually cold and wet climate over many years—a "little ice age" that brought small harvests, periodic food shortages, and even starvation. Not least, the combination of war, increased taxation, and economic suffering triggered social unrest and widespread peasant revolts, which were both a cause and an effect of profound dislocation.

The many-sided crisis of the seventeenth century posed a grave challenge to European governments: how were they to maintain order? The most common response of monarchical governments was to seek more power to deal with the problems and the threats that they perceived. Thus at the same time that powerful governments were emerging and evolving in Asia—such as the Qing Dynasty in China, the Tokugawa Shogunate in Japan, and the Mughal Empire in India—European rulers generally sought to attain *absolute,* or complete, power and build absolutist states. Thus monarchs regulated religious sects, and they abolished the liberties long held by certain areas, groups, or provinces. Absolutist rulers also created new state bureaucracies to enhance their power and to direct the economic life of the country in the interest of the monarch. Above all, monarchs fought to free themselves from the restrictions of custom, competing institutions, and powerful social groups. In doing so, they sought freedom from the nobility and from traditional representative bodies—most commonly known as Estates or Parliament—that were usually dominated by the nobility.

The monarchical demand for freedom of action upset the status quo and led to bitter political battles. Nobles and townspeople sought to maintain their traditional rights, claiming that monarchs could not rule at will but rather had to respect representative bodies and follow established constitutional practices. Thus opponents of absolutism argued for *constitutionalism*—the limitation of the state by law. In seventeenth-century Europe, however, advocates of constitutionalism generally lost out, and would-be absolutists triumphed in most countries.

Thus in the period between roughly 1589 and 1725 two basic patterns of government emerged in Europe: absolute monarchy and the constitutional state. Almost all subsequent governments in the West have been modeled on one of these patterns, which have also influenced greatly the rest of the world in the past three centuries.

- How and why did Louis XIV of France lead the way in forging the absolute state?
- How did Austrian, Prussian, and Russian rulers in eastern Europe build absolute monarchies—monarchies that proved even more durable than that of Louis XIV?
- How did the absolute monarchs' interaction with artists, architects, and writers contribute to the splendid cultural achievements of both western and eastern Europe in this period?
- How and why did the constitutional state triumph in Holland and England?

This chapter will explore these questions.

FRANCE: THE MODEL OF ABSOLUTE MONARCHY

France had a long history of unifying and centralizing monarchy, although the actual power and effectiveness of the French kings had varied enormously over time. Passing through a time of troubles and civil war after the death of Henry II in 1559, both France and the monarchy recovered under Henry IV and Cardinal Richelieu in the early seventeenth century. They laid the foundations for fully developed French absolutism under the "Great Monarch," Louis XIV. Providing inspiration for rulers all across Europe, Louis XIV and the mighty machine he fashioned deserve special attention.

The Foundations of French Absolutism

Henry IV, the ingenious Huguenot-turned-Catholic, ended the French religious wars with the Edict of Nantes in 1598 (see page 475). The first of the Bourbon dynasty, Henry IV and his great minister Maximilian de Béthune, duke of Sully (1560–1641), then laid the foundations of later French absolutism.

Henry denied influence on the royal council to the nobility, which had harassed the countryside for half a

527

Philippe de Champaigne: Cardinal Richelieu   This portrait, with its penetrating eyes, expression of haughty and imperturbable cynicism, and dramatic sweep of red robes, suggests the authority, grandeur, and power that Richelieu wished to convey as first minister of France. *(Reproduced by courtesy of the Trustees, The National Gallery, London)*

After the death of Henry IV, the queen-regent Marie de' Medici led the government for the child-king Louis XIII (r. 1610–1643), but feudal nobles and princes of the blood dominated the political scene. In 1624 Marie de' Medici secured the appointment of Armand Jean du Plessis—Cardinal Richelieu (1585–1642)—to the council of ministers. It was a remarkable appointment. The next year Richelieu became president of the council, and after 1628 he was first minister of the French crown. Richelieu used his strong influence over King Louis XIII to exalt the French monarchy as the embodiment of the French state.

Richelieu's aim was the total subordination of all groups, individuals, and institutions to the monarchy. He ruthlessly crushed conspiracies staged by the nobility—long the greatest threat to the centralizing efforts of the monarchy—and refused to call the Estates General, which was dominated by the nobility. To impose monarchical policy in the provinces, he installed royal commissioners *(intendants)* in charge of each of France's thirty-two districts. Members of the upper middle class or minor nobility, they owed their position to the king; they had the power to "decide, order, and execute all they see good to do." They recruited soldiers for the army, collected taxes, kept tabs on the local nobility, administered the law, and regulated the local economy. Finally, Richelieu broke the power of Protestantism, which had often served as a cloak for the political ambitions of the nobles. After the Huguenot revolt of 1625 was suppressed, Richelieu abolished fortified cities. No longer would Huguenots have the means to be an independent party.

French foreign policy under Richelieu was aimed at the destruction of the fence of Habsburg territories that surrounded France. Consequently, in the Thirty Years' War Richelieu supported the Habsburgs' enemies, like the Lutheran king Gustavus Adolphus (see page 477). French influence became an important factor in the political future of the German Empire.

These new policies, especially war, cost money. Richelieu fully realized the need for greater revenues through increased taxation. But seventeenth-century France remained "a collection of local economies and local societies dominated by local elites." The rights of assemblies in some provinces to vote their own taxes; the hereditary exemption from taxation of many wealthy members of the nobility and the middle class; and the royal pension system drastically limited the government's power to tax. Richelieu—and later Louis XIV—temporarily solved his financial problems by se-

century. Maintaining that "if we are without compassion for the people, they must succumb and we all perish with them," Henry also lowered taxes paid by the overburdened peasantry. Sully reduced the crushing royal debt accumulated during the era of religious conflict, encouraged French trade, and started a countrywide highway system. Within twelve years Henry IV and his minister had restored public order in France and laid the foundation for economic prosperity. Unfortunately, the murder of Henry IV in 1610 by a crazed fanatic led to a severe crisis.

curing the cooperation of local elites. Even in France royal absolutism was restrained by its need to compromise with the financial interests of well-entrenched groups.[1]

Richelieu persuaded Louis XIII to appoint his protégé Jules Mazarin (1602–1661) as his successor. Governing for the child-king Louis XIV, Mazarin became the dominant power in the government. He continued the centralizing policies of Richelieu, but in 1648 his unpopular attempts to increase royal revenues and expand the state bureaucracy resulted in a widespread rebellion known as the Fronde. Bitter civil war ensued between the monarchy and the opposition, led by the nobility and middle class. Riots and turmoil wracked Paris and the nation. Violence continued intermittently for the next twelve years.

Conflicts during the Fronde had a traumatic effect on the young Louis XIV. The king and his mother were frequently threatened and sometimes treated as prisoners by aristocratic factions. This period formed the cornerstone of Louis's political education and of his conviction that the sole alternative to anarchy was to concentrate as much power as possible in his own hands. Yet Louis XIV also realized that he would have to compromise with the bureaucrats and social elites who controlled local institutions and constituted the state bureaucracy. And he did so.

The Monarchy of Louis XIV

In the reign of Louis XIV (r. 1643–1715), the longest in European history, the French monarchy reached the peak of its absolutist development. In the magnificence of his court, in his absolute power, in the brilliance of the culture over which he presided and which permeated all of Europe, and in his remarkably long life, the "Sun King" dominated his age. It was said that when Louis sneezed, all Europe caught cold.

Born in 1638, king at the age of five, Louis entered into personal, or independent, rule in 1661. Always a devout Catholic, Louis believed that God had established kings as his rulers on earth. The royal coronation consecrated Louis to God's service, and he was certain that although kings were a race apart, they had to obey God's laws and rule for the good of the people.

Louis's education was more practical than formal. He learned statecraft by direct experience. The misery he suffered during the Fronde gave him an eternal distrust of the nobility and a profound sense of his own isolation. Accordingly, silence, caution, and secrecy became political tools for the achievement of his goals. His characteristic answer to requests of all kinds became the enigmatic "Je verrai" (I shall see).

Louis XIV installed his royal court at Versailles, an old hunting lodge ten miles from Paris. His architects, Le Nôtre and Le Vau, turned what the duke of Saint-Simon called "the most dismal and thankless of sights" into a veritable paradise. Louis XIV required all the great nobility of France—at the peril of social, political, and sometimes economic disaster—to live at Versailles for at least part of the year. Versailles became a model of rational order, the center of France, and the perfect symbol of the king's power. In the gigantic Hall of Mirrors hundreds of candles illuminated the domed ceiling, where allegorical paintings celebrated the king's victories. Louis skillfully used the art and architecture of Versailles to overawe his subjects and visitors and reinforce his power. (See the feature "Listening to the Past: The Court at Versailles" on pages 558–559.) Many monarchs subsequently imitated Louis XIV's example, and French became the language of diplomatic exchange and of royal courts all across Europe.

Historians have often said that Louis XIV was able to control completely the nobility, which historically had opposed the centralizing goals of the French monarchy. The duke of Saint-Simon, a high-ranking noble and fierce critic of the king, wrote in his memoirs that Louis XIV

reduced everyone to subjection, and brought to his court those very persons he cared least about. Whoever was old enough to serve did not dare demur. It was still another device to ruin the nobles by accustoming them to equality and forcing them to mingle with everyone indiscriminately.[2]

As Saint-Simon suggests, the king did use court ceremonial to curb the great nobility. By excluding the highest nobles from his councils, he also weakened their ancient right to advise the king and to participate in government. They became mere instruments of policy, their time and attention occupied with operas, balls, gossip, and trivia.

Recent research, however, has demonstrated that Louis XIV actually secured the active collaboration of the nobility. For example, Louis persuaded the nobles of Languedoc to support an ambitious canal project, with increased taxation, in return for royal support of local industries and oppressive measures against Huguenots in the region. Thus Louis separated power from status and grandeur at Versailles: he secured the nobles' cooperation, and the nobility enjoyed their

Hall of Mirrors, Versailles   The grandeur and elegance of the Sun King's reign are reflected in the Hall of Mirrors at the Versailles palace. The king's victories were celebrated in paintings on the domed ceiling. Hundreds of candles lit up the dome. *(Giraudon/Art Resource, NY)*

status and the grandeur in which they lived. The nobility agreed to participate in projects that both exalted the monarchy and reinforced their own ancient aristocratic prestige. Thus French government in the seventeenth century rested on a social and political structure in which the nobility continued to exercise great influence.[3]

In day-to-day government Louis utilized several councils of state, which he personally attended, and the intendants, who acted for the councils throughout France. A stream of questions and instructions flowed between local districts and Versailles, and under Louis XIV a uniform and centralized administration was imposed on the country. The councilors of state came from the upper middle class or from the recently ennobled, who were popularly known as "nobility of the robe" (because of the long judicial robes many of them wore). These ambitious professional bureaucrats served the state in the person of the king.

Throughout Louis's long reign and despite increasing financial problems, he never called a meeting of the Estates General. Thus his critics had no means of united action. French government remained highly structured, bureaucratic, centered at Versailles, and responsible to Louis XIV.

Economic Management and Religious Policy

Louis XIV's bureaucracy, court, and army cost a great amount of money, and the French method of collecting taxes consistently failed to produce the necessary revenue. An old agreement between the Crown and the nobility permitted the king to tax the common people if he did not tax the nobles. The nobility thereby relinquished a role in government: since nobles did not pay taxes, they could not legitimately claim a say in how taxes were spent. Because many among the rich and prosperous classes were exempt, the tax burden fell heavily on those least able to pay: the poor peasants.

The king named Jean-Baptiste Colbert (1619–1683), the son of a wealthy merchant-financier, as controller general of finances. Colbert came to manage the entire royal administration and proved himself a financial genius. His central principle was that the French economy should serve the state, and he rigorously applied to France the system called mercantilism.

Mercantilism is a collection of government policies for the regulation of economic activities, especially commercial activities, by and for the state. In the seventeenth and eighteenth centuries a nation's international power was thought to be based on its wealth—specifically on the gold so necessary for fighting wars. To accumulate gold, economic theory suggested, a country should always sell more goods abroad than it bought. Colbert insisted that France should be self-sufficient, able to produce within its borders everything needed by the subjects of the French king. If France were self-sufficient, the outflow of gold would be halted, debtor states would pay in bullion, and, with the wealth of the nation increased, France's power and prestige would be enhanced.

Colbert attempted to accomplish self-sufficiency through state support for both old industries and newly created ones. New factories in Paris manufactured mirrors to replace Venetian imports, for example. To ensure a high-quality finished product, Colbert set up a system of state inspection and regulation. He compelled all craftsmen to organize into guilds, and he encouraged skilled foreign craftsmen and manufacturers to immigrate to France. To improve communications, he built roads and canals. To protect French products, he placed high tariffs on foreign goods. His most important accomplishment was the creation of a powerful merchant marine to transport French goods. This merchant marine would then closely connect France with its colonial holdings in North America. Colbert tried to organize and regulate the entire French economy for the glory of the French state as embodied in the king.

Colbert's achievement in the development of manufacturing was prodigious. The commercial classes prospered, and between 1660 and 1700 their position steadily improved. The national economy, however, rested on agriculture. Although French peasants were not serfs, as were the peasants of eastern Europe, they were mercilessly taxed. After 1685 other hardships afflicted them: savage warfare, poor harvests, continuing deflation of the currency, and fluctuation in the price of grain. Many peasants emigrated. A totally inadequate

The Spider and the Fly   In reference to the insect symbolism *(upper left)*, the caption on the lower left side of this illustration states, "The noble is the spider, the peasant the fly." The other caption *(upper right)* notes, "The more people have, the more they want. The poor man brings everything—wheat, fruit, money, vegetables. The greedy lord sitting there ready to take everything will not even give him the favor of a glance." This satirical print summarizes peasant grievances. *(New York Public Library)*

tax base and heavy expenditure for war in the later years of Louis's reign made Colbert's goals unattainable.

Economic policy was complicated in 1685 by Louis XIV's revocation of the Edict of Nantes. The new law ordered the destruction of churches, the closing of schools, the Catholic baptism of Huguenots, and the exile of Huguenot pastors who refused to renounce their faith. Why did Louis, by revoking the edict, persecute some of his most loyal and industrially skilled subjects?

Recent scholarship has convincingly shown that Louis XIV was basically tolerant. He insisted on religious unity not for religious but for political reasons. His goal was "one king, one law, one faith." He hated division within the realm and insisted that religious unity was essential to his royal dignity and to the security of the state. Thus after permitting religious liberty in the early years of his reign, Louis finally decided to crack down on Protestants.

Although France's large Catholic majority applauded Louis XIV, writers in the eighteenth century and later damned him for intolerance and for the adverse impact that revocation of the Edict of Nantes had on the economy and foreign affairs. They claimed that tens of thousands of Huguenot craftsmen, soldiers, and business people emigrated, depriving France of their skills and tax revenues and carrying their bitterness to Holland, England, and Prussia. Although the claims of economic damage were exaggerated, the revocation certainly aggravated Protestant hatred for Louis and for his armies.

French Classicism

Artists and writers of the age of Louis XIV deliberately imitated the subject matter and style of classical antiquity, for which their work is called "French classicism." French art of this period possesses the classical qualities of discipline, balance, and restraint. The principles of absolutism molded these artistic ideals. Individualism was not allowed, and artists glorified the state, personified by the king. Precise rules governed all aspects of culture.

Contemporaries said that Louis never ceased playing the role of grand monarch on the stage of his court, and he used music and theater as a backdrop for court ceremonial. He favored the works of Jean-Baptiste Lully (1632–1687), whose orchestral works, ballets, and operatic productions attained wide influence. French classicism also achieved heights in plays, an art form the king loved. Playwright, stage manager, director, and actor Jean-Baptiste Poquelin, known as Molière (1622–1673), produced satirical comedies that exposed the hypocrisies and follies of society, being careful to attack only the bourgeoisie and never the nobility. One of his contemporaries, Jean Racine (1639–1699), wrote restrained, balanced tragedies that used classical settings to explore the power of love and the conflict of good and evil.

The Wars of Louis XIV

Visualizing himself as a great military hero, Louis XIV used almost endless war to exalt himself above the other rulers of Europe. His secretary of war created a professional army, which was modern in the sense that the French state, rather than nobles, employed the soldiers. The army was built on a rational system of recruitment, training, and promotion; equipped with standardized weapons and uniforms; and led by a commissariat, taking the place of the traditional practice of living off the countryside, a truly revolutionary innovation. With this new military machine, one national state, France, was able to dominate the politics of Europe for the first time.

In 1667 Louis used a dynastic excuse to invade Flanders, part of the Spanish Netherlands, and Franche-Comté. He gained twelve towns, including important commercial centers (Map 17.1). Another war gained him more Flemish towns and all of Franche-Comté, and in 1681 he seized the city of Strasbourg. After that victory Louis's military fortunes faded. The wars of the 1680s and 1690s brought no new territorial gains. The Habsburg emperor; the kings of England, Spain, and Sweden; and the electors of Bavaria, Saxony, and the Palatinate united against Louis in the League of Augsburg to check his advance. By the end of the War of the League of Augsburg, fought to a draw, France was financially exhausted.

At the same time a series of bad harvests between 1688 and 1694 brought catastrophe. Cold, wet summers reduced the harvests by an estimated one-third to two-thirds, and in many provinces the death rate rose to several times the normal figure. Rising grain prices, new taxes, a slump in manufacturing, and the constant nuisance of pillaging troops—all these meant great suffering for the French people. France wanted peace at any price. Louis XIV granted a respite for five years while he prepared for the conflict later known as the War of the Spanish Succession.

This struggle (1701–1713) involved the dynastic question of the succession to the Spanish throne. When Charles II (r. 1665–1700) died in 1700, his will left the Spanish crown and the worldwide Spanish Empire to Philip of Anjou, Louis XIV's grandson. By accepting this will, Louis obviously would gain power in Spain; he would also be reneging on an earlier treaty to divide the vast Spanish possessions between himself and the Holy Roman emperor. He accepted the will, thereby provoking a great war.

The Dutch and the English would not accept French acquisition of the Spanish Netherlands and of the rich trade with the Spanish colonies, which would make France too strong in Europe and in North America. Thus in 1701 they joined with the Austrians and Prussians in the Grand Alliance. In the ensuing series of conflicts, Louis suffered major defeats and finally sued for peace.

The war was concluded at Utrecht in 1713, where the principle of partition was applied. Louis's grandson

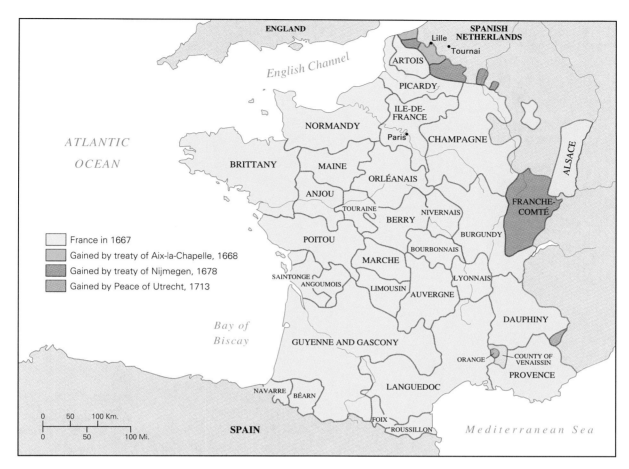

MAP 17.1 The Acquisitions of Louis XIV, 1668–1713   The desire for glory and the weakness of his German neighbors encouraged Louis's expansionist policy, but he paid a high price for his acquisitions.

Philip remained the first Bourbon king of Spain on the understanding that the French and Spanish crowns would never be united. France surrendered Newfoundland, Nova Scotia, and the Hudson Bay territory to England, which also acquired Gibraltar, Minorca, and control of the African slave trade from Spain. The Dutch gained little because Austria received the former Spanish Netherlands (Map 17.2).

The Peace of Utrecht represented the balance-of-power principle in operation, setting limits on the extent to which any one power, in this case France, could expand. The treaty completed the decline of Spain as a Great Power. It expanded the British Empire. The Peace of Utrecht also marked the end of French expansionist policy. In Louis's thirty-five-year quest for military glory, his main territorial acquisition after 1678 was Strasbourg. Even revisionist historians sympathetic

to Louis acknowledge "that the widespread misery in France during the period was in part due to royal policies, especially the incessant wars."[4] The news of Louis's death in 1715 brought rejoicing throughout France.

THE DECLINE OF ABSOLUTIST SPAIN IN THE SEVENTEENTH CENTURY

Spanish absolutism and greatness had preceded that of the French. In the sixteenth century Spain (or, more precisely, the kingdom of Castile) had developed the standard features of absolute monarchy: a permanent professional bureaucracy, a standing army, and national taxes that fell most heavily on the poor. Spanish absolutism was based on silver bullion extracted from its colonial possessions, especially Peru. But by the 1590s

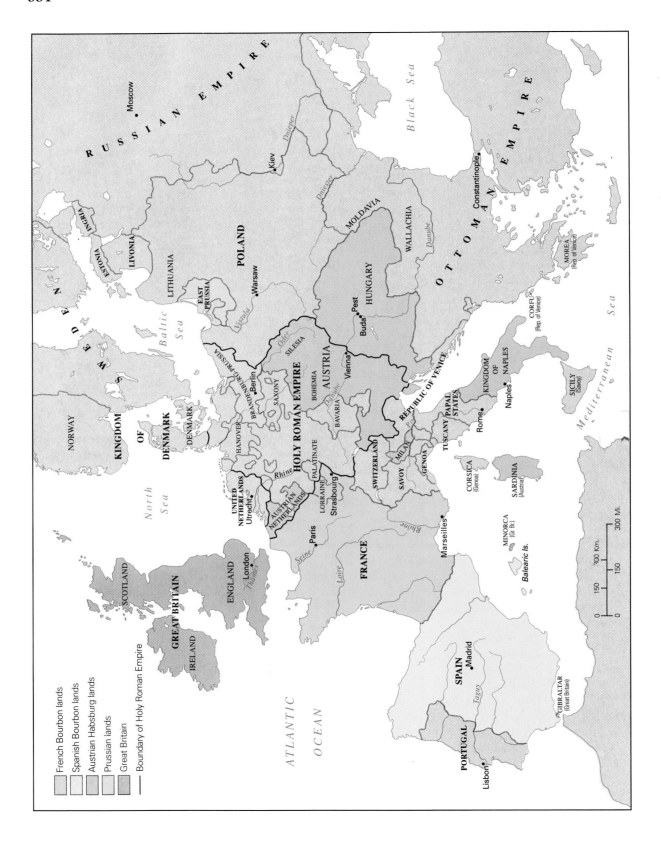

RUSSIAN EMPIRE

Moscow

Dnieper

Kiev

Dniester

POLAND

Warsaw

LITHUANIA

EAST PRUSSIA

Vistula

INGRIA

ESTONIA

LIVONIA

SWEDEN

Baltic Sea

NORWAY

KINGDOM OF DENMARK

DENMARK

North Sea

HANOVER

BRANDENBURG-PRUSSIA

Berlin

SAXONY

Oder

SILESIA

Rhine

HOLY ROMAN EMPIRE

BOHEMIA

AUSTRIA

Danube

BAVARIA

PALATINATE

Strasbourg

LORRAINE

UNITED NETHERLANDS

Utrecht

AUSTRIAN NETHERLANDS

Paris

Seine

Loire

FRANCE

Rhône

Marseilles

Vienna

SWITZERLAND

SAVOY

MILAN

GENOA

TUSCANY

PAPAL STATES

Rome

REPUBLIC OF VENICE

Po

MOLDAVIA

WALLACHIA

HUNGARY

Buda

Pest

Danube

OTTOMAN EMPIRE

Constantinople

Black Sea

MOREA
(Rep. of Venice)

CORFU
(Rep. of Venice)

KINGDOM OF NAPLES

Naples

SICILY
(Savoy)

Mediterranean Sea

CORSICA
(Genoa)

SARDINIA
(Austria)

MINORCA
(Gr. Br.)

Balearic Is.

GREAT BRITAIN

SCOTLAND

ENGLAND

London

Thames

IRELAND

ATLANTIC OCEAN

SPAIN

Madrid

Tagus

GIBRALTAR
(Great Britain)

PORTUGAL

Lisbon

French Bourbon lands
Spanish Bourbon lands
Austrian Habsburg lands
Prussian lands
Great Britain
Boundary of Holy Roman Empire

300 Mi.
300 Km.
150
150
0
0

the seeds of disaster were sprouting, and in the seventeenth century Spain experienced a steady decline. The lack of a strong middle class, agricultural crisis and population decline, failure to invest in productive enterprises, intellectual isolation and psychological malaise—by 1715 all combined to reduce Spain to a second-rate power.

The fabulous flow of silver from Mexico and Peru had led Philip II to assume the role of defender of Roman Catholicism in Europe (see page 476). But when the "Invincible Armada" went down in 1588, a century of Spanish pride and power went with it. After 1590 a spirit of defeatism and disillusionment crippled most reform efforts.

Philip II's Catholic crusade had been financed by the revenues of the Spanish-Atlantic economy. In the early seventeenth century the Dutch and English began to trade with the Spanish colonies, and Mexico and Peru developed local industries. Between 1610 and 1650 Spanish trade with the colonies fell 60 percent, and the American silver lodes started to run dry. Yet in Madrid royal expenditures remained high. The result was chronic deficits and frequent cancellations of Spain's national debt. These brutal cancellations—a form of bankruptcy—shook public confidence in the state.

Spain, in contrast to the other countries of western Europe, developed only a tiny middle class. Public opinion, taking its cue from the aristocracy, condemned moneymaking as vulgar and undignified. Those with influence or connections sought titles of nobility and social prestige, or they became priests, monks, and nuns. The flood of gold and silver had produced severe inflation, and many businessmen found so many obstacles in the way of profitable enterprise that they simply gave up. The expulsion of the Jews and Moors had also deprived Spanish society of a significant proportion of middle-class people.

Spanish aristocrats, attempting to maintain an extravagant lifestyle that they could no longer afford, increased the rents on their estates. High rents and heavy taxes in turn drove the peasants from the land. Agricultural production suffered, and the peasants departed for the large cities, where they swelled the ranks of beggars.

Their most Catholic majesties, the kings of Spain, had no solutions to these dire problems. Philip IV (r. 1622–1665) left the management of his several kingdoms to Count Olivares. An able administrator, the count devised new sources of revenue, but he clung to the grandiose belief that the solution to Spain's difficulties rested in a return to the imperial tradition. Unfortunately, the imperial tradition demanded the revival of war with the Dutch in 1622 and a long war with France over Mantua (1628–1659). These conflicts, on top of an empty treasury, brought disaster. The Treaty of the Pyrenees of 1659, which ended the French-Spanish wars, compelled Spain to surrender extensive territories to France. After this treaty, Spain's decline as a Great Power became irreversible.

In the brilliant novel *Don Quixote,* the Spanish writer Miguel de Cervantes (1547–1616) produced one of the masterpieces of world literature. *Don Quixote* delineates the whole fabric of sixteenth-century Spanish society. The main character, Don Quixote, lives in a dream world, traveling about the countryside seeking military glory. A leading scholar wrote, "The Spaniard convinced himself that reality was what he felt, believed, imagined. He filled the world with heroic reverberations. Don Quixote was born and grew."[5]

ABSOLUTISM IN EASTERN EUROPE: AUSTRIA, PRUSSIA, AND RUSSIA

The rulers of eastern Europe also labored to build strong absolutist states in the seventeenth century. But they built on social and economic foundations different from those in western Europe. These foundations were laid between 1400 and 1650, when the princes and the landed nobility of eastern Europe rolled back the gains made by the peasantry during the High Middle Ages and reimposed serfdom on the rural masses. The nobility also enhanced its power as the primary social force by reducing the importance of the towns and the middle classes.

Despite the strength of the nobility, strong kings did begin to emerge in many eastern European lands in the course of the seventeenth century. There were endless wars, and in this atmosphere of continuous military emergency monarchs found ways to reduce the political

MAP 17.2 Europe in 1715 The series of treaties commonly called the Peace of Utrecht (April 1713–November 1715) ended the War of the Spanish Succession and redrew the map of Europe. A French Bourbon king succeeded to the Spanish throne on the understanding that the French would not attempt to unite the French and Spanish crowns. France surrendered to Austria the Spanish Netherlands (later Belgium), then in French hands, and France recognized the Hohenzollern rulers of Prussia. Spain ceded Gibraltar to Great Britain, for which it has been a strategic naval station ever since. Spain also granted to Britain the *asiento,* the contract for supplying African slaves to America.

power of the landlord nobility. Cautiously leaving the nobles the unchallenged masters of their peasants, eastern monarchs gradually monopolized political power in three key areas. They taxed without consent; maintained permanent standing armies, which policed their subjects in addition to fighting abroad; and conducted relations with other states as they pleased.

There were important variations on the absolutist theme in eastern Europe. The royal absolutism created in Prussia was stronger and more effective than that established in Austria. This advantage gave Prussia a thin edge over Austria in the struggle for power in east-central Europe in the eighteenth century, and it prepared the way for Prussia's unification of the German people in the nineteenth century. As for Russia, it developed its own form of autocratic government at an early date, and its political absolutism was quite different from that of France or even Prussia.

Lords and Peasants

Lords and peasants were the basic social groups in eastern Europe, a vast region including Bohemia, Silesia, Hungary, eastern Germany, Poland, Lithuania, and Russia. Peasants in eastern Europe had done relatively well in the period from roughly 1050 to 1300, a time of gradual economic expansion and population growth. Eager to attract German settlers to their sparsely populated lands, the rulers and nobles of eastern Europe had offered potential newcomers economic and legal incentives. Large numbers of incoming settlers had obtained land on excellent terms and gained much personal freedom. These benefits were gradually extended to the local Slavic populations, even those of central Russia. Thus by 1300 serfdom had all but disappeared in eastern Europe. Peasants were able to bargain freely with their landlords and move about as they pleased.

After about 1300, however, as Europe's population and economy declined grievously, mainly because of the Black Death, noble landlords sought to solve their tough economic problems by more heavily exploiting the peasantry. In western Europe this attempt generally failed, but in the vast region east of the Elbe River in Germany the landlords were successful in degrading peasants. By 1500 eastern peasants were on their way to becoming serfs again.

Punishing Serfs   This seventeenth-century illustration from Adam Olearius's famous *Travels to Moscovy* suggests what Eastern serfdom really meant. The scene is set in eastern Poland. There, according to Olearius, a common command of the lord was, "Beat him till the skin falls from the flesh." *(University of Illinois Library, Champaign)*

ABSOLUTISM AND CONSTITUTIONALISM IN EUROPE

1237–1242	Mongol invasion and conquest of Russia
1400–1650	The nobility reimposes serfdom in eastern Europe
ca 1480	Ivan III rejects Mongol overlordship and begins to use the title of tsar
1533–1584	Rule of Tsar Ivan IV (the Terrible); subjugation of the boyar aristocracy
1581	Formation of the Republic of the United Provinces of the Netherlands
1588	Defeat of the Spanish Armada
1589–1610	Reign of Henry IV of France; lays foundation for absolutist rule
1598	Edict of Nantes: Henry IV ends the French wars of religion
1598–1613	Time of Troubles in Russia; ends with the election of Michael Romanov as tsar
1618–1648	Thirty Years' War; Richelieu dominant figure in French government
1629–1640	Charles I attempts to rule England without Parliament
1640–1688	Rule of Frederick William, the Great Elector, in Brandenburg-Prussia
1642–1649	English civil war; Charles I executed in 1649
1643–1715	Reign of Louis XIV; began independent rule in 1661
1648–1660	The Fronde: French nobility opposes centralizing efforts of monarchy
1652	Patriarch Nikon's reforms split the Russian Orthodox church
1653–1658	Cromwell rules England as military dictator
1659	Treaty of the Pyrenees forces Spain to cede extensive territories to France
1660	Restoration of the English monarchy: Charles II returns from exile
ca 1663–1683	Colbert directs Louis XIV's mercantilist economic policy
1670–1671	Cossack revolt of Stenka Razin in Russia
1682–1725	Rule of Tsar Peter the Great; St. Petersburg becomes capital of Russia
1683	Siege of Vienna by the Ottoman Turks
1685	Louis XIV revokes the Edict of Nantes
1685–1688	James II rules England; attempts to restore Roman Catholicism as state religion
1688	The Glorious Revolution establishes a constitutional monarchy in England
1701–1713	War of the Spanish Succession completes the decline of Spain as a Great Power
1713–1740	Rule of King Frederick William I in Prussia

Eastern lords triumphed because they made their kings and princes issue laws that restricted the right of their peasants to move to take advantage of better opportunities elsewhere. In Prussian territories by 1500, the law required that runaway peasants be hunted down and returned to their lords, and a runaway servant was to be nailed to a post by one ear and given a knife to cut himself loose. Moreover, lords steadily took more and more of their peasants' land and arbitrarily imposed heavier and heavier labor obligations. By the early 1500s lords in many territories could command their peasants to work for them without pay for as many as six days a week.

The gradual erosion of the peasantry's economic position was bound up with manipulation of the legal system. The local lord was also the local prosecutor, judge, and jailer. There were no independent royal officials to provide justice or uphold the common law.

Between 1500 and 1650 the social, legal, and economic conditions of peasants in eastern Europe continued to decline. The consolidation of serfdom was accompanied by the growth of estate agriculture, particularly in Poland and eastern Germany. In the sixteenth century European economic expansion and population growth resumed after the great declines of the late Middle Ages. Eastern lords had powerful economic incentives to increase the production of their estates, and they did so. Generally, the estates were inefficient and technologically backward, but they nevertheless succeeded in squeezing sizable surpluses out of the impoverished peasants. These surpluses were sold to foreign merchants, who exported them to the growing cities of wealthier western Europe.

The re-emergence of serfdom in eastern Europe in the early modern period was a momentous human development. Above all, it reflected the fact that eastern lords enjoyed much greater political power than their western counterparts. In the late Middle Ages, when much of eastern Europe was experiencing innumerable wars and general political chaos, the noble landlord class had greatly increased its political power at the expense of the ruling monarchs. Moreover, the Western concept and reality of sovereignty, as embodied in a king who protected the interests of all his people, were not well developed in eastern Europe before 1650.

Finally, with the approval of weak kings, the landlords systematically undermined the medieval privileges of the towns and the power of the urban classes. For example, instead of selling their products to local merchants in the towns, as required in the Middle Ages, the landlords often sold directly to foreign capitalists. Eastern towns also lost their medieval right of refuge and were compelled to return runaways to their lords. The population of the towns and the urban middle classes declined greatly. This development both reflected and promoted the supremacy of noble landlords in most of eastern Europe in the sixteenth century.

Austria and the Ottoman Turks

The Habsburgs of Austria emerged from the Thirty Years' War impoverished and exhausted. The effort to root out Protestantism in the German lands had failed utterly, and the authority of the Holy Roman Empire and its emperors had declined almost to the vanishing point. Yet defeat in central Europe opened new vistas. The Habsburg monarchs were forced to turn inward and eastward in an attempt to fuse their diverse holdings into a strong, unified state.

An important step in this direction had actually been taken in Bohemia during the Thirty Years' War. Protestantism had been strong among the Czechs, a Slavic people concentrated in Bohemia. In 1618 the Czech nobles who controlled the Bohemian Estates—the representative body of the different legal orders—had risen up against their Habsburg king. This revolt was crushed, and then the Czech nobility was totally restructured to ensure its loyalty to the monarchy. With the help of this new nobility, the Habsburgs established strong direct rule over Bohemia. The condition of the enserfed peasantry worsened, Protestantism was stamped out, and religious unity began to emerge. The reorganization of Bohemia was a giant step toward royal absolutism.

After the Thirty Years' War, Ferdinand III (r. 1637–1657) centralized the government in the hereditary German-speaking provinces, most notably Austria, Styria, and the Tyrol. The king created a permanent standing army ready to put down any internal opposition. The Habsburg monarchy was then ready to turn toward the vast plains of Hungary, in opposition to the Ottoman Turks.

The Ottomans had come out of Anatolia, in present-day Turkey, to create one of history's greatest military empires (see Chapter 21). Their armies had almost captured Vienna in 1529, and for more than 150 years thereafter the Ottomans ruled all of the Balkan territories, almost all of Hungary, and part of southern Russia. In the late seventeenth century, under vigorous reforming leadership, the Ottoman Empire succeeded in marshaling its forces for one last mighty blow at Christian Europe. A huge Turkish army surrounded Vienna and

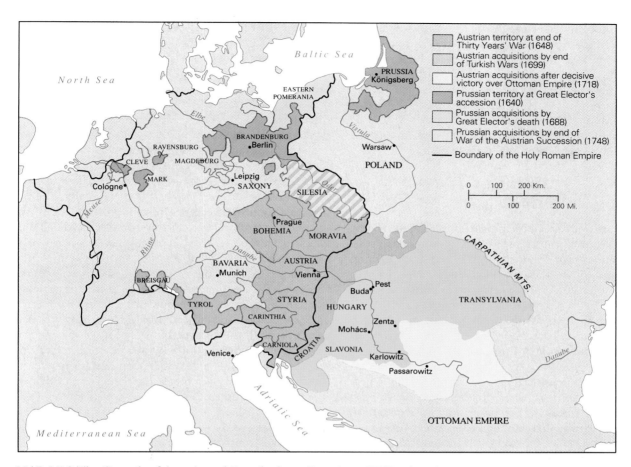

MAP 17.3 The Growth of Austria and Brandenburg-Prussia to 1748 Austria expanded to the southwest into Hungary and Transylvania at the expense of the Ottoman Empire. It was unable to hold the rich German province of Silesia, however, which was conquered by Brandenburg-Prussia.

laid siege to it in 1683. After holding out against great odds for two months, the city was relieved at the last minute, and the Ottomans were forced to retreat. The Habsburgs then conquered all of Hungary and Transylvania (part of present-day Romania) by 1699 (Map 17.3).

The Turkish wars and this great expansion strengthened the Habsburg army and promoted some sense of unity in the Habsburg lands. But Habsburg efforts to create a fully developed, highly centralized, absolutist state were only partly successful. The Habsburg state remained a composite of three separate and distinct territories: the old "hereditary provinces" of Austria, the kingdom of Bohemia, and the kingdom of Hungary. Each part had its own laws, culture, and political life, for the noble-dominated Estates continued to exist, though with reduced powers. Above all, the Hungarian

nobility effectively thwarted the full development of Habsburg absolutism. Time and again throughout the seventeenth century, Hungarian nobles rose in revolt against the attempts of Vienna to impose absolute rule. They never triumphed decisively, but neither were they ever crushed.

The Hungarians resisted because many of them were Protestants, especially in the area long ruled by the more tolerant Turks, and they hated the heavy-handed attempts of the Habsburgs to re-Catholicize everyone. Moreover, the lords of Hungary and even part of the Hungarian peasantry had become attached to a national ideal long before most of the other European peoples. They were determined to maintain as much independence and local control as possible. Thus when the Habsburgs were bogged down in the War of the

Spanish Succession (see page 532), the Hungarians rose in one last patriotic rebellion under Prince Francis Rákóczy in 1703. Rákóczy and his forces were eventually defeated, but this time the Habsburgs had to accept many of the traditional privileges of the Hungarian aristocracy in return for Hungarian acceptance of hereditary Habsburg rule. Thus Hungary, unlike Austria or Bohemia, never came close to being fully integrated into a centralized, absolute Habsburg state.

The Emergence of Prussia

As the status of east German peasants declined steadily after 1400, local princes lost political power, and a revitalized landed nobility became the undisputed ruling class. The Hohenzollern family, which ruled through different branches as the electors of Brandenburg and the dukes of Prussia, were little more than the largest landowners in a landlord society. Nothing suggested that the Hohenzollerns and their territories would ever play an important role in European or even German affairs.

Brandenburg was a helpless spectator in the Thirty Years' War, its territory alternately ravaged by Swedish and Habsburg armies. Yet the country's devastation prepared the way for Hohenzollern absolutism, because foreign armies dramatically weakened the political power of the Estates. The weakening of the Estates helped the very talented young elector Frederick William (r. 1640–1688), later known as the "Great Elector," to ride roughshod over traditional constitutional liberties and to take a giant step toward royal absolutism.

When Frederick William came to power in 1640, the twenty-year-old ruler was determined to unify his three quite separate provinces and to add to them by diplomacy and war. These provinces were Brandenburg itself, the area around Berlin; Prussia, inherited in 1618 when the junior branch of the Hohenzollern family died out; and scattered holdings along the Rhine in western Germany (see Map 17.3). Each province was inhabited by Germans, but each had its own Estates.

The struggle between the Great Elector and the provincial Estates was long, complicated, and intense. After the Thirty Years' War the representatives of the nobility zealously reasserted the right of the Estates to vote taxes, a right the Swedish armies of occupation had simply ignored. Yet first in Brandenburg and then in Prussia, the Great Elector eventually had his way. To

pay for the permanent standing army that he first established in 1660, Frederick William forced the Estates to accept the introduction of permanent taxation without consent. The soldiers doubled as tax collectors and policemen, becoming the core of the expanding state bureaucracy. The power of the Estates declined rapidly thereafter, and the Great Elector turned the screws of taxation. State revenue tripled and the size of the army leaped about tenfold during his reign.

In accounting for the Great Elector's fateful triumph, two factors appear central. First, as in the formation of every absolutist state, war was a decisive factor. The ongoing struggle between Sweden and Poland for control of the Baltic after 1648 and the wars of Louis XIV in western Europe created an atmosphere of permanent crisis. It was no accident that, except in commercially minded Holland, constitutionalism won out only in England, the only major country to escape devastating foreign invasions in the seventeenth century.

Second, the nobility had long dominated the government through the Estates, but only for its own narrow self-interest. When, therefore, the Great Elector reconfirmed the nobility's freedom from taxation and its unlimited control over the peasants in 1653 and after, the nobility accepted a self-serving compromise. While Frederick William reduced the nobility's political power, the bulk of the Great Elector's new taxes fell on towns, and royal authority stopped at the landlords' gates.

By the time of his death in 1688, the Great Elector had created a single state out of scattered principalities. But his new creation was still small and fragile. It was Frederick William I, the "Soldiers' King" (r. 1713–1740), who truly established Prussian absolutism and gave it its unique character. A dangerous psychoneurotic as well as a talented reformer, Frederick William I created the best army in Europe, for its size, and he infused military values into a whole society.

Frederick William's attachment to the army and military life was intensely emotional. He had, for example, a bizarre, almost pathological love for tall soldiers, whom he credited with superior strength and endurance. Like some fanatical modern-day basketball coach in search of a championship team, he sent his agents throughout both Prussia and all of Europe, tricking, buying, and kidnapping top recruits. Neighboring princes sent him their giants as gifts to win his gratitude. Prussian mothers told their sons, "Stop growing or the recruiting agents will get you."[6] Frederick William's love of the army was also based on a hard-headed conception of the struggle for power and a dog-eat-dog view of international politics. He never wavered in his conviction that the welfare of king and state depended above all else on the army.

As in France, the cult of military power provided the rationale for a great expansion of royal absolutism. As the ruthless king himself put it, "I must be served with life and limb, with house and wealth, with honour and conscience, everything must be committed except eternal salvation—that belongs to God, but all else is mine."[7] To make good these extraordinary demands, Frederick William created a strong and exceptionally honest bureaucracy, which administered the country and tried to develop it economically. The last traces of the parliamentary Estates and local self-government vanished.

The king's grab for power brought him into considerable conflict with the noble landowners, the Junkers. In the end the Prussian nobility responded to a combination of threats and opportunities and became the officer caste. By 1739 all but 5 of 245 officers with the rank of major or above were aristocrats. A new compromise had been worked out: the nobility imperiously commanded the peasantry in the army as well as on its estates.

Coarse and crude, penny-pinching and hard-working, Frederick William achieved results. Above all, he built a first-rate army out of third-rate resources. Twelfth in Europe in population, Prussia had the fourth largest army by 1740, behind France, Russia, and Austria. Soldier for soldier the Prussian army became the best in Europe, astonishing foreign observers with its precision, skill, and discipline. Curiously, the king loved his "blue boys" so much that he hated to "spend" them. This most militaristic of kings was, paradoxically, almost always at peace.

Nevertheless, the Prussian people paid a heavy and lasting price for the obsessions of the royal drillmaster. Civil society became rigid and highly disciplined. Prussia became the "Sparta of the North"; unquestioning obedience was the highest virtue. As a Prussian minister later summed up, "To keep quiet is the first civic duty."[8] Thus the absolutism of Frederick William I combined with harsh peasant bondage and Junker tyranny to lay the foundations for probably the most militaristic country of modern times.

The Rise of Moscow

In the ninth century the Vikings, those fearless warriors from Scandinavia, appeared in the lands of the eastern

A Prussian Giant Grenadier   Frederick William I wanted tall, handsome soldiers. He dressed them in tight, bright uniforms to distinguish them from the peasant population from which most soldiers came. He also ordered several portraits of his favorites from his court painter, J. C. Merk. Grenadiers wore the distinctive miter cap instead of an ordinary hat so that they could hurl their heavy hand grenades unimpeded by a broad brim. *(The Royal Collection © Her Majesty Queen Elizabeth II)*

Slavs. Called "Varangians" in the old Russian chronicles, the Vikings were interested primarily in international trade. In order to increase and protect their international commerce, they declared themselves the rulers of the eastern Slavs. The Varangian ruler Oleg (r. 878–912) established his residence at Kiev. He and his successors ruled over a loosely united confederation of Slavic territories—the Kievan state—which reached its height under Prince Iaroslav the Wise (r. 1019–1054).

After Iaroslav's death in 1054 Kiev disintegrated into competing units, each ruled by a prince. A given prince owned a certain number of farms or landed estates and had them worked directly by his people, mainly slaves, called *kholops* in Russian. Outside of these estates the prince exercised limited authority in his principality. Excluding the clergy, two kinds of people lived there: the noble boyars and the commoner peasants.

Like the Germans and the Italians, the eastern Slavs might have emerged from the Middle Ages weak and politically divided had it not been for the Mongol conquest. Wild nomadic tribes from present-day Mongolia, the Mongols were temporarily unified in the thirteenth century by Chinggis Khan (1162–1227), one of history's greatest conquerors. In five years his armies subdued all of China (see Chapter 11). His successors then wheeled westward, smashing everything in their path and reaching the plains of Hungary before they pulled back in 1242. The Mongol army—the Golden Horde—was savage in the extreme, often slaughtering entire populations of cities before burning them to the ground.

The Mongols ruled the eastern Slavs for more than two hundred years. They forced all the bickering Slavic princes to submit to their rule. If the conquered peoples rebelled, the Mongols were quick to punish with death and destruction. Thus the Mongols unified the eastern Slavs, for the Mongol khan was acknowledged by all as the supreme ruler.

Beginning with Alexander Nevsky in 1252, the previously insignificant princes of Moscow became particularly adept at serving the Mongols. They loyally put down popular uprisings and collected the khan's harsh taxes. By way of reward, the princes of Moscow emerged as hereditary great princes. Eventually the Muscovite princes were able to destroy their princely rivals and even to replace the khan as supreme ruler.

One of the more important Muscovite princes was Ivan I (r. 1328–1341), popularly known as "Ivan Mon-eybags." Extremely stingy, Ivan I built up a large personal fortune and increased his influence by loaning money to less frugal princes to pay their Mongol taxes. Ivan's most serious rival was the prince of Tver, who joined his people in 1327 in a revolt against Mongol oppression. Appointed commander of a large Russian-Mongol army, Ivan laid waste to Tver and its lands. For this proof of devotion the Mongols made Ivan the general tax collector for all the Slavic lands they had subjugated and named him great prince. Ivan also convinced the metropolitan of Kiev, the leading churchman of all eastern Slavs, to settle in Moscow. Ivan I thus gained greater prestige.

Over the next century or so, the great princes of Moscow significantly increased their holdings. Ivan III (r. 1462–1505) completed the process of consolidating power around Moscow and won Novgorod, gaining access to the Baltic Sea (Map 17.4).

The prince of Moscow became an absolute ruler: the *tsar,* the Slavic word for "caesar," with all its connotations. This imperious conception of absolute power was reinforced by two developments. First, about 1480 Ivan III stopped acknowledging the Mongol khan as a supreme ruler, but he and his successors assimilated the Mongol concept of kingship as the exercise of unrestrained and unpredictable power. Second, after the fall of Constantinople to the Turks in 1453, the tsars saw themselves as the heirs of both the caesars and Orthodox Christianity, the one true faith. This idea was promoted by Orthodox clergy, who spoke of "holy Russia" as the "third Rome." Ivan's marriage to the daughter of the last Byzantine emperor further enhanced an aura of imperial inheritance for Moscow.

As peasants had begun losing their freedom of movement in the fifteenth century, so had the noble boyars begun losing power and influence. For example, when Ivan III conquered the principality of Novgorod in the 1480s, he confiscated fully 80 percent of the land, executing the previous owners or resettling them nearer Moscow. He then kept more than half of the confiscated land for himself and distributed the remainder to members of a newly emerging service nobility, who held the tsar's land on the explicit condition that they serve in the tsar's army. Moreover, Ivan III began to require boyars outside Novgorod to serve him if they wished to retain their lands.

The rise of the new service nobility accelerated under Ivan IV (r. 1533–1584), the famous "Ivan the Terrible." Having ascended the throne at age three, Ivan suffered insults and neglect at the hands of the haughty

Ivan the Terrible Ivan IV, the first to take the title tsar of Russia, executed many Muscovite boyars and their peasants and servants. His ownership of all the land, trade, and industry restricted economic development. *(National Museum, Copenhagen, Denmark)*

boyars after his mother died. But at age sixteen he suddenly pushed aside his hated boyar advisers and crowned himself. Selecting the beautiful and kind Anastasia of the popular Romanov family for his wife and queen, the young tsar soon declared war on the remnants of Mongol power. He defeated the faltering khanates of Kazan and Astrakhan between 1552 and 1556, adding vast new territories to Russia. In the course of these wars Ivan virtually abolished the old distinction between hereditary boyar private property and land granted temporarily for service. All nobles, old and new, had to serve the tsar in order to hold any land.

This transformation was completed in the second part of Ivan the Terrible's reign. In 1557 Ivan began an exhausting, unsuccessful twenty-five-year war primarily with the large Polish-Lithuanian state. Quarreling with the boyars and blaming them for the sudden death of his beloved Anastasia in 1560, Ivan turned to strike down all who stood in his way. He reduced the ancient Muscovite boyar families with a reign of terror. Leading

boyars, their relatives, and even their peasants were executed en masse. Large estates were confiscated and reapportioned to the lower service nobility.

Ivan also took giant strides toward making all commoners servants of the tsar. As the service nobles demanded more from their peasants, more and more peasants fled toward the wild, recently conquered territories to the east and south. There they formed free groups and outlaw armies known as Cossacks. The Cossacks maintained a precarious independence beyond the reach of the oppressive landholders and the tsar's hated officials. The solution to this problem was to complete the tying of the peasants to the land, making them serfs perpetually bound to serve the noble landholders, who were bound in turn to serve the tsar.

In the time of Ivan the Terrible, urban traders and artisans were also bound to their towns and jobs so that the tsar could tax them more heavily. The urban classes had no security in their work or property and remained weak and divided. Even the wealthiest merchants were basically dependent agents of the tsar.

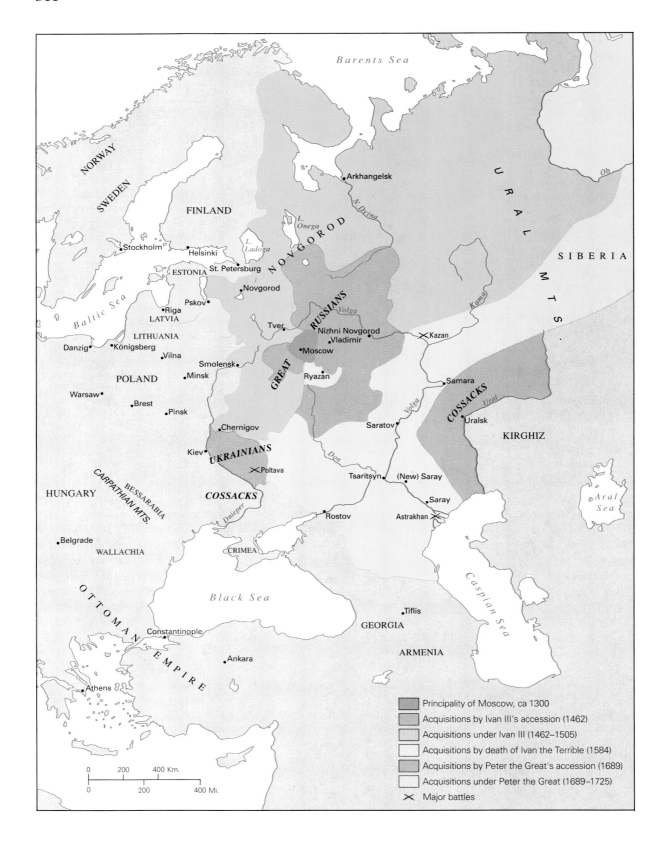

Barents Sea

NORWAY

SWEDEN

FINLAND

Arkhangelsk

L. Onega

L. Ladoga

Stockholm

Helsinki

St. Petersburg

ESTONIA

Novgorod

Pskov

Riga

LATVIA

LITHUANIA

Danzig

Königsberg

Vilna

Smolensk

Minsk

POLAND

Warsaw

Brest

Pinsk

Chernigov

Kiev

UKRAINIANS

COSSACKS

HUNGARY

CARPATHIAN MTS.

BESSARABIA

Belgrade

WALLACHIA

CRIMEA

Black Sea

OTTOMAN EMPIRE

Constantinople

Ankara

Athens

NOVGOROD

N. Dvina

GREAT RUSSIANS

Tver

Nizhni Novgorod

Vladimir

Moscow

Ryazan

Volga

Kazan

Samara

COSSACKS

Uralsk

Saratov

Volga

Don

Tsaritsyn

(New) Saray

Saray

Rostov

Astrakhan

Poltava

Dnieper

GEORGIA

Tiflis

ARMENIA

Caspian Sea

URAL MTS.

Ob

Kama

SIBERIA

Ural

KIRGHIZ

Aral Sea

	Principality of Moscow, ca 1300
	Acquisitions by Ivan III's accession (1462)
	Acquisitions under Ivan III (1462–1505)
	Acquisitions by death of Ivan the Terrible (1584)
	Acquisitions by Peter the Great's accession (1689)
	Acquisitions under Peter the Great (1689–1725)
✕	Major battles

0   200   400 Km.

0   200   400 Mi.

As has so often occurred in Russia, the death of an iron-fisted tyrant—in this case, Ivan the Terrible in 1584—ushered in an era of confusion and violent struggles for power. Events were particularly chaotic after Ivan's son Theodore died in 1598 without an heir. The years 1598 to 1613 are aptly called the Time of Troubles.

Close relatives of the deceased tsar intrigued against and murdered each other, alternately fighting and welcoming the invading Swedes and Poles, who even occupied Moscow. Most serious for the cause of autocracy, there was a great social upheaval as Cossacks marched northward, rallying peasants and slaughtering nobles and officials. This social explosion from below, which combined with a belated surge of patriotic opposition to the Polish invaders, brought the nobles to their senses. In 1613 they elected Ivan's sixteen-year-old grandnephew, Michael Romanov, the new hereditary tsar and rallied around him in the face of common internal and external threats.

Michael's reign saw the gradual re-establishment of tsarist autocracy. The recently rebellious peasants were ground down further, while Ivan's heavy military obligations on the nobility were relaxed considerably. The result was a second round of mass upheaval and protest.

In the mid-seventeenth century the unity of the Russian Orthodox church was torn apart by the religious reforms of the patriarch Nikon, a dogmatic purist who wished to bring "corrupted" Russian practices of worship into line with the Greek Orthodox model. The self-serving church hierarchy quickly went along, but the intensely religious common people resisted. Great numbers left the church and formed illegal communities of "Old Believers," who were hunted down and persecuted. After the great split the Russian masses were alienated from the established church, which became totally dependent on the state for its authority.

Again the Cossacks revolted against the state, which was doggedly trying to catch up with them on the frontiers and reduce them to serfdom. Under the leadership of Stenka Razin they moved up the Volga River in 1670 and 1671, attracting a great undisciplined army of peasants, murdering landlords, and high church officials, and proclaiming freedom from oppression. This rebellion was finally defeated by the government. (See the feature "Individuals in Society: Stenka Razin, Russian Rebel.") In response the thoroughly scared upper classes tightened the screws of serfdom even further.

The Reforms of Peter the Great

It is now possible to understand the reforms of Peter the Great (r. 1682–1725) and his kind of monarchical absolutism. Contrary to some historians' assertions, Peter was interested primarily in military power and not in some grandiose westernization plan. A giant for his time, at six feet seven inches, and possessing enormous energy and determination, Peter was determined to increase Russia's power and to continue the territorial expansion that had gained a large part of the Ukraine in 1667 and had completed the conquest of Siberia in the seventeenth century. Little wonder that the forty-three years of Peter's rule knew only one year of peace.

When Peter took full control in 1689, the heart of his part-time army still consisted of cavalry made up of boyars and service nobility. The Russian army was lagging behind the professional standing armies being formed in Europe in the seventeenth century. The core of such armies was a highly disciplined infantry—an infantry that fired and refired rifles as it fearlessly advanced, before charging with fixed bayonets. Such a large, permanent army was enormously expensive. Given Peter's desire to conquer more territory, his military problem was serious.

Peter's solution was, in essence, to tighten up Muscovy's old service system and really make it work. He put the nobility back in harness with a vengeance. Every nobleman, great or small, was once again required to serve in the army or in the civil administration—for life. Since a more modern army and government required skilled technicians and experts, Peter created schools and even universities. One of his most hated reforms required five years of compulsory education away from home for every young nobleman. Peter established a merit-based military-civilian bureaucracy in which some people of non-noble origin rose to high positions. He also searched out talented foreigners—twice in his reign he went abroad to study and observe—and placed them in his service. These measures combined to make the army and government more powerful and efficient.

Peter also greatly increased the service requirements of the commoners. He established a regular standing army of more than 200,000 soldiers. The departure of a drafted peasant boy was regarded by his family and village as almost like a funeral, as indeed it was, since the

MAP 17.4 The Expansion of Russia to 1725   After the disintegration of the Kievan state and the Mongol conquest, the princes of Moscow and their descendants gradually extended their rule over an enormous territory. Ivan the Terrible acquired more territory than Peter the Great.

Individuals in Society

Stenka Razin, Russian Rebel

Stenka Razin in Cossack dress, from a contemporary engraving. *(Novosti)*

The Don Cossack Stenka Razin led the largest peasant rebellion in Europe in the seventeenth century, a century rich in peasant revolt. Who was this Cossack leader who challenged Moscow, this outlaw who grew into a social revolutionary?

Descended from fugitives who fled to the turbulent southern frontier in search of freedom, Razin epitomized the old Cossack spirit of liberty and self-rule. Sharing the Cossack love of fighting and adventure, Razin also felt great sympathy for northern "have-nots" who had lost out and could not escape their fate. Why this was so remains a mystery. His family belonged to the Cossack establishment, which had settled the lower Don Valley long ago and received annual payments from the tsar in return for friendship and defense. One folk story tells of a hatred kindled by a Russian prince who unjustly hanged an older brother leading a Cossack detachment in Poland. True or not, rebel leaders like Razin have often come from comfortable backgrounds. As Paul Avrich notes, "Seldom have the oppressed themselves led the way, but rather those who have been aroused by their suffering and degradation."[1]

Whatever his motivation, Stenka Razin was a born leader. A striking personality with violent emotions, he was also shrewd and generous. He understood the lower classes and how to move them. The crowds called him a magician—a magician who hated the privileged and whom they felt compelled to follow.

Razin was a seasoned warrior of about forty years of age when in 1667 he led his first campaign. With an armed band of poor and rootless Cossacks, recent fugitives living upstream from the well-settled Cossacks, Razin sailed down the Volga River and seized a rich convoy of Russian merchant ships. He reportedly told survivors they were free to go or join him as free Cossacks. "I have come to fight only the boyars and the wealthy lords. As for the poor and the plain folk, I shall treat them as brothers."[2] Moving on to plunder Persian commerce on the Caspian Sea, Razin's forces returned home loaded with booty, which they divided equally according to Cossack custom. Gaining immense popularity and responding to threats from Moscow, Razin and his movement changed. The gang of outlaws became a rebel army.

In early 1670 Razin marched north with seven thousand Don Cossacks. His leaflets proclaimed that he was entering Russia "to establish the Cossack way, so that all men will be equal." Shrewdly blaming treacherous nobles and officials, and not the divinely appointed tsar, for the exploitation of the people, Razin's agents infiltrated the fortified towns along the Volga. Some towns resisted, but many threw open their gates, as the urban poor rose up against the "traitors and bloodsuckers." Peasants joined the revolt, killing lords and burning manor houses.

Frightened but unified, Russia's tiny elite mobilized all its strength. In late 1670 crack cavalry units of service nobility finally repulsed the swollen, ill-equipped army of the poor at Simbirsk on the upper Volga. The insurgents had to retreat. Fighting until the end, Razin was captured, hideously tortured, and chopped into pieces on the execution block. His followers and sympathizers were slaughtered with ferocious cruelty.

A fearless leader in the struggle against tsarist absolutism, Stenka Razin nurtured a myth of rebellion that would inspire future generations with dreams of freedom. He became Russia's most celebrated folk hero. He lived in story and song, an immortal superman who would someday ride out of the forest and deliver the people from oppression.

Questions for Analysis

1. What did Stenka Razin do? Why did his rebellion inspire future generations?

2. How would you interpret Razin? Was he a great hero, a common criminal, or something else?

1. Paul Avrich, *Russian Rebels, 1600–1800* (New York: Schocken Books, 1972), p. 67. This account is based on Avrich's masterful study.

2. Quoted ibid., p. 70.

recruit was drafted for life. The peasantry also served with its taxes, which increased threefold during Peter's reign. Serfs were arbitrarily assigned to work in the growing number of factories and mines.

The constant warfare of Peter's reign consumed from 80 to 85 percent of all revenues but brought only modest territorial expansion. Yet after initial losses in the Great Northern War with Sweden, which lasted from 1700 to 1721, Peter's new war machine crushed Sweden's smaller army in the Ukraine at Poltava in 1709, one of the most significant battles in Russian history. Sweden never really regained the offensive. Annexing Estonia and much of present-day Latvia (see Map 17.4), Russia became the dominant power on the Baltic Sea and very much a European Great Power. If victory or defeat is the ultimate historical criterion, Peter's reforms were a success.

There were other important consequences of Peter's reign. Because of his feverish desire to use modern technology to strengthen the army, many Westerners and Western ideas flowed into Russia for the first time. A new class of educated Russians began to emerge. At the same time, vast numbers of Russians, especially among the poor and weak, hated Peter's massive changes. The split between the enserfed peasantry and the educated nobility thus widened, even though all were caught up in the endless demands of the sovereign.

A new idea of state interest began to take hold. Peter claimed to act for the common good, and he attached explanations to his decrees in an attempt to gain the support of the populace. The tsar, of course, decided what the common good was.

In sum, Peter built primarily on the service obligations of old Muscovy. His monarchical absolutism was truly the culmination of the long development of a unique Russian civilization. Yet the creation of a more modern army and state introduced much that was new and Western to that civilization. This development paved the way for Russia to move much closer to the European mainstream in its thought and institutions during the Enlightenment under Catherine the Great.

Absolutism and the Baroque

The rise of royal absolutism in eastern Europe had major cultural consequences. Inspired in part by Louis XIV of France, the great and not-so-great rulers called on the artistic talent of the age to glorify their power and magnificence. This exaltation of despotic rule was particularly striking in architecture and city planning.

As soaring Gothic cathedrals expressed the idealized spirit of the High Middle Ages, so dramatic baroque palaces symbolized the age of absolutist power. By 1700 palace building had become an obsession for the rulers of central and eastern Europe. Their baroque palaces were clearly intended to overawe the people with the monarch's strength. One such palace was Schönbrunn, an enormous Viennese Versailles begun in 1695 by Emperor Leopold I to celebrate Austrian military victories and Habsburg might.

Petty princes and important nobles also contributed mightily to the mania of palace building. Palaces like Schönbrunn and Würzburg (see the accompanying illustration) were magnificent examples of the baroque style. They expressed the baroque delight in bold, sweeping statements intended to provide a dramatic emotional experience. To create this experience, baroque masters dissolved the usual artistic frontiers: the architect permitted the painter and the artisan to cover the undulating surfaces with wildly colorful paintings, graceful sculptures, and fanciful carvings. Space was used in a highly original way, to blend everything together in a total environment.

Not content with fashioning ostentatious palaces, absolute monarchs and baroque architects remodeled existing capital cities or built new ones to reflect royal magnificence and the centralization of political power. Karlsruhe, founded in 1715 as the capital city of a small German principality, is one extreme example. There broad, straight avenues radiated out from the palace, so that all roads—like all power—were focused on the ruler. More typically, the monarch's architects added new urban areas alongside the old city, and these areas became the real heart of the expanding capital.

The distinctive features of the new additions were their broad avenues, their imposing government buildings, and their rigorous mathematical layout. Along major thoroughfares the nobles built elaborate townhouses; stables and servants' quarters were built on the alleys behind. Under arcades along the avenues appeared smart and expensive shops, the first department stores, with plate-glass windows and fancy displays. The additions brought reckless speed to the European city. Whereas everyone had walked through the narrow, twisting streets of the medieval town, the high and mighty raced down the broad boulevards in elegant carriages. A social gap opened between the wealthy riders and the gaping, dodging pedestrians.

No city illustrates better than St. Petersburg the close ties among politics, architecture, and urban development in this period. In 1702 Peter the Great's armies

Würzburg, the Prince-Bishop's Palace   The baroque style brought architects, painters, and sculptors together in harmonious, even playful, partnership. This magnificent monumental staircase, designed by Johann Balthasar Neumann in 1735, merges into the vibrant ceiling frescos by Giovanni Battista Tiepolo. A man is stepping out of the picture, and a painted dog resembles a marble statue. *(Erich Lessing/Art Resource, NY)*

seized a desolate Swedish fortress on one of the water-logged islands at the mouth of the Neva River on the Baltic Sea. Within a year the tsar had decided to build a new city there and to make it, rather than ancient Moscow, his capital. The land was swampy and inhospitable. But for Peter it was a future metropolis gloriously bearing his name. After the decisive Russian victory at Poltava in 1709, he moved into high gear. In one imperious decree after another, he ordered his people to build a new city, his "window on Europe."

Peter believed that it would be easier to reform the country militarily and administratively from such a city than from Moscow, and his political goals were reflected in his architectural ideas. First Peter wanted a comfortable, "modern" city. Modernity meant broad, straight, stone-paved avenues, houses built in a uniform line, large parks, canals for drainage, stone bridges, and street lighting. Second, all building had to conform strictly to detailed architectural regulations set down by the government. Finally, each social group—the nobility, the merchants, the artisans, and so on—was to live in a certain section of town. In short, the city and its population were to conform to a carefully defined urban plan of the baroque type.

Peter used the methods of Russian autocracy to build his modern capital. The creation of St. Petersburg was just one of the heavy obligations he dictatorially imposed on all social groups in Russia. The peasants bore the heaviest burdens. Just as the government drafted peasants for the army, it also drafted from twenty-five thousand to forty thousand men each summer to labor in St. Petersburg for three months, without pay. Peasants hated forced labor in the capital, and each year from one-fourth to one-third of those sent risked brutal punishment and ran away. Many peasant construction workers died each summer from hunger, sickness, and accidents. Beautiful St. Petersburg was built on the shoveling, carting, and paving of a mass of conscripted serfs.

Peter also drafted more privileged groups to his city, but on a permanent basis. Nobles were summarily ordered to build costly stone houses and palaces in St. Petersburg and to live in them most of the year. Merchants and artisans were also commanded to settle and build in St. Petersburg. These nobles and merchants were then required to pay for the city's avenues, parks, canals, embankments, pilings, and bridges. The building of St. Petersburg was, in truth, an enormous direct tax levied on the wealthy, who in turn forced the peasantry to do most of the work. No wonder so many Russians hated Peter's new city.

Yet the tsar had his way. By the time of his death in 1725, there were at least six thousand houses and numerous impressive government buildings in St. Petersburg. Under the remarkable women who ruled Russia throughout most of the eighteenth century, St. Petersburg blossomed as a majestic and well-organized city, at least in its wealthy showpiece sections. Chief architect Bartolomeo Rastrelli combined Italian and Russian traditions into a unique, wildly colorful St. Petersburg style in many noble palaces and government buildings. All the while St. Petersburg grew rapidly, and its almost 300,000 inhabitants in 1782 made it one of the world's largest cities. A magnificent and harmonious royal city, St. Petersburg proclaimed the power of Russia's rulers and the creative potential of the absolutist state.

ENGLAND: THE TRIUMPH OF CONSTITUTIONAL MONARCHY

In 1588 Queen Elizabeth I of England exercised great personal power, but by 1689 the power of the English monarchy was severely limited. Change in England was anything but orderly. Yet out of this tumultuous century England built the foundations for a strong and enduring constitutional monarchy.

In the middle years of the seventeenth century, the problem of sovereignty was vigorously debated. In *Leviathan* the English philosopher and political theorist Thomas Hobbes (1588–1679) maintained that sovereignty is ultimately derived from the people, who transfer it to the monarchy by implicit contract. The power of the ruler is absolute, Hobbes said, but kings do not hold their power by divine right. This abstract theory pleased no one in the seventeenth century, but it did stimulate fruitful thinking about England's great seventeenth-century problem—the problem of order and political power.

The Decline of Absolutism in England (1603–1660)

Elizabeth I's extraordinary success was the result of her political shrewdness and flexibility, her careful management of finances, her wise selection of ministers, her clever manipulation of Parliament, and her sense of royal dignity and devotion to hard work. After her Scottish cousin James Stuart succeeded her as James I (r. 1603–1625), Elizabeth's strengths seemed even greater.

King James was learned and, with thirty-five years' experience as king of Scotland, politically shrewd. But he was not as interested in displaying the majesty and mystique of monarchy as Elizabeth had been, and he lacked the common touch. Moreover, James was a dogmatic proponent of the theory of divine right of kings. "There are no privileges and immunities," said James, "which can stand against a divinely appointed King." This absolutist notion implied total royal jurisdiction over the liberties, persons, and properties of English men and women. Such a view ran directly counter to many long-standing English ideas, including the belief that a person's property could not be taken away without due process of law. And in the House of Commons the English had a strong representative body to question these absolutist pretensions.

The House of Commons guarded the state's pocketbook, and James and later Stuart kings badly needed to open that pocketbook. James I looked on all revenues as a windfall to be squandered on a lavish court and favorite courtiers. The extravagance displayed in James's court, as well as the public flaunting of his male lovers, weakened respect for the monarchy. These actions also stimulated the knights and burgesses who sat in the House of Commons at Westminster to press for a thorough discussion of royal expenditures, religious reform, and foreign affairs. In short, the Commons aspired to sovereignty—the ultimate political power in the realm.

During the reigns of James I and his son Charles I (r. 1625–1649) the English House of Commons was very different from the assembly that Henry VIII had manipulated into passing his Reformation legislation. The class that dominated the Commons during the Stuarts' reign wanted political power corresponding to its economic strength. A social revolution had brought about this change. The dissolution of the monasteries and the sale of monastic land had enriched many people. Agricultural techniques like the draining of wasteland had improved the land and increased its yield. In the seventeenth century old manorial common land was enclosed and profitably turned into sheep runs. Many invested in commercial ventures at home, such as the expanding cloth industry, and in foreign trade. Many also made prudent marriages. These developments increased social mobility. The typical pattern was for the commercially successful to set themselves up as country gentry. This elite group possessed a far greater proportion of the land and of the nation's wealth in 1640 than in 1540. Increased wealth resulted in a better-educated and more articulate House of Commons.

In England, unlike France, no social stigma was attached to paying taxes, although the House of Commons wanted some say in state spending and state policies. The Stuart kings, however, considered such ambitions intolerable presumption and a threat to their divine-right prerogative. Consequently, at every Parliament between 1603 and 1640, bitter squabbles erupted between Crown and Commons. Like the Great Elector in Prussia, Charles I tried to govern without Parliament (1629–1640) and to finance his government by arbitrary levies, measures that brought intense political conflict.

Religion was another source of conflict. In the early seventeenth century increasing numbers of English people felt dissatisfied with the Church of England established by Henry VIII. Many Puritans remained committed to "purifying" the Anglican church of Roman Catholic elements—elaborate vestments and ceremonies, even the giving and wearing of wedding rings.

Many Puritans were also attracted by the socioeconomic implications of John Calvin's theology. Calvinism emphasized hard work, sobriety, thrift, competition, and postponement of pleasure, and it tended to link sin and poverty with weakness and moral corruption. These attitudes, which have frequently been called the "Protestant ethic," "middle-class ethic," or "capitalist ethic," fit in precisely with the economic approaches and practices of many (successful) business people and farmers. These "Protestant virtues" represented the prevailing values of members of the House of Commons.

James I and Charles I both gave the impression of being highly sympathetic to Roman Catholicism. Charles supported the policies of Archbishop of Canterbury William Laud (1573–1645), who tried to impose elaborate ritual and rich ceremonial on all churches. In 1637 Laud attempted to impose Anglican organization and a new prayer book in Scotland. The Scots revolted. To finance an army to put down the Scots, King Charles was compelled to summon Parliament in November 1640. It was a fatal decision.

For eleven years Charles I had ruled without Parliament, financing his government through extraordinary stopgap levies considered illegal by most English people. Most members of Parliament believed that such taxation without consent amounted to absolutist despotism. Accordingly, the Parliament summoned in November 1640 (commonly called the Long Parliament because it sat from 1640 to 1660) enacted legislation that limited the power of the monarch and made arbitrary government impossible.

In 1641 the Commons passed the Triennial Act, which compelled the king to summon Parliament every three years. The Commons also impeached Archbishop Laud and abolished the House of Lords and the ecclesiastical Court of High Commission. King Charles reluctantly accepted these measures. But understanding and peace were not achieved, and an uprising in Ireland precipitated civil war.

Ever since Henry II had conquered Ireland in 1171, English governors had mercilessly ruled the land, and English landlords had ruthlessly exploited the Irish people. The English Reformation had made a bad situation worse: because the Irish remained Catholic, religious differences united with economic and political oppression. Without an army Charles I could neither come to terms with the Scots nor put down the Irish rebellion, and the Long Parliament remained unwilling to place an army under a king it did not trust. Charles thus recruited an army drawn from the nobility and the nobility's cavalry staff, the rural gentry, and mercenaries. The parliamentary army that rose in opposition was composed of the militia of the city of London, country squires with business connections, and men with a firm belief that serving was their spiritual duty.

The English civil war (1642–1649) tested whether ultimate political power in England was to reside in the king or in Parliament. The civil war did not resolve that problem, although it ended in 1649 with the execution of King Charles on the charge of high treason and thus dealt a severe blow to the theory of divine-right, absolute monarchy in England. Kingship was abolished in England, and a *commonwealth,* or republican form of government, was proclaimed.

In fact, the army that had defeated the royal forces controlled the government, and Oliver Cromwell controlled the army. Indeed, the period from 1649 to 1660, known as the Interregnum because it separated two monarchical periods, was a transitional time of military dictatorship, and for most of that time Cromwell was head of state.

Oliver Cromwell (1599–1658) came from the country gentry, and he was a member of the Long Parliament. Cromwell rose in the parliamentary army and achieved nationwide fame by infusing the army with his Puritan convictions and molding it into a highly effective military machine, called the New Model Army. In 1653 the army prepared a constitution that invested executive power in a lord protector (Cromwell) and a council of state. The instrument gave Parliament the sole power to raise taxes. But after repeated disputes Cromwell tore up the document and proclaimed quasi-martial law.

On the issue of religion Cromwell favored broad toleration, and the Instrument of Government gave all Christians, except Roman Catholics, the right to practice

Cartoon of 1649: "The Royall Oake of Brittayne"   The "Royall Oake" is chopped down, ending royal authority, stability, Magna Carta (see page 357), and the rule of law. As pigs graze (representing the unconcerned common people), being fattened for slaughter, Oliver Cromwell, with his feet in Hell, quotes Scripture. This is a royalist view of the collapse of Charles I's government and the rule of Cromwell. *(Courtesy of the Trustees of the British Museum)*

their faith. In 1649 he crushed rebellion in Ireland with merciless savagery, leaving a legacy of Irish hatred for England. He also rigorously censored the press, forbade sports, and kept the theaters closed in England.

Cromwell pursued mercantilist economic policies. He enforced a navigation act requiring that English goods be transported on English ships, which was a great boost to the development of an English merchant marine and brought about a short but successful war with the Dutch.

Military government collapsed when Cromwell died in 1658. The English longed for a return to civilian government, restoration of the common law, and social and religious stability. Moreover, the strain of creating a community of puritanical saints proved too psychologically exhausting. Government by military dictatorship was an experiment in absolutism that the English never forgot or repeated. By 1660 they were ready to try a restoration of monarchy.

The Restoration of the English Monarchy

The Restoration of 1660 re-established the monarchy in the person of Charles II (r. 1660–1685), eldest son of Charles I. At the same time both houses of Parliament were also restored, together with the established Anglican church. The Restoration failed to resolve two serious problems. What was to be the attitude of the state toward Puritans, Catholics, and dissenters from the established church? And what was to be the constitutional relationship between the king and Parliament?

Charles II, a relaxed, easygoing, and sensual man, was not much interested in religious issues. But the new members of Parliament were, and they proceeded to enact a body of laws that sought to compel religious uniformity. Those who refused to receive the sacrament of the Church of England could not vote, hold public office, preach, teach, attend the universities, or even assemble for meetings, according to the Test Act of 1673.

In politics Charles II was at first determined to get along with Parliament and share power with it. His method for doing so had profound importance for later constitutional development. The king appointed a council of five men who served both as his major advisers and as members of Parliament, thus acting as liaison agents between the executive and the legislature. It gradually came to be accepted that the council of five was answerable in Parliament for the decisions of the king.

Harmony between the Crown and Parliament rested on the understanding that Charles would summon Parliament frequently and Parliament would vote him sufficient revenues. However, although Parliament believed that Charles should have large powers, it did not grant him an adequate income. Accordingly, in 1670 Charles entered into a secret agreement with Louis XIV. The French king would give Charles £200,000 annually. In return Charles would relax the laws against Catholics, gradually re-Catholicize England, support French policy against the Dutch, and convert to Catholicism himself.

When the details of this secret treaty leaked out, a wave of anti-Catholic fear swept England. Charles had produced only bastards, and therefore it appeared that his brother and heir, James, duke of York, an avowed Catholic, would inaugurate a Catholic dynasty. The combination of hatred for the French absolutism embodied in Louis XIV and hostility to Roman Catholicism led the Commons to pass an exclusion bill denying the succession to a Roman Catholic. But Charles quickly dissolved Parliament, and the bill never became law.

James II (r. 1685–1688) succeeded his brother. Almost at once the worst English anti-Catholic fears, already aroused by Louis XIV's recent revocation of the Edict of Nantes, were realized. In direct violation of the Test Act, James appointed Roman Catholics to positions in the army, the universities, and local government. The king appeared to be reviving the absolutism of his father (Charles I) and grandfather (James I). He went further. Attempting to broaden his base of support with Protestant dissenters and nonconformists, James issued a declaration of indulgence granting religious freedom to all.

Two events gave the signals for revolution. First, seven bishops of the Church of England petitioned the king that they not be forced to read the declaration of indulgence because of their belief that it was an illegal act. They were imprisoned in the Tower of London but subsequently acquitted amid great public enthusiasm. Second, in June 1688 James's second wife produced a male heir. A Catholic dynasty seemed assured. The fear of a Roman Catholic monarchy, supported by France and ruling outside the law, prompted a group of eminent persons to offer the English throne to James's Protestant daughter, Mary, and her Dutch husband, Prince William of Orange. In December 1688 James II, his queen, and their infant son fled to France. In 1689 William and Mary were crowned king and queen of England.

The English call the events of 1688 to 1689 the "Glorious Revolution." It replaced one king with another with a minimum of bloodshed, and it represented the destruction, once and for all, of the idea of divine-right absolutism in England. William and Mary accepted the English throne from Parliament and in so doing explicitly recognized the supremacy of Parliament.

The men who brought about the revolution quickly framed their intentions in the Bill of Rights, the cornerstone of the modern British constitution. The basic principles of the Bill of Rights were formulated in direct response to Stuart absolutism. Law was to be made in Parliament; once made, it could not be suspended by the Crown. Parliament had to be called at least every three years. Both elections to and debate in Parliament were to be free, in the sense that the Crown was not to interfere in them. Judges would hold their offices "during good behavior," a provision that assured judicial independence.

In striking contrast to the states of continental Europe, there was to be no standing army that could be used against the English population in peacetime. Moreover, the Bill of Rights granted Protestants the right to possess firearms. Additional legislation granted freedom of worship to Protestant dissenters and nonconformists and required that the English monarch always be Protestant.

The Glorious Revolution found its best defense in John Locke's *Second Treatise of Civil Government* (1690). The political philosopher Locke (1632–1704) maintained that people set up civil governments in order to protect life, liberty, and property. A government that oversteps its proper function—protecting the natural rights of life, liberty, and property—becomes a tyranny. (By "natural" rights, Locke meant rights basic to all men because all have the ability to reason.) Under a tyrannical government the people have the natural right to rebellion. Recognizing the close relationship between economic and political freedom, Locke linked economic liberty and private property with political freedom.

Locke served as the great spokesman for the liberal English revolution of 1688 to 1689 and for representative government. His idea—that there are natural or universal rights equally valid for all peoples and societies—played a powerful role in eighteenth-century Enlightenment thought.

The events of 1688 to 1689 did not constitute a *democratic* revolution. The revolution formalized Parliament's power, and Parliament represented the upper classes. The great majority of English people had little say in their government. The English revolution established a constitutional monarchy; it also inaugurated an age of aristocratic government.

In the course of the eighteenth century the cabinet system of government evolved out of Charles II's old council-of-five system. The term *cabinet* derives from the small private room in which English rulers consulted their chief ministers. In a cabinet system, the leading ministers formulate common policy and conduct the business of the country. During the administration of one royal minister, Sir Robert Walpole, who led the Cabinet from 1721 to 1742, the idea developed that the Cabinet was responsible to the House of Commons. Walpole enjoyed the favor of the monarchy and of the House of Commons and came to be called the king's first, or "prime," minister. In the English cabinet system, both legislative and executive powers are held by the leading ministers, who form the government.

THE DUTCH REPUBLIC IN THE SEVENTEENTH CENTURY

In the late sixteenth century the seven northern provinces of the Netherlands, of which Holland and Zeeland were the most prosperous, had thrown off Spanish domination (see pages 475–477). The seventeenth century then witnessed an unparalleled flowering of Dutch scientific, artistic, and literary achievement. In this period, often called the golden age of the Netherlands, Dutch ideas and attitudes played a profound role in shaping a new and modern world-view.

The Republic of the United Provinces of the Netherlands represents a variation in the development of the modern constitutional state. Within each province an oligarchy of wealthy merchants called regents handled domestic affairs in the local Estates. The provincial Estates held virtually all the power. A federal assembly, or States General, handled matters of foreign affairs, such as war, but all issues had to be referred back to the local Estates for approval. The regents in each province jealously guarded local independence and resisted efforts at centralization. Nevertheless, Holland, which had the largest navy and the most wealth, dominated the republic and the States General.

The government of the United Provinces conforms to none of the standard categories of seventeenth-century political organization. The Dutch were not monarchical but fiercely republican. The government was controlled by wealthy merchants and financiers.

Room from Het Scheepje (The Little Ship)   A retired sea captain who became a successful brewer in Haarlem owned the house (adjacent to his brewery) that included this room. The brass chandelier, plates, tiles, Turkish rug on the table (probably from Transylvania in the then Ottoman Empire), oak mantelpiece, and paneling make this a superb example of Dutch domestic interiors during the Golden Age. A bed, built into the wall paneling, was warmed at night by coals in the pan hanging by the fireplace. *(Room from Het Scheepje, Haarlem, The Netherlands, early 17th century. Philadelphia Museum of Art, Gift of Edward W. Bok. 1928-66-1)*

Though rich, their values were not aristocratic but strongly middle class. The political success of the Dutch rested on their phenomenal commercial prosperity. The moral and ethical bases of that commercial wealth were thrift, hard work, and simplicity in living.

John Calvin had written, "From where do the merchant's profits come except from his own diligence and industry." This attitude undoubtedly encouraged a sturdy people who had waged a centuries-old struggle against the sea. Louis XIV's hatred of the Dutch was proverbial. They represented all that he despised— middle-class values, religious toleration, and independent political institutions.

Alone of all European peoples in the seventeenth century, the Dutch practiced religious toleration. Peoples of all faiths were welcome within their borders. Jews enjoyed a level of acceptance and absorption in Dutch business and general culture unique in early modern Europe. It is a testimony to the urbanity of Dutch society that in a century when patriotism was closely identified with religious uniformity, the Calvinist province of Holland allowed its highest official, Jan van Oldenbarnevelt, to continue to practice his Roman Catholic faith.

Toleration paid off. It attracted a great amount of foreign capital and business expertise. The Bank of Amsterdam became Europe's best source of cheap credit and commercial intelligence and the main clearinghouse for bills of exchange. People of all races and creeds traded in Amsterdam, at whose docks on the Amstel River five thousand ships were berthed. Joost van den Vondel, the poet of Dutch imperialism, exulted:

God, God, the Lord of Amstel cried, hold every conscience free;
And Liberty ride, on Holland's tide, with billowing sails to sea,
And run our Amstel out and in; let freedom gird the bold,

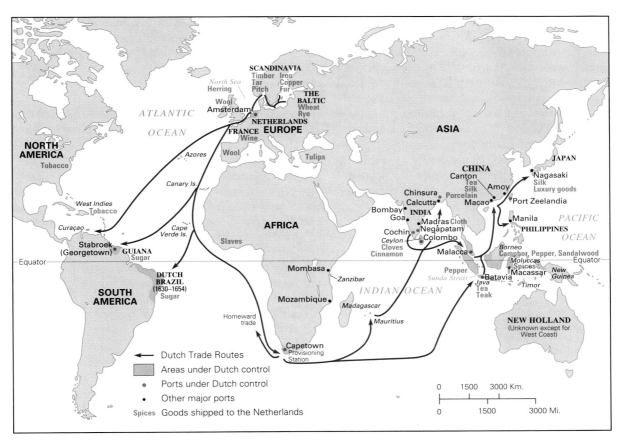

MAP 17.5 Seventeenth-Century Dutch Commerce   Dutch wealth rested on commerce, and commerce depended on the huge Dutch merchant marine, manned by perhaps forty-eight thousand sailors. The fleet carried goods from all parts of the globe to the port of Amsterdam.

And merchant in his counting house stand elbow deep in gold.[9]

The fishing industry was a cornerstone of the Dutch economy. For half of the year, from June to December, fishing fleets combed the dangerous English coast and the North Sea, raking in tiny herring. Profits from herring stimulated shipbuilding, and even before 1600 the Dutch were offering the lowest shipping rates in Europe. In 1650 the Dutch merchant marine was the largest in Europe, accounting for roughly half of the European total. All the wood for these ships had to be imported: the Dutch bought whole forests from Norway. They controlled the Baltic grain trade, buying entire wheat and rye crops in Poland, east Prussia, and Swedish Pomerania. Foreign merchants coming to Amsterdam could buy anything from precision lenses for the newly invented microscope to muskets for an army of five thousand.

In 1602 a group of the regents of Holland formed the Dutch East India Company, a joint stock company. Each investor received a percentage of the profits proportional to the amount of money he had put in. Within a half century, the Dutch East India Company had cut heavily into Portuguese trading in East Asia. The Dutch seized the Cape of Good Hope, Ceylon, and Malacca and established trading posts in each place. In the 1630s the Dutch East India Company was paying its investors about a 35 percent annual return on their investments. The Dutch West India Company, founded in 1621, traded extensively with Latin America and Africa (Map 17.5).

Trade and commerce brought the Dutch prodigious wealth. In the seventeenth century the Dutch enjoyed the highest standard of living in Europe, perhaps in the world. Amsterdam and Rotterdam built massive granaries where the surplus of one year could be stored against possible shortages the next. Thus food prices fluctuated very little. By the standards of Cologne, Paris, or London, salaries were high for all workers, except women. All classes of society, including unskilled laborers, ate well. The low price of bread meant that, compared with other places in Europe, a higher percentage of a worker's income could be spent on fish, cheese, butter, vegetables, even meat. A leading scholar has described the Netherlands as "an island of plenty in a sea of want."[10]

Dutch economic leadership was eventually sapped by wars, beginning with those with France and England in the 1670s. The long War of the Spanish Succession, in which the Dutch supported England against France, was a costly drain on Dutch manpower and financial resources. The peace signed in 1713 to end that war marked the beginning of Dutch economic decline.

SUMMARY

War, religious strife, economic depression, and peasant revolts were all aspects of a deep crisis in seventeenth-century Europe. Rulers responded by aggressively seeking to expand their power, which they claimed was essential to meet emergencies and quell disorders. Claiming also that they ruled by divine right, monarchs sought the freedom to wage war, levy taxes, and generally make law as they saw fit. Although they were limited by technology and inadequate financial resources, monarchical governments on the European continent succeeded to a large extent, overpowering organized opposition and curbing the power of the nobility and the traditional representative institutions.

The France of Louis XIV led the way to royal absolutism. France developed a centralized bureaucracy, a professional army, and a state-directed economy, all of which Louis personally supervised. The king saw himself as the representative of God on earth and accountable to no one here below. His majestic bearing and sumptuous court dazzled contemporaries. Yet behind the grand façade of unchallenged personal rule and obedient bureaucrats working his will there stood major limitations on Louis XIV's power. Most notable were the financial independence of some provinces and the nobility's traditional freedom from taxation, which Louis himself was compelled to reaffirm.

Within a framework of resurgent serfdom and entrenched nobility, Austrian and Prussian monarchs also fashioned absolutist states in the seventeenth and early eighteenth centuries. These monarchs won absolutist control over standing armies, permanent taxes, and legislative bodies. But they did not question the underlying social and economic relationships. Indeed, they enhanced the privileges of the nobility, which furnished the leading servitors for enlarged armies and growing government bureaucracies.

In Russia social and economic trends were similar to those in Austria and Prussia. Unlike those two states, however, Russia had a long history of powerful princes. Tsar Peter the Great succeeded in tightening up Russia's traditional absolutism and modernizing it by reforming the army, the bureaucracy, and the defense industry. In Russia and throughout eastern Europe war and the needs of the state in time of war weighed heavily in the triumph of absolutism.

Triumphant absolutism interacted spectacularly with the arts. It molded the ideals of French classicism, which glorified the state as personified by Louis XIV. Baroque art, which had grown out of the Catholic Reformation's desire to move the faithful and exalt the faith, admirably suited the secular aspirations of eastern European rulers. Thus baroque art attained magnificent heights in eastern Europe, symbolizing the ideal and harmonizing with the reality of imperious royal absolutism.

Holland and England defied the general trend toward absolute monarchy. While Holland prospered under a unique republican confederation that placed most power in the hands of the different provinces, England—fortunately shielded from continental armies and military emergencies by its navy and the English Channel—evolved into the first modern constitutional state. The bitter conflicts between Parliament and the first two Stuart rulers, James I and Charles I, tested where supreme power would rest in the state. The resulting civil war deposed the king, but it did not settle the question. A revival of absolutist tendencies under James II brought on the Glorious Revolution of 1688, and the people who made that revolution settled three basic issues. Power was divided between king and Parliament, with Parliament enjoying the greater share. Government was to be based on the rule of law. And the liberties of English people were to be made explicit in written form, in the Bill of Rights. This constitutional settlement marked an important milestone in world history, although the framers left to later generations the task of making constitutional government work.

NOTES

1. J. B. Collins, *Fiscal Limits of Absolutism: Direct Taxation in Early Seventeenth Century France* (Berkeley: University of California Press, 1988), pp. 1, 3–4, 215–222.

2. S. de Gramont, ed., *The Age of Magnificence: Memoirs of the Court of Louis XIV by the Duc de Saint Simon* (New York: Capricorn Books, 1964), pp. 141–145.

3. W. Beik, *Absolutism and Society in Seventeenth Century France: State Power and Provincial Aristocracy in Languedoc* (Cambridge: Cambridge University Press, 1985), pp. 279–302.

4. W. F. Church, *Louis XIV in Historical Thought: From Voltaire to the Annales School* (New York: W. W. Norton, 1976), p. 92.

5. B. Bennassar, *The Spanish Character: Attitudes and Mentalities from the Sixteenth to the Nineteenth Century,* trans. B. Keen (Berkeley: University of California Press, 1979), p. 125.

6. Quoted in R. Ergang, *The Potsdam Fuhrer: Frederick William I, Father of Prussian Militarism* (New York: Octagon Books, 1972), pp. 85, 87.

7. Quoted in R. A. Dorwart, *The Administrative Reforms of Frederick William I of Prussia* (Cambridge, Mass.: Harvard University Press, 1953), p. 226.

8. Quoted in H. Rosenberg, *Bureaucracy, Aristocracy, and Autocracy: The Prussian Experience, 1660–1815* (Boston: Beacon Press, 1966), p. 38.

9. Quoted in D. Maland, *Europe in the Seventeenth Century* (New York: Macmillan, 1967), pp. 198–199.

10. S. Schama, *The Embarrassment of Riches: An Interpretation of Dutch Culture in the Golden Age* (New York: Knopf, 1987), pp. 165–170.

SUGGESTED READING

Students who wish to explore the problems presented in this chapter will find a rich and exciting literature. G. Parker, *Europe in Crisis, 1598–1618* (1980), provides a sound introduction to the social, economic, and religious tensions of the period, as does R. S. Dunn, *The Age of Religious Wars, 1559–1715,* 2d ed. (1979). P. Anderson, *Lineages of the Absolutist State* (1974), is a stimulating Marxist interpretation of absolutism in western and eastern Europe.

Louis XIV and his age have attracted the attention of many scholars. J. Wolf, *Louis XIV* (1968), remains the best available biography. P. Burke, *The Fabrication of Louis XIV* (1992), explores the representations of the Sun King. Two works of W. H. Lewis, *The Splendid Century* (1957) and *The Sunset of the Splendid Century* (1963), make delightful light reading. The advanced student will want to consult the excellent historiographical analysis by Church mentioned in the Notes, *Louis XIV in Historical Thought.* P.

Goubert's heavily detailed *The Ancien Régime: French Society, 1600–1750,* 2 vols. (1969–1973) contains invaluable material on the lives and work of ordinary people. R. Bonney, *The King's Debts: Finance and Politics in France, 1589–1661* (1981), and A. Trout, *Jean-Baptiste Colbert* (1978), consider economic and financial conditions. R. Hatton, *Europe in the Age of Louis XIV* (1979), is a splendidly illustrated survey of many aspects of seventeenth-century European culture.

For Spain, M. Defourneaux, *Daily Life in Spain in the Golden Age* (1976), is extremely useful. See also C. R. Phillips, *Ciudad Real, 1500–1750: Growth, Crisis, and Readjustment in the Spanish Economy* (1979), a significant case study. A. Pagden, *Spanish Imperialism and the Political Imagination* (1990), explores Spanish ideas of empire. V. L. Tapie, *The Age of Grandeur: Baroque Art and Architecture* (1960), emphasizes the relationship between art and politics with excellent illustrations. Art and architecture are also treated admirably in E. Hempel, *Baroque Art and Architecture in Central Europe* (1965), and G. Hamilton, *The Art and Architecture of Russia* (1954).

The best study on early Prussian history is still F. L. Carsten, *The Origin of Prussia* (1954). Rosenberg, *Bureaucracy, Aristocracy, and Autocracy,* cited in the Notes, is a masterful analysis of the social context of Prussian absolutism. Ergang, *The Potsdam Fuhrer,* also cited in the Notes, is an exciting and critical biography of ramrod Frederick William I. G. Craig, *The Politics of the Prussian Army, 1640–1945* (1964), expertly traces the great influence of the military on the Prussian state over three hundred years. R. J. Evans, *The Making of the Habsburg Empire, 1550–1770* (1979), analyzes the development of absolutism in Austria, as does A. Wandruszka, *The House of Habsburg* (1964). D. McKay and H. Scott, *The Rise of the Great Powers, 1648–1815* (1983), is a good general account. R. Vierhaus, *Germany in the Age of Absolutism* (1988), offers a thorough survey of the different German states.

On eastern European peasants and serfdom, D. Chirot, ed., *The Origins of Backwardness in Eastern Europe: Economics and Politics from the Middle Ages Until the Twentieth Century* (1989), is a wide-ranging introduction. E. Levin, *Sex and Society in the World of the Orthodox Slavs, 900–1700* (1989), carries family history to eastern Europe. J. Blum, *Lord and Peasant in Russia from the Ninth to the Nineteenth Century* (1961), provides a good look at conditions in rural Russia, and P. Avrich, *Russian Rebels, 1600–1800* (1972), treats some of the violent peasant upheavals that those conditions produced. R. Hellie, *Enserfment and Military Change in Muscovy* (1971), is outstanding. In addition to the fine survey by N. V. Riasanovsky, *A History of Russia* (1963), J. Billington, *The Icon and the Axe* (1970), is a stimulating history of early Russian intellectual and cultural developments. B. H. Sumner, *Peter the Great and the Emergence of Russia* (1962), is a good brief introduc-

(continued on page 560)

The Court at Versailles

Although the duke of Saint-Simon (1675–1755) was a soldier, courtier, and diplomat, his enduring reputation rests on his Memoirs *(1788), an eyewitness account of the personality and court of Louis XIV. A nobleman of ancient lineage, Saint-Simon resented Louis's "domestication" of the nobility and his promotion of the bourgeoisie. His* Memoirs, *excerpted here, remains a monument of French literature and an indispensable historical source, partly for its portrait of the court at Versailles.*

Very early in the reign of Louis XIV the Court was removed from Paris, never to return. The troubles of the minority had given him a dislike to that city; his enforced and surreptitious flight from it still rankled in his memory; he did not consider himself safe there, and thought cabals would be more easily detected if the Court was in the country, where the movements and temporary absences of any of its members would be more easily noticed. . . . No doubt that he was also influenced by the feeling that he would be regarded with greater awe and veneration when no longer exposed every day to the gaze of the multitude.

His love-affair with Mademoiselle de la Vallière, which at first was covered as far as possible with a veil of mystery, was the cause of frequent excursions to Versailles. . . . The visits of Louis XIV becoming more frequent, he enlarged the *château* by degrees till its immense buildings afforded better accommodation for the Court than was to be found at St. Germain, where most of the courtiers had to put up with uncomfortable lodgings in the town. The Court was therefore removed to Versailles in 1682, not long before the Queen's death. The new building contained an infinite number of rooms for courtiers, and the King liked the grant of these rooms to be regarded as a coveted privilege.

He availed himself of the frequent festivities at Versailles, and his excursions to other places, as a means of making the courtiers assiduous in their attendance and anxious to please him; for he nominated beforehand those who were to take part in them, and could thus gratify some and inflict a snub on others. He was conscious that the substantial favours he had to bestow were not nearly sufficient to produce a continual effect; he had therefore to invent imaginary ones, and no one was so clever in devising petty distinctions and preferences which aroused jealousy and emulation. The visits to Marly later on were very useful to him in this way; also those to Trianon [Marly and Trianon were small country houses], where certain ladies, chosen beforehand, were admitted to his table. It was another distinction to hold his candlestick at his *coucher;* as soon as he had finished his prayers he used to name the courtier to whom it was to be handed, always choosing one of the highest rank among those present. . . .

Not only did he expect all persons of distinction to be in continual attendance at Court, but he was quick to notice the absence of those of inferior degree; at his *lever* [formal rising from bed in the morning], his *coucher* [preparations for going to bed], his meals, in the gardens of Versailles (the only place where the courtiers in general were allowed to follow him), he used to cast his eyes to right and left; nothing escaped him, he saw everybody. If any one habitually living at Court absented himself he insisted on knowing the reason; those who came there only for flying visits had also to give a satisfactory explanation; any one who seldom or never appeared there was certain to incur his displeasure. If asked to bestow a favour on such persons he would reply haughtily: "I do not know him"; of such as rarely presented themselves he would say, "He is a man I never see"; and from these judgements there was no appeal.

He always took great pains to find out what was going on in public places, in society, in private houses, even family secrets, and maintained an immense number of spies and tale-bearers. These were of all sorts; some did not know that their reports were carried to him; others did know it; there were others, again, who used to write to him directly, through channels which he prescribed; others who were admitted by the backstairs and saw him in his private room. Many a man in all ranks of life was ruined by these methods, often very unjustly, without ever being able to discover the reason; and when the King had once taken a prejudice against a man, he hardly ever got over it. . . .

No one understood better than Louis XIV the art of enhancing the value of a favour by his manner of bestowing it; he knew how to make the most of a word, a smile, even of a glance. If he addressed any one, were it but to ask a trifling question or make some commonplace remark, all eyes were turned on the person so honored; it was a mark of favour which always gave rise to comment. . . .

He loved splendour, magnificence, and profusion in all things, and encouraged similar tastes in his Court; to spend money freely on equipages [the king's horse carriages] and buildings, on feasting and at cards, was a sure way to gain his favour, perhaps to obtain the honour of a word from him. Motives of policy had something to do with this; by making expensive habits the fashion, and, for people in a certain position, a necessity, he compelled his courtiers to live beyond their income, and gradually reduced them to depend on his bounty for the means of subsistence. This was a plague which, once introduced, became a scourge to the whole country, for it did not take long to spread to Paris, and thence to the armies and the provinces; so that a man of any position is now estimated entirely according to his expenditure on his table and other luxuries. This folly, sustained by pride and ostentation, has already produced widespread confusion; it threatens to end in nothing short of ruin and a general overthrow.

Painting of Louis XIV by Mignard Pierre (1612–1695). *(Galleria Sabauda, Turin/Scala/Art Resource, NY)*

Questions for Analysis

1. How would you define the French court? Why did Louis XIV move it to Versailles?

2. By what means did Louis control the nobility at Versailles? Why did he use those particular means?

3. Consider the role of ritual and ceremony in some modern governments, such as the U.S. government. How does it compare to Louis XIV's use of ceremony, as portrayed by Saint-Simon?

4. Saint-Simon faulted Louis for encouraging the nobles' extravagance. Is that a justifiable criticism?

Source: F. Arkwright, ed., *The Memoirs of the Duke de Saint-Simon,* vol. 5 (New York: Brentano's, n.d.), pp. 271–274, 276–278.

tion, which may be compared with N. V. Riasanovsky, *The Image of Peter the Great in Russian History and Thought* (1985).

English political and social issues of the seventeenth century are considered by M. Ashley, *The House of Stuart: Its Rise and Fall* (1980); C. Hill, *A Century of Revolution* (1961); and K. Wrightson, *English Society, 1580–1680* (1982). Comprehensive treatments of Parliament include C. Russell, *Crisis of Parliaments, 1509–1660* (1971). L. Stone, *The Causes of the English Revolution* (1972), and B. Manning, *The English People and the English Revolution* (1976), are recommended. D. Underdown, *Revel, Riot, and Rebellion* (1985), discusses the extent of popular involvement. For English intellectual currents, see J. O. Appleby, *Economic Thought and Ideology in Seventeenth Century England* (1978). Other recommended works include P. Collinson, *The Religion of Protestants* (1982); R. Thompson, *Women in Stuart England and America* (1974); and A. Fraser, *The Weaker Vessel* (1985). For Cromwell and the Interregnum, A. Fraser, *Cromwell, the Lord Protector* (1973), is valuable. C. Hill, *The World Turned Upside Down* (1972), discusses radical thought during the period. For the Restoration and the Glorious Revolution, see R.

Hutton, *Charles II: King of England, Scotland and Ireland* (1989); J. Childs, *The Army, James II, and the Glorious Revolution* (1980); and L. G. Schwoerer, *The Declaration of Rights, 1689* (1981), a fine assessment of that fundamental document. The ideas of John Locke are analyzed by J. P. Kenyon, *Revolution Principles: The Politics of Party, 1689–1720* (1977).

On Holland, K. H. D. Haley, *The Dutch Republic in the Seventeenth Century* (1972), is a splendidly illustrated appreciation of Dutch commercial and artistic achievements, and Schama, *The Embarrassment of Riches,* cited in the Notes, is a lively recent synthesis. R. Boxer, *The Dutch Seaborne Empire* (1980), is useful for Dutch overseas expansion. V. Barbour, *Capitalism in Amsterdam in the Seventeenth Century* (1950), and D. Regin, *Traders, Artists, Burghers: A Cultural History of Amsterdam in the Seventeenth Century* (1977), focus on the leading Dutch city. The leading statesmen of the period may be studied in these biographies: H. H. Rowen, *John de Witt, Grand Pensionary of Holland, 1625–1672* (1978); S. B. Baxter, *William the III and the Defense of European Liberty, 1650–1702* (1966); and J. den Tex, *Oldenbarnevelt,* 2 vols. (1973).

18 Toward a New World-View in the West

Painting by Jean-Honoré Fragonard of Denis Diderot, one of the editors of the *Encyclopedia,* the greatest intellectual achievement of the Age of Enlightenment. *(Louvre © Photo R.M.N.)*

Most people are not philosophers, but they nevertheless have a basic outlook on life, a more or less coherent world-view. At the risk of oversimplification, one may say that the world-view of medieval and early modern Europe was primarily religious and theological. Not only did Christian or Jewish teachings form the core of people's spiritual and philosophical beliefs, but religious teachings also permeated all the rest of human thought and activity. Political theory relied on the divine right of kings, for example, and activities ranging from marriage and divorce to eating habits and hours of business were regulated by churches and religious doctrines.

In the course of the eighteenth century, this religious and theological world-view underwent a fundamental transformation among the European upper and comfortable classes. Economically secure and increasingly well educated, these privileged groups of preindustrial Europe often came to see the world primarily in secular and scientific terms. And while few individuals abandoned religious beliefs altogether, the role of churches and religious thinking in earthly affairs and in the pursuit of knowledge was substantially reduced. Among many in the aristocracy and solid middle classes, a new critical, scientific, and very modern world-view took shape.

- Why did this momentous change occur?
- How did this new world-view affect the way people thought about society and human relations?
- What impact did this new way of thinking have on political developments and monarchical absolutism?

This chapter will focus on these questions.

 THE SCIENTIFIC REVOLUTION

The foremost cause of the change in world-view was the scientific revolution. Modern science—precise knowledge of the physical world based on the union of experimental observations with sophisticated mathematics—crystallized in the seventeenth century. Whereas science had been secondary and subordinate in medieval intellectual life, it became independent and even primary for many educated people in the eighteenth century.

To be sure, other civilizations developed early forms of scientific inquiry. For example, the West did not have a monopoly on the study of astronomy, which played a key role in scientific development, as we shall see. Many other cultures collected data on the heavens. The Maya of Central America constructed exceptionally accurate calendars based on astronomical observations and maintained a view of the universe not substantially different from that of Ptolemy. Ulugh Beg (r. 1447–1449), grandson of the famous Tamerlane, was a Central Asian astronomer-king who ordered the creation of the Samarkand Tables, the most accurate compilation of astronomical data ever made, based on the evidence collected at his huge observatory. Yet although other cultures conducted extensive observations of the heavens, it was only in the West that such observations became part of a systematic approach to the study of the physical universe, the scientific method.

The emergence of modern science was a development of tremendous long-term significance. A noted historian has even said that the scientific revolution of the late sixteenth and seventeenth centuries "outshines everything since the rise of Christianity" and was "the real origin both of the modern world and the modern mentality."[1]

This statement is an exaggeration, but not much of one. Of all the great civilizations, only that of the West developed modern science. Moreover, it was with the scientific revolution that Western society began to acquire its most distinctive traits. Let us examine the milestones on this fateful march toward modern science first and then search for the nonscientific influences along the route.

Scientific Thought in 1500

Since developments in astronomy and physics were at the heart of the scientific revolution, one must begin with the traditional European conception of the universe and movement within it. In the early 1500s traditional European ideas about the universe were still based primarily on the ideas of Aristotle, the great Greek philosopher of the fourth century B.C. These ideas had been recovered gradually during the Middle Ages and then brought into harmony with Christian doctrines by medieval theologians. According to this revised Aristotelian view, a motionless earth was fixed at the center of the universe. Around it moved ten separate transparent crystal spheres. In the first eight spheres were embedded, in turn, the moon, the sun, the five known planets, and the fixed stars. Then followed two spheres that theologians added during the Middle Ages to account for slight changes in the positions of the stars over the centuries. Beyond the tenth sphere was Heaven, with the throne of God and the souls of the saved. Angels kept these perfect spheres moving in perfect circles.

Aristotle's views also dominated thinking about physics and motion on earth—the sublunar world. The sublunar world was made up of four imperfect, changeable elements. The "light" elements (air and fire) naturally moved upward; the "heavy" elements (water and earth) naturally moved downward. These natural directions of motion did not always prevail, however, for elements were often mixed together and could be affected by an outside force such as a human being. Aristotle and his followers also believed that a uniform force moved an object at a constant speed and that the object would stop as soon as that force was removed.

Aristotle's science as interpreted by Christian theologians fit neatly with Christian doctrines. It established a home for God and a place for Christian souls. It put human beings at the center of the universe and made them the critical link in a "great chain of being" that stretched from the throne of God to the most lowly insect on earth. Thus science was primarily a branch of theology, and it reinforced religious thought.

The Copernican Hypothesis

The desire to explain and thereby glorify God's handiwork led to the first great departure from the medieval system. This departure was the work of the Polish clergyman and astronomer Nicolaus Copernicus (1473–1543). As a young man Copernicus studied church law and astronomy in various European universities. He saw how professional astronomers still depended for their most accurate calculations on the work of Ptolemy, the last great ancient astronomer, who had lived in Alexandria in the second century A.D. Ptolemy's achievement had been to work out complicated rules to help stargazers and astrologers to track the planets with greater precision. Many people then (and now) believed that the changing relationships between planets and stars influence and even determine the future.

The young Copernicus was uninterested in astrology and felt that Ptolemy's cumbersome and occasionally

The Geometry Room at Cracow The young Copernicus sat in this classroom at the University of Cracow, where he first studied astronomy and mathematics and began to ponder the universe. Diagrams illustrating principles of Euclidean geometry were permanently painted on the walls. *(Erich Lessing/Art Resource, NY)*

inaccurate rules detracted from the majesty of a perfect Creator. He preferred an old Greek idea being discussed in Renaissance Italy—the idea that the sun, rather than the earth, was at the center of the universe. Working on his hypothesis from 1506 to 1530, Copernicus indeed theorized that the stars and planets, including the earth, revolve around a fixed sun. Yet Copernicus was a cautious man. Fearing the ridicule of other astronomers, he did not publish his *On the Revolutions of the Heavenly Spheres* until 1543, the year of his death.

Copernicus's theory had enormous scientific and religious implications, many of which the conservative Copernicus did not anticipate. Perhaps most significant from a religious standpoint was that by characterizing the earth as just another planet in an immense universe, Copernicus destroyed the basic idea of Aristotelian physics—the idea that the earthly world was quite different from the heavenly one. Where were Heaven and the throne of God?

The Copernican theory quickly brought sharp attacks from religious leaders, especially Protestants. Hearing of Copernicus's work even before it was published, Martin Luther spoke of him as the "new astrologer who wants to prove that the earth moves and goes round. . . . The fool wants to turn the whole art of astronomy upside down." Luther noted that "as the Holy Scripture tells us, so did Joshua bid the sun stand still and not the earth."[2] Catholic reaction was milder at first, but in 1616 the church officially declared the Copernican theory false.

Astronomical phenomena also cast doubts on traditional astronomical ideas. In 1572 a new star appeared and shone very brightly for almost two years. The new star, which was actually a distant exploding star, made an enormous impression on people. It seemed to contradict the idea that the heavenly spheres were unchanging and therefore perfect. In 1577 a new comet suddenly moved through the sky, cutting a straight path across the supposedly impenetrable crystal spheres. It was time, as a typical scientific writer put it, for "the radical renovation of astronomy."[3]

From Brahe to Galileo

One astronomer who agreed was Tycho Brahe (1546–1601) of Denmark. He established himself as Europe's leading astronomer with his detailed observations of the new star of 1572. For twenty years thereafter he meticulously observed the stars and planets with the naked eye. An imposing man who had lost a piece of his nose in a duel and replaced it with a special bridge of gold and silver alloy, Brahe's great contribution was his mass of data. His limited understanding of mathematics, however, prevented him from making much sense out of his data. That was left to his brilliant young assistant, the German Johannes Kepler (1571–1630).

Working and reworking Brahe's mountain of observations in a staggering sustained effort, Kepler formulated three famous laws of planetary motion. First, building on Copernican theory, he demonstrated in 1609 that the orbits of the planets around the sun are elliptical rather than circular. Second, he demonstrated that the planets do not move at a uniform speed in their orbits. Third, in 1619 he showed that the time a planet takes to make its complete orbit is precisely related to its distance from the sun. Kepler's contribution was monumental. Whereas Copernicus had speculated, Kepler proved mathematically the precise relations of a sun-centered (solar) system. His work demolished the old system of Aristotle and Ptolemy, and in his third law he came close to formulating the idea of universal gravitation.

While Kepler was unraveling planetary motion, a young Florentine named Galileo Galilei (1564–1642) was challenging all the old ideas about motion. Like so many early scientists, Galileo was a poor nobleman first marked for a religious career. However, he soon became fascinated by mathematics. A brilliant student, Galileo became a professor of mathematics in 1589 at age twenty-five. He proceeded to examine motion and mechanics in a new way. Indeed, his great achievement was the elaboration and consolidation of the modern experimental method: rather than speculate about what might or should happen, Galileo conducted controlled experiments to find out what actually *did* happen.

In his famous acceleration experiment, by rolling brass balls down an inclined plane, he showed that a uniform force—in this case, gravity—produces a uniform acceleration. With this and other experiments, Galileo went on to formulate the law of inertia: rather than rest being the natural state of objects, an object continues in motion forever unless stopped by some external force. Aristotelian physics was in a shambles.

On hearing details about the invention of the telescope in Holland, Galileo made one for himself and trained it on the heavens. He quickly discovered the first four moons of Jupiter, providing new evidence for the Copernican theory, in which Galileo already believed. Galileo then pointed his telescope at the moon. He wrote in 1610 in *Siderus Nuncius:*

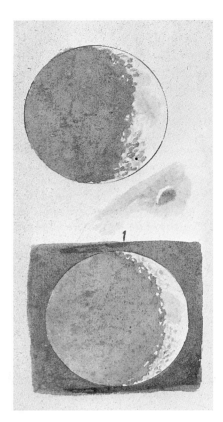 

Galileo's Paintings of the Moon When Galileo published the results of his telescopic observations of the moon, he added these paintings to illustrate the marvels he had seen. Galileo made two telescopes, which are shown here. The larger one magnifies fourteen times, the smaller twenty times. *(Biblioteca Nazionale Centrale, Florence; Museum of Science, Florence/Scala/Art Resource, NY)*

I feel sure that the moon is not perfectly smooth, free from inequalities, and exactly spherical, as a large school of philosophers considers with regard to the moon and the other heavenly bodies. On the contrary, it is full of inequalities, uneven, full of hollows and protuberances, just like the surface of the earth itself.... The next object which I have observed is the essence or substance of the Milky Way. By the aid of a telescope anyone may behold this in a manner which so distinctly appeals to the senses that all the disputes which have tormented philosophers through so many ages are exploded by the irrefutable evidence of our eyes.... For the galaxy is nothing else but a mass of innumerable stars planted together in clusters.[4]

Reading these famous lines, one feels a crucial corner in Western civilization being turned. The traditional religious and theological world-view, which rested on identifying and accepting the proper established authority, was beginning to give way in certain fields to a critical, scientific method. This new method of learning and investigating was the greatest accomplishment of the entire scientific revolution, for it proved capable of great extension. A historian investigating documents of the past, for example, is not so different from a Galileo studying stars and rolling balls.

Galileo's work eventually aroused the ire of some theologians. After the publication in Italian of his widely read *Dialogue on the Two Chief Systems of the World* in 1632, which openly lampooned the traditional views of Aristotle and Ptolemy and defended those of Copernicus, Galileo was tried for heresy by the papal Inquisition. Imprisoned and threatened with torture, the aging Galileo recanted, "renouncing and cursing" his Copernican errors. Galileo's trial later became for some writers the perfect symbol of the inherent conflict between religious belief and scientific knowledge.

Newton's Synthesis

The accomplishments of Kepler, Galileo, and other scientists had taken effect by about 1640. The old astronomy and physics were in ruins, and several fundamental breakthroughs had been made. The fusion of the new findings in a new synthesis, a single explanatory system that would comprehend motion both on earth and in the skies, was the work of Isaac Newton (1642–1727).

Newton was born into lower English gentry and attended Cambridge University. Fascinated by alchemy, he sought the elixir of life and a way to change base metals into gold and silver. Newton was also intensely religious. He had a highly suspicious nature, and in 1693 suffered a nervous breakdown from which he later recovered. He was far from being the perfect rationalist so endlessly eulogized by writers in the eighteenth and nineteenth centuries.

Of his intellectual genius and incredible powers of concentration there can be no doubt, however. Arriving at some of his most basic ideas about physics in 1666 at age twenty-four, but unable to prove these theories mathematically, he attained a professorship and studied optics for many years. In 1684 Newton returned to physics for eighteen extraordinarily intensive months. Seldom leaving his room, he neglected even the meals sent up, his mind fastened like a vise on the laws of the universe. He opened the third book of his immortal *Principia,* published in Latin in 1687, with these lines: "In the preceding books I have laid down the principles . . . [that] are the laws of certain motions, and powers or forces. . . . It remains that from the same principles I now demonstrate the frame of the System of the World."

Newton made good his grandiose claim. He integrated the astronomy of Copernicus, as corrected by Kepler's laws, with the physics of Galileo and his predecessors. Newton did this by means of a set of mathematical laws that explain motion and mechanics. These laws of dynamics are complex, and it took scientists and engineers two hundred years to work out all their implications. The key feature of the Newtonian synthesis was the law of universal gravitation. According to this law, every body in the universe attracts every other body in the universe in a precise mathematical relationship, based on mass and distance. The whole universe—from Kepler's elliptical orbits to Galileo's rolling balls—was unified in one majestic system.

Isaac Newton This portrait suggests the depth and complexity of the great genius. Is the powerful mind behind those piercing eyes thinking of science or of religion, or perhaps of both? *(Scala/Art Resource, NY)*

Causes of the Scientific Revolution

With a charming combination of modesty and self-congratulation, Newton once wrote, "If I have seen further [than others], it is by standing on the shoulders of Giants."[5] Surely the path from Copernicus to Newton confirms the "internal" view of the scientific revolution as the product of towering individual genius. Yet there were certainly broader causes as well.

First, the long-term contribution of medieval intellectual life and medieval universities to the scientific revolution was considerable. By the thirteenth century permanent universities with professors and large student bodies had been established in western Europe to train the lawyers, doctors, and church leaders that society required. By 1300 philosophy had taken its place alongside law, medicine, and theology. Medieval philosophers developed a limited but real independence from theologians and a sense of free inquiry. They

The Observatory at Nuremberg   The quest for scientific knowledge in the seventeenth century was already an expensive undertaking that required teamwork and government support, as this encyclopedic illustration suggests. Nuremberg was a historic center of commerce and culture in southern Germany, and its observatory played a pioneering role in early astronomical advance. *(Kunstsammlungen der Veste Coburg)*

nobly pursued a body of knowledge and tried to arrange it meaningfully by means of abstract theories.

Within this framework science was able to emerge as a minor but distinct branch of philosophy. In the fourteenth and fifteenth centuries leading universities established new professorships of mathematics, astronomy, and physics (natural philosophy) within their faculties of philosophy. Although the prestige of the new fields was low among both professors and students, rational, critical thinking was applied to scientific problems by a permanent community of scholars. And an outlet existed for the talents of a Galileo or a Newton: all the great pathfinders either studied or taught at universities.

Second, the Renaissance also stimulated scientific progress. The recovery of the finest works of Greek mathematics—a byproduct of Renaissance humanism's ceaseless search for the knowledge of antiquity—greatly improved European mathematics well into the early seventeenth century. In the Renaissance pattern of patronage, especially in Italy, various rulers and wealthy business people supported scientific investigations, as the Medicis of Florence did those of Galileo.

The navigational problems of long sea voyages in the age of overseas expansion were a third factor in the scientific revolution. As early as 1484 the king of Portugal appointed a commission of mathematicians to perfect tables to help seamen find their latitude. This resulted in the first European navigation manual. The problem of fixing longitude was much more difficult, but a union of leading merchants and top scientists, who were sponsored by the English government through the Royal Navy, was able to solve it. This collaborative effort led to the establishment in 1662 of the Royal Society of London, which published scientific papers and sponsored scientific meetings.

Navigational problems were also critical in the development of many new scientific instruments, such as the telescope, barometer, thermometer, pendulum clock, microscope, and air pump. Better instruments, which permitted more accurate observations, were part of a fourth factor in the scientific revolution, the development of better ways of obtaining knowledge about the world. Two important thinkers, Francis Bacon (1561–1626) and René Descartes (1596–1650), represented key aspects of this improvement in scientific methodology.

The English politician, writer, and courtier Francis Bacon was the greatest early propagandist for the new experimental method. He argued that new knowledge had to be pursued through empirical, experimental research. A researcher who wants to learn more about rocks should not speculate but collect a multitude of specimens and compare and analyze them, he said.

Descartes in Sweden   Queen Christina of Sweden encouraged art and science, and she invited many foreign artists and scholars to visit her court. She speaks here with French mathematician and philosopher René Descartes in 1649. The daughter of Protestant hero Gustavus Adolphus, Christina rejected marriage, abdicated in 1654, converted to Catholicism, and died in Rome. *(Versailles/Bulloz)*

General principles will then emerge. Bacon formalized Brahe's and Galileo's empirical method into the general theory of inductive reasoning known as empiricism. He claimed that the empirical method would produce highly practical, useful knowledge, giving a new and effective justification for the pursuit of science.

French philosopher René Descartes began as a mathematician and remained more systematic and mathematical than Bacon. Descartes decided it was necessary to doubt everything that could reasonably be doubted and then, as in geometry, use deductive reasoning from self-evident principles to ascertain scientific laws. Bacon's inductive experimentalism and Descartes's deductive, mathematical rationalism are combined in the

modern scientific method, which began to crystallize in the late seventeenth century and which relies on both these intellectual approaches.

Finally, there is the question of the role of religion in the development of science. Just as some historians have argued that Protestantism led to the rise of capitalism, others have concluded that Protestantism, by supposedly making scientific inquiry a question of individual conscience and not of religious doctrine, was a fundamental factor in the rise of modern science. However, all religious authorities in the West—Catholic, Protestant, and Jewish—opposed the Copernican system to a greater or lesser extent until about 1630, by which time the scientific revolution was definitely in progress. The Catholic church was initially less hostile than Protestant and Jewish religious leaders, and Italian scientists played a crucial role in scientific progress right up to the trial of Galileo in 1633. Thereafter, the Counter-Reformation church became more hostile to science in Italy (but not in Catholic France). At the same time, some Protestant countries became quite proscience, especially if the country lacked a strong religious authority capable of imposing religious orthodoxy on scientific questions, as did Protestant England after 1630. English religious conflicts became so intense that the authorities could not impose religious unity on anything, including science. Neutral and useful, science became an accepted part of life and developed rapidly in England after about 1640.

Some Consequences of the Scientific Revolution

The rise of modern science had many consequences, some of which are still unfolding. First, it went hand in hand with the rise of a new and expanding social group—the international scientific community. Members of this community were linked together by common interests and shared values as well as by journals and the learned scientific societies founded in many countries in the later seventeenth and eighteenth centuries. Expansion of knowledge was the primary goal of this community, and scientists' material and psychological rewards depended on their success in this endeavor. Thus science became quite competitive, and even more scientific advance was inevitable.

Second, the revolutionary modern scientific method, in addition to being both theoretical and experimental, was highly critical, and it differed profoundly from the old way of getting knowledge about nature. It refused to base its conclusions on tradition and established sources, on ancient authorities and sacred texts.

The scientific revolution had few consequences for economic life and the living standards of the masses until the late eighteenth century at the very earliest. True, improvements in the techniques of navigation facilitated overseas trade and helped enrich leading merchants, but science had relatively few practical economic applications. The close link between theoretical, or pure, science and applied technology, which we take for granted today, simply did not exist before the nineteenth century. Thus the scientific revolution of the seventeenth century was first and foremost an intellectual revolution. For more than a hundred years its greatest impact was on how people thought and believed.

 # THE ENLIGHTENMENT

The scientific revolution was the single most important factor in the creation of the new world-view of the eighteenth-century Enlightenment. This world-view, which played a large role in shaping the modern mind, grew out of a rich mix of ideas. These ideas were diverse and often conflicting, for the talented (and not-so-talented) writers who espoused them competed vigorously for the attention of a growing public of well-educated but fickle readers, who remained a small minority of the population. Despite this diversity, three central concepts stand at the core of Enlightenment thinking.

The most important and original idea of the Enlightenment was that the methods of natural science could and should be used to examine and understand all aspects of life. This was what intellectuals meant by *reason,* a favorite word of Enlightenment thinkers. Nothing was to be accepted on faith. Everything was to be submitted to the rational, critical, scientific way of thinking. This approach often brought the Enlightenment into a head-on conflict with established churches, which rested their beliefs on the special authority of the Bible and Christian theology. A second important Enlightenment concept was that the scientific method was capable of discovering the laws of human society as well as those of nature. Thus was social science born. Its birth led to the third key idea, that of progress. Armed with the proper method of discovering the laws of human existence, Enlightenment thinkers believed it was at least possible for human beings to create better societies and better people. Their belief was strengthened by some modest improvements in economic and social life during the eighteenth century.

The Enlightenment was therefore thoroughly secular. It revived and expanded the Renaissance concentration on worldly explanations. In the course of the eighteenth century the Enlightenment had a profound impact on the thought and culture of the urban middle classes and the aristocracy. It did not, however, have much appeal for the urban poor and the peasants, who were preoccupied with the struggle for survival and who often resented the Enlightenment attack on traditional popular beliefs (see Chapter 19).

The Emergence of the Enlightenment

Loosely united by certain key ideas, the European Enlightenment was a broad intellectual and cultural move-

Popularizing Science The frontispiece illustration of Fontenelle's *Conversations on the Plurality of Worlds* invites the reader to share the pleasures of astronomy with an elegant lady and an entertaining teacher. The drawing shows the planets revolving around the sun. *(By permission of the Syndics of Cambridge University Library)*

ment that gained strength gradually and did not reach its maturity until about 1750. Yet it was the generation that came of age between the publication of Newton's *Principia* in 1687 and the death of Louis XIV in 1715 that tied the crucial knot between the scientific revolution and a new outlook on life. Talented writers of that generation popularized hard-to-understand scientific achievements for the educated elite.

The most famous and influential popularizer was a versatile French man of letters, Bernard de Fontenelle (1657–1757). He set out to make science witty and entertaining for a broad nonscientific audience—as easy to read as a novel. This was a tall order, but Fontenelle

largely succeeded. His most famous work, *Conversations on the Plurality of Worlds* (1686), begins with two elegant figures walking in the gathering shadows of a large park. One is a woman, a sophisticated aristocrat, and the other is her friend, perhaps even her lover. They gaze at the stars, and their talk turns to a passionate discussion of . . . astronomy! He confides that "each star may well be a different world," then gently stresses how error is giving way to truth. At one point he explains:

There came on the scene . . . one Copernicus, who made short work of all those various circles, all those solid skies, which the ancients had pictured to themselves. . . . Fired with the noble zeal of a true astronomer, he took the earth and spun it very far away from the center of the universe, where it had been installed, and in that center he put the sun, which had a far better title to the honor.[6]

Rather than despair at this dismissal of traditional understanding, Fontenelle's lady rejoices in the knowledge that the human mind is capable of making great progress. The concept of progress was a late-seventeenth-century creation. Unlike their medieval and Renaissance predecessors, Fontenelle and like-minded writers had come to believe that progress was very possible.

Fontenelle and other writers of his generation were instrumental in bringing science into conflict with religion. Many seventeenth-century scientists, both Catholic and Protestant, believed that their work exalted God. Fontenelle, in contrast, was skeptical about absolute truth and cynical about the claims of organized religion. His antireligious ideas, drawn from the scientific revolution, reflected a crisis in European thought that had its roots in several intellectual uncertainties. The nature of religious truth was one such uncertainty, highlighted by the destructive wars of religion fought in early-seventeenth-century Europe. Both Catholics and Protestants had believed that religious truth was absolute and that a strong state required unity of religious faith. Yet the disastrous results of the many attempts to impose such religious unity led some to ask if it was really necessary and others to doubt that religious truth could ever be known with absolute certainty.

The most famous of these skeptics was Pierre Bayle (1647–1706), a French Huguenot refugee who despised Louis XIV. Bayle concluded that nothing can ever be known beyond all doubt and that in religion, as in philosophy, humanity's best hope is open-minded toleration. Bayle's skeptical views were very influential.

The rapidly growing travel literature on non-European lands and cultures was another cause of uncertainty. Europeans were learning that the peoples of China, India, Africa, and the Americas all had their own very different beliefs and customs. Europeans shaved their faces and let their hair grow. Turks shaved their heads and let their beards grow. In Europe a man bowed before a woman to show respect. In Siam a man turned his back on a woman when he met her because it was disrespectful to look directly at her. Countless similar examples discussed in the travel accounts helped change the perspective of educated Europeans. They began to look at truth and morality in relative, rather than absolute, terms. If anything was possible, who could say what was right or wrong?

A third cause and manifestation of European intellectual turmoil was John Locke's epoch-making *Essay Concerning Human Understanding.* Published in 1690—the same year Locke published his *Second Treatise of Civil Government* (see page 553)—Locke's essay brilliantly set forth a new theory about how human beings learn and form their ideas. In doing so, he rejected the prevailing view of Descartes, who had held that all people are born with certain basic ideas and ways of thinking. Locke insisted that all ideas are derived from experience. The human mind at birth is like a blank tablet *(tabula rasa)* on which the environment writes the individual's understanding and beliefs. Human development is therefore determined by education and social institutions, for good or for evil. Locke's *Essay* was, along with Newton's *Principia,* one of the dominant intellectual inspirations of the Enlightenment.

The Philosophes and the Public

By the time Louis XIV died in 1715, many of the ideas that would soon coalesce into the new world-view had been assembled. Yet Christian Europe was still strongly attached to its traditional beliefs, as witnessed by the powerful revival of religious orthodoxy in the first half of the eighteenth century (see Chapter 19). By the outbreak of the American Revolution in 1775, however, a large portion of western Europe's educated elite had embraced many of the new ideas. This acceptance was the work of one of history's most influential groups of intellectuals, the *philosophes.* It was the philosophes who proudly and effectively proclaimed that they, at long last, were bringing the light of knowledge to their ignorant fellow creatures in an Age of Enlightenment.

Philosophe is the French word for "philosopher," and it was in France that the Enlightenment reached its highest development. The French philosophes were indeed philosophers, asking fundamental philosophical questions about the meaning of life, God, human nature, good and evil, and cause and effect. Not content with abstract arguments or ivory-tower speculations, they were determined to reach and influence all the economic and social elites, whom they perceived as the educated or enlightened public, or simply the "public."

As a wealth of recent scholarship has shown, this public was quite different from the great majority of the population, which was known as the common people, or simply the "people." French philosophe Jean le Rond d'Alembert (1717–1783) characteristically made a sharp distinction between "the truly enlightened public" and "the blind and noisy multitude."[7] The philosophes believed that the great majority of the common people were doomed to superstition and confusion because they lacked the money and leisure to look beyond their bitter struggle with grinding poverty (see Chapter 19).

The great philosophes and their imitators were not free to write as they wished, for it was illegal in France to criticize openly either church or state. Their most radical works had to circulate in manuscript form. Knowing that direct attacks would probably be banned or burned, the philosophes wrote novels and plays, histories and philosophies, dictionaries and encyclopedias, all filled with satire and double meanings to spread their message to the public.

One of the greatest philosophes, the baron de Montesquieu (1689–1755), brilliantly pioneered this approach in *The Persian Letters,* an extremely influential social satire published in 1721. Montesquieu's work consisted of amusing letters supposedly written by Persian travelers, who see European customs in unique ways and thereby cleverly criticize existing practices and beliefs. Having gained fame by using wit as a weapon against cruelty and superstition, Montesquieu settled down on his family estate to study history and politics. Inspired by the example of the physical sciences, he set out to apply the critical method to the problem of government in *The Spirit of Laws* (1748). The result was a complex comparative study of republics, monarchies, and despotisms.

Dismayed by the triumph of royal absolutism under Louis XIV, Montesquieu focused on the conditions that would promote liberty and prevent tyranny. He argued that despotism could be avoided if political power was divided and shared by a variety of classes and legal orders holding unequal rights and privileges. Apprehensive about the uneducated poor, Montesquieu was clearly no democrat, but his theory of separation of powers had a great impact on France's wealthy, well-educated elite. The constitutions of the young United States in 1789 and of France in 1791 were based in large part on this theory.

The most famous and in many ways most representative philosophe was François Marie Arouet, who was known by the pen name Voltaire (1694–1778). In his long career this son of a comfortable middle-class family wrote more than seventy witty volumes, hobnobbed

Madame du Châtelet Fascinated by the new world system of Isaac Newton, Madame du Châtelet helped to spread Newton's ideas in France by translating his *Principia* and by influencing Voltaire, her companion for fifteen years until her death. *(Private Collection/Bulloz)*

with kings and queens, and died a millionaire because of shrewd business speculations. His early career, however, was turbulent. In 1717 Voltaire was imprisoned for eleven months in the Bastille in Paris for insulting the regent of France. In 1726 a barb from his sharp tongue led a great French nobleman to have him beaten and arrested. This experience made a deep impression on Voltaire. All his life he struggled against legal injustice and unequal treatment before the law. Released from prison after promising to leave the country, Voltaire lived in England for three years and came to share Montesquieu's enthusiasm for English institutions.

Returning to France and soon threatened again with prison in Paris, Voltaire had the great fortune of meeting Gabrielle-Emilie Le Tonnelier de Breteuil, marquise du Châtelet (1706–1749), an intellectually gifted woman from the high aristocracy with a passion for science. Inviting Voltaire to live in her country house at Cirey in Lorraine and becoming his long-time companion (under the eyes of her tolerant husband), Madame du Châtelet studied physics and mathematics and published scientific articles and translations.

Perhaps the finest representative of a small number of elite French women and their scientific accomplishments during the Enlightenment, Madame du Châtelet suffered nonetheless because of her gender. Excluded on principle from the Royal Academy of Sciences and from stimulating interchange with other scientists because she was a woman, she depended on private tutors for instruction and became uncertain of her ability to make important scientific discoveries. Madame du

Châtelet therefore concentrated on spreading the ideas of others, and her translation of Newton's *Principia* into French for the first time, with an accompanying commentary, was her greatest work. But she had no doubt that women's limited scientific contributions in the past were due to limited and unequal education. If she were a ruler, Madame du Châtelet wrote, "I would reform an abuse which cuts off, so to speak, half the human race. I would make women participate in all the rights of humankind, and above all in those of the intellect."[8]

While living at Cirey, Voltaire wrote various works praising England and popularizing English scientific progress. Typical of the Enlightenment, Voltaire mixed the glorification of science and reason with an appeal

Voltaire   Voltaire leans forward (at left) to exchange ideas with King Frederick the Great (in the center of the picture), as Prussian officials look on. As this painting suggests, Voltaire's radicalism was mainly intellectual and philosophical, not social or political. The men and women of the Enlightenment prized witty, spirited conversation. *(Bildarchiv Preussischer Kulturbesitz)*

for better individuals and institutions. Yet like almost all of the philosophes, Voltaire was a reformer, not a revolutionary, in social and political matters. He began a long correspondence with Frederick the Great, and although the two men later quarreled, Voltaire always admired Frederick as a free thinker and an enlightened monarch.

Unlike Montesquieu, Voltaire pessimistically concluded that the best one could hope for in the way of government was a good monarch since human beings "are very rarely worthy to govern themselves." Nor did he believe in social and economic equality in human affairs, which he considered "absurd and impossible." The only realizable equality, Voltaire thought, was that "by which the citizen only depends on the laws which protect the freedom of the feeble against the ambitions of the strong."[9]

Voltaire's philosophical and religious positions were much more radical. In the tradition of Bayle, Voltaire's voluminous writings challenged, often indirectly, the Catholic church and Christian theology at almost every point. Though he was considered by many devout Christians to be a shallow blasphemer, Voltaire's religious views were influential and quite typical of the mature Enlightenment. Voltaire clearly believed in a God, but his was a distant, deistic God, a great Clockmaker who built an orderly universe and then stepped aside and let it run. Above all, Voltaire and most of the philosophes hated all forms of religious intolerance, which, they believed, often led to fanaticism and savage, inhuman action. Simple piety and human kindness—as embodied in Christ's great commandments to "love God and your neighbor as yourself"—were religion enough, even Christianity enough, as may be seen in Voltaire's famous essay on religion. (See the feature "Listening to the Past: Voltaire on Religion" on pages 588–589.)

The philosophes' greatest and most representative intellectual achievement was, quite fittingly, a group effort—the seventeen-volume *Encyclopedia: The Rational Dictionary of the Sciences, the Arts, and the Crafts,* edited by Denis Diderot (1713–1784) and Jean le Rond d'Alembert. Diderot and d'Alembert set out to teach people how to think critically and objectively about all matters. As Diderot said, he wanted the *Encyclopedia* to "change the general way of thinking."[10]

The editors of the *Encyclopedia* had to conquer innumerable obstacles. After the appearance in 1751 of the first volume, which dealt with such controversial subjects as atheism, the soul, and blind people, the government temporarily banned publication. The work was placed on the Catholic church's index of banned books. Later the timid publisher watered down some of the articles in the last ten volumes without the editors' consent. Yet Diderot's unwavering belief in the importance of his mission held the encyclopedists together for fifteen years, and the enormous work was completed in 1765. Hundreds of thousands of articles by leading scientists, famous writers, skilled workers, and progressive priests treated every aspect of life and knowledge.

Not every article was daring or original, but the overall effect was little short of revolutionary. Science and the industrial arts were exalted, religion and immortality questioned. Intolerance, legal injustice, and out-of-date social institutions were openly criticized. The encyclopedists were convinced that greater knowledge would result in greater human happiness, for knowledge was useful and made possible economic, social, and political progress. The *Encyclopedia,* widely read and extremely influential throughout western Europe, summed up the new world-view of the Enlightenment.

The Later Enlightenment

After about 1770 the harmonious unity of the philosophes and their thought began to break down. As the new world-view became increasingly accepted by the educated public, some thinkers sought originality by exaggerating certain Enlightenment ideas to the exclusion of others. These latter-day philosophes often built rigid, dogmatic systems.

In his *System of Nature* (1770) the wealthy German-born but French-educated Baron Paul d'Holbach (1723–1789) argued that human beings were machines completely determined by outside forces. Free will, God, and immortality of the soul, he claimed, were foolish myths. D'Holbach's atheism and determinism dealt the unity of the Enlightenment movement a severe blow.

Even so, one of d'Holbach's associates whose carefully argued skepticism had a powerful long-term influence was the Scottish philosopher David Hume (1711–1776). Building on Locke's teachings on learning, Hume argued that the human mind is really nothing but a bundle of impressions. These impressions originate only in sense experiences and our habits of joining these experiences together. Reason, therefore, cannot tell us anything about questions that cannot be verified by sense experience (in the form of controlled experiments or mathematics), such as the origin of the universe or the existence of God. Paradoxically, Hume's rationalistic inquiry ended up undermining the Enlightenment's faith in the power of reason.

Another French aristocrat, Marie-Jean Caritat, the marquis de Condorcet (1743–1794), transformed the Enlightenment belief in gradual, hard-won progress into fanciful utopianism. In his *Progress of the Human Mind,* written in 1793 during the French Revolution, Condorcet hypothesized and tracked nine stages of human progress that had already occurred, and he predicted that the tenth would bring perfection.

Other thinkers and writers after about 1770 began to attack the Enlightenment's faith in reason, progress, and moderation. The most famous of these was the Swiss Jean-Jacques Rousseau (1712–1778), a brilliant but difficult thinker, an appealing but neurotic individual. Born into a poor family of watchmakers in Geneva, Rousseau went to Paris and was greatly influenced by Diderot and Voltaire. Always extraordinarily sensitive and suspicious, Rousseau came to believe that his philosophe friends and the women of the Parisian salons were plotting against him. In the mid-1750s he broke with them personally and intellectually, living thereafter as a lonely outsider with his uneducated common-law wife and going in his own highly original direction.

Like other Enlightenment thinkers, Rousseau was passionately committed to individual freedom. Unlike them, however, he attacked rationalism and civilization as destroying, rather than liberating, the individual. Warm, spontaneous feeling had to complement and correct cold intellect, he believed. Moreover, the basic goodness of the individual and the unspoiled child had to be protected from the cruel refinements of civilization. These ideas greatly influenced the early romantic movement (see Chapter 25), which rebelled against the culture of the Enlightenment. Rousseau's ideas also had a powerful impact on the development of child psychology and modern education (see pages 618–619).

Rousseau's contribution to political theory in *The Social Contract* (1762) was equally significant. It was based on two fundamental concepts: the general will and popular sovereignty. According to Rousseau, the general will is sacred and absolute, reflecting the common interests of all the people, who have displaced the monarch as the holder of sovereign power. The general will is not necessarily the will of the majority, however. At times the general will may be the authentic, long-term needs of the people as correctly interpreted by a farseeing minority. Little noticed before the French Revolution, Rousseau's concept of the general will appealed greatly to democrats and nationalists after 1789. The concept has also been used since 1789 by many dictators claiming that they, rather than some momen-

tary majority of the voters, represent the general will and thus the true interests of democracy and the sovereign masses.

Urban Culture and Public Opinion

The writings and press campaigns of the philosophes were part of a profound cultural transformation. The object of impressive ongoing research and scholarly debate in recent years, this transformation had several interrelated aspects.

Of great importance, the European market for books grew dramatically in the eighteenth century. In Germany the number of new titles appearing annually grew substantially and at an accelerating rate, from roughly six hundred new titles in 1700 to about eleven hundred in 1764 and about twenty-six hundred in 1780. France witnessed an explosive growth in book consumption. While a modest increase in literacy among the popular classes had some impact (see Chapter 19), the solid and upper middle classes, the clergy, and the aristocracy accounted for most of the change. The number of books in the hands of these privileged groups increased eight- to tenfold between the 1690s and the 1780s. Moreover, the number of religious and devotional books published legally in Paris declined precipitously. History and law held constant, while the proportion of legally published books treating the arts and sciences surged.

In addition, France's unpredictable but pervasive censorship caused many books to be printed abroad and then smuggled back into the country for "under-the-cloak" sale. Experts believe that perhaps the majority of French books produced between 1750 and 1789 came from publishing companies located outside France. These publishers also smuggled forbidden books in French and other languages into the absolutist states of central, southern, and eastern Europe. The recently discovered catalogues of some of these foreign publishers reveal a massive presence of the famous French philosophes, reaffirming the philosophes' central role in the spread of critical secular attitudes.

The illegal book trade in France also featured an astonishing growth of scandalmongering denunciations of high political figures and frankly pornographic works. These literary forms frequently came together in scathing pornographic accounts of the moral and sexual depravity of the French court, allegedly mired in luxury, perversion, and adultery. A favorite theme was the way that some beautiful but immoral aristocratic women used their sexual charms to gain power over weak rulers and high officials, thereby corrupting the process of government. Spurred by repeated royal directives, the French police did their best to stamp out this underground literature, but new slanders kept cropping up, like the wild tabloid fantasies at checkout counters in today's supermarkets.

Reading more books on many more subjects, the educated public in France and throughout Europe increasingly approached reading in a new way. The result was what some German scholars have called a "reading revolution." The old style of reading in Europe had been centered on sacred texts read aloud slowly with the audience reverently savoring each word. Now reading involved many texts, which were constantly changing and commanded no special respect. Reading became individual, silent, and rapid. The well-educated classes were reading insatiably, skeptically, and carelessly. Subtle but profound, the reading revolution was closely linked to the rise of a critical world-view.

As the reading public developed, it joined forces with the philosophes to call for the autonomy of the printed word. Outside Prussia, the Netherlands, and Great Britain, however, censorship was the rule. And the philosophes and the public resorted to discussion and social interchange in order to circumvent censorship and create an autonomous cultural sphere. Indeed, sparkling conversation in private homes spread Enlightenment ideas to Europe's upper middle class and aristocracy. Paris set the example, and other French and European cities followed. In Paris a number of talented and often rich women presided over regular social gatherings in their elegant drawing rooms, or *salons*. There they

Enlightenment Culture   The culture of the Enlightenment was elegant, intellectual, and international. This painting shows the seven-year-old Austrian child prodigy Wolfgang Amadeus Mozart (1756–1791) playing his own composition at an "English tea" given by the Princess de Conti near Paris. Mozart's phenomenal creative powers lasted a lifetime, and he produced a vast range of symphonies, operas, and chamber music. *(Versailles/Bulloz)*

encouraged the exchange of witty, uncensored observations on literature, science, and philosophy.

Elite women also exercised an unprecedented feminine influence on artistic taste. Soft pastels, ornate interiors, sentimental portraits, and starry-eyed lovers protected by hovering Cupids were all hallmarks of the style they favored. This style, known as the rococo, was popular throughout Europe in the eighteenth century. Some philosophes championed greater rights and expanded education for women, claiming that the position and treatment of women were the best indicators of a society's level of civilization and decency.[11] To be sure, to these male philosophes greater rights for women did not mean equal rights, and the philosophes were not particularly disturbed by the fact that elite women remained legally subordinate to men in economic and political affairs. Elite women lacked many rights, but so did most men.

One of the most famous salons was that of Madame Geoffrin, the unofficial godmother of the *Encyclopedia*. Madame Geoffrin was married by arrangement at fifteen to a rich and boring businessman of forty-eight. After dutifully raising her children, and in spite of her husband's loud protests, she developed a twice-weekly salon that counted Fontenelle and Montesquieu among its regular guests. Inheriting a large fortune after her husband's death, Madame Geoffrin gave the encyclopedists generous financial aid and helped save their enterprise from collapse. Corresponding with the king of Sweden and Catherine the Great of Russia, Madame Geoffrin remained her own woman, a practicing Christian who would not tolerate attacks on the church in her house.

The salons created an independent cultural realm free from religious dogma and political censorship. There educated members of the intellectual, economic, and social elites could debate issues and form their own ideas, their own *public opinion*. In this gracious atmosphere the *public* of philosophes, the French nobility, and the prosperous middle classes intermingled and increasingly influenced one another. Critical thinking about almost any question became fashionable and flourished with hopes for human progress through greater knowledge and enlightened public opinion.

THE ENLIGHTENMENT AND ABSOLUTISM

How did the Enlightenment influence political developments? To this important question there is no easy

answer. On the one hand, the French philosophes and kindred spirits in most European countries were primarily interested in converting people to critical, scientific thinking and were not particularly concerned with politics. On the other hand, such thinking naturally led to political criticism and interest in political reform as both possible and desirable.

Some Enlightenment thinkers, led by the nobleman Montesquieu, argued for curbs on monarchical power in order to promote liberty. Until the American Revolution, however, most Enlightenment thinkers outside England and the Netherlands believed that political change could best come from above—from the ruler—rather than from below, especially in central and eastern Europe. Royal absolutism was a fact of life, and the kings and queens of Europe's leading states clearly had no intention of giving up their great power. Therefore, the philosophes and their sympathizers realistically concluded that a benevolent absolutism offered the best opportunities for improving society. Critical thinking was turning the art of good government into an exact science. It was necessary only to educate and "enlighten" the monarch, who could then make good laws and promote human happiness. Enlightenment thinkers also turned toward rulers because rulers seemed to be listening, treating them with respect, and seeking their advice. Finally, the philosophes distrusted "the people," who they believed were deluded by superstitions and driven by violent passions, little children in need of firm parental guidance.

Encouraged and instructed by the philosophes, many absolutist rulers of the later eighteenth century tried to govern in an "enlightened" manner. Yet the actual programs and accomplishments of these rulers varied greatly. Let us therefore examine the evolution of monarchical absolutism at close range before trying to form any overall judgment about the Enlightenment's effect on it.

Absolutism in Central and Eastern Europe

Enlightenment teachings inspired European rulers in small as well as large states in the second half of the eighteenth century. Yet by far the most influential of the new-style monarchs were in Prussia, Russia, and Austria, and they deserve primary attention.

Frederick the Great of Prussia   Frederick II (r. 1740–1786), commonly known as Frederick the Great, built masterfully on the work of his father, Frederick William I (see pages 540–541). This was somewhat surprising, for like many children with tyrannical parents, he rebelled against his family's wishes in his early years. Rejecting the crude life of the barracks, Frederick embraced culture and literature, even writing poetry and fine prose in French, a language his father detested. After trying unsuccessfully to run away in 1730 at age eighteen, he was virtually imprisoned and compelled to watch his companion in flight beheaded at his father's command. Yet like many other rebellious youths, Frederick eventually reached a reconciliation with his father, and by the time he came to the throne ten years later, Frederick was determined to use the splendid army that his father had left him.

Therefore, when the ruler of Austria, Charles VI, also died in 1740 and his young and charismatic daughter, Maria Theresa, inherited the Habsburg dominions, Frederick suddenly and without warning invaded her rich, mainly German province of Silesia. This action defied solemn Prussian promises to respect the Pragmatic Sanction, which guaranteed Maria Theresa's succession. Maria Theresa's ethnically diverse army was no match for Prussian precision. In 1742, as other greedy powers were falling on her lands in the general European War of the Austrian Succession (1740–1748), she was forced to cede almost all of Silesia to Prussia (see Map 17.3 on page 539). In one stroke Prussia doubled its population to 6 million people. Now Prussia unquestionably towered above all the other German states and stood as a European Great Power.

Though successful in 1742, Frederick had to spend much of his reign fighting against great odds to save Prussia from total destruction. Maria Theresa was determined to regain Silesia, and when the ongoing competition between Britain and France for colonial empire brought renewed conflict in 1756, Austria fashioned an aggressive alliance with France and Russia. During the Seven Years' War (1756–1763) the aim of the alliance was to conquer Prussia and divide up its territory. Frederick led his army brilliantly, striking repeatedly at vastly superior forces invading from all sides. At times he believed all was lost, but he fought on with stoic courage. In the end he was miraculously saved: Peter III came to the Russian throne in 1762 and called off the attack against Frederick, whom he greatly admired.

In the early years of his reign Frederick II had kept his enthusiasm for Enlightenment culture strictly separated from a brutal concept of international politics. He wrote:

Of all States, from the smallest to the biggest, one can safely say that the fundamental rule of government is the principle of extending their territories. . . . The passions of rulers have no other curb but the limits of their power. Those are the fixed laws of European politics to which every politician submits.[12]

But the terrible struggle of the Seven Years' War tempered Frederick and brought him to consider how more humane policies for his subjects might also strengthen the state.

Thus Frederick went beyond a superficial commitment to Enlightenment culture for himself and his circle. He tolerantly allowed his subjects to believe as they wished in religious and philosophical matters. He promoted the advancement of knowledge, improving his country's schools and permitting scholars to publish their findings. Moreover, Frederick tried to improve the lives of his subjects more directly. As he wrote his friend Voltaire, "I must enlighten my people, cultivate their manners and morals, and make them as happy as human beings can be, or as happy as the means at my disposal permit." He energetically promoted the reconstruction of agriculture and industry following the Seven Years' War. Prussia's laws were simplified, torture of prisoners was abolished, and judges decided cases quickly and impartially. Prussian officials became famous for their hard work and honesty. Frederick himself set a good example. He worked hard and lived modestly, claiming that he was "only the first servant of the state." Thus Frederick justified monarchy in terms of practical results and said nothing of the divine right of kings.

Frederick's dedication to high-minded government went only so far, however. He never tried to change Prussia's existing social structure. True, he condemned serfdom in the abstract, but he accepted it in practice. He accepted and extended the privileges of the nobility, which he saw as his primary ally in the defense and extension of his realm. The Junker nobility remained the backbone of the army and the entire Prussian state.

Nor did Frederick listen to thinkers such as Moses Mendelssohn (1729–1786), who urged that Jews be given freedom and civil rights. (See the feature "Individuals in Society: Moses Mendelssohn and the Jewish Enlightenment.") As in other German states, Jews in Prussia remained an oppressed group. Frederick opposed steadfastly any general emancipation for the Jews, as he did for the serfs.

Catherine the Great of Russia   Catherine the Great of Russia (r. 1762–1796) was one of the most remarkable rulers who ever lived, and the French philosophes adored her. Catherine was a German princess from

Individuals in Society

Moses Mendelssohn and the Jewish Enlightenment

Lavater (on the right) attempts to convert Mendelssohn, in a painting by Moritz Oppenheim of an imaginary encounter. *(Collection of the Judah L. Magnes Museum, Berkeley)*

In 1743 a small, humpbacked Jewish boy with a stammer left his poor parents in Dessau in central Germany and walked eighty miles to Berlin, the capital of Frederick the Great's Prussia. According to one story, when the boy reached the Rosenthaler Gate, the only one through which Jews could pass, he told the inquiring watchman that his name was Moses, and that he had come to Berlin "to learn." The watchman laughed and waved him through. "Go Moses, the sea has opened before you."[1] Embracing the Enlightenment and seeking a revitalization of Jewish religious thought, Moses Mendelssohn did point his people in a new and uncharted direction.

Turning in Berlin to a learned rabbi he had previously known in Dessau, the young Mendelssohn studied Jewish law and eked out a living copying Hebrew manuscripts in a beautiful hand. But he was soon fascinated by an intellectual world that had been closed to him in the Dessau ghetto. There, like most Jews throughout central Europe, he had spoken Yiddish—a mixture of German, Polish, and Hebrew. Now, working mainly on his own, he mastered German; learned Latin, Greek, French, and English; and studied mathematics and Enlightenment philosophy. Word of his exceptional abilities spread in Berlin's Jewish community (1,500 of the city's 100,000 inhabitants). He began tutoring the children of a wealthy Jewish silk merchant, and he soon became the merchant's clerk and later his partner. But his great passion remained the life of the mind and the spirit, which he avidly pursued in his off hours.

Gentle and unassuming in his personal life, Mendelssohn was a bold thinker. Reading eagerly in Western philosophy since antiquity, he was, as a pious Jew, soon convinced that Enlightenment teachings need not be opposed to Jewish thought and religion. Indeed, he concluded that reason could complement and strengthen religion, although each would retain its integrity as a separate sphere.[2] Developing his idea in his first great work, "On the Immortality of the Soul" (1767), Mendelssohn used the neutral setting of a philosophical dialogue between Socrates and his followers in ancient Greece to argue that the human soul lived forever. In refusing to bring religion and critical thinking into conflict, he was strongly influenced by contemporary German philosophers who argued similarly on behalf of Christianity. He reflected the way the German Enlightenment generally supported established religion, while the French Enlightenment attacked it. This was the most important difference in Enlightenment thinking between the two countries.

Mendelssohn's treatise on the human soul captivated the educated German public, which marveled that a Jew could have written a philosophical masterpiece. In the excitement, a Christian zealot named Lavater challenged Mendelssohn in a pamphlet to accept Christianity or to demonstrate how the Christian faith was not "reasonable." Replying politely but passionately, the Jewish philosopher affirmed that all his studies had only strengthened him in the faith of his fathers, although he certainly did not seek to convert anyone not born into Judaism. Rather, he urged toleration in religious matters. He spoke up courageously for his fellow Jews and decried the oppression they endured, and he continued to do so for the rest of his life.

Orthodox Jew and German philosophe, Moses Mendelssohn serenely combined two very different worlds. He built a bridge from the ghetto to the dominant culture over which many Jews would pass, including his novelist daughter Dorothea and his famous grandson, the composer Felix Mendelssohn.

Questions for Analysis

1. How did Mendelssohn seek to influence Jewish religious thought in his time?
2. How do Mendelssohn's ideas compare with those of the French Enlightenment?

1. H. Kupferberg, *The Mendelssohns: Three Generations of Genius* (New York: Charles Scribner's Sons, 1972), p. 3.
2. D. Sorkin, *Moses Mendelssohn and the Religious Enlightenment* (Berkeley: University of California Press, 1996), pp. 8ff.

Anhalt-Zerbst, a totally insignificant principality sandwiched between Prussia and Saxony. Her father commanded a regiment of the Prussian army, but her mother was related to the Romanovs of Russia, and that relationship proved to be Catherine's chance.

Peter the Great had abolished the hereditary succession of tsars so that he could name his successor and thus preserve his policies. This move opened a period of palace intrigue and a rapid turnover of rulers until Peter's youngest daughter, Elizabeth, came to the Russian throne in 1741. A shrewd but crude woman—one of her official lovers was an illiterate shepherd boy—Elizabeth named her nephew Peter heir to the throne and chose Catherine to be his wife in 1744. It was a mismatch from the beginning. The fifteen-year-old Catherine was intelligent and attractive; her husband was stupid and ugly, his face badly scarred by smallpox. Ignored by her childish husband, Catherine carefully studied Russian, endlessly read writers such as Bayle and Voltaire, and made friends at court. Soon she knew what she wanted. "I did not care about Peter," she wrote in her *Memoirs,* "but I did care about the crown."[13]

As the old empress Elizabeth approached death, Catherine plotted against her unpopular husband. She selected as her new lover a tall, dashing young officer named Gregory Orlov, who with his four officer brothers commanded considerable support among the soldiers stationed in St. Petersburg. When Peter came to the throne in 1762, his decision to withdraw Russian troops from the coalition against Prussia alienated the army. At the end of six months Catherine and her military conspirators deposed Peter III in a palace revolution. Then the Orlov brothers murdered him. The German princess became empress of Russia.

Catherine had drunk deeply at the Enlightenment well. Never questioning the common assumption that absolute monarchy was the best form of government, she set out to rule in an enlightened manner. She had three main goals. First, she worked hard to bring the sophisticated culture of western Europe to backward Russia. To do so, she imported Western architects, sculptors, musicians, and intellectuals. She bought masterpieces of Western art in wholesale lots and patronized the philosophes. An enthusiastic letter writer, she corresponded extensively with Voltaire and praised him as the "champion of the human race." When the French government banned the *Encyclopedia,* she offered to publish it in St. Petersburg. She sent money to Diderot when he needed it. With these and countless similar actions, Catherine won good press in the West

for herself and for her country. Moreover, this intellectual ruler, who wrote plays and loved good talk, set the tone for the entire Russian nobility. Peter the Great westernized Russian armies, but it was Catherine who westernized the thinking of the Russian nobility.

Catherine's second goal was domestic reform, and she began her reign with sincere and ambitious projects. Better laws were a major concern. She appointed a special legislative commission to prepare a new law code. No new unified code was ever produced, but Catherine did restrict the practice of torture and allowed limited religious toleration. She also tried to improve education and strengthen local government. The philosophes applauded these measures and hoped more would follow.

Such was not the case. In 1773 a Cossack soldier named Emelian Pugachev ignited a violent and bloody revolt of the serfs. Catherine's noble-led army was able to suppress it, but the event was a turning point in the empress's domestic policy. On taking the throne she had condemned serfdom, but the revolt put an end to any thoughts she may have had of reforming society. The peasants were dangerous, and the nobles were her allies. After 1775 she gave the nobles absolute control over their serfs. Ten years later she freed nobles forever from taxes and state service.

Catherine's third goal was territorial expansion, and in this she was extremely successful. Her armies subjugated the last descendants of the Mongols, the Crimean Tartars, and began the conquest of the Caucasus. Her greatest coup by far was the partitioning of Poland, whose fate in the late eighteenth century demonstrated the dangers of failing to build a strong absolutist state. All important decisions continued to require the unanimous agreement of all nobles elected to the Polish Diet, which meant that nothing could ever be done to strengthen the state. When Frederick of Prussia proposed that Prussia, Austria, and Russia each take a gigantic slice of Polish territory, Catherine jumped at the chance. The first partition of Poland took place in 1772. Two more partitions, in 1793 and 1795, gave all three powers more Polish territory, and the ancient republic of Poland simply vanished from the map.

The Austrian Habsburgs   In Austria two talented rulers did manage to introduce major reforms, although traditional power politics was more important than Enlightenment teachings. One was Joseph II (r. 1780–1790), a fascinating individual. For an earlier generation of historians he was the "revolutionary emperor," a tragic hero whose lofty reforms were undone

Pugachev and Catherine This haunting portrait of Pugachev was painted over an existing portrait of Catherine the Great, who seems to be peeking over the rebel leader's head. Painting from life in 1773, the artist may have wanted to represent Pugachev's legitimacy as Catherine's rightful successor. *(From* Pamiatniki Kul'tury, *No. 32, 1961)*

by the landowning nobility he challenged. More recent scholarship has revised this romantic interpretation and stressed how Joseph II continued the state-building work of his mother, the empress Maria Theresa (r. 1740–1780), a remarkable but old-fashioned absolutist.

Emerging from the long War of the Austrian Succession in 1748 with only the serious loss of Silesia, Maria Theresa and her closest ministers were determined to introduce reforms that would make the state stronger and more efficient. Three aspects of these reforms were most important. First, Maria Theresa introduced measures aimed at limiting the papacy's political influence in her realm. Second, a whole series of administrative

reforms strengthened the central bureaucracy, smoothed out some provincial differences, and revamped the tax system, taxing even the lands of nobles without special exemptions. Third, the government sought to improve the lot of the agricultural population, cautiously reducing the power of lords over their hereditary serfs and their partially free peasant tenants.

Coregent with his mother from 1765 onward and a strong supporter of change, Joseph II moved forward rapidly when he came to the throne in 1780. He controlled the established Catholic church even more closely in an attempt to ensure that it produced better citizens. He granted religious toleration and civic rights to Protestants and Jews—a radical innovation that im-

Maria Theresa   In this family portrait by court painter Martin Meytens (1695–1770), Maria Theresa and her husband pose with eleven of their sixteen children at Schönbrunn palace. Joseph, the heir to the throne, stands at the center of the star pattern. Wealthy women often had very large families, in part because they seldom nursed their babies as poor women usually did. *(Kunsthistorisches Museum, Vienna)*

pressed his contemporaries. In even more spectacular peasant reforms, Joseph abolished serfdom in 1781, and in 1789 he decreed that all peasant labor obligations be converted into cash payments. This ill-conceived measure was violently rejected not only by the nobility but also by the peasants it was intended to help, for their primitive barter economy was woefully lacking in money. When a disillusioned Joseph died prematurely at forty-nine, the entire Habsburg Empire was in turmoil. His brother Leopold II (r. 1790–1792) was

forced to cancel Joseph's radical edicts in order to re-establish order. Peasants once again were required to do forced labor for their lords.

Absolutism in France

The Enlightenment's influence on political developments in France was complex. The monarchy maintained its absolutist claims, and some philosophes, such as Voltaire, believed that the king was still the best source of needed reform. At the same time, discontented nobles and learned judges drew on thinkers such as Montesquieu for liberal arguments. They sought with some success to limit the king's power, as France diverged from the absolutist states just considered.

When Louis XIV finally died in 1715, to be succeeded by his five-year-old great-grandson, Louis XV (r. 1715–1774), the Sun King's elaborate system of absolutist rule was challenged in a general reaction. Favored by the duke of Orléans (1674–1723), who governed as regent until 1723, the nobility made a strong comeback.

Most important, in 1715 the duke restored to the high court of Paris—the Parlement—the ancient right to evaluate royal decrees publicly before they were given the force of law. The restoration of this right, which had been suspended under Louis XIV, was a fateful step. The judges of the Parlement of Paris had originally come from the middle class. By the eighteenth century, however, these middle-class judges had risen to become hereditary nobles, which conferred much-desired social status on them. Moreover, the judicial positions became essentially private property, passed down from father to son. By allowing this well-entrenched and increasingly aristocratic group to evaluate the king's decrees, the duke of Orléans sanctioned a counterweight to absolute power.

These implications became clear when the heavy expenses of the War of the Austrian Succession plunged France into financial crisis. In 1748 Louis XV authorized a 5 percent income tax on every individual regardless of social status. The result was a vigorous protest from many sides, led by the Parlement of Paris. The monarchy retreated; the new tax was dropped.

After the disastrously expensive Seven Years' War, the conflict re-emerged. The government tried to maintain emergency taxes after the war ended. The Parlement of Paris protested and even challenged the basis of royal authority, claiming that the king's power had to be limited to protect liberty. Once again the government caved in and withdrew the wartime taxes in 1764. The judicial opposition then asserted that the king could not levy taxes without the consent of the Parlement of Paris acting as the representative of the entire nation.

Indolent and sensual by nature, more interested in his many mistresses than in affairs of state, Louis XV finally roused himself for a determined defense of his absolutist inheritance. "The magistrates," he angrily told the Parlement of Paris in a famous face-to-face confrontation, "are my officers. . . . In my person only does

the sovereign power rest."[14] In 1768 Louis appointed a tough career official named René de Maupeou as chancellor and ordered him to crush the judicial opposition.

Maupeou abolished the Parlement of Paris and exiled its members to the provinces. He created a new and docile Parlement of royal officials, and he began once again to tax the privileged groups. Most philosophes and educated public opinion as a whole sided with the old Parlement, however, and there was widespread criticism of "royal despotism." The illegal stream of scandalmongering, pornographic attacks on the king and his court became a torrent, and some scholars now believe these lurid denunciations ate away at the foundations of royal authority. Yet Maupeou and Louis XV would probably have prevailed—if the king had lived to a very ripe old age.

But Louis XV died in 1774. The new king, Louis XVI (r. 1774–1792), was a shy twenty-year-old with good intentions. Upon taking the throne, he is reported to have said, "What I should like most is to be loved."[15] The eager-to-please monarch decided to yield in the face of such strong criticism from so much of France's educated elite. He dismissed Maupeou and repudiated the strong-willed minister's work. The old Parlement of Paris was reinstated as enlightened public opinion cheered and anticipated moves toward more representative government. But such moves were not forthcoming. Increasingly locked in stalemate, the country was drifting toward renewed financial crisis and political upheaval.

The Overall Influence of the Enlightenment

Having examined the evolution of monarchical absolutism in four leading states, we can begin to look for meaningful generalizations and evaluate the overall influence of Enlightenment thought on politics.

France clearly diverged from its eastern neighbors in its political development in the eighteenth century. The capacity of the French monarch to govern in a truly absolutist manner declined substantially. The political resurgence of the French nobility after 1715 and the growth of judicial opposition drew crucial support from educated public opinion, which increasingly made the liberal critique of unregulated royal authority its own.

The situation in eastern and east-central Europe was different. The liberal critique of absolute monarchy remained an intellectual curiosity, and proponents of reform from above held sway. Moreover, despite differences, the leading eastern European monarchs of the later eighteenth century all claimed that they were acting on the principles of the Enlightenment. The philosophes generally agreed with this assessment and cheered them on. Beginning in the mid-nineteenth century historians developed the idea of a common "enlightened despotism" or "enlightened absolutism," and they canonized Frederick, Catherine, and Joseph as its most outstanding examples. More recent research has raised doubts about this old interpretation and has led to a fundamental re-evaluation.

There is general agreement that these absolutists, especially Catherine and Frederick, did encourage and spread the cultural values of the Enlightenment. They were proud of their intellectual accomplishments and good taste, and they supported knowledge, education, and the arts. Historians also agree that the absolutists believed in change from above and tried to enact needed reforms. Yet the results of these efforts brought only very modest improvements, and the life of the peasantry remained very hard in the eighteenth century. Thus some historians have concluded that these monarchs were not really sincere in their reform efforts. Others disagree, arguing that powerful nobilities blocked the absolutists' genuine commitment to reform. (The old interpretation of Joseph II as the tragic revolutionary emperor forms part of this argument.)

The emerging answer to this controversy is that the later Eastern absolutists were indeed committed to reform but that humanitarian objectives were of quite secondary importance. Above all, the absolutists wanted reforms that would strengthen the state and allow them to compete militarily with their neighbors. Modern scholarship has therefore stressed how Catherine, Frederick, and Joseph were in many ways simply continuing the state building of their predecessors, reorganizing armies and expanding bureaucracies to raise more taxes and troops. The reason for this continuation was simple. The international political struggle was brutal, and the stakes were high. First Austria under Maria Theresa and then Prussia under Frederick the Great had to engage in bitter fighting to escape dismemberment. Decentralized Poland was coldly divided and eventually liquidated.

Yet in this drive for more state power, the later absolutists were also innovators, and the idea of an era of enlightened absolutism retains a certain validity. Sharing the Enlightenment faith in critical thinking and believing that knowledge meant power, these absolutists really were more enlightened than their predecessors because they put state-building reforms in a new, broader perspective. Above all, the later absolutists considered how more humane laws and practices could help their populations become more productive and satisfied and thus able to contribute more substantially to the welfare of the state. It was from this perspective that they introduced many of their most progressive reforms, tolerating religious minorities, simplifying legal codes, and promoting practical education. Nevertheless, reforms had to be grafted onto existing political and social structures. Thus each enlightened absolutist sought greater state power, but each believed a different policy would attain it.

The eastern European absolutists of the later eighteenth century combined old-fashioned state building with the culture and critical thinking of the Enlightenment. In doing so, they succeeded in expanding the role of the state in the life of society. Unlike the successors of Louis XIV, they perfected bureaucratic machines that were to prove surprisingly adaptive and capable of enduring into the twentieth century.

SUMMARY

This chapter has focused on the complex development of a new world-view in Western civilization. This new view was essentially critical and secular, drawing its inspiration from the scientific revolution and crystallizing in the Enlightenment.

Decisive breakthroughs in astronomy and physics in the seventeenth century, which demolished the imposing medieval synthesis of Aristotelian philosophy and Christian theology, had only limited practical consequences despite the expectations of scientific enthusiasts. Yet the impact of new scientific knowledge on intellectual life became great. Interpreting scientific findings and Newtonian laws in an antitraditional, antireligious manner, the French philosophes of the Enlightenment extolled the superiority of rational, critical thinking. This new method, they believed, promised not just increased knowledge but even the discovery of the fundamental laws of human society. Although they reached different conclusions when they turned to social and political realities, they did stimulate absolute monarchs to apply reason to statecraft and the search for useful reforms. Above all, the philosophes succeeded in shaping an emerging public opinion and spreading their radically new world-view. These were momentous accomplishments.

NOTES

1. H. Butterfield, *The Origins of Modern Science* (New York: Macmillan, 1951), p. viii.

2. Quoted in A. G. R. Smith, *Science and Society in the Sixteenth and Seventeenth Centuries* (New York: Harcourt Brace Jovanovich, 1972), p. 97.

3. Quoted in Butterfield, *The Origins of Modern Science,* p. 47.

4. Quoted in Smith, *Science and Society in the Sixteenth and Seventeenth Centuries,* p. 120.

5. Quoted in A. R. Hall, *From Galileo to Newton, 1630–1720* (New York: Harper & Row, 1963), p. 290.

6. Quoted in P. Hazard, *The European Mind, 1680–1715* (Cleveland: Meridian Books, 1963), pp. 304–305.

7. Quoted in R. Chartier, *The Cultural Origins of the French Revolution* (Durham, N.C.: Duke University Press, 1991), p. 27.

8. Quoted in L. Schiebinger, *The Mind Has No Sex? Women in the Origins of Modern Science* (Cambridge, Mass.: Harvard University Press, 1989), p. 64.

9. Quoted in G. L. Mosse et al., eds., *Europe in Review* (Chicago: Rand McNally, 1964), p. 156.

10. Quoted in P. Gay, "The Unity of the Enlightenment," *History* 3 (1960): 25.

11. E. Fox-Genovese, "Women in the Enlightenment," in *Becoming Visible: Women in European History,* 2d ed., ed. R. Bridenthal, C. Koonz, and S. Stuard (Boston: Houghton Mifflin, 1987), esp. pp. 252–259, 263–265.

12. Quoted in L. Krieger, *Kings and Philosophers, 1689–1789* (New York: W. W. Norton, 1970), p. 257.

13. Quoted in G. P. Gooch, *Catherine the Great and Other Studies* (Hamden, Conn.: Archon Books, 1966), p. 15.

14. Quoted in R. R. Palmer, *The Age of Democratic Revolution,* vol. 1 (Princeton, N.J.: Princeton University Press, 1959), pp. 95–96.

15. Quoted in G. Wright, *France in Modern Times,* 4th ed. (New York: W. W. Norton, 1987), p. 34.

SUGGESTED READING

The first three authors cited in the Notes—Butterfield, Smith, and Hall—have written excellent general interpretations of the scientific revolution. These may be compared with an outstanding work by M. Jacob, *The Cultural Meaning of the Scientific Revolution* (1988), which has a useful bibliography. Schiebinger's work, cited in the Notes, provides a brilliant analysis of how the new science gradually excluded women interested in science, a question completely neglected in older studies. A. Debus, *Man and Nature in the Renaissance* (1978), is good on the Copernican revolution, whereas M. Boas, *The Scientific Renaissance, 1450–1630* (1966), is especially insightful about the influence of magic on science. S. Drake, *Galileo* (1980), is a good short biography. T. Kuhn, *The Structure of Scientific Revolutions* (1962), is a challenging, much-discussed attempt to understand major breakthroughs in scientific thought over time. E. Andrade, *Sir Isaac Newton* (1958), is a good brief biography, which may be compared with F. Manuel, *The Religion of Isaac Newton* (1974), and R. Westfall, *Never at Rest: A Biography of Isaac Newton* (1993).

Hazard, listed in the Notes, is a classic study of the formative years of Enlightenment thought, and his *European Thought in the Eighteenth Century* (1954) is also recommended. Important recent works from a cultural perspective include D. Goodman, *The Republic of Letters: A Cultural History of the Enlightenment* (1994), and A. Farge, *Subversive Worlds: Public Opinion in Eighteenth Century France* (1994). P. Gay has written several major studies on the Enlightenment: *Voltaire's Politics* (1959) and *The Party of Humanity* (1971) are two of the best. J. Sklar, *Montesquieu* (1987), is an engaging biography. F. Baumer, *Religion and the Rise of Skepticism* (1969); H. Payne, *The Philosophes and the People* (1976); and H. Chisick, *The Limits of Reform in the Enlightenment: Attitudes Toward the Education of the Lower Classes in Eighteenth-Century France* (1981), are interesting studies of important aspects of Enlightenment thought. D. van Kley, *The Religious Origins of the French Revolution* (1996), is a stimulating interpretation. The changing attitudes of the educated public are imaginatively analyzed by Chartier, cited in the Notes, and in *French Historical Studies* (Fall 1992). R. Danton, *The Literary Underground of the Old Regime* (1982), provides a fascinating glimpse of low-life publishing. On women, see the stimulating study by Fox-Genovese cited in the Notes, as well as E. Goldsmith and D. Goodman, eds., *Going Public: Women and Publishing in Early Modern France* (1995); S. Spencer, ed., *French Women and the Age of Enlightenment* (1984); and K. Rogers, *Feminism in Eighteenth-Century England* (1982). J. Landes, *Women and the Public Sphere in the Age of the French Revolution* (1988), is a fascinating and controversial study of women and politics. Above all, one should read some of the philosophes themselves. Two good anthologies are C. Brinton, ed., *The Portable Age of Reason* (1956), and F. Manuel, ed., *The Enlightenment* (1951). Voltaire's most famous and very amusing novel, *Candide,* is highly recommended, as is S. Gendzier, ed., *Denis Diderot: The Encyclopedia: Selections* (1967).

In addition to the works mentioned in the Suggested Reading for Chapter 17, the monarchies of Europe are carefully analyzed in H. Scott, *Enlightened Absolutism* (1990); C. Tilly, ed., *The Formation of National States in Western Europe* (1975); and J. Gagliardo, *Enlightened Despotism* (1967), all of which have useful bibliographies. M. Anderson, *Historians and Eighteenth-Century Europe* (1979), is a valuable introduction to modern scholarship, and C. Behrens, *Society, Government, and the Enlighten-ment: The Experience of Eighteenth-Century France and Prus-sia* (1985), is a stimulating comparative study. E. Le Roy Ladurie, *The Ancien Régime* (1996), is an excellent synthe-sis by a leading French historian. J. Lynch, *Bourbon Spain, 1700–1808* (1989), and R. Herr, *The Eighteenth-Century Revolution in Spain* (1958), skillfully analyze the impact of Enlightenment thought in Spain. Important works on Austria include C. Macartney, *Maria Theresa and the House of Austria* (1970), and T. Blanning, *Joseph II and Enlight-ened Absolutism* (1970). There are several fine works on Russia. J. Alexander, *Catherine the Great: Life and Legend* (1989), is the best biography of the famous ruler. I. de Madariaga, *Russia in the Age of Catherine the Great* (1981), and P. Dukes, *The Making of Russian Absolutism, 1613–1801* (1982), are strongly recommended. The ambitious

reader should also look at A. N. Radishchev, *A Journey from St. Petersburg to Moscow* (English trans., 1958), a fa-mous 1790 attack on Russian serfdom and an appeal to Catherine the Great to free the serfs, for which Radishchev was exiled to Siberia.

The culture of the time may be approached through A. Cobban, ed., *The Eighteenth Century* (1969), a richly illus-trated work with excellent essays, and C. B. Behrens, *The Ancien Régime* (1967). T. Crow, *Painters and Public Life in Eighteenth-Century Paris* (1985), examines artists and cul-tural politics. C. Rosen, *The Classical Style: Haydn, Mozart, Beethoven* (1972), brilliantly synthesizes music and society, as did Mozart himself in his great opera *The Marriage of Fi-garo,* where the count is the buffoon and his servant the hero.

Voltaire on Religion

Voltaire was the most renowned and probably the most influential of the French philosophes. His biting, satirical novel Candide *(1759) is still widely assigned in college courses, and his witty yet serious* Philosophical Dictionary *remains a source of pleasure and stimulation. The* Dictionary *consists of a series of essays on topics ranging from Adam to Zoroaster, from certainty to circumcision. The following passage is taken from the essay on religion.*

Voltaire began writing the Philosophical Dictionary *in 1752, at the age of fifty-eight, after arriving at the Prussian court in Berlin. Frederick the Great applauded Voltaire's efforts, but Voltaire put the project aside after leaving Berlin, and the first of several revised editions was published anonymously in 1764. It was an immediate, controversial success. Snapped up by an "enlightened" public, it was denounced by religious leaders as a threat to the Christian community and was burned in Geneva and Paris.*

I meditated last night; I was absorbed in the contemplation of nature; I admired the immensity, the course, the harmony of those infinite globes which the vulgar do not know how to admire.

I admired still more the intelligence which directs these vast forces. I said to myself: "One must be blind not to be dazzled by this spectacle; one must be stupid not to recognize its author; one must be mad not to worship the Supreme Being. What tribute of worship should I render Him? Should not this tribute be the same in the whole of space, since it is the same Supreme Power which reigns equally in all space?

"Should not a thinking being who dwells on a star in the Milky Way offer Him the same homage as a thinking being on this little globe of ours? Light is the same for the star Sirius as for us; moral philosophy must also be the same. If a feeling, thinking animal on Sirius is born of a tender father and mother who have been occupied with his happiness, he owes them as much love and care as we owe to our parents. If someone in the Milky Way sees a needy cripple, and if he can aid him and does not do so, then he is guilty toward all the globes.

"Everywhere the heart has the same duties: on the steps of the throne of God, if He has a throne; and in the depths of the abyss, if there is an abyss."

I was deep in these ideas when one of those genii who fill the spaces between the worlds came down to me. I recognized the same aerial creature who had appeared to me on another occasion to teach me that the judgments of God are different from our own, and how a good action is preferable to a controversy.

The genie transported me into a desert all covered with piles of bones. . . . He began with the first pile. "These," he said, "are the twenty-three thousand Jews who danced before a calf, together with the twenty-four thousand who were killed while fornicating with Midianitish women. The number of those massacred for such errors and offences amounts to nearly three hundred thousand.

"In the other piles are the bones of the Christians slaughtered by each other because of metaphysical disputes. They are divided into several heaps of four centuries each. One heap would have mounted right to the sky; they had to be divided."

"What!" I cried, "brothers have treated their brothers like this, and I have the misfortune to be of this brotherhood!"

"Here," said the spirit, "are the twelve million native Americans killed in their own land because they had not been baptized."

"My God! . . . Why assemble here all these abominable monuments to barbarism and fanaticism?"

"To instruct you. . . . Follow me now." [The genie takes Voltaire to the "heroes of humanity, who tried to banish violence and plunder from the world," and tells Voltaire to question them.]

[At last] I saw a man with a gentle, simple face, who seemed to me to be about thirty-five years old. From afar he looked with compassion upon those piles of whitened bones, through which I had been led to reach the sage's dwelling place. I was astonished to find his feet swollen and bleeding, his hands likewise, his side pierced, and his ribs laid bare by the cut of the lash. "Good God!" I said to him, "is it possible for a just man, a sage, to be in this state? I have just seen one who was treated in a very hateful way, but there is no comparison between his torture and yours. Wicked priests and wicked judges poisoned him; is it by priests and judges that you were so cruelly assassinated?"

With great courtesy he answered, "Yes."

"And who were these monsters?"

"They were hypocrites."

"Ah! that says everything; I understand by that one word that they would have condemned you to the cruelest punishment. Had you then proved to them, as Socrates did, that the Moon was not a goddess, and that Mercury was not a god?"

"No, it was not a question of planets. My countrymen did not even know what a planet was; they were all arrant ignoramuses. Their superstitions were quite different from those of the Greeks."

"Then you wanted to teach them a new religion?"

"Not at all; I told them simply: 'Love God with all your heart and your neighbor as yourself, for that is the whole of mankind's duty.' Judge yourself if this precept is not as old as the universe; judge yourself if I brought them a new religion." . . .

"But did you say nothing, do nothing that could serve them as a pretext?"

"To the wicked everything serves as pretext."

"Did you not say once that you were come not to bring peace, but a sword?"

"It was a scribe's error; I told them that I brought peace and not a sword. I never wrote anything; what I said can have been changed without evil intention."

"You did not then contribute in any way by your teaching, either badly reported or badly interpreted, to those frightful piles of bones which I saw on my way to consult with you?"

"I have only looked with horror upon those who have made themselves guilty of all these murders."

. . . [Finally] I asked him to tell me in what true religion consisted.

"Have I not already told you? Love God and your neighbor as yourself."

"Is it necessary for me to take sides either for the Greek Orthodox Church or the Roman Catholic?"

"When I was in the world I never made any difference between the Jew and the Samaritan."

"Well, if that is so, I take you for my only master." Then he made a sign with his head that filled

An impish Voltaire, by the French sculptor Houdon. *(Courtesy of Board of Trustees of the Victoria & Albert Museum)*

me with peace. The vision disappeared, and I was left with a clear conscience.

Questions for Analysis

1. Why did Voltaire believe in a Supreme Being? Does this passage reflect the influence of Isaac Newton's scientific system?

2. Was Voltaire trying to entertain or teach or do both? Was he effective? Why or why not?

3. If Voltaire was trying to convey serious ideas about religion and morality, what were those ideas? What was he attacking?

4. If a person today thought and wrote like Voltaire, would that person be called a defender or a destroyer of Christianity? Why?

Source: F. M. Arouet de Voltaire, *Oeuvres completes,* vol. 8, trans. J. McKay (Paris: Firmin-Didot, 1875), pp. 188–190.

The Changing Life of the People in Europe

Market in Piazza San Carlo, Turin (detail), by Michele Graneri (1736–1778). *(Museo Civico, Turin/Madeline Grimaldi)*

The world of European absolutism and aristocracy, a combination of raw power and elegant refinement, was a world apart from that of common people. Weakness and uncertainty, poverty and pain—these enduring realities weighed heavily on the vast majority. Yet the common people in Western societies were by no means helpless victims of fate, ignorance, and inequality. With courage and intelligence, with hard work and family loyalties, ordinary men and women struggled and survived. There is a dignity in these efforts that is deeply moving.

This, then, is the story of those ordinary lives at a time when the idea of far-reaching scientific and material progress was only the sweet dream of a privileged elite in fashionable salons.

- How did the common people of Europe wring a living out of the land, and how was cottage industry growing to complement these efforts?
- What changes occurred in marriage and the family in the course of the eighteenth century?
- What was life like for children, and how did attitudes toward children evolve?
- What did people eat, and how did changes in diet and medical care affect their lives?
- What were the patterns of popular religion and culture? How did these patterns come into contact—and conflict—with the critical world-view of the educated public and thereby widen the cultural divide between rich and poor in the era of the Enlightenment?

Such questions help us better understand how the peasant masses and urban poor really lived in western Europe before the age of revolution opened at the end of the eighteenth century. These questions will be the focus of this chapter.

AGRICULTURE AND POPULATION

At the end of the seventeenth century at least 80 percent of the people of all western European countries, with the possible exception of Holland, drew their livelihood from agriculture. In eastern Europe the percentage was considerably higher. Men and women lavished their attention on the land, and the land repaid their efforts, yielding the food and most of the raw materials for industry that made life possible. But the land was stingy and capricious. Yields were low even in good years, finding enough to eat was an endless challenge, and disease or starvation was the price of failure. As a result, most peasant communities had learned to keep family size under control. If total population grew even modestly, as it did in the eighteenth century, people had to find new sources of food and income.

Working the Land

The greatest accomplishment of medieval agriculture was the open-field system of village agriculture developed by European peasants. That system divided the land to be cultivated by the peasants into a few large fields that in turn were cut up into long narrow strips. The fields and strips were not enclosed. An individual peasant family—if it was fortunate—held a number of strips scattered throughout the large fields. The land of those who owned but did not till—primarily the nobility, the clergy, and wealthy townsmen—was also in scattered strips. The peasants farmed each large field as a community, plowing, sowing, and harvesting in accordance with tradition and the village leaders.

The ever-present problem was exhaustion of the soil. If a community planted wheat year after year in the same field, the nitrogen in the soil was soon depleted, and crop failure and starvation were certain. Since the supply of manure for fertilizer was limited, the only way for land to recover its life-giving fertility was for a field to lie fallow for a period of time. In the early Middle Ages a year of fallow was alternated with a year of cropping, so that in any given year half of the land stood idle. Eventually, three-year rotations were introduced. This system permitted a year of wheat or rye followed by a year of oats or beans or peas and then a year of fallow. The results of this change were modest, however. In a rich agricultural region like the Po Valley in northern Italy, every bushel of wheat sown yielded on average only five or six bushels of grain at harvest during the seventeenth century. Such yields were no more than those attained in fertile, well-watered areas in the thirteenth century or in ancient Greece. By modern standards output in 1700 was distressingly low. (Today an American or French farmer with similar land can expect roughly fifty bushels of wheat for each bushel of wheat sown.) Only awareness of the tragic consequences of continuous cropping forced undernourished populations to let a third of their land lie idle at any given time.

Traditional rights reinforced the traditional pattern of farming. In addition to rotating the field crops in a uniform way, villages held open meadows in common to provide animals with hay and natural pasture. After the harvest, the people of the village also pastured their animals on the wheat or rye stubble. In many places such pasturing followed a brief period, also established by tradition, for the gleaning of grain. Poor women would go through the fields picking up the few single grains that had fallen to the ground in the course of the harvest providing the slender margin of survival for some people in the winter months.

State and landlord levied heavy taxes and high rents as a matter of course. In so doing, they stripped the peasants of much of their meager earnings. Generally speaking, the peasants of eastern Europe were worst off. As discussed in Chapter 17, they were serfs, bound to their lords in hereditary service. Five or six days of unpaid work per week on the lord's land was not uncommon.

Social conditions were considerably better in western Europe. Peasants were generally free from serfdom. In France and western Germany they owned land and could pass it on to their children. Yet life was hard, and poverty was the great reality for most people. In the Beauvais region of France at the beginning of the eighteenth century, only a tenth of the peasants could live satisfactorily off the fruits of their landholdings. Own-

Millet: The Gleaners   Poor French peasant women search for grains and stalks that the harvesters (in the background) have missed. The open-field system seen here could still be found in parts of Europe in 1857, when this picture was painted. Millet is known for his great paintings expressing social themes. *(Louvre © Photo R.M.N.)*

ing less than half of the land, the peasants had to pay heavy royal taxes, the church's tithe, and dues to the lord, as well as set aside seed for the next season. Left with only half of their crop for their own use, they had to toil for others and seek work far afield in a constant scramble for a meager living.

Technological progress offered a possible way for European peasants to improve their difficult position by producing more. The uncultivated fields were the heart of the matter. If peasants could replace the fallow with crops, they could increase the land under cultivation by 50 percent. The secret was to eliminate the fallow by alternating grain with certain nitrogen-storing crops, such as turnips and potatoes, clovers and grasses, which rejuvenate the soil while still giving produce.

Technological progress, however, did not come easily. To wait for the entire village to agree to a new crop rotation might mean waiting forever. Thus an innovating agriculturalist sought to enclose and consolidate his scattered holdings into a compact, fenced-in field, and he also sought to enclose his share of the natural pasture—known as the common. But because the common rights, like gleaning, were precious to many rural people, only powerful social and political pressures could overcome the traditionalism of rural communities. The old system of open fields held on tenaciously. Indeed, until the end of the eighteenth century the promise of the new system was extensively realized only in the Low Countries and in England. Across the rest of Europe technological progress was limited largely to the introduction of a single new but extremely important crop—the potato (see page 606).

The Balance of Numbers

Until 1700 the total population of Europe grew slowly much of the time and by no means constantly (Figure 19.1). In seventeenth-century Europe births and deaths were in a crude but effective balance. The birthrate—annual births as a proportion of the population—was fairly high but far lower than it would have been if all women had been having as many children as biologically possible. The death rate in normal years was also high, though somewhat lower than the birthrate. As a result, the population grew modestly in normal years at a rate of perhaps 0.5 to 1 percent. Yet even fairly modest population growth of 1 percent per year produces a large increase over a long period—a fourfold increase in 150 years, for example. Such gigantic increases did not occur in agrarian Europe because in certain tragic periods, many more people died than were born; total population fell sharply, even catastrophically.

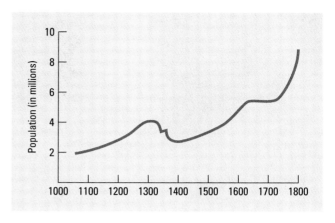

FIGURE 19.1 The Growth of Population in England, 1000–1800 England is a good example of both the uneven increase of European population before 1700 and the third great surge of growth, which began in the eighteenth century. *(Source: E. A. Wrigley,* Population and History. *Copyright © 1969 by McGraw-Hill. Reprinted by permission.)*

The grim reapers of demographic crisis were famine, epidemic disease, and war. Famine, the inevitable result of poor farming methods and periodic crop failures, was particularly murderous because it was accompanied by disease. With a brutal one-two punch, famine stunned and weakened a population, and disease finished it off. Disease, including epidemics of bubonic plague, dysentery, and smallpox, could also ravage independently, even in years of adequate harvests.

As for war, the indirect effects were more harmful than the organized killing. War spread disease. Soldiers and camp followers passed venereal disease throughout the countryside to scar and kill. Armies requisitioned scarce food supplies for their own use and disrupted the agricultural cycle. The Thirty Years' War witnessed all possible combinations of distress. In the German states the number of inhabitants declined by more than *two-thirds* in some large areas and by at least one-third almost everywhere else.

In the eighteenth century the population of Europe began to grow markedly, and similar growth occurred at the same time in most parts of the world. Thus Asian countries, especially China, experienced substantial increases, as did both North and South America. Africa was an exception to this powerful global trend, in part because of the depopulating ravages of the slave trade. Only in the later nineteenth century did Africa's population begin to grow significantly.

In Europe the eighteenth-century increase in numbers affected all areas: western and eastern, northern and southern. Growth was especially dramatic after

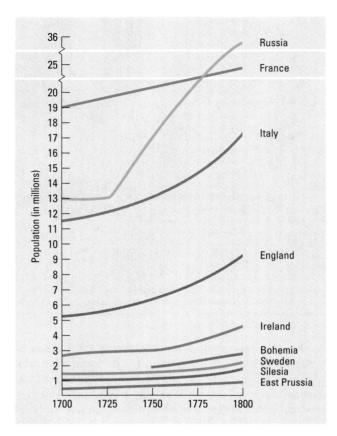

FIGURE 19.2 The Increase of Population in Europe in the Eighteenth Century France's large population continued to support French political and intellectual leadership. Russia emerged as Europe's most populous state because natural increase was complemented by growth from territorial expansion.

about 1750 (see Figure 19.2). Why was this so? In some areas some women did have more babies than before because new opportunities for employment in rural industry allowed them to marry at an earlier age (see page 600). But the basic cause for Europe as a whole was a decline in mortality—fewer deaths.

The bubonic plague mysteriously disappeared. After the Black Death in the fourteenth century plagues had remained a part of the European experience, striking again and again with savage force, particularly in towns. As late as 1720 an epidemic swept southern France, killing one-third, one-half, even three-fourths of those in the larger towns. But the epidemic passed, and that was the last time plague fell on western and central Europe. The final disappearance of plague was due in part to stricter measures of quarantine in plague-prone Mediterranean ports and along the Austrian border

with Turkey. Chance and plain good luck were more important, however.

After 1600, for reasons unknown, a new rat of Asiatic origin—the brown, or wander, rat—began to drive out and eventually eliminate the black rat, whose flea is the principal carrier of the plague bacillus. Although the brown rat also carries the plague bacillus, another kind of flea is its main parasite. That flea carries the plague poorly and, for good measure, has little taste for human blood.

Advances in medical knowledge did not contribute much to reducing the death rate in the eighteenth century (see pages 607–610). However, improvements in the water supply and sewerage promoted somewhat better public health and helped reduce such diseases as typhoid and typhus in some urban areas of western Europe. These improvements and the drainage of many swamps and marshes reduced the large population of flies and mosquitoes that helped spread serious epidemics and common diseases, especially those striking children and young adults.

Human beings also became more successful in their efforts to safeguard the supply of food and protect against famine. The eighteenth century was a time of considerable canal and road building in western Europe. These advances in transportation, which were among the more positive aspects of strong absolutist states, lessened the impact of local crop failure and famine. Emergency supplies could be brought in. The age-old spectacle of localized starvation became less frequent. Wars became less destructive than in the seventeenth century and spread fewer epidemics. New foods, particularly the potato from South America, were introduced. In short, population grew in the eighteenth century primarily because years of abnormal death rates were less catastrophic.

The growth of population in the eighteenth century cannot be interpreted as a sign of human progress, however. Serious population pressures on resources were in existence by 1600 and continued throughout the seventeenth and eighteenth centuries. Only so much land was available, and tradition slowed the adoption of better farming methods. Thus agriculture could not provide enough work for the rapidly growing labor force, and poor people in the countryside had to look for new ways to make a living.

The Growth of Cottage Industry

The growth of population increased the number of rural workers with little or no land, and this in turn contributed to the development of industry in rural areas. To be sure, peasant communities had always made some clothing, processed some food, and constructed some housing for their own use. But in the Middle Ages peasants did not produce manufactured goods on a large scale for sale in a market. Instead, industry was dominated and organized by urban craft guilds and urban merchants, who jealously sought to maintain it as an urban monopoly. By the eighteenth century, however, the pressures of rural poverty and the need for employment in the countryside had proved too great, and a new system, the *putting-out system,* was expanding lustily.

The two main participants in the putting-out system were the merchant-capitalist and the rural worker. The merchant loaned or "put out" raw materials—raw wool, for example—to several cottage workers. Those workers processed the raw material in their own homes, spinning and weaving the wool into cloth in this case, and returned the finished product to the merchant. The merchant then paid the workers by the piece and sold the finished products. There were endless variations on this basic relationship. Sometimes rural workers would buy their own materials and work as independent producers before they delivered finished goods to the merchant. Sometimes several workers toiled together in a workshop to perform a complicated process. The relative importance of earnings from the land and from industry varied greatly for handicraft workers. In all cases, however, the putting-out system was a kind of capitalism. Merchants sold finished goods in distant markets, seeking to make profits and increase their capital.

The putting-out system grew because it offered competitive advantages. Underemployed rural labor was abundant, and poor peasants and landless laborers

The Weaver's Repose This painting by Decker Cornelis Gerritz (1594–1637) captures the pleasure of release from long hours of toil in cottage industry. The loom realistically dominates the cramped living space and the family's modest possessions. *(Musées Royaux des Beaux-Arts, Brussels. Copyright A.C.I.)*

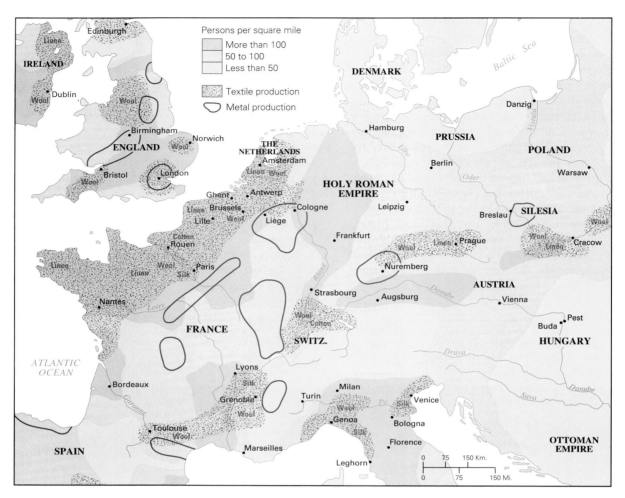

MAP 19.1 Industry and Population in Eighteenth-Century Europe The growth of cottage manufacturing in rural areas helped country people to increase their income and contributed to increases in the population. This putting-out system began in England, and much of the work was in the textile industry. Cottage industry was also strong in the Low Countries—modern-day Belgium and Holland.

would work for low wages. Since production in the countryside did not need to meet rigid guild standards, which maintained quality but discouraged the development of new methods, workers and merchants could change procedures and experiment as they saw fit. Textiles and all manner of everyday articles such as knives, forks, housewares, buttons, and gloves could be produced quite satisfactorily in the countryside.

Rural manufacturing did not spread across Europe at an even rate. It appeared first in England and developed most successfully there, particularly for the spinning and weaving of woolen cloth. Continental countries developed rural industry more slowly. In France at the

time of Louis XIV, Colbert had revived the urban guilds and used them as a means to control the cities and collect taxes (see page 531). But the pressure of rural poverty proved too great. In 1762 the special privileges of urban manufacturing were severely restricted in France, and the already-developing rural industries were given free rein from then on. Thus in France, as in Germany and other areas, the later eighteenth century witnessed a remarkable expansion of rural industry in certain densely populated regions (Map 19.1).

Cottage industry, like peasant agriculture from which it evolved, was based on family enterprise. All the members of the family helped in the work, especially in textiles, the most important cottage industry. Children and aged relatives carded and combed the cotton or wool, women and older daughters spun the thread, and the man of the house wove the cloth. The availability of work for everyone, even the youngest, encouraged cottage workers to marry early and have large families. After the dirt was beaten out of the raw material, for example, it had to be thoroughly cleaned with strong soap in a tub, where tiny feet took the place of the agitator in a washing machine. A famous English textile inventor recalled that "soon after I was able to walk I was employed in the cotton manufacture. . . . My mother tucked up my petticoats about my waist, and put me into the tub to tread upon the cotton at the bottom."[1] Each family member had a task, and family life overlapped with the work experience.

 ## MARRIAGE AND THE FAMILY

The family is the basic unit of social organization. It is within the structure of the family that human beings love, mate, and reproduce themselves. It is primarily the family that teaches each child, imparting values and customs that condition an individual's behavior for a lifetime. The family is also an institution woven into the web of history.

Extended and Nuclear Families

In many traditional Asian and African societies the typical family has often been an extended family. A newly married couple, instead of establishing a home, goes to live with either the bride's or the groom's family. The wife and husband raise their children while living under the same roof with their own brothers and sisters, who may also be married. The extended family is a big three- or four-generation clan. In China at this time, for example, Confucian principles stressed the importance of the family and reverence for one's elders and ancestors. In all but the poorest families (which tended to be nuclear), several generations of patrilineal relatives and their wives lived together. Authority was strictly patriarchal and absolute. In early African societies extended families made up larger social groups such as villages, which were organized into small kingdoms.

Extended families, it is often said, provide security for adults and children in traditional agrarian peasant economies. Everyone has a place within the extended family, from cradle to grave. Sociologists frequently assume that the extended family gives way to the nuclear family with the advent of industrialization and urbanization. In a society characterized by nuclear families, couples establish their own households when they marry, and they raise their children apart from their parents. Since Europe was once agrarian and preindustrial, it was believed that the extended family must also have prevailed in Europe before being destroyed by the Industrial Revolution.

More recently, innovative historians, analyzing previously neglected parish registers of births, deaths, and marriages, have greatly increased knowledge about the details of family life for the great majority of people before the nineteenth century. It seems clear that the extended, three-generation family was a rarity in western and central Europe by 1700. Indeed, the extended family may never have been common in Europe. When young European couples married, they normally established their own households and lived apart from their parents. When a three-generation household came into existence, it usually resulted from a parent moving in with a married child.

Most people did not marry young in the seventeenth and early eighteenth centuries. The average person, who was neither rich nor aristocratic, married surprisingly late, many years after reaching adulthood and many more after beginning to work. In one well-studied, apparently typical English village, both men and women married for the first time at an average age of twenty-seven or older in the seventeenth and eighteenth centuries. A similar pattern existed in early-eighteenth-century France. Moreover, a substantial portion of men and women never married at all.

The custom of late marriage in combination with a nuclear-family household was a distinctive characteristic of European society. It seems likely that the aggressiveness and creativity that have characterized European society have been due in part to a pattern of marriage and family that fosters and requires self-reliance and independence.

Why was marriage delayed? The main reason was that couples normally could not marry until they could support themselves economically. The land was still the main source of income. The peasant son often needed to wait until his father's death to inherit the family farm and marry his sweetheart. Similarly, the peasant daughter and her family needed to accumulate a small dowry to help her fiancé buy land or build a house.

There were also laws and community controls to temper impetuous love and physical attraction. In some areas couples needed the legal permission or tacit

Chardin: The Kitchen Maid   Lost in thought as she pauses in her work, this young servant may be thinking about her village and loved ones there. Chardin was one of eighteenth-century France's greatest painters, and his scenes from everyday life provide valuable evidence for the historian. *(National Gallery of Art, Washington, D.C. Samuel H. Kress Collection)*

approval of the local lord or landowner in order to marry, and poor couples had particular difficulty securing the approval of local officials. These officials believed that freedom to marry for the lower classes would mean more landless paupers, more abandoned children, and more money for welfare. Village elders often agreed. Thus prudence, law, and custom combined to postpone the march to the altar. This pattern helped society maintain some kind of balance between the number of people and the available economic resources.

Work Away from Home

Many young people worked within their families until they could start their own households. Boys plowed and wove; girls spun and tended the cows. Many others left home temporarily to work elsewhere. In the towns a lad might be apprenticed to a craftsman for seven or fourteen years to learn a trade. During that time he would not be permitted to marry. In most trades he earned little and worked hard, but if he was lucky, he might eventually be admitted to a guild and establish his economic independence. More often a young man would drift from one tough job to another, always subject to economic fluctuations and with unemployment a constant threat.

Girls also temporarily left their families to work, at an early age and in large numbers. The range of opportunities open to them was more limited, however. Service in another family's household was by far the most common job, and even middle-class families often sent their daughters into service. Thus a few years away from home as a servant were often a normal part of growing up.

The legions of young servant girls worked hard but had little real independence. Sometimes the employer paid the girl's wages directly to her parents. Constantly under the eye of her mistress, the servant girl found her tasks were many—cleaning, shopping, cooking, caring for the baby. Often the work was endless, for there were no laws to limit exploitation. Court records are full of complaints by servant girls of physical mistreatment by their mistresses. There were many others like the fifteen-year-old English girl in the early eighteenth century who told the judge that her mistress had not only called her "very opprobrious names, as Bitch, Whore and the like," but also "beat her without provocation and beyond measure."[2]

There was also the pressure of seducers and sexual attack. In theory domestic service offered protection and security, but in practice the servant girl was often the easy prey of a lecherous master, his sons, or his friends. Indeed, "the evidence suggests that in all European countries . . . the upper classes felt perfectly free to exploit sexually girls who were at their mercy."[3] If the girl became pregnant, she was quickly fired and thrown out in disgrace. Prostitution and petty thievery were often the harsh consequences of unwanted pregnancy. "What are we?" exclaimed a bitter Parisian prostitute. "Most of us are unfortunate women, without origins, without education, servants and maids for the most part."[4]

Premarital Sex and Community Controls

Did the plight of some former servant girls mean that late marriage in preindustrial Europe went hand in hand with premarital sex and many illegitimate children? For most of western and central Europe until at least 1750, the answer seems to be no. English parish registers seldom listed more than one bastard out of every twenty children baptized. Some French parishes in the seventeenth century had extraordinarily low rates of illegitimacy: less than 1 percent of all babies were born out of wedlock. Illegitimate babies were apparently a rarity, at least as far as the official church records are concerned.

At the same time, premarital sex was clearly commonplace. In one well-studied English village, 33 percent of all first children were conceived before the couple was married, and many were born within three months of the marriage ceremony. In the mid-eighteenth century 20 percent of the French women in the village of Auffay, in Normandy, were pregnant when they got married, although only 2 percent of all babies in the village were born to unwed mothers.

The combination of very low rates of illegitimate births and large numbers of pregnant brides reflected the powerful social controls of the traditional village. The prospect of an unwed (and therefore poor) mother with an illegitimate child was inevitably viewed as a grave threat to the economic, social, and moral stability of the closely knit community. Irate parents and anxious village elders, indignant priests and authoritative landlords, all combined to pressure any young people who wavered about marriage in the face of unexpected pregnancy. In the countryside premarital sex was not entered into lightly, and it was generally limited to those contemplating marriage.

Today uninvolved individuals are inclined to ignore the domestic disputes and marital scandals of others, but people in peasant communities gave such affairs the loudest and most unfavorable publicity, either at the time of the event or during the Carnival season (see page 615). Relying on degrading public rituals, the young men of the village would typically gang up on the person they wanted to punish and force him or her to sit astride a donkey facing backward and holding up the donkey's tail. They would parade the overly brutal spouse-beating husband (or wife), or the couple whose adultery had been discovered, all around the village, loudly proclaiming the offender's misdeeds with scorn and ridicule. The donkey ride and similar colorful humiliations ranging from rotten vegetables splattered on the doorstep to obscene and insulting midnight serenades were common punishments throughout much of Europe. They epitomized the community's far-reaching effort to police personal behavior and maintain community standards.

New Patterns of Marriage and Illegitimacy

In the second half of the eighteenth century the pattern of late marriage and few births out of wedlock began to

David Allan: The Penny Wedding (1795) The spirited merrymaking of a peasant wedding was a popular theme of European artists. In rural Scotland "penny weddings" like this one were common: guests paid a fee for the food and fun; the money left over went to the newlyweds to help them get started. Music, dancing, feasting, and drinking characterized these community parties, which led the Presbyterian church to oppose them and hasten their decline. *(National Galleries of Scotland)*

change and break down. The number of illegitimate births soared between about 1750 and 1850 as much of Europe experienced an "illegitimacy explosion." In Frankfurt, Germany, for example, illegitimate births rose steadily from about 2 percent of all births in the early 1700s to a peak of about 25 percent around 1850. In Bordeaux, France, 36 percent of all babies were being born out of wedlock by 1840. Small towns and villages experienced less startling climbs, but increases from a range of 1 to 3 percent initially to 10 to 20 percent between 1750 and 1850 were commonplace. Fewer young women were abstaining from premarital intercourse, and, more important, fewer young men were marrying the women they got pregnant. Thus a profound sexual and cultural transformation took place.

Historians are still debating the meaning of this transformation, but two interrelated ideas dominate most interpretations. First, the growth of cottage industry created new opportunities for earning a living, opportunities not tied to the land. Young people attained greater independence and did not have to wait to inherit a farm in order to get married and have children. A scrap of ground for a garden and a cottage for the loom and spinning wheel could be quite enough for a modest living. These circumstances worked against the businesslike, calculating peasant marriage that was often dictated by the needs of the couple's families. After 1750 courtship became more extensive and freer as cottage industry grew. It was easier to yield to the attraction of the opposite sex and fall in love. Sexual activity might follow, and in most cases marriage for love rather than economic considerations also did, as cottage workers blazed a path that factory workers would follow in the nineteenth century.

Second, the needs of a growing population sent many young villagers to towns and cities in search of temporary or permanent employment. Mobility in turn encouraged new sexual and marital relationships, which were less subject to village tradition and resulted in more illegitimate births. Yet most young women in urban areas found work only as servants or textile workers. Poorly paid, insecure, and with little possibility of living truly independent, "liberated" lives, they looked mainly to marriage and family life as an escape from hard work and as the foundation of a satisfying life.

Promises of marriage from a man of the working girl's own class led naturally enough to sex, which was widely viewed as part of serious courtship. In one medium-size French city from 1787 to 1788, the great majority of unwed mothers stated that sexual intimacy had followed promises of marriage. Their sisters in rural Normandy reported again and again that they had been "seduced in anticipation of marriage."[5] Many soldiers, day laborers, and male servants were no doubt sincere in their proposals. But their lives were also insecure, and many hesitated to take on the heavy economic burdens of wife and child.

Thus it became increasingly difficult for a woman to convert pregnancy into marriage, and in a growing number of cases the intended marriage did not take place. The romantic yet practical dreams and aspirations of many young working men and women in towns and villages were frustrated by low wages, inequality, and changing economic and social conditions. Old patterns of marriage and family were breaking down among the common people. Only in the late nineteenth century would more stable patterns reappear.

 ## CHILDREN AND EDUCATION

In the traditional framework of agrarian Europe women married late but then began bearing children rapidly. If a woman married before she was thirty, and if both she and her husband lived to forty-five, the chances were roughly one in two that she would give birth to six or more children. The newborn child entered a dangerous world. Infant mortality was high. One in five was sure to die, and one in three was quite likely to die in the poorest areas. Newborn children were very likely to catch mysterious infectious diseases of the chest and stomach, and many babies died of dehydration brought about by a bad bout of ordinary diarrhea. Even in rich families little could be done for an ailing child. Childhood itself was dangerous because of adult indifference, neglect, and even abuse.

Schools and formal education played only a modest role in the lives of ordinary children, and many boys and many more girls never learned to read. Nevertheless, basic literacy was growing among the popular classes, whose reading habits have been intensively studied in recent years.

Child Care and Nursing

Women of the lower classes generally breast-fed their infants and for a much longer period than is customary today. Breast-feeding decreases the likelihood of pregnancy for the average woman by delaying the resumption of ovulation. By nursing their babies, women limited their fertility and spaced their children—from two to three years apart. If a newborn baby died, nursing stopped and a new life could be created. Nursing also saved lives: an infant who was breast-fed and received precious immunity-producing substances with its mother's milk was more likely to survive than an infant who was given any other food. In many areas of Russia, where the common practice was to give a new child a sweetened (and germ-laden) rag to suck on for its subsistence, half of the babies did not survive the first year.

In contrast to the laboring poor, the women of the aristocracy and upper middle class seldom nursed their own children. The upper-class woman felt that breast-feeding was crude, common, and undignified. Instead, she hired a wet nurse to suckle her child. The urban mother of more modest means—the wife of a shopkeeper or an artisan—also commonly used a wet nurse in order to facilitate full-time work in the shop.

Wet-nursing was a very widespread and flourishing business in the eighteenth century, a dismal business within the framework of the putting-out system. The traffic was in babies rather than in wool and cloth, and two or three years often passed before the wet-nurse worker finished her task. In the process the poor wet-nurse worker was often exploited and abused.

Yet many observers stressed the flaws of wet nurses. It was a common belief that with her milk a nurse passed her bad traits to a baby. When a child turned out poorly, it was assumed that "the nurse had changed it." Many observers charged that nurses were often negligent and greedy. They claimed that there were large numbers of "killing nurses" with whom no child ever survived. Such a nurse let a child die quickly so that she could take another child and another fee.

Foundlings and Infanticide

In the ancient Mediterranean world it was not uncommon to allow or force newborn babies, particularly girl babies, to die when there were too many mouths to feed. In China, too, where male offspring were more highly valued, female infants born to poor families were sometimes abandoned; in Japan poor families sometimes sold their female children to entertainment houses. To its eternal credit, the early church in medieval Europe, strongly influenced by Jewish law, denounced infanticide as a pagan practice and insisted that every human life was sacred. The willful destruction of newborn children became a crime punishable by death. And yet, as the previous reference to killing nurses suggests, direct and indirect methods of eliminating un-

Abandoned Children At this French foundlings' home a desperate, secretive mother could give up her baby without any questions, day or night. She placed her child on the revolving table, and the nun on duty took it in. Similar practices existed in many countries. *(Jean-Loup Charmet)*

wanted babies did not disappear. There were, for example, many cases of "overlaying"—parents rolling over and suffocating the child placed between them in their bed. Such parents claimed they had been drunk and had acted unintentionally. Severe poverty, on the one hand, and increasing illegitimacy, on the other, conspired to force the very poor to thin their own ranks.

The young girl—very likely a servant—who could not provide for her child had few choices. If she would not have an abortion or employ the services of a killing nurse, she could bundle up her baby and leave it on the doorstep of a church. In the late seventeenth century Saint Vincent de Paul was so distressed by the number of babies brought to the steps of Notre Dame in Paris that he established a home for foundlings. Others followed his example. In England the government acted on a petition calling for a foundling hospital "to prevent the frequent murders of poor, miserable infants at birth" and "to suppress the inhuman custom of exposing newborn children to perish in the streets."

In much of Europe in the eighteenth century, foundling homes emerged as a favorite charity of the rich and powerful. Great sums were spent on them. At their best, foundling homes in the eighteenth century were a good example of Christian charity and social concern in an age of great poverty and inequality.

Yet the foundling home was no panacea. By the 1770s one-third of all babies born in Paris were immediately abandoned to the foundling home by their mothers. Fully one-third of all those foundlings were abandoned by married couples, a powerful commentary on the standard of living among the working poor, for whom an additional mouth to feed often meant tragedy.

Furthermore, great numbers of babies entered the foundling homes, but few left. Even in the best of these homes, 50 percent of the babies normally died within a year. In the worst, fully 90 percent did not survive, succumbing to the intentional and unintentional neglect of their wet nurses and the customary childhood illnesses. So great was the carnage that some contemporaries called the foundling hospitals "legalized infanticide."

Attitudes Toward Children

What were the typical circumstances of children's lives? Did the treatment of foundlings reflect the attitudes of typical parents? Although some scholars argue otherwise, it seems that the young child was often of little concern to its parents and to society in the eighteenth century. This indifference toward children was found in all classes. The practice of using wet nurses, who were casually selected and often negligent, is one example of how even the rich and the prosperous put the child out of sight and out of mind. One French moralist, writing in 1756 about how to improve humanity, observed that "one blushes to think of loving one's children." It has been said that the English gentleman of the period "had more interest in the diseases of his horses than of his children."[6]

Feelings toward children were greatly influenced by the terrible frequency of death among children of all classes. Doctors and clergymen urged parents not to become too emotionally involved with their children. Mothers especially did not always heed such warnings, but the risk of emotional devastation was very real for them. The great eighteenth-century English historian Edward Gibbon (1737–1794) wrote that "the death of a new born child before that of its parents may seem unnatural but it is a strictly probable event." Gibbon's father named all his boys Edward after himself, hoping that at least one of them would survive to carry his name. His prudence was not misplaced. Only Edward

the future historian and eldest survived. Five brothers and sisters who followed him all died in infancy.

The medical establishment was seldom interested in the care of children. One contemporary observer quoted a famous doctor as saying that "he never wished to be called to a young child because he was really at a loss to know what to offer for it." The best hope for children was often treatment by women healers and midwives, who helped many women deliver their babies and provided advice on child care. Nevertheless, children were still caught in a vicious circle: they were neglected because they were very likely to die, and they were likely to die because they were neglected.

Emotional detachment from children often shaded off into abuse. When parents and other adults did turn toward children, it was normally to discipline and control them. The novelist Daniel Defoe (1660?–1731), who was always delighted when he saw very young children working hard in cottage industry, coined the axiom "Spare the rod and spoil the child." He meant it. So did Susannah Wesley (1669–1742), mother of John Wesley, the founder of Methodism. According to her, the first task of a parent toward her children was "to conquer the will, and bring them to an obedient temper." She reported that her babies were "taught to fear the rod, and to cry softly."[7]

It was hardly surprising that when English parish officials dumped their paupers into the first factories late in the eighteenth century, the children were beaten and brutalized. That was part of the child-rearing pattern—considerable indifference, on the one hand, and strict physical discipline, on the other—that prevailed throughout most of the eighteenth century.

From the middle of the century this pattern came under increasing attack and began to change. Critics, led by Jean-Jacques Rousseau in his famous treatise *Emile,* called for greater love, tenderness, and understanding toward children, as well as child-based, experiential education. (See the feature "Listening to the Past: A New Way to Educate Children" on pages 618–619.) In addition to supporting foundling homes to discourage infanticide and urging wealthy women to nurse their own babies, these new voices ridiculed the practice of swaddling: wrapping youngsters in tight-fitting clothes and blankets was generally believed to form babies properly by "straightening them out." By the end of the eighteenth century small children were often being dressed in simpler, more comfortable clothing, allowing much greater freedom of movement. More parents expressed a delight in the love and intimacy of the child and found real pleasure in raising their offspring. These changes

Cultivating the Joy of Discovery
This English painting by Joseph Wright of Derby (1734–1797) reflects new attitudes toward child development and education, which advocated greater freedom and direct experience. The children rapturously watch a planetarium, which illustrates the movements and positions of the planets in the solar system. Wise teachers stand by, letting the children learn at their own pace. *(The Orrery, exh. 1766 by Joseph Wright of Derby. Derby Museum & Art Gallery, Derbyshire, UK/Bridgeman Art Library, London/New York)*

were part of the general growth of humanitarianism and cautious optimism about human potential that characterized the eighteenth-century Enlightenment.

Schools and Popular Literature

The role of schools and formal education outside the home was also growing more important. The aristocracy and the rich had led the way in the sixteenth century with special colleges, often run by Jesuits. But schools charged specifically with elementary education of the children of the common people usually did not appear until the seventeenth century. Unlike medieval schools, which mingled all age groups, these elementary schools specialized in boys and girls from seven to twelve, who were instructed in basic literacy and religion. The growth of popular education quickened in the eighteenth century, but there was no revolutionary acceleration, and many common people received no formal education.

Prussia led the way in the development of universal education, inspired by the old Protestant idea that every believer should be able to read and study the Bible in the quest for personal salvation and by the new idea of a population capable of effectively serving the state. As early as 1717 Prussia made attendance at elementary schools compulsory, and more Protestant German states, such as Saxony and Württemberg, followed in the eighteenth century. Religious motives were also extremely important elsewhere. From the middle of the seventeenth century, Presbyterian Scotland was convinced that the path to salvation lay in careful study of the Scriptures, and it established an effective network of parish schools for rich and poor alike. The Church of England and the dissenting congregations established "charity schools" to instruct the children of the poor, and in 1682 France began setting up Christian schools to teach the catechism and prayers as well as reading and writing. In 1774 Habsburg empress Maria Theresa established a general system of elementary education that called for compulsory education and a school in every community. Thus some elementary education was becoming a reality for European peoples, and schools were of growing significance in the life of the child.

The result of these efforts was a remarkable growth in basic literacy between 1600 and 1800, especially after 1700. Whereas in 1600 only one male in six was barely literate in France and Scotland, and one in four in England, by 1800 almost nine out of ten Scottish males, two out of three males in France, and more than half of English males were literate. In all three countries the bulk of the jump occurred in the eighteenth century. Women were also increasingly literate, although they lagged behind men in most countries.

The growth in literacy promoted a growth in reading, and historians have carefully examined what the common people read in an attempt to discern what they were thinking. One thing seems certain: the major philosophical works of the Enlightenment had little impact on peasants and workers, who could neither afford nor understand those favorites of the book-hungry educated public.

Although the Bible remained the overwhelming favorite, especially in Protestant countries, the staple of popular literature was short pamphlets known as chapbooks. Printed on the cheapest paper available, many chapbooks dealt with religious subjects. They featured Bible stories, prayers, devotions, and the lives of saints and other exemplary Christians. Promising happiness after death, devotional literature was also intensely practical. It gave the believer moral teachings and a confidence in God that helped in daily living.

Entertaining, often humorous stories formed a second element of popular literature. Fairy tales, medieval romances, fictionalized history, and fantastic adventures—these were some of the delights that filled the peddler's pack as he approached a village. Both heroes and villains possessed superhuman powers in this make-believe world, a world of danger and magic, of fairy godmothers and evil trolls. But the good fairies always triumphed over the evil ones in the stories' marvelous resolutions. The significance of these entertaining stories for the peasant reader is not clear, however. Many scholars see them reflecting a desire for pure escapism and a temporary flight from harsh everyday reality. Others see these tales reflecting ancient folk wisdom and counseling prudence in a world full of danger and evil, where wolves dress up like grandmothers and eat Little Red Riding Hoods.

Some popular literature was highly practical, dealing with rural crafts, household repairs, useful plants, and

similar matters. Much of such lore was stored in almanacs. With calendars listing secular, religious, and astrological events mixed in with agricultural schedules, bizarre bits of information, and jokes, the almanac was universal, noncontroversial, and highly appreciated, even by many in the comfortable classes. "Anyone who could would read an almanac."[8]

 ## FOOD AND MEDICAL PRACTICE

The European population increased rapidly in the eighteenth century. Plague and starvation gradually disappeared, and Europeans lived longer lives. What were the characteristics of diets and nutrition in this era of improving health and longevity? Although it played only a small part, what was medical practice like in the eighteenth century? What does a comparison of rich and poor reveal?

Diets and Nutrition

At the beginning of the eighteenth century ordinary men and women depended on grain as fully as they had in the past. Bread was quite literally the staff of life. Peasants in the Beauvais region of France ate two pounds of bread a day, washing it down with water, green wine, beer, or a little skim milk. Their dark bread was made from a mixture of roughly ground wheat and rye—the standard flour of the common people. The poor also ate grains in soup and gruel. In rocky northern Scotland, for example, people depended on oatmeal, which they often ate half-cooked so that it would swell in their stomachs and make them feel full.

Not surprisingly, an adequate supply of grain and an affordable price for bread loomed in the popular imagination. Peasants, landless laborers, and urban workers all believed in the old medieval idea of the "just price"—that is, a price that was "fair" to both consumers and producers. But in the later eighteenth century, this traditional, moral view of prices and the economy clashed repeatedly with the emerging free-market philosophy of unregulated supply and demand, which government officials, large landowners, and early economists increasingly favored. In years of poor harvests and soaring prices, this clash often resulted in food riots and popular disturbances. Peasants and workers would try to stop wagons loaded with grain from leaving their region, or they would seize grain held by speculators and big merchants accused of hoarding and rigging the

Le Nain: Peasant Family A little wine and a great deal of dark bread: the traditional food of the poor French peasantry accentuates the poetic dignity of this masterpiece, painted about 1640 by Louis Le Nain. *(Louvre © Photo R.M.N.—G. Blot/J. Schor)*

market. (Usually the tumultuous crowd paid what it considered to be a fair price for what it took.) Governments were keenly aware of the problem of adequate grain supplies, and they would sometimes try to control prices to prevent unrest in crisis years.

Although breadstuffs were all-important for the rural and urban poor, they also ate a fair quantity of vegetables. Indeed, vegetables were considered "poor people's food." Peas and beans were probably the most common and were eaten fresh in late spring and summer. Dried, they became the basic ingredients in the soups and stews of the long winter months. In most regions other vegetables appeared in season on the tables of the poor—primarily cabbages, carrots, and wild greens. Fruit was uncommon and limited to the summer months.

The common people of Europe loved meat and eggs, but they seldom ate their fill. Indeed, as the population surged in the sixteenth century, meat became more expensive, and the poor ate less meat in 1700 than in 1500. Moreover, in most European countries harsh game laws deprived the poor of the right to hunt and eat edible game such as rabbits, deer, and partridges. Only nobles and large landowners could legally kill game. Few laws were more bitterly resented—or more frequently broken—by ordinary people than those governing hunting.

Milk was rarely drunk. Perhaps because some individuals do suffer seriously from dairy allergies, it was widely believed that milk caused sore eyes, headaches, and a variety of ills, except among the very young and very old. Milk was used primarily to make cheese and butter, which the poor liked but could afford only occasionally. Medical and popular opinion considered whey, the watery liquid left after milk was churned, "an excellent temperate drink."

The diet of the rich—aristocrats, officials, and the comfortable bourgeoisie—was traditionally quite different from that of the poor. The men and women of the upper classes were rapacious carnivores. A truly elegant dinner among the great and powerful consisted of one rich meat after another: a chicken pie, a leg of lamb, a grilled steak, for example, perhaps followed by three fish courses, all complemented with sweets, cheeses, and nuts of all kinds. Fruits and vegetables were not often found on the tables of the rich.

There was also an enormous amount of overdrinking among the rich. The English squire who loved to hunt with his hounds loved to drink with a similar passion. With his dinner he drank red wine from France or white wine from the Rhineland, and with his dessert he took sweet but strong port or Madeira from Portugal. Sometimes he ended the evening under the table in a drunken stupor.

The diet of small traders, master craftsmen, minor bureaucrats—the people of the towns and cities—was generally less monotonous than that of the peasantry. The markets, stocked by market gardens on the outskirts, provided a substantial variety of meats, vegetables, and fruits, although bread and beans still formed the bulk of such families' diet.

There were also regional dietary differences in 1700. Generally speaking, northern, Atlantic Europe ate better than southern, Mediterranean Europe. The poor of England probably ate best of all. The Dutch were also considerably better fed than the average European, in large part because of their advanced agriculture and diversified gardens.

The Impact of Diet on Health

How were the poor and the rich served by their quite different diets? At first glance the diet of the laboring poor, relying as it did on grains and vegetables, might seem low in protein. However, the whole-grain wheat or rye flour used in eighteenth-century bread retained most of the bran—the ground-up husk—and the all-important wheat germ, which contains higher proportions of some minerals, vitamins, and good-quality proteins than does the rest of the grain. In addition, the field peas and beans eaten by poor people since the early Middle Ages contained protein that complemented the proteins in whole-grain bread. The proteins in whey, cheese, and eggs, which the poor ate at least occasionally, also supplemented the bread and vegetables.

The basic bread-and-vegetables diet of the poor *in normal times* was adequate. But a key dietary problem in some seasons, particularly in the late winter and early spring, was probably getting enough green vegetables (or milk) to ensure adequate supplies of vitamins A and C. A severe deficiency of vitamin C produces scurvy, a disease that leads to rotting gums, swelling of the limbs, and great weakness. Before the season's first vegetables, many people experienced shortages of vitamin C and suffered from mild cases of scurvy. (Scurvy was an acute problem for sailors on long voyages and by the end of the sixteenth century was being controlled on ships by a daily ration of lime juice for crew members.)

The practice of gorging on meat, sweets, and spirits caused the rich their own nutritional problems. Because of their great disdain for fresh vegetables, they too were very often deficient in vitamin C. Gout was also a common affliction of the overfed and underexercised rich. No wonder they were often caricatured as dragging their flabby limbs and bulging bellies to the table to stuff their swollen cheeks and poison their livers. People of moderate means, who could afford some meat and dairy products with fair regularity but who had not abandoned the bread and vegetables of the poor, were probably best off from a nutritional standpoint.

Patterns of food consumption changed rather markedly as the century progressed. More varied diets associated with new methods of farming were confined largely to the Low Countries and England, but a new food—the potato—came to the aid of the poor everywhere. Introduced into Europe from the Americas—along with corn, squash, tomatoes, and many other useful plants—the humble potato is an excellent food. Containing a good supply of carbohydrates, calories, and vitamins A and C (especially if it is not overcooked and the skin is eaten), the potato offset the lack of vitamins from green vegetables in the poor person's winter and early spring diet, and it provided a much higher caloric yield than grain for a given piece of land. Dietary changes resulting from the Columbian Exchange (see pages 513–516) also occurred in Asia and Africa, where New World staples such as maize and potatoes were introduced. Indeed, the widespread growth of the world population after 1700 has been attributed to the impact of the new staple crops from the Americas.

For some desperately poor peasants who needed to get every possible calorie from a tiny plot of land, the potato replaced grain as the primary food in the eighteenth century. This happened first in Ireland, where English (Protestant) repression and exploitation forced large numbers of poor (Catholic) peasants to live off tiny scraps of rented ground. Elsewhere in Europe potatoes took hold more slowly because many people did not like them. Thus potatoes were first fed to pigs and livestock, and there was even debate about whether they were fit for humans. By the end of the century, however, the potato had become an important dietary supplement in much of Europe.

There was also a general growth of market gardening, and a greater variety of vegetables appeared in towns and cities. In the course of the eighteenth century, the large towns and cities of maritime Europe began to receive semitropical fruits, such as oranges and lemons, from Portugal and the West Indies, although they were not cheap.

Not all changes in the eighteenth century were for the better, however. Bread began to change, most noticeably for the English and for the comfortable groups on the European continent. Rising incomes and new tastes led to a shift from whole-grain black or brown

Royal Interest in the Potato   Frederick the Great of Prussia, shown here supervising cultivation of the potato, used his influence and position to promote the new food on his estates and throughout Prussia. Peasants could grow potatoes with the simplest hand tools, but it was backbreaking labor, as this painting by R. Warthmüller suggests. *(Private Collection, Hamburg/AKG London)*

bread to "bread as white as snow" and started a decline in bread's nutritional value. The high-roughage bran and some of the dark but high-vitamin germ were increasingly sifted out by millers. This foretold further "improvements" in the nineteenth century, which would leave bread perfectly white and greatly reduced in nutritional value.

Another sign of nutritional decline was the growing consumption of sugar. Initially a luxury, sugar dropped rapidly in price as slave-based production increased in the Americas, and the sweetener was much more widely used in the eighteenth century. This development probably led to an increase in cavities and to other ailments as well, although the greater or lesser poverty of the laboring poor still protected most of them from the sugar-tooth virus of the rich and well-to-do.

Medical Practitioners

Although sickness, pain, and disease—intractable challenges built into the human condition—permeated the European experience in the eighteenth century, medical science played a very small part in improving the health of most people. Yet the Enlightenment's growing focus on discovering the laws of nature and on human problems did give rise to a great deal of research and experimentation. The century also saw a remarkable rise in the number of medical practitioners, and a high value was placed on their services. Therefore, when the great breakthroughs in knowledge came in the middle and late nineteenth century, they could be rapidly evaluated and diffused.

Care of the sick in the eighteenth century was the domain of several competing groups: faith healers, apothecaries (or pharmacists), surgeons, physicians, and midwives. Men and women had both been involved in the healing arts since the Middle Ages. But by 1700 women's options had been severely restricted, a result of their exclusion from medical colleges. In the course of the eighteenth century women faced increasing criticism and discrimination from the male-dominated medical profession, leading to their virtual exclusion from "scientific medicine" in the nineteenth century.

Cette Planche représente encore une fauße manœuvre en préferant de tirer l'enfant la face en devant plutôt que de lui avoir tourné par derrière, ce qui donne lieu au menton de l'enfant de s'accrocher sur les os Pubis et en continuant de le tirer dans cette position la tête se renversant en arrière la machoire peut se luxer, d'ailleurs l'occiput par ce renversement appuyant sur los Sacrum, il est impoßible de faire paßer la tête dans le détroit du petit baßin, il faut donc en repouñant l'enfant un peu en haut lui retourner la face en arrière.

Teaching Midwives   This plate from Madame du Coudray's manual for midwives, *The Art of Childbirth*, illustrates "another incorrect method of delivery." The caption tells the midwife that she should have rotated the baby within the womb to face the mother's back, so that the chin does not catch on the pubic bone and dislocate the jaw. *(Rare Books Division, Countway [Francis A.] Library of Medicine)*

Faith healers, who had been among the most important kinds of physicians in medieval Europe, remained active. They and their patients believed that demons and evil spirits caused disease by lodging in people and that the proper treatment was to exorcise, or drive out, the offending devil. Faith healing was particularly effective in the treatment of mental disorders where the link between attitude and illness is most direct.

In the larger towns and cities apothecaries sold a vast number of herbs, drugs, and patent medicines for every conceivable "temperament and distemper." Early pharmacists were seldom regulated, and they frequently diagnosed freely. Their prescriptions were incredibly complex and often very expensive. Some of the drugs and herbs undoubtedly worked, such as the strong laxatives given to the rich for their constipated bowels. But much purging was harmful, and only bloodletting was more effective in speeding patients to their graves. In the countryside people often turned to midwives and women healers for herbs and folk remedies.

Physicians, who were invariably men, were apprenticed in their teens to a practicing physician for several years of on-the-job training. This training was then rounded out with hospital work or some university courses. Because such prolonged training was expensive, physicians continued to come mainly from prosperous families, and they usually concentrated on urban patients from similar social backgrounds.

To their credit physicians in the eighteenth century were increasingly willing to experiment with new methods, but time-honored practices lay heavily on them. Physicians, like apothecaries, laid great stress on purging. And bloodletting was still considered a medical cure-all. It was the way "bad blood," the cause of illness, was removed and the balance of humors necessary for good health restored.

Surgeons, in contrast, made considerable medical and social progress. Long considered as ordinary artisans comparable to butchers and barbers, surgeons began studying anatomy seriously and improved their art. With endless opportunities to practice, army surgeons on gory battlefields led the way. They learned that a soldier with an extensive wound could perhaps be saved if the surgeon could obtain above the wound a flat surface that could be cauterized with fire. Thus if a soldier (or a civilian) had a broken limb and the bone stuck out, the surgeon amputated so that the remaining stump could be cauterized and the likelihood of death reduced.

The eighteenth-century surgeon (and patient) labored in the face of incredible difficulties. Almost all operations were performed without any painkiller, for the anesthesias of the day were hard to control and were believed too dangerous for general use. The terrible screams of people whose limbs were being sawed off echoed across battlefields and through hospitals. Surgery was also performed in the midst of filth and dirt, for there simply was no knowledge of bacteriology and the nature of infection. The simplest wound treated by a surgeon could fester and lead to death.

Midwives, the objects of suspicion and persecution during the witch-hunt craze of the sixteenth and seventeenth centuries, continued to deliver the overwhelming majority of babies. (See the feature "Individuals in Society: Martha Ballard, American Midwife.") The typ-

Individuals in Society

Martha Ballard, American Midwife

The journal of Martha Ballard. *(Maine State Archives)*

In the cold spring of 1789 Martha Ballard delivered fourteen babies in two months of high drama and unsung heroism. An American midwife in a small town on the Kennebec River in central Maine, Ballard attended women on both sides of the icy flooding river, paddling back and forth and braving the harsh and erratic weather. On her way to one patient, she and her terrified horse were caught in a violent rainstorm and almost struck by a falling tree. She recorded the outcome in her diary, which she kept for twenty-seven years: "Assisted by the same allmighty power I got safe thru and arrived unhurt. Mrs Hewins safe delivered at ten hours evening of a daughter."[1] Ballard had persevered and triumphed.

Exceptional in her meticulous record keeping, Ballard embodied many characteristics of the midwife in the eighteenth-century Western world. A mature woman of fifty when her diary opened in 1785, she had learned her trade on the job, assisting other midwives delivering the babies of friends and relatives. She had also learned birthing practices and compassion from her own experience, for she gave birth to nine children between 1756 and 1779. Ballard worked as she was trained, assisted by other women in each patient's own home. She received payment for services in money or in goods, such as food and cloth. In the 1790s the arrival of a young and inexperienced male doctor brought some competition, but the midwife continued to preside over the vast majority of births in the town.

The great adventures in Ballard's diary were her journeys to expectant mothers and her struggles with the elements. The deliveries themselves were described simply, in matter-of-fact terms. Ballard's women were "unwell," and their "illness" only increased as they passed into labor. Complications were rarely noted, and then only briefly in nontechnical language. Indeed, birthing tragedies hardly appeared in her everyday record. How, the modern reader may ask, can this be?

Part of the answer lies in Ballard's strength of constitution and character, her accepting nature, and her faith in God. Perhaps more lies in her skill, justifiable self-confidence, and enviable record of success. She attended more than eight hundred deliveries and lost not a single mother in birthing, although five died in the recovery period. Moreover, only nineteen babies died stillborn or within an hour or two of birth. These levels of maternal and infant death were not surpassed until 1930 in the United States. Ballard's success shows that if a woman had adequate nutrition (as in New England) and the care of an experienced midwife, childbirth at home was a natural physical process that normally ended well.

Tough and tender, Ballard also practiced as a nurse, physician, mortician, and pharmacist, relying on herbal medicines. For example, she administered mandrake and pinkroot as powerful laxatives and emetics to cause the expulsion of children's intestinal worms, which were contracted by playing in soil infected by human feces and which could grow up to fourteen inches in length.

A large portion of Ballard's time was occupied with laborious housecleaning, gardening, sewing, and bearing, nursing, raising, and teaching her children. Nursing for pay and simply helping her neighbors overlapped. In later life she endured the disasters of an alcoholic son and her husband's indifference to her fatigue and stomach pain. Unlike the women she assisted, she found relief from these trials only with death at age seventy-seven in 1812.

Questions for Analysis

1. Describe Martha Ballard. What kind of a person was she?

2. What challenges did Ballard face as a midwife? How successfully did she meet them?

1. L. Ulrich, *A Midwife's Tale: The Life of Martha Ballard, Based on Her Diary, 1785–1812* (New York: Alfred A. Knopf, 1990), p. 6. This section draws on Ulrich's pioneering study, a masterpiece of the biographer's art. Abbreviations have been spelled out.

ical midwife was older, often widowed, and of modest means and long experience. Usually trained by another practitioner, midwives not only delivered babies but also treated other female problems and ministered to small children.

The midwife orchestrated the delivery process, assisted by friends and relatives who offered encouragement to the pregnant woman in her own home. Excluded by tradition and modesty, the male surgeon (and husband) rarely entered this world, because most births were normal and spontaneous. With the invention of the forceps, which often helped in an exceptionally difficult birth, surgeon-physicians used their monopoly over this and other instruments to seek lucrative new business. They persuaded growing numbers of wealthy women of the superiority of their services and sought to undermine faith in midwives. Recent research has shown, however, that women practitioners successfully defended much, but not all, of their practice in the eighteenth century, as training was improved and professional certification instituted, often with the support of state and church. In general women remained dominant in the birthing trade, with a rate of successful deliveries that equaled that of male doctors.

While ordinary physicians were bleeding, apothecaries purging, surgeons sawing, faith healers praying, and midwives assisting, the leading medical thinkers were attempting to pull together and assimilate all the information and misinformation they had been accumulating. The attempt was ambitious: to systematize medicine around simple, basic principles, as Newton had done in physics. But the schools of thought resulting from such speculation and theorizing did little to improve medical care.

Hospitals and Medical Experiments

Hospitals were terrible places throughout most of the eighteenth century. There was no isolation of patients. Operations were performed in a patient's bed. Nurses were old, ignorant, greedy, and often drunk women. Fresh air was considered harmful, and infections of every kind were rampant. Diderot's article in the *Encyclopedia* on the Hôtel-Dieu in Paris, the "richest and most terrifying of all French hospitals," vividly describes normal conditions of the 1770s:

Imagine a long series of communicating wards filled with sufferers of every kind of disease who are sometimes packed three, four, five or even six into a bed, the living alongside the dead and dying, the air polluted by this mass

of unhealthy bodies, passing pestilential germs of their afflictions from one to the other, and the spectacle of suffering and agony on every hand. That is the Hôtel-Dieu.[9]

No wonder the poor of Paris hated hospitals and often saw confinement there as a plot to kill paupers.

In the last years of the century the humanitarian concern already reflected in Diderot's description of the Hôtel-Dieu led to a movement for hospital reform throughout western Europe. Efforts were made to improve ventilation and eliminate filth in the belief that bad air caused disease. The theory was wrong, but the results were beneficial, for the spread of infection was somewhat reduced.

Mental hospitals, too, were incredibly savage institutions. The customary treatment for mental illness was bleeding and cold water, administered more to maintain discipline than to effect a cure. Violent persons were chained to the wall and forgotten. A breakthrough of sorts occurred in the 1790s when William Tuke founded the first humane sanatorium in England.

In the eighteenth century all sorts of wildly erroneous ideas about mental illness circulated. One was that moonlight caused madness, a belief reflected in the word *lunatic*—someone harmed by lunar light. Another mid-eighteenth-century theory, which lasted until at least 1914, was that masturbation caused madness, not to mention acne, epilepsy, and premature ejaculation. Thus parents, religious institutions, and schools waged relentless war on masturbation by males, although they were curiously uninterested in female masturbation.

In the second half of the eighteenth century medicine in general turned in a more practical and experimental direction. Some of the experimentation was creative quackery involving the recently discovered phenomenon of electricity. One magnificent quack in London promoted sleep on a cure-all Celestial Bed, which was lavishly decorated with magnets and electrical devices. A single night on the bed cost a small fortune. The rich could buy expensive treatments, but they often got little for their money. Because so many treatments were harmful, the common people were probably much less deprived by their reliance on faith healers and folk medicine than one might think.

Experimentation and the intensified search for solutions to human problems led to some real advances in medicine after 1750, however. The eighteenth century's greatest medical triumph was the conquest of smallpox. With the progressive decline of bubonic plague, smallpox became the most terrible of the infectious diseases. It is estimated that 60 million Europeans

Hospital Life   Patients crowded into hospitals like this one in Hamburg in 1746 had little chance of recovery. A priest by the window administers last rites, while in the center a surgeon coolly saws off the leg of a man who has received no anesthesia. *(Germanisches Nationalmuseum, Nuremberg)*

died of smallpox in the eighteenth century. Fully 80 percent of the population was stricken at some point in life, and 25 percent of the total population was left permanently scarred. If ever a human problem cried out for solution, it was smallpox.

Inoculation against smallpox was already practiced in China and the Muslim lands of western Asia. This procedure had been demonstrated to the Jesuits in the seventeenth century. Something approaching mass inoculation took place in England in the 1760s, and the practice spread to the continent of Europe. However, the method of inoculation—using active smallpox to stimulate immunity—could cause a mild, and potentially infectious, case of the disease.

The final breakthrough against smallpox came at the end of the century. Edward Jenner (1749–1823), a talented country doctor, noted that in the English countryside there was a long-standing belief that dairy maids who had contracted cowpox did not get smallpox. Cowpox produces sores similar to those of smallpox on the cow's udder and on the hands of the milker, but the disease is mild and not contagious. In 1796 Jenner performed his first vaccination on a young boy. In the next two years he performed twenty-three successful vaccinations and in 1798 published his findings. After Austrian medical authorities replicated Jenner's results, the new method of treatment spread rapidly. Smallpox soon declined to the point of disappearance in Europe and then throughout the world. Jenner thus helped lay the foundation for the science of immunology in the nineteenth century.

 ## RELIGION AND POPULAR CULTURE

Though the critical spirit of the Enlightenment spread among the educated elite in the eighteenth century, the majority of ordinary men and women remained firmly committed to the Christian religion, especially in rural areas. Religion offered answers to life's mysteries and gave comfort and courage in the face of sorrow and fear. Religion also remained strong because it was usually embedded in local traditions, everyday social experience, and popular culture.

Yet the popular religion of village Europe was everywhere enmeshed in a larger world of church hierarchies and state power. These powerful outside forces sought to regulate religious life at the local level. Their efforts created tensions that helped set the scene for a vigorous religious revival in Germany and England. Similar tensions arose in Catholic countries, where powerful elites criticized and attacked popular religious practices that their increasingly rationalistic minds deemed foolish and superstitious.

The Institutional Church

As in the Middle Ages, the local parish church remained the basic religious unit all across Europe. Still largely coinciding with the agricultural village, the parish fulfilled many needs. Whether Catholic or Protestant, the parish church was the focal point of religious devotion and much more. Villagers came together at services and gossiped and swapped stories afterward, and neighbors joined in church for baptisms, marriages, funerals, and other special events. Thus the parish church was woven into the very fabric of community life.

Moreover, the local church had important administrative tasks. It is because priests and parsons kept such complete parish registers that historians have learned so much about population and family life. Parishes also normally distributed charity to the destitute, looked after orphans, and provided whatever primary education was available for the common people.

The many tasks of the local church were usually the responsibility of a resident priest or pastor, a full-time professional working with assistants and lay volunteers. All clerics—whether Roman Catholic, Protestant, or Orthodox—also shared the fate of middlemen in a complicated institutional system. Charged most often with ministering to poor peasants, the priest or parson was the last link in a powerful church-state hierarchy that was everywhere determined to control religion down to the grassroots. However, the regulatory framework of belief, which went back at least to the fourth century when Christianity became the official religion of the Roman Empire, had since 1500 undergone important changes, engendered by the Protestant Reformation.

As the Reformation gathered force, with peasant upheaval and doctrinal competition, German princes and monarchs in northern Europe put themselves at the head of official churches in their territories. Protestant authorities, with generous assistance from state-certified theologians, then proceeded to regulate their "territor-

ial churches" strictly, selecting personnel and imposing detailed rules. They joined with Catholics to crush the Anabaptists, who, with their belief in freedom of conscience and separation of church and state, had become the real revolutionaries. Thus the Reformation, initially so radical in its rejection of Rome and its stress on individual religious experience, eventually resulted in a bureaucratization of the church and local religious life in Protestant Europe.

The Reformation era also increased the practical power of Catholic rulers over "their" churches, but it was only in the eighteenth century that some Catholic monarchs began to impose striking reforms. These reforms, which had their counterparts in Orthodox Russia, had a very "Protestant" aspect. They increased state control over the Catholic church, making it less subject to papal influence. For instance, Spain, a deeply Catholic country with devout rulers, took firm control of ecclesiastical appointments. Papal proclamations could not even be read in Spanish churches without prior approval from the government. Spain also asserted state control over the Spanish Inquisition. In sum, Spain went far toward creating a "national" Catholic church, as France had done earlier.

Some Catholic rulers also turned their reforming efforts on certain religious orders and monasteries and convents. Following the earlier example of Portugal, the French king ordered the politically influential Jesuits out of France in 1763 and confiscated their property. Believing that the large monastic clergy should make a more practical contribution to social and religious life, Maria Theresa of Austria (see page 582) sharply restricted entry into "unproductive" orders, and her son Joseph II abolished contemplative orders, henceforth permitting only orders that were engaged in teaching, nursing, or other practical work. The state also expropriated the dissolved monasteries and used their great wealth for charitable purposes and higher salaries for ordinary priests.

Protestant Revival

In their attempt to recapture the vital core of the Christian religion, the Protestant reformers had rigorously suppressed all the medieval practices that they considered nonessential or erroneous because they were not founded on Scripture. Relics and crucifixes had been permanently removed from crypt and altar. Stained-glass windows had been smashed, walls and murals covered with whitewash, and processions and pilgrimages eliminated. Such revolutionary changes had often troubled ordinary churchgoers, but by the late seventeenth century the vast reforms of the Reformation had been completed and thoroughly routinized in most Protestant churches.

Indeed, official Protestant churches had generally settled into a smug complacency. In the Reformation heartland one concerned German minister wrote that the Lutheran church "had become paralyzed in forms of dead doctrinal conformity" and badly needed a return to its original inspiration.[10] This voice was one of many that would prepare and then guide a powerful and successful Protestant revival.

The Protestant revival began in Germany. It was known as Pietism, and three aspects account for its powerful appeal. First, Pietism called for a warm, emotional religion that everyone could experience. Enthusiasm—in prayer, in worship, in preaching, in life itself—was the key concept. "Just as a drunkard becomes full of wine, so must the congregation become filled with spirit," declared one exuberant writer. Another said simply, "The heart must burn."[11]

Second, Pietism reasserted the earlier radical stress on the priesthood of all believers, thereby reducing the wide gulf between the official clergy and the Lutheran laity. Bible reading and study were enthusiastically extended to all classes, and this provided a powerful spur for popular education as well as individual religious development. Third, Pietists believed in the practical power of Christian rebirth in everyday affairs. Reborn Christians were expected to lead good, moral lives and come from all social classes.

Pietism had a major impact on John Wesley (1703–1791), who served as the catalyst for popular religious revival in England. Wesley, who came from a long line of ministers, mapped a fanatically earnest "scheme of religion." As a teaching fellow at Oxford University, he organized a Holy Club for similarly minded students. They were soon known contemptuously as "Methodists" because they were so methodical in their devotion. Yet like the young Luther, Wesley remained intensely troubled about his own salvation, even after his ordination as an Anglican priest in 1728.

Wesley's anxieties related to grave problems of the faith in England. The government shamelessly used the Church of England to provide favorites with high-paying jobs and sinecures. The building of churches practically stopped even though the population was growing and in many parishes there was a grave shortage of pews. Services and sermons had settled into an uninspiring routine, while the skepticism of the Enlightenment was making inroads among the educated classes and deism was becoming popular.

Spiritual counseling from a sympathetic Pietist minister from Germany prepared Wesley for a mystical,

A Midsummer Afternoon with a Methodist Preacher   This detail from a painting by Philip James de Loutherbourg suggests in a humorous manner how Wesley and his followers took their optimistic Christianity to the people of England. Methodist ministers championed open-air preaching and weeklong revivals. *(National Gallery of Canada, Ottawa)*

emotional "conversion" in 1738. He described this critical turning point in his *Journal:*

In the evening I went to a [Christian] society in Aldersgate Street where one was reading Luther's preface to the Epistle to the Romans. About a quarter before nine, while he was describing the change which God works in the heart through faith in Christ, I felt my heart strangely warmed. I felt I did trust in Christ, Christ alone for salvation; and an assurance was given me that he had taken away my sins, even mine, and saved me from the law of sin and death.[12]

Wesley's emotional experience resolved his intellectual doubts.

Wesley took the good news to the people, traveling some 225,000 miles on horseback and preaching more than 40,000 sermons in 50 years. Faced with overcrowded churches and a hostile church-state establishment, Wesley preached in open fields. People came in large numbers. Of critical importance was Wesley's rejection of Calvinist predestination—the doctrine of salvation granted only to a select few. He preached that *all* men and women who earnestly sought salvation might be saved. It was a message of hope and joy, of free will and universal salvation. Wesley and his followers, the Methodists, also turned their attention to the social ills of the day, playing leading roles in the antislavery and temperance movements and reflecting Wesley's concern for the poor and downtrodden.

As Wesley had been inspired by Pietist revival in Germany, so evangelicals in the Church of England and the old dissenting groups followed his example, giving impetus to an even broader awakening among the lower classes. In Protestant countries religion remained a vital force in the lives of the people.

Catholic Piety

Religion also flourished in Catholic Europe around 1700, but there were important differences with Protestant practice. First of all, the visual contrast was striking. Baroque artists had lavished rich and emotionally exhilarating figures and images on Catholic churches; Protestants excluded such works from their places of worship. Catholics in Europe remained intensely religious.

The tremendous popular strength of religion in Catholic countries reflected religion's integral role in community life and popular culture. Thus although Catholics reluctantly confessed their sins to priests, they enthusiastically joined together in religious festivals to celebrate the passage of the liturgical year. In addition

to the great processional days—such as Palm Sunday, the joyful re-enactment of Jesus' triumphal entry into Jerusalem—each parish had its own saints' days, processions, and pilgrimages. Led by its priest, a congregation might march around the village or across the countryside to a local shrine or chapel, perhaps closing the event with an enormous picnic. Before each procession or feast day the priest explained its religious significance to kindle group piety. But processions were also part of folklore and tradition, an escape from work, and a form of recreation. A holiday atmosphere sometimes reigned on longer processions. People drank and danced, and couples disappeared into the woods.

Indeed, devout Catholics had many religious beliefs that were marginal to the Christian faith, often of obscure or even pagan origin. On the feast of Saint Anthony, for example, priests were expected to bless salt and bread for farm animals to protect them from disease. One saint's relics could help cure a child of fear, and there were healing springs for many ailments. Ordinary people combined a strong Christian faith with a wealth of time-honored superstitions.

Parish priests and Catholic hierarchies sought increasingly to "purify" popular religious practice and to detach that purified religion from everyday life in the eighteenth century. French priests particularly denounced the "various remnants of paganism" found in popular bonfire ceremonies during Lent in which young men, "yelling and screaming like madmen," tried to jump over the bonfires in order to help the crops grow and protect themselves from illness. One priest saw rational Christians regressing into pagan animals— "the triumph of Hell and the shame of Christianity."[13]

In contrast with Protestant reformers, who had already used the power of the territorial state to crush such practices, many Catholic priests and bishops preferred a compromise between theological purity and the people's piety, perhaps realizing that the line between divine truth and mere superstition is not easily drawn. Thus the severity of the formal attack on popular Catholicism varied widely by country and region. Where authorities pursued purification vigorously, as in Austria under Joseph II, pious peasants saw only an incomprehensible attack on the true faith and drew back in anger. Their reaction dramatized the growing tension between the educated elites and the common people.

Leisure and Recreation

The combination of religious celebration and popular recreation seen in festivals and processions was most strikingly displayed at Carnival, a time of reveling and excess in Catholic and Mediterranean Europe. Carnival preceded Lent—the forty days of fasting and penitence before Easter—and for a few days in January or February a wild release of drinking, masquerading, and dancing reigned. A combination of plays, processions, and rowdy spectacles turned the established order upside down. Peasants became nobles, fools turned into philosophers, and the rich were humbled. These once-a-year rituals gave people a much-appreciated chance to release their pent-up frustrations and aggressions before life returned to the usual pattern of leisure and recreation.

That pattern featured socializing in groups, for despite the spread of literacy the culture of the common people was largely oral rather than written. In the cold, dark winter months families gathered around the fireplace to talk, sing, tell stories, do craftwork, and keep warm. In some parts of Europe women gathered together in groups in someone's cottage to chat, sew, spin, and laugh. Sometimes a few young men would be invited so that the daughters (and mothers) could size up potential suitors in a supervised atmosphere. A favorite recreation of men was drinking and talking with buddies in public places. It was a sorry village that had no tavern. In addition to old favorites such as beer and wine, the common people turned with gusto toward cheap and potent hard liquor, which in the eighteenth century fell in price because of the greatly improved techniques for distilling grain.

Towns and cities offered a wide range of amusements. Participants had to pay for many of these because the eighteenth century saw a sharp increase in the commercialization of leisure-time activities—a trend that continues to this day. Urban fairs featured prepared foods, acrobats, freak shows, open-air performances, optical illusions, and the like. Such entertainments attracted a variety of social classes. So did the growing number of commercial, profit-oriented spectator sports. These ranged from traveling circuses and horse races to boxing matches and bullfights. Sports heroes such as hefty heavyweight champions and haughty matadors made their appearance on the historical scene.

"Blood sports," such as bullbaiting and cockfighting, remained popular with the masses. In bullbaiting a bull, usually chained to a stake in the courtyard of an inn, was attacked by ferocious dogs for the amusement of the innkeeper's guests. Eventually the maimed and tortured animal was slaughtered by a butcher and sold as meat. In a cockfight two roosters, carefully trained by their owners and armed with razor-sharp steel spurs, slashed and clawed each other in a small ring until the victor won—and the loser died. An added attraction of cockfighting was that the screaming spectators could bet on the lightning-fast combat and its uncertain outcome.

In trying to place the vibrant popular culture of the common people in broad perspective, historians have stressed the growing criticism levied against it by the educated elites in the second half of the eighteenth century. These elites, which had previously shared the popular enthusiasm for religious festivals, Carnival, drinking in taverns, blood sports, and the like, now tended to see only superstition, sin, disorder, and vulgarity.[14] The resulting attack on popular culture, which had its more distant origins in the Protestant clergy's efforts to eliminate frivolity and superstition, was intensified as educated elites embraced the critical world-view of the Enlightenment. This shift in cultural attitudes was yet another aspect of the widening separation between the common people and the educated public. The mutual hostility that this separation engendered played an important role in the emergence of sharp class conflict in the era of the French and the Industrial Revolutions.

SUMMARY

In recent years imaginative research has greatly increased the specialist's understanding of ordinary life and social patterns in the past. The human experience as recounted by historians has become richer and more meaningful, and many mistaken ideas have fallen by the wayside. This has been particularly true of eighteenth-century, predominately agrarian Europe, which combined a fascinating mixture of continuity and change.

The life of the people remained primarily rural and oriented toward the local community. Tradition, routine, and well-established codes of behavior framed much of the everyday experience of the typical villager. Thus just as the three-field agricultural cycle and its pattern of communal rights had determined traditional patterns of grain production, so did community values in the countryside strongly encourage a late age for marriage, a low rate of illegitimate births, and a strict attitude toward children. Patterns of recreation and leisure, from churchgoing and religious festivals to sewing and drinking in groups, also reflected and reinforced community ties and values. Many long-standing ideas and beliefs, ranging from obscure religious customs to support for fair prices, remained strong forces and sustained continuity in popular life.

Yet powerful forces also worked for change. Many of these came from outside and above, from the aggressive capitalists, educated elites, and government officials discussed in the last two chapters. Closely knit villages began to lose control over families and marital practices, as could be seen in the earlier, more romantic marriages of cottage workers and in the beginning of the explosion in illegitimate births. Although the new, less rigorous attitudes toward children that were emerging in elite culture did not reach the common people, the elite's belief in the usefulness of some education did result in growing popular literacy. The grain-based diet became more varied with the grudging acceptance of the potato, and the benefits of the spectacular conquest of smallpox began to reach the common people in the late eighteenth century. Finally, the common people found that their beliefs and customs were being increasingly attacked by educated elites, which thought they knew best. The popular reaction to these attacks generally remained muted in the eighteenth century, but the common people and their advocates would offer vigorous responses and counterattacks in the revolutionary era (see Chapter 23).

NOTES

1. Quoted in S. Chapman, *The Lancashire Cotton Industry* (Manchester, Eng.: Manchester University Press, 1903), p. 13.
2. Quoted in J. M. Beattie, "The Criminality of Women in Eighteenth-Century England," *Journal of Social History* 8 (Summer 1975): 86.
3. W. L. Langer, "Infanticide: A Historical Survey," *History of Childhood Quarterly* 1 (Winter 1974): 357.
4. Quoted in R. Cobb, *The Police and the People: French Popular Protest, 1789–1820* (Oxford: Clarendon Press, 1970), p. 238.
5. G. Gullickson, *Spinners and Weavers of Auffay: Rural Industry and the Sexual Division of Labor in a French Village, 1750–1850* (Cambridge: Cambridge University Press, 1986), p. 186.
6. Quoted in B. W. Lorence, "Parents and Children in Eighteenth-Century Europe," *History of Childhood Quarterly* 2 (Summer 1974): 1–2.
7. Quoted ibid., pp. 13, 16.
8. E. Kennedy, *A Cultural History of the French Revolution* (New Haven, Conn.: Yale University Press, 1989), p. 47.
9. Quoted in R. Sand, *The Advance to Social Medicine* (London: Staples Press, 1952), pp. 86–87.
10. Quoted in K. Pinson, *Pietism as a Factor in the Rise of German Nationalism* (New York: Columbia University Press, 1934), p. 13.
11. Quoted ibid., pp. 43–44.
12. Quoted in S. Andrews, *Methodism and Society* (London: Longmans, Green, 1970), p. 327.
13. Quoted in T. Tackett, *Priest and Parish in Eighteenth-Century France* (Princeton, N.J.: Princeton University Press, 1977), p. 214.
14. I. Woloch, *Eighteenth-Century Europe: Tradition and Progress, 1715–1789* (New York: W. W. Norton, 1982), pp. 220–221; see also pp. 214–220.

SUGGESTED READING

Social topics of the kind considered in this chapter have come into their own in recent years, and the reader is strongly advised to take time to look through recent volumes of journals such as *Journal of Social History, Past and Present, History of Childhood Quarterly,* and *Journal of Interdisciplinary History.*

Two fine books on the growth of population are C. Cipolla's short and lively *The Economic History of World Population* (1962) and T. McKeown's scholarly *The Modern Rise of Population* (1977). W. McNeill, *Plagues and Peoples* (1976), is also noteworthy. B. H. Slicher van Bath, *The Agrarian History of Western Europe,* A.D. *500–1850* (1963), is a wide-ranging general introduction to the gradual transformation of European agriculture. J. Blum, *The End of the Old Order in Rural Europe* (1978), is an impressive comparative study. E. L. R. Ladurie, *The Peasants of Languedoc* (1976), a brilliant and challenging study of rural life in southern France for several centuries, complements J. Goody et al., eds., *Family and Inheritance: Rural Society in Western Europe, 1200–1800* (1976). J. Brewer and R. Porter, eds., *Consumption and the World of Goods* (1993), reflects the growing historical interest in consumption. O. Hufton deals vividly and sympathetically with rural migration, work, women, and much more in *The Poor in Eighteenth-Century France* (1974). F. Braudel, *Civilization and Capitalism, 15th–18th Century* (1981–1984), is a monumental and highly recommended three-volume synthesis of social and economic development. Another exciting work is J. Nef, *War and Human Progress* (1968), which examines the impact of war on economic and industrial development in European history between about 1500 and 1800 and may be compared with M. Gutmann, *War and Rural Life in the Early Modern Low Countries* (1980).

Among general introductions to the history of the family, women, and children, J. Casey, *The History of the Family* (1989), is recommended. A. Imhof, *Lost Worlds: How Our European Ancestors Coped with Everyday Life and Why Life Is So Hard Today* (1996), sheds light on family ties. P. Laslett, *The World We Have Lost* (1965), is a pioneering investigation of England before the Industrial Revolution. L. Stone, *The Family, Sex and Marriage in England, 1500–*

1800 (1977), is a provocative general interpretation, and L. Tilly and J. Scott, *Women, Work and Family* (1978), is excellent. Two valuable works on women, both with good bibliographies, are M. Boxer and J. Quataert, eds., *Connecting Spheres: Women in the Western World, 1500 to the Present* (1987), and R. Bridenthal, C. Koonz, and S. Stuard, eds., *Becoming Visible: Women in European History,* 2d ed. (1987). P. Ariès, *Centuries of Childhood: A Social History of Family Life* (1962), is a famous study. E. Shorter, *The Making of the Modern Family* (1975), is a lively interpretation, which should be compared with the excellent study by M. Segalen, *Love and Power in the Peasant Family: Rural France in the Nineteenth Century* (1983). A. MacFarlane, *Origins of English Individualism: The Family, Property and Social Transition* (1978), is a major work. I. Pinchbeck and M. Hewitt, *Children in English Society* (1973), is a good introduction. B. Lorence-Kot, *Child-Rearing and Reform: A Study of Nobility in Eighteenth-Century Poland* (1985), stresses the harshness of parental discipline.

Various aspects of sexual relationships are treated imaginatively by M. Foucault, *The History of Sexuality* (1981), and R. Wheaton and T. Hareven, eds., *Family and Sexuality in French History* (1980). L. Moch, *Moving Europeans: Migration in Western Europe Since 1650* (1992), offers a rich, human, and highly recommended account of the movements of millions of ordinary people. J. Burnett, *A History of the Cost of Living* (1969), has a great deal of interesting information about what people spent their money on in the past and complements J. C. Drummond and A. Wilbraham, *The Englishman's Food: A History of Five Centuries of English Diet,* 2d ed. (1958). D. Porter and R. Porter, *Patient's Progress: Doctors and Doctoring in Eighteenth-Century England* (1989), and M. Romsey, *Professional and Popular Medicine in France, 1770–1830: The Social World of Medical Practice* (1988), are recommended. Good introductions to the evolution of medical practices include R. Porter, ed., *The Cambridge Illustrated History of Medicine* (1966), and A. Digby, *Making a Medical Living: Doctors and Patients in the English Market for Medicine, 1720–1991* (1994). M. Lindemann, *Health and Healing in Eighteenth-Century Germany* (1996), is a wide-ranging synthesis. H. Marland, ed., *The Art of Midwifery: Early Modern Midwives in Europe* (1993), discusses developments in several countries and complements L. Ulrich, *A Midwife's Tale: The Life of Martha Ballard, Based on Her Diary, 1785–1812* (1990), a superb reconstruction. W. Boyd, *History of Western Education* (1966), is a standard survey, whereas R. Houston, *Literacy in Early Modern Europe: Culture and Education, 1500–1800* (1988), is brief and engaging.

The study of popular culture is expanding. Among older studies, M. George, *London Life in the Eighteenth Century* (1965), is a delight, whereas D. Roche, *The People of Paris: An Essay in Popular Culture in the 18th Century* (1987), presents an unforgettable portrait of the Paris poor. I. Woloch, *Eighteenth-Century Europe: Tradition and Progress, 1715–1789* (1982), includes a survey of popular culture and a good bibliography. R. Malcolmson, *Popular Recreation in English Society, 1700–1850* (1973), provides a colorful account of boxers, bettors, bullbaiting, and more. L. Hunt, *The New Cultural History* (1989), provides an engaging discussion of conceptual issues. An important series edited by R. Forster and O. Ranuum considers neglected social questions such as diet, abandoned children, and deviants, as does P. Burke's excellent study, *Popular Culture in Early Modern Europe* (1978). J. Gillis, *For Better, for Worse: Marriage in Britain Since 1500* (1985), and R. Philips, *Untying the Knot: A Short History of Divorce* (1991), are good introductions to institutional changes.

Good works on religious life include J. Delumeau, *Catholicism Between Luther and Voltaire: A New View of the Counter-Reformation* (1977); B. Semmel, *The Methodist Revolution* (1973); and J. Bettey, *Church and Community: The Parish Church in English Life* (1979).

A New Way to Educate Children

Emile, by Jean-Jacques Rousseau, is one of history's most original books. Sometimes called a declaration of rights for children, Emile challenged existing patterns of child rearing and pleaded for humane treatment of children.

Rousseau's work also had a powerful impact on theories of education. As the following passage suggests, Emile argued that education must shield the unspoiled child from the corrupting influences of civilization and allow the child to develop naturally and spontaneously. It is eloquent testimony to Rousseau's troubled life that he neglected his own children and placed all five of them in orphanages.

Rousseau believed that the sexes are by nature intended for different occupations. Thus Emile might eventually tackle difficult academic subjects, but Sophie, his future wife in the book, needed to learn only how to manage the home and be a good mother and an obedient wife. The idea that girls and boys should be educated to operate in "separate spheres" was to gain wide acceptance in the nineteenth century.

A man must know many things which seem useless to a child, but need the child learn, or can he indeed learn, all that the man must know? Try to teach the child what is of use to a child and you will find that it takes all his time. Why urge him to the studies of an age he may never reach, to the neglect of those studies which meet his present needs? "But," you ask, "will it not be too late to learn what he ought to know when the time comes to use it?" I cannot tell; but this I do know, it is impossible to teach it sooner, for our real teachers are experience and emotion, and man will never learn what befits a man except under its own conditions. A child knows he must become a man; all the ideas he may have as to man's place in life are so many opportunities for his instruction, but he should remain in complete ignorance of those ideas which are beyond his grasp. My whole book is one continued argument in support of this fundamental principle of education.

As soon as we have contrived to give our pupil [Emile] an idea of the word "useful," we have got an additional means of controlling him, for this word makes a great impression on him, provided that its meaning for him is a meaning relative to his own age, and provided he clearly sees its relation to his own well-being. . . . "What is the use of that?" In the future this is the sacred formula, the formula by which he and I test every action of our lives. . . .

I do not like verbal explanations. Young people pay little heed to them, nor do they remember them. Things! Things! I cannot repeat it too often. We lay too much stress upon words; we teachers babble, and our students follow our example.

Suppose we are studying the course of the sun and the way to find our bearings, when all at once Emile interrupts me with the question, "What is the use of that?" What a fine lecture I might give [going on and on]! . . . When I have finished I shall have shown myself a regular pedant, I shall have made a great display of learning, and not one single idea has he understood. . . .

But Emile is educated in a simpler fashion. We take so much pains to teach him a difficult idea that he will have heard nothing of all this. At the first word he does not understand, he will run away, he will prance about the room, and leave me to speechify by myself. Let us seek a more commonplace explanation; my scientific learning is of no use to him.

We were observing the position of the forest to the north of Montmorency when he interrupted me with the usual question, "What is the use of that?" "You are right," I said. "Let us take time to think it over, and if we find it is no use we will drop it, for we only want useful games." We find something else to do and geography is put aside for the day.

Next morning I suggest a walk; there is nothing he would like better; children are always ready to run about, and he is a good walker. We climb up to the forest, we wander through its clearings and lose ourselves. . . . At last we [are exhausted and] sit down to rest and to consider our position. I assume that Emile has been educated like an ordinary child. He does not think, he begins to cry; he has no idea we are close to Montmorency, which is hidden from our view by a mere thicket. . . .

Jean-Jacques. "My dear Emile, what shall we do to get out?"

Emile. "I am sure I do not know. I am tired, I am hungry, I am thirsty, I cannot go any further."

Jean-Jacques. "Do you suppose I am any better off? I would cry too if I could make my lunch off tears. Crying is no use, we must look about us. What time is it?"

Emile. "It is noon and I am so hungry!"

Jean-Jacques. "I am so hungry too. . . . Unluckily my dinner won't come to find me. It is twelve o'clock. This time yesterday we were observing the position of the forest from Montmorency. If only we could see the position of Montmorency from the forest—"

Emile. "But yesterday we could see the forest, and here we cannot see the town."

Jean-Jacques. "That is just it. If we could only find it without seeing it. . . . Did not we say the forest was—"

Emile. "North of Montmorency."

Jean-Jacques. "Then Montmorency must lie—"

Emile. "South of the forest."

Jean-Jacques. "We know how to find the north at midday."

Emile. "Yes, by the direction of the shadows."

Jean-Jacques. "But the south?"

Emile. "What shall we do?"

Jean-Jacques. "The south is opposite the north."

Emile. "That is true; we need only find the opposite of the shadows. That is the south! That is the south! Montmorency must be over there! Let us look for it there!"

Jean-Jacques. "Perhaps you are right; let us follow this path through the wood."

Emile. (Clapping his hands.) "Oh, I can see Montmorency! there it is, quite plain, just in front of us! Come to lunch, come to dinner, make haste! Astronomy is some use after all."

Be sure that he thinks this if he does not say it; no matter which, provided I do not say it myself. He will certainly never forget this day's lesson as long as he lives, while if I had only led him to think of all this at home, my lecture would have been forgotten the next day. Teach by doing whenever you can, and only fall back upon words when doing is out of the question.

Jean-Jacques Rousseau (1712–1778), portrayed as a gentle teacher and a pensive philosopher in this contemporary illustration. *(The Granger Collection, New York)*

Questions for Analysis

1. What criticism did Rousseau direct at the social and educational practices of his time?

2. How did Rousseau propose to educate his pupil?

3. Do you think Rousseau's plan appealed to peasants and urban workers in the eighteenth century? Why or why not?

4. In what ways did Rousseau's plan of education and his assumptions on human nature reflect some major ideas of the Enlightenment?

Source: Slightly adapted from J.-J. Rousseau, *Emile, or Education,* trans. B. Foxley (New York: E. P. Dutton, 1911), pp. 141–144.

20

Africa and the World, ca 1400–1800

African-Portuguese ivory
saltcellar, ca 1490–1530.
*(Museo Preistorico e
Etnografico, Rome)*

African states and societies of the fifteenth through eighteenth centuries comprised hundreds of ethnic groups and a wide variety of languages, cultures, and kinds of economic and political development. Modern European intrusion into Africa beginning in the fifteenth century led to the transatlantic slave trade, one of the great forced migrations in world history. Africa made a substantial, though involuntary, contribution to the building of the West's industrial civilization. In the seventeenth century, an increasing desire for sugar in Europe resulted in an increasing demand for slave labor in South America and the West Indies. In the eighteenth century, Western technological changes created a demand for cotton and other crops that required extensive human labor. As a result, the West's "need" for slaves from Africa increased dramatically.

Africa's relationship with Asia, the Islamic world, and the West stretches back a very long time, but only recently have anthropologists, economists, and historians begun to ask critical questions about African societies in early modern times.

- What kinds of economic and social structures did African societies have?
- What impact did Islam have on African societies?
- What kinds of literary sources survive?
- What role did slavery play in African societies before European intrusion?
- What were the geographical and societal origins of the slaves involuntarily shipped to America and to Asia?

This chapter will explore these questions.

 ## SENEGAMBIA AND BENIN

In Africa in the mid-fifteenth century, there were societies held together by family or kinship ties, and there were kingdoms and states ruled by princes who governed defined areas through bureaucratic hierarchies. Along the two-thousand-mile west coast between Senegambia and the northeastern shore of the Gulf of Guinea, a number of kingdoms flourished. Because much of that coastal region is covered by tropical rain forest, in contrast to the western Sudan, it is called the West African Forest Region (Map 20.1). The Senegambian states in the north possessed a homogeneous culture and a common history. For centuries Senegambia—named for the Senegal and Gambia Rivers—had served as an important entrepôt for desert caravan contact with the Islamic civilizations of North Africa and the Middle East. Through the transatlantic slave trade, Senegambia contributed heavily to New World population in the early seventeenth century. That trade brought Senegambia into contact with the Americas and Europe. Thus Senegambia felt the impact of Islamic culture to the north and of European influences from the maritime West.

In the thirteenth century, the kingdoms of Ghana and Mali had incorporated parts of Senegambia. Mali's influence disintegrated after 1450, and successor kingdoms that were independent but connected to one another through family ties emerged. Stronger states rose and temporarily exercised power over weaker ones.

Scholars are still exploring the social and political structures of the various Senegambian states. The peoples of Senegambia spoke Wolof, Serer, and Pulaar, which all belong to the West African language group. Both the Wolof-speakers and the Serer-speakers had clearly defined social classes: royalty, nobility, warriors, peasants, low-caste artisans such as blacksmiths and leatherworkers, and slaves. Slaves were individuals who were pawned for debt, house servants who could not be sold, and people who were acquired through war or purchase. Senegambian slavery varied from society to society but generally was not a benign institution. In some places, the treatment of slaves was as harsh as treatment in the Western world later would be. However, many Senegambian slaves were not considered property to be bought and sold, and some served as royal advisers and enjoyed great power and prestige.[1]

The king of the Wolof was elected by the nobility. After his election, the king immediately acquired authority and a special religious charisma. He commanded contingents of soldier-slaves and appointed village chiefs. The king gained his revenue from the chiefs, from merchants, and from taxes levied on defeated peoples.[2] The Wolof had a well-defined government hierarchy.

Among the stateless societies of Senegambia, where kinship and lineage groups tended to fragment communities, age-grade systems evolved. Age-grades were groups of men and women whom the society initiated into adulthood at the same time. Age-grades cut across family ties, created community-wide loyalties, and provided a means of local law enforcement, because the

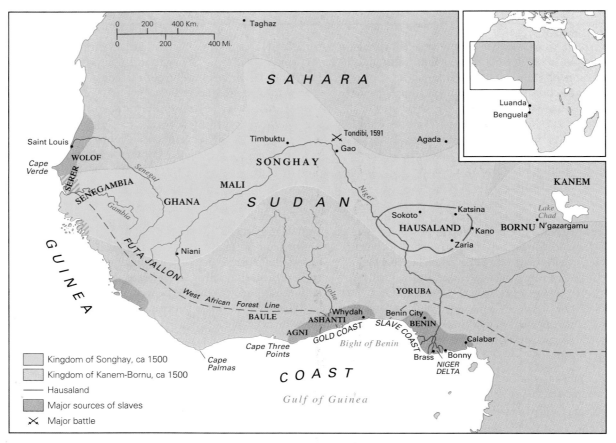

MAP 20.1 West African Kingdoms and the Slave Trade, ca 1500 to 1800   Consider the role that rivers and other geographical factors played in the development of the West African slave trade. Why were Luanda and Benguela the logical Portuguese sources for slaves?

group was responsible for the behavior of all its members.

The typical Senegambian community was a small self-supporting agricultural village of closely related families. Custom assigned a high value to cultivation of the land—the shared objective of the group. Fields were cut from the surrounding forest, and the average farm of six to eight acres supported a moderate-size family. Often the family worked the land for a common harvest; sometimes individuals had their own private fields. Millet and sorghum were the staple grains in northern Senegambia; farther south, forest dwellers cultivated yams as a staple. Senegambians supplemented their diet with plantains, beans, bananas, fish, oysters, and small game such as rabbits and monkeys. Along the Guinea coast, rice was the basic cereal, and okra, onions, melons, and pepper spiced the regular diet. Frequent fairs in neighboring villages served as markets for the exchange of produce and opportunities for receiving out-

side news and social diversion. As one scholar has put it, "Life was simple, government largely limited to the settlement of disputes by family heads or elders . . . social life centered on the ceremony accompanying birth, death, and family alliance."[3]

The fifteenth and sixteenth centuries saw the emergence of the great forest kingdom of Benin (see Map 20.1) in what is now southern Nigeria. Although scholars still know little about Benin's origins, its history seems to have been characterized by power struggles between the king and the nobility that neither side ever completely won. An elaborate court ceremonial exalted the position of the *oba,* or king, and brought stability to the state. In the later fifteenth century, the oba Ewuare played off his palace chiefs against the village chiefs and thereby maintained a balance of power. A great warrior, Ewuare strengthened his army and pushed Benin's borders as far as the Niger River in the east, westward into Yoruba country, and south to the Gulf of Guinea. Dur-

The Oba of Benin The walls of the Oba's palace were decorated with bronze plaques that date from about the sixteenth to eighteenth centuries. This plaque vividly conveys the Oba's power, majesty, and authority. The necklace (or choker) is his symbol of royalty. Attendants hold up his hands, and warriors raise shields over his head as sunshades. *(The Metropolitan Museum of Art, The Michael C. Rockefeller Memorial Collection, Gift of Nelson A. Rockefeller, 1965)*

ing the late sixteenth and seventeenth centuries, the office of the oba evolved from a warrior-kingship to a position of spiritual leadership.

At its height in the late sixteenth century, Benin controlled a vast territory, and European visitors described a sophisticated society. According to a modern historian, the capital, Benin City, "was a stronghold twenty-five miles in circumference, protected by walls and natural defenses, containing an elaborate royal palace and neatly laid-out houses with verandas and balustrades, and divided by broad avenues and smaller intersecting streets."[4] Visitors also noted that Benin City was kept scrupulously clean and had no beggars and that public security was so effective that theft was unknown. The period also witnessed remarkable artistic creativity in ironwork, in carved ivory, and especially in bronze portrait busts. Over nine hundred brass plaques survive, providing important information about Benin court life, military triumphs, and cosmological ideas.

In 1485 the Portuguese and other Europeans in pursuit of trade began to appear in Benin. A small exchange in pepper and slaves developed but never acquired importance in the Benin economy. Nor did the Portuguese have much success in converting the staunchly animistic people to Christianity. Europe's impact on Benin was minimal. In the early eighteenth century, as tributary states and stronger neighbors nibbled at Benin's frontiers, the kingdom underwent a crisis. Benin, however, survived as an independent entity until the British conquered and burned Benin City in 1898.

Women, Marriage, and Work

West Africa's need for population (see page 624) profoundly affected marriage patterns and family structure. Since wives and children could colonize and cultivate the land, and since they brought prestige, social support, and security in old age, the demand for them was strong. The result was intense competition for women, inequality of access to them, an emphasis on male virility and female fertility, slight concern for chastity, and serious tension between male generations. Polygyny was almost universal; scholars today project nineteenth-century evidence backward, and at that time two-thirds of rural wives were in polygynous marriages. The social taboo against sexual intercourse with a woman immediately after childbirth need not restrain a man with several wives.

Men acquired wives in two ways. First, artistic evidence and the evidence of European observers suggest that groups of young men formed subcultures that emphasized dress and personal adornment, virility, and aggression to attract girls' attention. Convinced of her interest, a young man abducted a girl, and they eloped and began a union. The second method was by bride wealth, in which a man's family paid the bride's family for the loss of her labor and fertility. Since it took time for a young man to acquire the bride wealth, most men married at an older age. Whereas women married at about the onset of puberty, all but the richest men delayed marriage until about age thirty, although that need not mean they were celibate.

The easy availability of land in Africa reduced the kinds of generational conflict that occurred in western Europe, where land was scarce (see page 398). The competition for wives between male generations, however, became "one of the most dynamic and enduring forces in African history."[5] On the one hand, myth and folklore stressed respect for the elderly, and the older men in a community imposed their authority over the younger ones by conducting painful rites of initiation into adulthood, such as circumcision. On the other hand, West African societies were not gerontocracies, as few people lived much beyond forty, and young men possessed the powerful asset of their labor, which could easily be turned into independence where so much land was available.

"Without children you are naked" goes a Yoruba proverb, and the production of children was the primary goal of marriage. Just as a man's virility determined his honor, so barrenness damaged a woman's status. A wife's infidelity was considered a less serious problem than her infertility. A woman might have six widely spaced pregnancies in her fertile years; the universal practice of breast-feeding infants for two, three, or even four years may have inhibited conception. Long intervals between births due to food shortages also may have limited pregnancies and checked population growth. Although little reliable evidence survives be-

fore the nineteenth century, scholars assume a very high infant mortality rate due to climate, poor nutrition, and infectious diseases.

Both extended and nuclear families seem to have been common in West Africa. The household of a Big Man (a man of power in the locality) included his wives, married and unmarried sons, unmarried daughters, poor relations, dependents, and scores of children. Extended families were common among the Hausa and Malinke peoples (see pages 627–628) and were the main colonizing groups in equatorial Africa. On the Gold Coast in the seventeenth century, a well-to-do man's household might number 150 people, in the Kongo region several hundred. Where one family cultivated extensive land, a large household of young adults, children, and slaves probably proved most efficient. Most families elsewhere, however, seemed to number only 5 or 6 people.

In agriculture men did the heavy work of felling trees and clearing the land; women performed the tedious chores of planting and weeding. All cooperated. Between 1000 and 1400, cassava (manioc), bananas, and plantains came to West Africa from Asia, leading to a reliance on cassava as the staple food. Cassava required little effort to grow, the tubers could be left unharvested for years, and they stored well, but they also had little nutritional value. In the sixteenth century, the Portuguese introduced maize (corn), sweet potatoes, and new varieties of yams from the Americas.[6] Fish supplemented the diet of people living in a region near a river or stream. Describing the food of his Ibo people in Benin in the mid-eighteenth century, Olaudah Equiano lists plantains, yams, beans, and Indian corn, along with stewed poultry, goat, or bullock (castrated steer) seasoned with peppers. Such a protein-rich diet was probably exceptional. Equiano also writes, "When our women are not employed with the men in tillage, their usual occupation is spinning and weaving cloth which they afterwards dye and make into garments."[7]

Disease posed perhaps the biggest obstacle to population growth. Malaria, spread by mosquitoes and rampant in West Africa (except in cool, dry Cameroon), was the greatest killer, especially of infants. West Africans developed a relatively high degree of immunity to malaria and other parasitic diseases, including hookworm (which enters the body through shoeless feet and attaches itself to the intestines); yaws (contracted by nonsexual contact and recognized by ulcerating lesions); sleeping sickness (the parasite enters the blood through the bite of the tsetse fly; symptoms are enlarged lymph nodes and, at the end, a comatose state);

Queen Mother and Attendants   As in Ottoman, Chinese, and European societies, so the mothers of rulers in Africa sometimes exercised considerable political power because of their influence on their sons. African kings granted the title "Queen Mother" as a badge of honor. In this figure, the long beaded cap, called "chicken's beak," symbolizes the mother's rank as do her elaborate neck jewelry and attendants. *(Metropolitan Museum of Art. Gift of Mr. and Mrs. Klaus G. Perls, 1991)*

and a mild nonsexual form of syphilis. As in Chinese and European communities in the early modern period, the sick depended on folk medicine. The Hausa people had several kinds of medical specialists: midwives, bone setters, exorcists using religious methods, and herbalists. Medical treatment consisted of herbal medication: salves, ointments, and purgatives. Modern anthropologists have great respect for African folk medicine, but disease was common where the diet was poor and lacked adequate vitamins. Slaves taken to the Americas grew much taller and broader than their African ancestors.

The devastating effects of famine, often mentioned in West African oral traditions, represent another major check on population growth. Drought, excessive rain, swarms of locusts, and rural wars that prevented the cultivation of land all meant later food shortages. In the 1680s, famine extended from the Senegambian coast to the Upper Nile, and many people sold themselves into slavery for food. In the eighteenth century, "slave exports" (see pages 634–639) "peaked during famines, and one ship obtained a full cargo merely by offering food." The worst disaster occurred from 1738 to 1756, when, according to one chronicler, the poor were reduced to cannibalism, an African metaphor for the complete collapse of civilization. The acute strains of smallpox introduced by Europeans certainly did not help population growth, nor did venereal syphilis, which originated in Latin America.[8]

Trade and Industry

As in all premodern societies, the West African economies rested on agriculture and the production of adequate food for local needs. There was some trade and industry, but population shortages encouraged local self-sufficiency, slowed transportation, and hindered exchange. There were very few large markets, and their relative isolation from the outside world and their failure to attract large numbers of foreign merchants limited technological innovation.

For centuries, black Africans had exchanged goods with North African merchants in centers such as Gao, Djenné, and Timbuktu. That long-distance trade was conducted and controlled by Muslim Berber merchants. Except as servants or slaves, black Africans did not make the long trek across the Sahara.

As elsewhere, the cheapest method of transportation was by water, and many small dugout canoes and larger trading canoes plied the Niger and its delta region (see Map 20.1). On land West African peoples used pack animals (camels or donkeys) rather than wheeled vehicles; south of the Sahara, only a narrow belt of land was suitable for animal-drawn carts. When traders reached an area infested with tsetse flies (see page 624), they transferred each animal's load to two human porters. Such difficulties in transport severely restricted long-distance trade, so most people relied on the regional exchange of local specialties.

West African communities had a well-organized market system. At informal markets on riverbanks, fishermen bartered fish for local specialties. More formal markets existed within towns and villages or on neutral ground between them. Markets also rotated among neighboring villages on certain days. People exchanged cotton cloth, thread, palm oil, millet, vegetables, and small articles for daily living. Olaudah Equiano says that foods constituted the main articles of commercial exchange. Local sellers were usually women; traders from afar were men.

Between the fifteenth and seventeenth centuries, salt represented West Africa's chief mineral product, its value worth more than the entire trans-Saharan trade. Salt is essential to human health; the Hausa language has more than fifty words for it. The main salt-mining center was at Taghaz (see Map 20.1) in the western Sahara, a desolate settlement about which the fourteenth-century traveler Ibn Battuta says, "This is a village with nothing good about it." In the most wretched conditions, slaves dug the salt from desiccated lakes and loaded heavy blocks onto camels' backs. The camels sometimes traveled in caravans of twenty thousand to thirty thou-

sand stretching over many miles. Tuareg warriors and later Moors (peoples of Berber and Arab descent) controlled the north–south trade; they traded their salt for gold, grain, slaves, and kola nuts, which were used by Muslims as stimulants or aphrodisiacs. Cowrie shells, imported from the Maldive Islands in the Indian Ocean by way of Gujarat (see page 497) and North Africa, served as the medium of exchange. (Shell money continued as a medium long after European intrusion.) Gold continued to be mined and shipped from Mali until South American bullion flooded Europe in the sixteenth century. Thereafter, its production in Africa steadily declined.

West African peoples engaged in many crafts, such as weaving various types of baskets. Ironworking, a specialized skill producing articles useful to hunters, farmers, and warriors, became hereditary in individual families; such expertise was regarded as family property. The textile industry had the greatest level of specialization. The earliest fabric in West Africa was made of vegetable fiber. Muslim traders introduced cotton and its weaving in the ninth century, as the fine-quality fabrics found in Mali reveal. By the fifteenth century, the Wolof and Malinke regions had professional weavers producing beautiful cloth, but this cloth was too expensive to compete in the Atlantic and Indian Ocean markets after 1500. Women who spun cotton used only a spindle and not a wheel, which slowed output. Women wove on inefficient broadlooms, men on less clumsy but unproductive narrow looms. These were the only machines that West Africans had.[9]

THE SUDAN: SONGHAY, KANEM-BORNU, AND HAUSALAND

The kingdom of Songhay, a successor state of Ghana and Mali, dominated the whole Niger region of the western and central Sudan (see Map 20.1). Muhammad Toure (1492–1528) completed the expansionist and administrative consolidation begun by his predecessors. Muhammad Toure's power rested on his successful military expeditions. From his capital at Gao, he extended his lordship as far north as the salt-mining center at Taghaz in the western Sahara and as far east as Agada and Kano. A convert to Islam, Muhammad made a pilgrimage to Mecca. Impressed by what he saw there, he tried to bring about greater centralization in his own territories. In addition to building a strong army and improving taxation procedures, he replaced local Songhay officials with more efficient Arab ones in an effort to substitute royal institutions for ancient kinship ties.

What kind of economy existed in the Songhay Empire? What social structures? What role did women play in Songhay society? What is known of Songhay education and culture? The paucity of written records and of surviving artifacts prevents scholars from satisfactorily exploring these questions. Some information is provided by Leo Africanus (ca 1465–1550), a Moroccan captured by pirates and given as a slave to Pope Leo X. Leo Africanus became a Christian, taught Arabic in Rome, and in 1526 published an account of his many travels, including a stay in the Songhay kingdom.

As a scholar, Leo was naturally impressed by Timbuktu, the second city of the empire, which he visited in 1513. "Here [is] a great store of doctors, judges, priests, and other learned men, that are bountifully maintained at the King's court," Leo reported.[10] Many of these Islamic scholars had studied in Cairo and other centers of Muslim learning. They gave Timbuktu a reputation for intellectual sophistication, religious piety, and moral justice.

Songhay under Muhammad Toure seems to have enjoyed economic prosperity. Leo Africanus noted the abundant food supply, which was produced in the southern Savanna and carried to Timbuktu by a large fleet of canoes controlled by the king. The Sudanese had large amounts of money to spend, and expensive North African and European luxuries were much in demand: clothes, copperware, glass and stone beads, perfumes, and horses. The existence of many shops and markets implies the development of an urban culture. At Timbuktu merchants, scholars, judges, and artisans constituted a distinctive bourgeoisie. The presence of many foreign merchants, including Jews and Italians, gave the city a cosmopolitan atmosphere. Jews largely controlled the working of gold.

Slaves played a very important part in the economy of Songhay. On the royal farms scattered throughout the kingdom, slaves produced rice—the staple crop—for the royal granaries. Although slaves could possess their own slaves, land, and cattle, they could not bequeath any of this property; the king inherited all of it. Muhammad Toure greatly increased the number of royal slaves through raids on the pagans (non-Muslims). He gave slaves to favorite Muslim scholars, who thus gained a steady source of income. Or the slaves were sold at the large market at Gao. Traders from North Africa bought them for sale in Cairo, Constantinople, Lisbon, Naples, Genoa, and Venice.

The kingdom of Songhay had considerable economic and cultural strengths, but it also had serious internal problems. Islamic institutions never took root in the countryside, and Muslim officials alienated the king

from his people. Muhammad Toure's reforms were a failure. He governed a diverse group of peoples—Tuareg, Malinke, Fulani, as well as Songhay—who were often hostile to one another, and no cohesive element united them. Finally, the Songhay never developed an effective method of transferring power. Revolts, conspiracies, and palace intrigues followed the deaths of every king, and only three of the nine rulers in the dynasty begun by Muhammad Toure died natural deaths. Muhammad himself was murdered by one of his sons. His death began a period of political instability that led to the slow disintegration of the kingdom.[11]

In 1582 the sultanate of Morocco began to press southward in search of a greater share of the trans-Saharan trade. The people of Songhay, lacking effective leadership and believing the desert to be a sure protection against invasion, took no defensive precautions. In 1591 a Moroccan army of three thousand soldiers—many of whom were slaves of European origin equipped with European muskets—crossed the Sahara and inflicted a crushing defeat on the Songhay at Tondibi. This battle spelled the end of the Songhay Empire. Although a moderate-size kingdom lingered on in the south for a century or so and weak political units arose, not until the eighteenth century did kingdoms able to exercise wide authority emerge again.

To the east of Songhay lay the kingdoms of Kanem-Bornu and Hausaland (see Map 20.1). Under the dynamic military leader Idris Alooma (1571–1603), Kanem-Bornu subdued weaker peoples and gained jurisdiction over an extensive area. Well drilled and equipped with firearms, camel-mounted cavalry and a standing army decimated warriors fighting with spears and arrows. Idris Alooma perpetuated the feudal pattern of government in which lands were granted to able fighters in return for loyalty and the promise of future military assistance. Meanwhile, agriculture occupied most people, peasants and slaves alike. Kanem-Bornu shared in the trans-Saharan trade, shipping eunuchs and young girls to North Africa in return for horses and firearms. A devout Muslim, Idris Alooma elicited high praise from ibn Fartura, who wrote a history of his reign called *The Kanem Wars:*

So he made the pilgrimage and visited Medina with delight. . . . Among the benefits which God . . . conferred upon the Sultan Idris Alooma was the acquisition of Turkish musketeers and numerous household slaves who became skilled in firing muskets. . . .

Among the most surprising of his acts was the stand he took against obscenity and adultery, so that no such thing took place openly in his time. Formerly the people had been

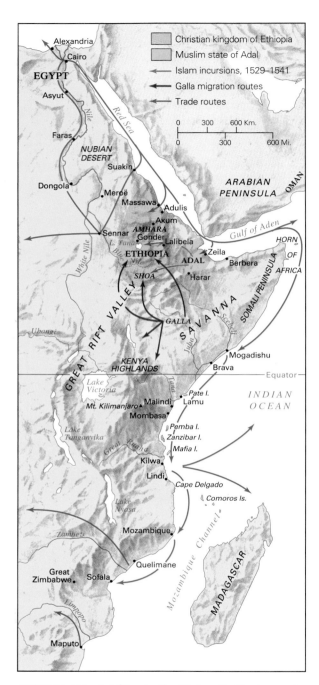

MAP 20.2 East Africa in the Sixteenth Century In early modern times, the Christian kingdom of Ethiopia, first isolated and then subjected to Muslim and European pressures, played an insignificant role in world affairs. But the East African city-states, which stretched from Sofala in the south to Mogadishu in the north, had powerfully important commercial relations with Mughal India, China, the Ottoman world, and southern Europe.

indifferent to such offences. . . . In fact he was a power among his people and from him came their strength.

The Sultan was intent on the clear path laid down by the Qur'an . . . in all his affairs and actions.[12]

Idris Alooma built mosques at his capital city of N'gazargamu and substituted Muslim courts and Islamic law for African tribunals and ancient customary law. His eighteenth-century successors lacked his vitality and military skills, however, and the empire declined.

Between Songhay and Kanem-Bornu were the lands of the Hausa. An agricultural people living in small villages, the Hausa grew millet, sorghum, barley, rice, cotton, and citrus fruit and raised livestock. Some Hausa merchants carried on a heavy trade in slaves and kola nuts with North African communities across the Sahara. Obscure trading posts evolved into important Hausa city-states like Kano and Katsina, through which Islamic influences entered the region. Kano and Katsina became Muslim intellectual centers and in the fifteenth century attracted scholars from Timbuktu. The Muslim chronicler of the reign of King Muhammad Rimfa of Kano (r. 1463–1499) records that Muhammad introduced the Muslim practices of *purdah,* or seclusion of women; of the *idal-fitr,* or festival after the fast of Ramadan; and of assigning eunuchs to the high offices of state.[13] As in Songhay and Kanem-Bornu, however, Islam made no strong imprint on the mass of the Hausa people until the nineteenth century.

 ## ETHIOPIA

At the beginning of the sixteenth century, the powerful East African Christian kingdom of Ethiopia extended from Massawa in the north to several tributary states in the south (Map 20.2). The ruling Solomonid Dynasty, however, faced serious troubles. Adal, a Muslim state along the southern base of the Red Sea, began incursions into Ethiopia, and in 1529 the Adal general Ahmad ibn-Ghazi inflicted a disastrous defeat on the Ethiopian emperor Lebna Dengel (r. 1508–1540). Ahmad followed up his victory with systematic devastation of the land, destruction of many Ethiopian artistic and literary works, and the forced conversion of thousands to Islam. Lebna Dengel fled to the mountains and appealed to Portugal for assistance. The Portuguese, eager for a share in the wealth of the East African coast and interested in the conversion of Ethiopia to Roman Catholicism, responded with a force of musketeers. In 1541 they decisively defeated the Muslims near Lake Tana.

Saint George in Ethiopian Art   This image of a black Saint George slaying a dragon, from a seventeenth-century Ethiopian manuscript, attests to the powerful and pervasive Christian influence in Ethiopian culture. *(The British Library)*

No sooner had the Muslim threat ended than Ethiopia encountered three more dangers. The Galla, Cushitic-speaking peoples, moved northward in great numbers, occupying portions of Harar, Shoa, and Amhara. The Ethiopians could not defeat them militarily, and the Galla were not interested in assimilation. For the next two centuries, the two peoples lived together in an uneasy truce. Simultaneous with the Galla migrations was the Ottoman Turks' seizure of Massawa and other coastal cities. Then the Jesuits arrived, eager to capitalize on earlier Portuguese support, and attempted to force Roman Catholicism on a proud people whose Coptic form of Christianity long antedated the European version. The overzealous Jesuit missionary Alphonse Mendez tried to revamp the Ethiopian liturgy, rebaptize the people, and replace ancient Ethiopian customs and practices with Roman ones. Since Ethiopian national sentiment was closely tied to Coptic Christianity, violent rebellion and anarchy ensued.

In 1633 the Jesuit missionaries were expelled. For the next two centuries, hostility to foreigners, weak po-

litical leadership, and regionalism characterized Ethiopia. Civil conflicts between the Galla and the Ethiopians erupted continually. The Coptic church, though lacking strong authority, survived as the cornerstone of Ethiopian national identity.

THE SWAHILI CITY-STATES

The word *Swahili,* meaning "People of the Coast," refers to the people living along the East African coast and on the nearby islands. Their history, unlike that of most African peoples, exists in writing. By the eleventh century, the Swahili had accepted Islam, and "its acceptance was the factor that marked the acquisition of 'Swahili' identity: Islam gave the society coherent cultural form."[14] The Swahili language is studied today by North Americans who want to identify themselves as having African ancestry, but slaves shipped from East Africa came from inland, not from Swahili-speaking coastal, peoples; virtually no Swahili people went to North America. As a people living on the shores of the Indian Ocean, the Swahili felt the influences of Indians, Indonesians, Persians, and especially Arabs.

Swahili civilization was overwhelmingly maritime. A fertile, well-watered, and intensely cultivated stretch of land no more than ten miles wide extends down the coast: it yielded rice, grains, citrus fruit, and cloves. The sea provided fish. But the considerable prosperity of the region rested on trade and commerce. The Swahili acted as middlemen in an Indian Ocean–East African protocapitalism, exchanging ivory, rhinoceros horn, tortoise shells, inlaid ebony chairs, copra (dried coconut meat that yields coconut oil), and inland slaves for Arabian and Persian perfumes, toilet articles, ink, and paper

and for Indian textiles, beads, and iron tools. In the fifteenth century, the city-states of Mogadishu, Pate, Lamu, Mombasa, and especially Kilwa enjoyed a worldwide reputation for commercial prosperity.[15] These cities were cosmopolitan, and their standard of living was very high.

The arrival of the Portuguese explorer Vasco da Gama (see Map 16.2 on page 502) in 1498 spelled the end of the Swahili cities' independence. Da Gama, lured by the spice trade, wanted to build a Portuguese maritime empire in the Indian Ocean, and between 1502 and 1507 the southern ports of Kilwa, Zanzibar, and Sofala fell before Portuguese guns and became Portuguese tributary states. (See the feature "Listening to the Past: Duarte Barbosa on the Swahili City-States" on pages 644–645.) The better-fortified northern cities, such as

Fort Jesus, Mombasa   Designed by the Milanese military architect Joao Batista Cairato in traditional European style, and built between 1593 and 1594, this great fortress still stands as a symbol of Portuguese military and commercial power in East Africa and the Indian Ocean in the sixteenth and seventeenth centuries. *(Wolfgang Kaehler/Liaison)*

Mogadishu, survived as important entrepôts for goods to India.

The Portuguese victory in the south proved hollow, however. Rather than accept Portuguese commercial restrictions, the residents deserted the towns, and the town economies crumbled. Large numbers of Kilwa's people, for example, immigrated to northern cities. The flow of gold from inland mines to Sofala slowed to a trickle. Swahili passive resistance successfully prevented the Portuguese from gaining control of the local coastal trade.

After the intermittent bombardment of several cities, Portugal finally won an administrative stronghold near Mombasa in 1589. Called Fort Jesus, it remained a Portuguese base for over a century. In the late seventeenth century, pressures from the northern European maritime powers—the Dutch, French, and English—aided greatly by the Arabs of Oman, combined with local African rebellions to bring about the collapse of Portuguese influence in Africa. A Portuguese presence remained only at Mozambique in the far south.

The Portuguese had no religious or cultural impact on the Swahili cities. Their sole effect was the cities' economic decline.

THE SLAVE TRADE

Slavery had a long history within Africa, and the transatlantic slave trade that began in the late fifteenth century is properly understood against that background. "Slavery was . . . fundamental to the social, political, and economic order of parts of the northern savanna, Ethiopia and the East African coast. . . . Enslavement was an organized activity, sanctioned by law and custom. Slaves were a principal commodity in trade, including the export sector, and slaves were important in the domestic sphere" as concubines, servants, soldiers, and ordinary laborers.[16]

Islam had heavily influenced African slavery. African rulers justified enslavement with the Muslim argument that prisoners of war could be sold; and since captured peoples were considered chattel, they could be used in the same positions that prevailed in the Muslim world. Between 650 and 1600, black as well as white Muslims transported perhaps as many as 4.82 million black slaves across the trans-Saharan trade route.[17] In the fourteenth and fifteenth centuries, the rulers and elites of Mali and Benin imported thousands of white slave women who had originally come from the eastern

KITCHIN STUFF.

Below Stairs The prints and cartoons of Thomas Rowlandson (1756–1827) testify to the sizable numbers of blacks in eighteenth-century London, where they worked in naval and military, as well as domestic, service. Here the household cook, maid, and footman relax before the kitchen fire. Interracial marriages were not uncommon. *(Courtesy of the Trustees of the British Museum)*

Mediterranean.[18] These women were signs of wealth and status symbols. In 1444, when Portuguese caravels landed 235 slaves at Algarve in southern Portugal, a contemporary observed that they seemed "a marvelous (extraordinary) sight, for, amongst them, were some white enough, fair enough, and well-proportioned; others were less white, like mulattoes; others again were black as Ethiops."[19]

Meanwhile, the flow of black people to Europe, begun during the Renaissance, continued. In the seventeenth and eighteenth centuries, perhaps as many as two hundred thousand Africans entered European societies. Some arrived as slaves, others as servants; the legal distinction was not always clear. Eighteenth-century

London, for example, had more than ten thousand blacks, most of whom arrived as sailors on Atlantic crossings or as personal servants brought from the West Indies. In England most were free, not slaves. Initially, a handsome black was a fashionable accessory, like a pedigreed pet, a rare status symbol. Later, English aristocrats considered black servants too ordinary. The duchess of Devonshire offered her mother an eleven-year-old boy, explaining that the duke did not want a Negro servant because "it was more original to have a Chinese page than to have a black one; everybody had a black one."[20] London's black population constituted a well-organized, self-conscious subculture, with black pubs, black churches, and black social groups assisting the black poor and unemployed. Some black people attained wealth and position, the most famous being Francis Barber, the literary giant Samuel Johnson's servant, who inherited Johnson's sizable fortune.

Scholars have commonly identified the slave trade exclusively with the transatlantic commerce in black slaves. Such a narrow geographical interpretation of the slave trade is inaccurate because enslaved Africans were transported to many destinations in the Middle East, India, and China, as well as to Europe and the Americas. Although little solid research has been done on the flow of black people to Asia, the evidence of a considerable amount of art (see, for example, page 514), though impressionistic, bears this out. Moreover, African people identified themselves ethnically—as Ibo, Wolof, or Yoruba—not regionally and certainly not nationally or continentally. Before the nineteenth or even the twentieth century, little African consciousness existed. Therefore, perhaps our late-twentieth-century use of the terms *African* and *African diaspora* is somewhat inaccurate.

Beginning in 1658, the Dutch in the Cape Colony of southern Africa imported large numbers of slaves, initially from India and Southeast Asia, then from Madagascar. By the late eighteenth century, Mozambique in East Africa (see Map 20.2) had become the largest supplier of slaves for the Cape Colony. They labored as domestic servants or field workers, producing wheat and wine. In 1780 only one farmer in the colony

Charles Davidson Bell (1813–1882): Schoolmaster Reading   In this watercolor print, a schoolmaster reads and explains the newspaper, *Zuid Afrikaan* (The South African), to the (probably illiterate) household, while black servants cook and fan. Chickens peck for crumbs on the floor. *(William Fehr Collection, Cape Town)*

admitted to possessing one hundred slaves, a small number by South or North American standards, but half of all white men there had at least one slave. That created a strong sense of racial and economic solidarity in the white master class.

Modern scholars consider slavery in the Cape Colony far more oppressive than that in the Americas or the Muslim world. Because male slaves greatly outnumbered female slaves in the Cape Colony, marriage and family life were almost nonexistent. There were few occupations requiring special skills, thus denying slaves a chance to earn manumission. In contrast to Muslim society, where the offspring of a freeman and a slave woman were free, in southern Africa such children were slaves. And in contrast to North and South America and Muslim societies, only a very tiny number of slaves in the Cape Colony won manumission. Most were women, suggesting a sexual or close personal relationship with their owners. While seventeenth- and eighteenth-century Holland enjoyed a European-wide reputation for its religious toleration and intellectual freedom (see page 554), in the Cape Colony the Dutch used a strict racial hierarchy and heavy paternalism to maintain control over native peoples and foreign-born slaves.[21]

The Savanna and Horn regions of East Africa experienced a great expansion of the slave trade in the late eighteenth century, and in the first half of the nineteenth century, slave exports from these areas and from the eastern coast amounted to perhaps thirty thousand a year. Why this demand? Merchants and planters wanted slaves to work the sugar plantations on the Mascarene Islands, located east of Madagascar, the clove plantations on Zanzibar and Pemba, and the food plantations along the Kenyan coast. The eastern coast also exported slaves to the Americas when Brazilian businessmen significantly increased their purchases. In the late eighteenth and early nineteenth centuries, precisely when the slave trade to North America and the Caribbean declined, the Eastern and Asian markets expanded. Only with colonial conquest by Great Britain, Germany, and Italy after 1870 did suppression of the trade begin. Slavery, however, persists even today. Reports from 1994 by the U.N. International Labor Organization, the British Anti-Slavery Society, and the U.S. Department of State reveal slavery on an extensive scale in Mauritania (northwestern Africa) and in the Sudan (eastern Africa).[22] The past isn't dead; it's not even past.

The Atlantic Slave Trade

Although the trade in African people was a worldwide phenomenon, the Atlantic slave trade was probably the most extensive aspect of it. This trade, extending from the early sixteenth to the late nineteenth century and involving the forced migration of millions of human beings, represents one of the most inhumane, unjust, and tragic blots on the history of human societies. The African diaspora immediately provokes a host of questions. What regions of Africa were the sources of slaves? What goods and business procedures were involved in the exchange of slaves? What were the economic, social, political, and demographic effects of the slave trades on African societies? In a period when serfdom was declining in western Europe, why were African peoples enslaved, when land was so widely available and much of the African continent had a labor shortage?

The answer to the last question seems to lie in a technical problem related to African agriculture. Partly because of the tsetse fly, which causes sleeping sickness and other diseases, and partly because of easily leached lateritic soils (containing high concentrations of oxides), farmers had great difficulty using draft animals. Tropical soils responded poorly to plowing, and most work had to be done with the hoe. Productivity, therefore, was low. Economists maintain that in most societies, the value of a worker's productivity determines the value of his or her labor. In precolonial Africa, the individual's agricultural productivity was low, so his or her economic value to society was less than the economic value of a European peasant in Europe. Slaves in the Americas were more productive than free producers in Africa. And European slave dealers were very willing to pay a price higher than the value of an African's productivity in Africa.

The incidence of disease in the Americas also helps to explain the enslavement of Africans. Smallpox took a terrible toll on native Americans (see page 516), and between 30 and 50 percent of Europeans exposed to malaria succumbed to that sickness. Africans had developed some immunity to both diseases, and in the New World they experienced the lowest mortality rate of any people. Europeans wanted workers for mines and sugar cane plantations. A coerced (or slave) labor force proved easier to exploit than a wage labor force.[23] As the demand for sugar increased, and as the technology for sugar production improved and shipping rates declined, the pressure for slave labor accelerated.

The search for a sea route to India led the Portuguese in the fifteenth century to explore the West African coast. Having "discovered" Brazil in 1500, the Portuguese founded a sugar colony at Bahia in 1551. Between 1551 and 1575, before the traffic to North America had gotten under way, the Portuguese delivered more African slaves to Brazil than would ever reach

City of Luanda, Angola   Founded by the Portuguese in 1575, Luanda was a center of the huge slave trade to Brazil. In this eighteenth-century print, offices and warehouses line the streets, and (right foreground) slaves are dragged to the ships for transportation to America. *(New York Public Library, Astor, Lenox, and Tilden Foundations)*

British North America (Table 20.1). Portugal essentially monopolized the slave trade until 1600 and continued to play a large role in the seventeenth century, though increasingly threatened by the Dutch, French, and English. From 1690 until the House of Commons abolished the slave trade in 1807, England was the leading carrier of African slaves.

Population density and supply conditions along the West African coast and the sailing time to New World markets determined the sources of slaves. As the demand for slaves rose, slavers moved down the West African coast from Senegambia to the more densely populated hinterlands of the Bight of Benin and the Bight of Biafra (see Map 16.4 on page 519). In the sixteenth and early seventeenth centuries, the Senegambian coast and the area near the mouth of the Congo River yielded the greatest numbers. By the late seventeenth century, the British found the Ivory Coast region the most profitable territory. A century later, the Bight of Benin and the Gold Coast had become the

largest suppliers. The abundant supply of slaves in Angola, the region south of the Congo River, and the quick passage from Angola to Brazil and the Caribbean established that region as the major coast for Portuguese slavers.

Transatlantic wind patterns partly determined the routes of exchange. Shippers naturally preferred the swiftest crossing—that is, from the African port nearest the latitude of the intended American destination. Thus Portuguese shippers carried their cargoes from Angola to Brazil, and British merchants sailed from the Bight of Benin to the Caribbean. The great majority of slaves were intended for the sugar and coffee plantations extending from the Caribbean islands to Brazil.[24]

Angola produced 26 percent of all African slaves and 70 percent of all Portuguese slaves. Trading networks extending deep into the interior culminated at two major ports on the Angolan coast, Luanda and Benguela (see inset to Map 20.1). Between the 1730s and 1770s, Luanda shipped between 8,000 and 10,000 slaves each year; at the end of the eighteenth century, Benguela's numbers equaled those of Luanda. In 1820, the peak year, 18,957 blacks left Luanda. The Portuguese acquired a few slaves through warfare but secured the vast majority through trade with African dealers. Whites did not participate in the inland markets.

Almost all Portuguese shipments went to satisfy the virtually insatiable Brazilian demand for slaves.[25] The transatlantic slave trade lasted for almost four centuries and involved the brutalization and exploitation of millions of human beings. Here is an excerpt from a Portuguese doctor's 1793 report on conditions in Luanda before the voyage across the Atlantic had begun:

Here takes place the second round of hardships that these unlucky people are forced to suffer. . . . their human nature entirely overlooked. The dwelling place of the slave is simply the dirt floor of the compound, and he remains there exposed to harsh conditions and bad weather, and at night there are only a lean-to and some sheds . . . which they are herded into like cattle.

Their food continues scarce as before . . . limited at times to badly cooked beans, at other times to corn. . . .

And when they reach a port . . . , they are branded on the right breast with the coat of arms of the king and nation, of whom they have become vassals. . . . This mark is made with a hot silver instrument in the act of paying the king's duties, and this brand mark is called a carimbo. . . .

In this miserable and deprived condition the terrified slaves remain for weeks and months, and the great number of them who die is unspeakable. With some ten or twelve thousand arriving at Luanda each year, it often happens that only six or seven thousand are finally transported to Brazil.[26]

Olaudah Equiano (see the feature "Individuals in Society: Olaudah Equiano") describes the experience of his voyage from Benin to Barbados in the Caribbean:

At last, when the ship we were in had got in all her cargo [of slaves], they made ready with many fearful noises, and we were all put under deck so that we could not see how they managed the vessel. . . . The stench of the hold while we were on the coast was so intolerably loathsome that it was dangerous to remain there for any time, and some of us had been permitted to stay on the deck for the fresh air; but now that the whole ship's cargo were confined together it became absolutely pestilential. The closeness of the place and the heat of the climate, added to the number in the ship, which was so crowded that each had scarcely room to turn himself, almost suffocated us. This produced copious perspirations, so that the air soon became unfit for respiration from a variety of loathsome smells, and brought on a sickness among the slaves, of which many died, thus falling

TABLE 20.1   Estimated Slave Imports by Destination, 1451–1870

Destination	Estimated Total Slave Imports
British North America	399,000
Spanish America	1,552,100
British Caribbean	1,665,000
French Caribbean	1,600,200
Dutch Caribbean	500,000
Danish Caribbean	28,000
Brazil	3,646,800
Old World	175,000
	9,566,100

Source: P. D. Curtin, The Atlantic Slave Trade: A Census *(Madison: University of Wisconsin Press, 1969), p. 268. Used with permission of The University of Wisconsin Press.*

victims to the improvident avarice, as I may call it, of their purchasers. This wretched situation was again aggravated by the galling of the chains, now become insupportable, and the filth of the necessary tubs [of human waste], into which the children often fell and were almost suffocated. The shrieks of the women and the groans of the dying rendered the whole a scene of horror almost inconceivable. Happily perhaps for myself I was soon reduced so low here that it was thought necessary to keep me almost always on deck, and from my extreme youth I was not put in fetters. . . . Two of my wearied countrymen who were chained together (I was near them at the time), preferring death to such a life of misery, somehow made through the nettings and jumped into the sea: immediately another quite dejected fellow, who on account of his illness was suffered to be out of irons, also followed their example. . . . Two of the wretches were drowned, but they got the other and afterwards flogged him unmercifully. . . . The want of fresh air, . . . and the stench of the necessary tubs carried off many. . . . At last we came in sight of the island of Barbados, at which the whites on board gave a great shout and made many signs of joy to us. . . . We soon anchored amongst them off Bridgetown. Many merchants and planters now came on board, though it was in the evening. They put us in separate parcels and examined us

Olaudah Equiano (1745–1797)

The transatlantic slave trade was a mass movement involving millions of human beings. It was also the sum of individual lives spent partly or entirely in slavery. Most of those lives remain hidden to us. Olaudah Equiano represents a rare ray of light into the slaves' obscurity; he is probably the best-known African slave.

Equiano was born in Benin (modern Nigeria) of Ibo ethnicity. His father, one of the village elders (or chieftains), presided over a large household that included "many slaves," prisoners captured in local wars. All people, slave and free, shared in the cultivation of family lands. One day, when all the adults were in the fields, two strange men and a woman broke into the family compound, kidnapped the eleven-year-old Olaudah and his sister, tied them up, and dragged them into the woods. Brother and sister were separated, and Olaudah was sold several times to various dealers before reaching the coast. As it took six months to walk there, his home must have been far inland. The sea, the slave ship, and the strange appearance of the white crew terrified the boy (see page 635). Equiano's master took him to Jamaica, Virginia, and then to England, where he placed him in the custody of a kind family. They gave him the rudiments of an education, and he was baptized a Christian.

Equiano soon went to sea as a captain's boy (servant), serving in the Royal Navy during the Seven Years' War. On shore at Portsmouth, England, after one battle, Equiano's master urged him to read, study, and learn basic mathematics. This education served him well, for after a voyage to the West Indies, his master sold him to a Philadelphia Quaker, Robert King, who was a rum and sugar merchant. Equiano worked as a clerk in King's warehouse, as a longshoreman loading and unloading cargo ships, and at sea where he developed good navigational skills; for his work, King paid him. Equiano became an entrepreneur himself, buying and selling small goods in the islands and mainland ports. Determined to buy his freedom, by 1766 Equiano had amassed enough money, and King signed the deed of manumission. Equiano was twenty-one years old; he had been a slave for ten.

He returned to London and used his remaining money to hire tutors to teach him hairdressing, mathematics, and how to play the French horn. When money was scarce, he found work as a merchant seaman, traveling to Portugal, Nice, Genoa, Naples, and Turkey. He participated in an Arctic expedition.

Olaudah Equiano, 1789, dressed as an elegant Englishman, his Bible open to the Book of Acts. *(New York Public Library, Schomburg Center for Research in Black Culture)*

Equiano's *Travels* (1788) reveals a complex and sophisticated man. He had a strong constitution and an equally strong character. His Christian faith undoubtedly sustained him. On the title page of his book, he cited a verse from Isaiah (12:2): "The Lord Jehovah is my strength and my song." The very first thought that came to his mind the day he was freed was a passage from Psalm 126: "I glorified God in my heart, in whom I trusted."

Equiano loathed the brutal slavery he saw in the West Indies and the vicious racism he experienced in the North American colonies. He respected the fairness of Robert King, admired British navigational and industrial technologies, and had many close white friends. He once described himself as "almost an Englishman." He was also involved in the black communities in the West Indies and in London. He joined free black Londoners' unanimous resolution not to return to Africa. *Travels* is a well-documented argument for the abolition of slavery and a literary classic that went through nine editions before his death.

Olaudah Equiano spoke to large crowds in the industrial cities of Manchester and Birmingham, arguing that it was in the business interests of manufacturers to support abolition, as Africa was a huge, virtually untapped market for English cloth. In 1808 the British Parliament abolished the slave trade.

Questions for Analysis

1. How typical was Olaudah Equiano's life as a slave? How atypical?
2. Describe his culture and his sense of himself.

Source: Equiano's Travels: The Interesting Narrative of the Life of Olaudah Equiano, ed. Paul Edwards (Portsmouth, N.H.: Heinemann, 1996).

Queen Njiga (also Nzinga) Mbandi Ana de Sousa (1582–1633)   Njiga of Ndongo (r. 1624–1629) is the most important female political figure in the history of early modern Angola. She used military force in her expansionist policy and participated fully in the slave trade, but she fiercely resisted Portuguese attempts to control that trade. Here she sits enthroned, wearing her crown (the cross a sign of her Christian baptism) and bracelets, giving an order. She has become a symbol of African resistance to colonial rule. *(Courtesy, Ezio Bassani)*

attentively. They also made us jump, and pointed to the land, signifying we were to go there. We thought by this we should be eaten by these ugly men, as they appeared to us. . . . They told us we were not to be eaten but to work, and were soon to go on land where we should see many of our country people. This report eased us much; and sure enough soon after we were landed there came to us Africans of all languages.[27]

Unlike Great Britain, France, and the Netherlands, Portugal did not have a strong mercantile class involved in slaving in the eighteenth century. Instead, the Portuguese colony of Brazil provided the ships, capital, and goods for the slave trade. Credit played a major role in the trade: Brazilian-controlled firms in Luanda extended credit to African operators, who had to make payments in slaves six or eight months later. Portuguese ironware and wine; Brazilian tobacco and brandies; and European and Asian textiles, firearms, and beads were the main goods exchanged for slaves. All commodities entered Angola from Brazil. The Luandan (or Benguelan) merchants pegged the value of the goods to the value of prime young slaves but then undervalued the worth of the slaves and overpriced the goods. As a result, the African operators frequently ended up in debt to the merchants.

Although the demand was great, Portuguese merchants in Angola and Brazil sought to maintain only a steady trickle of slaves from the African interior to Luanda and across the ocean to Bahia and Rio de Janeiro: a flood of slaves would have depressed the American market. Rio, the port capital through which most slaves

Slave Market at Rua do Valongo in Rio de Janeiro, Brazil   At one of the largest slave markets in the Western Hemisphere, women in the foreground sit cooking over a small fire, and men recline on the left, while a potential buyer, puffing a cheroot, casually examines the "goods." The dealer keeps accounts at his desk. *("Mercado de Escravos" by Joao Mauricio Rugendas. Courtesy, Harvard College Library)*

passed, commanded the Brazilian trade. Planters and mine operators from the provinces traveled to Rio to buy slaves. Between 1795 and 1808, approximately 10,000 Angolans per year stood in the Rio slave market. In 1810 the figure rose to 18,000; in 1828 it reached 32,000.[28]

The English ports of London, Bristol, and particularly Liverpool dominated the British slave trade. In the eighteenth century, Liverpool was the world's greatest slave-trading port. In all three cities, small and cohesive merchant classes exercised great public influence. The cities also had huge stores of industrial products for export, growing shipping industries, and large amounts of ready cash for investment abroad. Merchants generally formed partnerships to raise capital and to share the risks; each voyage was a separate enterprise or venture.

Slaving ships from Bristol searched the Gold Coast, the Bight of Benin, Bonny, and Calabar. The ships of Liverpool drew slaves from Gambia, the Windward Coast, and the Gold Coast. To Africa, British ships carried textiles, gunpowder and flint, beer and spirits, British and Irish linens, and woolen cloth. A collection of goods was grouped together into what was called the "sorting." An English sorting might include bolts of cloth, firearms, alcohol, tobacco, and hardware; this batch of goods would be traded for an individual slave or a quantity of gold, ivory, or dyewood. When Europeans added a markup for profit, Africans followed suit. Currency was not exchanged; it served as a standard of value and a means of keeping accounts.[29]

European traders had two systems for exchange. First, especially on the Gold Coast, they established factory-forts. These fortified trading posts were expensive to maintain but proved useful for fending off rival Europeans. In the second, or shore, method of trading, European ships sent boats ashore or invited African dealers to bring traders and slaves out to the ships. The English captain John Adams, who made ten voyages to Africa between 1786 and 1800, described the shore method of trading at Bonny:

This place is the wholesale market for slaves, as not fewer than 20,000 are annually sold here; 16,000 of whom are natives of one nation called Ibo. . . . Fairs where the slaves of the Ibo nation are obtained are held every five or six weeks at several villages, which are situated on the banks of the rivers and creeks in the interior, and to which the African traders of Bonny resort to purchase them.

. . . The traders augment the quantity of their merchandise, by obtaining from their friends, the captains of the slave ships, a considerable quantity of goods on credit. . . . Evening is the period chosen for the time of departure, when they proceed in a body, accompanied by the noise of drums, horns, and gongs. At the expiration of the sixth day, they generally return bringing with them 1,500 or 2,000 slaves, who are sold to Europeans the evening after their arrival, and taken on board the ships. . . .

It is expected that every vessel, on her arrival at Bonny, will fire a salute the instant the anchor is let go, as a compliment to the black monarch who soon afterwards makes his appearance in a large canoe, at which time, all those natives who happen to be alongside the vessel are compelled to proceed in their canoes to a respectful distance, and make way for his Majesty's barge. After a few compliments to the captain, he usually enquires after brother George, meaning the King of England, George III, and hopes he and his family are well. He is not pleased unless he is regaled with the best the ship affords. . . . His power is absolute; and the surrounding country, to a considerable distance, is subject to his dominion.[30]

The shore method of buying slaves allowed the ship to move easily from market to market. The final prices of the slaves depended on their ethnic origin, their availability when the shipper arrived, and their physical health when offered for sale in the West Indies or the North or South American colonies.

Meanwhile, according to one scholar, the northbound trade in slaves across the Sahara "continued without serious disruption until the late nineteenth century, and in a clandestine way and on a much reduced scale it survived well into the twentieth century."[31] The present scholarly consensus is that the trans-Saharan slave trade in the seventeenth and eighteenth centuries was never as important as the transatlantic trade.

Supplying slaves for the foreign market was in the hands of a small, wealthy merchant class, or it was a state monopoly. Gathering a band of raiders and the capital for equipment, guides, tolls, and supplies involved considerable expense. By contemporary standards, slave raiding was a costly operation. Only black entrepreneurs with sizable capital and labor could afford to finance and direct raiding drives. They exported slaves because the profits on exports were greater than the profits to be made from using labor in the domestic economy:

The export price of slaves never rose to the point where it became cheaper for Europeans to turn to alternative sources of supply, and it never fell to the point where it caused more than a temporary check to the trade. . . . The remarkable expansion of the slave trade in the eighteenth century provides a horrific illustration of the rapid response of producers in an underdeveloped economy to price incentives.[32]

Other factors that might result in slavery were kidnapping; judicial enslavement by the state for serious crimes, such as murder or threats to royal authority; state demand for slaves as tribute from subject peoples; destitution following a natural disaster, such as famine or plague, which might force parents to sell "surplus" children; and, as in Russia or China, severe debt, which might lead a person to surrender his or her freedom in return for settlement of the debt. Europeans initiated the Atlantic slave trade, but its continuation was made possible through an alliance between European shippers and African suppliers.

African peoples, captured and forcibly brought to the Americas, played an integral part in the formation of the Atlantic world. They had an enormous impact on the economics of the Portuguese and Spanish colonies of South America and in the Dutch, French, and British colonies of the Caribbean and North America. For example, on the sugar plantations of Mexico and the Caribbean; on the cotton, rice, and tobacco plantations of North America; and in the silver and gold mines of Peru and Mexico, slaves of African descent not only worked in the mines and fields but also filled skilled, supervisory, and administrative positions, as well as performed domestic service. African slaves also transmitted their cultures to the Americas. Through language, religion, music, and art, they contributed to the cultures of their particular regions and to the development of an Afro-Atlantic civilization.[33]

Consequences Within Africa

What economic impact did European trade have on African societies? Africans possessed technology well suited to their environment. Over the centuries, they had cultivated a wide variety of plant foods; developed plant and animal husbandry techniques; and mined, smelted, and otherwise worked a great variety of metals. Apart from firearms, American tobacco and rum, and the cheap brandy brought by the Portuguese, European goods presented no novelty to Africans. What made foreign products desirable to Africans was their price. Traders of handwoven Indian cotton textiles, Venetian imitations of African beads, and iron bars from European smelters could undersell African manufacturers. Africans exchanged slaves, ivory, gold, pepper, and animal skins for those goods. Their earnings usually did not remain in Africa. African states eager to expand or to control commerce bought European firearms, although the difficulty of maintaining guns often gave gun owners only marginal superiority over skilled bowmen.[34] The kingdom of Dahomey, however, built its power on the effective use of firearms.

The African merchants who controlled the production of exports gained from foreign trade. The king of Dahomey, for example, had a gross income in 1750 of £250,000 from the overseas export of slaves. A portion of his profit was spent on goods that improved the living standard of his people. Slave-trading entrepôts,

which provided opportunities for traders and for farmers who supplied foodstuffs to towns, caravans, and slave ships, prospered. But such economic returns did not spread very far.[35] International trade did not lead to the economic development of Africa. Neither technological growth nor the gradual spread of economic benefits occurred in Africa in early modern times.

As in the Islamic world (see page 653), women in sub-Saharan Africa also engaged in the slave trade. In Guinea the *signeres,* women slave merchants, acquired considerable riches in the business. One of them, Mae Correia, led a life famous in her region for its wealth and elegance.

The arrival of Europeans did cause basic social changes in some West African societies. In Senegambia chattel slavery seems to have been unknown before the

Three Traders This sixteenth-century brass plaque shows three traders, probably appointed to deal with Europeans. The one in the center carries his staff of office; the two on the sides hold manillas, an early form of currency. Just as the crocodile holding a fish represents power over the seas, so the traders symbolize royal authority over commerce with outsiders. *(Courtesy of the Trustees of the British Museum)*

growth of the transatlantic trade (see page 634). By the late eighteenth century, however, chiefs were using the slave labor of craftsmen, sailors, and farm workers. If the price was right, they were sold off. Those who committed crimes had traditionally paid fines, but because of the urgent demand for slaves, many misdemeanors became punishable by sale to slave dealers. Europeans introduced corn, pineapples, cassava, and sweet potatoes to West Africa, which had important consequences for population growth.

The intermarriage of French traders and Wolof women in Senegambia created a *métis,* or mulatto, class. In the emerging urban centers at Saint-Louis, this small class adopted the French language, the Roman Catholic faith, and a French manner of life. The métis exercised considerable political and economic power. When granted French citizenship in the late eighteenth century, its members sent Senegalese grievances to the Estates General of 1789.[36] However, European cultural influences did not penetrate West African society beyond the seacoast.

The political consequences of the slave trade varied from place to place. The trade enhanced the power and wealth of some kings and warlords in the short run but promoted conditions of instability and collapse over the long run. In the kingdom of the Congo, the perpetual Portuguese search for slaves undermined the monarchy, destroyed political unity, and led to constant disorder and warfare; power passed to the village chiefs. Likewise in Angola, which became a Portuguese proprietary colony, the slave trade decimated and scattered the population and destroyed the local economy. By contrast, the military kingdom of Dahomey, which entered into the slave trade in the eighteenth century and made it a royal monopoly, prospered enormously from trading in slaves. The economic strength of the state rested on the slave trade. The royal army raided deep into the interior, and in the late eighteenth century Dahomey became one of the major West African sources of slaves. When slaving expeditions failed to yield sizable catches, and when European demands declined, the resulting depression in the Dahomean economy caused serious political unrest. Iboland, inland from the Niger Delta, from whose great port cities of Bonny and Brass the British drained tens of thousands of slaves, experienced minimal political effects and suffered no permanent population loss. A high birthrate kept pace with the incursions of the slave trade, and Ibo societies remained demographically and economically strong.

What demographic impact did the slave trade have on Africa? In all, between approximately 1500 and 1900, about 12 million Africans were exported to the Ameri-

TABLE 20.2 The Trans-Atlantic Slave Trade, 1450–1900

Period	Volume	Percent
1450–1600	367,000	3.1
1601–1700	1,868,000	16.0
1701–1800	6,133,000	52.4
1801–1900	3,330,000	28.5
Total	11,698,000	100.0

Source: P. E. Lovejoy, Transformations in Slavery: A History of Slavery in Africa *(Cambridge: Cambridge University Press, 1983), p. 19. Used with permission.*

cas, 6 million were exported to Asia, and 8 million were retained within Africa. Tables 20.1 and 20.2 report the somewhat divergent findings of two careful scholars on the number of slaves shipped to the New World. Export figures do not include the approximately 10 to 15 percent who died during procurement or in transit.

Western and American markets wanted young male slaves. The Asian and African markets preferred young females. Women were sought for their reproductive value, as sex objects, and because their economic productivity was not threatened by the possibility of physical rebellion, as might be the case with young men. Consequently, two-thirds of those exported to the Americas were male, one-third female. The population on the western coast of Africa became predominantly female; the population in the East African Savanna and Horn regions was predominantly male. The slave trade therefore had significant consequences for the institutions of marriage, slavery itself, and the sexual division of labor—topics scholars have yet to explore. Although overall population may have shown modest growth from roughly 1650 to 1900, that growth was offset by declines in the Horn and on the eastern and western coasts. While Europe and Asia experienced considerable demographic and economic expansion in the eighteenth century, Africa suffered a decline.[37]

SUMMARY

In the early modern world, African kingdoms and societies represented considerable economic and political diversity. The communities of Wolof-, Serer-, and

Pulaar-speaking peoples in Senegambia had long known the trans-Saharan caravan trade, which along with goods brought Islamic, and later French, culture to the region. The West African kingdoms of Benin, Kanem-Bornu, and Hausaland maintained their separate existences for centuries. They also experienced strong Islamic influences, although Muslim culture affected primarily the royal and elite classes and seldom penetrated into the broad masses of people. In eastern Africa, Ethiopia had accepted Christianity long before northern and eastern Europe; Ethiopians practiced Coptic Christianity, which shaped their identity, and Jesuit attempts to substitute Roman liturgical forms met with fierce resistance. The wealthy Swahili city-states on the southeastern coast of Africa possessed a Muslim and mercantile culture. Cities such as Mogadishu, Kilwa, and Sofala used Arabic as the language of communication, and their commercial economies were tied to the trade of the Indian Ocean. The arrival of Europeans proved disastrous for those cities.

It is a brutal historical irony that Africa, so desperate for population, exported people in exchange for goods that chiefly benefited a small royal and commercial elite. The slave trade across the Atlantic and Indian Oceans greatly delayed population growth. We do not know how many Africans were exported to India, China, and Southeast Asia. Despite the export of as many as 12 million human beings to meet the labor needs of South and North America, European influences scarcely penetrated the African interior. The overall impact of the slave trade on Africa was devastating for some regions and societies but marginal for others.

But the Atlantic slave trade had another effect. When it declined after 1810, the search for slaves within Africa accelerated, and traders pressed ever deeper into the interior. Slaves were one part of the overall economy, which remained overwhelmingly agricultural. As the demand for workers to cultivate land rose, regions that possessed firearms traded them for slaves. In most places, such as Senegambia, the slaves went into agriculture. Thus the slave trade led to a wider use of slaves within Africa itself, and rather than promoting technological development in sub-Saharan Africa, slavery delayed it.

NOTES

1. P. D. Curtin, *Economic Change in Precolonial Africa: Senegambia in the Era of the Slave Trade* (Madison: University of Wisconsin Press, 1975), pp. 34–35; J. A. Rawley, *The Transatlantic Slave Trade: A History* (New York: W. W. Norton, 1981), p. 12.

2. R. W. July, *A History of the African People,* 3d ed. (New York: Scribner's, 1980), pp. 128–129.

3. R. W. July, *Precolonial Africa: An Economic and Social History* (New York: Scribner's, 1975), p. 99.

4. July, *A History of the African People,* p. 141.

5. J. Iliffe, *Africans: The History of a Continent* (Cambridge: Cambridge University Press, 1995), p. 95.

6. Ibid., pp. 66–67, 93–94.

7. *Equiano's Travels: The Interesting Narrative of the Life of Olaudah Equiano,* ed. P. Edwards (Portsmouth, N.H.: Heinemann, 1996), p. 4.

8. Iliffe, *Africans,* pp. 66–67.

9. Ibid., pp. 81–85.

10. Quoted in R. Hallett, *Africa to 1875* (Ann Arbor: University of Michigan Press, 1970), p. 151.

11. *The Cambridge History of Africa.* Vol. 3: *Ca 1050 to 1600,* ed. R. Oliver (Cambridge: Cambridge University Press, 1977), pp. 427–435.

12. A. ibn-Fartura, "The Kanem Wars," in *Nigerian Perspectives,* ed. T. Hodgkin (London: Oxford University Press, 1966), pp. 111–115.

13. "The Kano Chronicle," quoted in T. Hodgkin, ed., *Nigerian Perspectives* (London: Oxford University Press, 1966), pp. 89–90.

14. J. Middleton, *The World of Swahili: An African Mercantile Civilization* (New Haven, Conn.: Yale University Press, 1992), p. 27.

15. Ibid., pp. 35–38.

16. P. E. Lovejoy, *Transformations in Slavery: A History of Slavery in Africa* (Cambridge: Cambridge University Press, 1983), p. 19. This section leans heavily on Lovejoy's work.

17. See Table 2.1, "Trans-Saharan Slave Trade, 650–1600," ibid., p. 25.

18. Iliffe, *Africans,* p. 75.

19. Quoted in H. Thomas, *The Slave Trade* (New York: Simon and Schuster, 1997), p. 21.

20. G. Gerzina, *Black London: Life Before Emancipation* (New Brunswick, N.J.: Rutgers University Press, 1995), pp. 29–66, passim; the quotation is on p. 53.

21. Iliffe, *Africans,* pp. 121–126.

22. See Lori Grinker, "Disaster in the Sudan," *New York Times,* February 12, 1993, p. A33; Stanley Miller, "U.N. Agency Assails Mauritania on Slavery," *Los Angeles Times,* March 9, 1993, p. 3; Augustine Lado and Betty Hinds, "Where Slavery Isn't History," *Washington Post,* October 17, 1993, section 3, p. 13; Charles Jacobs and Mohamed Athie, "Bought and Sold," *New York Times,* July 13, 1994, p. A19.

23. P. Manning, *Slavery and African Life: Occidental, Oriental, and African Slave Trades* (New York: Cambridge University Press, 1990), pp. 31–37.

24. Rawley, *The Transatlantic Slave Trade,* p. 45.

25. Ibid., pp. 41–47.

26. R. E. Conrad, *Children of God's Fire: A Documentary History of Black Slavery in Brazil* (Princeton, N.J.: Princeton University Press, 1983), pp. 20–23.

27. *Equiano's Travels,* pp. 23–26.
28. Rawley, *The Transatlantic Slave Trade,* pp. 45–47.
29. July, *A History of the African People,* p. 208.
30. J. Adams, "Remarks on the Country Extending from Cape Palmas to the River Congo," in T. Hodgkin, ed., *Nigerian Perspectives* (London: Oxford University Press, 1966), pp. 178–180.
31. A. G. Hopkins, *An Economic History of West Africa* (New York: Columbia University Press, 1973), p. 83.
32. Ibid., p. 105.
33. J. Thornton, *Africa and Africans in the Making of the Atlantic World* (New York: Cambridge University Press, 1992), pp. 138–142.
34. July, *Precolonial Africa,* pp. 269–270.
35. Hopkins, *An Economic History of West Africa,* p. 119.
36. July, *A History of the African People,* pp. 201–202.
37. Manning, *Slavery and African Life,* pp. 22–23 and Chap. 3, pp. 38–59.

Suggested Reading

Perhaps the best general survey of African history is the title by Iliffe cited in the Notes; it is soundly researched and up-to-date, and it takes the history of population as its theme. Students wishing to explore more fully some of the issues raised in this chapter might begin with *African History: Text and Readings.* Vol. 1: *Western African History;* Vol. 2: *Eastern African History;* and Vol. 3: *Central and Southern African History* (1990), all edited by R. O. Collins. This work gives a useful introduction to the geography and history of the continent and brings together a solid collection of primary documents and scholarly commentaries. B. Davidson, ed., *African Civilization Revisited* (1991), also contains interesting source readings on many facets of African history and cultures from antiquity to the present. K. Shillington, *History of Africa* (1989), provides a soundly researched, highly readable, and well-illustrated survey, while R. Oliver, *The African Experience* (1991), traces African history through particular historical problems. Although many of the articles in *The Cambridge History of Africa.* Vol. 4: *From 1600–1790,* ed. R. Gray (1975), are now dated, the following articles are still useful: "The Central Sahara and Sudan," "North-West Africa," and "Southern Africa and Madagascar." V. B. Thompson, *Africa and Unity* (1969), offers an African and African-American response to the traditional Eurocentric interpretation of African history and culture.

J. Thornton, *Africa and Africans in the Making of the Atlantic World, 1400–1680* (1992), places African developments in an Atlantic context. Likewise, both A. L. Karras and J. R. McNeill, eds., *Atlantic American Societies: From Columbus Through Abolition, 1492–1888* (1992), and B. Solow, ed., *Slavery and the Rise of the Atlantic System* (1991), contain important and valuable articles on many of the economic and cultural factors that linked Africa and the Western Hemisphere. For Ethiopia, see H. G. Marcus, *A History of Ethiopia* (1994), a concise but highly readable study. The standard study of the Savanna is probably J. Vansina, *Kingdoms of the Savanna* (1966). For East Africa and the Horn region, see J. Middleton, *The World of Swahili: An African Mercantile Civilization* (1992), which provides an expert synthesis of recent scholarly literature by a social anthropologist. The older study by C. S. Nicholls, *The Swahili Coast* (1971), also is still useful. J. Knappert, *Four Centuries of Swahili Verse: A Literary History and Anthology* (1979), is a most interesting celebration of literary manifestations of Swahili culture.

The slave trade represents tropical Africa's first extensive relationship with the outside world, and the literature on slavery continues to grow. P. D. Curtin, *The Rise and Fall of the Plantation Complex: Essays in Atlantic History,* 2d ed. (1998), is broader in scope than the title implies, for in a series of stimulating articles, it treats most aspects of slavery in Europe and in the Americas from about 1300 to 1888. R. Segal, *The Black Diaspora: Five Centuries of the Black Experience Outside Africa* (1995), is narrower in scope than its title suggests, for it ignores the black experience in Asia and Europe. R. Blackburn, *The Making of New World Slavery: From the Baroque to the Modern, 1492–1800* (1997), describes the ways slavery in the Americas differed from earlier patterns, reflected distinctly modern business techniques, and contributed to a destructive pattern of human conduct. H. Thomas, *The Slave Trade* (1997), contains a mine of exciting information. Students seeking an understanding of African slave women and their reactions to slavery, work, and domestic situations might consult M. Morissey, *Slave Women in the New World: Gender Stratification in the Caribbean* (1989). In addition to the titles by Manning and Middleton cited in the Notes, see P. Manning, *Slavery, Colonialism and Economic Growth in Dahomey, 1640–1960* (1982), an in-depth study of the kingdom of Dahomey, which, after Angola, was the largest exporter of slaves to the Americas. J. F. Searing, *West African Slavery and Atlantic Commerce, 1700–1860* (1993), explores the effects of the Atlantic slave trade on the societies of the Senegal River valley. The theme of R. L. Stein's *The French Slave Trade in the Eighteenth Century: An Old Regime Business* (1979) is indicated by its title.

Although the emphasis in J. E. Harris, ed., *Global Dimensions of African Diaspora* (1982), is heavy on the United States and the Caribbean, with very little on South America, East Asia, or South Asia, some of the articles are very important: see especially those by J. E. Harris, L. W. Levine, and S. C. Drake. The highly important role of black sailors is treated in W. J. Bolster, *Black Jacks: African American Seamen in the Age of Sail* (1997). For the black experience in eighteenth- and early-nineteenth-century England, see Gerzina's work, cited in the Notes.

LISTENING TO THE
PAST

Duarte Barbosa on the Swahili City-States

The Portuguese linguist Duarte Barbosa made two voyages to India. Arriving first in 1500, he acted for five years as interpreter and translator in Cochin and Cananor in Kerala (in southwestern India on the Malabar Coast) and returned to Lisbon in 1506. On his second visit, in 1511, he served the Portuguese government as chief scribe in the factory of Cananor (a factory was a warehouse for the storage of goods, not a manufacturing center) and as the liaison with the local Indian rajah (prince). When Afonso de Albuquerque dismissed Barbosa, he went to Calicut. He returned to Cananor about 1520 and died there in 1545.

On the basis of his trips around the Indian Ocean in 1518, Barbosa completed his Libro des Coisas da India, *a geographical and ethnographic survey of peoples, lands, and commerce from the Cape of Good Hope to China. It was based largely on his personal observations. First published in Italian, the book won wide acclaim in Europe, and modern scholars consider the geographical information in it very accurate.*

Sofala

And the manner of their traffic was this: they came in small vessels named *zambucos* from the kingdoms of Kilwa, Mombasa, and Malindi, bringing many cotton cloths, some spotted and others white and blue, also some of silk, and many small beads, gray, red, and yellow, which things come to the said kingdoms from the great kingdom of Cambay [in Northwest India] in other greater ships. And these wares the said Moors who came from Malindi and Mombasa [purchased from others who bring them hither and] paid for in gold at such a price that those merchants departed well pleased; which gold they gave by weight.

The Moors of Sofala kept these wares and sold them afterwards to the heathen of the Kingdom of Benametapa, who came thither laden with gold which they gave in exchange for the said cloths without weighing it. These Moors collect also great store of ivory which they find hard by Sofala, and this also they sell in the Kingdom of Cambay at five or six cruzados the quintal. They also sell some ambergris, which is brought to them from the Hucicas, and is exceeding good. These Moors are black, and some of them tawny; some of them speak Arabic, but the more part use the language of the country. They clothe themselves from the waist down with cotton and silk cloths, and other cloths they wear over their shoulders like capes, and turbans on their heads. Some of them wear small caps dyed in grain in chequers and other woolen clothes in many tints, also camlets and other silks.

Their food is millet, rice, flesh and fish. In this river as far as the sea are many sea horses, which come out on the land to graze, which horses always move in the sea like fishes; they have tusks like those of small elephants, being whiter and harder, and it never loses color. In the country near Sofala are many wild elephants, exceeding great (which the country-folk know not how to tame), ounces, lions, deer and many other wild beasts. It is a land of plains and hills with many streams of sweet water. . . .

Kilwa

Going along the coast from [the] town of Mozambique, there is an island hard by the mainland which is called Kilwa, in which is a Moorish town with many fair houses of stones and mortar, with many windows after our fashion, very well arranged in streets, with many flat roofs. The doors are of wood, well carved, with excellent joinery. Around it are streams and orchards and fruit-gardens with many channels of sweet water. It has a Moorish king over it. From this place they trade with Sofala, whence they bring back gold, and from here they spread all over . . . the seacoast [which] is well peopled with villages and abodes of Moors.

Before the King our Lord sent out his expedition to discover India the Moors of Sofala, Cuama, Angoya and Mozambique were all subject to the king of Kilwa, who was the most mighty king among them. And in this town was great plenty of gold, as no ships passed towards Sofala without first coming to this island. . . .

This town was taken by force from its king by the Portuguese, as, moved by arrogance, he refused to obey the King our Lord. There they took many prisoners and the king fled from the island, and His Highness ordered that a fort should be built there, and kept it under his rule and governance. Afterwards he ordered that it should be pulled down, as its maintenance was of no value nor profit to him, and it was destroyed by Antonio de Saldanha. . . .

Malindi

. . . Journeying along the coast towards India, there is a fair town on the mainland lying along a strand, which is named Malindi. It pertains to the Moors and has a Moorish king over it; the which place has many fair stone and mortar houses of many stories, with great plenty of windows and flat roofs, after our fashion. The place is well laid out in streets. The folk are both black and white; they go naked, covering only their private parts with cotton and silk cloths. Others of them wear cloths folded like cloaks and waistbands, and turbans of many rich stuffs on their heads.

They are great barterers, and deal in cloth, gold, ivory, and divers other wares with the Moors and heathen of the great kingdom of Cambay; and to their haven come every year many ships with cargoes of merchandise, from which they get great store of gold, ivory and wax. In this traffic the Cambay merchants make great profits, and thus, on one side and the other, they earn much money. There is great plenty of food in this city, rice, millet, and some wheat which they bring from Cambay, and divers sorts of fruit, inasmuch as there is here abundance of fruit-gardens and orchards. Here too are plenty of round-tailed sheep, cows and other cattle and great store of oranges, also of hens.

The king and people of this place ever were and are friends of the King of Portugal, and the Portuguese always find in them great comfort and

Husuni Kubwa at Kilwa combined a royal palace, resting place for caravans, and enclosure for slaves held for later sale. *(Reprinted by permission from Peter S. Garlake,* The Early Islamic Architecture of the East African Coast, *Memoir 1 of the British Institute in Eastern Africa, Nairobi, 1966)*

friendship and perfect peace, and there the ships, when they chance to pass that way, obtain supplies in plenty.

Questions for Analysis

1. Locate on a map the city-states that Barbosa discusses.

2. What seems to have impressed Barbosa? What was his attitude toward the various peoples he saw? What Portuguese or Western prejudices do you discern?

3. What was the Portuguese relationship to the Swahili city-states at the time Barbosa saw them?

4. What was the source of Sofala's gold? Of Sofala's and Malindi's ivory? What did Cambay (that is, India) use ivory for?

Source: Basil Davidson, *The African Past: Chronicles from Antiquity to Modern Times* (Boston: Little, Brown, 1964). Copyright © 1964 by Basil Davidson. Reprinted by permission of Curtis Brown, Ltd.

21 West and South Asia: The Islamic World Powers, ca 1450–1800

Men carrying bolts of material, from "Prince Dara-Shikoh's Wedding." *(From the cover of* King of the World: The Padshah-nama *[Azimuth Editions—Sackler Gallery, 1997]. The Royal Collection © Her Majesty Queen Elizabeth II)*

Around 1450 the spiritual descendants of the Prophet Muhammad controlled three vast and powerful empires: the Ottoman Empire centered in Anatolia, the Safavid Empire of Persia, and the Mughal Empire of India. From West Africa to Central Asia, from the Balkans to Southeast Asia, Muslim armies pursued policies of territorial expansion. Between 1450 and 1800, these powerful Muslim kingdoms reached the zenith of their territorial extension and their intellectual and artistic vitality. With the conquest of Constantinople in 1453, the Ottoman Turks gained a nearly impregnable capital and the respect of all Islam. The Ottomans soon overran much of Anatolia, North Africa, and the Balkans. Lasting almost five hundred years (1453–1918), the Ottoman Empire was one of the largest, best-organized, and most enduring political entities in world history. In Persia the Safavid Dynasty created a theocracy and presided over a brilliant culture. A theological dispute between the Ottomans and the Safavids brought bitter division in the Islamic world and weakened both powers. Meanwhile, the Mughal leader Babur and his successors conquered the Indian subcontinent, and Mughal rule inaugurated a period of radical administrative reorganization in India and the flowering of intellectual and architectural creativity.

In 1450 all the great highways of international trade were in Muslim hands, and the wealth of the Muslim states derived largely from commerce. By 1750 the Muslims had lost that control, and the Muslim states were declining economically, politically, and culturally.

- What military and religious factors gave rise to the Ottoman, Safavid, and Mughal Empires? How were they governed?
- To what extent were these empires world powers?
- What intellectual developments characterized the Ottoman and Safavid Empires?
- How did Muslim government reform and artistic inspiration affect the dominant Hindu population in India?
- What domestic and external difficulties caused the decline of Ottoman Turkey, Safavid Persia, and Mughal India?

These are the questions this chapter will explore.

THE OTTOMAN TURKISH EMPIRE

The Ottomans took their name from Osman (1299–1326), the ruler of a Turkish-speaking people in western Anatolia who began expansionist moves in the fourteenth century. The Ottomans gradually absorbed other peoples on the Anatolian peninsula, and the Ottoman state emerged as one of many small Turkish states during the breakup of the empire of the Seljuk Turks. The first Ottoman state thus occupied the border between Islam and Byzantine Christendom. The Ottoman ruler called himself "border chief," or leader of the *gazis,* frontier fighters in the *jihad,* or holy war. The earliest Ottoman historical source, a fourteenth-century saga, describes the gazis as the "instrument of God's religion . . . God's scourge who cleanses the earth from the filth of polytheism . . . God's pure sword."[1]

Evolution of the Ottoman State

The holy war was intended to subdue, not destroy. The Ottomans built their empire by absorbing the Muslims of Anatolia and by becoming the protector of the Orthodox church and of the millions of Greek Christians in Anatolia and the Balkans. On the promise of obedience and the payment of a poll tax, the Muslims guaranteed the lives and property of Christians and Jews. Thus Serbs, Bosnians, Croats, and other Orthodox peoples submitted to the Ottoman rulers for the religious toleration, better administration (than the Byzantines), and tax breaks the Turks promised. Muslims had long practiced a religious toleration unknown in Christian Europe, and the Ottomans, preferring the voluntary submission of Christians to war against them, continued that policy. But when faced with determined opposition, the Ottomans could prove ruthless. The Ottoman Empire became a "frontier empire," a cosmopolitan state binding different ethnic groups and religious creeds in a single unified entity.[2] In 1389, in what is today the former Yugoslavia, the Ottomans defeated a combined force of Serbs and Bosnians. In 1396, on the Danube River in modern Bulgaria, they crushed King Sigismund of Hungary, who was supported by French, German, and English knights.

The reign of Sultan Mehmet II (r. 1451–1481) saw the end of all Turkish dynasties in Anatolia and the Ottoman conquest of Constantinople, capital of the

Byzantine Empire, which had lasted a thousand years. The six-week siege of Constantinople in 1453 remains one of the dramatic events in world history, because Constantinople symbolized the continuation of imperial Rome. The Byzantine emperor Constantine IX Palaeologus (r. 1449–1453), with only about ten thousand men, relied on the magnificent system of circular walls and stone fortifications that had protected the city for a thousand years. Mehmet II had more than one hundred thousand men and a large fleet, but iron chains spanning the harbor kept him out of the Golden Horn, the inlet of the Bosporus Strait that connects the Black and Marmora Seas and forms the harbor of Istanbul. Turkish ingenuity and Western technology eventually decided the battle. Mehmet's army carried boats over the steep hills to come in behind the chains blocking the harbor, then bombarded the city from the rear. A Transylvanian cannon founder who deserted the Greeks for the Turks cast huge bronze cannon on the spot (bringing raw materials to the scene of military action was easier than moving guns long distances).[3] When cannon shots shattered a city gate, the Turks entered the city. Mounting the dome of the church of Hagia Sophia and observing the ruined buildings, Mehmet recited poetic lines lamenting the glories of the past:

The spider serves as gatekeeper in the halls of Khosrau's
  dome,
The owl plays martial music in the palace of Afrasiyab.[4]

Victorious troops looted the city for three days, as was customary when a city did not surrender voluntarily. The Muslim historian Oruc describes the conquest:

Sultan Mehmet, the son of Sultan Murad, inspired by zeal, said "in the cause of God" and commanded plunder. The gazis, entering by force on every side, found a way in through the breaches in the fortress made by the guns and put the infidels in the fortress to the sword. . . . Mounting on the tower they destroyed the infidels who were inside and entered the city. They looted and plundered. They seized their money and possessions and made their sons and daughters slaves. The Muslims took so much booty that the wealth gathered in Istanbul (Constantinople) since it was built 2400 years before became the portion of the gazis. They plundered for three days, and after three days plunder was forbidden.[5]

The conquest of Constantinople inaugurated the imperial phase of the Ottoman state. The Ottoman sultans considered themselves successors of both the Byzantine and Seljuk emperors, as their title *Sultan-i-Rum* (Sultan of Rome) attests. The Arabic word *sultan,* originally used by the Seljuk Turks to mean "authority" or "dominion," was used by the Ottomans to connote political and military supremacy; it was carried by all members of the dynasty to stress that sovereign power was a family prerogative. The Ottomans renamed the city Istanbul.

Mehmet began the transformation of the city into an imperial Ottoman capital. He ordered Istanbul cleaned up and the walls repaired. He appointed officials to adapt the city administration to Ottoman ways and ordered wealthy Ottomans to participate in building mosques, markets, water fountains, baths, and other public facilities. He nominated the Greek patriarch as official representative of the Greek population, giving them protection and freedom of religion as long as they paid the *jitza,* a tax on non-Muslims. These appointments recognized non-Muslims as functioning parts of Ottoman society and economy, with all but a few posts within it open to them.

The population of Istanbul had declined in the decades before the conquest, and warfare, flight, and the sale of many survivors into slavery had decreased the population further. Therefore, Mehmet transplanted to the city inhabitants of other territories, granting them tax remissions and possession of empty houses. He wanted them to start businesses, make the city prosperous, and transform it into a microcosm of the empire. Jews cruelly oppressed in western Europe found Turkey "a paradise." In 1454 one Jewish resident, Isaac Sarfati, sent a circular letter to his coreligionists in the Rhineland, Swabia, Moravia, and Hungary, praising the happy conditions of the Jews under the crescent in contrast to the "great torture chamber" under the cross and urging them to come to Turkey.[6] A massive migration to Ottoman lands followed. When Ferdinand and Isabella of Spain expelled the Jews in 1492, many immigrated to the Ottoman Empire.

Expansion and Foreign Policy

The Ottomans continued to expand (Map 21.1). In 1453 they controlled only the northwest quadrant of Anatolia. Mehmet II completed the conquest of Anatolia. From Istanbul, their new capital, the Ottomans pushed down the Aegean and up the Adriatic. They so severely threatened Italy and southeastern Europe that the aged Pope Pius II himself shouldered the cross of the Crusader in 1464. In 1480 an Ottoman fleet took the Italian port of Otranto, and serious plans were laid for the conquest of all Italy. Only a disputed succession following the death

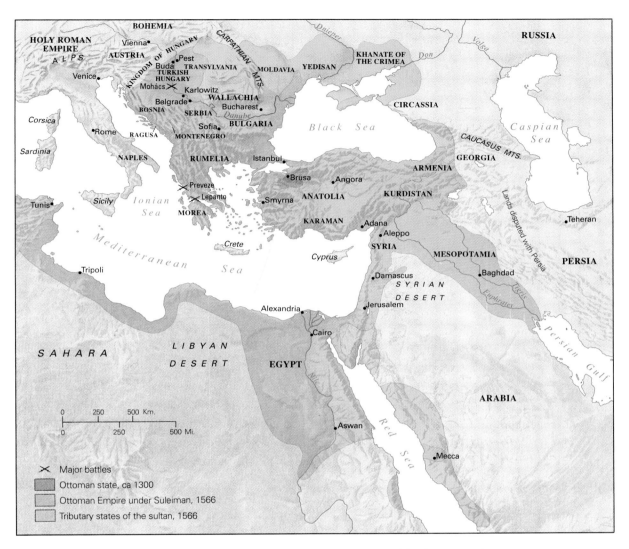

MAP 21.1 The Ottoman Empire at Its Height, 1566   The Ottomans, like their great rivals the Habsburgs, rose to rule a vast dynastic empire encompassing many different peoples and ethnic groups. The army and the bureaucracy served to unite the disparate territories into a single state.

of Mehmet II in 1481 caused the postponement of that conquest and, later, the cancellation of those plans. The Ottoman Turks inspired such fear that even in distant Iceland, the Lutheran Book of Common Prayer begged God for protection not only from "the cunning of the Pope" but also from "the terror of the Turk."

Bayezid II (r. 1481–1512) won the Ottoman throne by defeating his brother, Jem. Jem became a hostage of the pope, who used the threat of putting him on the Ottoman throne to keep Bayezid from attacking Europe. Bayezid devoted his energies to consolidating the empire and making war in the East until Jem's death.

Bayezid also strengthened the Ottoman navy, enabling it to play a major role in the Mediterranean. In the first half of the sixteenth century, the Ottomans gained control of shipping in the eastern Mediterranean, eliminated the Portuguese from the Red Sea and Persian Gulf, and supported Andalusian and North African Muslims in their fight against the Spanish *reconquista*. Selim I (r. 1512–1520) gained the title "the Grim" because he forced his father, Bayezid, to abdicate; executed his brother; and pursued inhumane policies. Selim was, however, a superb military commander. He wanted to pursue a more aggressive policy against the

Battle of Mohács The Süleymanname (Book of Suleiman), a biography, contains these wonderful illustrations of the battle that took place in Hungary on August 29, 1526. In the right panel, Suleiman in a white turban sits on a black horse surrounded by his personal guard, while janissaries fire cannon at the enemy. In the left panel, the Europeans are in disarray, in contrast to the Turks' discipline and order. Suleiman inflicted a crushing defeat and absorbed Hungary into the Ottoman Empire. The artist attempted to show the terrain and battle tactics. *(Topkapi Saray Museum, Istanbul)*

rising Safavids (see pages 660–662). Under Selim's leadership, the Ottomans defeated the Safavids and in 1514 turned them back from Anatolia. The Ottomans also added Syria and Palestine (1516) and Egypt (1517) to the empire, extending their rule across North Africa to Cyrenaica, Tripolitania, Tunisia, and Algeria. Selim's rule marks the beginning of four centuries when most Arabs were under Ottoman rule.

Suleiman (r. 1520–1566), who brought to the throne great experience as a provincial administrator and enormous energy as a soldier, extended Ottoman jurisdiction to its widest geographical extent (see Map 21.1). With Greece and the Balkans already under Ottoman domination, Suleiman's army crushed the Hun-garians at Mohács in 1526, killing the king and thousands of his nobles. Suleiman seems to have taken this victory entirely as his due. Not long after the battle, he recorded laconically in his diary, "The emperor, seated on a golden throne, receives the homage of the viziers and beys: massacre of 2,000 prisoners: the rains fall in torrents." Three years later, the Turks besieged the Habsburg capital of Vienna. Only an accident—the army's insistence on returning home before winter—prevented Muslim control of all central Europe. The Ottomans' military discipline, ability to coordinate cavalry and infantry, and capability in logistics were usually superior to those of the Europeans. In virtually every area, the Ottomans' success was due to the weakness and political disunity of their enemies and to the superiority of Turkish military organization and artillery. Gunpowder, invented by the Chinese and adapted to artillery use by the Europeans, played an influential role in the expansion of the Ottoman state.

Though victorious on land, the Ottomans did not enjoy complete dominion on the seas. The middle decades of the sixteenth century witnessed a titanic struggle between the Ottoman and Habsburg Empires for control of the Mediterranean. In September 1538, an Ottoman naval victory at Preveze, the chief Turkish port in Albania, ensured Turkish control of the Ionian and Aegean Seas. Meanwhile, Christian pirates' attacks from the island of Cyprus on Ottoman shipping in the eastern Mediterranean provoked the sultan to conquer Cyprus in 1570. He introduced Ottoman administration and settled thousands of Turks from Anatolia there. (Thus began the large Turkish presence on Cyprus that continues to the present day.) In response, Pope Pius V organized a Holy League against the Turks. Only an accident—the arrival of the Holy League's fleet so late that the Ottomans had already gone into port for the winter—brought temporary defeat. On October 7, 1571, a squadron of more than 200 Spanish, Venetian, and papal galleys smashed the Turks at Lepanto at the mouth of the Gulf of Patras in Greece (see Map 21.1). The victors lost about 7,000 men, the Turks lost about 15,000, and 10,000 Christian galley slaves were freed. Across western Europe, church bells signaled the victory, the first major Ottoman defeat by Christian forces. But Lepanto marked no decisive change in Turkish hegemony: the Turks remained supreme on land and quickly rebuilt their entire fleet.

From the late fourteenth to the early seventeenth century, from the Atlantic to the Indian Ocean, the Ottoman Empire exercised a decisive influence in world affairs. In western Europe, the Habsburg-Valois Wars worked to Ottoman advantage: they kept Europe divided. In 1525 Francis I of France and Suleiman struck an alliance; both believed that only their collaboration could prevent Habsburg hegemony in Europe. Suleiman's invasion of Hungary, culminating in his victory over the Habsburgs at Mohács in 1526, terrified Europe. The Habsburg emperor Charles V retaliated by seeking an alliance with Safavid Persia. Suleiman renewed the French agreement with Francis's son, Henry II (r. 1547–1559), and the French entente became the cornerstone of Ottoman policy in western Europe. Suleiman also allied with the German Protestant princes, forcing the Catholic Habsburgs to grant concessions to the Protestants. Ottoman pressure proved

Ottoman Helmet This mid-sixteenth-century helmet resembles a turban: conical shaped with sides tapering toward the apex, with ear and neck guards. Made of steel, the gold-inlaid and jeweled helmet was probably made for Suleiman the Magnificent. *(Topkapi Saray Museum, Istanbul)*

an important factor in the official recognition of Lutheran Protestants at the Peace of Augsburg in 1555. Suleiman believed that Protestants, including Calvinists, were similar to Muslims, since both had destroyed idols and opposed the pope. In addition to the rising tide of Protestantism, the Ottoman threat strengthened the growth of national monarchy in France.

In eastern Europe to the north of Ottoman lands stood the Grand Duchy of Moscow. In the fifteenth century, Ottoman rulers did not regard it as a threat; in 1497 they even gave Russian merchants freedom of trade within the empire. But in 1547 Grand Prince Ivan IV (the Terrible) assumed the title of tsar, or emperor, and after conquering the Muslim khanates of Kazan and Astrakhan from the Tartars (1552–1556), he brought under Russian control the entire Volga region (see Map 21.1). In 1557 Ivan's ally, the Cossack chieftain Dimitrash, tried to take Azov, the northernmost Ottoman fortress. Russian influence thus entered

Ottoman territories in the Caucasus and Black Sea regions.

Preoccupied with war against the Habsburgs, Suleiman delayed action. Grand Vizier Sokullu Mehmet prepared a large expedition to retake Astrakhan, use it as the center of a fortified defense system in the area, and build a canal between the Volga and the Don that would unite the Black and Caspian Seas. The object of this plan was to drive the Russians from the Volga basin and to encircle Persia (see Map 21.1). The proposal only succeeded in uniting Russia, Persia, and the pope against the Turks. Field commanders failed to receive adequate supplies, and the scheme failed. But Sokullu did expand Turkish influence in Moldavia, Wallachia, and Poland, thereby blocking Russian influence east of the Black Sea.

To the east, war with Persia occupied the sultans' attention throughout the sixteenth century. Several issues lay at the root of the long and exhausting conflicts: religious antagonism between the Sunni Ottomans and the Shi'ite Persians; disputes over territories south and west of the Caspian Sea; the Ottoman goal of controlling the international trade routes bringing silks from Persia and spices from the East, which yielded huge customs revenues to the Ottoman treasury; and Persian diplomatic alliances with the Habsburgs while the Ottomans supported the French. The Balkan conflicts and declining revenues prevented the sultans from winning a decisive victory. Finally, in 1638, Sultan Merad IV captured Baghdad, and the treaty of Kasr-I-Shirim established a permanent border between the two powers.

Meanwhile, in South Asia the Ottomans fought the Portuguese and Spanish for control of the Indian Ocean trade. An Ottoman fleet secured from some cities on the East African coast, such as Mombasa, recognition of Ottoman supremacy. In the face of tough Iberian naval power, however, Ottoman influence collapsed, and in the early seventeenth century the Dutch and the English came to dominate the Indian Ocean. For centuries the European powers had imported spices and silks via the Indian Ocean and western Asia. In the seventeenth century, those products went to Europe by the Atlantic route. Loss of supremacy on the seas and the sharp decline in customs duties contributed to Ottoman economic decline.[7]

Ottoman Society

The Ottoman social and administrative systems reached their classic form under Suleiman I. The seventeenth-century Ottoman historian Mustafa Naima divided Muslim society into producers of wealth, Muslim and non-Muslim, and the military. In Naima's view, there could be no state without the military, wealth was needed to support the military, the state's subjects raised the wealth, subjects could prosper only through justice, and without the state there could be no justice.[8]

All authority flowed from the sultan to his public servants: provincial governors, police officers, military generals, heads of treasuries, viziers. Under Suleiman I, the Ottoman ruling class consisted in part of descendants of Turkish families that had formerly ruled parts of Anatolia and in part of people of varied ethnic origins who rose through the bureaucratic and military ranks. All were committed to the Ottoman way: Islamic in faith, loyal to the sultan, and well versed in the Turkish language and the culture of the imperial court. In return for their services to the sultan, they held *timars* (landed estates) for the duration of their lives. The ruling class had the legal right to use and enjoy the profits, but not the ownership, of the land. Since all property belonged to the sultan and reverted to him on the holder's death, Turkish nobles, unlike their European counterparts, could not put down roots. The absence of a hereditary nobility and private property in agricultural land differentiates the Ottoman system from European feudalism.[9]

Modern scholarship has provided little information about the lives and public activities of ordinary women in the Ottoman world, but we know a fair amount about royal and wealthy women. Royal women resided in seclusion in the harem. In Muslim culture, the Arabic word *harem* means a sacred place; a sanctuary; a place of honor, respect, and religious purity. The word was often applied to the holy cities of Mecca and Medina. Just as the sultan's private quarters in the imperial palace was a kind of harem, so in the fifteenth century another set of chambers for his mother, wife, concubines, unmarried sisters, and royal children gained the same name. (In the seventeenth century, as absolute monarchy evolved in Europe, Europeans developed the myth of Muslim tyranny, and the sultan's harem was the crux of that tyranny. In the Western imagination, "Orgiastic sex became a metaphor for power corrupted."[10]) The Ottoman harem was *not* a stable of sexual partners for the sultan.

Because Muslim "histories rarely mention women" and "virtually ignore concubinage,"[11] it is difficult for students to penetrate the walled harem to get at the personalities and activities of the royal ladies. In the fourteenth and early fifteenth centuries, marriage served as a tool of diplomacy. Ottoman marriages were arranged as part of the negotiations ending a war to symbolize the defeated party's acceptance of subordinate status. After the conquest of Constantinople and the Ottoman claim to world empire, no foreigner was seen as worthy of so intimate a bond as marriage; the sultan had to occupy a position of visible superiority. By the reign of Selim I, the principle was established that the sultan did not contract legal marriage but perpetuated himself through concubinage. Slave concubinage served as the central element of Ottoman reproductive policy. Since in Muslim law, a child held the legal status of its father, the sons of a slave concubine were just as eligible for the throne as those of a free woman. With a notable exception (see the feature "Individuals in Society: Hürrem"), the sultans preferred to continue the dynasty through concubines. They could have none of the political aspirations or leverage that a native or foreign-born noblewoman had. Nor could a slave concubine press legal claims on the sultan, as a legal wife could. The latter also could demand a ceremonial deference, which a concubine could not.[12]

Other Muslim dynasties, such as the Abbasids, had practiced slave concubinage, but the Ottomans carried the institution beyond anything that had previously existed. Slave concubinage paralleled the Ottoman development of the janissary system (see page 655), whereby slave boys were trained for imperial service. Slave viziers, slave generals, and slave concubines held positions entirely at the sultan's pleasure, owed loyalty solely to him, and thus were more reliable than a hereditary nobility, as existed in Europe. Great social prestige, as well as the opportunity to acquire power and wealth, was attached to being a slave of the imperial household. Being a slave in the Ottoman world did not carry the demeaning social connotations connected with slavery in the Western Hemisphere.

When one of the sultan's concubines became pregnant, her status and her salary increased. If she delivered a boy, she raised the child until the age of ten or eleven. Then the child was given a province to govern under his mother's supervision. She accompanied him there, was responsible for his good behavior, and worked through imperial officials and the janissary corps to promote his interests. Since succession to the throne was open to all the sultan's sons, at his death fratricide often resulted, and the losers were blinded or executed. If a woman produced a girl, she raised her daughter until the girl married. Within the Ottoman dynasty, motherhood was the source of female power.[13]

Ottoman women of wealth and property—acquired through dowries, inheritance, gifts, salaries, and divorce—also possessed economic and social power. As society expected of them, wealthy women made charitable contributions by endowing religious foundations, freeing slaves (which the Qur'an called a meritorious act), and helping paupers, prisoners, and prostitutes. As in the Byzantine world, and as with rich Protestant women, Muslim women's assistance seems to have gone primarily to other women.

Evidence of women's charitable and business activities in the eighteenth and nineteenth centuries is more plentiful. For example, we know that in 1881 eighteen of the forty-two slave dealers in Istanbul (almost one-half) were women. Wealthy upper-class women in large harems bought Circassian girls, trained them in proper etiquette, and later sold them to the imperial harem or other large harems. These women dealers enjoyed financial profit in a society where the demand for slaves remained strong, as it did well into the twentieth century (although slavery was theoretically abolished).[14]

Recent scholars have demonstrated what European ambassadors and tourists had long speculated about: the prevalence of homosexual activity in the imperial palace, the janissary corps, and Ottoman society in general. Selected for "their bodily perfection, muscular strength, and intellectual ability," palace pages commonly had intimate sexual relationships with court officials and the sultan himself.[15] Ibrahim Pasa ascended the chain of offices—grand falconer, governor of Ruyelia, vizier, grand vizier (1523–1536)—through his mental acumen and relationship with Suleiman. His marriage to the daughter of Selim I suggests his prestige. Accused of aspiring to the sultanate, Ibrahim was executed by strangulation, an event that marked the ascendancy of Hürrem (see page 654). Ibrahim's successor as grand vizier, the Croatian-born page Rustem, won considerable wealth because of his relationship with Suleiman. A slave himself, he owned seventeen hundred slaves at his death. Earlier, in 1475, the Genoese visitor Jacopo de Promontoria ascribed the low birthrate among noble Turks in Anatolia to "the infinite lechery of various slaves and young boys to whom they give themselves."[16] With the prevalence of homosexuality in Genoa,[17] Jacopo was in no position to criticize. Moreover, in the fifteenth and sixteenth centuries, the Turkish population vastly increased,[18] rather than declined. Other writers at the time and through the nineteenth century, however, confirmed Jacopo's impression of sodomitical activity.

Slaves who had been purchased from Spain, North Africa, and Venice; captured in battle; or acquired through the system known as *devshirme*—by which the

Individuals in Society

Hürrem (ca 1505?–1558)

She was born in the western Ukraine (then part of Poland), the daughter of a Ruthenian priest, and given the Polish name Aleksandra Lisowska. After she acquired fame, Europeans called her Roxelana, the Polish term for "Ruthenian maiden." When Tartar raiders took Rogatin, a town on the Dniester River near Lvov, they captured and enslaved her. The next documented incident in her life dates from September 1520, when she was given as a gift to Suleiman on the occasion of his accession to the throne. The Venetian ambassador (probably relying on second- or third-hand information) described her as "young, graceful, petite, but not beautiful." She was given the Turkish name Hürrem, meaning "joyful."

Hürrem apparently brought joy to Suleiman. Their first child was born in 1521; by 1525 they had five children (four sons), and sources note that by that year Suleiman visited no other woman. But he waited eight or nine years before breaking Ottoman dynastic tradition. In 1533 or 1534, he made Hürrem his legal wife, the first slave concubine so honored. For the rest of her life, Hürrem played a highly influential role in the political, diplomatic, and philanthropic life of the Ottoman state. First, great power flowed from her position as mother of the prince, the future sultan Selim II (r. 1566–1574). Then, as the intimate and most trusted adviser of the sultan, she was Suleiman's closest confidant. He was frequently away in the far-flung corners of his multiethnic empire. Hürrem wrote him long letters filled with her love and longing for him, her prayers for his safety in battle, and political information about affairs in Istanbul, the activities of the grand vizier, and the attitudes of the janissaries. At a time when some people believed that the sultan's absence from the capital endangered his hold on the throne, Hürrem acted as his eyes and ears for potential threats.

Hürrem was the sultan's contact with her native Poland, which sent more embassies to Istanbul than any other power. Through her correspondence with King Sigismund I, peace between Poland and the Ottomans was maintained. When Sigismund II succeeded his father in 1548, Hürrem sent congratulations on his accession, along with two pairs of pajamas (originally a Hindu garment, but commonly worn in southwestern Asia) and six handkerchiefs. By sending the shah of Persia gold-embroidered sheets and shirts she had sewn herself, Hürrem sought to display the wealth of the sultanate and to keep peace between the Ottomans and the Safavids.

Hürrem and her ladies in the harem. (*Bibliothèque Nationale, Paris*)

The enormous stipend that Suleiman gave Hürrem permitted her to participate in his vast building program. In Jerusalem (in the Ottoman province of Palestine), she founded a hospice for fifty-five pilgrims that included a soup kitchen that fed four hundred pilgrims a day. In Istanbul Suleiman built and Hürrem endowed the Haseki (meaning "royal favorite concubine") mosque complex and a public bath for women near the Women's Market. We do not know whether these charitable benefactions reflected genuine concern for the poor, were intended to show the interests of the dynasty, or were meant to court favorable public opinion, for contemporaries hated and reviled Hürrem and thought she had bewitched Suleiman.

Perhaps Hürrem tried to fulfill two functions hitherto distinct in Ottoman political theory: those of the sultan's favorite and mother of the prince. She also performed the conflicting roles of slave concubine and imperial wife.

Questions for Analysis

1. Compare Hürrem to other powerful fifteenth- or sixteenth-century women, such as Isabella of Castile, Catherine de' Medici of France, Elizabeth of England, and Mary Queen of Scots.
2. What was Hürrem's "nationality"? What role did it play in her life?

Source: Leslie P. Pierce, *The Imperial Harem: Women and Sovereignty in the Ottoman Empire* (New York: Oxford University Press, 1993).

sultan's agents swept the provinces for Christian youths—were recruited for the imperial civil service and the standing army. Southern Europeans did not shrink from selling Christians into slavery, and as the Ottoman frontier advanced in the fifteenth and sixteenth centuries, Albanian, Bosnian, Wallachian, and Hungarian slave boys filled Ottoman imperial needs. Moreover, because devshirme recruitment often meant social advancement, some Christian parents bribed government officials to accept their children. All these children were converted to Islam. The brightest 10 percent entered the palace school. There they learned to read and write Arabic, Ottoman Turkish, and Persian; received special religious instruction; and were trained for the civil service. Other boys were sent to Turkish farms, where they acquired physical toughness in preparation for military service. Known as *janissaries* (Turkish for "recruits"), they formed the elite army corps. Thoroughly indoctrinated and absolutely loyal to the sultan, the janissary slave corps eliminated the influence of old Turkish families and played the central role in Ottoman military affairs in the sixteenth century.

Cultural Flowering

The reign of Suleiman I witnessed an extraordinary artistic flowering and represents the peak of Ottoman influence and culture. In Turkish history, Suleiman is known as *Kanuni* (Lawgiver) because of his profound influence on the civil law. He ordered Lütfi Paşa (d. 1562), a poet of slave origin and a juridical scholar, to draw up a new general code of laws. Published in Suleiman's name, this sultanic legal code prescribed penalties for routine criminal acts such as robbery, adultery, and murder. It also sought to reform bureaucratic and financial corruption in areas such as harem intervention in administrative affairs, foreign merchants' payment of bribes to avoid customs duties, imprisonment without trial, and promotion in the provincial administration because of favoritism rather than ability. The legal code also introduced the idea of balanced financial budgets. The head of the religious establishment, Hoja Sadeddin Efendi, was given the task of reconciling sultanic law with Islamic law. Suleiman's legal acts influenced many legal codes, including that of the United States. Today, Suleiman's image, along with the images of Solon, Moses, Thomas Jefferson, and other great lawgivers, appears in the chamber of the U.S. House of Representatives.

Europeans called Suleiman "the Magnificent" because of the grandeur of his court. With annual state revenues of about $80 million (at a time when Elizabeth I of England could expect $150,000 and Francis I of France perhaps $1 million), with thousands of servants to cater to his whims, and with a lifestyle no European monarch could begin to rival, Suleiman was indeed magnificent. He used his fabulous wealth to adorn Istanbul with palaces, mosques, schools, and libraries. The building of hospitals, roads, and bridges and the reconstruction of the water systems of the great pilgrimage sites at Mecca and Jerusalem benefited his subjects.

The Ottomans under Suleiman demonstrated splendid creativity in carpet weaving, textiles, ceramics, and, above all, architecture. In the buildings of Pasha Sinan (1491–1588), a Greek-born devshirme recruit who rose to become imperial architect, the Ottoman spirit is powerfully expressed. A contemporary of Michelangelo, Sinan designed 312 public buildings—mosques, schools, hospitals, public baths, palaces, and burial chapels. His masterpieces, the Shehzade and Suleimaniye mosques in Istanbul, which rivaled the Byzantine church of Hagia Sophia, represented solutions to spatial problems unique to domed buildings and expressed the discipline, power, and devotion to Islam that characterized the Ottoman Empire under Suleiman. With pardonable exaggeration, Suleiman began a letter to the king of France, with whom he was allied, by saying, "I who am the sultan of sultans, the sovereign of sovereigns, the dispenser of crowns to the monarchs on the face of the earth . . . to thee who are Francis, King of the land of France."[19]

The cultural explosion of Suleiman's reign rivaled the artistic and literary achievements of the European Renaissance. In addition to architecture, Ottoman scholars and artists showed great distinction in poetry, painting, history, mathematics, geographical literature, astronomy, medicine, and the religious sciences.

Poetry, rather than prose, was the main vehicle of Ottoman literary expression. *Diwan* poetry, so called because it consisted of collections of poems, though written by intellectuals in Turkish, followed classical Islamic (Arabic) forms and rules and addressed the ruling class. Sxeyhi of Kütahya (d. 1429) compiled a large Diwan collection and in his *Book of the Donkey* used animals to personify and satirize his political enemies. Modern scholars consider Bursah Ahmet Pasa, an imperial judge and confidential adviser to the sultan Mehmet II, to be the greatest Ottoman poet of the fifteenth century. Bursah Ahmet Pasa's beautiful odes and diversified style won him widespread popularity.

Folk literature, produced by traveling troubadours, described the traditions and wisdom of the people in

Lady Mary Wortley Montagu Famous in her own time for her letters from Constantinople and, after her return to England, for her efforts to educate the English public about inoculation against smallpox, Lady Mary is praised by twentieth-century scholars as a brilliant and urbane woman struggling for emancipation. *(Boston Athenaeum)*

humorous short stories and anecdotes. The folk collection of Dede Korkut, set down in Turkish prose, includes tribal epics describing the conflicts with the Georgians, Circassians, and Byzantines and serves as a source for the history of the fourteenth century. Just as Western historical writing in the early modern period often served to justify the rights of ruling dynasties, so Ottoman historical scholarship under Mehmet II and Suleiman promoted the claims of the family of Osman. Perhaps the greatest historian of the early sixteenth century was Ahmet Semseddin ibn-I-Kemal, or Kemalpasazède (d. 1526), the Muslim judge and administrator whose *History of the House of Osman* gives original source material for the reigns through which he himself lived. Building on the knowledge of earlier Islamic writers and stimulated by Ottoman naval power, the geographer and cartographer Piri Reis produced a map incorporating Islamic and Western knowledge that

showed all the known world (1513); another of his maps detailed Columbus's third voyage to the New World. Piri Reis's *Book of the Sea* (1521) contained 129 chapters, each with a map incorporating all Islamic (and Western) knowledge of the seas and navigation and describing harbors, tides, dangerous rocks and shores, and storm areas. Takiyuddin Mehmet (1521–1585), who served as the sultan's chief astronomer, built an observatory at Istanbul. His *Instruments of the Observatory* catalogued astronomical instruments and described an astronomical clock that fixed the location of heavenly bodies with greater precision than ever before.

What medical treatment or health care was available to the sick in the Ottoman world? Muslim medical education was practical, not theoretical: students received their training not in the *madrasas,* or mosque schools, but by apprenticeship to experienced physicians or in the *bimaristans,* or hospitals. Under a senior's supervision, medical students studied the course of various diseases, learned the techniques of surgery, and especially mastered pharmacology—the preparation of drugs from plants. The Muslim knowledge of pharmacology derived from centuries-old traditions, and modern students of the history of medicine believe that pharmacology as an institution is an Islamic invention.

By the fifteenth century, Muslims knew the value of quarantine. Yet when devastating epidemics such as the bubonic plague struck the empire during Mehmet II's reign, he and the court fled to the mountains of the Balkans, and the imperial government did little to fight the plague. Under Suleiman, however, the imperial palace itself became a center of medical science, and the large number of hospitals established in Istanbul and throughout the empire testifies to his support for medical research and his concern for the sick. Abi Ahmet Celebi (1436–1523), the chief physician of the empire, produced a study on kidney and bladder stones and supported the research of the Jewish doctor Musa Colinus ul-Israil on the application of drugs. Celebi founded the first Ottoman medical school, which served as a training institution for physicians of the empire.[20] The sultans and the imperial court relied on a cadre of elite Jewish physicians.

To fight smallpox, the Chinese had successfully practiced inoculation in the sixteenth century, and the procedure spread to Turkey in the seventeenth. Lady Mary Wortley Montagu, wife of the British ambassador to Istanbul, had her son inoculated in 1717. Here is her description of the method:

The smallpox, so fatal and so general amongst us (in England), is here entirely harmless by the invention of engraft-

ing. . . . Every autumn . . . people send one another to know if any of their family has a mind to have the smallpox (get inoculated). . . . An old woman comes with a nutshell full of the matter of the best sort of smallpox and asks what veins you please (want) to have opened. She immediately rips open what you offer to her with a large needle (which gives you no more pain than a common scratch) and puts into the vein as much venom as can lie upon the head of the needle, and after binds up the little wound. . . . The children or young patients play together all the rest of the day and are in perfect health till the eighth. Then the fever begins to seize 'em and they keep their beds two days, very seldom three. They have very rarely twenty or thirty (pockmarks) in their faces, which never mark (leave a permanent scar), and in eight days' time they are as well as before their illness. . . . Every year thousands undergo this operation, and the French ambassador says pleasantly that they take the smallpox here by way of diversion as they take the waters in other countries (at spas). . . . There is no example of anyone that has died in it.[21]

This was eighty years before the English physician Edward Jenner (see page 611) tried the procedure using cowpox in England.

Lady Mary Wortley Montagu marveled at the splendor of Ottoman culture. Remarkably intelligent and fluent in several languages, Lady Mary, a pioneer feminist, also had a mind exceptionally open to different cultures. As an aristocrat, the wife of an official foreign representative, and a woman, she had access to people and places (such as the imperial *seraglio*, or harem) that were off-limits to ordinary tourists. Her many letters to relatives and friends in England provide a wealth of information about upper-class Ottoman society.

On January 19, 1718, Lady Mary gave birth to a daughter and described the experience in a letter to an English friend:

I was brought to bed of a daughter. . . . I must own that it was not half so mortifying here as in England, there being as much difference as there is between a little cold in the head, which sometimes happens here, and the consumptive coughs so common in London.[22]

The naturalness of childbirth in Turkey, Lady Mary suggests, may have been because Turkish women had much more experience of it than Englishwomen:

In this country 'tis more despicable to be married and not fruitful than 'tis with us to be fruitful before marriage. They have a notion that whenever a woman leaves off bearing children, 'tis because she is too old for that business, whatever her face says to the contrary, and this opinion makes the ladies here so ready to make proofs of their youth. . . .

Without any exaggeration, all the women of my acquaintance that have been married ten years have twelve or thirteen children, and the old ones boast of having had five and twenty or thirty apiece and are respected according to the number they have produced.[23]

Turkish women's sense of self-worth seems to have been closely tied to their production of children, as was common in many cultures at the time. As for Turkish morality, "'Tis just as 'tis with you; and the Turkish ladies don't commit one sin the less for not being Christians." In other words, Turkish women were neither better nor worse than European ones. Moreover,

'tis very easy to see that they have more liberty than we have, . . . and their shapes are wholly concealed by a thing they call a ferigee, which no woman of any sort (class) appears without. . . . You may guess how effectively this disguises them, that there is no distinguishing the great lady from her slave, and 'tis impossible for the most jealous husband to know his wife when he meets her, and no man dare either touch or follow a woman in the street.

This perpetual masquerade gives them entire liberty of following their inclinations without danger of discovery. The most usual method of intrigue is to send an appointment to the lover to meet the lady at a Jew's shop, which are as notoriously convenient as our Indian houses. . . .

You may easily imagine the number of faithful wives very small in a country where they have nothing to fear from their lovers' indiscretion. . . . Neither have they much to apprehend from the resentment of their husbands, those ladies that are rich having all their money in their own hands, which they take with 'em upon a divorce with an addition which he is obliged to give 'em. Upon the whole, I look upon the Turkish women as the only free people in the empire.[24]

In short, in spite of the legal restrictions of the harem, upper-class ladies found ways to go out and even to have affairs.

The Decline of Ottoman Power

In the fifteenth and early sixteenth centuries, government depended heavily on the sultan, and the matter of the dynastic succession posed a major political problem. Heirs to the throne had gained administrative experience as governors of provinces and military experience on the battlefield as part of their education. After Suleiman's reign, however, this tradition was abandoned. To prevent threats of usurpation, heirs were brought up in the harem and were denied a role in government. By the time a prince succeeded his father, years of dissipation were likely to have rendered the prince alcoholic, insane, or exhausted from excessive sexual activity. Selim II (r. 1566–1574), whom the Turks called "Selim the Drunkard," left the conduct of public affairs to his vizier while he pursued the pleasures of the harem. Turkish sources attribute his death to a fall in his bath caused by dizziness when he tried to stop drinking. A series of rulers who were incompetent or minor children left power in the hands of leading bureaucratic officials and the mothers of the heirs. Instead of a fight for the throne among the surviving sons of the dead sultan, the practice arose of granting the throne to the eldest male member of the dynasty. Political factions formed around viziers, military leaders, and palace women. In the contest for political favor, the devshirme was abandoned, and political and military ranks were filled by Muslims.

Under the competent vizier Mehmet Köprülü (r. 1656–1661), imperial fortunes revived. Köprülü abolished corruption, maintained domestic peace, and conducted a vigorous war with Venice. His son Ahmet succeeded as vizier and continued these policies. Ahmet's ambitious brother-in-law and successor, Kara Mustafa, pursued a more aggressive foreign policy: his objective was an attack on the Habsburg capital, Vienna. When battle came on September 12, 1683, the combination of a strong allied Christian force (see page 538) and Habsburg heavy artillery, which the Turks lacked, gave the Europeans the victory. The Ottomans rallied again, but defeat at Vienna and domestic disorders led to the decline of Ottoman power in the Balkans. In the words of one historian, "The Ottoman state was predicated upon, committed to, and organized for conquest. . . . An end to significant and sustained conquest rocked the entire state structure and sent aftershocks through all its institutions."[25]

The peace treaty signed at Karlowitz (1699) marks a watershed in Ottoman history. By its terms, the empire lost (to Austria) the major European provinces of Hungary and Transylvania, along with the tax revenues they had provided. Karlowitz also shattered Ottoman morale. Eighteenth-century wars against European powers—Venice (1714–1718), Austria and Russia (1736–1739), and Russia alone (1768–1774 and 1787–1792)—proved indecisive but contributed to general Ottoman internal disintegration.

As in parts of Europe, rising population without corresponding economic growth caused serious social problems. A long period of peace in the later sixteenth century and again in the mid-eighteenth century— while the War of the Austrian Succession (1740–1748)

and the Seven Years' War (1756–1763) were preoccupying the European powers (see page 579)—and a decline in the frequency of visits of the plague led to a doubling of the population. The land could not sustain so many people, nor could the towns provide jobs for the thousands of agricultural workers who fled to them. The return of demobilized soldiers aggravated the problem. Inflation, famine, and widespread revolts resulted. The economic center of gravity shifted from the capital to the provinces, and politically the empire began to decentralize as well. Local notables and military men, rather than central officials, exercised political power. Scholars regard this provincial autonomy as the precursor of nationalism.

European colonialism and worldwide economic changes isolated the Ottomans from the centers of growth in the Western Hemisphere and the East Indies. European trade with the Americas, Africa, and Asia by means of the Atlantic also meant that the old southwestern Asian trade routes were bypassed. Ottoman trade turned more to regional and local markets, where profits were lower and there was little growth. Meanwhile, Ottoman guilds set the prices of commodities such as wheat, wool, copper, and precious metals, and European willingness to pay high prices pulled those commodities out of the Ottoman Empire. The result was scarcity, which led to a decline in Turkish industrial production. Likewise in the craft industries, Europeans bought Ottoman raw materials, used them to manufacture textiles and metallurgical goods, and sold them in Turkish lands, thereby disrupting Ottoman craft industries in the early nineteenth century. Prices rose, inflation increased, and the government devalued the currency, causing new financial crises.

More than any other single factor, a series of agreements known as capitulations, which the Ottoman government signed with European powers, contributed to the Ottoman decline. A trade compact signed in 1536 and renewed in 1569 virtually exempted French merchants from Ottoman law and allowed them to travel and buy and sell throughout the sultan's dominions and to pay low customs duties on French imports and exports. In 1590, in spite of strong French opposition, a group of English merchants gained the right to trade in Ottoman territory in return for supplying the sultan with iron, steel, brass, and tin for his war with Persia. In 1615, as part of a twenty-year peace treaty, the capitulation rights already given to French and English businessmen were extended to the Habsburgs. These capitulations progressively gave European merchants an economic stranglehold on Ottoman trade and com-

Visit to the Lunatic Asylum   Beginning in the ninth century, Islamic hospitals had special wards for the insane. Therapy consisted of baths, massages, bleeding (for the violently agitated), and drugs given as sedatives, stimulants, or antidepressants. Fear that the violent would harm themselves or others led to shackling. In this scene from an album produced for Sultan Ahmed I (r. 1603–1617), three violent patients are chained; the nearly naked appearance of two of them (which would have shocked Muslim sensibilities) is a sure sign of their insanity. The Jewish doctor (right) is threatened with a knife; his assistant is caught in the stocks from which the third lunatic tries to escape. Two visitors observing the mayhem through the window put their forefingers to their mouths, a common gesture in Muslim society indicating astonishment and a defense against evil. *(Topkapi Saray Museum, Istanbul)*

merce; Europeans had greater military power. In the nineteenth century, the Ottoman Empire was beset by the loss of territory, the pressures of European capitalistic imperialism, and unresolved internal problems; Tsar Nicholas I of Russia (r. 1825–1855) called it "the sick man of Europe."[26]

 THE PERSIAN THEOCRATIC STATE

Describing the Mongol destruction of Persia in the thirteenth century, the Persian historian Juvaini wrote, "With one stroke, a world which billowed with fertility was laid desolate, and the regions thereof became a desert, and the greater part of the living dead, and their skin and bones crumbling dust."[27] Pursuing a

scorched-earth policy toward the land and a psychological reign of terror over the people, the Mongols, so modern demographers estimate, reduced the population of Persia, Khurasan, Iraq, and Azerbaijan (Map 21.2) from 2.5 million to 250,000. Mongol devastation represents the last great sweep of Turkish steppe nomads from Central Asia into the European and Islamic heartlands. Turkish tribes in Central Asia far outnumbered the ethnic Mongols. The Turks joined Chinggis Khan partly because he had defeated them and partly because westward expansion with the Mongols offered adventure and rich pasturelands for their herds of sheep and horses.[28]

The rehabilitation of Persia began under Ghazan (r. 1295–1304), the *Ilkhan,* as the Mongol rulers of Persia were called. A descendant of Chinggis Khan, Ghazan

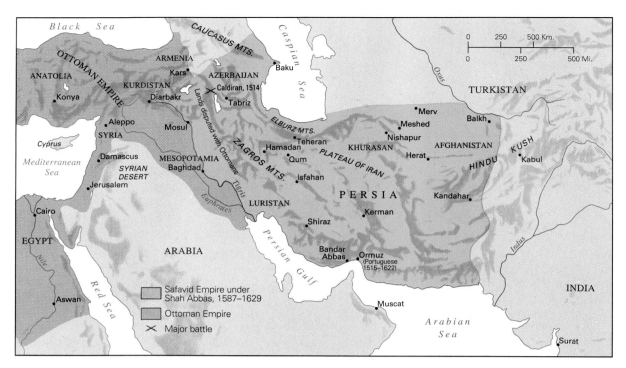

MAP 21.2 The Safavid Empire In the late sixteenth century, the power of the Safavid kingdom of Persia rested on its strong military force, its Shi'ite Muslim faith, and its extraordinarily rich trade in rugs and pottery. Many of the cities on the map, such as Tabriz, Qum, and Shiraz, were great rug-weaving centers.

reduced peasants' taxes and thereby encouraged their will to produce. He also worked to improve the fiscal and administrative systems. His declaration of Islam as the state religion had profound political and cultural consequences: native (and Muslim) Persians willingly served the state government; they alone had the literacy needed to run a bureaucracy. Turkish-Mongol soldiers adapted to Persian ways. The court patronized Persian art. The rehabilitation of Persia under Ghazan legitimated the Mongols as a Persian dynasty. Across the Central Asian heartlands, hundreds of Chinese doctors, engineers, artists, and potterymakers came seeking opportunity in the Persian-Mongol-Turkish capital at Tabriz. Chinese artistic influences left a permanent mark on Persian miniature painting, calligraphy, and pottery design.

But Mongol rule of Persia did not last long. While Mehmet II was extending Ottoman jurisdiction through eastern Anatolia, the Safavid movement advanced in Persia. The Safavid Dynasty, which takes its name from Safi al-Din (1252–1334), a supposed descendant of Ali (the fourth caliph), began as leaders of a contemplative Sufi sect. Gradually the dynasty evolved into a militant and (to the Sunni Muslims) heretical Shi'ite regime. The attraction of the masses to Shi'ism perhaps reflects the role of religion as a vehicle for the expression of political feeling—in this case, opposition to Mongol domination. It also shows the organizational role played by Sufi orders such as the Safavids in a society disrupted by conquest. In the early sixteenth century, Persia emerged as a powerful Muslim state under the Safavids. (Since 1935 Persia has been known as Iran.) Between 1502 and 1510, Ismail (r. 1502–1524) defeated petty Turkish leaders, united Persia under his sovereignty, and proclaimed himself *shah,* or king.

The strength of the early Safavid state rested on three crucial features. First, it had the loyalty and military support of Qizilbash nomadic tribesmen, many from Anatolia. (*Qizilbash,* a Turkish word meaning "redheads," was applied to these people because of the red hats they wore.) The shah secured the loyalty of the Qizilbash by granting them vast grazing lands, especially on the troublesome Ottoman frontier. In return, the Qizilbash supplied him with troops. Second, the Safavid state utilized the skills of urban bureaucrats and

Polo   Two teams of four on horseback ride back and forth on a grass field 200 by 400 yards, trying to hit a 4½-ounce wooden ball with a four-foot mallet through the opponents' goal. Because a typical match involves many high-speed collisions among the horses, each player has to maintain a string of expensive ponies in order to change mounts several times during the game. Students of the history of sports believe the game originated in Persia, as shown in this eighteenth-century miniature, whence it spread to India, China, and Japan. Brought from India to England, where it became very popular among the aristocracy in the nineteenth century, polo is a fine example of cross-cultural influences. *(Private Collection)*

made them an essential part of the civil machinery of government. The third source of Safavid strength was the Shi'ite faith. The Shi'ites claimed descent from Ali, Muhammad's cousin and son-in-law, and believed that leadership among Muslims rightfully belonged to the Prophet's descendants. Ismail claimed descent from a line of twelve infallible *imams* (leaders) beginning with Ali and was officially regarded as their representative on earth. When Ismail conquered Tabriz in 1501, he de-

clared Shi'ism the official and compulsory religion of his new empire under penalty of death. In the late twentieth century, Iran remained the only Muslim state in which Shi'ism was the official religion.

Shi'ism gradually shaped the cultural and political identity of Persia (and later Iran). Recent scholarship asserts that Ismail was not "motivated by cynical notions of political manipulation."[29] He imported Shi'ite *ulema* (scholars outstanding in learning and piety) from other Arab lands to instruct and guide his people, and he persecuted and exiled Sunni ulema. With its puritanical emphasis on the holy law and on self-flagellation in penance for any disloyalty to Ali, the Safavid state represented theocracy triumphant throughout the first half century of its existence.

Safavid power reached its height under Shah Abbas (r. 1587–1629), whose military achievements, support for trade and commerce, and endowment of the arts earned him the epithet "the Great." The Persian army had hitherto consisted of tribal units under tribal leadership. Using the Ottoman model, Shah Abbas built a national army composed of Armenian and Georgian recruits paid by and loyal to himself. Shah Abbas campaigned against the Turks and captured Baghdad, Mosul, and Diarbakr in Mesopotamia (see Map 21.2).

Military victories account for only part of Shah Abbas's claim to greatness. Determined to improve his country's export trade, he built the small cottage business of carpet weaving into a national industry. In the capital city of Isfahan alone, factories employed more than twenty-five thousand weavers, who produced woolen carpets, brocades, and silks of brilliant color, design, and quality. Armenians controlled the carpet industry; the Safavids had brought them to Isfahan to protect them from Turkish military attacks. Three hundred Chinese potters were imported to make glazed building tiles, which adorned the great Safavid buildings. They captured much of the European tile market.

The jewel of the empire was Isfahan, whose prosperity and beauty rested on trade and industry. A seventeenth-century English visitor described Isfahan's bazaar as "the surprisingest piece of Greatness in Honour of commerce the world can boast of." Besides splendid rugs, stalls displayed pottery and fine china, metalwork of exceptionally high quality, and silks and velvets of stunning weave and design. A city of perhaps 750,000 people, Isfahan contained 162 mosques, 48 schools where future members of the ulema learned the sacred Muslim sciences, 273 public baths, and the vast imperial palace. Private houses had their own garden courts, and public gardens, pools, and parks adorned the wide streets. Tales of the beauty of Isfahan circulated worldwide, attracting thousands of tourists annually in the seventeenth and eighteenth centuries.

Flowers represent a distinctive and highly developed feature of Persian culture. From the second century, and with the model of the biblical account of the Garden of Eden (Genesis 2 and 3), a continuous tradition of gardening had existed in Persia. A garden was a walled area with a pool in the center and geometrically laid-out flowering plants, especially roses. "In Arabic, paradise is simply *al janna*, the garden,"[30] and often as much attention was given to flowers as to food crops. First limited to the ruler's court, gardening soon spread among the wealthy citizens. Gardens served not only as centers of prayer and meditation but also as places of revelry and sensuality. A ruler might lounge near his pool as he watched the ladies of his harem bathe in it.

After the Abbasid conquest of Persia in 636–637, formal gardening spread west and east through the Islamic world, as illustrated by the magnificent gardens of Muslim Spain, southern Italy, and later southeastern Europe. The Mongol followers of Tamerlane (see page 664) took landscape architects from Persia back to Samarkand and adopted their designs to nomad encampments. In 1396 Tamerlane ordered the construction of a garden in a meadow, called House of Flowers. When Tamerlane's descendant Babur established the Mughal Dynasty in India (see the next section), he adapted the Persian garden to the warmer southern climate. Gardens were laid out near palaces, mosques, shrines, and mausoleums, the most famous being the Taj Mahal at Agra (see page 668).

Because it represented paradise, the garden played a large role in Muslim literature. Some scholars hold that to understand Arabic poetry, one must study Arabic gardening. The literary genres of flowers and gardens provided basic themes for Hispano-Arab poets and a model for medieval Christian Europe. The secular literature of Muslim Spain, rife with references such as "a garland of verses," influenced the lyric poetry of southern France, the troubadours, and the courtly love tradition.[31]

Gardens, of course, are seasonal. To remind themselves of "paradise" during the cold winter months, rulers, city people, and nomads ordered Persian carpets, which flower all year. Most Persian carpets of all periods use floral patterns and have a formal garden design. Because Islamic teaching holds that only God can create perfection, every carpet has some flaw or imperfection. Although Turkish, Caucasian, Indian, and other peoples produced carpets with their own local designs, motifs, patterns, and colors, so powerful was the Persian influence that Westerners came to label all carpets as "Persian." Carpets are always knotted; usually the smaller the knot, the more valuable the rug. Because the small hands of women and children can tie tinier knots than the large hands of men, women and children have often been used (and exploited) in the manufacture of expensive rugs. *Kilims,* floor or wall coverings or bags used on camels or horses, were woven.

Isfahan Tile   The embellishment of Isfahan under Shah Abbas I created unprecedented need for tiles—as had the rebuilding of imperial Istanbul after 1453, the vast building program of Suleiman the Magnificent, and a huge European demand. Persian potters learned their skills from the Chinese. By the late sixteenth century, Italian and Austrian potters had imitated the Persian and Ottoman tile makers. *(Courtesy of the Trustees of the Victoria & Albert Museum)*

The fifteenth century witnessed the acceleration of Eastern, especially Chinese, influences on West Asian art and culture. The naturalistic reproduction of lotus blossoms, peonies, chrysanthemums, birds, and even dragons, as well as tulips and carnations, appear in many carpets. The role of flowers and gardens in literature and life took on central significance. The Persian culture of flowers spread from the Islamic world to early modern Europe.[32]

Shah Abbas was succeeded by inept rulers whose heavy indulgence in wine and the pleasures of the harem weakened the monarchy and fed the slow disintegration of the state. Internal weakness encouraged increased foreign aggression. In the eighteenth century, the Turks, Afghans, and Russians invaded and divided Persia among themselves, and political anarchy and social chaos characterized Persian life.

INDIA, FROM MUGHAL DOMINATION TO BRITISH DOMINION (CA 1498–1805)

Of the three great Islamic empires of the early modern world, the Mughal Empire of India was the largest, wealthiest, and most populous. Extending over 1.2 million square miles at the end of the seventeenth century,

Tamerlane Contemplating an Ant A brilliant military tactician who used terror to frighten his enemies, Tamerlane (1336–1405), though permanently injured in an arm and a leg in an early battle, acquired a vast empire. He needed a steady flow of war booty to hold the loyalty of his armies. Resting in a garden, he watches an ant doggedly trying to climb a wall, despite falling again and again. The ant's persistence convinced Tamerlane to continue his campaign. The story has both humorous and moral aspects. *(Baron Maurice de Rothschild Collection)*

with a population between 100 million and 150 million, and with fabulous wealth and resources, the Mughal Empire surpassed Safavid Persia and Ottoman Turkey. Among the Mughal ruler's world contemporaries, only the Ming emperor of China could compare with him.[33]

In 1504 Babur (r. 1483–1530), the Turkish ruler of a small territory in Central Asia, captured Kabul and established the kingdom of Afghanistan. From Kabul he moved southward into India. In 1526, with a force of only twelve thousand men, Babur defeated the decrepit sultan of Delhi at Panipat. Babur's capture of the cities

of Agra and Delhi, key fortresses of the north, paved the way for further conquests in northern India. Babur and his son and successor, Humayun, after a bitter struggle with the Afghans, laid the foundations of the Mughal Empire. The center of their power rested in the Ganges plain of north India. Mughal rule lasted until the eighteenth century, when domestic disorder and incompetent government opened the door to European intervention on the subcontinent. The term *Mughal,* a variant of *Mogul,* is often used to refer to the Muslim empire of India, but the founders of Mughal India were primarily Turks, Afghans, and Persians, though Babur claimed remote descent from the Mongol conquerors Tamerlane and Chinggis Khan.

The Rule of the Mughals

Muslims first invaded India in the eighth century. The Turkish general Mahmud raided the Punjab (see Map 21.3) in the early eleventh century, and in the late twelfth century Turkish Muslim cavalry under Muhammad Bakhtiyar gained entrance to the royal city of Nudiya and overthrew the Hindu ruler of Bengal. In 1398 Central Asian forces under Tamerlane (Timur the Lame) swept down from the northwest, looted Delhi, and took thousands of slaves as booty. A contemporary wrote that he left Delhi completely destroyed, with "not a bird moving," and all India politically fragmented.

Babur's son Humayun reigned from 1530 to 1540 and from 1555 to 1556. When the Afghans of northern India rebelled, he lost most of the territories that his father had acquired. Humayun went into temporary exile in Persia, where he developed a deep appreciation for Persian art and literature. This interest led to a remarkable flowering of Mughal art under his son Akbar.

The reign of Akbar (r. 1556–1605) may well have been the greatest in the history of India. Under his dynamic leadership, the Mughal state took definite form. A boy of thirteen when he became *badshah,* or imperial ruler, Akbar was ably assisted during his early years by his father's friend Bairam Khan, a superb military leader. In 1555 Bairam Khan defeated Hindu forces at Panipat and shortly afterward recaptured Delhi and Agra. Before falling from power in 1560, Bairam Khan took the great fortress of Gwalior, annexed the rich city of Jaunpur, and prepared for war against Malwa. Akbar continued this expansionist policy throughout this time, gradually adding the territories of Malwa, Gondwana, and Gujarat. Because the Afghan tribesmen put up tremendous resistance, it took Akbar several years to acquire Bengal. The Mughal Empire under Akbar eventually included most of the subcontinent north of the Godavari River (see Map 21.3). No kingdom, or coalition of kingdoms, could long resist Akbar's armies. The once independent states of northern India were forced into a centralized political system under the sole authority of the Mughal emperor.

To govern this vast region, Akbar developed an administrative bureaucracy centered on four co-equal ministers: for finance and revenue; the army and intelligence; the judiciary and religious patronage; and the imperial household, which included roads, bridges, and infrastructure throughout the empire. Under Akbar's finance minister, Raja Todar Mal (a Hindu), a *diwan* (bureau of finance) and royal mint came into existence. Raja Todar Mal devised methods for the assessment and collection of taxes that were applied everywhere. In the provinces, imperial governors, appointed by and responsible solely to the emperor, presided over administrative branches modeled on those of the central government. The government, however, rarely interfered in the life of village communities. Whereas the Ottoman sultans recruited and utilized Balkan slaves (converted from Orthodox Christianity to Islam) for military and administrative positions, Akbar used the services of royal princes, *amirs* (nobles), and *mansabdars* (warrior-aristocrats). Initially these men were Muslims from Central Asia, but to reduce their influence, Akbar vigorously recruited Persians and Hindus. The Mughal nobility and the administration of the empire rested on a heterogeneous body of freemen, not slaves "who rose as their talents and the emperor's favor permitted."[34] Most were Sunni Muslims, but many also were Hindu. No single ethnic or religious faction could challenge the emperor.

Did the emperor have an official religious policy? How could a Muslim ruler win the active support of millions of Hindu subjects, representing the vast majority of the population? Conversion to any religion is usually a gradual and complex process, and recent scholars agree that the possibility of mass conversion, or forced Islamization, in India in the sixteenth century did not exist.[35] Moreover, the Ganges plain, the geographical area of the subcontinent most intensely exposed to Mughal rule and for the longest span of time, had, when the first reliable census was taken in 1901, a Muslim population of only 10 to 15 percent. In fact, "in the subcontinent as a whole there is an inverse relationship between the degree of Muslim political penetration and the degree of Islamization."[36]

Recent scholars disagree about Mughal religious policy. One scholar writes that it was one "of not interfer-ing with Hindu society," of maintaining a "hands-off policy towards non-Muslim religions."[37] Another holds that "the cultural and religious climate of [late] sixteenth-century India was more open and tolerant of change"; that Akbar took a personal interest in religious questions and theological speculation; and that the emperor's greatest difficulties came not from Hindus but from Muslim ulema, the scholars learned in Islamic law. The ulema argued that the emperor should lead a pious and devout life and ensure that all Muslims could live according to the Shari'a, or Islamic law.[38]

Akbar acted according to the principle of *sulahkul*, universal tolerance: the emperor was responsible for all his people, regardless of their religion. He celebrated important Hindu festivals, such as Diwali, the festival of lights. He wore his uncut hair in an Indian turban "as a concession to Indian usage and to please his Indian subjects."[39] Twice Akbar married Hindu princesses, one of whom became the mother of his heir, Jahangir. He appointed the Spanish Jesuit Antonio Monserrate (1536–1600) as tutor to his second son, Prince Murad. Hindus eventually totaled 30 percent of the imperial bureaucracy. In 1579 Akbar abolished the *jitza*, the property tax on non-Muslims. These actions, especially the abolition of the jitza, infuriated the ulema, and serious conflict erupted between them and the emperor. Ultimately, Akbar issued an imperial decree declaring that the Mughal emperor had supreme authority, even above the ulema, in all religious matters. This statement, resting on a policy of benign toleration, represented a severe defeat for the Muslim religious establishment. Although Muslim-Hindu tensions were by no means resolved, Akbar's policies served as the basis for Mughal administration for the next century.

Akbar often sought the spiritual advice of the Sufi mystic Shaykh Salim Chishti. The birth of a long-awaited son, Jahangir, which Akbar interpreted as fulfillment of the shaykh's prophecy, inspired Akbar to build a new city, Fatehpur-Sikri, to symbolize the regime's Islamic foundations. He personally supervised the construction of the new city. It combined the Muslim tradition of domes, arches, and spacious courts with the Hindu tradition of flat stone beams, ornate decoration, and solidity. According to Abu-l-Fazl, the historian of Akbar's reign, "His majesty plans splendid edifices, and dresses the work of his mind and heart in the garment of stone and clay."[40] Completed in 1578, the city included an imperial palace, a mosque, lavish gardens, and a hall of worship, as well as thousands of houses for ordinary people. Akbar placed Shaykh Salim Chishti's tomb inside the great mosque to draw on its presumed sanctity. Just as medieval European rulers

City of Fatehpur-Sikri   In 1569 Akbar founded the city of Fatehpur-Sikri to honor the Muslim holy man Shaikh Salim Chishti, who had foretold the birth of Akbar's son and heir, Jahangir. The red sandstone city, probably the finest example of Mughal architecture still intact, was Akbar's capital for fifteen years. *(Nrupen Madhvani/Dinodia Picture Agency, Bombay)*

such as Charlemagne and Philip the Fair sought to strengthen their political power through association with Christian saints, so Akbar tried to identify Mughal authority with a Muslim saint. Along with the ancient cities of Delhi and Agra, Fatehpur-Sikri served as an imperial capital and the center of Akbar's lavish court.

Akbar was gifted with a creative intellect and imagination. He replaced Barlas Turkish with Persian as the official language of the Mughal Empire. Persian remained the official language until the British replaced it with English in 1835. He enthusiastically supported artists who produced magnificent paintings and books in the Indo-Persian style. In Mughal India, as throughout the Muslim world, books were regarded as precious objects. Time, talent, and expensive materials went into their production, and they were highly coveted because

they reflected wealth, learning, and power. Akbar reportedly possessed twenty-four thousand books when he died. Abu-l-Fazl describes the library and Akbar's love of books:

His Majesty's library is divided into several parts. . . . Prose works, poetical works, Hindi, Persian, Greek, Kashmirian, Arabic, are all separately placed. In this order they are also inspected. Experienced people bring them daily and read them before His Majesty, who hears every book from beginning to end . . . and rewards the readers with presents of cash either in gold or silver, according to the number of leaves read out by them. Among books of renown there are few that are not read in His Majesty's assembly hall; and there are no historical facts of past ages, or curiosities of science, or interesting points of philoso-

phy, with which His Majesty, a leader of impartial sages, is unacquainted.[41]

Akbar's son Jahangir (r. 1605–1628) lacked his father's military abilities and administrative genius, but he did succeed in consolidating Mughal rule in Bengal. His patronage of the arts and lavish court have led scholars to characterize his reign as an "age of splendor."

Jahangir's son Shah Jahan (r. 1628–1658) launched fresh territorial expansion. Faced with dangerous revolts by the Muslims in Ahmadnagar and the resistance of the newly arrived Portuguese in Bengal, Shah Jahan not only crushed them but also strengthened his northwestern frontier. He reasserted Mughal authority in the Deccan and Golkunda.

All the Mughal emperors did some building, but Shah Jahan had the most sophisticated interest in architecture. The buildings in his capital at Agra suffered erosion, and its streets were too narrow for the large crowds that flocked there for festivals. In 1639 Shah Jahan, to distinguish himself from his predecessors and to leave a permanent mark on his era, decided to found a new capital city in the region of Delhi. Hindus considered the area especially sacred, and the site reflects their influence. In the design and layout of the buildings, however, Persian ideas predominated, an indication of the numbers of Persian architects and engineers who had flocked to the subcontinent. The walled palace-fortress alone extended over 125 acres. Built partly of red sandstone, partly of marble, it included private chambers for the emperor; mansions for the wives, widows, and concubines of the imperial household; huge audience rooms for the conduct of public business (treasury, arsenal, and military); baths; and vast gardens filled with flowers, trees, and thirty silver fountains spraying water. In 1650, with living quarters for guards, military officials, merchants, dancing girls, scholars, and hordes of cooks and servants, the palace-fortress housed 57,000 people. It also boasted a covered public bazaar (comparable to a modern mall), 270 feet long and 27 feet wide, with arcaded shops. It was probably the first roofed shopping center in India, although such centers were common in western Asia. The sight of the magnificent palace left contemporaries speechless, and the words of an earlier poet were inscribed on the walls:

If there is a paradise on the face of the earth,
It is this, it is this.

Beyond the walls, princes and aristocrats built mansions and mosques on a smaller scale. Muslim visitors called the Juma Masjid mosque one of the finest in Islam. They marveled at the broad thoroughfares. With a population between 375,000 and 400,000, Delhi gained the reputation of being one of the great cities of the Muslim world.[42]

But Delhi (also called Shahjahanabad) and cities in general were not typical of Indian society. As everywhere in the premodern world, most people lived in rural villages and engaged in some form of agriculture, especially rice and cotton production. Based on the evidence of one typical late-seventeenth-century tax roll from northern India, scholars believe that rural populations were divided roughly into three groups: perhaps 7 percent were wealthy grain or cotton merchants who controlled village society; about 19 percent were peasants tilling large amounts of land; and the largest group, roughly 74 percent, farmed small plots. Artisans, weavers, water carriers, and landless rustics worked on a seasonal or piecemeal basis and served the others.

Shah Jahan ordered the construction of the Peacock Throne. (See the feature "Listening to the Past: The Weighing of Shah Jahan on His Forty-Second Lunar Birthday" on pages 676–677.) This famous piece, actually a cot resting on golden legs, was encrusted with emeralds, diamonds, pearls, and rubies. It took seven years to fashion and cost the equivalent of $5 million. It served as the imperial throne of India until 1739, when the Persian warrior Nadir Shah seized it as plunder and carried it to Persia.

Shah Jahan's most enduring monument is the Taj Mahal, the supreme example of a garden tomb. The Mughals sought to bring their vision of paradise alive in the walled garden tombs in which they buried their dead. Twenty thousand workers toiled eighteen years to build this memorial in Agra to Shah Jahan's favorite wife, Mumtaz Mahal, who died giving birth to their fifteenth child. One of the most beautiful structures in the world, the Taj Mahal is both an expression of love and a superb architectural blending of Islamic and Indian culture. It also asserted the power of the Mughal Dynasty.

The Mughal state never developed a formal procedure for the imperial succession, and a crisis occurred toward the end of Shah Jahan's reign. Competition among his sons ended with the victory of Aurangzeb, who executed his elder brother and locked his father away until his death in 1666. A puritanically devout and strictly orthodox Muslim, a skillful general and a clever diplomat, Aurangzeb (r. 1658–1707) ruled more of India than did any previous badshah. His reign witnessed the culmination of Mughal power and the beginning of its decline (Map 21.3).

Taj Mahal at Agra This tomb is the finest example of Muslim architecture in India. Its white marble exterior is inlaid with semiprecious stones in Arabic inscriptions and floral designs. The oblong pool reflects the building, which asserts the power of the Mughal Dynasty. (*Ira Kirschenbaum/Stock, Boston*)

A combination of religious zeal and financial necessity seems to have prompted Aurangzeb to introduce a number of reforms. He appointed censors of public morals in important cities to enforce Islamic laws against gambling, prostitution, drinking, and the use of narcotics. He forbade *suttee*—the self-immolation of widows on their husbands' funeral pyres—and the castration of boys to be sold as eunuchs. He also abolished all taxes not authorized by Islamic law. This measure led to a serious loss of state revenues. To replace them, Aurangzeb in 1679 reimposed the jitza, the tax on non-Muslims. It fell mostly on the Hindu majority.

Regulating Indian society according to Islamic law meant modifying the religious toleration and cultural cosmopolitanism instituted by Akbar. Aurangzeb ordered the destruction of some Hindu temples. He required Hindus to pay higher customs duties than Muslims. Out of fidelity to Islamic law, he even criticized his mother's tomb, the Taj Mahal: "The lawfulness of a solid construction over a grave is doubtful, and there can be no doubt about the extravagance involved."[43] Aurangzeb employed more Hindus in the im-

perial administration than any previous Mughal ruler, but his religious policy proved highly unpopular with the majority of his subjects and created problems that weaker successors could not handle.

Aurangzeb's military ventures also had mixed results. A tireless general, he pushed the conquest of the south and annexed the Golkunda and Bijapur sultanates. The stiffest opposition came from the Marathas, a militant Hindu group centered in the western Deccan. From 1681 until his death in 1707 at the age of ninety, Aurangzeb led repeated sorties through the Deccan. He took many forts and won several battles, but total destruction of the Maratha guerrilla bands eluded him. After his death, they played an important role in the collapse of the Mughal Empire.

Aurangzeb's eighteenth-century successors faced formidable problems. They were less successful than the Ottomans at making the dynasty the focus of loyalty. Repeated disputes over the succession undermined the stability of the monarchy. Court intrigues replaced the battlefield as the testing ground for the nobility. Mughal provincial governors began to rule in-

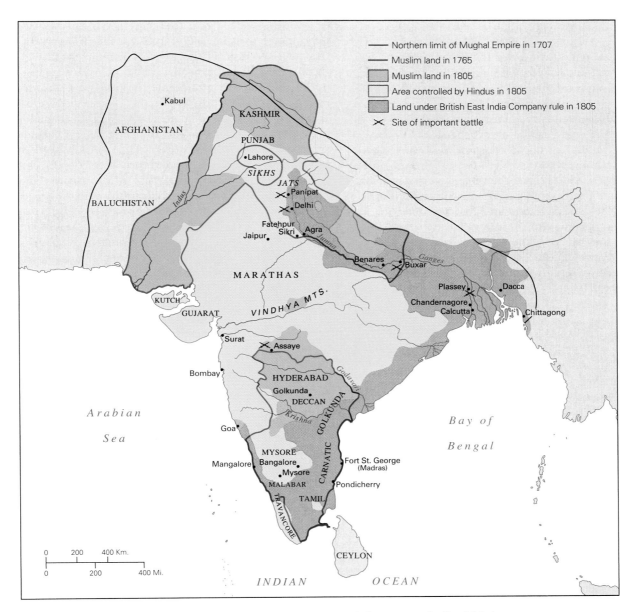

MAP 21.3 India, 1707–1805   In the eighteenth century, Mughal power gradually yielded to the Hindu Marathas and to the British East India Company.

dependently, giving only minimal allegiance to the bad-shah at Delhi. The Marathas, who revolted and pressed steadily northward, constituted the gravest threat to Mughal authority. No ruler could defeat them.

In 1739 the Persian adventurer Nadir Shah invaded India, defeated the Mughal army, looted Delhi, and af-ter a savage massacre carried off a huge amount of trea-sure, including the Peacock Throne. When Nadir Shah

withdrew to Afghanistan, he took with him the Mughal government's prestige. Constant skirmishes between the Afghans and the Marathas for control of the Punjab and northern India ended in 1761 at Panipat, where the Marathas were crushed by the Afghans. At that point, India no longer had any power capable of impos-ing order on the subcontinent or checking the penetra-tion of the rapacious Europeans.

Trade and Commerce

The Mughal period witnessed the growth of a thriving capitalist commercial economy on the Indian subcontinent. Although most people were involved in agriculture, from which most imperial revenue was derived, a manufacturing industry supported by a money economy and mercantile capitalism expanded.

Block-printed cotton cloth, produced by artisans working at home, was the chief export. Through an Islamic business device called the *sillim*, "contracts invoking prompt payment in return for a distant (future) delivery,"[44] banker-brokers supplied the material for production and the money that the artisans could live on while they worked; the cloth brokers specified the quality, quantity, and design of the finished product. This procedure resembles the later English "domestic"

or "putting-out" system (see page 595), for the very good reason that the English took the idea from the Indians. In and around the cities of Surat, Ahmedabad, Pattan, Baroda, and Broach, varieties of cloth were produced and shipped to Gujarat. Within India, the demand for cotton cloth, as well as food crops, was so great that Akbar had to launch a wide-scale road-building campaign. From Gujarat, Indian merchant bankers shipped their cloth worldwide: across the Indian Ocean to Aden and the Muslim-controlled cities on the east coast of Africa; across the Arabian Sea to Muscat and Hormuz and up the Persian Gulf to the cities of Persia; up the Red Sea to the Mediterranean; by sea also to Malacca, Indonesia, China, and Japan; by land across Africa to Ghana on the west coast; and to Astrakhan, Poland, Moscow, and even the Russian cities on the distant Volga River. In many of these places, Indian business-

Textile from Kalamkari Containing a rich variety of Persian, Hindu, Muslim, and Christian motifs, this superb example of seventeenth-century painted cotton suggests the beauty and complexity of Indian textile manufacture, as well as the diversity of influences in Indian culture itself. *(The Metropolitan Museum of Art)*

men had branch offices. All this activity represented enormous trade, which produced fabulous wealth for some Indian merchants. Some scholars have contrasted India's "international" trade in the sixteenth century with that of Italian firms, such as the Medici. The Indian trade actually extended over a far wider area. Since Indian merchants were often devout Hindus, Muslims, Buddhists, or Jains, the argument of some Western writers, notably Karl Marx (see page 785), that religion "retarded" Asia's economic development is patently false.[45]

European Rivalry for the Indian Trade

Shortly before Babur's invasion of India, the Portuguese under the navigator Pedro Alvares Cabral had opened the subcontinent to Portuguese trade. In 1510 they established the port of Goa on the Arabian Sea as their headquarters and through a policy of piracy and terrorism took control of Muslim shipping in the Indian and Arabian Oceans (see Map 21.3), charging high fees for passage. The Portuguese historian Barrões attempted to justify Portugal's seizure of commercial traffic that the Muslims had long dominated:

It is true that there does exist a common right to all to navigate the seas and in Europe we recognize the rights which others hold against us; but the right does not extend beyond Europe and therefore the Portuguese as Lords of the Sea are justified in confiscating the goods of all those who navigate the seas without their permission.[46]

In short, Western principles of international law did not apply in Asia. For almost a century, the Portuguese controlled the spice trade over the Indian Ocean.

In 1602 the Dutch formed the Dutch East India Company with the stated goal of wresting the enormously lucrative spice trade from the Portuguese. The scent of fabulous profits also attracted the English. With a charter signed by Queen Elizabeth, eighty London merchants organized the British East India Company. In 1619 Emperor Jahangir granted a British mission important commercial concessions at Surat on the west coast of India. Gifts, medical services, and bribes to Indian rulers enabled the British to set up twenty-seven other coastal forts. Fort St. George on the east coast became the modern city of Madras. In 1668 the city of Bombay—given to England when the Portuguese princess Catherine of Braganza married King Charles II—was leased to the company, marking the virtually total British absorption of Portuguese power in India. In 1690 the company founded a fort that became the city of Calcutta. Thus the three places that later became centers of British economic and political imperialism—Madras, Bombay, and Calcutta—existed before 1700. The Dutch concentrated their efforts in Indonesia.

Factory-Fort Societies

The British called their trading post at Surat a "factory," and the word was later used for all European settlements in India. The term did not signify manufacturing; it designated the walled compound containing the residences, gardens, and offices of British East India Company officials and the warehouses where goods were stored before being shipped to Europe. The company president exercised political authority over all residents.

Factory-forts existed to make profits from the Asian-European trade, and they evolved into flourishing centers of economic profit. The British East India Company sold silver, copper, zinc, lead, and fabrics to the Indians and bought cotton goods, silks, pepper and other spices, sugar, and opium from them. By the late seventeenth century, the company was earning substantial profits. Profitability increased after 1700, when the company began to trade with China. Some Indian merchants in Calcutta and Bombay made gigantic fortunes from trade within Asia.

Because the directors of the British East India Company in London discouraged all unnecessary expenses and financial risks, they opposed any interference in local Indian politics and even missionary activities. Conditions in India, however, brought about a fundamental change in the nature of the company's factories. The violent disorders and political instability that wracked India during Aurangzeb's reign and in the early eighteenth century caused the factories to evolve into defensive installations manned by small garrisons of native troops. When warlords appeared or an uprising occurred, people from the surrounding countryside flocked into the fort, and the company factory-forts gradually came to exercise political authority over the territories around them.

Indian and Chinese wares enjoyed great popularity in England and on the European continent in the late seventeenth and early eighteenth centuries. The middle classes wanted Indian textiles, which were colorful, durable, cheap, and washable. The upper classes desired Chinese wallpaper and porcelains and Indian silks and brocades. In the European economies, however, Asian goods created serious problems. As early as 1695, English manufacturers called for an embargo on Indian cloth, and silk weavers picketed the House of Commons.

English Factory at Surat   The factory began as a storage place for goods before they were bought and transported abroad; it gradually expanded to include merchants' residences and some sort of fortification. By 1650 the English had twenty-three factories in India. Surat, in the Gujarat region on the Gulf of Cambay, was the busiest factory and port until it was sacked by the Marathas in 1664. *(The Mansell Collection)*

Trade with Asia was one-way: Asians had little interest in European manufactured articles. Finding the Siamese (Thai) completely uninterested in traditional Dutch goods, the Dutch East India Company tried to interest them in collections of pornography. Europeans had to pay for everything they bought from Asia with precious metals. Thus there was insistent pressure in England, France, and the Netherlands against the importation of Asian goods. As one authority explains: "The root of the argument from which grew a tree of many branches was the old fear of the drain of gold."[47]

The Rise of the British East India Company

The French were the last to arrive in India. Louis XIV's financial wizard Colbert (see page 531) planned the French East India Company for trade in the Eastern Hemisphere, and in the 1670s the company established factories at Chandernagore in Bengal, Pondicherry, and elsewhere. Joseph Dupleix (1697–1764), who was ap-

pointed governor general at Pondicherry in 1742, made allies of Indian princes and built an army of native troops, called *sepoys,* who were trained as infantrymen. The British likewise built an army with Indian surrogates trained in Western military drill and tactics. War broke out at midcentury.

From 1740 to 1763, Britain and France were almost continually engaged in a tremendous global struggle. India, like North America in the Seven Years' War, became a battlefield and a prize. The French won land battles, but English sea power decided the first phase of the war. Then a series of brilliant victories destroyed French power in southern India. By preventing French reinforcements from arriving, British sea power again proved to be the determining factor, and British jurisdiction soon extended over the important northern province of Bengal. The Treaty of Paris of 1763 recognized British control of much of India, and scholars acknowledge the treaty as the beginning of the British Empire in India.

How was the vast subcontinent to be governed? Parliament believed that the British East India Company had too much power and considered the company responsible for the political disorders in India, which were bad for business. Parliament attempted to solve Indian problems with special legislation. The Regulating Act of 1773 created the office of governor general, with an advisory council, to exercise political authority over the territory controlled by the company. The India Act of 1784 required that the governor general be chosen from outside the company, and it made company directors subject to parliamentary supervision.

Implementation of these reforms fell to Warren Hastings, the governor of Bengal and first governor general (r. 1774–1785), with jurisdiction over Bombay and Madras. Hastings tried to build an effective administrative system and to turn the British East India Company into a government. He laid the foundations for the first Indian civil service, abolished tolls to facilitate internal trade, placed the salt and opium trades under government control, and planned a codification of Muslim and Hindu laws. He sought allies among Indian princes. The biggest problem facing Hastings's administration was a coalition of the rulers of Mysore and the Marathas aimed at the expulsion of the British. Hastings's skillful diplomacy offset this alliance temporarily.

Hastings's successor, Lord Charles Cornwallis, served as governor general of India from 1786 to 1794. Cornwallis continued the work of building a civil service and the war against Mysore. His introduction of the British style of property relations in effect converted a motley collection of former Mughal officers, tax collectors, and others into English-style landlords. The result was a new system of landholding, in which the rents of tenant farmers supported the landlords.

The third governor general, the marquess Richard Wellesley (r. 1797–1805), defeated Mysore in 1799 and four years later crushed the Marathas at the Battle of Assaye (see Map 21.3). Building on the work of his predecessors, he vastly extended British influence in India. Like most nineteenth-century British governors of India, Wellesley believed that British rule strongly benefited the Indians. With supreme condescension, he wrote that British power should be established over the Indian princes in order

to deprive them of the means of prosecuting any measure or of forming any confederacy hazardous to the security of the British empire, and to enable us to preserve the tranquility of India by exercising a general control over the restless spirit of ambition and violence which is characteristic of every Asiatic government.[48]

By the beginning of the nineteenth century, the authority and power of the British East India Company had yielded to the government in London. Subsequent British rule of India rested on three foundations: the support of puppet Indian princes who exercised the trappings but not the reality of power; a large army of sepoys of dubious loyalty; and an increasingly effective civil service, staffed largely by Englishmen, with Hindus and Muslims in minor positions.

SUMMARY

Pursuing a policy of territorial expansion, the Muslim Ottoman Turks captured the ancient Byzantine capital of Constantinople in May 1453. Renamed Istanbul, the city under Suleiman the Magnificent served as the administrative center of a vast multiethnic empire extending from the Atlantic to the Indian Ocean. Strong military organization and their enemies' disunity gave the Ottomans superiority. The wealth of the empire, based largely on commerce, provided the material basis for a great cultural efflorescence. In architecture, as shown in the many mosques, markets, schools, hospitals, and public baths; in poetry, folk literature, and historical writing; in ceramics, textiles, and carpet weaving; and in medical pharmacology, the splendid creativity of the early Ottomans is revealed. In the seventeenth century, economic, demographic, and political issues connected with the imperial succession all contributed to the weakening of Ottoman power.

Meanwhile, Shi'ite Persia under Safavid rule recovered from Mongol devastation. Under Shah Abbas, military success, strong domestic industry based on carpet weaving, and the talents of hundreds of Chinese immigrants from Central Asia led to a brilliant period of prosperity and artistic creativity.

For size of population, fabulous wealth, and sheer geographical extent, the Mughal Empire on the Indian subcontinent was the grandest of the three Muslim polities. The Turkish leader Babur's conquest of Delhi in the early sixteenth century laid the foundation for an enduring Muslim presence. Babur's grandson Akbar continued the policy of expansion, built a sound administrative bureaucracy, and conciliated his millions of Hindu subjects through a policy of universal religious toleration. Akbar's grandson left two powerful and enduring monuments—a new capital city in the region of Delhi and the Taj Mahal, a garden tomb in Agra in honor of his favorite wife. Indian textiles, much desired in Southeast Asia, China, and Europe, developed into a large industry. Manufacturing, in turn, attracted European businessmen. The inability of Indian leaders in the eighteenth century to resolve their domestic differences led first to British intervention and then to full British rule. Bitter hostility between Hindus and Muslims persisted as a dominant theme of Indian life and culture.

NOTES

1. Quoted in B. Lewis, *The Muslim Discovery of Europe* (New York: W. W. Norton, 1982), p. 29.
2. H. Inalcik, *The Ottoman Empire: The Classical Age, 1300–1600,* trans. N. Itzkowitz and C. Imber (London: Weidenfeld and Nicolson, 1975), pp. 6–7.
3. W. H. McNeill, *The Pursuit of Power: Technology, Armed Force, and Society Since A.D. 1000* (Chicago: University of Chicago Press, 1982), p. 87.
4. Quoted in P. Mansel, *Constantinople: City of the World's Desire, 1453–1924* (New York: St. Martin's Griffin, 1996), p. 4.
5. Quoted in Lewis, *The Muslim Discovery of Europe,* p. 30.
6. F. Babinger, *Mehmed the Conqueror and His Times,* trans. R. Manheim (Princeton, N.J.: Princeton University Press, 1978), p. 107.
7. Inalcik, *The Ottoman Empire,* Chap. 5.
8. F. Robinson, *Atlas of the Islamic World Since 1500* (New York: Facts on File, 1982), p. 72.
9. S. J. Shaw, *History of the Ottoman Empire and Modern Turkey.* Vol. 1: *Empire of the Gazis: The Rise and Decline of the Ottoman Empire, 1208–1808* (Cambridge: Cambridge University Press, 1988), pp. 139–151.
10. L. Pierce, *The Imperial Harem: Women and Sovereignty in the Ottoman Empire* (New York: Oxford University Press, 1993), p. 3.
11. Ibid., p. 31.
12. Ibid., pp. 32–47.
13. Ibid., pp. 47–72.
14. E. R. Tolendano, *The Ottoman Slave Trade and Its Suppression* (Princeton, N.J.: Princeton University Press, 1982), pp. 59–61.
15. S. O. Murray and W. Roscoe, *Islamic Homosexualities: Culture, History, and Literature* (New York: New York University Press, 1997), pp. 174–186; the quotation is on p. 175.
16. Ibid., footnote 10, p. 183.
17. See M. Rocke, *Forbidden Friendships: Homosexuality and Male Culture in Renaissance Florence* (New York: Oxford University Press, 1996), Chap. 1.
18. On the Ottoman Turkish population, see H. Inalcik and D. Quataert, *An Economic and Social History of the Ottoman Empire.* Vol. 1: *1300–1600* (Cambridge: Cambridge University Press, 1994), pp. 25–43. Although we lack data for the Muslim population of Andalusian Spain before 1520, between 1520 and 1580 the Muslim and non-Muslim population of western Asia Minor grew by 41.7 percent.

19. Quoted in P. K. Hitti, *The Near East in History* (Princeton, N.J.: Van Nostrand, 1961), p. 336.
20. Shaw, *History of the Ottoman Empire,* p. 148.
21. *The Selected Letters of Lady Mary Wortley Montagu,* ed. R. Halsband (London: Longman Group, 1970), pp. 98–99.
22. Ibid., p. 106.
23. Ibid., p. 105.
24. Ibid., pp. 96–97.
25. N. Itzkowitz, *Ottoman Empire and Islamic Tradition* (Chicago: University of Chicago Press, 1980), p. 95.
26. Shaw, *History of the Ottoman Empire,* pp. 171–175, 225, 246–247; V. H. Parry, H. Inalcik, A. N. Kurat, and J. S. Bromley, *A History of the Ottoman Empire to 1715* (New York: Cambridge University Press, 1976), pp. 126, 139–140.
27. Quoted in R. E. Dunn, *The Adventures of Ibn Battuta: A Muslim Traveler of the 14th Century* (Berkeley: University of California Press, 1986), p. 81.
28. Ibid., pp. 83–87. On population losses in Persia, see D. Morgan, *The Mongols* (Oxford: Basil Blackwell, 1987), pp. 149–151.
29. D. Morgan, *Medieval Persia, 1040–1797* (New York: Longman, 1988), pp. 112–113.
30. J. Goody, *The Culture of Flowers* (Cambridge: Cambridge University Press, 1993), p. 103.
31. Ibid., pp. 106–110.
32. Ibid., pp. 111–115.
33. J. F. Richards, *The New Cambridge History of India: The Mughal Empire* (Cambridge: Cambridge University Press, 1995), pp. 19–30.
34. Ibid., pp. 19–30, 59–60.
35. R. M. Eaton, *The Rise of Islam and the Bengal Frontier, 1204–1760* (Berkeley: University of California Press, 1993), Chap. 5; Richards, *The New Cambridge History of India,* p. 36.
36. Eaton, *The Rise of Islam,* p. 115.
37. Ibid., pp. 177–179.
38. Richards, *The New Cambridge History of India,* pp. 34–36; the quotation is on p. 34.
39. Quoted ibid., p. 45.
40. Quoted in V. A. Smith, *The Oxford History of India* (Oxford: Oxford University Press, 1967), p. 398.
41. Quoted in M. C. Beach, *The Imperial Image: Paintings for the Mughal Court* (Washington, D.C.: Freer Gallery of Art, Smithsonian Institution, 1981), pp. 9–10.
42. S. P. Blake, *Shahjahanabad: The Sovereign City in Mughal India, 1639–1739* (Cambridge: Cambridge University Press, 1991), Chaps. 1 and 2, pp. 1–82; the quotation is on p. 44.
43. Quoted in S. K. Ikram, *Muslim Civilization in India* (New York: Columbia University Press, 1964), p. 202.
44. J. Goody, *The East in the West* (Cambridge: Cambridge University Press, 1996), p. 93.
45. Ibid., pp. 91–96, 104 et seq.
46. Quoted in K. M. Panikkar, *Asia and Western Domination* (London: George Allen & Unwin, 1965), p. 35.

47. Quoted *ibid.,* p. 53.
48. Quoted in W. Bingham, H. Conroy, and F. W. Iklé, *A History of Asia,* vol. 2 (Boston: Allyn and Bacon, 1967), p. 74.

SUGGESTED READING

The curious student interested in the Ottoman world might begin with A. Wheatcroft, *The Ottomans* (1993), an excitingly written and beautifully illustrated popular account of many facets of Ottoman culture that separates Western myths from Turkish reality. P. Mansel, *Constantinople: City of the World's Desire, 1453–1924* (1995), is another broad popular survey, but better informed. In addition to the titles by Babinger, Inalcik, Itzkowitz, Pierce, and Shaw cited in the Notes, Chapters 13, 14, and 15 of A. Hourani, *A History of the Arab Peoples* (1991), should also prove helpful. Perhaps the best broad general studies of the material in this chapter are M. G. S. Hodgson, *The Venture of Islam.* Vol. 3: *The Gunpowder Empires and Modern Times* (1974), and Part 2 of I. M. Lapidus, *A History of Islamic Societies* (1989). For Suleiman the Magnificent, E. Atil, *The Age of Sultan Suleiman the Magnificent* (1987), is a splendidly illustrated celebration of the man and his times, while G. Necipoglu, *Architecture, Ceremonial and Power: The Topkapi Palace in the Fifteenth and Sixteenth Centuries* (1991), is broader than the title might imply and is valuable for many aspects of Ottoman culture. A. Bridge, *Suleiman the Magnificent, Scourge of Heaven* (1972), is a highly readable, if romantic, view with hoary myths. A. Stratton, *Sinan* (1972), is a well-written and highly informative biography of the great Ottoman architect. J. A. Levenson, ed., *Circa 1492: Art in the Age of Exploration* (1991), has several stimulating and nicely illustrated chapters on the Ottomans and Constantinople. For the later empire, see R. Dankoff, *The Intimate Life of an Ottoman Statesman* (1991), the memoirs of a seventeenth-century traveler; B. Masters, *The Origins of Western Economic Dominance in the Middle East* (1988); and S. J. Shaw, *Between Old and New: The Ottoman Empire Under Sultan Selim III, 1789–1807* (1971).

The literature on women is growing, though still largely restricted to the upper classes. In addition to the important work by Pierce cited in the Notes, see, for general background, L. Ahmed, ed., *Women and Gender in Islam* (1992), which is especially useful for Mamluk Egypt; F. Davis, *The Ottoman Lady: A Social History from 1718 to 1918* (1986); A. L. Croutier, *The World Behind the Veil* (1989); and *The Selected Letters of Lady Mary Wortley Montagu,* cited in the Notes.

For slavery and race, see B. Lewis, *Race and Slavery in the Middle East* (1990); E. R. Toledano, *The Ottoman Slave Trade and Its Suppression: 1840–1890* (1982), which, although dealing with a period later than this chapter, offers useful references to earlier centuries; and E. R. Toledano, ed., *Slavery and Abolition in the Ottoman Middle East* (1998), which has valuable source materials. The superb achievement of D. B. Davis, *Slavery and Human Progress* (1984), is the only work that explores slavery in a world context.

For Safavid Persia, see P. Jackson and L. Lockhart, eds., *The Cambridge History of Iran.* Vol. 6: *The Timurid and Safavid Periods* (1986), a standard reference work; C. Melville, ed., *Safavid Persia,* which contains useful source readings; and L. Lockhart, *Nadir Shah, a Critical Study* (1973), an interesting, if somewhat dated, political biography. Students interested in understanding Persian culture through its remarkable art should study A. Soudawar and M. C. Beach, *The Art of the Persian Courts* (1992), and Y. A. Petrosyan et al., *Pages of Perfection: Islamic Painting and Calligraphy from the Russian Academy of Sciences* (1995); these volumes are magnificently illustrated.

Perhaps the best general introduction to the history and civilization of India is S. Wolpert's elegant appreciation *India* (1990), but see also P. Spears, *A History of India,* vol. 2 (1986). The books by Blake, Eaton, and Richards cited in the Notes have up-to-date material and are highly recommended. The titles by Smith and Ikram cited in the Notes provide broad general treatments, as do P. M. Holt et al., eds., *The Cambridge History of India,* 2 vols. (1970); M. Mujeeb, *The Indian Muslims* (1967); and I. Habib, *The Agrarian System of Mughal India, 1556–1707* (1963), whose theme and scope are indicated by the title. Many of the essays in J. F. Richards, *Power, Administration and Finance in Mughal India* (1993), are useful and authoritative. For the decline of imperial authority in eighteenth-century India, see the important study of M. Alam, *The Crisis of Empire in Mughal North India: Awadh and the Punjab, 1707–48* (1986). Students wishing to study Indian culture through its architecture should consult two splendid and recent achievements: C. Tadgell, *The History of Architecture in India: From the Dawn of Civilization to the End of the Raj* (1995), and G. Mitchell, *The Royal Palaces of India* (1995). E. B. Findly, *Nur Jahan: Empress of Mughal India* (1993), provides a vivid picture of one powerful and influential woman. For Babur, see *The Baburnama: Memoirs of Babur, Prince and Emperor,* trans. and ed. by W. M. Thackston (1996), the well-annotated and beautifully illustrated diary of the founder of the Mughal Dynasty; and M. C. Beach and E. Koch, eds., *King of the World: The Padshahnama* (1997), a supremely elegant, learned, and splendidly illustrated study of the reign of Jahangir. E. Maclagan, *The Jesuits and the Great Mogul* (1932), discusses the Jesuits at the courts of Akbar, Jahangir, and Shah Jahan. B. Gascoigne, *The Great Moghuls* (1971), and G. Hambly, *The Cities of Mughal India: Delhi, Agra, and Fatehpur Sikri* (1968), are well illustrated and highly readable. For the impact of Portuguese, Dutch, and English mercantile activities in India, see M. N. Pearson, *Merchants and Rulers in Gujarat: The Response to the Portuguese in the Sixteenth Century* (1976). For Asian influences on European economic ideas and institutions, see J. Goody, *The East in the West* (1996).

The Weighing of Shah Jahan on His Forty-Second Lunar Birthday[1]

In 1799 the nawab (provincial governor) of Oudh in northern India sent to King George III of Great Britain the Padshahnama, *or official history of the reign of Shah Jahan. A volume composed of 239 folios on very high quality gold-flecked tan paper, with forty-four stunningly beautiful paintings illustrating the text, the* Padshahnama *represents both a major historical chronicle of a Mughal emperor's reign and an extraordinary artistic achievement. One of the great art treasures of the world, it now rests in the Royal Library at Windsor.*

All the Mughal emperors had a strong historical sense and the desire to preserve records of their reigns. They brought to India the traditional Muslim respect for books as sources of secular and religious knowledge and as images of their wealth and power. The Padshahnama, *in stressing Shah Jahan's descent from Tamerlane and his right to the throne, in celebrating his bravery and military prowess, and in magnifying his virtues, is one long glorification of Jahan's rule. The Persian scholar and calligrapher Abdul-Hamid Lahawri wrote the text. Many Persian artists painted the illustrations with detailed precision and an exactitude that art historians consider sensitive and faithful to the original.*

Since alms are beneficial for repelling bodily and psychic harm and for attracting spiritual and corporeal benefits, as all peoples, religions, and nations are agreed, His Majesty Arsh-Ashyani [Akbar] established the custom of weighing and had himself weighed twice [a year], once after the end of the solar year and the other after the end of the lunar year. In the solar weighing he was weighed twelve times, first against gold and then eleven other items, while in the lunar weighing he was weighed eight times, first against silver and then seven other items. . . . The amounts from the weighings were given away in alms.

. . . Inasmuch as it benefited the needy, His Majesty Jahanbani [Shah Jahan] has his perfect self weighed twice, and in his generosity he has ordered that gold and silver be used each time. . . .

. . . The lunar weighing ceremony for the end of the forty-third year of the Emperor's life was held. The Emperor, surrounded by a divine aura, was weighed against gold and the other usual things, and the skirt of the world was held out in expectation of gold and silver. On this auspicious day Muhammad-Ali Beg, the ambassador of Iran, was awarded a gold-embroidered robe of honor, a jeweled belt, an elephant, a female elephant, and four large ashrafis, one weighing 400 tolas [a measure of weight, slightly more than two mithcals], the second 300 tolas, the third 200 tolas, and the fourth 100 tolas, and four rupees also of the weights given above, and he was given leave to depart. From the time he paid homage until the time he set out to return he had been given 316,000 rupees in cash and nearly a lac of rupees in goods.

An earlier weighing ceremony of the Emperor Jahangir, on 1 September 1617, was described by the always observant, and usually skeptical, first English ambassador to the Mughal court, Sir Thomas Roe: "Was the Kings Birth-day, and the solemnitie of his weighing, to which I went, and was carryed into a very large and beautifull Garden; the square within all water; on the sides flowres and trees. . . . Here attended the Nobilitie, all sitting about it on Carpets, vntill the King came; who at last appeared clothed, or rather loden with Diamonds, Rubies, Pearles, and other precious vanities, so great, so glorious! . . . Suddenly hee entered into the scales, sate like a woman on his legges, and there was put against him many bagges to fit his weight, which were changed sixe times, and they say was siluer, and that I vnderstood his weight to be nine thousand *Rupias,* which are almost one thousand pound sterling."

Another official history of Shah Jahan's reign, the 'Amal-i-Salih, *describes the ceremonial weighing that took place another year.*

Since it is His Majesty's custom and habit to have beggars sought out, and his generous nature is always looking for a pretext to relieve those who are in need, therefore twice a year he sits, like the orient sun in majesty, in the pan of the scale of auspiciousness in the solar and lunar weighing ceremonies. Twice a year by solar and lunar calculation a magnificent celebration and a large-scale banquet is arranged by order of His Majesty. An amount equal to his weight in gold and silver is distributed among the destitute and the poor according to their deservedness and merits. Although this type of alms is not mentioned in the religious law, nonetheless since scholars of this country are all in agreement that such alms are the most perfect type of alms for repelling corporeal and spiritual catastrophes and calamities, therefore this pleasing method was chosen and established by His Majesty Arsh-Ashyani, whose personality was, like the world-illuminating sun, based upon pure effulgence. By this means the poor attained their wishes, and in truth the custom of *aqiqa*—which is an established custom in the law of the Prophet and his Companions, and in which on the seventh day after birth the equivalent weight of an infant's shaven hair in silver is given in alms, and a sacrificial animal is divided and distributed among the poor—has opened the way to making this custom permissible.

Questions for Analysis

1. Consider Shah Jahan's motives for the practice of ceremonial weighing. Does it have any theological basis?

2. Compare the Mughal practice to something similar in Ottoman, European, and South American societies.

1. A solar year is the time required for the earth to make one complete revolution around the sun (365 days). A lunar year equals 12 lunar months.

Source: King of the World. The Padshahnama. An Imperial Mughal Manuscript from the Royal Library, Windsor Castle, ed. Milo Cleveland Beach and Ebba Koch, trans. Wheeler Thackston (Washington, D.C.: Azimuth Editions—Sackler Gallery, 1997, pp. 39–43). Courtesy of the Arthur M. Sackler Gallery, Smithsonian Institution, Washington, D.C.

The "Weighing of Shah Jahan," who sits cross-legged on one plate of the scales, as bags of gold and silver wait to be placed on the other side. *(The Royal Collection © Her Majesty Queen Elizabeth II)*

22

Continuity and Change in East Asia, ca 1400–1800

Prosperous family, Ming Dynasty. *(Metropolitan Museum of Art, Anonymous Gift, 1942 [42.190.1]. Photograph © 1987 The Metropolitan Museum of Art)*

The period from about 1400 to 1800 witnessed growth and dynamic change in East Asia. In China, the native Ming Dynasty (1368–1644) replaced the Mongol Yuan Dynasty (1271–1368). Under the Ming, China saw agricultural reconstruction, commercial expansion, remarkable maritime expeditions abroad, and the production of magnificent porcelain, which was in high demand throughout Asia. By the later fifteenth century, however, incompetent emperors allowed corrupt and grasping eunuchs to gain control of commercial wealth and military power; friction between court factions paralyzed the state bureaucracy. The flood of Japanese and South American silver to China compounded a fiscal crisis. Meanwhile, the Manchus pressed along the northern frontier. In 1644, the Ming Dynasty collapsed and was replaced by the Qing.

The Manchus inaugurated a long period of peace, relative prosperity, and population expansion. In the Manchu, or Qing, period, the Chinese empire reached its greatest territorial extent, and literary and artistic creativity reached an apogee.

In the same centuries, the Korean peninsula saw the establishment of a new dynasty. Choson (Korea) achieved agricultural and commercial expansion that led to considerable social change. Korean culture was heavily influenced by the Chinese, and Korea several times felt the effects of Japanese aggression.

In the Japanese islands, united by Nobunaga and later the Tokugawa Shogunate (1600–1867), the feudal military aristocracy continued to evolve. Although Japan developed largely in isolation from outside influences, its sociopolitical system bore striking similarities to medieval European feudalism. The period of the Tokugawa Shogunate, like that of the Ming Dynasty in China, was marked by remarkable agricultural productivity and industrial growth.

- What features characterized the governments of the Ming and Qing Dynasties in China and the Tokugawa Shogunate?
- How did agricultural and commercial developments affect Chinese and Japanese societies?
- What significant political, economic, and cultural changes did Korea undergo?
- What developments occurred in literature, art, and drama in China and Japan under the Ming and Qing Dynasties and the Tokugawa Shogunate?

This chapter will explore these questions.

CHINA, FROM THE MING TO THE MID-QING (CA 1368–1795)

In the fourteenth century, a combination of military, natural, and epidemiological disasters dramatically weakened Yuan (Mongol) rule in China. Factions of local warlords fought among themselves; they, rather than the emperor, held real power. The flooding of the Yellow River did great damage and caused widespread famine. Beginning in 1353–1354, disease hit an already weak population. Modern scholars strongly suspect that this epidemic was the Black Death (bubonic plague), which spread to western Europe from Mongol territory. Revolts against Mongol rule in the southern provinces disrupted the transportation of rice on the Grand Canal from Beijing (Peking) to Nanjing (Nanking). Food shortages, which were aggravated by the issue of paper money, provoked terrible inflation. Still, the Mongols spent more time fighting each other for control of the central government than suppressing the large-scale revolts in the south. One rebel leader, Zhu Yuanzhang, leader of the Red Turbans, eventually emerged as master of all the others. His military skill and administrative ability won wide popular support. By 1359 he controlled the Nanjing region. In 1368 he proclaimed himself founder of the Ming Dynasty, taking the regnal name Hungwu (meaning "vast military power"). The Ming Dynasty (1368–1644) was the only dynasty that originated south of the Yangzi River (see Map 22.1).

Under the Ming, China experienced dynamic change. Agricultural and commercial reconstruction followed a long period of chaos and disorder. Hungwu revised social and political institutions. By the middle of the fifteenth century, however, his administrative framework had begun to decay. Externally, defeats in Mongolia in the later fifteenth century led to a long period of Chinese withdrawal. Nevertheless, the Ming period stands out because of its social and cultural achievements.

The Qing were not Chinese but Manchus from the north. Never more than 2 percent of the population, the Qing developed a centralized and authoritarian government, retaining the Ming administrative system but under Manchu supervision. Initially, this continuity brought prosperity and peace. By the mid-eighteenth century, however, the maintenance of the traditional Chinese position toward foreign "barbarians" and the refusal to trade with Westerners and to adopt Western

Imperial Seal   Seals on Chinese scrolls, letters, or artworks are the author's or artist's personal emblem or signature. A seal states the formal given name, or any of several personal names that a writer or artist (such as Hokusai; see page 705) adopted over a long career. Some Chinese scrolls and artworks also bear the seals of all their owners, which the Chinese view as items of interest and value. An emperor's seal, such as the one shown here, validated an edict. *(Reproduced by permission of the Commercial Press [Hong Kong] Limited, from the publication* Daily Life in the Forbidden City*)*

technology weakened imperial rule. It also left China at the mercy of European mercantile and imperialistic ambitions.

Ming Government

The character of Hungwu presents interesting paradoxes and odd contradictions. He was the youngest of six children, his father an itinerant laborer who fled Nanjing for defaulting on his taxes, his mother the daughter of a popular sorcerer. When most of the family died during a famine in 1344, the boy Zhu took refuge in a monastery, where he learned to read and write. At twenty-five, he joined the Red Turbans, a secret society contesting Mongol rule. He proved an excellent soldier and eventually married the leader's daughter.

As emperor, Hungwu displayed many qualities of a good political and military leader: he selected able officials, paid attention to detail, was decisive, and encouraged Confucian filial piety. He controlled the army, forbidding looting and rape under penalty of death. By contrast, he also seems to have been highly insecure. His family name, Zhu, means "pig," and Hungwu was reported to have had an ugly, porcine face. This feature, together with his humble background, made him extremely suspicious, especially of those he perceived to be of a higher station—the gentry and scholarly class. For all his pious and legal homilies (see below), Hungwu was a very violent man. For example, when he discovered his prime minister plotting against him, he had the man beheaded, together with his entire extended family—forty thousand people. Hungwu was the father of thirty-six sons and eighteen daughters, suggesting that he was also a very sensual man. When

he died, thirty-eight concubines were sacrificed and buried with him, in the Mongol tradition. A leading student of Chinese history writes that Hungwu's personality was a "disaster" for China and that his character shaped that of the entire dynasty.[1]

Hungwu attempted to rule the largest country in the world—a land of enormous geographical, economic, social, and religious diversity—with traditional Confucian teachings: loyalty to authority in a hierarchical social order; agriculture as the source of the country's wealth; the ideal of economically self-sufficient farm villages where frugality was the greatest virtue and the gentry helped the needy; commerce as base, parasitic, and to be discouraged; and taxes as an unfair burden on the peasantry. Holding rigidly to these beliefs, Hungwu flooded the country "with admonitions and regulations to guide his subjects' conduct—law codes, commandments, ancestral instructions, a series of grand pronouncements, village and government statutes and commercial regulations."[2] These ideals derive from the Song period, but Hungwu intended to enforce them in a society very different from that of the Song.

When Hungwu executed his prime minister, he abolished the central secretariat. He acquired absolute control of government administration and an impossible burden. One scholar estimates that 1,600 documents (called memorials), involving 3,391 issues to be resolved, arrived at the court every day. No one could cope with such a staggering amount of paperwork. The court became a bottleneck. Hungwu turned for help to members of his personal entourage, from which evolved the Embroidered Brocade Guards—bodyguards, clerical officials, and secret police. In 1382 the guards numbered 16,000; they gradually increased to 75,000.

Hungwu established China's capital at Nanjing (literally, "southern capital"), his old base on the Yangzi River. He stripped many wealthy people of their estates and divided the lands among the peasantry. Although Hungwu had been a monk, he confiscated many of the temples' tax-exempt lands, thereby increasing the proceeds of the state treasury. In the Song period, commercial taxes had fed the treasury. In the Ming and, later, the Manchu periods, imperial revenues came mainly from agriculture: farmers produced the state's resources.

Hungwu ordered a general survey of all China's land and several censuses of the population. The data gathered were recorded in official registers, which provided valuable information about the taxes that landlords, temples, and peasants owed. According to the registers, the capital was owed 8 million *shih,* or 160,000 tons, of rice per year. Such thorough fiscal information contributed to the efficient operation of the state.

To secure soldiers for the army and personnel for his administration and to generate revenue, Hungwu adopted the Yuan practice of requiring service to the state. Theoretically, the entire Chinese population was divided into three broad categories: peasants, artisans, and soldiers. Such a social structure may have appeared rational according to Confucian theory, but in reality there was great social mobility in the Ming period. For example, although each artisan household had to provide one artisan for the state workshops, the large majority of artisans were independent capitalists who were free to take on other work, as were their children. Ordinary people had the chance to rise through the examination system (see below). Farmers were not prohibited from trying to become scholars or merchants.

The Ministry of Finance oversaw the peasants, who provided the bulk of the taxes and performed public labor services (corvée). The Ministry of Public Works supervised artisans and people who had special skills and crafts in state workshops. The Ministry of the Army controlled the standing army of 2 million men. Each social category prevailed in a particular geographical region. Peasants lived in the countryside. Craftsmen lived mainly in the neighborhoods of the cities for which they produced goods. Army families lived along the coasts and lengthy frontiers that they defended. When a soldier died or proved unable to fight, his family had to provide a replacement.

The Ming emperors wielded absolute power, which in China was based on traditional Confucian teaching as it had been developed in the Song period. Confucian theory stresses that to achieve order and harmony in society, there has to be a hierarchical gradation of inferiors and superiors, that duties are more important than rights, and that the most important duty is loyalty. As a son owes loyalty and obedience to his father, public officials owed loyalty to the emperor, who was the Son of Heaven, the central divinity of the Chinese state and society. The emperor had to maintain political control over subordinate processes, such as economic growth and cultural diversification.

Access to the emperor's personal favor was the only means of acquiring privilege or some limited derivative power. The complex ceremonial and court ritual surrounding any public appearance by the emperor, the vast imperial palace staffed only by servile women and eunuchs, and the precise procedures of the imperial bureaucracy, which blamed any difficulties on the emperor's advisers—all lent the throne a rarefied aura and exalted the emperor's authority. In addition, Hungwu demanded that the military nobles (his old rebel comrades-in-arms) live at his court in Nanjing, where he could keep an eye on them. He raised many generals to the nobility, a position that bestowed honor and financial benefits but no political power whatsoever.

Late in his reign, Hungwu executed many nobles and divided China into principalities, putting one of his sons in charge of each. Suspicious even of his sons' loyalty, he carefully limited their power. Positions in the imperial administration were filled in part by means of civil service examinations, which Hungwu reinstituted. The examination system, which lasted until the twentieth century, later became the exclusive channel for official recruitment. Examinations were given every three years at the district, provincial, and state (imperial) levels; candidates had to pass the lower levels before trying for the imperial level, where the success rate in late imperial China was between 1 and 2 percent. The examinations required a minute and precise knowledge of the ancient Chinese classics, knowledge of and conformity to the commentaries on the Four Books by the Song Neo-Confucian scholar Zhu Xi, and a formal and precise literary style. (Neo-Confucianism centered on the family and involved an entire ethical, social, and political system. As harmony and order in the individual family depended on the obedience of children to their father, so good government depended on the moral character of the ruler, who was expected to display benevolence, righteousness, reverence, and wisdom. Neo-Confucianism as stated in Zhu Xi's Four Books became the accepted political philosophy of the Ming and Qing periods.) To prevent nepotism, corruption, and officials from using their positions to form a family base

Statue of Eunuch Official Hungwu forbade teaching eunuchs to read and write and declared that "eunuchs should not be allowed to interfere in affairs of state; death to the offender." But his son Yongle set up a palace school for the training of eunuchs and used them in the imperial administration as a counterbalance to regular officials. That move proved irreversible. (*Paolo Koch/Rapho-Guillemette*)

that could threaten the throne, civil service positions were filled according to the "Rule of Avoidance": a candidate could not be appointed to a place in his native province, nor could two members of the same family serve in the same province.

After 1426 the eunuch-dominated secret police controlled the palace guards and the imperial workshops, infiltrated the civil service, and headed all foreign missions. Through blackmail, espionage, and corruption, the secret police exercised enormous domestic power. How did eunuchs acquire such power? Often drawn from the lowest classes of society and viewed with distaste by respectable people, eunuchs had no hope of gaining status except by satisfying every whim of the emperor. Because they had access to the emperor's personal quarters, they had access to the emperor. By appearing to be totally submissive to the emperor, they won the emperor's absolute trust; thus they controlled many emperors and hence the machinery of government. Some eunuchs had been castrated by their families so that they could gain positions in the imperial palace. Some eunuchs married, adopted children, and had extended families. Several eunuchs—Wang Zhi in the 1500s and Zhongxian in the 1620s—gained dictatorial power when their emperors lost interest in affairs of state.

Fiscal disorders were the biggest problem of the Ming Dynasty. The imperial court made no distinction between the private household revenue of the emperor and public or state funds. Although Hungwu was a frugal man, under eunuch management the size of the imperial household steadily rose, and with it the costs to maintain the household. Imperial income derived largely from a 10 percent land tax—not a heavy burden. Most governments in the early modern world, such as those of France and England, had all state income delivered to a central treasury, and from there bills were paid. Because of the immense size of the Chinese empire, however, revenue was collected from specific sources and carried to the places of approved expenditure. A complex network of clerks and runners developed, and this network gradually "hardened into inflexible precedent." Because no single official or office had responsibility for the imperial finances, the considerable bribery and corruption that occurred along the financial road could not be policed and corrected. Fragmentation of revenue and expenditure drastically weakened the central government.[3]

A secondary problem, as in most governments in the early modern world, was that the maintenance of public infrastructure—roads, bridges, and canals—fell to local corvée service, not to the central government. This was true of the Grand Canal in China. Begun in the Sui period (518–618), the 1,250-mile-long Grand Canal was actually a series of canals from Hangzhou in the southwest to Yangzhou on the Yangzi River and northwest to Luoyang. Khubilai, with the labor of 2.5 million workers, extended it north to the Beijing region (see Map 22.1). The Grand Canal's purpose was to connect "the southern rice bowl" to the northern plains. In the fifteenth century, local soldiers had responsibility for its upkeep and for the transportation of grain. But because the soldiers were seldom paid, the troops depended for support on transporting private rice barges. Sections of the canal fell into disrepair.

Any emergency, such as a flood, required crisis management.

A third problem was the steady decline of the value of the currency. Unaware that the unlimited printing of paper money produces inflation, Hungwu's government continued issuing it. By 1425 paper money had less than one-fortieth of its original value and gradually went out of use. Although trade expanded and the need for copper coins increased, the Ming issued very few coins. Counterfeiters forged tons of coins, with the result that the value of copper coins steadily declined.

In the sixteenth century, China became part of the worldwide trade network (see pages 509–511). Demand for Chinese porcelain, silk, and later tea led to the massive flow of Japanese and South American silver into China. This potential wealth, however, did not lead to currency reform or fiscal stability. As silver entered the empire in vast quantities, its value declined and its buying power diminished, compounding inflation. Taxes customarily paid in rice were converted to payments of a fixed amount of silver. People owing local corvée services bought substitutes with silver. Between about 1575 and 1620, silver lost two-thirds of its value. The fiscal foundation of the Ming Dynasty eroded as China's tax revenues continually declined. Domestic price inflation in the late sixteenth and early seventeenth centuries destroyed the Ming's financial basis.

Economic, Social, and Cultural Change

China had experienced an agricultural revolution during the Song period. The civil wars that accompanied the breakdown of Yuan rule—with vast stretches of farmland laid waste or entirely abandoned and dikes, bridges, and canals rendered unusable—necessitated reconstruction. At the heart of this reconstruction was a radical improvement in methods of rice production.

More than bread in Europe, rice supplied almost the total nourishment of the population in central and south China. (In north China, wheat, made into steamed or baked bread or into noodles, served as the staple of the diet.) Terracing and irrigation of mountain slopes, introduced in the eleventh century, had increased rice harvests. The introduction of drought-resistant Indochinese, or Champa, rice proved an even greater boon. Although Champa rice was of lower nutritional quality than the native rice, it considerably increased the total output of food. Ming farmers experimented with Champa rice that required only sixty days from planting to harvesting instead of the usual hun-

TABLE 22.1   Land Reclamation in Early Ming China

Year	Reclaimed Land (in hectares; 1 hectare = 2.5 acres)
1371	576,000
1373	1,912,000
1374	4,974,000
1379	1,486,000

Source: J. Gernet, A History of Chinese Civilization, *trans. J. R. Foster (Cambridge: Cambridge University Press, 1982), p. 391. Used with permission.*

dred days. Peasants soon reaped two harvests a year, an enormous increase in production.

Other innovations also brought good results. Ming era peasants introduced irrigation pumps worked by pedals. Farmers began to stock the rice paddies with fish, which continuously fertilized the rice fields, destroyed malaria-bearing mosquitoes, and enriched the diet. Fish farming in the paddies eventually enabled large, previously uninhabitable parts of southern China to be brought under cultivation. Farmers discovered the possibilities of commercial cropping in cotton, sugar cane, and indigo. And new methods of crop rotation allowed for continuous cultivation and for more than one harvest per year from a single field.

The Ming rulers promoted the repopulation and colonization of devastated regions through massive transfers of people. Immigrants received large plots of land and exemption from taxation for many years. Table 22.1, based on fourteenth-century records of newly reclaimed land, helps tell the story.[4]

Reforestation was a dramatic aspect of the agricultural revolution. In 1391 the Ming government ordered 50 million trees planted in the Nanjing area. Lumber from the trees was intended for the construction of a maritime fleet. In 1392 each family holding colonized land in Anhui province had to plant 200 each of mulberry, jujube, and persimmon trees. In 1396 peasants in the present-day provinces of Hunan and Hupeh in the east planted 84 million fruit trees. Historians have estimated that 1 billion trees were planted during Hungwu's reign.[5]

Jade Fisherman The Chinese valued jade as the most precious of all gems, and they associated jade with good omens and the virtues of charity, wisdom, and justice. This magnificently sculptured piece shows a bearded fisherman with a basket, while children hold a carp. A fine example of artistic creativity among the Ming. *(The Avery Brundage Collection/ Laurie Platt Winfrey, Inc.)*

What were the social consequences of agricultural development? Increased food production led to steady population growth. Demographers date the start of the Chinese population boom at about 1550, as a direct result of improved methods of rice production. Increases in total yields differed fundamentally, however, from comparable agricultural growth in Europe: Chinese grain harvests were improved through intensification of peasant labor. This meant lower income per capita.

Population increase led to the multiplication of towns and small cities. Urbanization in the Ming era (and, later, in the Manchu period) meant the proliferation of market centers and small towns rather than the growth of "large" cities like those in Europe in the central Middle Ages and China in the Song period. Most people lived in tiny hamlets or villages that had no markets. What distinguished a village from a town was the existence of a market in the town.

The population density of a particular region determined the frequency of the markets there. In cities and larger towns, shops were open all the time, but not all on the same schedule. Smaller towns had periodic markets—some every five days, some every ten days, some only once a month. Town markets usually consisted of little open-air shops that sold essential goods—pins, matches, oil for lamps, candles, paper, incense, tobacco (after it was introduced from the Americas)—to country people from the surrounding hamlets. The market usually included a tearoom, sometimes a wine shop where tea and rice wine were sold, entertainers, and moneylenders and pawnbrokers. Sometimes the tearooms served the function of banks.

Tradesmen, who carried their wares on their backs, and craftsmen—carpenters, barbers, joiners, locksmiths—moved constantly from market to market. Itinerant salesmen depended on the city market for their wares. In large towns and cities, foodstuffs from the countryside and rare and precious goods from distant places were offered for sale. Cities gradually became islands of sophistication in the highly localized Chinese economy. Nanjing, for example, spread out enormously because the presence of the imperial court and bureaucracy generated a great demand for goods. The concentration of people in turn created a greater demand for goods and services. Industrial development was stimulated. Small businesses manufactured textiles, paper, and luxury goods such as silks and porcelains. Nanjing and Shanghai became centers for the production of cotton and silks; Xiangtan specialized in the grain and salt trade and in silver. Small towns remained embedded in peasant culture, but large towns and cities pursued contacts with the wider world.

Some cities in the late Ming period were large commercial centers where trade set the pattern of daily life. Some merchants accumulated vast fortunes and had elegant and luxurious lifestyles. Other cities were bureaucratic centers where busy officials carried out their tax-gathering and administrative duties. All cities had a bustling, energetic, thriving air.

In spite of grave political weakness and financial instability, commercial wealth in the later Ming period supported a remarkable flowering of artistic creativity. In novels, drama, short stories, poetry, landscape painting, and historical and medical works, Chinese artists and scholars produced some of the masterpieces of the world. The plays of the dramatist Tang Xianzu, for example, have been compared for richness and complexity of character and plot to those of Shakespeare. China's classic novel of adventure and religious quest, *The Journey to the West,* which describes the experiences of a

Transport of Chinese Porcelain   Chinese blue and white porcelain, especially the large covered jars shown here, enjoyed enormous popularity in southwestern Asia. This Turkish miniature painting depicts several such pieces, carried for public display in a filigreed cart in a wedding procession; the porcelain was probably part of the bride's dowry. *(Topkapi Saray Museum, Istanbul)*

clever monkey on his travels to India in search of Buddhist scriptures, was written in the 1590s. The tensions within an elite Chinese family are explored in the socially complex and sexually explicit anonymous novel *The Golden Lotus,* which can be analyzed on several levels. Printing, originally a Chinese invention using woodblocks (ca 1040) and then advanced by Koreans using movable type from metal molds in the early thirteenth century, achieved a technical excellence around 1550. This advance, plus Chinese expertise in paper manufacture, made cheap copies of classical, educational, and popular literature widely available.[6]

The better Ming porcelain dates from the fifteenth century, when ceramic factories at Jingdezhen in Jiangxi province, subsidized by the imperial treasury, poured out dishes, flasks, vases, and other objects with the underglaze blue decoration. Or they had green or red enamel ornamentations of flowers and dragons. When, in the late sixteenth and early seventeenth centuries, the imperial court spent what revenue it had on frontier defense against the Manchus, support for the porcelain factories ceased. Roughly potted from poorly prepared paste, Chinese ceramics declined in quality. This had no effect on the imperial court and elite classes, which continued to dine on gold, silver, or jade plates.[7]

Foreign Relations

Throughout the Ming period, Mongol nomads raided along China's northern frontier. Initially, Hungwu adopted a defensive strategy, absorbing thousands of Mongols into the Chinese army. By such recruitment, and by enlisting men from military households in southern China, the entire military force in 1392 totaled 1.2 million men, with 531,000 on the northern frontier. To supply this enormous force, Hungwu intended that the soldiers, under the officers' supervision, should raise their own food in peacetime. Hungwu boasted that he "had supported an army of one million men without using as much as one kernel of peasant-produced grain."[8] He spoke too soon. Because the land along the northern frontier was only partially arable, the soldiers were not interested in farming and were very inefficient, and the officers acted as landlords working soldier-tenants, the system failed. A self-supporting Chinese army did not work. The imperial government refused to allocate resources for it permanently, and Mongol attacks continued.

In the fifteenth century, an alternative solution arose. The Chinese could maintain a peaceful equilibrium on the frontier through extensive trade with the Mongols. Diplomatic ties with selected Mongol groups could be developed, the goal being the promotion of trade. But Ming emperors refused such commercial negotiations. Rather, they attempted to organize commercial relations with the Mongols of the steppe region according to the Chinese concept of the "tribute system." In return for elaborate gifts delivered to the Ming court and presented with the traditional acts of ritual subordination (the kowtow), the emperor would allow a limited amount of trade at specified times and places. This was the pattern of relations with Burma, Korea (see page 696), and Vietnam. But the Ming had never conquered Mongolia and really could not insist on tribute. Nor were the Mongols under such circumstances willing to pay it.

Thus, unable to defeat the Mongols militarily and unwilling to trade with them, the Ming in the sixteenth century tried to keep the nomads out by building walls. The Chinese had built border walls or fortifications since the seventh century B.C. Ming chroniclers called the fortifications that became China's great modern tourist attraction, the Great Wall, "border garrisons." In response to the path of nomad migrations, Ming wall building began in the west and moved eastward. Building was in brick and stone, which meant that masons had to be recruited; a network of brick kilns, quarries, and transportation routes had to be developed; and the dynasty had to finance this barrier. Towers, not for combat but for signaling by fire, smoke, or cannon blast, pierced the several thousand miles of fortifications. These fortifications slowed but never completely thwarted determined advance. Construction of them continued even as the dynasty fell. Today the Great Wall stands as China's symbol of patriotism and pride, but in the seventeenth century it represented futility and failure.[9]

Another dramatic development of the Ming period was the series of naval expeditions sent out between 1405 and 1433 under Yongle (r. 1403–1424) and his successors. China had a strong maritime history stretching back to the eleventh century, and these early-fifteenth-century voyages were a continuation of that tradition. The Ming expeditions established China as the greatest maritime power in the world—considerably ahead of Portugal, whose major seafaring reconnaissances began a half century later.

In contrast to Hungwu, Yongle broadened diplomatic and commercial contacts within the tribute system. He had two basic motives for launching overseas voyages. First, he sent them in search of Jian Wen, a serious contender for the throne whom he had defeated but who, rumor claimed, had escaped to Southeast Asia. Second, he launched the expeditions to explore and to expand the tribute system. Led by the Muslim eunuch admiral Zheng He and navigating by compass, seven fleets sailed to East and South Asia (see page 498).

These voyages had important consequences. They extended the prestige of the Ming Dynasty throughout Asia. Trade, in the form of tribute from as far as the west coast of southern India, greatly increased. Diplomatic contacts with the distant Middle East led to the arrival in Nanjing of embassies from Egypt. The maritime expeditions also led to the publication of geographical works such as the *Treatise on the Barbarian Kingdoms on the Western Oceans* (1434) and *The Marvels Discovered by the Boat Bound for the Galaxy* (1436). The information acquired from the voyages served as the basis of Chinese knowledge of the maritime world until the nineteenth century. Finally, these expeditions resulted in Chinese immigration to the countries of Southeast Asia and the ports of southern India. The voyages were terminated because Confucian court intellectuals persuaded the emperor that his quest for strange and exotic things signaled the collapse of the dynasty. After 1435 China returned to a policy of isolation. Xenophobia and anticommercialism triumphed.

Ming Decline

In the middle of the sixteenth century, China showed many signs of developing into an urban mercantile society. Merchants and businessmen had large amounts of capital, and they invested it not in land, as in the past, but in commercial and craft industries. Silkmaking, cotton weaving, porcelain manufacture, printing, and steel production assumed a definite industrial character. So many peasants seeking employment migrated to the towns that agriculture declined. Some businesses employed several hundred workers, many of them women. According to a French scholar, "Peasant women took jobs at Sung-chiang, southwest of Shanghai in the cotton mills. According to contemporary descriptions, in the big workshops the employees were already the anonymous labor force that we regard as characteristic of the industrial age."[10]

Technical treatises reveal considerable progress in manufacturing procedures. Silk looms had three or four shuttle winders. Printers could produce a sheet of paper with three or four different colors, similar to the page of a modern magazine. Chinese ceramics displayed astonishing technology—which helps explain the huge demand for them. Likewise, agricultural treatises described new machines for working the soil, sowing seed, and irrigation. Population, which stood at roughly 70 million at the start of the Ming period, increased to about 130 million by 1600.

In Confucian theory, wealth is thought to be based on agriculture, and from agriculture the state derived its taxes and the ruling class its income. Also, according to Confucian philosophy, any promotion of trade would encourage people to aspire to a different lifestyle and to a higher social status, and such aspirations would bring change and social disorder. Moreover, Chinese thinkers held that merchants produced nothing: they bought something from its grower or maker and sold it at a higher price than they had paid; thus they were parasites living off the labor of others. In addition, the proliferation of luxury goods, which people did not really need, would lead to extravagance and excessive consumption and in turn to moral decay.

Believing that virtue lies in frugality, vice in extravagance, the Ming emperors issued sumptuary laws restricting or prohibiting certain styles of clothing and tableware, means of conveyance, and articles of household decoration. The effect of these laws, however, was *increased* social stratification: the richer became richer, the poor poorer. Nevertheless, the Confucian ideal remained intact: a "successful merchant" was, by definition, one who had stopped trading and had invested his wealth in agriculture. Theory did not square with social reality.

Between about 1575 and 1625, a combination of problems led to the collapse of the Ming. The entire imperial administration revolved around the emperor, who was expected to carry out certain duties. Often he did not. The emperor Wanli (r. 1573–1620), for example, refused after 1589 to appear at imperial audiences; declined to see his eunuch grand secretaries, who gradually assumed his responsibilities; ignored issues he found unpleasant; and eventually refused to consider even pressing matters of defense and finance. Offices were left vacant for decades. The imperial bureaucracy slowed to a halt.

Military and defensive difficulties multiplied. In 1560 the Mongols invaded and occupied Qinghai. Between 1593 and 1598, China supported its tributary state, Korea, against Japanese invasion. And in 1599–1600, Chinese troops entered another tributary country, Burma, to quell rebels from southwestern China. To pay for these expensive campaigns, Wanli reopened Chinese silver mines and imposed new taxes on trade. From both these potential sources of income, greedy eunuch tax officials siphoned off much of the revenue. Likewise, the eunuchs skimmed off huge sums when the emperor tried to provide relief for areas hit by famines, floods, or earthquakes. As partisan factionalism divided court eunuchs, a desperate population resorted to banditry or rebellion.

As we have seen, the influx of Japanese and South American silver destabilized the currency. The extravagance of the imperial court aggravated a terrible financial situation. Sensual, vain, and self-indulgent, Wanli spent ninety thousand ounces of silver on his wedding clothes. Prodigious sums were spent on palaces and tombs: the Jesuit Matteo Ricci saw a convoy of wood two miles long, pulled by tens of thousands of workers, on the Grand Canal; the wood was brought from the southwest to Beijing to rebuild two palaces, and Ricci was told it would take four years to deliver it all.

As the Ming weakened, the Manchus from southeastern Manchuria grew stronger. In 1636 they occupied the Liaoning region in north China, selected Shenyang (Mukden) as their capital, and proclaimed a new dynasty with the Chinese name Qing (meaning "pure"). Helped by rebel opposition to the Ming, the Manchus captured Beijing in 1644. The entry of the Manchus' imperial armies into Yunnan in 1681 marked their complete military triumph.

Qing Rule

By purging the civil service of the old court eunuchs and troublesome factions, and by offering Chinese intellectuals positions in the bureaucracy, the Manchus gained the support of the influential academic and intellectual classes. Chinese scholars flocked to Beijing. The Manchu government, staffed by able and honest Chinese, became much more efficient than the Ming.

The Qing Dynasty ruled until 1912. In its heyday in the eighteenth century, the Qing Empire covered much of Asia—China proper, Manchuria, Mongolia, Tibet, and Xinjiang (Sinkiang)—and enjoyed tribute from Burma, Nepal, Laos, Siam, Annam, and Korea (Map 22.1). China had the largest population on earth and achieved an unprecedented degree of prosperity.

How did a million Manchus govern 350 million Chinese? The Qing Dynasty retained the basic structures of

The Scholar-Bureaucrat's Study, Qing Period   The study was located in the most private part of the scholar's house. Notice the carved rosewood desk with brass-edged corners *(rear left)*; the small stove for preparing tea for guests; the cushioned couch *(rear right)*; the rich carpet; the long narrow table for painting or studying scrolls, some of which stand in a holder on the tiled floor; and the birdcage on the window wall. The immaculate order, restrained elegance, and sense of calm tranquillity of this room incorporate the loftiest Confucian ideals for the highest class, the scholars. *(Philadelphia Museum of Art. Gift of Wright S. Ludington in memory of his father, Charles H. Ludington, 1929-30-1)*

Ming and Confucian government. The emperor, possessor of the Mandate of Heaven, governed as a supreme and autocratic ruler. The bureaucracies continued as they had in Ming and earlier times: the imperial household bureaucracy managed the emperor's palaces and households; the central bureaucracy administered his vast empire. Most positions in the empire were assigned on the basis of candidates' performances on the civil service examinations in the Confucian classics. The highest positions in Beijing and in the provinces of China were open to Chinese as well as to Manchus. These measures pacified the Chinese economic and intellectual elites. The Manchus, however, maintained a privileged status in society. They wore distinctive clothes, did not practice foot binding, retained their own language and alphabet, and maintained ethnic separatism by forbidding intermarriage with the Chinese. The Manchus required Chinese males to wear their hair in a pigtail as a sign of subservience.

Along with the agricultural improvements begun in the Ming period, internal peace, relative prosperity, and engineering methods that prevented flooding of the countryside contributed to a population explosion in the eighteenth century, as the statistics in Table 22.2 illustrate. But in the late eighteenth century, growth without increased agricultural output led to rebellions and uprisings that eventually weakened the Qing Dynasty.

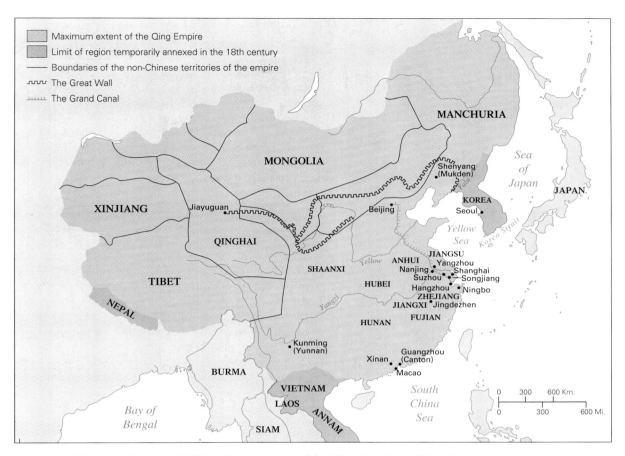

MAP 22.1 The Qing Empire, 1759   The sheer size of the Qing Empire in China almost inevitably led to its profound cultural influence on the rest of Asia. What geographical and political factors limited the extent of the empire?

The reign of the emperor Kangxi (r. 1662–1722) launched a period of great achievement. A contemporary of the Indian ruler Aurangzeb, the French king Louis XIV, and the Russian tsar Peter the Great, Kangxi demonstrated exceptional intelligence, energy, and concern for the welfare of his people. He also enjoyed much greater freedom of action than had the Ming emperor Wanli a century earlier. Whereas Wanli had been a captive of precedent, incapable of making changes, Kangxi cut both court expenses and taxes and traveled extensively throughout his domain. On these trips, he investigated the conduct of local bureaucrats in an effort to prevent them from oppressing the people. Kangxi squarely faced and thoroughly crushed a massive rebellion in southern China in 1678. He personally led an army into Mongolia and smashed the forces of the Mongol leader Galdan. This victory permanently

eliminated the danger of a reinvigorated Mongolian empire on China's borders.

Kangxi also cultivated the arts of peace. He invited scholars to his court and subsidized the compilation of a huge encyclopedia and two monumental dictionaries. *The Complete Library of the Four Treasuries,* a collection of all of Chinese literature, required the work of 15,000 calligraphers and 361 editors. It preserved the Chinese literary tradition. Kangxi's contributions to literature hold a distinguished place in the long history of Chinese culture. Europeans and Americans, however, appreciate this period primarily for its excellent porcelain. An imperial factory at Jiangxi (Kiangsi), directly controlled by Kangxi's court, produced porcelain masterpieces. Monochrome vases, bowls, and dishes in oxblood, pale green, and dark blue, and polychrome pieces in blue and white, enjoyed great popularity in

TABLE 22.2   Population of China, ca 1390–1790

ca 1390	150,000,000
ca 1585	100,000,000*
ca 1749	177,495,000
1767	209,840,000
1776	268,238,000
1790	301,487,000

*The catastrophic drop in China's overall population from the time of the Ming-Qing transition to the end of Kangxi's wars with three powerful rebels in 1681 was due to civil wars, foreign invasions, bandit actions, natural disasters, virulent epidemics, and the failure of irrigation systems.

Source: J. D. Spence, *The Search for Modern China* (New York: W. W. Norton, 1991), pp. 93–95.

Paris, London, New York, and Boston, although modern art collectors and museums rate the early Ming porcelain of higher quality.

The long reign of the emperor Qianlong (r. 1736–1795) marked the zenith of the Qing Dynasty. The cultivation of new crops from the Americas—white potatoes, corn, peanuts—on marginal lands helped to support the steadily expanding population. Chinese rule was extended into Central Asia. The imperial court continued to support arts and letters. In the last two decades of his reign, however, Qianlong showered titles, gifts, and offices on a handsome young Manchu named Heshen. Contemporaries considered Heshen uncultured, greedy, and ambitious. The corruption of the imperial civil service under Heshen, combined with heavy taxation, sparked revolts that continued to the end of the dynasty in 1912.

External Pressures

By the middle years of the eighteenth century, Qianlong also faced increasing foreign pressures. In the north and northwest, the region from which invaders had historically entered China, Mongols, Russians, and ethnic minority peoples pressed the borders. Christian missionaries, notably the Jesuits, wanted greater scope for their proselytizing activities. Nearby Asian countries that had many cultural affinities with China—Korea, Burma, Siam, Vietnam—desired greater trade with China. So, too, did European merchants: the European demand for Chinese silk, porcelain, and tea was enormous. The British East India Company, for example, had by 1740 become an international corporation with global activities, backed by eager investors in Great Britain. What was the response of the imperial government to these increasing foreign pressures?

The Qing government had no ministry of foreign affairs. Chinese relations with all foreign countries reflected the Chinese belief that China was the "central kingdom" and that all other countries were "peripheral" and removed from the cultural center of the universe. The Office of Border Affairs conducted relations with peoples in the northwest crescent (Mongols and Russians). It took police action when necessary and used the marriages of imperial daughters as the means of making alliances and maintaining peace in the north. Acting on the theory that religious evangelization by foreigners reflected on the prestige of the emperor, the imperial household itself supervised the activities of Jesuit missionaries. The Ministry of Rituals managed commercial relations with the nations of East Asia. Business delegations from Korea, Burma, and Siam were termed "tribute missions." As long as they used a language of subservience to the emperor and his ministers and made the ritual prostrations, they were allowed limited amounts of trade with China in precisely designated places and times—for Europeans, the port of Canton (Guangzhou) from October to March; for the Japanese, the city of Ningbo. As mentioned above, the Chinese value system did not respect business and commerce and distrusted traders.

Sniffing fat profits to be made from expanded trade, the aggressive merchants of London and Liverpool could not comprehend the Chinese attitude. Accordingly, the British East India Company, with the support of King George III's government, resolved on a personal appeal to Qianlong through a delegation headed by an experienced diplomat, Lord George Macartney. Three ships sailed from Portsmouth in September 1792 carrying rich gifts for the emperor: a huge imperial state coach fashioned after George III's own vehicle; a variety of heavily jeweled pocket, wrist, and neck watches; and a planetarium, a working model of the entire solar system. The dazzling array of gifts was intended to show that England was the most scientifically advanced and economically powerful nation on earth. Delivered

The Qianlong Emperor at an Archery Contest   Executed by the Italian Jesuit Giuseppe Castiglione, whose portraits and panoramas combine Chinese composition with Western perspective and coloration, this painting—with elegant garden, stately uniforms of the attendants, and dignified image of the emperor—suggests the formal ritual of the imperial court. Castiglione was a special favorite of the Qianlong emperor, who also supported Jesuit architects and designers. *(Private collection/Photo: Wan-go Weng)*

in a diamond-encrusted gift box, George III's respectful letter to the emperor stated in part:

His Most Sacred Majesty George III . . . to the Supreme Emperor of China Qianlong, worthy to live tens of thousands and tens of thousands thousand years, sendeth

Greeting . . .

We have been still more anxious to inquire into the arts and manners of countries where civilization has been perfected by the wise ordinances and virtuous examples of their Sovereigns thro a long series of ages; and, above all, Our ardent wish had been to become acquainted with those celebrated institutions of Your Majesty's populous and extensive Empire which have carried its prosperity to such a height as to be the admiration of all surrounding nations. . . .

We have the happiness of being at peace with all the World. . . . Many of our subjects have also frequented for a long time past a remote part of your Majesty's dominions for the purpose of Trade. No doubt the interchange of commodities between Nations distantly situated tends to their mutual convenience, industry, and wealth.[11]

The letter went on to ask for the establishment of permanent Chinese-British diplomatic relations; broader trade, including the opening of new ports for international commerce; and a fair system of tariffs or customs duties.

The mission that reached Canton in June 1793 (the long journey is an indication of the time involved in eighteenth-century travel) almost floundered over the issue of ritual and procedure. Court officials agreed that Macartney might see the emperor at his summer palace, if the British emissaries acknowledged that they came as a "tributary nation" and performed the *kowtow*—kneeling and striking their heads on the ground nine times in front of the emperor. Macartney protested that he was not required to show such obeisance even to George III. A compromise was finally reached when Macartney agreed to bow on one knee as he would bow to his English sovereign. Qianlong, however, was not pleased. The ruler of China considered himself supreme and all other kings his subordinates. Though thoroughly courteous to his guests, he denied all their requests. (See the feature "Listening to the Past: The Qianlong Emperor Responds to King George III" on pages 710–711.)

The Macartney mission represented the clash of two different cultures. On the one side was China, "an immobile empire," convinced of its superiority, opposed to all innovation, and certain that the ancient Confucian texts contained the answers to all problems. On the other side was Great Britain, equally convinced of its superiority "because it was modern: founded on science, the free exchange of ideas, and the mastery of commercial exchange."[12] Understanding and communication proved impossible.

The Life of the People

The family is the fundamental unit of every society. In Ming and Qing China, however, the family probably exercised greater social influence than it did anywhere else—and far more than in Western societies. The family directed the moral education of the child, the economic advancement and marriage of the young, and religious life through ceremonial rites honoring family ancestors. The Chinese family discharged many of the roles that the Christian church performed in Europe in the Middle Ages and that the state carries out today. It assumed total responsibility for the sick, the indigent, and the aged. The family expected and almost invariably received the full devotion and loyalty of its members. A person without a family had no material or psychological support.

Poor families tended to be nuclear: couples established their own households and raised their own children. The educated, the middle class, and the wealthy frequently resided in extended families: several generations of patrilineal relatives and their wives lived together in one large house or compound, individual families occupying different sections. In both kinds of families, the paternal head of the family held autocratic power over all members of the household. Apart from

crimes against the emperor and his family, the worst crimes were those committed by children against their parents. Fathers who harmed their sons received lighter punishment than sons who harmed (or even insulted) their fathers. In one instance, the Ministry of Punishments reviewed a local governor's sentence that a father be beaten for burying his son alive. The son had used foul language to his father. The ministry concluded that "although the killing (by the father) was done intentionally, it was the killing of a son who had committed a capital crime by reviling his father. The father was acquitted."[13] When a father died, his authority over the household passed to his eldest son.

The father led the family in the ancient Confucian rites honoring the family ancestors. If these ceremonies were not continued by the next generation, the family suffered social disgrace and, it was believed, the dead endured great misery. Thus marriage and childbearing were extremely important.

Although women in the Han and Tang periods had enjoyed a fair degree of freedom—to mingle socially with men and even, in the Song period, to inherit, if they had no brothers, a father's property—the Ming period stressed puritanical Neo-Confucian ideals of womanhood. A woman should be humble, diligent in her work, serene, and polite in serving her husband. Ming and Qing ideals emphasized female virginity and chastity, and a woman who had been raped could best prove her morality by committing suicide, thereby ensuring her fidelity to her husband. To what extent social reality conformed to these ideals, we do not know. Much evidence suggests that widows did commonly remarry, but was it from economic necessity, because in-laws pressured them to remarry so that they could claim the original dowry and their sons' property? We do not yet have definitive answers. One able scholar writes that "women were one of the most disparaged and exploited segments of society."[14]

Almost everyone married. Marriage was not intended to satisfy emotional longings or personal pleasures. Marriage promoted familial interests. Reverence for one's parents, maintenance of the family, and perpetuation of the line required that sons marry shortly after reaching puberty. The father and family elders discussed the possibilities and employed a local go-between to negotiate with the prospective bride's family. The go-between drew up a marriage contract specifying the property, furniture, clothing, and gifts that the two young people would bring to the union. As elsewhere, parents wanted to make the most economically and socially advantageous union for their children. The couple had no part in these arrangements. Often they did not meet each other until the groom lifted the bride's veil on their wedding day. But they were brought up to accept this custom.

A Chinese bride became part of her husband's family, subject to him and to her in-laws. Her first duty was to bear sons. If she did not, she might adopt a son. Failure to provide heirs gave her husband grounds for divorce, which brought great disgrace on her family. A woman, however, could not divorce her husband for any reason. Divorce was extremely rare in Chinese society, but a wealthy man with a "nonproductive" wife might bring concubines to live in the house along with his wife.

Men held a much higher position in society than did women. The desperately poor often killed girl babies or sold their daughters as servants or concubines. Young brides came under the direct control of their mothers-in-law, whose severity and cruelty are a common theme in Chinese literature. Once a strong-willed woman had sons, she gained increasing respect as the years went by. The Chinese deeply respected age. Some women of the wealthy classes, with servants to do the household chores, spent their days in semiseclusion nibbling dainties, smoking opium, and gambling. Women who brought large dowries to their marriages could dispose of part of those dowries as they wished. Some invested in profitable business activities. Poor women worked in the fields beside their husbands, in addition to bearing children and managing the household.

The educational system during the Ming and Qing periods had both virtues and weaknesses. Most villages and all towns and cities operated schools that prepared boys for the all-important civil service examinations. Boys learned to write with a brush the approximately three thousand commonly used characters of literary Chinese, and they learned the standard texts of Confucian philosophy, ethics, and history. The curriculum was very limited, and the instructional method stressed memorization and discouraged imagination. The civil service aspirant received no practical training in the work of government. But the system yielded a high percentage of literate men (relative to Europe at the same time) and gave Chinese society cohesion and stability. All educated Chinese shared the same basic ethical and literary culture, much as medieval Europeans were formed by Latin Christian culture.

In China, as in medieval Europe, educational opportunities for girls were limited. Rich men occasionally hired tutors for their daughters, and a few women achieved exceptional knowledge. Most women of all classes received training that prepared them for their

Ch'en Shu: The White Cockatoo   Like Italy and France in the early modern period, China and Japan can boast of distinguished women artists. This painting in ink and color on a hanging scroll depicts a highly prized species of parrot. The work of Ch'en Shu is very much in the Chinese artistic tradition. *(The Metropolitan Museum of Art, 13.220.31)*

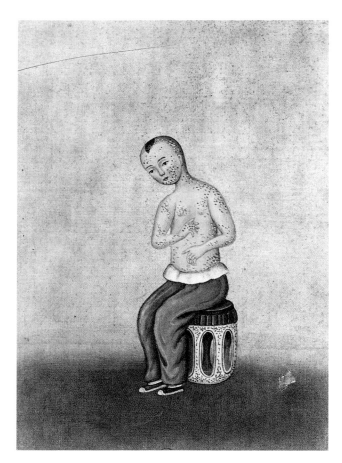

Chinese Victim of Syphilis   The growth of travel in the seventeenth and eighteenth centuries meant the worldwide transmission of disease, another consequence of the Columbian Exchange. *(Bibliothèque Nationale, Paris)*

roles as wives and mothers: courteous behavior, submission to their husbands, and the administration of a household.

In the late sixteenth century, when book publishing and educational facilities increased, women began to share in these opportunities. A few upper-class women, such as the poet/painter Lin Yiu (1618–1664) and the painter Ch'en Shu (1660–1736), gained considerable public recognition. We know of Ch'en Shu's life only because her eldest son, the prominent scholar/official Ch'ien Ch'en-ch'un, wrote her biography, casting her as a model of Confucian virtue.[15] Even in the early nineteenth century, only 1 to 10 percent of women were literate. By the criterion of education, the status of women in the Qing period may have fallen lower than at any other time in China's long history.[16]

What of health and medical care in imperial China? Although Egyptian and Babylonian medicine predates Chinese medicine by perhaps a millennium, the Chinese medical tradition is the oldest continuing usage in the world. Chinese medical theory deriving from the Han period (from the third century B.C. to the third century A.D.) attributed all ailments to a lack of harmony in the body; cure, then, rests on restoring harmony. Diagnosis of disease depended on visual observation, studying the case history, auditory symptoms, and taking the pulse. Physicians held that three spots along the wrist gave the pulse readings of different organs, and the experienced physician could diagnose the malfunction of any internal organ by checking the pulse. Two basic forms of therapy (treatment) existed. Medicinal therapy was based on the curative effects of herbs. This treatment entailed taking pills or powders in a boiled broth. The other therapy was acupuncture, the insertion of needles into specific parts of the body.

The theory behind acupuncture is that twelve channels run over the body close to the skin, each channel is related to a specific organ, and the needle stimulates a sluggish or pacifies an overactive organ. The early acupuncturist used fine needles and avoided vital organs. Certainly acupuncture was no more dangerous than the widespread European practice of bleeding.

Reliance on acupuncture and the Confucian principle that the body is the sacred gift of parents to child made dissection a terrible violation of filial piety and thus strongly discouraged serious surgery. Another factor militating against surgery was the Chinese culture's disdain for manual work of any kind. A "wise" doctor mastered a body of classical texts, prescribed medicine for treatment, and "did not lower himself to perform manual, surgical operations."[17] Nor should a doctor accept fees for service.

Confucian policy did not allow any experts with specialized knowledge to rise socially as a group: social mobility, it was thought, led to social tensions and demands for restructuring.[18] Thus, while physicians in the Islamic and European worlds enjoyed respect and sometimes modest wealth, the position of Chinese doctors was deemed insignificant, and they were considered mere artisans. Rather than consulting medical experts, each person had to acquire sufficient knowledge, including pharmacological knowledge, to help members of his or her family in times of illness.

Several emperors decreed that medical colleges should be established and that annual examinations should test physicians' skills so that the needs of the people, as well as the needs of the imperial court, would be served. But these orders were never implemented. As a result, although the idea of state-supported hospitals was an ancient one in China, the first institutions to provide medical care for the sick of a community were established by Christian medical missionaries in the nineteenth century.

In sharp contrast to Europe, China had few social barriers. The emperors fought the development of a hereditary aristocracy that could have undermined their absolute monarchy, and they granted very few titles of nobility in perpetuity. Though China had no legally defined aristocracy, it did have an "upper class" based on a *combination* of wealth, education, lineage, and bureaucratic position. Agricultural land remained the most highly prized form of wealth, but silver ingots, jade, libraries of classical works, porcelain, and urban real estate also indicated status. Wealth alone, however, did not bring status. Offices in the state bureaucracy provided opportunities and motivation for upward mobility. Family members encouraged intelligent sons to prepare for the civil service examinations, and the work and sacrifice of parents bore fruit in their sons' success. Positions in the bureaucracy brought salaries and gifts, which a family invariably invested in land. The competitive examinations with few exceptions were open to all classes, and that accessibility prevented the formation of a ruling caste. China did not develop a politically articulate bourgeoisie. Because everyone accepted the Confucian principle that the learned and civilized should rule the state, scholars ranked highest in the social order. They, along with Heaven, Earth, the emperor, and parents, deserved special veneration. With the possible exception of the Jewish people, no people have respected learning as much as the Chinese. Merchants tried to marry into the scholar class in order to rise in the world. At the bottom of society were actors, prostitutes, and beggars.

The Chinese found recreation and relaxation in many ways. All classes gambled at cards and simple numbers games. The teahouse served as the local meeting place for exchanging news and gossip and listening to the tales of professional storytellers, who enjoyed great popularity. The affluent indulged in an alcoholic drink made from fermented and distilled rice, and both men and women liked pipes and tobacco. Everyone who could afford to do so went to the theater. The actors, like their ancient Greek counterparts, wore happy and sad masks, and their gestures were formal and stylized. The plays typically dramatized episodes from Chinese history and literature. The Chinese associated athletics,

Chinese Cookery   Everywhere in the world, until very recently, meat was scarce and thus a luxury. In China, the shortage of meat encouraged great sophistication in the preparation of foods, especially vegetables. Although European travelers interpreted the frequent servings of vegetables and fish as a sign of poverty, the Chinese, if we can trust modern nutritionists, probably had a healthier diet than that of Europeans. Notice the variety of dishes. Women obviously ate separately from men. *(Roger-Viollet)*

riding, and horse racing with soldiers, at best a necessary evil, and regarded the active life as the direct antithesis of the scholarly contemplation they most valued.

The Qianlong emperor's reign saw the publication of China's greatest novel, *The Dream of the Red Chamber.* In 120 chapters with hundreds of characters, several levels of meaning, and echoes of the great Ming plays and novels, the author Cao Xuepin tells a tale of a wealthy extended family: its complex business dealings, varied religions, involvement in the imperial civil service, and loves and sexual liaisons, both heterosexual and homosexual. *The Dream of the Red Chamber* is both a love story and an account of one man's quest for identity and the meaning of life. Cao had not finished the book when he died in 1763; only in 1792 did a completed version appear. It achieved immediate success among all literate social classes and remains today one of the world's great literary classics.[19]

 # KOREA (CHOSON)

The peninsula of Korea juts out of the East Asian landmass, dividing the Yellow Sea to the west from the Sea of Japan to the east. Korea is bounded on the south by the Korea Strait and on the north by other natural barriers—the Yalu River and the Changpai Mountains, which separate Korea from China and Russia. With a highly indented coastline, Korea measures 600 miles in length and 135 miles in width. Because of a mountainous and rocky terrain, only about 20 percent of the soil is arable, and half of that arable land is given to the chief crop, rice. Surrounded on three sides by water, encompassing some of the best fishing areas in the world, Koreans have depended heavily on fish as their chief source of protein.

Political and Cultural Foundations

Korea was united as a kingdom in the seventh century B.C., but much of its history shows strong Chinese influences. From China, Buddhism entered Korea in the fourth century A.D. and became the official state religion. Likewise, in the tenth century, Confucianism came to Korea, and although Buddhism remained the state religion, Confucianism controlled the model of government. In 1231 Mongol forces from China invaded Korea, leading to thirty years of war and domestic turmoil. Only when the ruling Koryo Dynasty accepted Mongol rule and made an alliance with it did peace come.

Throughout the fourteenth century, Japanese marauders raided Korea's east coast and penetrated deep into the interior; towns in southern Korea especially felt the brunt of Japanese assault. In this crisis, a soldier from the northeastern frontier, Yi Song-gye (1335–1408) saved the country. His successive victories over the Japanese won him a national following. In 1392, with the support of the Ming rulers of China, who had just overthrown the Mongols (see page 679), Yi Song-gye staged a coup: he overthrew the Koryo and seized the throne. Yi Song-gye (r. 1392–1396) renamed the country Choson and founded the Choson Dynasty, which lasted until 1910, the longest dynasty of East Asian history.

The reign of Yi Song-gye launched a broad movement of Neo-Confucian reform. Confucianism replaced Buddhism as the state religion. Neo-Confucian ideals of the Chinese philosopher Zhu Xi (1130–1200) determined state policy in land reform, educational reconstruction, and cultural development. For example, the government confiscated the tax-exempt monastic lands, laicized the monks and nuns, and redistributed the lands to the peasants, whose produce (mainly rice) yielded revenue for the state. Scholars rewrote the law codes and redesigned government institutions along Confucian lines. A Korean phonetic alphabet and printing with movable metal type were developed. A system of state examinations for civil service positions, similar to the Chinese system, was set up. In 1392 Yi Song-gye turned the fortress and trade center at Seoul, on the Han River, into his capital.

In 1592 the Japanese military leader Hideyoshi (see page 700) attacked Korea. After broad devastation and destruction, the Koreans, with Chinese help, repulsed the invaders. Then, in 1637, the Manchus assailed Korea, and after the Ming collapse in 1644, Korea became a vassal state of the Manchus.

Although Koreans form a distinct ethnic people, Korean culture reflects strong Chinese cultural models. In the seventeenth and eighteenth centuries, Korea had a Chinese-style calendrical system, a script for writing adapted from Chinese models, similar dress and food, the practice of Buddhism and Confucianism, and a governmental administration similar to the Chinese. China held to the fixed assumption that it was "the central kingdom," the cultural center of the universe. It followed, by Chinese logic, that all other countries were marginal, removed from the center (see page 690). Thus Korea (along with Siam, renamed Thailand in 1938; Burma; and Annam) was a subordinate, or "tributary," state that had to acknowledge China's cultural and political pre-eminence. Korean diplomats, emissaries, and merchants had to use a language of submission and to kowtow when received by the Chinese emperors in imperial audiences. On a fixed annual schedule, Korea sent emissaries to Beijing and were allowed limited rights of trade. From the Chinese perspective, these were "tribute missions." The Chinese government had, as we have seen, no foreign office or department of state. Rather, the Ministry of Rituals had authority over all diplomatic and commercial relations with Korea, and that ministry stressed Korea's cultural inferiority.

Economic and Social Change

The Choson government relied for revenue on "tribute taxes" on many locally produced items. Inequitably levied and collected, these taxes imposed a heavy burden on all peasants and drove some off the land. The establishment of the Uniform Land-Tax Law—requiring payment of 1 percent of the harvest of each unit of land, payable in rice, cotton, or corn—effectively abolished the tribute system. First imposed in 1608, the Uniform Land-Tax Law was enforced throughout the country a century later.

Rubens: Korean Man (left) and Portrait of the Monk Sa-Myong Taesa (right)   The great Flemish master Peter Paul Rubens sketched the drawing on the left (ca 1617–1618) with black chalk and a little red chalk on the face. Scholars consider it one of the earliest representations of a Korean in the West and one of Rubens's most meticulous portraits. It is a fine example of cross-cultural interests. We do not know the name of the Korean or what he was doing in Antwerp, where Rubens encountered him. Roughly contemporaneous with the Rubens is this portrait of a Korean monk, painted in ink and colors on silk and mounted on a hanging scroll. Taesa had organized an army of monks to fight the Japanese invaders, and after their defeat he negotiated the peace treaty. Rubens relied on stark simplicity for effect, and the man's face on the left has a direct, inquiring expression. In contrast the Korean artist used rich colors and details, such as the chair panels. Taesa's facial expression is idealized, denoting his spirituality. *(Left: The J. Paul Getty Museum, Los Angeles. Accession number: 83.GB.384; Right: 17th century, Korea: Choson Dynasty. Museum of Fine Arts, Boston, Denman Waldo Ross Collection)*

The law had significant consequences. It reduced the tax burden on the peasantry; allowed government-designated merchants (kongin), who purchased goods for the government, to accumulate capital; and led to the emergence of independent artisans who manufactured goods for the kongin.

Beginning in the seventeenth century, advances in farming technology led to a great increase in agricultural yields. Farmers used a new technique for starting rice seedlings: they were first planted in a small seedbed. A winter barley crop went into the fields. After the barley was harvested, the fields were flooded and the rice seedlings were transferred to the paddy. This "double-cropping" method required large amounts of water, and reservoirs were constructed to supply it. By the late eighteenth century, six thousand reservoirs dotted the Korean countryside. These improvements reduced the amount of labor needed, and one farmer could cultivate a larger amount of land. "Enlarged-scale farming," as the new method was called, became widespread. The condition of tenant farmers, the great majority of Choson rustics, also improved. Their labor was more valuable, and rather than working under the supervision of the landowner, they could farm as they chose. Payment in cash gradually replaced payment in kind.[20]

The seventeenth and eighteenth centuries also witnessed a great expansion of commercial farming: the raising of specialized crops for (distant) domestic and foreign sale. Tobacco, introduced from the Americas in the early seventeenth century, had a big market in China, as well as in Korea; tobacco proved even more profitable than rice. Ginseng, a family of tropical herbs, was in great demand in China, both as a cure for various ailments and for use in the manufacture of fine rice paper. The acreage given to cotton production also expanded.

Korean rural society underwent considerable change. A new-rich class of peasant farmers, whose wealth derived from crops grown for distant commercial markets, appeared. Below them, the ranks of successful tenant farmers increased. At the bottom were the unemployed; some became wage laborers, and others joined roving bands of robbers.

Economic and social change accelerated in the eighteenth century. The kongin emerged as a class of specialized merchants, each dealing in a specific product. Private merchants—some transporting goods by boat, others by overland routes—extended their operations throughout the country. The capital city, Seoul, especially enjoyed the advantages of more and greatly varied goods. As Seoul's population grew, more than one thousand local markets also sprang up throughout the Korean countryside.

In 1976 deep-sea divers at Sinan off the Korean coast uncovered a Chinese ship. Dated about 1323, it had sailed from Ningbo in Zhejiang province in China to Japan with a stop in Korea. The wreck, containing a huge cargo of Chinese ceramics, provides valuable evidence about Korean trade in the early modern world.

Since at least the Song period of Chinese history, Koreans had shown a strong interest in Chinese porcelain and had imported large quantities of it. Ceramic dishes and jars for everyday use, together with perfume bottles, jugs, ink pots, vases, candlesticks, teapots, and bowls, arrived in Korean markets for sale to the elite and scholarly classes. Just as Persian, Turkish, and later English potters did, Korean craftsmen quickly copied Chinese porcelain figures, styles, and colors. Throughout the Ming and Qing periods, Koreans also bought ceramic building and roofing tiles from China, as well as silks. In return, Korea exported tobacco, paper—ordinary paper for business uses and printing, heavy writing paper for scholars—brushes, ginseng, and cotton. The large forests that constituted one of Korea's great natural resources supplied the wood for paper manufacture.

JAPAN (CA 1400–1800)

The Ashikaga Shogunate lasted from the middle of the fourteenth to the late sixteenth century. During this period, Japanese society experienced almost continual violence and civil war. Weak central governments could not maintain order. Throughout the islands, local strongmen took charge. Around 1450, 250 daimyos, or lords, held power; by 1600 only 12 survivors could claim descent from daimyo families of the earlier date. Successful military leaders carved out large territories and governed them as independent rulers. Political and social conditions in fifteenth- and sixteenth-century Japan strongly resembled conditions in western Europe in the tenth and eleventh centuries. Political power was in the hands of a small group of military leaders. Historians often use the same term—feudalism—to describe the Japanese and the European experiences. As in medieval Europe, feudalism paved the way for the rise of a strong centralized state in seventeenth-century Japan.

Feudalism in Japan

Feudalism played a powerful role in Japanese culture until the nineteenth century. The similarities between feudalism in Japan and that in medieval Europe have fascinated scholars, as have the very significant differences. In Europe, feudalism emerged out of the fusion of Germanic and Roman social institutions and flowered under the impact of Muslim and Viking invasions. In Japan, feudalism evolved from a combination of the native warrior tradition and Chinese Confucian ethics. Japanese society had adopted the Confucian emphasis on filial respect for the head of the family, for the local civil authorities, and for the supreme authority of the head of state.

The two constituent elements of Japanese feudalism appeared between the eighth and the twelfth centuries: (1) the *shoen* (private land outside imperial control) with its *shiki* (rights) and (2) the *samurai* (military warrior clique). Some scholars have equated the shoen with the European manor, but the comparison needs careful qualification. A manor usually corresponded to one composite village; a particular family's shoen was widely scattered. Those who held shoen possessed the shiki there—that is, the right to the income or rice produced by the land. But, just as several persons might hold rights—military, judicial, grazing—on a medieval European manor and all these rights yielded income, so several persons frequently held shiki rights on a Japanese estate.

By the sixteenth century, only a small proportion of samurai had attained the rank of daimyo and possessed a shoen. Most warriors were salaried fighters with no connection to land. From their daimyos, they received stipends in rice, not in land; and in this respect they resembled European knights, who were supported by cash or money fiefs.

The Japanese samurai warrior resembled the knight of twelfth-century France in other ways as well. Both were armed with expensive weapons, and both fought on horseback. Just as the knight was supposed to live according to the chivalric code, so Japanese samurai were expected to live according to *Bushido,* or "Way of the Warrior," a code that stressed military honor, courage, stoic acceptance of hardship, and, above all, loyalty. Disloyalty brought social disgrace, which the samurai could avoid only through *seppuku,* ritual suicide by slashing his belly. Both samurai and knights were highly conscious of themselves as aristocrats. But knights fought as groups, and samurai fought as individuals.

By the middle of the sixteenth century, Japanese feudalism had taken on other distinctive features. As the number of shoen decreased and the powerful daimyos consolidated their territories, the practice of *primogeniture,* keeping an estate intact under the eldest or ablest son, became common. Around 1540 the introduction of the musket from Europe made infantrymen effective against mounted samurai, and the use of Western cannon required more elaborately fortified castles. Thus, in addition to armed cavalrymen, daimyos began to employ large numbers of foot soldiers equipped with spears, and they constructed new castles. These military and social developments occurred during a century of turbulence and chronic disorder, out of which emerged a leader who ended the chaos and began the process of unification, laying the foundation of the modern Japanese national state.

Nobunaga and National Unification

Oda Nobunaga (1534–1582), a samurai of the lesser daimyo class, won control of his native province of Owari in 1559. He began immediately to extend his power, defeating a powerful daimyo in 1560 and eight years later seizing Kyoto, the capital city, where the emperor and his court resided. As a result, Nobunaga became the virtual ruler of central Japan.

Scholars have called the years from 1568 to 1600 the period of "national unification." During this time, Japan underwent aggressive and dynamic change. Adopting the motto "Rule the empire by force," Nobunaga set out to subdue all real and potential rivals and to replace them with his vassals. With the support of Toyotomi Hideyoshi (1537–1598), a brilliant general, he subdued first western and then eastern and northern Japan.

The great Buddhist temple-fortresses proved to be Nobunaga's biggest problem. Some of these monasteries possessed vast wealth and armed retainers. During the civil wars, the Buddhists had supported various daimyos in their private wars, but Nobunaga would tolerate no such interference. The strategically located monastery on Mount Hiei near Kyoto had long provided sanctuary for political factions. Previous daimyos had refused to attack it because it was sacred. Nobunaga, however, used fire to reduce it, and his men slaughtered thousands of its occupants.

Although Nobunaga won control of most of Japan by the sword, he backed up his conquests with government machinery and a policy of conciliation. He gave lands and subordinate positions in the army to his defeated enemies. Trusted daimyos received complete civil jurisdiction over entire provinces. At strategic points, such as Nijo near Kyoto and Azuchi on the shore of Lake Biwa, Nobunaga built castles to serve as key administrative and defensive centers for the surrounding territories. He opened the little fishing village of Nagasaki to foreign commerce; it soon grew into the nation's largest port. He standardized the currency, eliminated customs barriers, and encouraged the development of trade and industry. In 1582, when Nobunaga was murdered by one of his vassals, his general and staunchest adherent, Hideyoshi, carried on his work.

A peasant's son who had risen to power by his military bootstraps, Hideyoshi advanced the unification and centralization of Japan in two important ways. First, in 1582 he attacked the great fortress at Takamatsu. When direct assault failed, his troops flooded the castle and forced its surrender. When Takamatsu fell, so did the large province of Mori. A successful siege of the town of Kagoshima then brought the southern island of Kyushu under his domination. Hideyoshi soothed the vanquished daimyos as Nobunaga had done—with lands and military positions—but he also required them to swear allegiance and to obey him "down to the smallest particular."

Having reduced his most dangerous adversaries, Hideyoshi ordered a survey of the entire country. The military power of the unified Japanese state depended on a strong agricultural base, and Hideyoshi wanted to exploit the peasantry fully. His agents collected detailed information about the daimyos' lands and about towns, villages, agricultural produce, and industrial output all over Japan. This material enabled Hideyoshi to assess military quotas and taxable property. His surveys tied the peasant population to the land and tightened the collection of the land tax. With the country pacified, Hideyoshi embarked on an ill-fated attempt to conquer Korea. The expedition failed amid great bloodshed and devastation; it was the last Japanese medieval involvement in continental Asia. When Hideyoshi died in 1598, he left a strong centralized state. Brute force had created a unified Japan.

On his deathbed, the old soldier set up a council of regents to govern during the minority of his infant son. The strongest regent was Hideyoshi's long-time supporter Tokugawa Ieyasu (1543–1616), who ruled vast territories around Edo (modern-day Tokyo). Ieyasu quickly eliminated the young ruler and in 1600 at Sekigahara smashed a coalition of daimyo defenders of the heir. This battle was the beginning of the Tokugawa regime.

The Tokugawa Regime

Japanese children are taught that "Ieyasu ate the pie that Nobunaga made and Hideyoshi baked." As the aphorism suggests, Ieyasu took over and completed the work begun by his able predecessors. He took decisive steps to solidify his dynasty and control the feudal no-

bility and to maintain peace and prosperity in Japan. The Tokugawa regime that Ieyasu fashioned worked remarkably well, lasting until 1867.

Ieyasu obtained from the emperor the ancient title of *shogun,* or general-in-chief. Constitutionally, the emperor exercised sovereign authority. In practice, authority and power—both the legal right and the physical means—were held by the Tokugawa shogun. Ieyasu declared the emperor and his court at Kyoto "very precious and decorative, like gold and silver," and surrounded the imperial court with all the ceremonial trappings but none of the realities of power.

In a scheme resembling the later residency requirements imposed by Louis XIV (see page 529) and Peter the Great (see page 549), Ieyasu forced the feudal lords to establish "alternate residence" at his capital city of Edo, to spend part of each year there, and to leave their wives and sons there—essentially as hostages. This requirement had obvious advantages: the shogun could keep close tabs on the daimyos, control them through their children, and weaken them financially with the burden of maintaining two residences. Ieyasu justified this course of action by invoking the *Bushido* code, with its emphasis on loyalty. He forbade members of the nobility to marry without his consent, thus preventing the formation of dangerous alliances.

The early Tokugawa shoguns also restricted the construction of castles—symbols, in Japan as in medieval Europe, of feudal independence. Later, the practice of alternate residence led to considerable castle building—castles that represented demands for goods and services. The Tokugawa regime also enforced a policy of complete separation of samurai and peasants. Samurai were defined as those who could bear swords; peasants could not bear swords. Samurai had to live in castles (which evolved into castle-towns), and they depended on stipends from their lords, the daimyos. Samurai were effectively prevented from establishing ties to the land, so they could not become landholders. Gradually, the samurai turned into urban administrators or merchants; only members of the warrior class could hold official positions in the state bureaucracy. Likewise, merchants and artisans had to live in towns and could not own land. Japanese castle-towns evolved into bustling, sophisticated urban centers. Peasants had to live in villages and till the land. According to the Neo-Confucian theory of the Tokugawa regime, society had four strata: samurai, peasants, artisans, and merchants.[21]

As in medieval Europe and early modern China, the agricultural class held a respected position because its members provided Japanese society with sustenance.

Even so, farmers had to mind their betters, and they bore a disproportionate share of the tax load. According to the survey made by Hideyoshi, taxes were imposed on villages, not on individuals; the tax varied between 30 and 40 percent of the rice crop. Also as in Europe and China, the commercial classes in Japan theoretically occupied the lowest rungs on the social ladder because they profited from the toil of others.

Urbanization and Commercialization

In the early seventeenth century, Japanese society rested on agriculture—a rice-based economy. Peasants paid their taxes in rice. Both the *bakufu* (national government) and the daimyos needed to exchange their rice for cash. This need led to the growth of central markets where quantities of rice could be exchanged and cash received for the purchase of other goods and services. Osaka came to manage most of this rice trade. Other goods—cotton cloth, oil, sugar, salt, paper, and iron ore—also flowed into Osaka. Granted special privileges by the government, and with the facilities for large commodity exchange, Osaka became the commercial center of Japan. Wholesalers and brokers were concentrated there. The city was also closely tied to Kyoto, where the emperor and his court resided and which also represented a big demand for goods and services. Thus Osaka, "the kitchen of Japan," developed as the central market for the entire country. By the mid-eighteenth century, Osaka's population numbered about 1 million, Kyoto's 400,000. Edo, the center of government and the city where daimyos and their retainers had to spend part of each year according to the system of alternate residence, also expanded to about 400,000.

Other towns and cities sprang up. In contrast to western and eastern Europe, where cities grew out of religious centers (cathedrals), military camps (fortifications), or small marketplaces in the Middle Ages, Japanese towns in the seventeenth century trace their origins to a *political* factor: the daimyos' requirement that their vassals live at their castles. The concentration of vassals-in-residence, representing a consumer class and joined by commoners providing services, gave rise to castle-towns in Tokugawa Japan (Map 22.2). Two hundred fifty towns, most ranging in size from 3,000 to 20,000 people—but a few, such as Hiroshima, Kagoshima, and Nagoya, that had populations between 65,000 and 100,000 people—came into being. In most places, half of the people had samurai status; the other half were commoners. In addition, perhaps 200 transit towns along the roads and highways emerged to service the needs of men traveling on the alternate residence system. In the eighteenth century, perhaps 4 million people, 15 percent of the Japanese population, resided in cities or towns.

In most cities, merchant families with special privileges from the government controlled the urban economy. The founders of businesses had entered the cities as samurai and changed their status to merchants. Frequently, a particular family dominated the trade of a particular product; then that family branched out into other businesses. The family of Kōnoike Shinroku provides a typical example.

In 1600 he established a sake brewery in the village of Kōnoike (sake is an alcoholic beverage made from fermented rice). By 1604 he had opened a branch office in Edo, and in 1615 he opened an office in Osaka; that same year, he began shipping tax-rice (taxes paid in rice) from western Japan to Osaka. One of Shinroku's sons, Kōnoike Zen'amon (remember that the Japanese put the surname before the individual name) in 1656 founded a banking or money-changing business in Osaka. Forty years later, the Kōnoike family was doing business in thirty-two daimyo domains. Eventually, the Kōnoike banking house made loans to and handled the tax-rice for 110 daimyo families. The Kōnoike continued to expand their businesses. In 1705, with the interest paid from daimyo loans, the Kōnoike bought a tract of ponds and swampland, turned the land into rice paddies, and settled 480 households numbering perhaps 2,880 peasants on the land. Land reclamation under merchant supervision became a typical feature of Tokugawa business practices. Involved in five or six business enterprises, the "house of Kōnoike" had come a long way from brewing sake.

Recent scholarship demonstrates that the Tokugawa regime witnessed the foundations of modern Japanese capitalism: the development of a cash economy, the use of money to make more money, the accumulation of large amounts of capital available for investment in factory or technological enterprises, and the growth of business ventures operating over a national network of roads. That these developments occurred simultaneously with, but entirely independent of, similar changes in Europe fascinates and challenges historians.

Japanese merchant families also devised distinct patterns and procedures for their business operations. What today is called "Family Style Management Principles" determined the age of appointment or apprenticeship (between eleven and thirteen); the employee's detachment from past social relations and adherence to the norms of a particular family business; salaries;

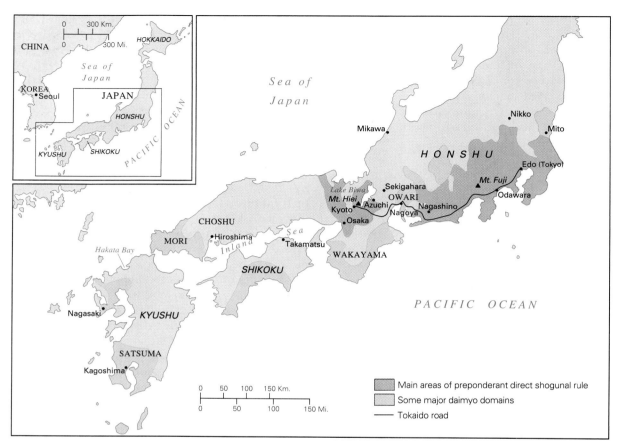

MAP 22.2 Tokugawa Japan   Consider the cultural and political significance of the fact that Japan is an island. How did the concentration of shogunate lands affect the shogunate's government of Japan?

seniority as the basis of promotion—though job performance at the middle rungs determined who reached the higher ranks; and the time for retirement. All employees in a family business were imbued with the "cardinal tenets" of Tokugawa business law: frugality, resourcefulness, and careful accounting. The successful employee also learned appropriate business behavior and a spirit of self-denial. These values formed the basis of what has been called the Japanese "industrious revolution." They help to explain how, after the Meiji Restoration of 1867 (see page 869), Japan was able to industrialize rapidly and to compete successfully with the West.[22]

The peace that the Tokugawa Shogunate imposed brought a steady rise in population and prosperity. As demand for goods grew, so did the numbers of merchants. To maintain stability, the early Tokugawa shoguns froze the four ancient social categories: imperial court nobility, samurai, peasants, and merchants. Laws rigidly prescribed what each class could and could not do. Nobles, for example, were "strictly forbidden, whether by day or by night, to go sauntering through the streets or lanes in places where they have no business to be." Daimyos were prohibited from moving troops outside their frontiers, making alliances, and coining money. Designated dress and stiff rules of etiquette distinguished one class from another. As intended, this stratification protected the Tokugawa shoguns from daimyo attack and inaugurated a long era of peace.

In the interests of stability and peace, Ieyasu's descendants also imposed measures called *sakoku*. This "closed country policy" sealed Japan's borders around 1639. Japanese were forbidden to leave the country. Foreigners were excluded.

In 1549 the Jesuit missionary Francis Xavier landed at Kagoshima. He soon made many converts among the poor and even some among the daimyos. By 1600 there were 300,000 baptized Christians in Japan. Most of them lived on Kyushu, the southernmost island (see Map 22.2), where the shogun's power was weakest and the loyalty of the daimyos most doubtful. In 1615 bands of Christian samurai supported Ieyasu's enemies at the fierce Battle of Osaka. In 1637, 30,000 peasants in the heavily Catholic area of northern Kyushu revolted. The shoguns thus came to associate Christianity with domestic disorder and feudal rebellion. Accordingly, what had been mild persecution of Christians became ruthless repression after 1639. Foreign priests were expelled or tortured, and thousands of Japanese Christians suffered crucifixion. The "closed country policy" remained in force for almost two centuries. The shogunate kept Japan isolated—but not totally.

Through the Dutch factory on the tiny island of Deshima in Nagasaki harbor (see page 513), a stream of Western ideas and inventions trickled into Japan in the eighteenth century. Western writings, architectural illustrations, calendars, watches, medicine, and paintings deeply impressed the Japanese. Western portraits and other paintings introduced the Japanese to perspective and shading. When the Swedish scientist C. P. Thunberg, physician to the Dutch at Deshima, visited Nagasaki and Edo, the Japanese looked on him as a scientific oracle and plied him with questions. Japanese scholars believed that Western inventions were more efficient than their Japanese equivalents and that these inventions contributed to the prosperity of European nations. Japanese curiosity about things Western gave rise to an intellectual movement known as *rangaku*, foreign studies, which urged that these Western ideas and inventions be adopted by the Japanese.

Japanese understanding of the West was severely limited and often fanciful, as was Western knowledge of Asian civilizations. Like eighteenth-century Europeans who praised Chinese and Persian customs to call attention to shortcomings at home, Japanese scholars idealized Western conditions. Both peoples wanted to create within their countries the desire for reform and progress.[23]

The Life of the People

The Tokugawa Shogunate subdued the nobility by emasculating it politically. Stripped of power and required to spend part of each year at Edo, the daimyos and samurai passed their lives pursuing pleasure. They spent frantically on fine silks, paintings, concubines, boys, the theater, and the redecoration of their castles. Around 1700 one scholar observed that the entire military class was living "as in an inn, that is, consuming now and

paying later."[24] Eighteenth-century Japanese novels, plays, and histories portray the samurai engrossed in tavern brawls and sexual orgies. These frivolities, plus more sophisticated pleasures and the heavy costs of maintaining an alternate residence at Edo, gradually ruined the warrior class.

In traditional Japanese society, women were subordinate to men, and the civil disorders of the sixteenth century strengthened male domination. Parents in the samurai class arranged their daughters' marriages to advance family interests. Once a woman married, her life centered on her children and domestic chores. The management of a large household with several children and many servants imposed heavy responsibilities on women. An upper-class wife rarely left home unchaperoned. "Middle-class" women, however, began to emerge from the home. The development of an urban commercial culture in the cities (see page 701) in the Tokugawa period led to the employment of women in silk and textile manufacture, in publishing, in restaurants and various shops, and especially in entertainment.

All major cities contained places of amusement for men—teahouses, theaters, restaurants, houses of prostitution. Desperately poor parents sometimes sold their daughters to entertainment houses (as they did in medieval Europe), and the most attractive or talented girls, trained in singing, dancing, and conversational arts, became courtesans, called *geishas,* or "accomplished persons," in modern times. The Tokugawa period saw the beginnings for men of the separation of family and business life on the one hand, and leisure and amusement on the other. That separation is still evident in Japanese society.[25]

The samurai spent heavily on kabuki theater. (See the feature "Individuals in Society: Katsushika Hokusai.") An art form created by townspeople, kabuki consisted of crude, bawdy skits dealing with love and romance or aspects of prostitution, an occupation in which many actors and actresses had professional experience. Performances featured elaborate costumes, song, dance, and poetry. Because actresses were thought to be corrupting the public morals, the Tokugawa government banned them from the stage in 1629. From that time on, men played all the parts. Male actors in female dress and makeup performed as seductively as possible to entice the burly samurai who thronged the theaters. Homosexuality, long accepted in Japan, was widely practiced among the samurai, who pursued the actors and spent profligately on them. According to one seventeenth-century writer, "'Youth's kabuki' began with beautiful youths being made to sing and dance, whereupon droll fools . . . had their hearts captivated

Women Weaving Often working at home, women made an enormous contribution to the Japanese silk industry: their small, delicate hands (in contrast to the larger and possibly callused hands of men) seemed suited to working with fine silk threads. In an age when public-assisted child care was not dreamed of, working mothers relied on the help of female relatives, or, as here, infants were tied to mothers' backs—an added burden for mothers and probably not ideal for the child. Notice the spinning wheel in the corner and various spindles on the floor. *(By kind permission of the East-West Gallery, New Hope, Penn.)*

and their souls stolen. . . . There were many of these men who soon had run through their fortunes."[26] Some moralists and bureaucrats complained from time to time, but the Tokugawa government decided to accept kabuki and prostitution as necessary evils. The practices provided employment, gratified the tastes of samurai and townspeople, and diverted former warriors from potential criminal and political mischief.[27] The samurai paid for their costly pleasures in the way their European counterparts did—by fleecing the peasants and borrowing from the merchants.

According to Japanese tradition, farmers deserved respect. In practice, peasants were sometimes severely oppressed and led miserable lives. It was government policy to tax them to the level of bare subsistence, and official legislation repeatedly redefined their duties. In 1649 every village in Japan received these regulations:

Peasants are people without sense or forethought. Therefore they must not give rice to their wives and children at

harvest time, but must save food for the future. They should eat millet, vegetables, and other coarse food instead of rice. Even the fallen leaves of plants should be saved as food against famine. . . . During the seasons of planting and harvesting, however, when the labor is arduous, the food taken may be a little better. . . .

They must not buy tea or sake [a fermented liquor made from rice] to drink nor must their wives.

The husband must work in the fields, the wife must work at the loom. Both must do night work. However good-looking a wife may be, if she neglects her household duties by drinking tea or sightseeing or rambling on the hillsides, she must be divorced.

Peasants must wear only cotton or hemp—no silk. They may not smoke tobacco. It is harmful to health, it takes up time, and costs money. It also creates a risk of fire.[28]

The conspicuous consumption of the upper classes led them during the seventeenth and eighteenth centuries to increase taxes from 30 or 40 percent of the rice

Individuals in Society

Katsushika Hokusai (1760–1849)

Today some of Katsushika Hokusai's paintings and prints sell for hundreds of thousands of dollars; in his lifetime, he knew mainly want and poverty. In spite of a very long and often tragic life, his art is filled with wit and humor. Although he wanted to be an artist from age six, he realized his potential and produced his greatest art only after age eighty. When dying in his eighty-ninth year, he prayed that God would give him just five more years to perfect his art.

Hokusai was born to a lower-middle-class family in Edo, but probably because he was an expendable younger child, he was put out for adoption and taken in by an important artisan family. As a boy, he did all kinds of work: running errands, engraving the backs of metal mirrors, which he later adapted to cutting woodblocks; peddling wood, books, and calendars; selling red peppers and hot sweet potatoes on the streets. A long apprenticeship in the workshop of a famous Edo woodblock artist, Katsukawa Shunsho (1726–1792), launched Hokusai's artistic career. Following Japanese tradition, he was given the formal art name Katsukawa Shunro, but he used more than fifty names before settling on the one by which we know him.

Hokusai married twice and had five children, but they brought him slight consolation. A son and a grandson implicated him in financial difficulties from which he was never able to extricate himself. As an old man at the height of his powers, when he should have been an honored citizen of Edo, he lived in a rural hovel and had to walk miles into the city, "sneaking into his publishers after dark to check upon the prints which were later to bedazzle the world." Hokusai's youngest daughter, Oci, was his only solace. An able artist herself, Oci took care of him in his long old age.

Hokusai belonged to the *ukiyo-e* ("pictures of the floating world") movement, a seventeenth- to nineteenth-century art movement devoted to recording transient everyday life, with an emphasis on leisure pursuits. He produced thousands of street scenes, as well as scenes from Japanese history, legend, and kabuki theater and scenes of the culture of rice; of women—tending children, as prostitutes, and as nuns; of sports and games; of erotic situations; of fat,

thin, and blind people; and of fauna—real and fantastic—and flora. He illustrated many novels and short stories, and his thirteen-volume *Manga* (sketches or drawings) represents a rich collection of cartoons, figure studies, and fabulous beasts. His most famous landscapes are the dramatic *Thirty-Six Views of Mount Fuji,* showing the

Hokusai self-portrait. In his later years Hokusai often used the pen name Gakyojin, "old man mad about drawing." *(Musée Guimet © R.M.N.)*

volcanic mountain in Honshu province in a wide range of seasonal and weather conditions. The richness of his imagination and the quality of his humor appealed to the Japanese bourgeoisie who bought his works. (Most people could afford his inexpensive woodblock prints.)

Hokusai's unsentimental love for animals and the natural world inspired the Victorian illustrator Beatrix Potter *(The Tale of Peter Rabbit).* His technical excellence and careful representation of ordinary life influenced the French artists Edouard Manet and Edgar Degas, and they in turn influenced Toulouse-Lautrec and Picasso. Hokusai was not just a great Japanese artist; with Michelangelo and Titian, his nearest rivals for longevity, he was one of the great artists of the world.

Questions for Analysis

1. Where did Hokusai find the models for his art?
2. Consider Hokusai's art in light of Charlie Chaplin's remark, "There are more valid facts and details in works of art than there are in history books."

Sources: James A. Michener, *The Hokusai Sketch-Books: Selections from the Manga* (Rutland, Vt., and Tokyo: Charles E. Tuttle, 1989); The *Random House Library of Painting and Sculpture.* Vol. 4: *Dictionary of Artists and Art Terms* (New York: Random House, 1981).

crop to 50 percent. Merchants who bought farm produce fixed the price of rice so low that it seemed to farmers that the more they produced, the less they earned. They found release only by flight or revolt.

After 1704 peasant rebellions were chronic. Oppressive taxation provoked eighty-four thousand farmers in the province of Iwaki to revolt in 1739. After widespread burning and destruction, their demands were met. In other instances, the shoguns ordered savage repression.

Natural disasters also added to the peasants' misery. In the 1770s fires, floods, and volcanic eruptions hit all parts of Japan. Drought and torrential rain led to terrible famines between 1783 and 1788 and again between 1832 and 1836. Taxation, disaster, and oppression often combined to make the lot of peasants one of unrelieved wretchedness.

This picture of the Japanese peasantry tells only part of the story, however. Scholarship has demonstrated that in the Tokugawa period, peasant society was "a pyramid of wealth and power . . . that rose from the tenant farmer at the bottom through small landholders to wealthy peasants at the top."[29] Agricultural productivity increased substantially, and assessed taxes were fixed, though they remained high. Peasants who im-

proved their lands and increased their yields continued to pay the same assessed tax and could pocket the surplus as profit. Their social situation accordingly improved. By the early nineteenth century, there existed a large class of relatively wealthy, educated, and ambitious peasant families who resembled the middle ranks of the warrior class.

Likewise, local economic conditions and family social status shaped the lives of Japanese women. The existence of a rich peasant's wife, daughter, or sister differed considerably from that of poor peasant women. The well-to-do seem to have made few distinctions in the early upbringing of male and female children. Regional prosperity determined the amounts of money spent on the education of both sexes in their early years. In the early nineteenth century, the regions around flourishing Edo and Kyoto spent far more than the poor Tohoku region, and parents in thriving areas devoted considerable sums on their daughters' education. Girls from middle-level peasant families may have had from two to five years of formal schooling. But they were thought incapable of learning the difficult Chinese characters, so their education focused on moral instruction intended to instill the virtue of obedience. Daughters of wealthy peasant families learned penmanship, the

A Male Prostitute   A male prostitute writes a poem as a female prostitute massages their patron's back. Notice the elaborate hairstyles, the rich material of the kimonos, and the boxes of writing instruments. *(The Fine Arts Museums of San Francisco. Achenbach Foundation for Graphic Arts purchase, 1969, 32.20)*

Chinese classics, poetry, and the proper forms of correspondence, and they rounded off their education with travel.[30]

Scholars of the Japanese family, like students of the late medieval and early modern European family (see pages 597–600), have explored the extent of premarital sex, the age at which people married, the frequency with which they married someone from another village, and the level of divorce. For Tokugawa Japan, considerable regional variations make broad generalizations dangerous; research continues. It is clear, however, that marriage linked families of equal status and class; Japanese marriages, therefore, strengthened economic and social divisions.

On the Japanese bride fell the responsibility of bringing harmony to the household. Harmony "meant that she had to refrain from quarreling with the members of her new household, do the work expected of her position, and conform to family custom."[31] Both samurai and peasant teachings stressed that "the married couple was the foundation of morality" and that the basis for harmony in the couple rested on good connubial relations. Once, the author of *Observations of Agricultural Practices,* a study of rural life, stayed overnight at a farmhouse. Newlyweds in the family went to bed early and, separated from the others by only a screen, began noisy lovemaking. "Outrageous," exclaimed the guest, whereupon the old woman of the family got angry. "Harmony between husband and wife is the basis for prosperity for the descendants. . . . I permit this coupling day and night. People who laugh at their passion are themselves outrageous. Get out!"[32] Domestic harmony and social necessity were closely linked.

A peasant wife shared with her husband responsibility for the family's economic well-being. If of poor or middling status, she worked alongside her husband in the fields, doing the routine work while he did the heavy work. If they were farm hands and worked for salaries, the wife invariably earned half or a third less than her husband. Wives of prosperous farmers never worked in the fields, but they spun silk, wove cloth, helped in any family business, and supervised the maids. Whatever their economic status, Japanese women, like women everywhere in the world, tended the children; children were women's special responsibility. The production of children, especially sons, strengthened a wife's prestige, but among well-to-do Japanese farm women, the bride's skill in prudent household management was the most desired talent.

How was divorce initiated, and how frequent was it? Customs among the noble class differed considerably from peasant practices. Widows and divorcées of the samurai aristocracy—where female chastity was the core of fidelity—were not expected to remarry. The husband alone could initiate divorce by ordering his wife to leave or by sending her possessions to her natal home. The wife could not prevent divorce or ensure access to her children.

Among the peasant classes, divorce seems to have been fairly common—at least 15 percent in the villages near Osaka in the eighteenth century. Women as well as men could begin the procedure. Wives' reasons were husbands' drunkenness, physical abuse, or failure to support the family. Many women secured divorce from temples whose function was to dissolve marriages: if a married woman entered the temple and performed its rites for three years, her marriage bond was dissolved. Sometimes Buddhist temple priests served as divorce brokers: they went to the village headman and had him force the husband to agree to a divorce. News of the coming of temple officials was usually enough to produce a letter of separation. A poor woman wanting a divorce simply left her husband's home. Opportunities for remarriage were severely limited. Divorce in samurai society carried a social stigma; it did not among the peasantry.[33]

The Tokugawa period witnessed a major transformation of agriculture, a great leap in productivity and specialization. The rural population increased, but the agricultural population did not; surplus labor was drawn to other employment and to the cities. In fact, Japan suffered an acute shortage of farm labor from 1720 to 1868. In some villages, industry became almost as important as agriculture. At Hirano near Osaka, for example, 61.7 percent of all arable land was sown in cotton. The peasants had a thriving industry: they ginned the cotton locally before transporting it to wholesalers in Osaka. In many rural places, as many peasants worked in the manufacture of silk, cotton, or vegetable oil as in the production of rice.[34] In theory, the urban commercial classes, scorned for benefiting from the misery of the peasants and the appetites of the samurai, occupied the bottom rung of the social ladder. Merchants had no political power, but they accumulated wealth, sometimes great wealth. They also demonstrated the possibility of social mobility and thus the inherent weakness of the regime's system of strict social stratification.

The commercial class grew in response to the phenomenal development of urban life. In the seventeenth century, the surplus rural population, together with underemployed samurai and the ambitious and

Hokusai Manga Hokusai produced fifteen fat volumes of *manga* (random sketches or cartoons), testimony to his incredible energy and vitality. They have been called "a record of the people of Japan" and "a major art treasure." This charming scene of children playing with toys gives the lie to the view that Hokusai was a crusty irascible old man. *(Private collection)*

adventurous, thronged to the cities. All wanted a better way of life than could be found in the dull farming villages. Japan's cities grew tremendously: Kyoto, home to the emperor and his pleasure-loving court; Edo (modern Tokyo), the political capital, with its multitudes of government bureaucrats, daimyos in alternate residence, intellectuals, and police; and Osaka, by this time the greatest commercial city in Japan, with its huge grain exchange and commercial banks. In the eighteenth century, Edo's population of almost a million represented the largest demand for goods and services in the world.

The Tokugawa shoguns turned the samurai into urban consumers by denying them military opportunities. Merchants stood ready to serve them. Towns offered all kinds of luxury goods and catered to every extravagant and exotic taste. By marketing the daimyos' grain, town merchants gave the aristocrats the cash they needed to support their rich establishments. Merchants formed guilds and banks and lent money to the samurai. Those who defaulted on their debts found themselves cut off from further credit.[35]

As the ruling samurai with their fixed stipends became increasingly poorer, the despised merchants grew steadily wealthier. By contemporary standards anywhere in the world, the Japanese "middle" class lived very well. In 1705 the shogunate confiscated the property of a merchant in Osaka "for conduct unbecoming a member of the commercial class." In fact, the confiscation was at the urging of influential daimyos and samurai who owed the merchant gigantic debts. The government seized 50 pairs of gold screens, 360 carpets, several mansions, 48 granaries and warehouses scattered around the country, and hundreds of thousands of gold pieces. This merchant possessed fabulous wealth, but other merchants also enjoyed a rich lifestyle.[36]

SUMMARY

In the eighteenth century, China experienced a rapid increase in both prosperity and population. The Qing rulers were not Chinese but Manchus from the north. Never more than 2 percent of the population, the Qing developed a centralized and authoritarian government, retaining the Ming administrative system but under Manchu supervision. Initially, this continuity brought peace and relative affluence. Over the centuries, however, the maintenance of the traditional Chinese position toward foreign "barbarians" and the refusal to trade with Westerners and to adopt Western technology weakened imperial rule and left China, in the nineteenth century, at the mercy of European mercantile and imperialistic ambitions.

In Korea, commercial expansion brought into being a new class of wealthy peasants. Chinese culture influenced the Koreans in many ways.

In 1800 Tokugawa Japan was reaping the rewards of two centuries of peace and social order. Steady economic growth and improved agricultural technology had swelled the population. The samurai had been transformed into peaceful city dwellers and civil bureaucrats. The wealth of the business classes grew, and the samurai, dependent on fixed agricultural rents or stipends in rice in a time of rising standards of living, fell into debt. The Tokugawa regime formed submissive citizens whose discipline is apparent even today.

Although the shogunate maintained a policy of national isolation and no foreign power influenced Japan's political or social life, Japan was not really cut off from outside cultural contacts. Through the port of Nagasaki, Western scientific ideas and some Western technology entered Japan in response to the persistent interest of Japanese scholars. The Japanese readily absorbed foreign technological ideas.

NOTES

1. J. K. Fairbank, *China: A New History* (Cambridge, Mass.: Harvard University Press, 1992), p. 128.
2. Ibid., p. 129.
3. Ibid., p. 133.
4. J. Gernet, *A History of Chinese Civilization,* trans. J. R. Foster (New York: Cambridge University Press, 1982), p. 391.
5. Ibid.
6. J. D. Spence, *The Search for Modern China* (New York: W. W. Norton, 1991), pp. 9–10.
7. S. J. Vainker, *Chinese Pottery and Porcelain: From Prehistory to the Present* (New York: G. Braziller, 1991), Chap. 5, pp. 134–159.
8. A. Waldron, *The Great Wall of China: From History to Myth* (New York: Cambridge University Press, 1990), p. 83.
9. Ibid., pp. 140–164.
10. Gernet, *A History of Chinese Civilization,* pp. 425–426.
11. Quoted in A. Peyrefitte, *The Immobile Empire,* trans. J. Rothschild (New York: Knopf, 1992), pp. 195–196.
12. Ibid., p. 539.
13. Quoted in Spence, *The Search for Modern China,* p. 125.
14. L. E. Eastman, *Family, Fields, and Ancestors: Constancy and Change in China's Social and Economic History, 1550–1949* (New York: Oxford University Press, 1988), p. 20.
15. M. Weidner, ed., *Flowering in the Shadows: Women in the History of Chinese and Japanese Painting* (Honolulu: University of Hawaii Press, 1990), pp. 123–154.
16. Eastman, *Family, Fields, and Ancestors.*
17. See R. C. Croizier, *Traditional Medicine in Modern China* (Cambridge, Mass.: Harvard University Press, 1968), pp. 19–27.
18. P. U. Unschuld, *Medicine in China: A History of Pharmaceutics* (Berkeley: University of California Press, 1986), p. 4.
19. Spence, *The Search for Modern China,* pp. 106–110.
20. C. J. Eckert et al., *Korea, Old and New: A History* (Cambridge, Mass.: Harvard University Press, 1980), pp. 155–164.
21. C. Nakane, "Tokugawa Society," in *Tokugawa Japan: The Social and Economic Antecedents of Modern Japan,* ed. C. Nakane and S. Ōishi (Tokyo: University of Tokyo Press, 1991), pp. 213–214.
22. Y. Sakudo, "The Management Practices of Family Business," in *Tokugawa Japan: The Social and Economic Antecedents of Modern Japan,* ed. C. Nakane and S. Ōishi (Tokyo: University of Tokyo Press, 1991), pp. 147–166.
23. D. Keene, *The Japanese Discovery of Europe, 1720–1830* (Stanford, Calif.: Stanford University Press, 1969), pp. 24–25, Chap. 4, and passim.
24. Quoted in D. H. Shively, "Bakufu Versus Kabuki," in *Studies in the Institutional History of Early Modern Japan,* ed. J. W. Hall (Princeton, N.J.: Princeton University Press, 1970), p. 236.
25. E. O. Reischauer and A. M. Craig, *Japan: Tradition and Transformation,* rev. ed. (Boston: Houghton Mifflin, 1989), pp. 104–105.
26. Quoted in Shively, "Bakufu Versus Kabuki," pp. 241–242.
27. Ibid.
28. Quoted in G. B. Sansom, *A History of Japan, 1615–1867,* vol. 3 (Stanford, Calif.: Stanford University Press, 1978), p. 99.
29. T. C. Smith, "The Japanese Village in the Seventeenth Century," in *Studies in the Institutional History of Early Modern Japan,* ed. J. W. Hall (Princeton, N.J.: Princeton University Press, 1970), p. 280.

(continued on page 712)

The Qianlong Emperor Responds to King George III

Lord George Macartney's embassy to China (1792–1794) sought to establish permanent diplomatic relations between China and Great Britain and to expand trade between the two countries. The mission failed when the emperor rejected the British proposals for the reasons that he states in the letter that follows. Although Macartney later wrote, "Nothing could be more fallacious than to judge of China by any European standard," the British refused to recognize the right of Chinese civilization to be different. The Macartney mission thus serves as a parading of the cultural clashes between the West and Asia that marked the next two centuries.

You, O King, from afar have yearned after the blessings of our civilization, and in your eagerness to come into touch with our converting influence have sent an Embassy across the sea bearing a memorial.[1] I have already taken note of your respectful spirit of submission, have treated your mission with extreme favor and loaded it with gifts. . . .

Yesterday your Ambassador petitioned my Ministers to memorialize me regarding your trade with China, but his proposal is not consistent with our dynastic usage and cannot be entertained. Hitherto, all European nations, including your own country's barbarian merchants, have carried on their trade with our Celestial Empire at Canton. Such has been the procedure for many years, although our Celestial Empire possesses all things in prolific abundance and lacks no product within its own borders. There was therefore no need to import the manufactures of outside barbarians in exchange for our own produce. But as the tea, silk and porcelain which the Celestial Empire produces, are absolute necessities to European nations and to yourselves, we have permitted, as a signal mark of favor, that foreign *hongs*[2] should be established at Canton, so that your wants might be supplied and your country thus participate in our beneficence. But your Ambassador has now put

forward new requests which completely fail to recognize the Throne's principle to "treat strangers from afar with indulgence," and to exercise a pacifying control over barbarian tribes, the world over. Moreover, our dynasty, swaying the myriad races of the globe, extends the same benevolence towards all. Your England is not the only nation trading at Canton. If other nations, following your bad example, wrongfully importune my ear with further impossible requests, how will it be possible for me to treat them with easy indulgence? Nevertheless, I do not forget the lonely remoteness of your island, cut off from the world by intervening wastes of sea, nor do I overlook your excusable ignorance of the usages of our Celestial Empire. I have consequently commanded my Ministers to enlighten your Ambassador on the subject, and have ordered the departure of the mission. . . .

Your request for a small island near Chusan,[3] where your merchants may reside and goods be warehoused, arises from your desire to develop trade. As there are neither foreign *hongs* nor interpreters in or near Chusan, where none of your ships have ever called, such an island would be utterly useless for your purposes. Every inch of the territory of our Empire is marked on the map and the strictest vigilance is exercised over it all: even tiny islets and far-lying sand-banks are clearly defined as part of the provinces to which they belong. Consider, moreover, that England is not the only barbarian land which wishes to establish . . . trade with our Empire. . . .

The next request, for a small site in the vicinity of Canton city, where your barbarian merchants may lodge or, alternatively, that there be no longer any restrictions over their movements at Aomen,[4] has arisen from the following causes. Hitherto, the barbarian merchants of Europe have had a definite locality assigned to them at Aomen for residence and trade, and have been forbidden to encroach an inch beyond the limits assigned to that locality. . . . If these restrictions were withdrawn, friction would inevitably occur between the Chinese and your barbarian subjects, and the results would militate against the benevolent regard that I feel towards you. From every point of view, therefore, it is best that the regulations now in force should continue unchanged. . . .

Regarding your nation's worship of the Lord of Heaven, it is the same religion as that of other European nations. Ever since the beginning of history, sage Emperors and wise rulers have bestowed on China a moral system and inculcated a code, which from time immemorial has been religiously observed by the myriads of my subjects.[5] There has been no hankering after heterodox doctrines. Even the European (missionary) officials in my capital are forbidden to hold intercourse with Chinese subjects; they are restricted within the limits of their appointed residences, and may not go about propagating their religion. The distinction between Chinese and barbarian is most strict, and your Ambassador's request that barbarians shall be given full liberty to disseminate their religion is utterly unreasonable.

It may be, O King, that the above proposals have been wantonly made by your Ambassador on his own responsibility, or peradventure you yourself are ignorant of our dynastic regulations and had no intention of transgressing them when you expressed these wild ideas and hopes. . . . If, after the receipt of this explicit decree, you lightly give ear to the representations of your subordinates and allow your barbarian merchants to proceed to Chêkiang and Tientsin,[6] with the object of landing and trading there, the ordinances of my Celestial Empire are strict in the extreme, and the local officials, both civil and military, are bound reverently to obey the law of the land. Should your vessels touch the shore, your merchants will assuredly never be permitted to land or to reside there, but will be subject to instant expulsion. In that event your barbarian merchants will have had a long journey for nothing. Do not say that you were not warned in due time! Tremblingly obey and show no negligence! A special mandate!

Questions for Analysis

1. Consider the basic premises of eighteenth-century European Enlightenment culture and the premises of Chinese culture.

Lord Macartney tries to impress the emperor Qianlong with an array of expensive presents. *(National Maritime Museum, London)*

2. What reasons does the emperor give for denying Britain's requests? What is the basis for the emperor's position?

3. How does the emperor view China's economic and cultural position in the world?

1. Memorandum.
2. Groups of merchants.
3. A group of islands in the East China Sea at the entrance to Hangzhou Bay.
4. A city some forty-five miles to the south of Canton, at the lower end of the Pearl (Zhu) River delta.
5. The reference is to Confucianism.
6. Two Chinese port cities.

Source: A. J. Andrea and J. H. Overfield, eds., *The Human Record: Sources of Global History*, vol. 2 (Boston: Houghton Mifflin, 1990), pp. 262–264. Reprinted from E. Backhouse and J. O. P. Brand, *Annals and Memoirs of the Court of Peking* (Boston: Houghton Mifflin, 1914), pp. 325–331.

30. A. Walthall, "The Life Cycle of Farm Women in Toku-gawa Japan," in *Recreating Japanese Women, 1600–1945,* ed. G. L. Bernstein (Berkeley: University of California Press, 1991), pp. 46–47.

31. Ibid., pp. 55–56.

32. Quoted ibid., p. 56.

33. Ibid., pp. 60–62.

34. Smith, "The Japanese Village."

35. Nakane, "Tokugawa Society."

36. G. B. Sansom, *Japan: A Cultural History,* rev. ed. (New York: Appleton-Century-Crofts, 1962), p. 472.

SUGGESTED READING

All the titles cited in the Notes represent solid scholarship; the books by Eastman, Fairbank, Spence, and Waldron are especially recommended. Fairbank was probably the most distinguished American Sinologist of the past half century. The many works of J. D. Spence also include *The Chan's Great Continent: China in Western Minds* (1998), a fascinating study of how Europeans and Americans have perceived China; *Chinese Roundabout* (1992), a collection of excellent essays on such diverse topics as Matteo Ricci, Ming life, food, medicine, and gambling, and the great scholars who shaped the study of Chinese history in North America; and *Emperor of China: Self-Portrait of Kang-Hsi* (1988), described as a "masterpiece." For Ming government, the enterprising student should also see C. Hucker, ed., *Chinese Government in Ming Times* (1969); R. Huang, *1587, A Year of No Significance: The Ming Dynasty in Decline* (1981); and *The Cambridge History of China.* Vol. 7: *The Ming Dynasty, 1368–1644* (1988). J. Spence and J. Wills, eds., *From Ming to Ch'ing: Conquest, Region, and Continuity in Seventeenth Century China* (1979), is also valuable. For the importance of commercialization in the social and economic history of the period, see T. Brook, *The Confusions of Pleasure: Commerce and Culture in Ming China* (1998). M. Elwin, *The Pattern of the Chinese Past* (1973), offers a broad but difficult survey of premodern China, with particular attention to China's failure to maintain its technological superiority.

The following titles should prove useful for serious study of the Qing period: B. S. Bartlett, *Monarchs and Ministers: The Grand Council in Mid-Ch'ing China, 1723–1820* (1991); S. Naquin and E. Rawski, *Chinese Society in the Eighteenth Century* (1987); W. Yeh-Chien, "The Sprouts of Capitalism," in *Ming and Qing Historical Studies in the People's Republic of China,* ed. F. Wakeman (1981); and S. Min-hsiung, *The Silk Industry in Ch'ing China* (1976). The latter two works are very helpful for understanding China's economic development.

For aspects of everyday life, see K. C. Chang, ed., *Food in Chinese Culture: Anthropological and Historical Perspectives* (1977); C. Clunas, *Superfluous Things: Material Culture and Social Status in Early Modern China* (1991); and P. Huard and M. Wong, *Chinese Medicine* (1972).

The literature on the history of women steadily expands. S. Mann, *Precious Records: Women in China's Long Eighteenth Century* (1997), discusses many aspects of gender relations in the period 1683–1839 and revises traditional interpretations of women in China's patriarchial society. F. Bray, *Technology and Gender: Fabrics of Power in Late Imperial China* (1997), explores the everyday life of women in the history of technology, as well as intimate aspects of women's lives such as childbearing and child rearing. J. D. Spence, *The Death of Woman Wang* (1978), is a masterpiece of historical reconstruction. P. B. Ebrey, "Women, Marriage, and the Family in Chinese History," in *Heritage of China: Contemporary Perspectives on Chinese Civilization,* ed. P. S. Ropp (1990); C. Furth, "Rethinking van Gulik: Sexuality and Reproduction in Traditional Chinese Medicine," in *Engendering China: Women, Culture, and the State,* eds. C. K. Gilmartin, G. Hershatter, L. Rofel, and T. White (1994); and V. Ng, "Ideology and Sexuality: Rape Laws in Qing China," *Journal of Asian Studies* 46 (1987): 57–70, should also prove helpful.

For Korea, R. Tennant, *A History of Korea* (1996), is an informed and highly readable survey, helpful to the tourist as well as the student. C. J. Eckert et al., *Korea, Old and New: A History* (1990), focuses on the political-cultural background from which modern Korea emerged, while Ki-baik Lee, *A New History of Korea,* trans. E. W. Wagner (1984), is a very detailed political history.

The titles by Reischauer and Craig, Sansom, and Smith cited in the Notes are highly recommended for Japan. P. Duus, *Feudalism in Japan* (1976), contrasts Japanese and European feudalism and explores the political-social background of the Tokugawa regime. H. Ooms, *Tokugawa Ideology: Early Constructs, 1570–1680* (1985), treats the Buddhist, Shinto, and Neo-Confucian intellectual foundations of the Tokugawa regime. R. P. Toby, *State and Diplomacy in Early Modern Japan: Asia in the Development of the Tokugawa Bakufu* (1983), revises the standard interpretation that Tokugawa Japan existed in virtual isolation from the rest of the world, arguing that Japan's foreign policy sought to maintain the nation's security in a hostile world. For the Japanese understanding of the West, see D. Keene, *The Japanese Discovery of Europe, 1720–1830,* rev. ed. (1969), and for the West's early perception of Japan, see D. Massarella, *A World Elsewhere: Europe's Encounter with Japan in the Sixteenth and Seventeenth Centuries* (1990). An important work of social history, H. P. Bix, *Peasant Protest in Japan, 1590–1884* (1986), discusses concepts of class, status, and exploitation and the different forms of peasant protest. The essays in C. Nakane and S. Ōishi, eds., *Tokugawa Japan: The Social and Economic Antecedents of Modern Japan,* trans. C. Totman (1991), is invaluable for the study of the beginnings of Japanese capitalism. Perhaps the best general survey of the Tokugawa period is C. Totman, *Japan Before Perry: A Short History* (1981). G. Bernstein, ed., *Recreating Japanese Women, 1600–1945* (1991), contains exciting, informed, and very readable essays on many aspects of women's lives.

23

The Revolution in Western Politics, 1775–1815

The Planting of a Liberty Tree, by Pierre Antoine Leseur. *(Giraudon/Art Resource, NY)*

The last years of the eighteenth century were a time of great upheaval in the West. A series of revolutions and revolutionary wars challenged the old order of monarchs and aristocrats. The ideas of freedom and equality, ideas that have not stopped shaping the world since that era, flourished and spread. The revolutionary era began in North America in 1775. Then in 1789 France, the most influential country in Europe, became the leading revolutionary nation. It established first a constitutional monarchy, then a radical republic, and finally a new empire under Napoleon. The armies of France also joined forces with patriots and radicals abroad in an effort to establish throughout much of Europe new governments based on new principles.

The French and American Revolutions were in many ways world-historical events, for their impact was felt far beyond Europe and long after the late eighteenth and early nineteenth centuries. The universal nature of the aspirations of the French revolutionaries in particular soon inspired revolutionary movements, such as the Haitian Revolution in the Caribbean and the independence struggles in Latin America in the early nineteenth century. And in the course of the nineteenth century the revolutionary ideals of individual liberty, representative government, and nationalism would find adherents around the world, contributing eventually to the emergence of independence movements in Asia and Africa. The modern pattern of domestic and international politics was born.

- What caused this era of revolution?
- What were the ideas and objectives of the men and women who rose up violently to undo the established system?
- What were the gains and losses for privileged groups and for ordinary people in a generation of war and upheaval?

These are the questions underlying this chapter's examination of the revolutionary era.

 ## LIBERTY AND EQUALITY

While the economic distress of the French laboring classes and France's outdated social hierarchy played a significant role in determining the course of events in France, certain concepts associated with the new worldview of the Enlightenment were also critical. Indeed, two ideas fueled the revolutionary period in both America and Europe: liberty and equality. What did eighteenth-century politicians and other people mean by liberty and equality, and why were those ideas so radical and revolutionary in their day?

The call for liberty was first of all a call for individual human rights. Even the most enlightened monarchs customarily claimed that it was their duty to regulate what people wrote and believed. Liberals of the revolutionary era protested such controls. They demanded freedom to worship, an end to censorship, and freedom from arbitrary laws and from judges who simply obeyed orders from the government. The Declaration of the Rights of Man, issued at the beginning of the French Revolution, proclaimed, "Liberty consists in being able to do anything that does not harm another person." In theory, therefore, a citizen's rights had "no limits except those which assure to the other members of society the enjoyment of these same rights." In the context of the monarchical and absolutist forms of government then dominating Europe, this was a truly radical idea.

The call for liberty was also a call for a new kind of government. Revolutionary liberals believed that the people were sovereign—that is, that the people alone had the authority to make laws limiting an individual's freedom of action. In practice this system of government meant choosing legislators who represented the people and were accountable to them.

Equality was a more ambiguous idea. Eighteenth-century liberals argued that, in theory, *all* citizens should have identical rights and civil liberties, regardless of birth. However, liberals accepted some well-established distinctions.

First, most eighteenth-century liberals were *men* of their times, and they generally shared with other men the belief that equality between men and women was neither practical nor desirable. Women played an important political role in the French Revolution at several points, but the men of the French Revolution limited formal political rights—the right to vote, to run for office, to participate in government—to men.

Second, liberals never believed that everyone should be equal economically. Quite the contrary. As Thomas Jefferson wrote in an early draft of the American Declaration of Independence (before he changed "property" to the more noble-sounding "happiness"), everyone was equal in "the pursuit of property." Jefferson and

The Marquis de Lafayette   The most famous great noble to embrace the liberal revolution is shown here directing a battle in the American Revolution. He later returned to France to champion liberty and equality there. The elegant black man is Lafayette's servant, a free man in an age of widespread slavery. *(Jean-Loup Charmet)*

Although the ideas of liberty and equality—the central ideas of classical liberalism—had firm roots in Western history dating back to ancient Greece and the Judeo-Christian tradition, classical liberalism first crystallized at the end of the seventeenth century and during the Enlightenment. Liberal ideas reflected the Enlightenment's stress on human dignity, personal liberty, and human happiness on earth and its faith in science, rationality, and progress.

Certain English and French thinkers were mainly responsible for joining the Enlightenment's concern for personal freedom and legal equality to a theoretical justification of liberal self-government. The two most important were John Locke and the baron de Montesquieu. Locke maintained that England's long political tradition rested on "the rights of Englishmen" and on representative government through Parliament. He argued that if a government oversteps its proper function of protecting the natural rights of life, liberty, and private property, it becomes a tyranny. Montesquieu was also inspired by English constitutional history. He, too, believed that powerful "intermediary groups"—such as the judicial nobility of which he was a proud member—offered the best defense of liberty against despotism.

The belief that representative institutions could defend their liberty and interests appealed powerfully to well-educated, prosperous groups, which historians have traditionally labeled as the bourgeoisie. Yet liberal ideas about individual rights and political freedom also appealed to much of the hereditary nobility, at least in western Europe. Representative government did not mean democracy, which liberal thinkers tended to equate with mob rule. Rather, they envisioned voting for representatives as being restricted to those who owned property—those with "a stake in society." England had shown the way. After 1688 it had combined a parliamentary system and considerable individual liberty with a restricted franchise and unquestionable aristocratic pre-eminence. In the course of the eighteenth century, many leading French nobles, led by a judicial nobility inspired by the doctrines of Montesquieu, were increasingly eager to follow the English example. Thus eighteenth-century liberalism found broad support among the prosperous, well-educated elites in western Europe.

What liberalism lacked from the beginning was strong popular support. At least two reasons account for the people's wary attitude. First, for common people the great questions were not theoretical and political but immediate and economic; getting enough to eat

other liberals certainly did not expect equal success in that pursuit. Great differences in wealth and income between rich and poor were perfectly acceptable to liberals. The essential point was that everyone should legally have an equal chance.

In eighteenth-century Europe, however, such equality of opportunity was a truly revolutionary idea. Society was still legally divided into groups with special privileges, such as the nobility and the clergy, and groups with special burdens, such as the peasantry. And in most countries, various middle-class groups—professionals, business people, townspeople, and craftsmen—enjoyed privileges that allowed them to monopolize all sorts of economic activity. Liberals criticized not economic inequality itself but this kind of economic inequality based on artificial legal distinctions.

was a crucial challenge. Second, some of the traditional practices and institutions that liberals wanted to abolish were dear to peasants and urban workers. Comfortable elites had already come into conflict with the people in the eighteenth century over the enclosure of common lands and the regulation of food prices. This conflict would sharpen in the revolutionary era as differences in outlook and well-being led to many misunderstandings and disappointments for both groups.

THE AMERICAN REVOLUTION (1775–1789)

The era of liberal political revolution began in the New World. The thirteen mainland colonies of British North America revolted against their home country and then succeeded in establishing a new unified government.

The American revolutionaries believed that they were demanding only the traditional rights of English men and women. But those traditional rights were liberal rights, and in the American context they had very strong democratic and popular overtones that made them quite radical. In founding a government firmly based on liberal principles, the Americans set an example that had a forceful impact on Europe and sped up political development there.

The Origins of the Revolution

The American Revolution had its immediate origins in a squabble over increased taxes. The British government had fought and decisively won the Seven Years' War on the strength of its professional army and navy. The high cost of the war to the British, however, had led to a doubling of the British national debt. Anticipating further expense defending its recently conquered western lands from native American uprisings, the British government in London set about reorganizing the empire with a series of bold, largely unprecedented measures, including the maintenance of a large army in North America after peace was restored in 1763. Moreover, they sought to exercise strict control over their newly conquered western lands and to tax the colonies directly. In 1765 the government pushed through Parliament the Stamp Act, which levied taxes on a long list of commercial and legal documents, diplomas, pamphlets, newspapers, almanacs, dice, and playing cards.

This effort to increase taxes seemed perfectly reasonable to the British. Americans were being asked to pay only a share of their own defense costs. Moreover, Americans had been paying only very low local taxes. The Stamp Act would have doubled taxes to about 2 shillings per person per year. In contrast, the British paid the highest taxes in the Western world—26 shillings per person. The colonists protested the Stamp Act vigorously and violently, however, and after rioting and boycotts against British goods, Parliament reluctantly repealed the new tax.

As the fury over the Stamp Act revealed, much more was involved than taxes. The key questions were political. To what extent could the home government reassert its power while limiting the authority of colonial legislatures and their elected representatives? Who had the right to make laws for Americans? While a troubled majority of Americans searched hard for a compromise, some radicals began to proclaim that "taxation without representation is tyranny." The British government replied that Americans were represented in Parliament, albeit indirectly (like most English people themselves), and that the absolute supremacy of Parliament could not be questioned. Many Americans felt otherwise. As John Adams of Massachusetts put it, "A Parliament of Great Britain can have no more rights to tax the colonies than a Parliament of Paris." At risk were Americans' existing liberties and time-honored institutions.

Americans had long exercised a great deal of independence and gone their own way. The colonial assemblies made the important laws. The right to vote was much more widespread than in England. In many parts of colonial Massachusetts, for example, as many as 95 percent of the adult males could vote. Moreover, greater political equality was matched by greater social and economic equality. Neither a hereditary nobility nor a hereditary serf population existed, although the slavery of the Americas consigned blacks to a legally oppressed caste. Independent farmers were the largest group in the country and set much of its tone. In short, the colonial experience had slowly formed a people who felt themselves separate and distinct from the home country. The controversies over taxation intensified those feelings of distinctiveness and separation and brought them to the fore.

The efforts of Britain to restructure its empire and increase direct control were mirrored in Latin America. There the Spanish monarchy tightened control over its colonies, exacerbating tensions between *peninsulares* (Spaniards), who monopolized the imperial bureaucracy, and *creoles* (people of Spanish blood born in the New World). These tensions set the stage for the

Toward Revolution in Boston   The Boston Tea Party was one of many angry confrontations between British officials and Boston patriots. On January 27, 1774, an angry crowd seized a British customs collector and then tarred and feathered him. This French engraving from 1784 commemorates the defiant and provocative action. *(The Granger Collection, New York)*

independence movements of the early nineteenth century (see Chapter 28).

In 1773 the dispute over taxes and representation flared up again. The British government had permitted the financially hard-pressed East India Company to ship its tea from China directly to its agents in the colonies. Thus the company secured a monopoly on the tea trade, and colonial merchants were suddenly excluded from a highly profitable business. The colonists were quick to protest.

In Boston men disguised as Indians had a rowdy "tea party" and threw the company's tea into the harbor. Parliament responded with the so-called Coercive Acts, which closed the port of Boston, curtailed local elections and town meetings, and greatly expanded the royal governor's power. County conventions in Massachusetts protested vehemently and urged that the acts be "rejected as the attempts of a wicked administration

to enslave America." Other colonial assemblies joined in the denunciations. In September 1774 the First Continental Congress met in Philadelphia, where the more radical members argued successfully against concessions to the Crown. Compromise was also rejected by the British Parliament, and in April 1775 fighting began in Massachusetts, at Lexington and Concord.

Independence

The fighting spread, and the colonists moved slowly but inevitably toward open rebellion and a declaration of independence. The uncompromising attitude of the British government and its use of German mercenaries went a long way toward dissolving long-standing loyalties to the home country and rivalries among the separate colonies. *Common Sense* (1775), a brilliant attack by the recently arrived English radical Thomas Paine (1737–1809), also mobilized public opinion in favor of independence. A runaway bestseller, Paine's tract ridiculed the idea of a small island ruling a great continent. In his call for freedom and republican government, Paine expressed Americans' growing sense of separateness and moral superiority.

On July 4, 1776, the Second Continental Congress adopted the Declaration of Independence, which boldly listed the tyrannical acts committed by King George III (r. 1760–1820) and confidently proclaimed the natural rights of mankind and the sovereignty of the American states. Sometimes called the world's greatest political editorial, the Declaration of Independence in effect universalized the traditional rights of English people and made them the rights of all mankind. It stated "that all men are created equal; that they are endowed by their Creator with certain unalienable rights; that among these are life, liberty, and the pursuit of happiness." No other American political document has ever caused such excitement, either at home or abroad. It would provide the model for a similar landmark declaration in revolutionary France.

Many American families remained loyal to Britain; many others divided bitterly. After the Declaration of Independence, the conflict often took the form of a civil war pitting patriots against those who remained loyal to the king. The Loyalists tended to be wealthy and politically moderate. Many patriots, too, were wealthy—individuals such as John Hancock and George Washington—but willingly allied themselves with farmers and artisans in a broad coalition. This coalition harassed the Loyalists and confiscated their property to help pay for the American war effort. The broad social base of the revolutionaries tended to make the liberal revolu-

The Signing of the Declaration of Independence, July 4, 1776   John Trumbull's famous painting shows the dignity and determination of America's revolutionary leaders. An extraordinarily talented group, they succeeded in rallying popular support without losing power to more radical forces in the process. *(Yale University Art Gallery)*

tion democratic. State governments extended the right to vote to many more men in the course of the war and re-established themselves as republics.

On the international scene the French sympathized with the rebels from the beginning. They wanted revenge for the humiliating defeats of the Seven Years' War. Officially neutral until 1778, they supplied the great bulk of guns and gunpowder used by the American revolutionaries, very much as foreign Great Powers have supplied weapons for "wars of national liberation" in our time. By 1777 French volunteers were arriving in Virginia, and a dashing young nobleman, the marquis de Lafayette (1757–1834), quickly became one of Washington's most trusted generals. In 1778 the French government offered a formal alliance, and in 1779 and 1780 the Spanish and Dutch declared war on Britain. Catherine the Great of Russia helped organize the League of Armed Neutrality in order to protect neutral shipping rights, which Britain refused to recognize.

Thus by 1780 Great Britain was engaged in an imperial war against most of Europe as well as the thirteen colonies. In these circumstances, and in the face of se-

vere reverses in India, in the West Indies, and at Yorktown in Virginia, a new British government decided to cut its losses. American negotiators in Paris were receptive. They feared that France wanted a treaty that would bottle up the new United States east of the Allegheny Mountains and give British holdings west of the Alleghenies to France's ally, Spain. Thus the American negotiators separated themselves from their French allies and accepted the extraordinarily favorable terms Britain offered.

By the Treaty of Paris of 1783 Britain recognized the independence of the thirteen colonies and ceded all its territory between the Allegheny Mountains and the Mississippi River to the Americans. Out of the bitter rivalries of the Old World, the Americans snatched dominion over almost half a continent.

Framing the Constitution

The liberal program of the American Revolution was consolidated by the federal Constitution, the Bill of Rights, and the creation of a national republic.

Assembling in Philadelphia in the summer of 1787, the delegates to the Constitutional Convention were determined to end the period of economic depression, social uncertainty, and very weak central government that had followed independence. In secret deliberations the delegates decided to grant the federal, or central, government important powers: regulation of domestic and foreign trade, the right to levy taxes, and the means to enforce its laws.

Strong rule would be placed squarely in the context of representative self-government. Senators and congressmen would be the lawmaking delegates of the voters, and the president of the republic would be an elected official. The central government would operate in Montesquieu's framework of checks and balances. The executive, legislative, and judicial branches would systematically balance one another. The power of the federal government would in turn be checked by the powers of the individual states.

When the draft constitution was presented to the states for ratification, a great public debate began. The opponents of the proposed constitution—the Antifederalists—charged that the new document took too much power from the individual states, made the federal government too strong, and endangered the personal liberties and individual freedoms for which they had just fought. In order to overcome these objections, the Federalists solemnly promised to spell out these basic freedoms as soon as the new constitution was adopted. The result was the first ten amendments to the Constitution, the Bill of Rights, passed in March 1789. These amendments formed an effective safeguard for the individual. Most of them—trial by jury, due process of law, right to assemble, freedom from unreasonable search—had their origins in English law and the English Bill of Rights of 1689. Others—the freedoms of speech, the press, and religion—reflected natural-law theory and the American experience.

The American Constitution and the Bill of Rights exemplified the great strengths and the limits of what came to be called classical liberalism. Liberty meant individual freedoms and political safeguards. Liberty also meant representative government but did not necessarily mean democracy, with its principle of one person, one vote. Equality—slaves excepted—meant equality before the law, not equality of political participation or economic well-being. Indeed, economic inequality was resolutely defended by the elite that framed the Constitution. The radicalism of liberal revolution in America was primarily legal and political, *not* economic or social.

THE FRENCH REVOLUTION (1789–1791)

In Europe hundreds of books, pamphlets, and articles analyzed and romanticized the American upheaval. Thoughtful Europeans noted, first of all, its enormous long-term implications for international politics. A secret report by the Venetian ambassador to Paris in 1783 stated what many felt: if the new nation survived in unity, it might "become the most formidable power in the world."[1] More generally, American independence fired the imaginations of those aristocrats who were uneasy with their hereditary privileges and those commoners who yearned for equality. Many Europeans believed that the world was advancing and that America was leading the way. As one French writer put it in 1789, "This vast continent which the seas surround will soon change Europe and the universe." The Americans had shown how rational beings could assemble together to exercise sovereignty and write a permanent constitution—a new social contract. All this gave greater reality to the concepts of individual liberty and representative government and reinforced one of the primary ideas of the Enlightenment: that a better world was possible.

No country felt the consequences of the American Revolution more directly than France. Hundreds of French officers served in America and were inspired by the experience. The most famous of these, the young and impressionable marquis de Lafayette, left home as a great aristocrat determined to fight only France's traditional foe, England. He returned with a love of liberty and firm republican convictions. French intellectuals and publicists engaged in passionate analysis of the federal and state constitutions. The American Revolution undeniably hastened upheaval in France.

Yet the French Revolution did not mirror the American example. It was more radical and more complex, more influential and more controversial, more loved and more hated. For Europeans and most of the rest of the world, it was the great revolution of the eighteenth century, *the* revolution that opened the modern era in politics.

The Breakdown of the Old Order

Like the American Revolution, the French Revolution had its immediate origins in the financial difficulties of the government. With both the high court of Paris—the Parlement—and public opinion successfully resisting increased taxes, the government was forced to finance all of its enormous expenditures during the American war with borrowed money. As a result, the national debt and the annual budget deficit soared. By the 1780s fully 50 percent of France's annual budget went for interest on the ever-increasing debt. Another 25 percent went to maintain the military, while 6 percent was absorbed by the costly and extravagant king and his court at Versailles. Less than 20 percent of the entire national budget was available for the productive functions of the state, such as transportation and general administration. This was an impossible financial situation.

One way out would have been for the government to declare partial bankruptcy, forcing its creditors to accept greatly reduced payments on the debt. Both the Spanish and the French monarchies had done this in earlier times. By the 1780s, however, the French debt was being held by an army of aristocratic and bourgeois creditors, and the French monarchy, though absolute in theory, had become far too weak for such a drastic and unpopular action.

Nor could the king and his ministers, unlike modern governments, print money and create inflation to cover their deficits. Unlike England and Holland, which had far larger national debts relative to their populations, France had no central bank, no paper currency, and no means of creating credit. French money was good gold coin. Therefore, when a depressed economy and a lack of public confidence made it increasingly difficult for the government to obtain new gold loans in 1786, it had no alternative but to try increasing taxes. But since France's tax system was unfair and out-of-date, increased revenues were possible only through fundamental reforms. Such reforms, which would affect all groups in France's complex and fragmented society, opened a Pandora's box of social and political demands.

Legal Orders and Social Realities

As in the Middle Ages, France's 25 million inhabitants were still legally divided into three orders, or *estates*—the Roman Catholic clergy, the nobility, and everyone else. As the nation's first estate, the clergy numbered about 100,000 and had important privileges. It owned about 10 percent of the land and paid only a "voluntary gift," rather than regular taxes, to the government every five years. Moreover, the church levied a tax (the tithe) on landowners, which averaged somewhat less than 10 percent. Much of the church's income was actually drained away from local parishes by political appointees and worldly aristocrats at the top of the church

The Three Estates   In this political cartoon from 1789 a woman of the third estate struggles under the burden of a nun and an aristocrat. The third estate is being represented in a new way as the true nation, oppressed by the parasitic clergy and nobility. *(Musée Carnavalet/Photo Bulloz)*

hierarchy—to the intense dissatisfaction of the poor parish priests.

The second legally defined estate consisted of some 400,000 noblemen and noblewomen. The nobles owned outright about 25 percent of the land and were taxed very lightly. Moreover, nobles continued to enjoy certain manorial rights, or privileges of lordship, that dated back to medieval times and allowed them to tax the peasantry for their own profit. They did this by means of exclusive rights to hunt and fish, village monopolies on baking bread and pressing grapes for wine, fees for justice, and a host of other "useful privileges." In addition, nobles had "honorific privileges," such as the right to precedence on public occasions and the right to wear a sword. These rights conspicuously proclaimed the nobility's legal superiority and exalted social position.

Everyone else was a commoner, legally a member of the third estate. A few commoners—prosperous merchants or lawyers and officials—were well educated and rich, and might even buy up manorial rights as profitable investments. Many more commoners were urban artisans and unskilled day laborers. The vast majority of the third estate consisted of the peasants and agricultural workers in the countryside. Thus the third estate was a conglomeration of vastly different social groups united only by their shared legal status as distinct from the nobility and clergy.

In discussing the long-term origins of the French Revolution, historians have long focused on growing tensions between the nobility and the comfortable members of the third estate, usually known as the *bourgeoisie,* or middle class. A dominant historical interpretation, which has held sway for at least two generations, maintains that the bourgeoisie was basically united by economic position and class interest. Aided by a general economic expansion, the middle class grew rapidly in the eighteenth century, tripling to about 2.3 million persons, or about 8 percent of France's population. Increasing in size, wealth, culture, and self-confidence, this rising bourgeoisie became progressively exasperated by archaic "feudal" laws and customs that restrained the economy and their needs and aspirations. As a result, the French bourgeoisie eventually rose up to lead the entire third estate in a great social revolution, a revolution that destroyed feudal privileges and established a capitalist order based on individualism and a market economy.

In recent years a flood of new research has challenged these accepted views and prompted a heated scholarly debate. Above all, revisionist historians have questioned the existence of a growing social conflict between a progressive capitalistic bourgeoisie and a reactionary feudal nobility in eighteenth-century France. Rather than standing as unified blocs against each other, nobility and bourgeoisie—both fragmented and ridden with internal rivalries—formed two parallel social ladders increasingly linked together at the top by wealth, marriage, and Enlightenment culture.

Revisionist historians stress three developments in particular. First, the nobility remained a fluid and relatively open order. Throughout the eighteenth century substantial numbers of successful commoners continued to seek and obtain noble status through government service and purchase of expensive positions conferring nobility. Thus the nobility continued to attract the wealthiest members of the middle class and to permit social mobility. Second, key sections of the nobility and the prosperous bourgeoisie formed together the core of the book-hungry Enlightenment public. Both groups saw themselves as forming part of the educated elite and standing well above the common

people—the peasants and the urban poor. Both groups were also equally liberal until revolution actually began, and they generally supported the judicial opposition to the government. Third, the nobility and the bourgeoisie were not really at odds in the economic sphere. Both looked to investment in land and to government service as their preferred activities, and the goal of the merchant capitalist was to gain enough wealth to live nobly as a large landowner. At the same time, wealthy nobles often acted as aggressive capitalists, investing especially in mining, metallurgy, and foreign trade.

The revisionists have clearly shaken the interpretation of the bourgeoisie and the nobility as inevitably locked in growing conflict before the French Revolution. But in stressing the similarities between the two groups, especially at the top, revisionists have also reinforced the view, long maintained by historians, that the Old Regime had ceased to correspond with social reality by the 1780s. Legally, society was still based on rigid orders inherited from the Middle Ages. But France had moved far toward being a society based on wealth and education, where an emerging elite that included both aristocratic and bourgeois notables was frustrated by a bureaucratic monarchy that continued to claim the right to absolute power.

The Formation of the National Assembly

The Revolution was under way by 1787, though no one could have realized what was to follow. Spurred by a depressed economy and falling tax receipts, Louis XVI's minister of finance convinced the king to call an assembly of notables to gain support for a general tax on all landed property. The assembled notables, mainly important noblemen and high-ranking clergy, responded that such sweeping tax changes required the approval of the Estates General, the representative body of all three estates, which had not met since 1614.

Facing imminent bankruptcy, the king tried to reassert his authority. He dismissed the notables and established new taxes by decree. In stirring language the Parlement of Paris promptly declared the royal initiative null and void. When the king tried to exile the judges, a tremendous wave of protest swept the country. Frightened investors also refused to advance more loans to the state. Finally, in July 1788, a beaten Louis XVI bowed to public opinion and called for a spring session of the Estates General. Absolute monarchy was collapsing.

What would replace it? Throughout the unprecedented election campaign of 1788 and 1789 that question excited France. All across the country clergy,

The Oath of the Tennis Court   This painting, based on an unfinished work by Jacques-Louis David (1748–1825), enthusiastically celebrates the revolutionary rupture of June 20, 1789. Locked out of their assembly hall at Versailles and joined by some sympathetic priests, the delegates of the third estate have moved to an indoor tennis court and are swearing never to disband until they have written a new constitution and put France on a firm foundation. *(Musée Carnavalet/Photo Bulloz)*

nobles, and commoners met together in their respective orders to draft petitions for change and to elect their respective delegates to the Estates General. The local assemblies of the clergy chose two-thirds of the delegates from among the poorer parish priests, who were commoners by birth. Among the nobles, already badly split by wealth and education, a conservative majority was drawn from the poorer and more numerous provincial nobility. But fully one-third of the nobility's representatives were liberals committed to major changes.

As for the third estate, there was great popular participation in the elections. Almost all male commoners ages twenty-five years and older had the right to vote. Still, most of the representatives finally selected were well-educated, prosperous lawyers and government officials. There were no delegates elected from the great mass of laboring poor, an exclusion that would encourage the peasants and also the urban artisans to intervene directly and dramatically at numerous points in the Revolution, as we shall see.

The petitions for change coming from the three estates showed a surprising degree of consensus on most issues. There was general agreement that royal absolutism should give way to constitutional monarchy, in which the Estates General, meeting regularly, should pass all laws and taxes; that individual liberties should be guaranteed by law; and that general reforms, such as the abolition of internal tariffs, should be introduced to promote economic development. The striking similarities in the grievance petitions of the clergy, nobility, and third estate reflected the broad commitment of France's educated elite to liberalism.

Yet an increasingly bitter quarrel undermined this consensus during the intense electoral campaign. *How* would the Estates General vote, and precisely *who* would lead in the political reorganization that was generally desired? The Estates General of 1614 had sat as three separate houses. Any action had required the agreement of at least two branches, a requirement that had virtually guaranteed control by the nobility and the clergy. The aristocratic Parlement of Paris ruled that the Estates General should once again sit separately. Certain middle-class intellectuals and some liberal nobles demanded instead a single assembly dominated by representatives of the third estate. The government agreed that the third estate should have as many delegates as the clergy and the nobility combined. When it then rendered this act meaningless by upholding voting by separate order, middle-class leaders saw fresh evidence of an aristocratic conspiracy.

The Estates General opened in May 1789 at Versailles with twelve hundred delegates. The estates were almost immediately deadlocked. Delegates of the third estate refused to transact any business until the king ordered the clergy and nobility to sit with them in a single body. Finally, after a six-week war of nerves, the third estate on June 17 voted to call itself the National Assembly. On June 20 the delegates of the third estate, excluded from their hall because of "repairs," moved to a large indoor tennis court. There they swore the Oath of the Tennis Court, pledging not to disband until they had written a new constitution.

The indecisive king's actions were then somewhat contradictory. On June 23 he made a conciliatory speech urging reforms to a joint session and ordered the three estates to meet together. Then, apparently following the advice of relatives and court nobles that he dissolve the Estates General by force, the king called an army of eighteen thousand troops toward Versailles. On July 11 he dismissed his finance minister and his other more liberal ministers. Having resigned himself to bankruptcy, Louis XVI belatedly sought to reassert his historic "divine right" to rule. The middle-class delegates and their allies from the liberal nobility had done their best, but they were resigned to being disbanded at bayonet point. One third-estate delegate reassured a worried colleague, "You won't hang—you'll only have to go back home."[2]

The Revolt of the Poor and the Oppressed

While the delegates of the third estate pressed for symbolic equality with the nobility and clergy in a single legislative body at Versailles, economic hardship gripped the common people of France in a tightening vise. Grain was the basis of the diet of ordinary people in the eighteenth century, and in 1788 the harvest had been extremely poor. The price of bread, which had been rising gradually since 1785, began to soar. By July 1789 it had climbed as high as 8 sous per pound in the provinces. In Paris, where bread was regularly subsidized by the government in an attempt to prevent pop-

ular unrest, the price rose to 4 sous, a price at which a laborer with a wife and three children had to spend most of his wages to buy the family's bread.

Harvest failure and high bread prices unleashed a classic economic depression of the preindustrial age. With food so expensive and with so much uncertainty, the demand for manufactured goods collapsed, resulting in thousands of artisans and small traders being thrown out of work. By the end of 1789 almost half of the French people were in need of relief. In Paris the situation was so desperate in July 1789 that perhaps 150,000 of the city's 600,000 people were without work.

Against this background of dire poverty and excitement generated by the political crisis, the people of Paris entered decisively onto the revolutionary stage. They believed in a general, though ill-defined, way that the economic distress had human causes. They believed that they should have steady work and enough bread at fair prices to survive. Specifically, they feared that the dismissal of the king's moderate finance minister would put them at the mercy of aristocratic landowners and grain speculators. Stories like that quoting the wealthy financier Joseph François Foulon as saying that the poor "should eat grass, like my horses" and rumors that the king's troops would sack the city began to fill the air. Angry crowds formed, and passionate voices urged action. On July 13 the people began to seize arms for the defense of the city, and on July 14 several hundred of the most determined people marched to the Bastille to search for gunpowder.

The governor of the medieval fortress-prison refused to hand over the powder, panicked, and ordered his men to fire, killing ninety-eight people attempting to enter. Cannon were brought to batter the main gate, and fighting continued until the prison surrendered. The governor of the prison was later hacked to death, and his head was stuck on a pike and paraded through the streets. The next day a committee of citizens appointed the marquis de Lafayette commander of the city's armed forces. Paris was lost to the king, who was forced to recall the finance minister and disperse his troops. The popular uprising had saved the National Assembly.

As the delegates resumed their long-winded and inconclusive debates at Versailles, the people in the countryside sent them a radical and unmistakable message. Sparked by rumors of vagabonds and outlaws roaming the countryside, called the Great Fear by contemporaries, peasants all across France began to rise in spontaneous, violent, and effective insurrection against their lords. Neither middle-class landowners nor the larger, more prosperous farmers were spared. In some areas

Storming the Bastille   This representation by an untrained contemporary artist shows civilians and members of the Paris militia—the "conquerors of the Bastille"—on the attack. This successful action had enormous practical and symbolic significance, and July 14 has long been France's most important national holiday. *(Musée Carnavalet/Photo Hubert Josse)*

peasants reinstated traditional village practices, undoing recent enclosures and reoccupying old common lands. Peasants seized forests, and taxes went unpaid. Rebellion raced through the countryside.

Faced with chaos yet afraid to call on the king to restore order, some liberal nobles and middle-class delegates at Versailles responded to peasant demands with a surprise maneuver on the night of August 4, 1789. The duke of Aiguillon, one of France's greatest noble landowners, declared that

in several provinces the whole people forms a kind of league for the destruction of the manor houses, the ravaging of the lands, and especially for the seizure of the archives where the title deeds to feudal properties are kept. It seeks to throw off at last a yoke that has for many centuries weighted it down.[3]

He urged equality in taxation and the elimination of feudal dues. In the end, all the old exactions imposed

on the peasants—serfdom where it still existed, village monopolies, the right to make peasants work on the roads, and a host of other dues—were abolished. They never paid feudal dues again. Thus the French peasantry, which already owned about 30 percent of all the land, achieved a great and unprecedented victory in the early days of revolutionary upheaval. Henceforth, the French peasants would seek mainly to protect and consolidate their triumph, becoming a force for order and stability.

A Limited Monarchy

The National Assembly moved forward. On August 27, 1789, it issued the Declaration of the Rights of Man, which stated, "Men are born and remain free and equal in rights." The declaration also maintained that mankind's natural rights are "liberty, property, security, and resistance to oppression." As for law, "it is an expression of the general will; all citizens have the right to concur personally or through their representatives in its formation. . . . Free expression of thoughts and opinions is one of the most precious rights of mankind: every citizen may therefore speak, write, and publish freely." In short, this clarion call of the liberal revolutionary ideal guaranteed equality before the law, representative government for a sovereign people, and individual freedom. This revolutionary credo, only two pages long, was propagandized throughout France and the rest of Europe and around the world.

Moving beyond general principles to draft a constitution proved difficult. The questions of how much power the king should retain led to another deadlock. Once again the decisive answer came from the poor—in this instance, the poor women of Paris.

Women customarily bought the food and managed the poor family's slender resources. In Paris great numbers of women also worked for wages. In the general economic crisis, increasing unemployment and hunger put tremendous pressure on household managers, and the result was another popular explosion.

On October 5 some seven thousand desperate women marched the twelve miles from Paris to Versailles to demand action. This great crowd invaded the National Assembly, "armed with scythes, sticks and pikes." One tough old woman directing a large group of younger women defiantly shouted into the debate, "Who's that talking down there? Make the chatterbox shut up. That's not the point: the point is that we want bread."[4] Hers was the genuine voice of the people, essential to any understanding of the French Revolution.

The women invaded the royal apartments, slaughtered some of the royal bodyguards, and furiously searched for the queen, Marie Antoinette, who was widely despised for her lavish spending and supposedly immoral behavior. "We are going to cut off her head, tear out her heart, fry her liver, and that won't be the end of it," they shouted, surging through the palace in a frenzy. It seems likely that only the intervention of Lafayette and the National Guard saved the royal family. But the only way to calm the disorder was for the king to go and live in Paris, as the crowd demanded. With this victory the women clearly emerged as a major and enduring element in the Parisian revolutionary crowd.[5]

The National Assembly followed the king to Paris, and the next two years, until September 1791, saw the consolidation of the liberal revolution. Under middle-class leadership, the National Assembly abolished the French nobility as a legal order and pushed forward with the creation of a constitutional monarchy, which Louis XVI reluctantly agreed to accept in July 1790. In the final constitution the king remained the head of state, but all lawmaking power was placed in the hands of the National Assembly, elected by the economic upper half of French males.

New laws broadened women's rights to seek divorce, to inherit property, and to obtain financial support from fathers for illegitimate children. But women were not allowed to vote or hold political office. The great majority of comfortable, well-educated males in the National Assembly believed that women should be limited to child raising and domestic duties and should leave politics and most public activities to men. The delegates to the National Assembly also believed that excluding women from politics would free the political system from the harmful effects of the sexual intrigue common at court; and pure, home-focused wives would raise the high-minded sons needed to govern and defend the nation.

The National Assembly replaced the complicated patchwork of historic provinces with eighty-three departments of approximately equal size. It replaced the jumble of weights and measures that varied from province to province with the simple, rational metric system in 1793. It prohibited monopolies, guilds, and workers' combinations, and it abolished barriers to trade within France in the name of economic liberty. Thus the National Assembly applied the critical spirit of the Enlightenment to reform France's laws and institutions completely.

The National Assembly also nationalized the Catholic church's property and abolished monasteries as useless relics of a distant past. The government sold all former church property in an attempt to put the state's finances on a solid footing. Peasants eventually purchased much of this land when it was subdivided. The purchases strengthened their attachment to the revolutionary state. These actions, however, brought the new government into conflict with the Catholic church and with many sincere Christians, especially in the countryside.

Many delegates to the National Assembly, imbued with the rationalism and skepticism of the eighteenth-century philosophes, harbored a deep distrust of popular piety and "superstitious religion." They were interested in the church only to the extent that they could seize its land and use the church to strengthen the new state. Thus they established a national church and a Civil Constitution of the clergy, requiring priests to be chosen by voters. In the face of widespread resistance, the National Assembly then required the clergy to take a loyalty oath to the new government. The Catholic clergy became just so many more employees of the state. The pope formally condemned this attempt to subjugate the church. Only half of the priests of France took the oath of allegiance, and confusion and hostility among French Catholics were pervasive. The attempt to remake the Catholic church, like the National Assembly's abolition of guilds and workers' combinations, sharpened the division between the educated classes and the common people that had been emerging in the eighteenth century. This policy toward the church was the revolutionary government's first important failure.

WORLD WAR AND REPUBLICAN FRANCE (1791–1799)

When Louis XVI accepted the final version of the completed constitution in September 1791, a young and still obscure provincial lawyer and member of the National Assembly named Maximilien Robespierre (1758–1794) evaluated the work of two years and concluded, "The Revolution is over." Robespierre was both right and wrong. He was right in the sense that the most constructive and lasting reforms were in place. Nothing substantial in the way of liberty and equality would be gained in the next generation. He was wrong in the sense that a much more radical stage lay ahead. New heroes and new ideologies were to emerge in revolutionary wars and international conflict.

Foreign Reactions and the Beginning of War

The outbreak and progress of the French Revolution produced great excitement and a sharp division of opinion in Europe and the United States. Liberals and radicals saw a mighty triumph of liberty over despotism. In Great Britain especially, they hoped that the French example would lead to a fundamental reordering of the political system that had placed Parliament in the hands of the aristocracy and a few wealthy merchants, with the great majority of people having little say in the government. Conservative leaders such as Edmund Burke (1729–1797) were deeply troubled by the aroused spirit of reform. In 1790 Burke published *Reflections on the Revolution in France,* one of the great intellectual defenses of European conservatism. Defending inherited privileges, he glorified the unrepresentative Parliament and predicted that thoroughgoing reform like that occurring in France would lead only to chaos and tyranny. Burke's work sparked vigorous debate.

One passionate rebuttal came from a young writer in London, Mary Wollstonecraft (1759–1797). Born into the middle class, Wollstonecraft was schooled in adver-

Mary Wollstonecraft   Painted by an unknown artist when Mary Wollstonecraft was thirty-two and writing her revolutionary *Vindication of the Rights of Woman,* this portrait highlights the remarkable strength of character that energized Wollstonecraft's brilliant intellect. *(The Board of Trustees of the National Museums and Galleries on Merseyside, Walker Art Gallery)*

sity by a mean-spirited father who beat his wife and squandered his inherited fortune. Determined to be independent in a society that generally expected women of her class to become homebodies and obedient wives, she struggled for years to earn her living as a governess and teacher—practically the only acceptable careers for single, educated women—before attaining success as a translator and author. Interested in politics and believing that "a desperate disease requires a powerful remedy" in Great Britain as well as France, Wollstonecraft was incensed by Burke's book. She immediately wrote a blistering, widely read attack, *A Vindication of the Rights of Man* (1790).

Then, fired up on controversy and commitment, she made a daring intellectual leap. She developed for the first time the logical implications of natural-law philosophy in her masterpiece, *A Vindication of the Rights of Woman* (1792). To fulfill the still-unrealized potential of the French Revolution and to eliminate the many-sided sexual inequality she had felt so keenly, she demanded that

the Rights of Women be respected . . . [and] JUSTICE for one-half of the human race. . . . It is time to effect a revolution in female manners, time to restore to them their lost dignity, and make them, as part of the human species, labor, by reforming themselves, to reform the world.

Setting high standards for women, Wollstonecraft advocated rigorous coeducation, which would make women better wives and mothers, good citizens, and even economically independent people. Women could manage businesses and enter politics if only men would give them the chance. Men themselves would benefit from women's rights, for Wollstonecraft believed that "the two sexes mutually corrupt and improve each other."[6] Wollstonecraft's analysis testified to the power of the Revolution to excite and inspire outside France. Paralleling ideas put forth independently in France by Olympe de Gouges (1748–1793), a self-taught writer and woman of the people (see the feature "Listening to the Past: Revolution and Women's Rights" on pages 742–743), Wollstonecraft's work marked the birth of the modern women's movement for equal rights, and it was ultimately very influential.

The kings and nobles of continental Europe, who had at first welcomed the Revolution in France as weakening a competing power, began to feel threatened. At their courts they listened to the diatribes of great court nobles who had fled France and were urging intervention in France's affairs. When Louis XVI and Marie Antoinette were arrested and returned to Paris after trying unsuccessfully to slip out of France in June 1791, the monarchs of Austria and Prussia, in the Declaration of Pillnitz, declared their willingness to intervene in France in certain circumstances.

But the crowned heads of Europe did not deter the revolutionary spirit in France. When the National Assembly disbanded, it decreed that none of its members would be eligible for election to the new Legislative Assembly. This meant that when the new representative body convened in October 1791, it had a different character. The great majority of the legislators were still prosperous, well-educated, middle-class men, but they were younger and less cautious than their predecessors. Loosely allied and known as Jacobins, after the name of their political club, the representatives to the Legislative Assembly were passionately committed to liberal revolution.

The Jacobins increasingly lumped "useless aristocrats" and "despotic monarchs" together and easily whipped themselves into a patriotic fury with bombastic oratory. If the courts of Europe were attempting to incite a war of kings against France, then "we will incite a war of people against kings. . . . Ten million Frenchmen, kindled by the fire of liberty, armed with the sword, with reason, with eloquence would be able to change the face of the world and make the tyrants tremble on their thrones."[7] Only Robespierre and a very few others argued that people would not welcome liberation at the point of a gun. Such warnings were brushed aside. France would "rise to the full height of her mission," as one deputy urged. In April 1792 France declared war on Francis II, the Habsburg monarch.

France's crusade against tyranny went poorly at first. Prussia joined Austria in the Austrian Netherlands (present-day Belgium), and French forces broke and fled at their first encounter with armies of this First Coalition. The road to Paris lay open, and it is possible that only conflict between the eastern monarchs over the division of Poland saved France from defeat.

Military reversals and Austro-Prussian threats caused a wave of patriotic fervor to sweep France. In this supercharged wartime atmosphere rumors of treason by the king and queen spread in Paris. Once again, the common people of Paris acted decisively. On August 10, 1792, a revolutionary crowd captured the royal palace at the Tuileries after heavy fighting. The king and his family fled for their lives to the nearby Legislative Assembly, which suspended the king from all his functions, imprisoned him, and called for a new National Convention to be elected by universal male suffrage. Monarchy in France was on its deathbed, mortally wounded by war and popular upheaval.

The Second Revolution

The fall of the monarchy marked a rapid radicalization of the Revolution, a phase that historians often call the "second revolution." Louis's imprisonment was followed by the September Massacres. Wild stories seized the city that imprisoned counter-revolutionary aristocrats and priests were plotting with the allied invaders. As a result, angry crowds invaded the prisons of Paris and summarily slaughtered half of the men and women they found. In late September 1792 the new, popularly elected National Convention proclaimed France a republic.

The republic sought to create a new popular culture to ensure its future and fashioned compelling symbols that broke with the past and glorified the new order. It adopted a brand-new revolutionary calendar, which eliminated saints' days and renamed the days and the months after the seasons of the year. The republic energetically promoted broad, open-air, democratic festivals that sought to redirect the people's traditional enthusiasm for Catholic religious celebrations to secular holidays. Instilling republican virtue and a love of nation, these spectacles were less successful in villages than in cities, where popular interest in politics was greater and Catholicism was weaker.

All of the members of the National Convention were Jacobins and republicans, and the great majority continued to come from the well-educated middle class. But the Convention was increasingly divided into two bitterly competitive groups—the Girondists, named after a department in southwestern France, and the Mountain, led by Robespierre and another young lawyer, Georges Jacques Danton. The Mountain was so called because its members sat on the uppermost left-hand benches of the assembly hall.

This division was clearly apparent after the National Convention overwhelmingly convicted Louis XVI of treason. By a single vote 361 of the 720 members of the Convention then unconditionally sentenced him to death in January 1793. Louis died with tranquil dignity

on the newly invented guillotine. One of his last statements was "I am innocent and shall die without fear. I would that my death might bring happiness to the French, and ward off the dangers which I foresee."[8]

Both the Girondists and the Mountain were determined to continue the "war against tyranny." After stopping the Prussians at the indecisive Battle of Valmy on September 20, 1792, republican armies successfully invaded Savoy and the German Rhineland. To the north the revolutionary armies won their first major battle at Jemappes and by November 1792 were occupying the entire Austrian Netherlands. Everywhere they went, French armies of occupation chased the princes, "abolished feudalism," and found support among some peasants and middle-class people.

But the French armies also lived off the land, requisitioning food and supplies and plundering local treasures. The liberators looked increasingly like foreign invaders. In February 1793 the National Convention, at war with Austria and Prussia, declared war on Britain, Holland, and Spain as well. Republican France was now at war with almost all of Europe, a great war that would last almost without interruption until 1815.

The End of Louis XVI   The executioner holds up the severed head of the dead king for the soldiers and the crowd to see in the large, central square of Paris, which is now known as the Place de la Concorde. The execution of the king was a victory for the radicals in Paris, but it horrified Europe's monarchs and conservatives and strengthened their opposition to the French Revolution. *(Musée Carnavalet/Laurie Platt Winfrey, Inc.)*

As the forces of the First Coalition drove the French from the Austrian Netherlands, peasants in western France revolted against being drafted into the army. They were supported and encouraged in their resistance by devout Catholics, royalists, and foreign agents.

In Paris the quarrelsome National Convention found itself locked in a life-and-death political struggle between the Girondists and the Mountain. Both groups hated privilege and wanted to temper economic liberalism with social concern. Yet personal hatreds ran deep. The Girondists feared a bloody dictatorship by the Mountain, and the Mountain was no less convinced that the more moderate Girondists would turn to conservatives and even royalists in order to retain power. With the middle-class delegates so bitterly divided, the laboring poor of Paris emerged as the decisive political factor.

The laboring men and women of Paris always constituted—along with the peasantry in the summer of 1789—the elemental force that drove the Revolution forward. It was they who had stormed the Bastille, marched on Versailles, driven the king from the Tuileries, and carried out the September Massacres. The petty traders and laboring poor were often known as the *sans-culottes,* "without breeches," because the men wore trousers instead of the knee breeches of the aristocracy and the solid middle class. The immediate interests of the sans-culottes were mainly economic, and in the spring of 1793 the economic situation was as bad as the military situation. Rapid inflation, unemployment, and food shortages were again weighing heavily on poor families.

By the spring of 1793 sans-culottes men and women, encouraged by the so-called angry men, were demanding radical political action to guarantee them their daily bread. At first the Mountain joined the Girondists in violently rejecting these demands. But in the face of military defeat, peasant revolt, and hatred of the Girondists, Robespierre's group joined with sans-culottes activists in the city government to engineer a popular uprising, which forced the Convention to arrest thirty-one Girondist deputies for treason on June 2. All power passed to the Mountain.

Robespierre and others from the Mountain joined the recently formed Committee of Public Safety, to which the Convention had given dictatorial power to deal with the national emergency. These developments in Paris triggered revolt in leading provincial cities, such as Lyons and Marseilles, where moderates denounced Paris and demanded a decentralized government. The peasant revolt spread, and the republic's armies were driven back on all fronts. By July 1793 defeat appeared imminent.

Total War and the Terror

A year later, in July 1794, the Austrian Netherlands and the Rhineland were once again in the hands of conquering French armies, and the First Coalition was falling apart. This remarkable change of fortune was due to the revolutionary government's success in harnessing, for perhaps the first time in history, the explosive forces of a planned economy, revolutionary terror, and modern nationalism in a total war effort.

Robespierre and the Committee of Public Safety advanced with implacable resolution on several fronts in 1793 and 1794. First, in an effort to save revolutionary France, they continued to collaborate with the fiercely patriotic and democratic sans-culottes, who retained the common people's traditional faith in fair prices and a moral economic order, distrusting wealthy capitalists and all aristocrats. Thus Robespierre and his coworkers established, as best they could, a planned economy with egalitarian social overtones. Rather than let supply and demand determine prices, the government decreed the maximum allowable prices for a host of key products. Though the state was too weak to enforce all its price regulations, it did fix the price of bread in Paris at levels the poor could afford. Bakers were permitted to make only the "bread of equality"—a brown bread made of a mixture of all available flours. White bread and pastries were outlawed as frivolous luxuries. The poor of Paris may not have eaten well, but at least they ate.

They also worked, mainly to produce arms and munitions for the war effort. Craftsmen and small manufacturers were told what to produce and when to deliver. The government nationalized many small workshops and requisitioned raw materials and grain from the peasants. Seldom if ever before had a government attempted to manage an economy so thoroughly. The second revolution and the ascendancy of the sans-culottes had produced an embryonic emergency socialism, which thoroughly frightened Europe's propertied classes and had great influence on the subsequent development of socialist ideology.

Second, while radical economic measures supplied the poor with bread and the armies with weapons, the Reign of Terror (1793–1794) was solidifying the home front. Special revolutionary courts responsible only to Robespierre's Committee of Public Safety tried rebels and "enemies of the nation" for political crimes. Drawing on popular, sans-culottes support, these local courts

The Last Roll Call   Prisoners sentenced to death by revolutionary courts listen to an official solemnly reading the names of those selected for immediate execution. After being bound, the prisoners will ride standing up in a small cart through the streets of Paris to the nearby guillotine. As this painting highlights, both women and men were executed for political crimes under the Terror. *(Mansell/Time Inc.)*

ignored normal legal procedures and judged severely. Some 40,000 French men and women were executed or died in prison. Another 300,000 suspects crowded the prisons.

Robespierre's Reign of Terror was one of the most controversial phases of the French Revolution. Most historians now believe that the Reign of Terror was not directed against any single class but was a political weapon directed impartially against all who might oppose the revolutionary government. For many Europeans of the time, however, the Reign of Terror represented a terrifying perversion of the generous ideals that had existed in 1789.

The third and perhaps most decisive element in the French republic's victory over the First Coalition was its ability to continue drawing on the explosive power of patriotic dedication to a national state and a national mission. This is the essence of modern nationalism, and it was something new in history. With a common language and a common tradition newly reinforced by the ideas of popular sovereignty and democracy, the French people were stirred by a common loyalty. The shared danger of foreign foes and internal rebels unified all

classes in a heroic defense of the nation. Everyone had to participate in the national effort. According to a famous decree of August 23, 1793:

The young men shall go to battle and the married men shall forge arms. The women shall make tents and clothes, and shall serve in the hospitals; children shall tear rags into lint. The old men will be guided to the public places of the cities to kindle the courage of the young warriors and to preach the unity of the Republic and the hatred of kings.

Like the wars of religion, war in 1793 was a crusade, a life-and-death struggle between good and evil. This war, however, was fought for a secular, rather than a religious, ideology.

Because all unmarried young men were subject to the draft, the French armed forces swelled to a million men in fourteen armies. A force of this size was unprecedented in the history of European warfare. The soldiers were led by young, impetuous generals who had often risen rapidly from the ranks and personified the opportunities the Revolution seemed to offer gifted sons of the people. These generals used mass attacks at bayonet point by their highly motivated forces to overwhelm

May 5, 1789	Estates General convenes at Versailles.
June 17, 1789	Third estate declares itself the National Assembly.
June 20, 1789	Oath of the Tennis Court is sworn.
July 14, 1789	Storming of the Bastille occurs.
July–August 1789	Great Fear ravages the countryside.
August 4, 1789	National Assembly abolishes feudal privileges.
August 27, 1789	National Assembly issues Declaration of the Rights of Man.
October 5, 1789	Women march on Versailles and force royal family to return to Paris.
November 1789	National Assembly confiscates church lands.
July 1790	Civil Constitution of the Clergy establishes a national church. Louis XVI reluctantly agrees to accept a constitutional monarchy.
June 1791	Royal family is arrested while attempting to flee France.
August 1791	Austria and Prussia issue the Declaration of Pillnitz.
April 1792	France declares war on Austria.
August 1792	Parisian crowd attacks the palace and takes Louis XVI prisoner.
September 1792	September Massacres occur. National Convention declares France a republic and abolishes monarchy.
1793–1794	Reign of Terror darkens Paris and the provinces.
January 1793	Louis XVI is executed.
February 1793	France declares war on Britain, Holland, and Spain. Revolts take place in some provincial cities.
March 1793	Bitter struggle occurs in the National Convention between Girondists and the Mountain.
April–June 1793	Robespierre and the Mountain organize the Committee of Public Safety and arrest Girondist leaders.
September 1793	Price controls are instituted to aid the sans-culottes and mobilize the war effort.
Spring 1794	French armies are victorious on all fronts.
July 1794	Robespierre is executed. Thermidorian reaction begins.
1795	Economic controls are abolished, and suppression of the sans-culottes begins.
1795–1799	Directory rules.
1797	Napoleon defeats Austrian armies in Italy and returns triumphant to Paris.
1798	Austria, Great Britain, and Russia form the Second Coalition against France.
1799	Napoleon overthrows the Directory and seizes power.

the enemy. By the spring of 1794 French armies were victorious on all fronts. The republic was saved.

The Thermidorian Reaction and the Directory (1794–1799)

The success of the French armies led Robespierre and the Committee of Public Safety to relax the emergency economic controls, but they extended the political Reign of Terror. Their lofty goal was increasingly an ideal democratic republic where justice would reign and there would be neither rich nor poor. Their lowly means were unrestrained despotism and the guillotine, which struck down any who might seriously question the new order. In March 1794, to the horror of many sans-culottes, Robespierre's Terror wiped out many of the angry men, who had been criticizing Robespierre for being soft on the wealthy. Two weeks later several of Robespierre's long-standing collaborators, led by the famous orator Danton, marched up the steps to the guillotine. A strange assortment of radicals and moderates in the Convention, knowing that they might be next, organized a conspiracy. They howled down Robespierre when he tried to speak to the National Convention on 9 Thermidor (July 27, 1794). On the following day, it was Robespierre's turn to be shaved by the revolutionary razor.

As Robespierre's closest supporters followed their leader, France unexpectedly experienced a thorough reaction to the despotism of the Reign of Terror. In a general way this "Thermidorian reaction" recalled the early days of the Revolution. The respectable middle-class lawyers and professionals who had led the liberal revolution of 1789 reasserted their authority, drawing support from their own class, the provincial cities, and the better-off peasants. The National Convention abolished many economic controls, printed more paper currency, and let prices rise sharply. And all the while wealthy bankers and newly rich speculators celebrated the sudden end of the Terror with an orgy of self-indulgence and ostentatious luxury, an orgy symbolized by the shockingly low-cut gowns that quickly became the rage among their wives and mistresses.

The collapse of economic controls, coupled with runaway inflation, hit the working poor very hard. The gaudy extravagance of the rich wounded their pride. The sans-culottes accepted private property, but they believed passionately in small business, decent wages, and economic justice. Increasingly disorganized after Robespierre purged radical leaders, the common people of Paris finally revolted against the emerging new order in early 1795. The Convention quickly used the army to suppress these insurrections. For the first time since the fall of the Bastille, uprisings by Parisians were effectively put down by a government that made no concessions to the poor. In the face of all these catastrophes, the revolutionary fervor of the laboring poor in Paris finally subsided.

In villages and small towns there arose a great cry for peace and a turning toward religion, especially from women, who had seldom experienced the political radicalization of sans-culottes women in the big cities. Instead, these women had frequently and tenaciously defended their culture and religious beliefs. As the frustrated government began to retreat on the religious question from 1796 to 1801, the women of rural France brought back the Catholic church and the open worship of God. In the words of a leading historian, these women worked constructively and effectively for a return to a normal and structured lifestyle:

Peacefully but purposefully, they sought to re-establish a pattern of life punctuated by a pealing bell and one in which the rites of passage—birth, marriage, and death—were respected and hallowed. The state had intruded too far and women entered the public arena to push it back and won. It was one of the most resounding political statements made by the populace in the entire history of the Revolution.[9]

As for the middle-class members of the National Convention, in 1795 they wrote yet another constitution, which they believed would guarantee their economic position and political supremacy. The mass of the population voted only for electors, who were men of means. Electors then elected the members of a reorganized Legislative Assembly, as well as key officials throughout France. The new assembly also chose a five-man executive—the Directory.

The Directory continued to support French military expansion abroad. War was no longer so much a crusade as a means to meet ever-present, ever-unsolved economic problems. Large, victorious French armies reduced unemployment at home and were able to live off the territories they conquered and plundered.

The unprincipled action of the Directory reinforced widespread disgust with war and starvation, and the national elections of 1797 returned a large number of conservative and even monarchist deputies who favored peace at almost any price. The members of the Directory, fearing for their skins, used the army to nullify the elections and began to govern dictatorially. Two years later Napoleon Bonaparte ended the Directory in a coup d'état and substituted a strong dictatorship for a weak one. The effort to establish stable representative government had failed.

THE NAPOLEONIC ERA (1799–1815)

For almost fifteen years, from 1799 to 1814, France was in the hands of a keen-minded military dictator of exceptional ability. One of history's most fascinating leaders, Napoleon Bonaparte (1769–1821) realized the need to put an end to civil strife in France in order to create unity and consolidate his rule. And he did. But Napoleon saw himself as a man of destiny, and the glory of war and the dream of universal empire proved irresistible.

Napoleon's Rule of France

In 1799 when he seized power, young General Napoleon Bonaparte was a national hero. Born in Corsica into an impoverished noble family in 1769, Napoleon left home and became a lieutenant in the French artillery in 1785. After a brief and unsuccessful adventure fighting for Corsican independence in 1789, he returned to France as a French patriot and a dedicated revolutionary. Rising rapidly in the new army, Napoleon was placed in command of French forces in Italy and won brilliant victories there in 1796 and 1797. His next campaign, in Egypt, was a failure, but Napoleon made his way back to France before the fiasco was generally known. His reputation remained intact.

Napoleon soon learned that some prominent members of the Legislative Assembly were plotting against the Directory. The dissatisfaction of these plotters stemmed not so much from the fact that the Directory was a dictatorship as from the fact that it was a weak dictatorship. Ten years of upheaval and uncertainty had made firm rule much more appealing than liberty and popular politics to these disillusioned revolutionaries. They wanted a strong military ruler, and the flamboyant thirty-year-old Napoleon was ideal. Thus the conspirators and Napoleon organized a takeover. On November 9, 1799, they ousted the Directors, and the following day soldiers disbanded the Legislative Assembly at bayonet point. Napoleon was named first consul of the republic, and a new constitution consolidating his position was overwhelmingly approved in a plebiscite in December 1799. Republican appearances were maintained, but Napoleon was already the real ruler of France.

The essence of Napoleon's domestic policy was to use his great and highly personal powers to maintain order and put an end to civil strife. He did so by working out unwritten agreements with powerful groups in France. In 1800, Napoleon and the leading bankers of Paris established the privately owned Bank of France, which loyally served the interests of both the state and the financial oligarchy. Napoleon's bargain with the solid middle class was codified in the Civil Code of 1804, which reasserted two of the fundamental principles of the liberal and essentially moderate revolution of 1789: equality of all male citizens before the law and absolute security of wealth and private property. Napoleon's defense of the new economic order also appealed successfully to the peasants, who had gained both land and status from the revolutionary changes.

At the same time, Napoleon accepted and strengthened the position of the French bureaucracy. Building on the solid foundations that revolutionary governments had inherited from the Old Regime, he perfected a thoroughly centralized state. A network of prefects, subprefects, and centrally appointed mayors depended on Napoleon and served him well. Napoleon also granted amnesty to émigrés on the condition that they return to France and take a loyalty oath. Members of this returning elite soon ably occupied many high posts in the expanding centralized state. Napoleon also created a new imperial nobility in order to reward his most talented generals and officials.

Napoleon's great skill in gaining support from important and potentially hostile groups is illustrated by his treatment of the Catholic church in France. Personally uninterested in religion, Napoleon wanted to heal the religious division so that a united Catholic church in France could serve as a bulwark of order and social peace. After long and arduous negotiations, Napoleon and Pope Pius VII (r. 1800–1823) signed the Concordat of 1801. The pope gained for French Catholics the precious right to practice their religion freely, but Napoleon gained political power: his government now nominated bishops, paid the clergy, and exerted great influence over the church in France.

The domestic reforms of Napoleon's early years were his greatest achievement. Much of his legal and administrative reorganization has survived in France to this day. More generally, Napoleon's domestic initiatives gave the great majority of French people a welcome sense of order and stability. And when Napoleon added the glory of military victory, he rekindled a spirit of national unity.

Order and unity had their price: Napoleon's authoritarian rule. Women, who had often participated in revolutionary politics, lost many of the gains they had made in the 1790s under the new Napoleonic Code. Under the law women were dependents of either their fathers or their husbands. Indeed, Napoleon and his advisers aimed at re-establishing a "family monarch,"

The Coronation of Napoleon, 1804 (detail)   In this grandiose painting by Jacques-Louis David, Napoleon prepares to crown his beautiful wife, Josephine, in an elaborate ceremony in Notre Dame Cathedral. Napoleon, the ultimate upstart, also crowned himself. Pope Pius VII, seated glumly behind the emperor, is reduced to being a spectator. *(Louvre © Photo R.M.N.)*

where the power of the husband and father was as absolute over the wife and the children as that of Napoleon was over his subjects.

Free speech and freedom of the press—fundamental rights of the liberal revolution enshrined in the Declaration of the Rights of Man—were continually violated. Napoleon constantly reduced the number of newspapers in Paris. By 1811 only four were left, and they were little more than organs of government propaganda. The occasional elections were a farce.

These changes in the law were part of the creation of a police state in France. Since Napoleon was usually busy making war, this task was largely left to Joseph Fouché, an unscrupulous opportunist who had earned a reputation for brutality during the Reign of Terror. As minister of police, Fouché organized a ruthlessly efficient spy system, which kept thousands of citizens under continual police surveillance. People suspected of

subversive activities were arbitrarily detained, placed under house arrest, or even consigned to insane asylums. After 1810 political suspects were held in state prisons, as they had been during the Terror. There were about twenty-five hundred such political prisoners in 1814.

Napoleon's Wars and Foreign Policy

Napoleon was above all a military man, and a great one. After coming to power in 1799, he sent peace feelers to Austria and Great Britain, the two remaining members of the Second Coalition, which had been formed against France in 1798. When these overtures were rejected, French armies led by Napoleon decisively defeated the Austrians. Once more, as in 1797, the British were alone—and war-weary, like the French. Still seeking to consolidate his regime domestically, Napoleon concluded the Treaty of Amiens with Great Britain in

1802. France remained in control of Holland, the Austrian Netherlands, the west bank of the Rhine, and most of the Italian peninsula. The Treaty of Amiens was clearly a diplomatic triumph for Napoleon, and peace with honor and profit increased his popularity at home.

In 1802 Napoleon was secure but unsatisfied. Ever a romantic gambler as well as a brilliant administrator, he could not contain his power drive. He aggressively threatened British interests in the eastern Mediterranean and tried to restrict British trade with all of Europe. Deciding to renew war with Britain in May 1803, Napoleon began making preparations to invade England. But Great Britain remained dominant on the seas. When Napoleon tried to bring his Mediterranean fleet around Gibraltar to northern France, a combined French and Spanish fleet was, after a series of mishaps, virtually annihilated by Lord Nelson at the Battle of Trafalgar on October 21, 1805. A cross-Channel invasion of England was henceforth impossible. Renewed fighting had its advantages, however, for the first consul used the wartime atmosphere to have himself proclaimed emperor in late 1804.

Austria, Russia, and Sweden joined with Britain to form the Third Coalition against France shortly before the Battle of Trafalgar. Both Alexander I of Russia and Francis II of Austria were convinced that Napoleon was a threat to their interests and to the European balance of power. Yet the Austrians and the Russians were no match for Napoleon, who scored a brilliant victory over them at the Battle of Austerlitz in December 1805. Alexander I decided to pull back, and Austria accepted large territorial losses in return for peace as the Third Coalition collapsed.

Victorious at Austerlitz, Napoleon proceeded to reorganize the German states to his liking. He established by decree the German Confederation of the Rhine, a union of fifteen German states minus Austria, Prussia, and Saxony. Naming himself "protector" of the confederation, Napoleon firmly controlled western Germany. His intervention in German affairs alarmed the Prussians, who mobilized their armies after more than a decade of peace with France. Napoleon attacked and won two more brilliant victories in October 1806, at Jena and Auerstädt. The war with Prussia, now joined by Russia, continued into the spring. After Napoleon's larger armies won another victory, Alexander I of Russia wanted peace. In the subsequent treaties of Tilsit in 1807, Prussia lost half of its population, while Russia accepted Napoleon's reorganization of western and central Europe. Alexander also promised to enforce Napoleon's recently decreed economic blockade against British goods.

Napoleon now saw himself as the emperor of Europe and not just of France. The so-called Grand Empire he built had three parts. The core, or first part, was an ever-expanding France, which by 1810 included Belgium, Holland, parts of northern Italy, and much German territory on the east bank of the Rhine. Beyond French borders were a number of dependent satellite kingdoms, on the thrones of which Napoleon placed (and replaced) the members of his large family. The third part comprised the independent but allied states of Austria, Prussia, and Russia. Both satellites and allies were expected after 1806 to support Napoleon's continental system and cease trade with Britain.

The impact of the Grand Empire on the peoples of Europe was considerable. In the areas incorporated into France and in the satellites (Map 23.1), Napoleon introduced many French laws, abolishing feudal dues and serfdom where French revolutionary armies had not already done so. Some of the peasants and middle class benefited from these reforms. Yet while he extended progressive measures to his cosmopolitan empire, Napoleon had to put the prosperity and special interests of France first in order to safeguard his power base. Levying heavy taxes in money and men for his armies, Napoleon came to be regarded more as a conquering tyrant than as an enlightened liberator.

The first great revolt occurred in Spain. In 1808 a coalition of Catholics, monarchists, and patriots rebelled against Napoleon's attempts to make Spain a French satellite with a Bonaparte as its king. French armies occupied Madrid, but the foes of Napoleon fled to the hills and waged uncompromising guerrilla warfare. Resistance to French imperialism was growing. Yet Napoleon pushed on, determined to hold his empire together.

In 1810, when the Grand Empire was at its height, Britain still remained at war with France, helping the guerrillas in Spain and Portugal. Napoleon's continental system, organized to exclude British goods from the European continent and force that "nation of shopkeepers" to its knees, was a failure. Instead, it was France that suffered from Britain's counter-blockade, which created hard times for French artisans and the middle class. Perhaps looking for a scapegoat, Napoleon turned on Alexander I of Russia, who had been giving only lukewarm support to Napoleon's war of prohibitions against British goods.

Napoleon's invasion of Russia began in June 1812 with a force that eventually numbered 600,000, probably the largest force yet assembled in a single army. Only one-third of this force was French, however; nationals of all the satellites and allies were drafted into the operation. (See the feature "Individuals in Society:

Goya: The Third of May 1808   This great painting screams in outrage at the horrors of war, which Goya witnessed in Spain. Spanish rebels, focused on the Christ-like figure at the center, are gunned down by anonymous French soldiers, grim forerunners of modern death squads and their atrocities. *(Museo del Prado, Madrid)*

Jakob Walter, German Draftee with Napoleon.") Originally planning to winter in the Russian city of Smolensk if Alexander did not sue for peace, Napoleon reached Smolensk and recklessly pressed on toward Moscow. The great Battle of Borodino that followed was a draw, and the Russians retreated in good order. Alexander ordered the evacuation of Moscow, which then burned, and he refused to negotiate. Finally, after five weeks in the burned-out city, Napoleon ordered a retreat. That retreat was one of the great military disasters in history. The Russian army and the Russian winter cut Napoleon's army to pieces. When the frozen remnants staggered into Poland and Prussia in December, 370,000 men had died, and another 200,000 had been taken prisoner.[10]

Leaving his troops to their fate, Napoleon raced to Paris to raise yet another army. When he refused to accept a France reduced to its historical size—the proposal offered by Austria's foreign minister, Prince Klemens von Metternich—Austria and Prussia deserted Napoleon and joined with Russia and Great Britain in forming the Quadruple Alliance. All across Europe patriots called for a "war of liberation" against Napoleon's oppression, and the well-disciplined regular armies of Napoleon's enemies closed in for the kill. Less than a month later, on April 4, 1814, a defeated, abandoned Napoleon abdicated his throne. After this unconditional abdication, the victorious allies granted Napoleon the island of Elba off the coast of Italy as his own tiny state.

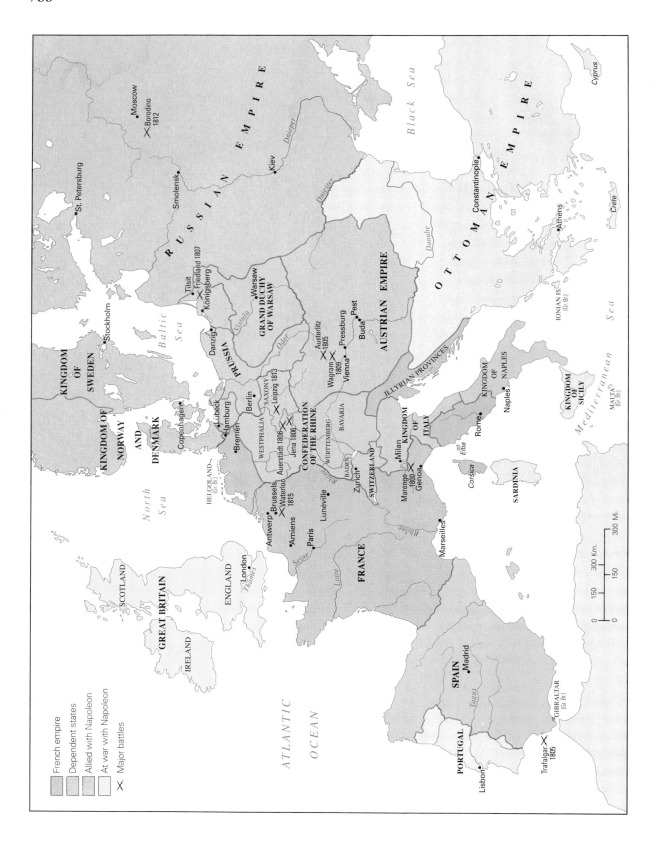

Moscow
•Borodino 1812

St. Petersburg

RUSSIAN EMPIRE

BLACK Sea

Dnieper

Kiev•

Smolensk•

Constantinople•

OTTOMAN EMPIRE

Danube

Athens•

Cyprus

Crete

IONIAN IS.
(Gr. Br.)

KINGDOM OF SWEDEN

KINGDOM OF NORWAY AND DENMARK

Stockholm•

Baltic Sea

Tilsit•
•Friedland 1807
•Königsberg

Danzig•

PRUSSIA

Vistula

Warsaw•

GRAND DUCHY OF WARSAW

Oder

Pest•
•Pressburg
Austerlitz 1805
Buda•

AUSTRIAN EMPIRE

Wagram 1809
Vienna•

ILLYRIAN PROVINCES

KINGDOM OF NAPLES

Naples•

KINGDOM OF SICILY

MALTA (Gr. Br.)

Mediterranean Sea

Copenhagen•

Lübeck•
Hamburg•
Bremen•
•Berlin

WESTPHALIA

SAXONY
Leipzig 1813

Auerstädt 1806
Jena 1806

CONFEDERATION OF THE RHINE

BAVARIA

WÜRTEMBERG

Rhine

BADEN

Zurich•

SWITZERLAND

KINGDOM OF ITALY

Milan•

Marengo 1800
Genoa•

Rome•

Elba

Corsica

SARDINIA

HELGOLAND (Gr. Br.)

North Sea

Antwerp•
•Brussels
•Waterloo 1815

Amiens•

Lunéville•

Paris•

Seine

Loire

FRANCE

Marseilles•

Rhône

ATLANTIC OCEAN

SCOTLAND

GREAT BRITAIN

ENGLAND
•London
Thames

IRELAND

SPAIN

•Madrid

Tagus

PORTUGAL

Lisbon•

GIBRALTAR (Gr. Br.)

Trafalgar 1805

French empire
Dependent states
Allied with Napoleon
At war with Napoleon
Major battles

300 Mi.

300 Km.

150

150

0

0

THE NAPOLEONIC ERA

November 1799	Napoleon overthrows the Directory.
December 1799	French voters overwhelmingly approve Napoleon's new constitution.
1800	Napoleon founds the Bank of France.
1801	France defeats Austria and acquires Italian and German territories in the Treaty of Lunéville. Napoleon signs the Concordat with the pope.
1802	France signs the Treaty of Amiens with Britain.
December 1804	Napoleon crowns himself emperor.
October 1805	Britain defeats the French and Spanish fleets at the Battle of Trafalgar.
December 1805	Napoleon defeats Austria and Russia at the Battle of Austerlitz.
1807	Napoleon redraws the map of Europe in the treaties of Tilsit.
1810	The Grand Empire is at its height.
June 1812	Napoleon invades Russia with 600,000 men.
Fall–Winter 1812	Napoleon makes a disastrous retreat from Russia.
March 1814	Russia, Prussia, Austria, and Britain form the Quadruple Alliance to defeat France.
April 1814	Napoleon abdicates and is exiled to Elba.
February–June 1815	Napoleon escapes from Elba and rules France until he is defeated at the Battle of Waterloo.

The allies also agreed to the restoration of the Bourbon dynasty. The new monarch, Louis XVIII (r. 1814–1824), issued the Constitutional Charter, which accepted many of France's revolutionary changes and guaranteed civil liberties. Indeed, the Charter gave France a constitutional monarchy roughly similar to that established in 1791, although far fewer people had the right to vote for representatives to the resurrected Chamber of Deputies. Moreover, in an attempt to strengthen popular support for Louis XVIII's new government, France was treated leniently by the allies, who agreed to meet in Vienna to work out a general peace settlement (see pages 777–779).

Louis XVIII—old, ugly, and crippled by gout—totally lacked the glory and magic of Napoleon. Hearing of political unrest in France and diplomatic tensions in Vienna, Napoleon staged a daring escape from Elba in February 1815. Landing in France, he issued appeals for support and marched on Paris with a small band of followers. Many veterans responded to the call. Louis XVIII fled, and once more Napoleon took command. But Napoleon's gamble was a desperate long shot, for the allies were united against him. At the end of a frantic period known as the Hundred Days, they crushed

MAP 23.1 Napoleonic Europe in 1810   Only Great Britain remained at war with Napoleon at the height of the Grand Empire. Many British goods were smuggled through Helgoland, a tiny but strategic British possession off the German coast.

Individuals in Society

Jakob Walter, German Draftee with Napoleon

In January 1812 a young German named Jakob Walter (1788–1864) was recalled to active duty in the army of Württemberg, a Napoleonic satellite in the Confederation of the Rhine. Stonemason and common draftee, Walter later wrote a rare enlisted man's account of the Russian campaign, a personal history that testified to the terrible price paid by the common people for a generation of war.

Napoleon's invasion of Russia was a desperate gamble from the beginning. French armies were accustomed to living off well-developed local economies, but this strategy did not work well in poor, sparsely populated eastern Europe. Scrounging for food dominated Walter's recollection of earlier fighting in Poland, and now, in 1812, the food situation was much worse. Crossing into Russia, Walter and his buddies found the nearby villages half-burned and stripped of food. Running down an occasional hog, they greedily tore it to pieces and ate it raw. Strangled by dust and thirst and then pelted for days by cold rain, the Great Army raced to catch the retreating Russians and force them into battle. When the famished troops stopped, the desperate search for food began.

In mid-August Walter's company helped storm the city of Smolensk in heavy fighting. From there onward the road was littered with men, horses, and wagons, and all the towns and villages had been burned by the Russians to deprive the enemy of supplies. Surrounded by all these horrors, Walter almost lost his nerve, but he drew on his Catholic faith and found the courage "to go on trustingly to meet my fate."[1] Fighting at the great Battle of Borodino, "where the death cries and the shattering gunfire seemed a hell," he and the allied troops entered a deserted and fire-damaged Moscow in mid-September. But food, liquor, and fancy silks were there for the taking, and the weather was warm.

On October 18 the reprieve was over, and the retreating allied infantrymen re-entered hell. Yet Walter, "still alert and spirited," was asked by an officer to be his attendant and received for his services a horse to ride. The horse proved a lifesaver. It allowed Walter to forage for food farther off the highway, to flee from approaching Cossacks, and to conserve his strength as vicious freezing winter weather set in. Yet food found at great peril could be quickly lost. Once Walter fought off some French soldiers with the help of some

The retreat from Moscow; detail of engraving by G. Küstler. Soldiers strip the sick of their blankets and boots, leaving them to die in the cold. *(New York Public Library, Slavonic Division)*

nearby Germans, who then robbed him of his bread. But what, he reflected later, could one expect? The starving men had simply lost their humanity. "I myself could look cold-bloodedly into the lamenting faces of the wounded, the freezing, and the burned," he wrote. When his horse was stolen as he slept, he silently stole someone else's. Struggling on in this brutal every-man-for-himself environment, Walter reached Poland in late December and hobbled home, a rare survivor. He went on to recover, marry, and have ten children.

Why did Jakob Walter survive? Pure chance surely played a large part. So did his robust constitution and street smarts. His faith in God also provided strength to meet each day's challenges. The beautiful vision of returning home and seeing his family offered equal encouragement. Finally, he lacked hatred and animosity, whether toward the Russians, the French, or whomever. He accepted the things he could not change and concentrated on those he could.

Questions for Analysis

1. Why was obtaining food such a problem for Jakob Walter and his fellow soldiers?

2. What impresses you most about Walter's account of the Russian campaign?

1. Jakob Walter, *The Diary of a Napoleonic Foot Soldier,* ed. with an introduction by M. Raeff (New York: Penguin Books, 1993), p. 53. Also pp. 54, 66.

his forces at Waterloo on June 18, 1815, and imprisoned him on the rocky island of St. Helena, far off the western coast of Africa. Old Louis XVIII returned again—"in the baggage of the allies," as his detractors scornfully put it—and recommenced his reign. The allies now dealt more harshly with the apparently incorrigible French (see page 779). And Napoleon, doomed to suffer crude insults at the hands of sadistic English jailers on distant St. Helena, could take revenge only by writing his memoirs, skillfully nurturing the myth that he had been Europe's revolutionary liberator, a romantic hero whose lofty work had been undone by oppressive reactionaries. An era had ended.

SUMMARY

The French Revolution left a compelling and many-sided political legacy. This legacy included, most notably, liberalism, assertive nationalism, radical democratic republicanism, embryonic socialism, and self-conscious conservatism. It also left a rich and turbulent history of electoral competition, legislative assemblies, and even mass politics. Thus the French Revolution and conflicting interpretations of its significance presented a whole range of political options and alternative visions of the future. For this reason it was truly *the* revolution in modern European politics.

The revolution that began in America and spread to France was a liberal revolution. Revolutionaries on both sides of the Atlantic wanted to establish civil liberties and equality before the law within the framework of representative government, and they succeeded. In France liberal nobles and an increasingly class-conscious middle class overwhelmed declining monarchical absolutism and feudal privilege, thanks to the intervention of the common people—the sans-culottes and the peasants. France's new political system reflected a social structure based increasingly on wealth and achievement rather than on tradition and legal privileges.

After the establishment of the republic, the radical phase of the Revolution during the Terror, and the fall of Robespierre, the educated elites and the solid middle class reasserted themselves under the Directory. And though Napoleon sharply curtailed representative institutions and individual rights, he effectively promoted the reconciliation of old and new, of centralized bureaucracy and careers open to talent, of noble and bourgeois in a restructured property-owning elite. Louis XVIII had to accept the commanding position of this restructured elite, and in granting representative government and civil liberties to facilitate his restoration to the throne in 1814, he submitted to the rest of the liberal triumph of 1789 to 1791. The liberal core of the French Revolution had successfully survived a generation of war and dictatorship.

The lived experience of the French Revolution and the wars that went with it exercised a pervasive influence on politics and the political imagination in the nineteenth century, not only in France but also throughout Europe and even the rest of the world. The radical legacy of the embattled republic of 1793 and 1794, with its sans-culottes democratic republicanism and its egalitarian ideology and embryonic socialism, would inspire republicans, democrats, and early socialists. Indeed, revolutionary upheaval encouraged generations of radicals to believe that political revolution might remake society and even create a new humanity. At the same time, there was a legacy of a powerful and continuing reaction to the French Revolution and to aggressive French nationalism. Monarchists and traditionalists believed that 1789 had been a tragic mistake. They concluded that democratic republicanism and sans-culottes activism led only to war, class conflict, and savage dictatorship. Conservatives and many comfortable moderates were profoundly disillusioned by the revolutionary era. They looked with nostalgia toward the supposedly ordered world of benevolent monarchy, firm government, and respectful common people.

NOTES

1. Quoted in R. R. Palmer, *The Age of the Democratic Revolution,* vol. 1 (Princeton, N.J.: Princeton University Press, 1959), p. 239.
2. Quoted in G. Lefebvre, *The Coming of the French Revolution* (New York: Vintage Books, 1947), p. 81.
3. P. H. Beik, ed., *The French Revolution* (New York: Walker, 1970), p. 89.
4. G. Pernoud and S. Flaisser, eds., *The French Revolution* (Greenwich, Conn.: Fawcett, 1960), p. 61.
5. O. Hufton, *Women and the Limits of Citizenship in the French Revolution* (Toronto: University of Toronto Press, 1992), pp. 3–22.
6. Quotations from Wollstonecraft are drawn from E. W. Sunstein, *A Different Face: The Life of Mary Wollstonecraft* (New York: Harper & Row, 1975), pp. 208, 211; and H. R. James, *Mary Wollstonecraft: A Sketch* (London: Oxford University Press, 1932), pp. 60, 62, 69.
7. Quoted in L. Gershoy, *The Era of the French Revolution, 1789–1799* (New York: Van Nostrand, 1957), p. 150.
8. Pernoud and Flaisser, *The French Revolution,* pp. 193–194.
9. Hufton, *Women and the Limits of Citizenship in the French Revolution,* p. 130.

(continued on page 744)

LISTENING TO THE
PAST

Revolution and Women's Rights

The 1789 Declaration of the Rights of Man was a revolutionary call for legal equality, representative government, and individual freedom. But the new rights were strictly limited to men; Napoleon tightened further the subordination of French women.

Among those who saw the contradiction in granting supposedly universal rights to only half the population was Marie Gouze (1748–1793), known to history as Olympe de Gouges. The daughter of a provincial butcher and peddler, she pursued a literary career in Paris after the death of her husband. Between 1790 and 1793 she wrote more than two dozen political pamphlets under her new name. De Gouges's great work was her "Declaration of the Rights of Woman" (1791). Excerpted here, de Gouges's manifesto went beyond the 1789 Rights of Man. It called on males to end their oppression of women and give women equal rights. A radical on women's issues, de Gouges sympathized with the monarchy and criticized Robespierre in print. Convicted of sedition, she was guillotined in November 1793.

. . . Man, are you capable of being just? . . . Tell me, what gives you sovereign empire to oppress my sex? Your strength? Your talents? Observe the Creator in his wisdom . . . and give me, if you dare, an example of this tyrannical empire. Go back to animals, consult the elements, study plants . . . and distinguish, if you can, the sexes in the administration of nature. Everywhere you will find them mingled; everywhere they cooperate in harmonious togetherness in this immortal masterpiece.

Man alone has raised his exceptional circumstances to a principle. . . . [H]e wants to command as a despot a sex which is in full possession of its intellectual faculties; he pretends to enjoy the Revolution and to claim his rights to equality in order to say nothing more about it.

DECLARATION OF THE RIGHTS OF WOMAN AND THE FEMALE CITIZEN

For the National Assembly to decree in its last sessions, or in those of the next legislature:

Preamble

Mothers, daughters, sisters and representatives of the nation demand to be constituted into a national assembly. Believing that ignorance, omission, or scorn for the rights of woman are the only causes of public misfortunes and of the corruption of governments, [the women] have resolved to set forth in a solemn declaration the natural, inalienable, and sacred rights of woman. . . .

. . . the sex that is as superior in beauty as it is in courage during the sufferings of maternity recognizes and declares in the presence and under the auspices of the Supreme Being, the following Rights of Woman and of Female Citizens:

I. Woman is born free and lives equal to man in her rights. Social distinctions can be based only on the common utility.

II. The purpose of any political association is the conservation of the natural and imprescriptible rights of woman and man; these rights are liberty, property, security, and especially resistance to oppression.

III. The principle of all sovereignty rests essentially with the nation, which is nothing but the union of woman and man. . . .

IV. Liberty and justice consist of restoring all that belongs to others; thus, the only limits on the exercise of the natural rights of woman are perpetual male tyranny; these limits are to be reformed by the laws of nature and reason.

V. Laws of nature and reason proscribe all acts harmful to society. . . .

VI. The law must be the expression of the general will; all female and male citizens must contribute either personally or through their representatives to its formation; it must be the same for all: male and female citizens, being equal in the eyes of the law, must be equally admitted to all honors, positions, and public employment according to their capacity and without other distinctions besides those of their virtues and talents.

VII. No woman is an exception; she is accused, arrested, and detained in cases determined by law. Women, like men, obey this rigorous law.

VIII. The law must establish only those penalties that are strictly and obviously necessary. . . .

IX. Once any woman is declared guilty, complete rigor is [to be] exercised by the law.

X. No one is to be disquieted for his very basic opinions; woman has the right to mount the scaffold; she must equally have the right to mount the rostrum, provided that her demonstrations do not disturb the legally established public order.

XI. The free communication of thoughts and opinions is one of the most precious rights of woman, since that liberty assures the recognition of children by their fathers. Any female citizen thus may say freely, I am the mother of a child which belongs to you, without being forced by a barbarous prejudice to hide the truth. . . .

XIII. For the support of the public force and the expenses of administration, the contributions of woman and man are equal; she shares all the duties . . . and all the painful tasks; therefore, she must have the same share in the distribution of positions, employment, offices, honors, and jobs. . . .

XIV. Female and male citizens have the right to verify, either by themselves or through their representatives, the necessity of the public contribution. This can only apply to women if they are granted an equal share, not only of wealth, but also of public administration. . . .

XV. The collectivity of women, joined for tax purposes to the aggregate of men, has the right to demand an accounting of his administration from any public agent.

XVI. No society has a constitution without the guarantee of rights and the separation of powers; the constitution is null if the majority of individuals comprising the nation have not cooperated in drafting it.

XVII. Property belongs to both sexes whether united or separate; for each it is an inviolable and sacred right. . . .

Postscript

Women, wake up. . . . Discover your rights. . . . Oh, women, women! When will you cease to be

The late-eighteenth-century French painting *La Liberté. (Bibliothèque Nationale/Giraudon/Art Resource, NY)*

blind? What advantage have you received from the Revolution? A more pronounced scorn, a more marked disdain. . . . [If men persist in contradicting their revolutionary principles,] courageously oppose the force of reason to the empty pretensions of superiority . . . and you will soon see these haughty men, not groveling at your feet as servile adorers, but proud to share with you the treasure of the Supreme Being. Regardless of what barriers confront you; it is in your power to free yourselves; you have only to want to. . . .

Questions for Analysis

1. On what basis did de Gouges argue for gender equality? Did she believe in natural law?
2. What consequences did "scorn for the rights of woman" have for France, according to de Gouges?
3. Did de Gouges stress political rights at the expense of social and economic rights? If so, why?

Source: Olympe de Gouges, "Declaration of the Rights of Woman," in Darline G. Levy, Harriet B. Applewhite, and Mary D. Johnson, eds., *Women in Revolutionary Paris, 1789–1795* (Urbana: University of Illinois Press, 1979), pp. 87–96. Copyright © 1979 by the Board of Trustees, University of Illinois. Used with permission.

10.   D. Sutherland, *France, 1789–1815: Revolution and Counterrevolution* (New York: Oxford University Press, 1986), p. 420.

SUGGESTED READING

For fascinating eyewitness reports on the French Revolution, see the edited works by Beik and by Pernoud and Flaisser mentioned in the Notes. In addition, A. Young, *Travels in France During the Years 1787, 1788 and 1789* (1969), offers an engrossing contemporary description of France and Paris on the eve of revolution. E. Burke, *Reflections on the Revolution in France,* first published in 1790, is the classic conservative indictment. The intense passions the French Revolution has generated may be seen in nineteenth-century French historians, notably the enthusiastic J. Michelet, *History of the French Revolution;* the hostile H. Taine; and the judicious A. de Tocqueville, whose masterpiece, *The Old Regime and the French Revolution,* was first published in 1856. Important general studies on the entire period include the work of Palmer, cited in the Notes, which paints a comparative international picture; E. J. Hobsbawm, *The Age of Revolution, 1789–1848* (1962); C. Breunig, *The Age of Revolution and Reaction, 1789–1850* (1970); O. Connelly, *French Revolution—Napoleonic Era* (1979); and L. Dehio, *The Precarious Balance: Four Centuries of the European Power Struggle* (1962).

Revisionist study has created a wealth of new scholarship and interpretation. A. Cobban, *The Social Interpretation of the French Revolution* (1964), and F. Furet, *Interpreting the French Revolution* (1981), are major reassessments of long-dominant ideas, which are admirably presented in N. Hampson, *A Social History of the French Revolution* (1963), and in the volume by Lefebvre listed in the Notes. E. Kennedy, *A Cultural History of the French Revolution* (1989), beautifully written and handsomely illustrated, and W. Doyle, *Origins of the French Revolution,* 3d ed. (1988), are excellent on long-term developments. P. Jones, ed., *The French Revolution in Social and Political Perspective* (1996), offers a representative sampling of recent scholarship, while T. Tackett, *Becoming a Revolutionary* (1996), is an important attempt at a new synthesis. Among studies that are often quite critical of revolutionary developments, several are noteworthy: J. Bosher, *The French Revolution* (1988); S. Schama, *Citizens: A Chronicle of the French Revolution* (1989); W. Doyle, *The Oxford History of the French Revolution* (1989); and D. Sutherland, *France, 1789–1815: Revolution and Counterrevolution* (1986).

Two valuable anthologies concisely presenting a range of interpretations are F. Kafker and J. Laux, eds., *The French Revolutions: Conflicting Interpretations,* 4th ed. (1989), and G. Best, ed., *The Permanent Revolution: The French Revolution and Its Legacy, 1789–1989* (1988). G. Rudé makes the men and women of the great days of upheaval come alive in *The Crowd in the French Revolution*

(1959), whereas R. R. Palmer studies sympathetically the leaders of the Terror in *Twelve Who Ruled* (1941). Four other particularly interesting, detailed works are B. Shapiro, *Revolutionary Justice in Paris, 1789–1790* (1993); D. Jordan, *The Revolutionary Career of Maximilien Robespierre* (1985); J. P. Bertaud, *The Army of the French Revolution: From Citizen-Soldier to Instrument of Power* (1988); and C. L. R. James, *The Black Jacobins* (1938, 1980), on black slave revolt in Haiti. Other significant studies on aspects of revolutionary France include P. Jones's pathbreaking *The Peasantry in the French Revolution* (1979), and L. Hunt's innovative *Politics, Culture, and Class in the French Revolution* (1984). Two major reinterpretations of the era's continuous wars are T. Blanning, *The French Revolutionary Wars, 1787–1802* (1966), and O. Connelly, *Blundering to Glory: Napoleon's Military Campaigns* (1987).

An ongoing explosion of studies on women in the French Revolution is increasing knowledge and also raising conflicting interpretations. These developments may be seen by comparing two particularly important works: J. Landes, *Women and the Public Sphere in the Age of the French Revolution* (1988), and Hufton's work, listed in the Notes. D. Outram, *The Body and the French Revolution: Sex, Class and Political Culture* (1989), and L. Hunt, *The Family Romance of the French Revolution* (1992), also provide innovative analyses of the gender-related aspects of revolutionary politics and are recommended. D. Levy, H. Applewhite, and M. Johnson, eds., *Women in Revolutionary Paris, 1789–1795* (1979), is a valuable collection of contemporary documents with helpful commentaries. Mary Wollstonecraft's dramatic life is the subject of several good biographies, including those by Sunstein and James cited in the Notes.

Two important works placing political developments in a comparative perspective are P. Higonnet, *Sister Republics: The Origins of French and American Republicanism* (1988), and E. Morgan, *Inventing the People: The Rise of Popular Sovereignty in England and America* (1988). B. Bailyn, *The Ideological Origins of the American Revolution* (1967), is also noteworthy.

The best synthesis on Napoleonic France is L. Bergeron, *France Under Napoleon* (1981). E. Arnold, Jr., ed., *A Documentary Survey of Napoleonic France* (1944), includes political and cultural selections. K. Kafker and J. Laux, eds., *Napoleon and His Times: Selected Interpretations* (1989), is an interesting collection of articles, which may be compared with R. Jones, *Napoleon: Man and Myth* (1977). Good biographies are J. Thompson, *Napoleon Bonaparte: His Rise and Fall* (1952); F. Markham, *Napoleon* (1964); and V. Cronin, *Napoleon Bonaparte* (1972). Wonderful novels inspired by the period include Raphael Sabatini's *Scaramouche,* a swashbuckler of revolutionary intrigue with accurate historical details; Charles Dickens's fanciful *Tale of Two Cities;* and Leo Tolstoy's monumental saga of Napoleon's invasion of Russia (and much more), *War and Peace.*

Index

Abbas, Shah (Safavid Empire), 662, 663
Abbasid Empire: slave concubinage in, 653; Persia and, 662
Abbess (prioress), 387
Abdul-Hamid Lahawri (scholar), 676–677
Abélard, Peter, 372
Abi Ahmet Celebi (Ottoman physician), 656
Abolition, Equiano and, 636
Aborigines (Australia), 518
Absenteeism, of Catholic clergy, 459
Absolutism, 527; in France, 456, 475, 527–533, 583–584; in Latin American colonies, 517; in Spain, 533–535; in eastern Europe, 535–549; and baroque, 547–549, 548(illus.); Enlightenment and, 578–585; of Austrian Habsburgs, 581–583; reform and, 585
Abu-l-Fazl (historian), 665
Acamapichti (Aztec), 426
Act for the Submission of the Clergy (England), 468
Act in Restraint of Appeals (England), 468
Acupuncture, 694
Adal (state), 628
Adams, John (captain), 638–639
Adams, John (U.S.), 717
Administration: of Latin American colonies, 517; of Ottoman Empire, 650. See also Government
Admonition to Peace, An (Luther), 463–464
Adoration of the Magi (Mantegna), 448(illus.)
Aegean Sea, 651
Afghans and Afghanistan, 669; India and, 664–665
Africa, 620(illus.); European knowledge of, 455; Portugal and, 500, 509; spice trade and, 500; Columbian Exchange and, 515; slave trade and, 517–520, 519(map), 631–641; Dutch trade with, 555; family in, 597; Senegambia and, 621–622; Benin and, 622–623; Songhay Empire, 626–627; Sudan and, 626–628; East Africa, 628(map); Swahili city-states in, 629–631. See also Blacks; West Africa; specific countries
African Americans, see Blacks
African slaves, see Slaves and slavery
Against the Murderous, Thieving Hordes of the Peasants (Luther), 464
Age, see Elderly

Age-grade systems, in Senegambia, 621–622
Age of Discovery, 499–509
Age of Expansion, 499
Age of Reconnaissance, 499
Agincourt, Battle of, 395
Agriculture: medieval, 377–381; Black Death and, 390; in Mexico, 415; in Peru, 415; of Maya, 417–418; in Andes, 432–433; in Southeast Asia, 493(illus.); Columbian Exchange and, 513–516; slavery and, 519–520; in Europe, 591–593; technology and, 593; in Senegambia, 622; gender and labor in West Africa, 624; African slave trade and, 633; in Ottoman society, 652; in Ming China, 681, 683–684; in China, 687; in Korea, 698; in Japan, 707
Ahmed I (Ottoman Empire), 659
Ahmet (Ottoman Empire), 658
Aiguillon, duke of, 725
Akan people, 500
Akbar (Mughal Empire), 664–667
Albert (Archbishop), 461, 462
Alberti, Leon Battista, 445
Albigensians, 389(illus.)
Albuquerque, Afonso de, 501, 644
Alcohol, see Drinking
Alembert, Jean le Rond d', 573, 575
Ale production, women and, 380
Alexander I (Russia), 736
Alexander VI (Pope), 444, 457, 459–461
Allan, David, 599(illus.)
Alooma, Idris (Kanem-Bornu), 627–628
Alphabet, Korean, 696
Alsace, French control of, 479
Alva, duke of, 475
Alvarado, Pedro (Spanish soldier), 508
Ambassadors, see Diplomacy
Amendments, to U.S. Constitution, 720
America(s): sex and sexuality in, 398; pre-Columbian, 412–438, 412(illus.); naming of, 413; geography and peoples of, 413–415; reasons for exploring, 503–505; Columbus and, 505–506; exploration of, 505–509; Columbian Exchange and, 513–516; slavery and, 518–520, 519(map); disease and, 633; slave trade and, 633, 637–638; impact of African slaves on, 639. See also Mesoamerica
American Revolution, 717–720
Amerindians, 415. See also Native Americans

Amesbury Priory, convent at, 386–387
Amiens, Treaty of, 735–736
Amsterdam, 511, 554, 556
Anabaptists, 467
Anatolia: Ottomans and, 648. See also Turkey
Ancestors: among Inca, 434, 435; in China, 512, 692
Andalusia, courtly tradition of, 375
Andes Mountains, 413, 432
Anesthesia, 608
Anglican church, 469. See also Church of England
Angola: slave trade and, 634, 634(illus.); Queen Njiga of Ndongo in, 637(illus.)
Angry men (France), 730, 733
Anguissola, Sofonisba, 454, 454(illus.)
Animals: Maya cultivation of, 418; Columbian Exchange and, 513, 514–516
Annam, 696
Anne (wife of Richard II of England), 397
Antiquity, Renaissance study of, 446
Anti-Semitism, see Jews and Judaism
Antwerp, 475–476
Apothecaries, 608
Appeal to the Christian Nobility of the German Nation (Luther), 465
Aqueduct, of Tenochtitlán, 430
Aquitaine: Hundred Years' War and, 393; French reconquest of, 396
Arabian Ocean, piracy in, 671
Arab people: Granada reconquest and, 457; Ottoman control of, 650. See also Islam; Muslims
Aragon, Spain, kingdom of Naples and, 444
Archbishop of Canterbury, Laud as, 550
Architecture: medieval cathedrals and, 372–374; Gothic, 373; Romanesque, 373; in Italian Renaissance, 447; in northern Renaissance, 451–452; baroque, 547–549; in Mughal Empire, 665; of Shah Jahan (Mughal Empire), 667
Ardennes mountains, 476
Aretino, Pietro, 480
Aristocracy: European children and, 384; medieval widows and, 385–386; Hundred Years' War and, 393; in England, 456; in Spain, 535; in China, 695; in French Revolution, 728
Aristotle, astronomy and, 563–564
Armada (Spain), 476–477, 535
Armed forces: Aztec, 423; in France, 456; in Prussia, 541; in Russia, 545–547; in

Armed forces (cont.)
England, 550–551; in Ming China, 681, 685–686. See also Military
Arms and armaments, see Weapons
Arouet, François Marie, see Voltaire
Art and artists: in Italian Renaissance, 447–449; status in Renaissance, 448–449; Bellini and, 450, 450(illus.); baroque, 483–484, 547–549; French classicism and, 532; in Enlightenment, 578; in Ottoman Empire, 655; Persian, 660, 662–663, 663(illus.); in Mughal Empire, 664, 666–667; in China, 684–686; Chinese women as, 693(illus.)
Arthur (legendary king), 375
Artisans, in Ming China, 681
Ashikaga Shogunate (Japan), 698
Asia: trade and, 491–493, 509; Columbian Exchange and, 515; economic impact of European discoveries, 521; world trade and, 521; governments in, 527; population growth in, 593; Ottomans and, 652; European trade with, 671–672; Qing Empire in, 687. See also East Asia
Assemblies, see Estates General (France)
Astrakhan, 651, 652
Astrolabe, 503
Astronomy: of Maya, 563; scientific revolution and, 563–567, 571(illus.); observatory at Nuremberg, 568(illus.); in Ottoman Empire, 656
Atauhualpa (Inca), 436, 438, 509
Athletics, see Sports
Atlantic region: trade in, 509; slave trade in, 633–639, 635(table)
Audiencia (judges), 517
Auerstädt, battle at, 736
Augsburg, Peace of, 465, 477, 651
Aurangzeb (Mughal Empire), 667–668, 671
Austerlitz, Battle of, 736
Austria: Habsburgs in, 458–459, 581–583; Ottoman Turks and, 538–540; growth to 1748, 539(map); Maria Theresa and, 579, 582, 583(illus.); religious toleration in, 582–583; French Revolution and, 728; Napoleon and, 735, 736. See also Metternich, Klemens von
Austrian Netherlands, 736; France and, 728, 729, 730
Austronesian languages, 493
Authority: Christian, 463; Enlightenment and, 584–585
Authorized (King James) Bible, 482, 483
Autocracy, Russian tsarist, 545
Avignon, papal court in, 397
Avison-Christine (Christine de Pisan), 405
Aymara people, 413
Ayullu (Inca clan), 437
Azov, 651
Aztec Empire, 413; Quetzalcoatl and, 421;

empire of (1519), 422(map); youth of, 426(illus.); cities of, 430–431; Cortés on, 431–432; Spanish conquest of, 506–508
Aztlan, 422

Babur (Mughal Empire), 664; Persia and, 662
Babylonian Captivity, of Catholic church, 397
Bach, Johann Sebastian, 484
Bacon, Francis, 568–569
Baghdad, 652
Bahia, 633
Bairam Khan (India), 664
Bakufu (Japan), 701
Balance of power: in Italian city-states, 444–445; Napoleon and, 736
Balkan region, Ottoman Empire and, 652
Ball, John, 401(illus.)
Ballard, Martha, 609
Baltic region, Russia and, 542
Bank of France, 734
Banks and banking: in Renaissance Florence, 443(illus.); in Amsterdam, 554
Baptists, Anabaptists and, 467
Barber, Francis, 632
Barbosa, Duarte, 644–645
Baroque arts, 483–484, 547–549
Barrões (historian), 671
Bastille, storming of, 724, 725(illus.)
Batista Cairato, Joao, 630(illus.)
Battles, see specific battles
Bayezid II (Ottoman Empire), 649
Bayle, Pierre, 572
Beatrice of Dia, 375
Beg, Ulugh, 563
Beijing (Peking), 679
Belgium: Spanish Netherlands as, 476; France and, 736. See also Austrian Netherlands; Low countries; Netherlands
Bell, Charles Davidson, 632(illus.)
Bellini, Gentile, 447(illus.), 450, 450(illus.)
Benefices, 459
Bengal, see India
Benguela, Angola, 622(map), 634–635
Benin, 622–623, 631
Benin City, 623
Berbers, 381; West Africa trade and, 626
Berdaches: in Aztec society, 428; in Native American society, 428; Sioux and, 429(illus.)
Bering Strait, 413
Berlin, 540. See also Germany
Betanzos, Juan de, 440–441
Betel, 494(illus.)
Béthune, Maximilian de (duke of Sully), 527
Bible: Maya, 420; Christian, 451, 464, 482; reading of, 604
Bigarny, Felipe, 458(illus.)
Bight of Benin, slave trade and, 634

Bight of Biafra, slave trade and, 634
Bill of Rights: in England, 553; in United States, 720
Birthrate: in Europe, 593, 594; slave trade and, 641
Black Death: in Europe, 390–393, 390(map), 594; China and, 679. See also Bubonic plague
Blacks: in Renaissance Europe, 454–455, 455(illus.); in London, 631(illus.); Americas and, 639. See also Africa; Skin color; Slaves and slavery; Slave trade
Black Sea region, 652
Blockades, in Napoleonic wars, 736
Bloodletting, 608
Blood sports, 615
Boats, see Ships and shipping
Boccaccio, Giovanni, 392
Bohemia, 405, 538
Bohemian phase, of Thirty Years' War, 477
Boleyn, Anne, 468
Bolivia, see Potosí
Bologna, University of, 371
Bombay, India, 671
Bonaparte, Napoleon, see Napoleon I (Bonaparte, France)
Boniface VIII (Pope), 389
Book(s): in French Enlightenment, 576–577; in Mughal Empire, 666–667; in China, 694. See also Literature
Book of Common Prayer, 468, 649
Book of Revelations (New Testament), Middle Ages and, 371
Book of the City of Ladies, The (Christine de Pisan), 405, 410–411
Book of the Donkey (Sxeyhi of Kütahya), 655
Book of the Sea (Piri Reis), 656
Book of Three Virtues, The (Christine de Pisan), 405
Bora, Katharine von, 464
Borgia family: Cesare, 444; Rodrigo (Pope Alexander VI), 459–461
Borneo, 495
Borodino, Battle of, 737
Boston, Revolution and, 718(illus.)
Boston tea party, 718
Bourbon Dynasty, 533, 534(map), 739
Bourgeoisie: in China, 695; French Revolution and, 722. See also Middle classes
Bow and arrow, longbow and, 393–394
Boyars (Russia), 542–543
Boys: Aztec cross-gendered, 428; work of, 598. See also Men
Bradford, William, 517
Brahe, Tycho, 565
Brandenburg-Prussia, 540–541; growth to 1748, 539(map)
Brazil, 517; Portugal and, 509; blacks in, 520; slave trade and, 633–634, 635, 637–638, 638(illus.)

Brazilian Highlands, 413
Bread, 604–605, 606–607
Breteuil, Gabrielle-Emilie Le Tonnelier de, *see* Châtelet, Madame du
Brethren of the Common Life, 461
Bride wealth, 494, 624
Britain, *see* England (Britain)
British Anti-Slavery Society, 633
British East India Company, 671–673; China and, 690
British Empire: expansion of, 533; in India, 672. *See also* England (Britain)
Brothels, 398, 481. *See also* Prostitutes and prostitution
Brunelleschi, Filippo, 447
Bruni, Leonardo, 446
Brussels, 475
Bubonic plague, 391, 392; in Ottoman Empire, 656. *See also* Black Death
Buddhism: in Southeast Asia, 495; in Korea, 696; in Japan, 699
Bullion, ocean trade and, 511
Bureaucracy, in Napoleonic France, 734
Burgundy, Habsburgs and, 458–459
Burke, Edmund, 727
Burma, 696; China and, 687
Bursah Ahmet Pasa, 655
Bushido (Japan), 699, 700
Business: in Japan, 701–702, 708. *See also* Commerce; Merchants; Trade

Cabinet system, in England, 553
Cabral, Pedro Alvares, 500, 671
Caciques (Aztec chieftans), 428
Calais, as English property, 396
Calcutta, India, 671
Calendar: Christianity and, 382; Maya, 420; in French republic, 728–729
Calicut, 501
Calpullis, in Aztec Mexico, 424
Calvin, John, 466–467(illus.), 473, 486–487
Calvinism, 466–467; France and, 473; in Low countries, 475; after Thirty Years' War, 479; England and, 550
Cambridge University, 372
Camels, West African trade and, 626
Cameroon, 624
Canals, in Ming China, 682
Canary Islands, 501, 506
Candide (Voltaire), 588
Cannibalism, in African famine, 625
Cannon, 501
Canterbury Tales (Chaucer), 403, 404
Cao Xuepin (China), 695
Cape Colony, slaves in, 632–633
Cape of Good Hope, 500, 555
Capitalism: putting-out system and, 595; in Mughal Empire, 670; in Tokugawa Japan, 701
Capitalist ethic, 550

Capitulations, by Ottoman Empire, 658
Caraffa (Cardinal), 471
Caravan trade: collapse of route, 496–497; Senegambia and, 621; Berbers and, 626. *See also* Trans-Saharan trade
Caravel, 501–503
Cardinals, church reform and, 397
Caribbean region: geography of, 413; Columbus and, 506; slaves in, 634
Carib people, 413
Caritat, Marie-Jean (marquis de Condorcet), 576
Carnival, 615
Carpet industry, Persia and, 662
Caspian Sea, 652
Castiglione, Baldassare, 452, 454
Castiglione, Giuseppe, 691(illus.)
Castile, 533. *See also* Isabella of Castile (Spain); Spain and Spaniards
Castle(s): defense of, 386(illus.); in Japan, 700, 701
Casualties: of Hundred Years' War, 396; in Napoleonic invasion of Russia, 737
Cateau-Cambrésis, Treaty of, 471–472
Catechisms (Luther), 464
Cathedrals: Gothic, 371; medieval, 372–373; secular and religious purposes of, 374
Catherine of Aragon, 468
Catherine of Braganza (Portugal), 671
Catherine the Great (Russia), 579–581, 582(illus.), 719
Catholicism, *see* Roman Catholic church
Catholic League, 477
Catlin, George, 429(illus.)
Caucasus region, 652
Celibacy: of Catholic priests, 459; Christian, 496
Cellini, Benvenuto, 445
Central America: Columbian Exchange and, 514. *See also* America(s); Latin America
Central Asia, *see* Asia
Central Europe: Thirty Years' War and, 477–480; absolutism in, 578–579, 581–583; Muslims in, 650. *See also* Europe
Centralization, of European states, 499
Central Middle Ages, 375–389
Ceramics, in China, 687
Ceremonies, Olmec, 416
Cervantes, Miguel de, 535
Ceuta, Morocco, 499
Ceylon, 555
Chamber of Deputies (France), 739
Champaigne, Philippe de, *see* Richelieu (Cardinal)
Champa rice, 683
Changpai Mountains, 696
Chapbooks, 604
Chardin, Jean-Baptiste-Siméon, 598(illus.)

Charity: foundling homes and, 601–602; in Ottoman Empire, 653
Charles I (England), 550; execution of, 551
Charles II (England), 552, 671
Charles II (Spain), 532
Charles V (Habsburg), 651
Charles V (Holy Roman Empire), 397; sack of Rome by, 445; European empire of, 459, 460(map); Luther and, 463; Protestantism and, 465; Council of Trent and, 470; Low Countries and, 475; slave trade and, 519–520
Charles VI (Austria), 579
Charles VII (France), 395, 456
Charles IX (France), 474
Châtelet, Madame du, 573–574, 573(illus.)
Chaucer, Geoffrey, 385, 403, 404
Ch'en Shu (China), 693, 694
Chibcha people, 413
Chichén Itzá, 418
Chichimeca people, 413, 422
Chieftains (societies), 415
Ch'ien Ch'en-ch'un (China), 694
Childbirth: in Aztec society, 427. *See also* Midwives
Child care, 600–601
Children: of medieval European peasants, 380, 381; abandonment of, 383; as oblates, 383–384; European nobility as, 383–385; nursing of, 600–601; in 18th-century Europe, 600–603; infanticide and, 601; foundlings, 601–602, 601(illus.); education of, 602, 618–619. *See also* Education; Family life; Illegitimacy; Schools
Chile, Inca in, 435
China, 679; Zheng He and, 497, 498; European trade with, 509, 511; scientific contributions to West, 512–513; Western world and, 512–513; Columbian Exchange and, 515; racism in, 520; silver trade and, 521; world trade and, 521; family life in, 597, 692–695; babies in, 601; Persian culture and, 663, 663(illus.); Ming Dynasty in, 679, 680–687; Qing Empire in, 679–680, 687–695; from 1400 to 1800, 679–695; imperial seal in, 680(illus.); Korea and, 696. *See also* Asia; Language(s)
Chinampas, 415
Chinggis Khan (Mongols), 659; Russia and, 542
Chivalric code: Hundred Years' War and, 393; in Japan, 699
Choson Dynasty (Korea), 696. *See also* Korea
Chrétien de Troyes, 375
Christianity: Gothic cathedrals and, 371; Thomas Aquinas and, 372; cathedrals and, 372–374; of medieval peasants,

Christianity (cont.)
381–383; challenge to authority and, 389; conversion of Maya to, 420; Renaissance secularism and, 446–447; humanists and, 451; Jewish conversos and, 457; in Indian Ocean region, 493(map); in Southeast Asia, 495–496; Portuguese exploration and, 499; European exploration and, 503–504, 505–506; China and, 512–513; Japan and, 513, 702–703; in Latin America, 516–517; racism and, 520; science and, 563–564; in 18th-century Europe, 611–614; in Ethiopia, 628

Christian IV (Denmark), 477

Christina (Sweden), 569(illus.)

Christine de Pisan, 405, 410–411, 411(illus.)

Chumu people (Peru), 435(illus.)

Church(es): role in medieval life, 382; marriage and, 398–399; Christian definition of, 463; institutional, 612. See also Cathedrals; Monks and monasteries

Church of England, 468–469, 550, 552, 613

Cicero, 446

Ciompi revolt, in Florence, 401

Cities and towns: in medieval Europe, 377; plague in, 391–392; migration to, 402; Aztec, 430–431; St. Petersburg and, 547–549; in Mughal Empire, 667; in Ming China, 684; in Japan, 701. See also Urbanization

Citizenship, in Italian Renaissance, 444

City of Ladies, see Book of the City of Ladies, The (Christine de Pisan)

City-states: Maya, 417(map); in Italian Renaissance, 444–445; Hausa, 628; East African, 628(map); Swahili, 629–631

Civilization(s): of Americas, 412–438, 412(illus.); of Olmecs, 415–417; Inca, 435–437; contacts among, 491; of Indian Ocean region, 491–497; spreading European, 505; Swahili, 629–631. See also Culture(s); Society

Civil rights and liberties, 715–716

Civil service, in China, 682, 687, 688

Civil war: in Inca Empire, 436, 509; English Wars of the Roses, 456; in France, 474–475, 529

Clans, in Inca society, 437

Classes: in medieval Europe, 375–377, 376(illus.); serfs as, 376; in Aztec society, 425, 426; in Inca society, 437; in Renaissance Italy, 444; in Spain, 457; Lutheranism and, 463–464; nobility of the robe (France) as, 473, 530; France and, 474–475; in Reformation Europe, 481; diet and, 605–606; separation between, 615; in Senegambia, 621; in Ottoman Empire, 652; in Ming China, 681;

in China, 687, 694, 695; in Korea, 698; in Japan, 700–701, 702. See also Estates (French orders); French Revolution; Working classes

Classical liberalism, 720. See also Liberalism

Classical period: in Mesoamerica, 417. See also China

Classicism, in France, 532

Clement V (Pope), 397

Clement VII (Pope), 397, 468, 470

Clergy: in central Middle Ages, 375; in medieval parishes, 382–383; reforms of, 459; Lutheranism and, 465; Council of Trent and, 470; as French class, 473; Christian vs. Muslim, 496; in 18th-century Europe, 612; in France, 721. See also Monks and monasteries; Priesthood; Religion(s)

Climate, in 17th century Europe, 527

Cloves, 501

Cockfights, 615

Code (Justinian law), 371

Codes of law, see Law codes

Coercive Acts, 718

Cohin, 501

Coins, in China, 683

Coke, Edward, 481

Colbert, Jean-Baptiste, 531, 596, 672

Coligny, Gaspard de, 474

Collected Works (Christine de Pisan), 411(illus.)

College of Cardinals, Great Schism and, 397

Colleges, see Universities and colleges

Cologne, Germany, 399

Colombia, 435

Colonial empires, see Empires

Colonialism, see Colonies and colonization; Empires

Colonies and colonization: by Europeans, 499–509; in Latin America, 517; slave trade and, 518–520; French, 531; Spanish, 533, 535; Frederick the Great and, 579; Ottomans and, 658; American Revolution and, 717–720

Color, see Skin color

Columbian Exchange, 513–516; Native American holocaust and, 516–517; European diet and, 606

Columbus, Christopher, 501, 505–506; first voyage of, 524–525

Commerce: Olmec, 416–417; in Italian Renaissance, 443–445; in Southeast Asia, 497; seaborne trade and, 509–512, 510(map); slave trade and, 518; French, 531; Russian, 543; Dutch, 554, 555–556, 555(map); in Swahili city states, 630; Muslims and, 647; of Persian Empire, 662; China and, 690; in Japan, 701–703, 707–708. See also Trade

Committee of Public Safety (France), 730, 733

Commoners: as French third estate, 722; in France, 733. See also Classes; Elites; Middle classes; Peasants; Working classes

Common Sense (Paine), 718

Commonwealth, in England, 551

Communication(s), in Inca Empire, 436

Communities: in Senegambia, 622. See also Cities and towns

Compass, 503

Complete Library of the Four Treasuries, The, 689

Conciliar movement, 398, 459

Conciliar theory, of church government, 470, 473

Concordat of 1801, 734

Concordat of Bologna, 473

Concubines, in Ottoman Empire, 653

Condorcet, marquis de, see Caritat, Marie-Jean (marquis de Condorcet)

Confucius and Confucianism: in Southeast Asia, 495; in China, 680, 681, 687; in Korea, 696; Japan and, 699

Congregationalists, Anabaptists and, 467

Conquests: European voyages of discovery and, 502(map). See also Colonies and colonization; Expansion and expansionism; Exploration

Conscription, see Draft (military)

Conservatism, Burke and, 727

Consistory (Geneva), 466–467

Constance, Council of (1414–1418), 397

Constantine IX Palaeologus (Byzantine emperor), 648

Constantinople (Istanbul): siege of (1453), 501, 647–648; as Ottoman Istanbul, 648

Constitution: in England, 553; in United States, 719–720; in France, 723, 733

Constitutional Charter (France), 739

Constitutional Convention (1787), 720

Constitutionalism, 527

Constitutional monarchy: in England, 549–553; in France, 723. See also Republic

Continental Congress, 718

Convention (France), see National Convention (France)

Convents, 386–387, 481

Conversations on the Plurality of Worlds (Fontenelle), 571–572, 571(illus.)

Conversion: in Southeast Asia, 495. See also Missions and missionaries

Conversos (Spain), 457, 458

Cook, Sherbourne, 423

Copán, 418

Copernicus, Nicolaus, 564–565, 564(illus.)

Coptic Christianity, 629

Corn, see Maize (corn)

Cornwallis, Charles (England), 673

Corregidores (tax officials), 517

Corsica, 734

Cortés, Hernando: Quetzalcoatl and, 421; Aztecs and, 425, 506–508; on Tenochtitlán, 431; search for gold and, 505
Cortes (Spanish assembly), 396
Cossacks, 543, 545, 581; Stenka Razin and, 545, 546, 546(illus.)
Cottage industry, in Europe, 594–597
Councils (Roman Catholic church): at Basel, 397; of Constance, 397; at Ferrara-Florence, 397; at Pisa, 397; of Trent, 470
Counter-Reformation, 469–471; scientific revolution and, 570
Courier, The (Castiglione), 452
Courtesans, in Japan, 703
Courtly tradition: troubadour poetry and, 375; in medieval Europe, 385
Court of Star Chamber (England), 457
Courts: in Renaissance Italian cities, 444; of Louis XIV, 529; at Versailles, 558–559
Craft guilds: women and, 399. *See also* Guilds
Cranach, Lucas (the Younger), 462(illus.)
Cranmer, Thomas, 468
Creativity, in central Middle Ages, 371
Crécy, Battle of, 393–394, 395(illus.)
Credit, in France, 721
Creoles, 717
Cromwell, Oliver, 551–552, 551(illus.)
Cromwell, Thomas, 468
Crop rotation, 377, 591, 593
Crops: in medieval Europe, 377; of Maya, 417–418; in Southeast Asia, 493–494; Columbian Exchange and, 514–516; yields of, 591; fallow and, 593; in West Africa, 624; in Qing China, 690; in Korea, 698. *See also* Agriculture
Crossbow, 395
Crucifixion, Mary and, 383
Crusades, European exploration and, 499
Cuckhold, in medieval Europe, 385
Cultivating the Joy of Discovery (Wright), 603(illus.)
Cultivation: in Americas, 415. *See also* Agriculture; Crops; Farms and farming
Cult of the royal mummies (Inca), 434, 435, 436, 437, 508, 509
Culture(s): race, ethnicity, and, 401–403; of Native Americans, 414(map); of Monte Albán, 420; Aztec, 423–425; Inca, 432–438; of Renaissance Europe, 443–459; of Indian Ocean region, 491–495; European, 499–509; urban Enlightenment, 576–578; in Ottoman Empire, 655–657; in Safavid Empire, 660–663; in Ming China, 684–685; Korean, 696; of French republic, 728–729. *See also* Civilization(s); Enlightenment; Intellectual thought; Popular culture
Currency: in China, 683, 687; in Japan, 699

Cushitic-speaking people, 629
Cuzco region, 432, 433, 508–509
Cyprus, 651
Czech people: language of, 405; Austria and, 538

Da Gama, Vasco, *see* Gama, Vasco da
Dahomey (kingdom), 640
Daimyos (Japan), 698, 700, 701
Dancing, in medieval Europe, 399(illus.)
Danish phase, of Thirty Years' War, 477
Dante Alighieri, 403–404; *Inferno* of, 370(illus.)
Danton, Georges Jacques, 729, 733
Dark Ages, use of term, 445
Dauphin of France, Charles VII as, 395
David, Gerard, 452(illus.)
David, Jacques-Louis, 723(illus.), 735(illus.)
David (Michelangelo's statue), 449(illus.)
Death(s): from Black Death, 392; Maya and, 418(illus.); rituals in Southeast Asia, 495
Death rate: in post-Columbian Latin America, 517; in Europe, 593
Debt, *see* National debt
Decameron, The (Boccaccio), 392
Deccan region (India), 668
Decimal system, of Maya, 420
Declaration of Independence (U.S.), 719, 719(illus.)
Declaration of Pillnitz, 728
Declaration of the Rights of Man (France), 715, 725–726, 742
Declaration of the Rights of Woman and the Female Citizen (France), 742–743
Defenestration of Prague, 477
Defoe, Daniel, 602
Deities, *see* Gods and goddesses
Delhi, 667
Demesne, 377
Democracy, England and, 553
Dengel, Lebna (Ethiopia), 628
De Paul, Vincent (Saint), 601
Descartes, René, 568, 569–570, 569(illus.)
Despotism: in France, 584; French Revolution and, 727; monarchs and, 728
Despots, of Italian city-states, 455–456
Devshirme system, 653–655
Dialogue on the Two Chief Systems of the World (Galileo), 566
Diaz, Bartholomew, 500
Díaz, Bernal, 430
Diderot, Denis, 562(illus.), 575, 610
Diet: of medieval European peasants, 380–381; of Mexicans, 420; of Incas, 433; in Southeast Asia, 493–494; of Muslims, 496; Columbian Exchange and, 514–516; population growth and, 516; in Dutch Republic, 556; nutrition and, 604–606; health and, 606–607; in

Senegambia, 622; in West Africa, 624; in China, 683; in Korea, 696. *See also* Foods
Diet (German assembly), 396
Diet at Worms, 463
Dimitrash (Cossack), 651
Diplomacy: in Italian city-states, 444–445; China and, 691–692
Directory (France), 733
Discovery, *see* Expansion and expansionism
Discrimination, against Irish, 402
Disease: of medieval European peasants, 381; Columbian Exchange and, 516; Native American holocaust and, 516–517; population and, 593; smallpox and, 610–611; in West Africa, 624; African slave trade and, 633; in Ottoman Empire, 656; in China, 679, 694, 694(illus.)
Distribution of wealth, *see* Wealth
Diversity: of Native Americans, 413; of Southeast Asia religions, 495–496
Divine Comedy (Dante), 370(illus.), 403–404
Divine right of kings, 724; in England, 549, 551
Divorce: Christian marriage and, 398–399; in Southeast Asia, 495; in China, 693; in Japan, 707
Diwan (Islamic financial bureau), 665
Diwan poetry, 655
Djenné (Jenne), 626
Doctors, *see* Physicians
Domestic policy, of Napoleon, 734
Dominic (Saint), 389(illus.)
Dominicans, 516
Donatello, 448
Don Cossacks, *see* Cossacks
Don Quixote (Cervantes), 535
Dowry: in medieval Europe, 385. *See also* Bride wealth
Draft (military), in revolutionary France, 731
Drama: Shakespeare and, 482–483; in France, 532
Dream of the Red Chamber, The (Cao Xuepin), 695
Drinking, among European rich, 605
Dualism, legal, 401–402
Dupleix, Joseph, 672
Dutch, 475; seaborne trade of, 509, 511; Japanese trade with, 513; Spanish war with, 535; commerce of, 554, 555–556, 555(map); Cape Colony slaves and, 632; Indian Ocean trade and, 652; Japan and, 703. *See also* Holland; Low Countries; Netherlands; United Provinces of the Netherlands
Dutch East India Company, 504, 511, 555, 671, 672
Dutch East Indies, *see* Indonesia

Dutch Republic, *see* United Provinces of the Netherlands
Dutch West India Company, 520, 555
Dynastic wars, 471–473
Dynasties, *see* Empires

Earth, astronomy and, 563–564
East Africa: kingdoms in, 628–629, 628(map); in 16th Century, 628(map); slave trade and, 633; Ottomans and, 652
East Asia: Ming Dynasty family in, 678(illus.); from 1400 to 1800, 679. *See also* specific countries
Eastern Europe, absolutism in, 535–549, 579–581
Ecclesiastical History of England and Normandy (Vitalis), 386
Economy: in Europe, 377, 527; plague and, 392; of Tenochtitlán, 430–431; of Renaissance Italy, 446; European exploration and, 520–521; in France, 528–529, 532, 720–721, 730, 733; Louis XIV and, 530–531; of Spain, 535; in Songhay Empire, 627; in Ottoman Empire, 658–659; in China, 682; in Korea, 696–697; in Japan, 701. *See also* Agriculture
Ecuador, 435
Edict of Nantes, 475, 527, 531, 532
Edict of Restitution, 477
Education: in Renaissance, 452–454; of Lutheran women, 464; Rousseau and, 576, 618–619; formal, 600; in 18th-century Europe, 603–604; in Ottoman Empire, 656; in China, 693–695; of Japanese women, 706–707. *See also* Philosophy; Schools; Universities and colleges
Education of a Christian Prince, The (Erasmus), 451
Edward (Black Prince, England), 395
Edward I (England), 389
Edward III (England), 393; Parliament and, 396
Edward IV (England), 456
Edward VI (England), Protestant Reformation and, 468, 469(illus.)
Egypt (modern), Ottomans and, 650
Ekkehard of Aura, 386
Elba, 737
Elderly: in West Africa, 624; Chinese respect for, 693
Elections: in France, 722–723. *See also* Voting
Electors, of Brandenburg, 540
Elementary education, 603–604
Elites: of Maya, 419; in Renaissance Italy, 444; in France, 528–529; in Enlightenment, 577–578; nursing and, 601; popular culture and, 615. *See also* Classes
Elizabeth (Russia), 581

Elizabeth I (England), 476–477, 549, 671; Protestantism of, 468–469
Elizabethan literature, 482–483
Elizabethan Settlement, 469
Embroidered Brocade Guards (China), 680
Emigrants and emigration: from China, 686. *See also* Immigrants and immigration
Emile (Rousseau), 602, 618–619
Emperor(s): Aztec, 428; Inca, 437. *See also* Japan
Empires: in pre-Columbian Americas, 413; German, 465, 528; commercial, 509–512; of Napoleon, 736. *See also* Islam; Kingdoms
Encomienda system, 516
Encyclopedia (Diderot) and Encyclopedists, 562(illus.), 575, 578
Engineering, in Tenochtitlán, 430
England (Britain): troubadours in, 375; Hundred Years' War and, 393–396; French holdings in Hundred Years' War, 394(map); Peasants' Revolt in, 400; serfdom in, 400; discrimination against Irish by, 402; schools in, 405; Renaissance politics in, 456–457; Protestant Reformation in, 467–469; witch scare in, 481–482; slave trade and, 520, 634, 636, 638; acquisition of French territories by, 533; constitutional monarchy in, 549–553; commonwealth in, 551; Restoration in, 552; Voltaire and, 574–575; population growth in, 593(fig.); charity schools in, 603; blacks in, 631(illus.), 632; Indian Ocean trade and, 652; India and, 671, 672–673; American Revolution and, 717–719; French Revolution and, 727; France and, 729, 736; Napoleon and, 735–736. *See also* British Empire
English Channel, Armada and, 476–477
Enlarged-scale farming (Korea), 698
Enlightenment, 570–578; absolutism and, 578–585; Jewish thought and, 580; influence of, 584–585; freedom, equality, and, 716
"Enterprise of the Indies, The," as Columbus' expedition, 506
Entertainment: literature as, 604. *See also* Leisure; Recreation
Epidemics, 516–517. *See also* Disease
Equality: of opportunity, 715–716; concept of, 715–717; political, 717; in France, 725–726
Equatorial Africa, 624
Equiano, Olaudah, 624, 626; on slave trade, 635–637, 636(illus.)
Erasmus, Desiderius, 451
Ericson, Leif, 499
Eric the Red, 499
Essay Concerning Human Understanding (Locke), 572

Estate agriculture, 538
Estates (agricultural), medieval, 385–386
Estates (assembly): in Bohemia, 538, 539; in Germany, 540
Estates (French orders), 721–722
Estates General (France), 528, 530, 722, 723–724. *See also* National Assembly (France)
Estonia, 547
Ethiopia and Ethiopians, 628–629, 628(map); Christianity in, 628, 629
Ethnic cleansing, 424
Ethnicity: and European frontiers, 401–403; in Aztec Empire, 436; in Inca Empire, 436, 437; of African people, 632; in Ottoman Empire, 647
Eucharist: Lollards and, 397; transubstantiation and, 468; Calvin on, 486–487
Euclidean geometry, 564(illus.)
Eunuchs: Zheng He as, 498; in Mughal Empire, 668; in China, 682, 682(illus.), 687
Europe: universities and colleges in, 371; central Middle Ages in, 375–389; Black Death in, 390–393, 390(map); Hundred Years' War in, 393–396; Renaissance in, 442; Italian Renaissance in, 443–449; Northern Renaissance in, 449–452; Protestantism in north of, 465–469; after Thirty Years' War, 478(map); Age of Discovery in, 499–509; technology, exploration, and, 501–503; global trade networks and, 509–512; inflation in, 521; absolutism in, 526; in 1715, 534(map); agriculture in, 591–593; population of, 593–594; labor in, 594–597; marriage and family in, 597–600; children in, 600–603; education in, 603–604; food and diet in, 604; medicine in, 607–611; religion in, 611–614; popular culture in, 614–615; Africans in, 631–632; impact on African slavery, 640–641; Ottomans and, 648–649, 652, 658–659; Muslims in, 650; Indian trade and, 671; French Revolution and, 728; Grand Empire in, 736, 738(map). *See also* Central Europe; Christianity; Eastern Europe; specific countries
Evangelicals, Methodists and, 614
Ewuare (Senegambia), 622
Exclusion bill (England), 552
Excommunication, of Luther, 462
Executions: of witches, 481–482; in revolutionary France, 731(illus.)
Expansion and expansionism: by Inca, 436; of Europe, 499–509, 502(map); Christian missionaries and, 512–513; of France, 532–533, 533(map); of Ottoman Turks, 538–540; of Russia, 544(map); of Ottoman Empire, 648–652. *See also*

Colonies and colonization; Exploration; Imperialism; Migrants and migration

Exploration: by Vikings, 499; European voyages of discovery, 499–501, 502(map); by Europeans, 499–509; by Diaz, 500; technology and, 501–503; motives of explorers, 503–505; government sponsorship of, 504; Columbian Exchange and, 513–516; economic effects of European, 520–521; Columbus' first voyage and, 524–525; by China, 686

Extended family: in Europe, 597; in West Africa, 624

Factory-forts (India), 671–672, 672(illus.)

Fairs, 615

Faith healers, 608

Family life: of medieval European peasants, 380; in 18th-century Europe, 597–598; in Senegambia, 622; in West Africa, 623–624; of Cape Colony slave, 633; in Ming Dynasty, 678(illus.); in China, 692–695; in Japan, 707; under Napoleon, 734–735

Famine, 594; population and, 593; in West Africa, 625

Farms and farming: in Europe, 377–381, 591–593; yields and, 378; of Maya, 417–418; diet and, 606; in Ming China, 681, 683; in Korea, 698; in Japan, 700, 704–706. See also Agriculture

Farnese, Alexander, 475, 476

Fatehpur-Sikri, India, 665, 666(illus.)

Fathers: in China, 692. See also Family life; Men

Ferdinand II (Holy Roman Empire), 475

Ferdinand III (Holy Roman Empire), 538

Ferdinand of Aragon (Spain), 456, 457, 458(illus.), 499; Inquisition and, 389(illus.), 458; Jews and, 457; Columbus and, 505–506

Fertility: nursing and, 600–601; in West Africa, 624

Fertilizers, 591

Feudalism: in Japan, 698–699; Ieyasu and, 700

Fighters, see Warrior class

Finances, see Economy; Taxation

Firearms, slave trade and, 640

First Coalition, 728, 730–731

First estate (clergy), 721

Fish and fishing: in Southeast Asia, 493; in China, 683, 684(illus.); Korea and, 696

Flagellants, Black Death and, 393

Flanders: Hundred Years' War and, 393; strikes and riots in, 399; French invasion of, 532. See also Low Countries

Flemish tapestries, 374(illus.). See also Low countries

Florence: ciompi revolt in, 401; in Renaissance, 443–444, 443(illus.), 445

Flowers, in Persian culture, 662

Folk literature, Ottoman, 655–656

Folk medicine, 381; in West Africa, 625

Fontenelle, Bernard de, 571–572, 571(illus.)

Foods: for Maya, 418; human bodies as, 424; in Indian Ocean region, 493–494; Columbian Exchange and, 514–516; and nutrition, 604–606; in Ming China, 684. See also Diet

Foreign affairs: in Ming China, 685–686; in Qing China, 690. See also Balance of power

Foreigners, expulsion from Japan, 703

Foreign policy: of Ottoman Empire, 648–652; of Napoleon, 735–741

Foreign trade, see Trade

Forests, in Ming China, 683

Fort Jesus, Mombasa, 630(illus.), 631

Forts. See also specific forts

Forts, British, in India, 671

Fouché, Joseph, 735

Foundlings, 601–602, 601(illus.)

Four Books (Zhu Xi), 681

Fragonard, Jean-Honoré, 562(illus.)

France: medieval cathedrals in, 372–373; Gothic architecture in, 373; troubadours in, 375; Black Death in, 391; Hundred Years' War and, 393–396; English holdings in Hundred Years' War, 394(map); representative government and, 396; peasant riots in, 400; Renaissance politics in, 456; Burgundy and, 458–459; Charles V and, 459; Habsburg wars with, 465; political difficulties in, 473–474; religious riots and civil war in, 474–475; absolutism in, 475, 527–533, 583–584; Thirty Years' War and, 477; under Louis XIV, 529–533; economy of, 530–531; surrender of American colonies, 533; rural industry in, 596; Seven Years' War and, 671; political revolution in, 715–716; French Revolution and, 720–727; reorganization of, 726; as Republic, 728–729; Napoleonic Era in, 734–741; Grand Empire of, 736, 738(map)

Franche-Comté, 532

Francis I (France), 473, 474(illus.), 651

Francis II (Habsburg), 728

Francis II (Holy Roman Empire), 736

Franciscans, 516; in China, 512

Francis Xavier (Saint), 513

Françoise of Florence, 398

Fratricide, in Ottoman Empire, 653

Frederick II (Holy Roman Empire), church and, 459

Frederick II (the Great, Prussia), 578–579, 581; Voltaire and, 574(illus.), 575, 579; potato and, 607(illus.)

Frederick of Saxony, Luther and, 462, 462(illus.), 463

Frederick William (Great Elector, Brandenburg), 540

Frederick William I (Soldiers' King, Prussia), 540–541, 541(illus.), 578

Freedom: in medieval Europe, 377; manumission of serfs and, 379; Luther on, 464; Rousseau and, 576; under Napoleon, 735. See also Abolition; Slaves and slavery

Free will, 575

French East India Company, 672

French Revolution, 720–727; Rousseau and, 576; monarchy and, 721, 722–723, 725–726; outbreak of, 727–728; wars during, 728; second revolution in, 728–730; resistance to, 730; Thermidorian Reaction and Directory in, 733; women's rights and, 742–743, 743(illus.)

Fronde, 529

Frontiers, race and ethnicity along European, 401–403

Frossart, Jean, 393

Fugger family, 461

Fust, Johann, 453

Galdan (Mongols), 689

Galilei, Galileo, 565–566, 566(illus.)

Galla people, 629

Galleys, 501

Gama, Vasco da, 500, 505, 630

Gao, 626

Gays and lesbians, see Homosexuality

Geishas, 703

Gender: child abandonment and, 383; in Aztec society, 428; in Renaissance society, 453–454; infanticide and, 601; of physicians, 608; and labor in West Africa, 624; of African slaves, 641. See also Men; Women

General History of the Indies (Oviedo), 504–505

Geneva, Calvin in, 466–467

Genoa, 444, 518

Geography: of Americas, 413–415; Andean, 433; exploration and, 504–505; Ottoman Empire and, 656; Chinese voyages and, 686; of Korea, 695–696

Geometry, Copernicus and, 564(illus.)

George III (England): letter to Qianlong emperor, 690, 710–711; American independence and, 718

Ge people, 413

German Confederation of the Rhine, 736

German Empire: fragmentation of, 465; France and, 528

German language, Luther and, 464

Germany: troubadours and, 375; Hildegard of Bingen in, 387(illus.); peasant revolts in, 401; Renaissance politics in, 458–459; Lutheranism in, 465; authority of

Germany (cont.)
princes in, 477–479; after Thirty Years' War, 479–480; serfdom in, 538; Jews in, 579; population in, 593; Protestant revival in, 613–614. See also Brandenburg-Prussia; German Empire; Holy Roman Empire; Prussia
Gerontocracies, 624
Gerritz, Decker Cornelis, 595(illus.)
Gertrude (Saxony), 386
Gesù (church), 483–484
Ghana (Gold Coast), 500, 624; kingdom of, 621; slave trade and, 634
Ghazan the Ilkhan (Persia), 659–660
Ghent, 475
Gheselin de Busbecq, Ogier, 505
Ghiberti, Lorenzo, 447
Gibbon, Edward, 602
Gibraltar, 533
Giotto, 448
Giovanni Arnolfini and His Bride (Van Eyck), 451
Girls: work of, 598. See also Women
Girondists (France), 729, 730
Glanvill (English writer), 376–377
Gleaners, The (Millet), 592(illus.)
Globalization: worldwide contacts and, 491–521; trade networks and, 509–512; Latin American discoveries and, 520–521; travel and, 572
Glorious Revolution (England), 552–553
Goa, 501, 509, 671
Gods and goddesses, of Aztecs, 423
Gold: Portuguese search for, 499; from Africa, 500; exploration and, 505; of Inca, 509; in Latin America, 517
Gold Coast, see Ghana (Gold Coast)
Golden Age, of Dutch Republic, 554(illus.)
Golden Horde, see Mongols
Golden Legend, 391(illus.)
Golden Lotus, The, 685
Gonzaga family (Mantua), 448(illus.)
Gothic cathedrals, 371, 373
Gouges, Olympe de, 728, 742–743
Gout, 606
Gouze, Marie, see Gouges, Olympe de
Government: of Montezuma II (Aztec), 425; of Renaissance European states, 455–459; Lutheranism and, 465; French absolutism, 527–533; constitutional monarchy as, 549–553; of United Provinces, 553–554; Locke on, 572; Voltaire on, 574–575; in Ottoman Empire, 652; of Mughal Empire, 665; British, in India, 673; of Ming China, 680–683; of Qing China, 687–690; in Japan, 699–700; liberty, equality, and, 715–716; of United States, 720; in Napoleonic France, 734–735. See also Absolutism; Law(s); Law codes; Politics and political thought; Society

Goya y Lucientes, Francisco de, 737(illus.)
Grains, 604–605; diet and, 606. See also Agriculture
Granada, Spain, 457
Grand Alliance, in War of the Spanish Succession, 532
Grand Canal (China), 682–683, 687
Grand Duchy of Kiev, see Kiev
Grand Duchy of Moscow, 651
Grand Empire (Napoleon), 736, 738(map)
Grand Testament (Villon), 403
Graneri, Michele, 590(illus.)
Gravitation: Galileo and, 565; Kepler on, 565; Newton on, 567
Great Britain, see England (Britain)
Great Elector, see Frederick William (Great Elector, Brandenburg)
Great Fear (France), 724
Great Northern War, 547
Great Pyramid, Olmec, 417
Great Schism, 397
Great Wall (China), 686
Greenland, 499
Gregory (Saint), 391(illus.)
Gregory XI (Pope), 397
Grien, Hans Baldung, 481(illus.)
Guanajuato, 516, 521
Guarani people, 413
Guatemala, Maya and, 417
Guibert of Nogent, 384–385
Guilds, 374; of professors, 372; craft, 399; Ottoman, 658
Guillotine, Louis XVI and, 729, 729(illus.)
Guise family (France), 474
Gujarat, trade and, 626
Gulf of Guinea, 621, 622
Gunpowder, 473, 651
Gustavus Adolphus, 477; France and, 528
Gutenberg, Johann, 453
Gynecology, 381

Habsburg Dynasty: Renaissance politics and, 458–459; France and, 459, 465, 528; Ottoman Turks and, 538–540; Austrian absolutism and, 581–583; Ottomans and, 658; French Revolution and, 728
Habsburg-Valois Wars, 465, 471–472, 651; cost to France, 473
Hagia Sophia, 655
Hair, in Qing China, 688
Hall of Mirrors (Versailles), 529, 530(illus.)
Hancock, John, 718
Harem, in Ottoman society, 652, 653
Harrow, 377
Hastings, Warren (England), 673
Hausa: people, 624; language, 626
Hausaland, 627–628
Health and health care: of medieval European peasants, 381; diet and, 606–607;

in China, 694, 694(illus.). See also Disease; Medicine; Pharmacology; Physicians
Hebrew people. See also Jews and Judaism
Helgoland, 739(map)
Henry II (England), villeins and, 376–377
Henry II (France), 473, 474, 527, 651
Henry III (France), 474, 475
Henry IV (France), 475, 527–528
Henry V (England), 395
Henry VII (England), 455–456, 457
Henry VIII (England), 451, 456, 540; Protestant Reformation and, 467–469, 469(illus.)
Henry of Guise, 474
Henry of Navarre, 474, 475
Henry the Navigator (Portugal), 499–500, 504, 518
Heresies and heretics: Joan of Arc as, 396. See also Inquisition
Hermandades (brotherhoods), 457
Hersendis (French lady), 385
Heshen (China), 690
Heterosexuality, see Homosexuality; Sex and sexuality
Hideyoshi, Toyotomi (Japan), 696, 699
Hierarchical society, of Maya, 419
Hieroglyphic writing, of Maya, 419
Higher education, see Education; Universities and colleges
Hildegard of Bingen (nun), 387, 387(illus.)
Hindus and Hinduism: in Southeast Asia, 495; in Mughal Empire, 665, 668. See also India
Hiroshima, 701
Hispaniola, Columbus and, 506
Historians and historiography: Ekkehard of Aura, 386; Jean Frossart, 393; Sherbourne Cook, 423; historical time divisions and, 445; Valla, 446; Ibn Khaldun, 520; on Louis XIV, 529; Ibn Battuta, 626; Ibn Fartura, 627–628; Mustafa Naima, 652; Juvaini and, 659; Abu-l-Fazl, 665; on French Revolution, 722. See also Polo, Marco
History of the House of Osman (Ahmet Semseddin-ibn-I-Kemal), 656
Hobbes, Thomas, 549
Hohenzollern Dynasty, 540
Hokusai (Japan), 705, 705(illus.), 708(illus.)
Holbach, Paul d', 575
Holland, 553; religious reform in, 461; Protestantism in, 476; France and, 729, 736. See also Belgium; Dutch; Low countries; Netherlands
Holy League, against Turks, 651
Holy Roman Empire, 538; Low Countries, Spain, and, 475–477; Thirty Years' War and, 477–480. See also Austria; Germany
Holy wars, see Crusades; Jihad (Islamic holy war)

Homosexuality: Native American berdaches, 428–429; in Ottoman Empire, 653; in Tokugawa Japan, 703
Horses, for farming, 377–378
Hospitals, 610–611, 611(illus.); in China, 695
Hôtel-Dieu (Paris), 610
Households, of medieval European peasants, 380
House of Commons (England), 549–550; Cabinet and, 553
Housing, of medieval European peasants, 380
Huascar (Inca), 436, 508–509
Huaylas, 432
Huayna Capac (Inca), 435, 436, 508
Hudson Bay region, 533
Huguenots: Calvin and, 467; French religious wars and, 474–475; Edict of Nantes and, 475; in France, 528; Louis XIV and, 529
Huitzilopotchtli (god), 421, 423, 424, 425; pyramid of, 431; Spaniards and, 507–508
Humanists: in Italian Renaissance, 445–446; in northern Renaissance, 451; Luther and, 464
Humanitarianism: children and, 603; hospitals and, 610
Human sacrifice: by Olmecs, 416; Maya blood sacrifice and, 419(illus.); of Aztecs, 423–424
Humayun (Mughal Empire), 664
Hume, David, 575
Hundred Days, of Napoleon, 739–741
Hundred Years' War, 393–396; Battle of Crécy in, 393–394, 395(illus.); English and French holdings in, 394(map); England and, 456; gunpowder and, 473
Hungary, 539–540, 539(map); Ottomans and, 650, 650(illus.), 658
Hungwu (China), 679–681, 685–686
Hürrem (Ottoman Empire), 653, 654, 654(illus.)
Hus, Jan, 397
Husuni Kubwa, Kilwa, slave trade and, 645(illus.)
Hygiene: plague and, 392. See also Disease; Health and health care

Iaroslav the Wise (Kiev), 542
Iberian Peninsula, see Portugal; Spain and Spaniards
Ibn Battuta, 626
Ibn Fartura, 627–628
Ibn-Ghazi, Ahmad (Adal), 628
Ibn Khaldun, 520
Iboland, slave trade and, 641
Ibrahim Pasa (Ottoman Empire), 653
Ieyasu, Tokugawa (Japan), 700
Île-de-France, Gothic architecture and, 373

Illegitimacy, 383; in Europe, 599–600
Illness, see Disease; Health and health care
Imam, Ismail (Persia) as, 661
Immigrants and immigration: within China, 683. See also Emigrants and emigration; Migrants and migration
Immunology, Jenner and, 611
Imperialism: of Incas, 433–437; Portuguese, 501
Inca, use of term, 508
Inca Empire, 413, 432–438, 432(map); imperialism of, 433–437; language of, 435–436; society in, 437–438; Inca Yupanque and, 440; Spanish conquest of, 508–509; royal succession in, 509
Inca Mancu Yupanque (Inca), 438
Inca Tupac Amaru II (Inca), 438
Inca Yupanque (Inca): death of, 440–441. See also Pachacuti Inca
Independence, of British American colonies, 718–719
Index of Prohibited Books, 471, 575
India: Cabral and, 500; Da Gama in, 505; European trade with, 509, 511; Mughal Empire in, 663–673; in 18th century, 669, 669(map); British East India Company and, 671–673; British in, 671–673. See also Asia
Indian Ocean region: civilizations of, 491–497; trade and, 493(map), 496–497; vessels in, 497(illus.); Muslim control of, 501; Columbian Exchange and, 515; slave trade and, 517–518; Portuguese trade and, 630; Ottomans and, 652; piracy in, 671
Indians: use of term, 413. See also Amerindians; Native Americans
Indies, see Expansion and expansionism; Exploration
Individualism, in Renaissance, 445
Indonesia, 493, 495; Dutch and, 511
Indulgences, Luther and, 461, 462
Indus River region, see India
Industry: cottage, 594–597; in 18th-century Europe, 596(map); in West Africa, 626; in China, 686–687; in Japan, 707
Inertia, 565
Infanticide, in Europe, 383, 601, 602
Infant mortality: in European nobility, 383–385; midwives and, 609; in West Africa, 624
Infants, see Children
Inferno (Dante), 370
Inflation: after Thirty Years' War, 479–480; in Europe, 521; in China, 683; in France, 733
Infrastructure, in Ming China, 682–683
Inoculation, against smallpox, 611
Inquisition, 389(illus.), 471; in Spain, 458; Galileo and, 566

Institutes of the Christian Religion, The (Calvin), 466, 467, 473
Institutional church, 612
Instrument of Government (England), 551–552
Instruments of the Observatory (Takiyuddin Mehmet), 656
Intellectual thought: Scholastics and, 372; monasteries and, 386; in Renaissance, 452–453; scientific revolution and, 563–570; Enlightenment and, 570–578; Japanese rangaku movement, 703. See also Religion(s); Universities and colleges; Writing
Intendants, in France, 528
Intermarriage: in medieval Europe, 403; métis in Senegambia, 641
International phase, of Thirty Years' War, 477
International trade, see Trade
Interregnum, 551
Ionian Sea, Ottoman control of, 651
Iran, see Persia
Ireland: England and, 402, 550, 552; potato in, 606
Iron and iron industry, farming and, 377
Iroquois Confederacy, 429
Isabella of Castile (Spain), 456, 457, 458(illus.), 499; Inquisition and, 389(illus.), 458; Jews and, 457; motives for exploration and, 503–504; Columbus and, 505–506
Isfahan, Persia, 662
Islam: in Indian Ocean region, 493(map); in Southeast Asia, 495–496; Christian expansionism and, 503–504; racism of, 520; in Songhay, 627; in Hausaland, 628; Swahili city-states and, 629; African slavery and, 631; wedding procession and, 646(illus.); Safavid Empire and, 660–663; empires in India and, 663–673. See also Muslims; Ottoman Turkish Empire; Safavid Empire
Islamic law, in Mughal Empire, 668
Islands, in Indian Ocean, 493
Ismail (Persia), 660–661
Istanbul, see Constantinople (Istanbul)
Italy: medieval universities in, 371; Black Death in, 391; peasant revolts in, 401; Renaissance in, 443–449; Charles V (Holy Roman Empire) and, 459; slave trade and, 518; France and, 736
Ivan I (Ivan Moneybags, Russia), 542
Ivan III (Russia), 542
Ivan IV (the Terrible, Russia), 542–543, 543(illus.), 651
Ivory Coast, slave trade and, 634

Jacobean literature, 482
Jacobins, 728; in National Convention, 729
Jacopo de Promontoria, 653

Jacquerie, 400
Jahangir (Mughal Empire), 665, 667, 671
James I (England), 549
James II (England), 552
Janissaries, 655
Japan, 679; European trade with, 509, 511, 513; Jesuits in, 513, 514(illus.); Western world and, 513; Portuguese and, 514(illus.); babies in, 601; Korea and, 696; feudalism in, 698–699; in 1400–1800, 698–709; national unification period in, 699; Nobunaga in, 699–700; Hideyoshi in, 700; Tokugawa regime in, 700–701; Meiji Restoration in, 702; Christianity in, 702–703; Western influences on, 703; lifestyle in, 703–708; prostitution in, 706(illus.). *See also* Asia
Jean Mouflet of Sens, 379
Jefferson, Thomas, 715–716
Jehovah (god), 443
Jem (Ottoman Empire), 649
Jemappes, battle at, 729
Jena, battle at, 736
Jenner, Edward, 611, 657
Jesuits, 471; Edict of Restitution and, 477; in China, 512–513; Japan and, 513, 514(illus.); in Latin America, 516; Ethiopia and, 629; China and, 690
Jewelry, of Moche period (Peru), 437(illus.)
Jews and Judaism: Black Plague and, 392; peasant revolts and, 401; at European frontiers, 402; in Spain, 457–458; in Southeast Asia, 495; in Dutch Republic, 554; in Prussia, 579; Enlightenment and, 580; in Songhay, 627; in Ottoman Empire, 648, 656
Jian Wen (China), 686
Jihad (Islamic holy war), 647
Jiménez, Francisco, 461
Jizya (tax), 665
Joanna of Castile, 458, 459
Joan of Arc (France), 395–396
John II (Portugal), 500
John of Cracow (bishop), 402
John of Drazic (bishop), 402
Johnson, Samuel, 632
Joseph II (Austria), 581–583, 585, 612
Journal (Columbus), 505–506
Journal (Wesley), 614
Journey to the West, The (Tang Xianzu), 684–685
Julius II (Pope), 446, 461, 468
Junkers (Prussia), 541, 579
Justice, in medieval Europe, 385
Justinian I (Byzantine Empire), *Code* of, 371
Juvaini (historian), 659

Kabuki theater, 703–704
Kagoshima, Japan, 701

Kanem-Bornu, 627–628
Kanem Wars, The (ibn Fartura), 627–628
Kangnido map, 500(map)
Kangxi (China), 689
Kano (city-state), 628
Kara Mustafa (Ottoman Empire), 658
Karlowitz, treaty at, 658
Karlsruhe, Germany, 547
Kasr-I-Shirim, Treaty of, 652
Katsina (city-state), 628
Kazan, 651
Kenya, slave trade and, 633
Kepler, Johannes, 565
Khan, *see* Khanates
Khanates, Muslim, 651
Kholops (slaves), 542
Khubilai (Mongols), 682
Kiev, 542
Kilims, 662
Kilwa (city-state), 630, 631; slave trade in, 645(illus.)
Kingdom of Naples, in Renaissance, 444
Kingdoms: of Senegambia, 621; of Benin, 622–623; Songhay, 626–627; Hausaland, 627–628; Kanem-Bornu, 627–628. *See also* Empires; Kings
King James Bible, 482, 483
Kings: of European states, 455–456. *See also* Empires; Kingdoms; Monarchs and monarchies
Kinship: in Senegambia, 621. *See also* Family life
Kisowska, Aleksandra, *see* Hürrem (Ottoman Empire)
Kitchen Maid, The (Chardin), 598(illus.)
Knighting, 385
Knights: samurai and, 699. *See also* Warrior class
Kongin (Korea), 698
Kongo region, 624
Korea, 679, 695–698; world map from, 500(map); China and, 687; Buddhism in, 696; culture of, 696; Japan and, 696, 700; Rubens sketch and, 697(illus.); trade of, 698
Korkut, Dede, 656
Koryo Dynasty (Korea), 696
Kunturkanki, Jose Gabriel (Peru), 438
Küstler, G., 740(illus.)
Kyoto, Japan, 699
Kyushu, Japan, 700, 703

Labor: in medieval Europe, 375–383, 400–401; of Aztec women, 427–428; in Inca Empire, 437, 438; after Thirty Years' War, 479–480; of Native Americans, 506; *encomienda* system, 516; slavery and, 518–520, 627; European cottage industry and, 594–597; in 18th century Europe, 598; in West Africa, 624, 626; in China, 684, 686; and French Revolution,

730; inflation and, 733. *See also* Industry; Women; Working classes
Lafayette, marquis de, 716(illus.), 719, 724
Laguna de los Cerros, Olmecs in, 416
La Liberté (painting), 743(illus.)
Lamu (city-state), 630
Lancastrians (England), 456
Land: in West Africa, 624; Ottoman control of, 652; in British India, 673; in China, 681; reclamation in Ming China, 683(table); in Japan, 699, 700. *See also* Agriculture; Farms and farming
Land bridge, 413–415
Landlords: serfdom and, 538; in England, 550
Landscapes, in Persia, 662
Language(s): European national, 402; European vernacular literature and, 403–404; of Native Americans, 414(map); in Andes valleys, 435; Luther and, 464; Austronesian, 493; Scriptures translated into, 496; Yiddish, 580; of Senegambia, 621; in Mughal Empire, 666. *See also* Writing
La Plata, territory of, 517
Las Casas, Bartolomé de, 516, 517, 519
Later Middle Ages, crises of, 389–398
Latin America: Columbian Exchange and, 513–516, 515(illus.); colonial administration in, 517; economic effects of European discoveries and, 520–521; Dutch trade with, 555. *See also* America(s); Central America; South America
Latin Christendom, *see* Roman Catholic church
Latin classics, in Renaissance, 446
Latin language: Mass in, 382; in Chinese Christian missions, 512
Latin Quarter (Paris), 371
Latvia, 547
Laud, William, 550
Lavater (Christian zealot), 580
La Venta, Olmecs in, 416, 417
Law(s): of Justinian, 371; Roman, 371; toward natives and newcomers, 401–402; English, 553; in Ottoman Empire, 655; of Suleiman I, 655; of Napoleon, 734–735. *See also* Law codes
Law(s) (social and scientific): of inertia, 565; of planetary motion, 565; of universal gravitation, 567; of human existence, 570
Law codes: of Justinian, 371; of Suleiman I, 655; of Napoleon, 734–735
Law schools, in medieval Europe, 371
League of Armed Neutrality, 719
Learning: monasteries and, 386; China and, 695. *See also* Education; Intellectual thought
Lectures, in universities, 372
Legal pluralism/dualism, 401–402

Legazpi, Miguel Lopez de, 511
Legislative Assembly (France), 728
Legislatures, Hundred Years' War and, 396
Leisure, in 18th-century Europe, 614–615
Le Nain, Louis, 605(illus.)
Lent, 615
Leo X (Pope), 461
Leo Africanus, 627
Leonardo da Vinci, 447
Leopold I (Austria), 547
Leopold II (Austria), 583
Lepanto, battle at, 651
Leseur, Pierre Antoine, 714(illus.)
Leviathan (Hobbes), 549
Liberalism, 715–717; popular support
    for, 716–717; American Revolution
    and, 717, 719–720; classical, 720.
    See also French Revolution;
    Revolution(s)
Liberty, concept of, 715–717
Libro des Coisas (Barbosa), 644–645
Lifestyle: in central Middle Ages Europe,
    375–389; in medieval manor, 378–381;
    in monasteries, 387–388; of Olmecs,
    415–417; of Maya, 418; of Aztecs, 425–
    428; of European children, 602–603; in
    Ottoman Empire, 655; in Tokugawa
    Japan, 703–708
Linguistics, *see* Language(s)
Lin Yiu (China), 694
Lisbon, trade and, 500–501
Literacy, 600; for European nobility, 385;
    in 14th century, 405; movable type and,
    453; in 18th-century Europe, 604
Literature: Hildegard of Bingen and, 387;
    Black Death and, 393; vernacular, 403–
    404; of Renaissance, 446; in Reformation
    Europe, 482–483; Cervantes and, 535;
    in Enlightenment, 571–572; French ille-
    gal book trade and, 576–577; popular,
    603–604; in Ottoman Empire, 655–656;
    Persian, 662; in Mughal Empire, 666–
    667; in Ming China, 684; in China, 689.
    See also Art and artists
Lithuania, *see* Poland-Lithuania
Livestock, 740
Locke, John, 553, 572, 716
Lollards, 397
London, blacks in, 631(illus.), 632
Longbow, 393–394
Longitude, 568
Long Parliament, 550, 551
Lords, *see* Nobility; Vassals
Louis VII (France), 373
Louis IX (France), Sainte-Chapelle and,
    373(illus.)
Louis XI (France), 455, 456, 473
Louis XIII (France), 529
Louis XIV (France), 527, 528, 529–533,
    672; Versailles and, 526(illus.), 529,
    530(illus.), 558–559; acquisitions of,

532–533, 533(map); England and, 552;
    death of, 584
Louis XV (France), 584
Louis XVI (France), 584; French Revolu-
    tion and, 722, 724, 727, 728, 729,
    729(illus.)
Louis XVIII (France), 739, 741
Loutherbourg, Philip James de, 613(illus.)
Low Countries, 476(map); Hundred Years'
    War in, 393–394; division of, 475–476.
    See also Belgium; Holland; Netherlands
Lower classes, *see* Classes
Loyalists, in America, 718
Loyalty oath: for French clergy, 726–727;
    Napoleon and, 734
Loyola, Ignatius, 471
Luanda, Angola, 622(map), 634–635,
    634(illus.)
Lully, Jean-Baptiste, 532
Lunatic: use of term, 610; Islamic asylums
    and, 659(illus.)
Lütfi Pasa, 655
Luther, Martin: theology of, 461–463;
    Protestantism and, 461–465;
    Lutheranism and, 463–465; doctrines of,
    464; on Copernicus, 565. *See also*
    Protestants and Protestantism

Macanas (Aztec weapons), 426–427
Macao, trade and, 509
Macartney, George, 690, 691, 693, 710,
    711(illus.)
Maceualtin (Aztec working class), 427
Machiavelli, Niccolò, 444, 452–453
Machu Picchu, 438
Madagascar, slave trade and, 633
Madeira Islands, 518
Madras, India, 671
Magellan, Christianization of Southeast
    Asia and, 496
Magna Carta, 551(illus.)
Maize (corn), 417, 515, 606; in Africa, 624
Malacca, 495, 497, 555; Portugal and, 501,
    509
Malaria, 624
Malaya (Malaysia), 493
Malay Peninsula, 491; trade and, 509
Malbar Coast, 501
Mali: kingdom of, 621; slavery and, 631
Malinke people, 624, 627
Managed economy, in revolutionary
    France, 730
Manchus (China), 679, 687; Korea and,
    696
Manco Capic (Inca king), 434–435
Manila: Spanish occupation of, 495; found-
    ing of, 511
Manor: peasants on, 377; life on, 378–381
Mantegna, Andrea, 448(illus.)
Mantua, 535
Manuel (Portugal), 500

Manufacturing: in France, 531; in rural Eu-
    rope, 596; in China, 687. *See also* Com-
    merce; Industry; Trade
Manumission: of Jean Mouflet, 379, 379(il-
    lus.); Cape Colony and, 633
Maps: Kangnido, 500(map); improvements
    in, 503; in Ottoman Empire, 656
Mapuche people, 413
Marathas (Mughal Empire), 669
Marcus Tullius Cicero, *see* Cicero
Margaret of Valois, 474
Maria Theresa (Austria), 579, 582, 583(il-
    lus.); compulsory education and, 603–
    604; religious orders and, 612
Marie Antoinette (France), 726, 728
Marie of Champagne, 375
Maritime trade: European global, 509–512,
    510(map); Portugal and, 630; of China,
    686. *See also* Trade
Markets: in Senegambia, 622; in West
    Africa, 626; in Ming China, 684
Marriage: of medieval European peasants,
    380; dowry and, 385; divorce and, 398–
    399; in later Middle Ages, 398–399; in-
    termarriage in Europe and, 403; in Aztec
    Empire, 427; in Inca society, 437–438; in
    Italian Renaissance, 444; Lutheranism
    and, 464–465; Catholic, 470; in Refor-
    mation Europe, 480, 481; in Southeast
    Asia, 494–495; by Muslim clergy, 496;
    age and, 594; in 18th-century Europe,
    597–598; illegitimacy and, 599–600; in
    West Africa, 623; interracial, 631(illus.);
    of Cape Colony slaves, 633; in Ottoman
    Empire, 652–653; in China, 692–693; in
    Japan, 707
Married women, *see* Marriage; Women
Martin V (Pope), 397–398
*Marvels Discovered by the Boat Bound for the
    Galaxy, The,* 686
Marx, Karl, on Asia, 671
Mary, in medieval Christian religion, 383
Mary I (Tudor, England), 465, 468
Mary II (England), Glorious Revolution
    and, 552–553
Mary, Queen of Scots, 476
Mary of Burgundy, 458–459
Masaccio, Florentine, 448
Mass, in Latin, 382
Massawa, 628
Masturbation, 610
Mathematics: of Maya, 417, 420; in scien-
    tific revolution, 568
Maupeou, René de, 584
Mauritania, slavery in, 633
Maximilian I (Habsburg), 458–459
Maya, 413, 417–420; world of, 417(map);
    writing of, 419; sciences of, 420; astron-
    omy and, 563
Mayflower (ship), 517
Mazarin, Jules, 529

Measles, 516
Mechanics, Newton on, 567
Medici family: Cosimo de', 449; Giovanni de' (Pope Leo X), 461; Giulio (Clement VII), 470; Marie de', 528
Medicine: schools of, 371; women and, 381; death rate and, 594; children and, 602; European, 607–610; advances in, 610–611; in West Africa, 625; Ottoman education in, 656; Islamic lunatic asylum, 659(illus.); in China, 694. *See also* Midwives
Medieval Europe, *see* Middle Ages
Mediterranean region: Ottoman Turks in, 499; slave trade and, 518, 519(map); Ottomans vs. Habsburgs in, 651; Napoleon and, 736
Mehmet, Takiyuddin, 656
Mehmet II (Ottoman Empire), 647–648, 649, 656
Mehmet Köprülü (Ottoman Empire), 658
Meiji Restoration (Japan), 702
Memoirs (Catherine the Great), 581
Memoirs (Saint-Simon), 558–559
Men: in medieval religious life, 382; medieval European monasteries of, 387; and marriage in later Middle Ages, 398–399; Aztec cross-gendered, 428; in Inca society, 437–438; Renaissance education of, 454; medicine and, 607; in Western India, 624; in China, 693; in Japanese theater, 703; prostitution and, 706(illus.). *See also* Gender; Kingdoms; Kings; Monarchs and monarchies
Mendelssohn, Felix, 580
Mendelssohn, Moses, 579, 580
Mendez, Alphonse, 629
Mental hospitals, 610. *See also* Lunatic
Merad IV (Ottoman Empire), 652
Mercantilism: in Spanish America, 517; in France, 531; England and, 551
Merchant capitalism, *see* Capitalism
Merchants: slave trade and, 639, 640, 640(illus.); China and, 687; in Korea, 698; in Japan, 701–702, 707–708. *See also* Caravan trade
Merchant's Tale, The (Chaucer), 385
Merici, Angela, 471
Merk, J. C., 541(illus.)
Mesoamerica, 413; Olmecs in, 415–417; Classic period in, 417; Maya in, 417–420; Zapotecs in, 418, 420; Teotihuacán, 420; Time of Troubles in, 420–422; Aztec Empire in, 421(map); human sacrifice in, 423–424. *See also* Human sacrifice
Metals, *see* Mines and mining
Methodism, 613–614. *See also* Wesley, John
Métis, in Senegambia, 641
Metternich, Klemens von, 737

Mexica: use of term, 422; Spaniards and, 507(illus.). *See also* Aztec Empire; Mexico
Mexico: geography of, 413; Amerindians in, 415; Olmec civilization in, 415–417; Teotihuacán in, 420, 421, 421(illus.); Aztec lifestyle in, 425–428; Spanish conquest of, 506–508; trade and, 511; population drop in, 516; silver in, 521
Mexico City, *see* Tenochtitlán
Meytens, Martin, 583(illus.)
Michael Romanov (Russia), 545
Michelangelo, 447; Sistine Chapel and, 442(illus.); St. Peter's dome and, 446; *David* (statute) of, 449(illus.)
Middle Ages: central and later period in, 370(illus.), 371–405; life in Christian Europe, 375–389; popular religion in, 381–383; crises of later period, 389–398; Black Death, 390–393; Hundred Years' War and, 393–396; religious crisis in, 396–398; Renaissance and, 445; slavery in, 518. *See also* Monks and monasteries
Middle classes: in France, 529, 722, 733; in Spain, 535; in Japan, 703, 708. *See also* Classes
Middle Passage, *see* Slave trade
Midwives, 610; Aztec, 427; in Europe, 608(illus.); Martha Ballard as, 609. *See also* Obstetrics
Migrants and migration: in late 13th century, 402; of Europeans, 499; within China, 683. *See also* Immigrants and immigration
Mije-speaking people, 418
Milan, in Renaissance, 444, 445
Military: Aztec, 426–427; Inca, 432, 435; in Brandenburg-Prussia, 541; in Russia, 545; janissaries in, 655; Safavid Empire and, 662; in Mughal Empire, 665, 668; sepoys in India, 672; in Ming China, 685–686; in revolutionary France, 731–733; Napoleon and, 734. *See also* Armed forces; Warrior class
Milk, 605
Millet, Jean-François, 592(illus.)
Milpa system of agriculture, 417, 418
Mines and mining, in Latin America, 516, 517
Ming Dynasty (China), 679; economy of, 521; family and, 678(illus.); government of, 680–683; economic, social, and cultural change and, 683–685; decline of, 686–687
Minorca, 533
Minorities, *see* Ethnicity
Missions and missionaries: racial and national hostilities and, 402; and European expansion, 512–513; Christianization of Latin America, 516–517; in China, 690; Christian: in Southeast Asia, 495

Mita system (Inca), 437
Mitima (Inca colonization), 436
Moche civilization (Peru), 432, 433(illus.), 435(illus.), 437(illus.)
Mogadishu (city-state), 628(map), 630, 631
Mogul, *see* Mughal Empire (India)
Mohács, Battle of, 650, 650(illus.), 651
Mohammed II (Ottoman Turks), 499; siege of Constantinople by, 501
Mohican people, 429
Moldavia, 652
Molière, 532
Moluccas (Maluku), 495
Mombasa (city-state), 630, 652; Portugal and, 630(illus.), 631
Monarchical theory, of church government, 473
Monarchs and monarchies: in Eastern Europe, 535–536; constitutional monarchy in England, 549–553; Enlightenment and, 584–585; French Revolution and, 721, 722–723, 725–726. *See also* Kingdoms; Kings
Monasticism, *see* Monks and monasteries
Money: shell, 626; Japanese capitalism and, 701; in France, 721
Money economy, serfs and, 377
Mongolia, China and, 686
Mongols: China and, 490(illus.), 679, 687; Golden Horde and, 542; Russia and, 542, 543; Persia and, 659–660; trade and, 686; in Korea, 696
Monks and monasteries: secular universities and, 371; in medieval Europe, 375, 386–389; oblates and, 384, 385(illus.); English Reformation and, 468; in Korea, 696. *See also* Religious orders
Monserrate, Antonio, 665
Montagu, Mary Wortley, 656–657, 656(illus.)
Montaigne, Michel de, 482
Monte Albán, 420
Monte Cassino, monastery at, 388(illus.)
Montesquieu, baron de, 573, 716, 720
Montezuma I (Aztec), 428
Montezuma II (Aztec), 423, 424, 425; coronation stone of, 425(illus.); Cortés and, 507–508
Montpellier, France, 371, 398
Monuments: Olmec, 416(illus.); Maya, 418
Moon: Galileo and, 565–566, 566(illus.). *See also* Astronomy; Universe
Moors, 626
More, Thomas, 451
Mori, Japan, 700
Morison, Samuel Eliot, 505
Morocco: Portuguese control in, 499; Songhay and, 627
Mortality, *see* Death rate; Infant mortality
Moscow: as Russian capital, 548; Napoleon

and, 737, 740, 740(illus.). *See also* Grand Duchy of Moscow; Muscovy state

Mosques: Suleiman I and, 655; in Mughal Empire, 665

Mothers: in 18th-century Europe, 602; in Africa, 625(illus.); in Ottoman Empire, 653. *See also* Family life; Women

Motion, *see* Astronomy; Universe

Mountain (French revolutionaries), 729, 730

Movable type, 453

Mozambique, slaves from, 632

Mozart, Wolfgang Amadeus, 577(illus.)

Mughal Empire (India), 663–671; trade with, 511; Akbar in, 664–667; succession in, 667; trade and commerce in, 670–671

Muhammad Rimfa of Kano, 628

Mummies, Inca, 434, 436, 508, 509

Mumtaz Mahal (India), 667

Musa Colinus ul-Israil (doctor), 656

Muscovy state, 542–549

Music: baroque, 483–484; in Enlightenment, 577(illus.)

Muslim Arabs, *see* Arab people; Caravan trade; Muslims

Muslims: clergy of, 496; Zheng He as, 498; Ottoman Turks as, 499; Indian Ocean and, 501; Ethiopia and, 628; literature of, 662. *See also* India; Islam; Ottoman Turkish Empire

Mysore, India, 673

Mysticism, of Hildegard of Bingen, 387(illus.)

Nadir Shah (Persia), 667, 669

Nagoya, Japan, 701

Nahuatl-speaking people, Aztecs and, 424

Naima, Mustafa, 652

Nanjing (Nanking), 679, 681, 684

Naples (kingdom), 444

Napoleon I (Bonaparte, France), 734–741; Directory and, 733; wars and foreign policy of, 735–741; coronation of, 735(illus.); Grand Empire of, 736; invasion of Russia, 736–737, 740; in Elba, 737; Hundred Days and, 739–741; Europe and (1810), 739(map); in St. Helena, 741

Napoleonic Code, 734–735

Narrative of the Incas (Betanzos), 440–441

National Assembly (France), 724, 725–726; disbanding of, 728

National Convention (France), 728–730

National debt, in France, 721

Nationalism, after Hundred Years' War, 396

National unification period, in Japan, 699

Nation-state: in Renaissance, 455–459; in Russia, 547. *See also* Nationalism

Native Americans: as Indians, 413; Columbian Exchange and, 513–516, 515(illus.); Christianization of Latin American, 516–517; disease and, 516–517, 633; slavery and, 518(illus.), 519–520. *See also* Amerindians

Natural rights, Locke on, 553

Navarre, Spanish reconquest of, 457

Navigation: improvements in, 503, 503(illus.); portolans and, 506; scientific revolution and, 568

Navigation Acts (England), 552

Navy: of Zheng He, 497, 498; Ottoman, 649, 651; in Ming China, 686; Battle of Trafalgar and, 736

Nelson, Horatio (Lord), 736

Neo-Confucianism, 681; in Korea, 696; in Japan, 700

Netherlands: revolt of, 475–476; wars with Spain, 475–476; United Provinces of, 476; trading companies and, 504; Dutch Republic and, 553. *See also* Austrian Netherlands; Belgium; Dutch

Neumann, Johann Balthasar, 548(illus.)

Nevsky, Alexander, 542

Newfoundland, 533

New Granada, 517

New learning, in Renaissance, 446

New Model Army, 551

New Spain, 517

Newton, Isaac, 567, 567(illus.), 571; translation of *Principia,* 573(illus.), 574

New World, *see* America(s); Western Hemisphere (New World)

N'gazargamu, Kanem-Bornu, 628

Nicholas I (Russia), 659

Nicholas V (Pope), 446

Nigeria, 622

Niger River region, 626

Ninety-five theses (Luther), 462–463

Njiga of Ndongo (Queen), 637(illus.)

Nobility: in medieval Europe, 375, 383–386; chivalric code and, 393; Aztec, 425; Inca, 438; urban, 444; in Catholic church, 459; in France, 474–475, 527–528, 529–530, 531(illus.), 584, 721; in eastern Europe, 536–538; in Russia, 542–543. *See also* Aristocracy

Nobility of the robe (France), 473, 530

Nobunaga, Oda (Japan), 679, 699

Nocturnal (instrument), 503(illus.)

Nödlingen, Battle of, 477

Nomadic people, Amerindians as, 415

North Africa: West African trade and, 626; Ottoman control of, 650

North America: Viking discovery of, 499; European diseases in, 517; French colonies in, 531. *See also* America(s); Latin America; Native Americans

Northmen, *see* Vikings

Notre Dame (Paris), cathedral school of, 371–372

Nova Scotia, 533

Novels and novelists, *see* Literature

Novgorod, 542

Nuclear family: in Europe, 597–598; in West Africa, 624; in China, 692

Nuns: Ursuline order of, 471; in Middle Ages, 481

Nuremberg, observatory at, 568(illus.)

Nursing: fertility and, 600–601. *See also* Medicine

Nutmeg, 501

Nutrition, *see* Agriculture; Diet; Foods

Oath of the Tennis Court (France), 723(illus.)

Oaxaca, Zapotecan-speaking people in, 420

Oba (Benin kingship), 622–623, 623(illus.)

Oblates, 383–384; Hildegard of Bingen as, 387

Observations of Agricultural Practices (Japan), 707

Observatory, at Nuremberg, 568(illus.)

Obsidian: Olmecs and, 416–417; Aztec weapons and, 426–427

Obstetrics, 381. *See also* Midwives

Occupations, *see* Labor; Professions

Of Plymouth Plantation (Bradford), 517

Older people, *see* Elderly

Old Regime, Napoleon and, 734

Olearius, Adam, 536(illus.)

Oleg (Varangian), 542

Oligarchies: and Italian Renaissance cities, 444; and Italian city-states, 455–456

Olivares (Count), 535

Olmecs, 415–417

On Christian Liberty (Luther), 463

On Pleasure (Valla), 446

On the Dignity of Man (Pico della Mirandola), 446

On the False Donation of Constantine (Valla), 446

"On the Immortality of the Soul" (Mendelssohn), 580

On the Revolutions of the Heavenly Spheres (Copernicus), 565

Open-field system, 377, 591

Oregones (Inca nobility), 428, 438

Orinoco River region, 413

Orléans, Battle of, 395–396

Orlov, Gregory, 581

Orthodox Christianity: Russia and, 542, 545; Ottomans and, 647

Osaka, Japan, 701, 707; Battle of, 703

Osman (Anatolia), 647

Otoni people, 413

Ottoman Turkish Empire, 647–659; expansion of, 499; Austria and, 538–540; Ethiopia and, 629; evolution of, 647–648; expansion and foreign policy of, 648–652; in 1566, 649(map); society in, 652–655; culture in, 655–657; decline of, 657–659. *See also* Turkey

Ottoman Turks, *see* Ottoman Turkish Empire
Otumba, battle at, 508
Overseas exploration and conquest, by Europe, 499–501
Oviedo, 504–505
Oxford University, 372

Pachacuti Inca, 435, 437, 440–441
Pacific region, trade in, 511
Padshahnama, 676
Pagans and paganism, Catholics and, 614
Paine, Thomas, 718
Painting: in Italian Renaissance, 447–448; in northern Renaissance, 451; baroque in, 484; of social themes, 592(illus.); of Katsushika Hokusai, 705. *See also* Art and artists
Palenque, 418
Palestine, Ottomans and, 650
Pampa de las Llamas-Moxeke, Peru, 432
Pamphlets, chapbooks as, 604
Papacy, *see* Popes; specific popes
Papal States, in Renaissance, 444, 445
Paris: cathedral school in, 371–372; hospitals in, 610. *See also* Paris, Treaty of; Parlement (Paris)
Paris, Treaty of: in 1763, 672; in 1783, 719
Paris, University of, 381
Parish: in later Middle Ages, 398–399; church in, 612
Parlement (Paris), 584, 720–721, 722, 723
Parliament (England), 396, 456, 457, 717; English Reformation and, 468; constitutional monarchy and, 549–553; Restoration and, 552; role of, 553
Parma, duke of, *see* Farnese, Alexander
Partition, of Poland (1772, 1793, 1795), 581
Pata (city-state), 630
Patriarchal society, women and, 480
Patriots, in America, 718–719
Paul III (Pope), 470, 471
Paul of Tarsus (Saint Paul), letters of, 461
Paupers, 602. *See also* Poverty
Peace of Augsburg, 465, 477, 651
Peace of Utrecht, 532–533, 534(map)
Peace of Westphalia, 473, 477–479
Peacock Throne, 667, 669
Peanuts, 437(illus.)
Peasant Family (Le Nain), 605(illus.)
Peasants: in medieval Europe, 375–378; manorial life of, 378–381; noble's control over, 385; marriage and, 399; revolts in Europe, 400–401; Lutheranism and revolts of, 463; in France, 531, 531(illus.), 725, 726; in Spain, 535; in eastern Europe, 536–538; in Russia, 542; Russian military and, 545–547; in Austria, 583; European agriculture and, 591–593; potato crops and, 606; in Ming

China, 681; in Japan, 704–707. *See also* Serfs and serfdom
Peasants' Revolt (England, 1381), 400
Pemba, 633
Peninsulares, 717
Penny Wedding, The (Allan), 599(illus.)
Peoples: of Americas, 413–415, 414(map); of Indian Ocean region, 491–495
Pepper, 504(illus.); trade in, 501
Persia: Safavid Empire in, 647; Ottomans and, 652; theocratic state in, 659–663. *See also* Safavid Empire
Persian carpets, 662
Persian language, in Mughal Empire, 666
Persian Letters, The (Montesquieu), 573
Peru, 415; mask from, 412(illus.); Incas of, 432–438; population drop in, 516; colonial administration of, 517. *See also* Inca Empire
Peter III (Russia), 579, 581
Peter the Great (Russia), 545–549, 581
Petrarch, Francesco, 445
Pharmacists, 608
Pharmacology, Ottomans and, 656
Philadelphia, Constitutional Convention in, 720
Philip II (Spain), 475, 476, 521, 532; Armada and, 476–477
Philip VI (France), 393
Philip of Burgundy, 458, 459
Philippine Islands, 493, 495; Islam and, 496; trade and, 509, 511
Philip the Fair (France), 389; Babylonian Captivity and, 397
Philosophes, 572–575, 585
Philosophical Dictionary (Voltaire), 588–589
Philosophy: world-view of West and, 563; scientific revolution and, 567; Enlightenment and, 570–578; *Philosophes* and, 572–575
Physicians, 608–611; in medieval Europe, 381; Aztec women as, 427. *See also* Medicine
Physics: Newton and, 567. *See also* Science(s); Scientific revolution
Pico della Mirandola, 446
Piedras Negras, 418
Pietism, 613–614
Pigs, Islam and, 496
Pilgrimage of Grace, 468
Piracy, of Muslim shipping, 671
Pisa: Council at (1409), 397; in Renaissance, 444
Pius II (Pope), Ottomans and, 648
Pius IV (Pope), 481
Pius VI (Pope), Holy League against Turks and, 651
Pius VII (Pope), Napoleon and, 734
Pizarro, Francisco, Inca Empire and, 436–437, 438, 508, 509

Plague: in Europe, 390–393, 390(map); in 18th-century Europe, 594
Planets: Kepler on, 565. *See also* Astronomy; Universe
Planting of a Liberty Tree (Leseur), 714(illus.)
Plant life, Columbian Exchange and, 513–516
Playwrights, *see* Drama
Plowing: in medieval Europe, 377, 378(illus.). *See also* Agriculture; Farms and farming
Pluralism, legal, 401–402
Pneumonic plague, 391
Poets and poetry: of troubadours, 374–375; *Romance of Tristan and Isolde,* 375, 385; Arabic, 662
Poitiers, Battle of, 393, 395
Poland: serfdom in, 538; partitions of, 581; Russian conquest of, 581; Ottomans and, 652, 654
Poland-Lithuania, Russia and, 543
Political organization: in Korea, 696. *See also* Government
Politics and political thought: Machiavelli and, 452–453; in Renaissance, 452–459; Lutheranism and, 465; after dynastic wars, 473; in France, 473–474; in Netherlands, 475–476; Thirty Years' War and, 477–480. *See also* Conservatism; Liberalism; Reign of Terror; Revolution(s); Socialism
Politiques (France), 474
Polo (sport), 661(illus.)
Polo, Marco, 505, 506
Poltava, Battle of, 547
Polygyny: in Aztec society, 428; in West Africa, 624
Popes: supremacy of, 389; in Avignon, 397; Great Schism and, 397; Henry VIII and, 468; France and, 473. *See also* Papal States; specific popes
Pòpolo, in Italian Renaissance, 444
Popular culture, 614–615
Popular literature, 603–604
Population: Black Death and European, 392; and Hundred Years' War, 396; of Tenochtitlán, 425, 430; in England, 456, 593(fig.); after Hundred Years' War, 473; of Southeast Asia, 494; diet and, 516; of Native Americans, 516–517; of Asia, 593; in Europe, 593–594, 594(fig.), 596(map); illegitimacy and, 600; in Africa, 624, 641; of Mughal India, 664; in China, 684, 687, 690(table); in Japan, 701, 702
Popul Vuh (Maya Book of Council), 420
Poquelin, Jean-Baptiste, *see* Molière
Porcelein: in China, 685, 685(illus.), 689–690; in Korea, 698
Pork, Muslim restrictions on, 496

Portolans, 506

Portraits: in Renaissance, 448. *See also* Painting

Portugal: slave trade and, 454–455, 520, 622(map), 623, 631, 633–634, 637–638; Malacca and, 495; exploration by, 499–501; caravel and, 501–503; commercial empire of, 509, 511; Japanese trade and, 513, 514(illus.); Latin American colonies of, 517; Africa and, 620(illus.); Ethiopia and, 628; Swahili city-states and, 630–631; India and, 671

Post-Olmec people, 418

Potato, 515, 606; Andean people and, 433; in Europe, 593; Frederick the Great and, 607(illus.)

Potosí, 516, 520–521

Potter, Beatrix, 705

Poverty: child abandonment and, 383; infanticide and, 601; in revolutionary France, 724, 730

Power (political), of medieval nobility, 385–386

Pragmatic Sanction of Bourges, 456, 579

Prague, defenestration of, 477

Praise of Folly, The (Erasmus), 451, 459

Prat, Antoine du, 459

Prayer, in medieval Christian monasteries, 387–388

Pre-Columbian Americas, 412–438, 412(illus.); sex and sexuality in, 398

Pregnancy: illegitimacy, marriage, and, 600. *See also* Birthrate; Illegitimacy

Premarital sex, 598–599

Presbyterian church, Calvin and, 467

Prester John, 499

Preveze, battle at, 651

Priesthood, in Aztec society, 428

Prime minister, in England, 553

Primogeniture, in Japan, 699

Prince, The (Machiavelli), 444, 452–453

Principia (Newton), 567, 571; translation of, 573(illus.), 574

Printing: movable type and, 453; in China, 687

Priories, *see* Monks and monasteries

Products: of Tenochtitlán, 430–431; in African slave trade, 639–640

Professions, Aztec women in, 427–428

Progress: Enlightenment concept of, 570; population growth and, 594

Property: equality and, 715–716. *See also* Wealth

Prophetic religions, *see* Christianity; Islam; Jews and Judaism

Proposal to Geneva Town Council (Calvin), 486–487

Prostitutes and prostitution, 398; Aztec, 428; berdaches as, 428; in Europe, 480–481; male and female (Japan), 706(illus.)

Protein, *see* Diet

Protestant ethic, 550

Protestant Reformation, 461–469, 473(map); Luther and, 461–465; growth and spread of, 465–469

Protestants and Protestantism: Luther and, 461–465; meaning of term, 463; in Germany, 465; Calvin and, 466–467; Anabaptists and, 467; English Reformation and, 467–469; Catholic Reformation, Counterreformation, and, 469–471; in France, 473–474, 528; United Provinces of the Netherlands and, 476; Louis XIV and, 531–532; in Holy Roman Empire, 538; in England, 553; institutional church and, 612; revival in, 612–614; Pietism and, 613–614; Ottomans and, 651. *See also* Scientific revolution

Protestant Union, 477

Provinces, *see* Colonies and colonization

Prussia, 538; emergence of, 540–541; Junkers in, 541; Frederick the Great in, 578–579; universal education in, 603; French Revolution and, 728; France and, 729, 736. *See also* Brandenburg-Prussia; Germany

Ptolemy (astronomer), 563, 564

Public health, in Europe, 381

Public offices, sale in France, 473

Public opinion, in Enlightenment, 578

Pueblo people, 413

Pugachev, Emelian, 581, 582(illus.)

Pulaar language, 621

Punjab region, 669. *See also* India

Purdah (seclusion), 628

Purging, 608

Puritans, 468–469; Calvin and, 467; in England, 550

Putting-out system, 595–596, 670

Pyramids: Olmec (La Venta), 417; in Teotihuacán, 420; in Tenochtitlán, 423, 431

Pyrenees, Treaty of, 535

Qianlong emperor (China), 690–692, 691(illus.), 695; response to letter from George III, 710–711, 711(illus.)

Qing Empire (China), 521, 679, 687–695; scholar-bureaucrat's study in, 688(illus.); in 1759, 689(illus.)

Qizilbash people, 660

Quadruple Alliance, 737

Quakers, Anabaptists and, 467

Quattrocento, 447. *See also* Renaissance (European)

Quechua (Inca language), 435–436

Queens, *see* Kingdoms; Kings; specific rulers

Quetzalcoatl (god), 420, 421, 421(illus.); Spaniards and, 507

Quibayasa people, 413

Race and racism: in European frontiers, 401–403; in Americas, 517–520; of Europeans, 520; religion and, 520

Racine, Jean, 532

Radicalism: of Voltaire, 574–575; of liberalism, 720. *See also* French Revolution; Liberalism; Revolution(s); Socialism

Rain forests, in South America, 413

Raised-field system of agriculture, Maya and, 418

Raja Todar Mal (Mughal Empire), 665

Rákóczy, Francis, 540

Rangaku (Japan), 703

Raphael, 447

Rastrelli, Bartolomeo, 549

Rationalism: of Newton, 567; Rousseau and, 576

Raymond of Toulouse, 389(illus.)

Razin, Stenka, 545, 546, 546(illus.)

Reading, *see* Literacy; Literature

Realism, in Renaissance painting, 448

Reason, *see* Enlightenment

Rebellions: in England, 468; of Japanese peasants, 706. *See also* Revolts; Revolution(s)

Reconquista (Spain), 457

Recreation: in medieval Europe, 399; dancing as, 399(illus.); in 18th-century Europe, 614–615; in China, 695. *See also* Entertainment; Leisure

Red-light districts, 398

Red Sea region, 501

Red Turbans, 679

Reflections on the Revolution in France (Burke), 727

Reforestation, in China, 683

Reform and reformers: in Catholic church, 397, 459, 461, 469–471; in Russia, 581; in Austria, 581–582; absolutism and, 585; in Mughal Empire, 668; in Korea, 696. *See also* Reformation

Reformation: Protestant, 461–469, 473(map); Catholic, 469–471, 473(map); institutional church and, 612

Reformed religion, Calvinism as, 467, 473, 474

Refugees, religious, 467

Regulating Act (1773), 673

Reign of Terror (France), 730–731, 733

Reis, Piri, 656

Religion(s): in Ghana, 288–289; popular, in medieval Europe, 381–383; challenge to authority of, 389; medieval crisis in, 396–398; Maya, 420; Aztec, 423–425; Inca, 433–434; art and, 447–448; in Spanish state, 457–458; Catholic reforms and, 461; Protestant Reformation and, 461–469; Lutheranism, 463–465; Calvinism, 466–467; Catholic Reformation, Counterreformation, and, 469–471; French riots, civil war, and, 474–475; in Low

Religion(s) *(cont.)*
Countries, 475; Thirty Years' War and, 477; baroque arts and, 483–484; in Southeast Asia, 495–496; exploration and, 503–504; in Inca Empire, 508; in China, 512–513; in Japan, 512–513; Islam and, 520; Louis XIV and, 531–532; in England, 550, 551–552; in United Provinces, 554; science and, 563–566, 569–570, 572; Enlightenment and, 570; Voltaire on, 575, 588–589; in 18th-century Europe, 611–614; Methodism as, 613–614; Pietism in, 613–614; in Mughal Empire, 665, 668; French Revolution and, 726–727, 733. *See also* Gods and goddesses; Monks and monasteries
Religious orders: Jesuits as, 471; Ursuline, 471; Franciscans, 512, 516; reform of, 612
Religious toleration, 554, 582–583; in Ottoman Empire, 647; in Mughal Empire, 665
Remonstrance, from Irish princes, 402
Renaissance (European), 443–459; Michelangelo and, 442(illus.); Italy and, 443–449; intellectual thought in, 445–452; northern Europe and, 449–452; social change during, 452–455; blacks in, 454–455, 455(illus.). *See also* Scientific revolution
Representative government, 716; Hundred Years' War and, 396; in America, 717, 718
Republic, in France, 728–729
Restoration (England), 552
Revenue, *see* Economy; Taxation
Revolts: of European peasants, 400–401; Lutheranism, peasants, and, 464; by French poor, 733. *See also* Rebellions; Revolution(s)
Revolution(s): in 18th century, 715; American, 717–720; in France, 720–727. *See also* Scientific revolution
Revolutionaries, in Paris, 724
Rhineland, France and, 729, 730
Ricci, Matteo, 512, 687
Rice: in Southeast Asia, 493–494; in China, 683; in Japan, 704–706
Richard II (England), 397; Peasants' Revolt and, 400
Richelieu (Cardinal), 527, 528, 528(illus.)
Rights: civil, 716; in U.S. Bill of Rights, 720; of women, 727–728
Riots, in France, 474–475, 724–725
"Rites Controversy," in China, 512
Rituals: in medieval European religion, 382; in Southeast Asia, 495
Ritual slaughter, by Aztecs, 423–424
Robert of Geneva, *see* Clement VII (Pope)

Robespierre, Maximilien, 727, 728, 729, 730, 733
Roger II (Sicily), 371
Roman Catholic church: Thomas Aquinas and, 372; oblates in, 383–384; challenge to authority of, 389; Babylonian Captivity and, 397; Great Schism in, 397; Spanish monarchs and, 457; in Renaissance, 459–461; in Germany, 465; English Reformation and, 467–469; Catholic Reformation, Counterreformation, and, 469–471, 473(map); as French state religion, 473; in Spanish Netherlands, 476; marriage and, 480; in France, 532, 721; in Spain, 535; in England, 550, 551, 552; in Ireland, 550; institutional church and, 612; piety in, 614; Ottomans and, 651; French Revolution and, 726–727, 733; Napoleon and, 734. *See also* Monks and monasteries; Reformation; Scientific revolution
Romance of Tristan and Isolde, 375, 385
Romanesque architecture, 373
Roman law, medieval universities and, 371
Romano, Francesca, 381
Romanov Dynasty, 543; Michael and, 545
Romantic movement, Rousseau and, 576
Romantic poetry, of troubadours, 375
Rome (city), papal court in, 397
Rotation of crops, *see* Crop rotation
Rotterdam, 556
Rousseau, Jean-Jacques, 576, 602, 619(illus.)
Rowlandson, Thomas, 631(illus.)
Royal African Company (England), 520
Royal council, in France, 527–528
Rubens, Peter Paul, 484, 697(illus.)
Rule of Avoidance, in China, 682
Rulers: of Inca, 437–438; in Italian cities, 444; Machiavelli on, 452–453; Renaissance politics and, 455–459
Rural areas: putting-out system in, 595–596; in Korea, 698
Russia: Muscovy and, 541–548; Mongols and, 542; expansion to 1725, 544(map); Peter the Great and, 545–549, 581; Great Northern War and, 547; Peter III and, 579; Catherine the Great and, 579–581; Ottomans and, 651; France and, 736; Napoleon's invasion of, 736–737, 740
Russian Orthodox Christianity, *see* Orthodox Christianity
Rustem (Ottoman Empire), 653

Sacrament, marriage as, 480
Sacred Congregation of the Holy Office, 471
Sacrifices: Maya blood sacrifice, 419(illus.); Aztec mass sacrifices, 423. *See also* Human sacrifice

Safavid Empire, 647, 648, 660–663, 660(map)
Safi al-Din (Persia), 660
Sahagún, Bernardino de, 428
Saint Albans monastery, 388–389
Saint Bartholomew's Day massacre, 474
Saint-Denis, Suger as abbot of, 373
Sainte-Chapelle, La (Paris), 373(illus.)
St. Helena, Napoleon at, 741
St. Paul, *see* Paul of Tarsus (Saint Paul)
St. Peter's Basilica (Rome), 446
St. Petersburg, 547–549
Saints, in medieval Europe, 382
Saint-Simon, duke of (Louis de Rouvroy), 529, 558–559
Sake (Japanese rice wine), 701
Sakoku (Japan), 702
Salerno, medical school in, 371
Salons (gatherings), in Enlightenment, 577–578
Salt, 626
Salvation: Luther on, 463; by faith, 464; Wesley on, 614
Samarkand Tables, 563
Samurai (Japan), 699, 700, 701, 708; lifestyle of, 703
San Lorenzo: Olmecs in, 416, 416(illus.); destruction of, 417
San Salvador, Columbus and, 501
Sans-culottes, 730, 733
Sarfati, Isaac, 648
Satellite states, of Napoleonic France, 736
Savigny abbey (Normandy), 388
Savoy, 729
Schöffer, Peter, 453
Scholarship, *see* Intellectual thought; Learning
Scholastics, 372
Schönbrunn (Vienna), 547
Schools: literacy and, 405; in 18th-century Europe, 603–604. *See also* Education
Science(s): medieval universities and, 372; of Maya, 420; Jesuit contributions to China, 512; in 1500, 563–564; Enlightenment and, 570; popularizing, 571(illus.); medicine and, 610; in Ottoman Empire, 656. *See also* Medicine; Religion(s); Scientific revolution; Technology
Scientific instruments, 568
Scientific revolution, 563–570; causes of, 567–570
Scotland, Anglicans and, 550
Script: of Maya language, 420. *See also* Writing
Sculpture: Olmec, 416. *See also* Art and artists
Scurvy, 606
Sea of Japan, 695–696
Secondat, Charles-Louis de, *see* Montesquieu, baron de
Second Coalition, 735

Second Continental Congress, 718
Second estate (France), 721
Second Treatise of Civil Government (Locke), 553, 572
Secret police, in China, 682
Secularism, in Italian Renaissance, 446–447, 448–449
Secular states, medieval universities and, 371–372
Sedentary people, Amerindians as, 415
Selective breeding, 740
Self-government, 716; in United States, 720
Selim I (Ottoman Empire), 649–650, 653
Selim II (Ottoman Empire), 658
Senegambia, 621–622; métis in, 641
Seoul, Korea, 698
Sepoys (India), 672
Seppuku (Japan), 699
September Massacres (France), 728
Seraglio, 656. *See also* Harem
Serer language, 621
Serfs and serfdom, 375–376; manumission of, 379; in England, 400; Aztec, 427; in France, 473, 725; in eastern Europe, 535, 536–538, 536(illus.); in Russia, 581; abolition in Austria, 583
Servants, 598. *See also* Slaves and slavery
Settlements: of Amerindians, 415; in Inca Peru, 432; Viking, 499
Seven Years' War, 579, 658, 717, 719; France and, 584
Sex and sexuality: in later Middle Ages, 398; homosexuality in Aztec society, 428; and gender in Renaissance, 454; Luther and, 464–465; in Reformation Europe, 480; in Southeast Asia, 494–495; servant girls and, 598; premarital and controls of, 598–599; illegitimacy, marriage, and, 599–600; Ottoman harem and, 652. *See also* Homosexuality
Sforza, Isabella, 455
Shah (Persia, Iran): Abbas as, 660; Ismail as, 660
Shah Jahan (Mughal Empire), 667, 676–677, 677(illus.)
Shakespeare, William, 482
Shanghai, 684
Shaykh Salim Chishti (Sufi), 665, 666(illus.)
Shell money, 626
Shenyang (Mukden), China, 687
Shi'ite Muslims, 652, 660–662, 660(map). *See also* Sunni Muslims
Shiki (Japan), 699
Shimroku, Kōnoike (Japan), 701
Ships and shipping: Zheng He and, 497, 498; in Indian Ocean, 497(illus.); cannon mounted on, 501; exploration and, 501–503; global seaborne trade and, 509–512, 511(map); England and, 552;

Dutch, 555, 555(map); slave trade and, 634–637; Ottoman, 649. *See also* Spanish Armada; Trade
Shoen (Japan), 699
Shogun (Japan), 700
Shunsho, Katsukawa (Japan), 705
Siam (Thailand), 672, 696
Sick man of Europe, Ottoman Empire as, 659
Siderus Nuncius (Galileo), 565–566
Siena, in Renaissance, 444
Sigismund (Germany), 397
Sigismund (Hungary), Ottomans and, 647
Sigismund II (Poland), 654
Signori (Italy), 444
Silesia, 539(map), 579, 582
Silk and silk industry: trade in, 511; in China, 687
Silk Road, collapse of, 496–497
Silver: Japanese trade and, 511; from Latin America, 516, 517, 520–521; Chinese economy and, 683, 687
Sioux people, Catlin and, 429(illus.)
Sipán, Peru, 432
Sistine Chapel, 442(illus.)
Sixtus V (Pope), 476
Skeptics and skepticism, 572; Bayle and, 572; Hume and, 575; Voltaire and, 575
Skilled workers, *see* Working classes
Skin color, racism and, 401
Slaves and slavery: origin of term, 376; in Aztec Empire, 427; in Renaissance Europe, 454–455; in Latin America, 517; in Americas, 517–520; contemporary, 518, 633; sources of, 518–519, 519(map); Mongols and, 542; Russian peasants and, 542; Senegambia and, 621; in Songhay, 627; economic value of, 633; in Ottoman society, 653; devshirme system and, 653–655; janissary corps as, 655. *See also* Africa; Slave trade
Slave trade, 517–520, 519(map), 631–641; Portugal and, 509, 511(map); English control of, 533; Senegambia and, 621; West Africa and, 622(map); in Songhay, 627; extent of, 632–633; suppression of, 633; Atlantic, 633–639; imports by destination, 635(table); exchange systems for, 638–639; products involved in, 639–640; volume of trans-Atlantic, 641(table)
Slavic people: serfdom and, 536; eastern, 542
Sleeping sickness, 633
Smallpox, 516, 517, 610–611; in West Africa, 625; African slave trade and, 633; in Ottoman Empire, 656–657
Social classes, *see* Classes
Social Contract, The (Rousseau), 576
Socialism, in France, 730
Social science, Enlightenment and, 570
Society: in central Middle Ages Europe,

375–389; Black Death and, 392–393; Hundred Years' War and, 396; in pre-Columbian Americas, 412–438; Maya, 419; Aztec, 422–431; Inca, 437–438, 508; in Renaissance, 445–455; blacks in Renaissance, 455; Luther and, 463–465; in Reformation Europe, 480–482; spread of European, 499–509; motives for exploration and, 503–505; in Dutch Republic, 556; in 18th-century Europe, 591–615; peasants in western Europe, 592–593; in Senegambia, 621–622; in Benin, 622–623; in Sudan, 627–628; in Ottoman Empire, 652–655; Indian factory-fort, 671–672; in Ming China, 684; in Korea, 698; feudal, in Japan and, 698–699; in Japan, 700–701, 703–708; in France, 721–722. *See also* Classes; Men; Women
Society of Jesus, *see* Jesuits
Sofala (city-state), 628, 630
Sokullu Mehmet (Ottoman), 652
Solar system: sun-centered, 565; Galileo on, 565–566
Soldiers: pillaging by, 479(illus.); in China, 681; in Napoleonic wars, 740, 740(illus.). *See also* Military; Warrior class
Solomonid Dynasty (Ethiopia), 628
Songhay Empire, 626–627
Soto, Hernando de, 517
South America: geography of, 413; people of, 414(map); Vasco da Gama and, 500; Columbian Exchange and, 513–516. *See also* America(s); Latin America
Southeast Asia: trade and, 491–493, 496–497; agriculture in, 493(illus.); population of, 494; religion in, 495–496; commerce and, 497. *See also* Indian Ocean region; specific countries
Sovereignty, Hobbes on, 549
Spain and Spaniards: peasant revolts in, 401; Maya and, 420; Inca and, 436–437; Jews and, 457–458, 458, 521; Renaissance politics in, 457–458; Charles V and, 459; Philip II of, 475; Low Countries and, 475–476; Netherlands wars with, 475–476; consolidation of, 499; Columbus and, 501, 505–506; Aztecs and, 506–508; Incas and, 508–509; commercial empire of, 509–511; Columbian Exchange and, 513–516; *encomienda* system and, 516; economic effects of discoveries, 520–521; inflation in, 521; Muslims and, 521; War of the Spanish Succession and, 532–533; Bourbon kings in, 533, 534(map); absolutism in, 533–535; church in, 612; American colonies and, 717–718; France and, 729; Napoleon and, 737(illus.)
Spanish Armada, 476–477

Spanish Netherlands (Belgium), 476, 553; France and, 532, 533

Spice trade, 497; Portugal and, 500, 671; pepper and, 501, 504; importance of, 505; Dutch monopoly over, 511; global seaborne trade and, 511

Spider King, see Louis XI (France)

Spirit of Laws, The (Montesquieu), 573

Sports, 615

Spy system, in Napoleonic France, 735

Stamp Act (1765), 717

Starvation, see Famine

State, see Nation-state

States General (Dutch Republic), 553

Statute of Kilkenny (Ireland), 403

Statute of Laborers (England), 400

Staupitz, John, 461

Strasbourg, France and, 532

Stuart family, in England, 549–550

Sub-Saharan Africa, see Africa

Succession: in Inca Empire, 509; in Ottoman Empire, 653, 657–658; in Mughal Empire, 667

Sudan, 621, 626–628; slavery in, 633

Suffrage, see Voting

Sufis, Mughal Empire and, 665

Sugar: cane, 493; trade in, 509; in Brazil, 517; slavery and, 518–519; consumption of, 607; slave trade and, 633

Suger (abbot of Saint-Denis), 373

Sui Dynasty (China), 682

Suleiman I (the Magnificent, Ottoman Empire): Southeast Asia and, 495; Ottoman Empire under, 650–652, 655–657; Hürrem and, 654

Süleymanname (Book of Suleiman), 650(illus.)

Sultan, Ottoman, 648, 652, 653

Summa Theologica (Thomas Aquinas), 372

Sunni Muslims: in Mughal Empire, 665. See also Shi'ite Muslims

Sunni Ottomans, 652

Supremacy Act (England), 468

Surgeons, 608

Suttee (self-immolation), 668

Swahili city-states, 629–631

Sweden, 479; Great Northern War and, 547; Napoleon and, 736

Swedish phase, of Thirty Years' War, 477

Swidden agriculture, of Maya, 417

Swinka, Jakub (bishop of Gniezno), 402

Sxeyhi of Kütahya, 655

Syphilis, 516; in West Africa, 625; in China, 694(illus.)

Syria, Ottomans and, 650

System of Nature (Holbach), 575

Tabriz (Persian Empire), 660, 661

Tabula rasa, Locke on, 572

Taesa, Sa-Myong (Korea), 697(illus.)

Taille (tax), 473

Taj Mahal (Agra), 662, 667, 668(illus.)

Takamatsu, Japan, 700

Tamerlane, 563, 662, 664, 664(illus.)

Tametsi (decree), 470

Tang Xianzu (China), 684–685

Tapestries, of Tournai, Belgium, 374(illus.)

Tariffs, in France, 531

Tartars, see Mongols

Taxation: French peasants and, 400; in England, 456, 550; in France, 456, 473, 528, 584; by Louis XIV, 530–531; on landowners and peasants, 592–593; in Mughal Empire, 665, 668; in China, 683; in Korea, 696; in Japan, 701, 704–706; of American colonies, 717, 718; by French church, 721

Technology: exploration and, 501–503. See also Science(s)

Telescope, 565–566, 568

Temples: Aztec, 428; Inca, 436

Temujin, see Chinggis Khan (Mongols)

Tennis Court Oath (France), 723(illus.)

Tenochtitlán, 425, 430–431, 430(illus.); Aztec sacrifice at, 423; Cortés in, 507–508

Teotihuacán, 420

Terror, the (France), 730–731, 733

Test Act (England), 552

Textiles and textile industry: Maya, 418; Moche, 433, 433(illus.); Latin American trade and, 521; in West Africa, 626; in Mughal Empire, 670(illus.)

Tezcatlipoca (god), 421

Thailand, see Siam (Thailand)

Theater: Shakespeare and, 482–483; in China, 695; in Japan, 703

Theocracy, in Persia, 659–663

Theodore (Russia), 545

Theology: Gothic cathedrals and, 374; of Luther, 461–463; of Calvin, 466, 467; science and, 563–564; Voltaire and, 575. See also Religion(s)

Thermidorian reaction (France), 733

Third Coalition, 736

Third estate (France), 721–722; Tennis Court Oath and, 723(illus.)

Thirty Years' War, 477–480; phases of, 477; Europe after, 478(map); France and, 528

Thomas Aquinas (Saint), 372

Tiepolo, Giovanni Battista, 548(illus.)

Tikal, 418

Tile, Persian, 662, 663(illus.)

Tilsit, Treaty of, 736

Timars (landed estates), 652

Timbuktu, 626, 627, 628

Time of Troubles (Mesoamerica), 420–422

Time of Troubles (Russia), 545

Timucua people, 429

Titicaca, 432

Tlalmaitl (Aztec serf class), 427

Tlazolteotl (god), 424(illus.)

Tobacco, in Korea, 698

Tokugawa regime (Japan), 511, 679, 700–701, 702(map)

Tokyo, 700

Toliptzin (Toltec king), 421, 422

Toltecs, 420–422

Tondibi, battle at, 627

Topa Inca (Inca), 435, 437

Totonacs, 507

Toure, Muhammad, 626–627

Tournai, Belgium, tapestry in, 374(illus.)

Towns, see Cities and towns

Trade: in medieval Europe, 375, 377; Olmec, 416; Maya, 418–419; Aztec, 423; with Indian Ocean region, 491–493, 493(map); Southeast Asian colonies and, 495; Muslims and, 496; of Southeast Asia, 496–497; in Malacca, 497; Chinese, 498, 683, 687, 690; Portuguese-African, 500; exploration and, 504; global seaborne networks of, 509–512, 511(map); Japan and, 513, 699–700, 701; Portuguese American colonies and, 517; Spanish American colonies and, 517; slave trade, 517–520, 519(map); world economy and, 520–521; in France, 531; Russian, 543; Dutch, 555, 555(map); in West Africa, 625; of Songhay, 627; Kanem-Bornu and, 627–628; of Hausa, 628; Swahili, 629; Muslim control of, 647; in Indian Ocean region, 652; Ottoman, 652, 658–659; of Safavid Empire, 662; in Mughal Empire, 670–671; Dutch East India Company and, 671; Portugal and, 671; British East India Company and, 671–673; by Qing China, 679–680; trade and, 686; Korean, 698. See also Spice trade

Trades (skills), in Ming China, 684

Trading companies, 504

Trading posts: for slave trade, 638–639; factory-fort society and, 671–672

Trafalgar, Battle of, 736

Transportation: by Maya, 419; in Europe, 594; in West African trade, 626; in Ming China, 682–683

Trans-Saharan trade: in slaves, 518; Kanem-Bornu and, 627; of Hausa, 628. See also Caravan trade; Slave trade

Transubstantiation doctrine, 468

Transvestites, in Native America cultures, 428–429

Transylvania, 539(map); Ottomans and, 658

Travel, literature about, 572

Travels (Equiano), 637

Travels (Marco Polo), 505, 506

Treason, religious heresy as, 471

Treasury, in China, 682

Treaties, see specific treaties

Treatise on the Barbarian Kingdoms on the Western Oceans, 686
Trent, Council of, 470
Tres Zapotes, Olmecs in, 416, 417
Tribute, in China, 686, 690, 692
Triennial Act (England), 550
Triptych with the Nativity (Gerard David), 452(illus.)
Troeltsch, Ernst, 463
Troubadour poetry, 374–375
Trouvères (France), 375
Trumbull, John, 719(illus.)
Truth, *see* Philosophy
Tsar (Russia), 542; Michael as, 545; Ivan IV as, 651
Tuareg people, 626, 627
Tuberculosis, 517
Tudor Dynasty (England), 456–457
Tuileries, fighting in, 728
Tuke, William, 610
Tula, 422
Tulelo people, 429
Tupis people, 413
Turkey: Ottomans and, 538, 648. *See also* Anatolia; Ottoman Turkish Empire
Turkish Empire, *see* Ottoman Turkish Empire
Turkish people: in Cyprus, 651. *See also* Ottoman Turkish Empire
Type (printing), movable, 453
Tzeltalan people, 417

Uaxactún, 418
Ukraine, 547
Ulema (religious scholars), 661–662
Unam Sanctam (1302), 389
Unification, in Japan, 699
Uniform Land-Tax Law (Korea), 696
Union of Utrecht, 476
United Nations (UN), International Labor Organization, 633
United Provinces of the Netherlands, 476, 477, 479, 553–556; commerce of, 555–556, 555(map)
United States: Montesquieu and, 573, 716, 720; Constitution in, 719–720. *See also* America(s); American Revolution; North America
Universal education, 603–604
Universe: Aristotle on, 563–564; Copernicus on, 565; sun-centered solar system in, 565. *See also* Astronomy
Universities and colleges, medieval European, 371–372
Upper classes: women in, 481; in China, 695; in Japan, 704–706. *See also* Elites
Urban VI (Pope), 397
Urban areas: plague in, 391–392; nobility in, 444
Urban culture: of Amerindians, 415; in Enlightenment, 576–578

Urbanization: in Ming China, 684; in Japan, 700, 701–703
Ursuline order of nuns, 471
Utopia (More), 451
Utrecht, 534(map). *See also* Peace of Utrecht
Uxmal, 418

Vaccinations, 611
Valla, Lorenzo, 446
Valley of Mexico, Aztecs in, 422–423
Valmy, Battle of, 729
Valois Dynasty (France), 465
Van den Vondel, Joost, 554
Van der Weyden, Rogier, 451
Van Eyck, Jan, 451
Varangians, 542
Vassals: nobles as, 385; in Japan, 701
Vegetables, 605, 606
Velázquez, Juan de Paraeja, 483(illus.)
Venereal disease, 593
Venice, 447(illus.); in Renaissance, 444, 445; slave trade and, 518
Veracruz, 428; Cortés in, 506
Vergerio, Peter Paul, 452
Vernacular languages, literature in, 403–404
Versailles, 526(illus.), 529, 530(illus.), 558–559; Estates General at, 724
Vespucci, Amerigo, 413
Viceroyalties, Spanish, 517
Vienna, 538–539; Ottomans and, 650; battle at, 658
Vikings: voyages of exploration, 499; in Russia, 542
Villages, *see* Cities and towns
Villeins, in England, 376–377
Villon, François, 403
Vindication of the Rights of Man, A (Wollstonecraft), 727
Vindication of the Rights of Woman, A (Wollstonecraft), 727–728
Violence, in medieval recreation, 399
Virgil, Dante and, 403–404
Virocha (Inca god), 508
Vitalis, Orderic (monk), 386
Vitamins, 606
Vitry, Jacques de, 400
Vocations, of clerics, 470
Volga region, 546, 651
Voltaire, 573–575, 574(illus.), 589(illus.); on religion, 588–589
Voting, in France, 728

Waldseemüller, Martin, 413
Wallace, William, 399
Wallachia, 652
Walpole, Robert, 553
Walter, Jakob, 737, 740
Wang Zhi (China), 682
Wan-li (China), 512, 687

War of the Austrian Succession, 579, 582, 584, 658
War of the League of Augsburg, 532
War of the Spanish Succession, 532, 539–540; Dutch in, 556
War of the Three Henrys, 474
Warrior class: in medieval Europe, 375, 376(illus.), 383–386; Aztec, 426–427; in Japan, 699, 703. *See also* Nobility
Wars and warfare: training of European nobility in, 385; Aztec, 423, 425; Inca, 436; gunpowder and, 473; civil war in France, 474–475; Aztec vs. Spanish, 508; under Louis XIV, 532–533; population and, 593; Ottomans and, 658; during French Revolution, 728, 729; of revolutionary France, 728, 729–730; Napoleon and, 735–741. *See also* Jihad (Islamic holy war); specific wars
Wars of the Roses, 456
Warthmüller, R., 607(illus.)
Washington, George, 718
Waterloo, Battle of, 741
Waterways, *see* Canals; specific rivers
Way of the Warrior (Japan), 699
Wealth: of medieval monasteries, 388; Maya trade and, 419; of Aztec Empire, 423; in Renaissance Italy, 443–444, 446; of Catholic church, 459; European exploration and expansion and, 505; Ottoman women and, 652, 653; in Confucianism, 687; in China, 695; equality and, 716. *See also* Elites; Mercantilism; Merchants; Upper classes
Weapons: longbow as, 393–394; crossbow as, 395; Aztec, 426–427; gunpowder and, 473; in siege of Constantinople, 501; in Japan, 699
Weaver's Repose, The (Gerritz), |595(illus.)
Weaving: of medieval tapestries, 374(illus.); in West Africa, 626; in Japan, 704(illus.)
Wedding(s): church ceremonies and, 399; of Inca, 438
Wedding Procession of Prince Dara-Shikoh, The, 646(illus.)
"Weighing of Shah Jahan on His Forty-Second Lunar Birthday," 676–677, 677(illus.)
Wellesley, Richard (England), 673
Wesley, John, 602, 613–614
Wesley, Susannah, 602
West, *see* Western world
West Africa: Portugal and, 500; Senegambia in, 621–622; Benin in, 622–623; slave trade and, 622(map), 634; women, marriage, and work in, 623–625; trade and industry in, 626
West African Forest Region, 621
Western Christian church, *see* Roman Catholic church

Western Europe, *see* Europe; Western world

Western Hemisphere (New World): pre-Columbian civilizations in, 412–438, 412(illus.). *See also* America(s)

Western world: China and, 512–513; Japan and, 513, 703; Russia and, 547; world-view in, 563; Catherine the Great and, 581; political revolution in (1775–1815), 714

West Indies, blacks from, 632

Westphalia, *see* Peace of Westphalia

Wet nurses, 601, 602

Wheat, in China, 683

White(s), as slaves, 518

White Mountain, Battle of the, 477

Widows: medieval aristocratic, 385–386. *See also* Women

William of Orange (England), 552–553

William of Orange (the Silent), 475

Witch scare, 481–482, 481(illus.)

Wittenberg, Luther and, 461, 462

Wives: in West Africa, 624. *See also* Family life; Marriage; Men; Women

Wollstonecraft, Mary, 727–728, 727(illus.)

Wolof language, 621

Women: as troubadours, 374–375; on medieval European manor, 380; medicine and, 381, 607; in medieval religious life, 382; marriageable age in Europe, 385; and medieval estates, 385, 386(illus.); monasticism and, 386–387; as Lollards, 397; and marriage in later Middle Ages,

398–399; craft guilds and, 399; in Aztec Empire, 427; in Inca society, 438; in Renaissance, 453–454; Lutheranism and, 464–465; as Anabaptists, 467; in Reformation Europe, 480–482; witchcraft charges and, 481–482; in Southeast Asia, 494; in Enlightenment, 573–574, 578; farming by, 592; population growth and, 594; in West Africa, 623–624, 625(illus.), 626; in Songhay Empire, 627; and slave trade, 640; in Ottoman society, 652, 653; in China, 692–694, 693(illus.); in Japan, 703, 704(illus.), 706–707; in French Revolution, 726, 733; Wollstonecraft on, 727–728; in France, 734. *See also* Family life; Gender; Midwives; Monarchs and monarchies; Mothers; Nuns; Wives

Women's rights, French Revolution and, 727–728, 742–743, 743(illus.)

Wool industry: Hundred Years' War and, 393; in Florence, 444; Low Countries, England, and, 476; cottage industry and, 595

Workers, *see* Labor; Working classes

Working classes, women in, 481

World, *see* Globalization

World-view: in West, 563; scientific view of universe and, 565–567. *See also* Enlightenment; Scientific revolution

Worms, diet at, 463

Wright, Joseph, of Derby, 603(illus.)

Writers, *see* Literature

Writing: of Maya, 417, 419. *See also* Script

Würzburg, palace at, 547, 548(illus.)

Wyclif, John, 397

Xavier, Francis (Saint), 495, 702–703

Xiangtan, China, 684

Yalu River, 696

Yellow Sea, 695

Yiddish language, 580

Yi Song-gye (Korea), 696

Yongle (China), 498, 682(illus.), 686

Yorkists (England), 456

Yoruba people, 622

Youth: of European nobility, 383–385; Aztec, 426(illus.), 427

Yuan Dynasty (China), 490(illus.), 679

Yucatán: Maya and, 417, 420; Spanish in, 420

Yugoslavia, ethnic cleansing and, 424

Yves (Saint), 382

Zacatecas, 516, 521

Zamna (god), 417

Zanzibar, 630, 633

Zapotec people, 413, 418; in Oaxaca, 420

Zeeland, 475, 553

Zheng He (China), 497, 498, 498(illus.), 686

Zhongxian (China), 682

Zhu Xi (Chinese philosopher), 681, 696

Zhu Yuanzhang (China), 679, 680. *See also* Hungwu (China)

Zwingli, Ulrich, 464

A History of World Societies: A Brief Overview

Period (CA 10,000–CA 400 B.C.)	Africa and the Middle East	The Americas
10,000 B.C.	New Stone Age culture, ca 10,000–3500	Migration into Americas begins, ca 20,000
5000 B.C.	Farming begins in Tigris-Euphrates and Nile River Valleys, ca 6000 First writing in Sumeria; city-states emerge, ca 3500 Unification of Egypt, 3100–2660	Maize domesticated in Mexico, ca 5000
2500 B.C.	Egypt's Old Kingdom, 2660–2180 Akkadian empire, ca 2331–2200 Egypt's Middle Kingdom, 2080–1640 Hyksos "invade" Egypt, 1640–1570 Hammurabi, 1792–1750 Hebrew monotheism, ca 1700	First pottery in Americas, Ecuador, ca 3000 First metalworking in Peru, ca 2000
1500 B.C.	Egypt's New Kingdom; Egyptian empire, ca 1570–1075 Hittite Empire, ca 1475–1200 Akhenaten institutes worship of Aton, ca 1360 Moses leads Hebrews out of Egypt, ca 1300–1200 Political fragmentation of Egypt; rise of small kingdoms, ca 1100–700 United Hebrew kingdom, 1020–922	Olmec civilization, Mexico, ca 1500 B.C.–A.D. 300
1000 B.C.	Ironworking spreads throughout Africa, ca 1000 B.C.–A.D. 300 Assyrian Empire, 900–612 Zoroaster, ca 600 Babylonian captivity of Hebrews, 586–539 Cyrus the Great founds Persian Empire, 550 Persians conquer Egypt, 525 Darius and Xerxes complete Persian conquest of Middle East, 521–464	Chavin civilization in Andes, ca 1000–200 B.C. Olmec center at San Lorenzo destroyed, ca 900; power passes to La Venta
500 B.C.		
400 B.C.	Alexander the Great extends empire, 334–331 Death of Alexander (323): Ptolemy conquers Egypt, Seleucus rules Asia	

East Asia	India and Southeast Asia	Europe
Farming begins in Yellow River Valley, ca 4000	Indus River Valley civilization, ca 2800–1800; capitals at Mohenjo-daro and Harappa	
Horse domesticated in China, ca 2500		Greek Bronze Age, 2000–1100 Arrival of Greeks in peninsular Greece Height of Minoan culture, 1700–1450
Shang Dynasty, first writing in China, ca 1500–ca 1050	Aryans arrive in India; Early Vedic Age, ca 1500–1000 Vedas, oldest Hindu sacred texts	Mycenaeans conquer Minoan Crete, ca 1450 Mycenaean Age, 1450–1200 Trojan War, ca 1180 Greek Dark Age, ca 1100–800
Zhou Dynasty, promulgation of the Mandate of Heaven, ca 1027–256 Confucius, 551–479 First written reference to iron, ca 521	Later Vedic Age, solidification of caste system, ca 1000–500 Upanishads; foundation of Hinduism, 700–500 Persians conquer parts of India, 513 Maharira, founder of Jainism, 540–486 Siddhartha Gautama (Buddha), 528–461	Greek Lyric Age; rise of Sparta and Athens, 800–500 Origin of Greek polis, ca 700 Roman Republic founded, 509
		Persian Wars, 499–479 Athenian Empire; flowering of art and philosophy, 5th century Peloponnesian War, 431–404
Warring States Period in China, 403–221 Zhuangzi and development of Daoism, 369–268	Alexander invades India, 327–326 Chandragupta founds Mauryan Dynasty, 322–ca 185	Plato, 426–347 Roman expansion, 390–146 Conquests of Alexander the Great, 334–323

Period (CA 300 B.C.–A.D. 700)	Africa and the Middle East	The Americas
300 B.C.	Arsaces of Parthia begins conquest of Persia, ca 250–137 Scipio Africanus defeats Hannibal at Zama, 202	Fall of La Venta, 300; Tres Zapotes becomes leading Olmec site
200 B.C.		Andean peoples intensify agriculture, ca 200
100 B.C.	Meroë becomes iron-smelting center, 1st century B.C. Dead Sea Scrolls Pompey conquers Syria and Palestine, 63	
A.D. 100	Jesus Christ, ca 4 B.C.–A.D. 30 Bantu migrations begin Jews revolt; Romans destroy temple in Jerusalem: end of Hebrew state, 70	Moche civilization flourishes in Peru, ca 100–800
A.D. 200	Camel first used for trans-Saharan transport, ca 200 Expansion of Bantu peoples, ca 200–900 Axum (Ethiopia) controls Red Sea trade, ca 250	
A.D. 300	Axum accepts Christianity, ca 4th century	Maya civilization in Central America, ca 300–1500 Classic period of Teotihuacán civilization in Mexico, ca 300–900
A.D. 500	Political and commercial ascendancy of Axum, ca 6th–7th centuries Muhammad, 570–632; the *hijra*, 622 African Mediterranean slave trade, ca 600–1500 Umayyad Dynasty, 661–750; continued expansion of Islam	Mayan civilization reaches peak, ca 600–900 Tiahuanaco civilization in South America, ca 600–1000
A.D. 700	Berbers control trans-Saharan trade, ca 700–900 Abbasid Dynasty, 750–1258; Islamic capital moved to Baghdad Decline of Ethiopia, ca 9th century Golden age of Muslim learning, ca 900–1100 Kingdom of Ghana, ca 900–1100	Teotihuacán, Monte Alban destroyed, ca 700 "Time of Troubles" in Mesoamerica, 800–1000 Toltec hegemony, ca 980–1000

East Asia	India and Southeast Asia	Europe
Development of Legalism, ca 250–208 Qin Dynasty unifies China; Great Wall begun, Confucian literature destroyed, 221–210 Han Dynasty, 206 B.C.–A.D. 220	Ashoka, 269–232	Punic Wars, destruction of Carthage, 264–146
	Greeks invade India, ca 183–145 Mithridates creates Parthian empire, ca 171–131	Late Roman Republic, 133–27
China expands, ca 111 Silk Road opens to Parthia, Rome; Buddhism enters China, ca 104 First written reference (Chinese) to Japan, A.D. 45	First Chinese ambassadors to India and Parthia, ca 140 Bhagavad Gita, ca 100 B.C.–A.D. 100 Shakas and Kushans invade eastern Parthia and India, 1st century A.D.	Julius Caesar killed, 44 Octavian seizes power, rules imperial Rome as Augustus, 27 B.C.–A.D. 14
Chinese invent paper, 105 Emperor Wu, 140–186	Kushan rule in northwestern India, 2d–3d century Roman attacks on Parthian empire, 115–211	Roman Empire at greatest extent, 117 Breakdown of pax Romana, ca 180–284
Creation of Yamato state in Japan, ca 3d century Buddhism gains popularity in China and Japan, ca 220–590 Fall of Han Dynasty, 220; Period of Division, 220–589	Fall of the Parthian empire, rise of the Sassanids, ca 225	Reforms by Diocletian, 284–305
Three Kingdoms Period in Korea, 313–668 China divides into northern, southern regimes, 316	Chandragupta I founds Gupta Dynasty in India, ca 320–480 Gupta expansion, trade with Middle East and China, ca 400 Huns invade India, ca 450	Constantine, 306–337; Edict of Milan, 313; founding of Constantinople, 324; Council of Nicaea, 325 Theodosius recognizes Christianity as official state religion, 380 Germanic raids of western Europe, 400s Clovis rules Gauls, 481–511
Sui Dynasty restores order in China, 581–618 Shotoku's "Constitution" in Japan, 604 Tang Dynasty, 618–907; cultural flowering Korea unified, 668	Sanskrit drama, ca 600–1000 Muslim invasions of India, ca 636–1206	Saint Benedict publishes his *Rule,* 529 Code of Justinian, 529 Synod of Whitby, 664
Taika Reforms in Japan, 646 Nara era, creation of Japan's first capital, 710–794 Heian era in Japan, 794–1185; literary flowering Era of the Five Dynasties in China, 907–960 Song Dynasty, 960–1279	Islam reaches India, 713 Khmer Empire (Kampuchea) founded, 802	Charles Martel defeats Muslims at Tours, 733 Charlemagne rules, 768–814 Viking, Magyar invasions, 845–900 Treaty of Verdun divides Carolingian Empire, 843 Cluny monastery founded, 910

Period (CA 1000–1600)	Africa and the Middle East	The Americas
1000	Seljuk Turks take Baghdad, 1055 Islam penetrates sub-Saharan Africa, ca 11th century Great Zimbabwe built, flourishes, ca 1100–1400 Kingdom of Benin, ca 1100–1897	Inca civilization in South America, ca 1000–1500 Toltec state collapses, 1174
1200	Kingdom of Mali, ca 1200–1450 Mongol invasion of Middle East, ca 1220 Mongols conquer Baghdad, 1258; fall of Abbasid Dynasty	Manco Capac, first Inca king, ca 1200
1300	Rise of Yoruba states, West Africa, ca 1300 Height of Swahili (East African) city-states, ca 1300–1500 Mansa Musa rules Mali, 1312–1337 Ottomans invade Europe, 1356	Aztecs arrive in Valley of Mexica, found Tenochtitlán (Mexico City), ca 1325
1400	Arrival of Portuguese in Benin, ca 1440 Songhay Empire, ca 1450–1591 Atlantic slave trade, ca 1450–1850 Ottoman Empire, 1453–1918 Da Gama reaches East Africa, 1498	Height of Inca Empire, 1438–1493 Reign of Montezuma I, 1440–1468; height of Aztec culture Columbus reaches Americas, 1492
1500	Portugal dominates East Africa, ca 1500–1650 Safavid Empire in Persia, 1501–1722; height of power under Shah Abbas, 1587–1629 Peak of Ottoman power under Suleiman, 1520–1566 Height of Kanem-Bornu, 1571–1603 Battle of Lepanto, 1571, signals Ottoman naval weakness in the eastern Mediterranean	Mesoamerican and South American holocaust, ca 1500–1600 First African slaves brought to Americas, ca 1510 Cortés arrives in Mexico, 1519; Aztec Empire falls, 1521 Pizarro reaches Peru, conquers Incas, 1531
1600	Dutch West India Co. supplants Portuguese in West Africa, ca 1630 Dutch settle Cape Town, 1651	British settle Jamestown, 1607 Champlain founds Quebec, 1608 Dutch found New Amsterdam, 1624 Black slave labor allows tenfold increase in production of Carolinian rice and Virginian tobacco, ca 1730–1760

East Asia	India and Southeast Asia	Europe
China divided into Song, Jin empires, 1127 Kamakura Shogunate, 1185–1333	Vietnam gains independence from China, ca 1000 Construction of Angkor Wat, ca 1100–1150 Muslim conquerors end Buddhism in India, 1192	Yaroslav the Wise, 1019–1054; peak of Kievan Russia Latin, Greek churches split, 1054 Norman Conquest of England, 1066 Investiture struggle, 1073–1122 Crusades, 1096–1270 Growth of trade and towns, ca 1100–1400 Barbarossa invades Italy, 1154–1158
Mongol conquest of China begins, 1215 Yuan (Mongol) Dynasty, 1271–1368 Unsuccessful Mongol invasions of Japan, 1274, 1281 Marco Polo arrives at Kublai Khan's court, ca 1275	Peak of Khmer Empire in Southeast Asia, ca 1200 Turkish sultanate at Delhi, 1206–1526; Indian culture divided into Hindu and Muslim	Magna Carta, 1215 Aquinas, *Summa Theologica,* 1253 Nevsky recognizes Mongol overlordship of Moscow, 1252
Ashikaga Shogunate, 1336–1408 Hung Wu defeats Mongols, 1368; founds Ming Dynasty, 1368–1644	Tamerlame conquers the Punjab, 1398	Babylonian Captivity of papacy, 1307–1377 Tver revolt in Russia, 1327–1328 Hundred Years' War, 1337–1453 Bubonic plague, 1347–1700 Beginnings of representative government, ca 1350–1500
Ming policy encourages foreign trade, ca 15th century Ming maritime expeditions to India, Middle East, Africa, 1405–1433	Sultan Mehmed II, 1451–1481 Da Gama reaches India, 1498	Italian Renaissance, ca 1400–1530 Voyagers of discovery, ca 1450–1600 Ottomans capture Constantinople, 1453; end of Byzantine Empire War of the Roses in England, 1453–1471 Unification of Spain completed, 1492
Portuguese trade monopoly in East Asia, ca 16th century Christian missionaries active in China and Japan, ca 1550–1650 Unification of Japan, 1568–1600	Barbur defeats Delhi sultanate, 1526–1527; founds Mughal Empire Akbar expands Mughal Empire, 1556–1605 Spanish conquer the Philippines, 1571	Luther's Ninety-five Theses, 1517 Charles V elected Holy Roman emperor, 1519 English Reformation begins, 1532 Council of Trent, 1545–1563 Dutch declare independence, 1581 Spanish Armada, 1588
Tokugawa Shogunate, 1600–1867 Japan expels all Europeans, 1637 Manchus establish Qing Dynasty, 1644–1911 Height of Qing Dynasty under K'ang-hsi, 1662–1722	Height of Mughal Empire under Shah Jahan, 1628–1658 British found Calcutta, 1690	Romanov Dynasty in Russia, 1613 Thirty Years' War, 1618–1648 English Civil War, 1642–1649 Louis XIV, king of France, 1643–1715 Growth of absolutism in central and eastern Europe, ca 1680–1790 The Enlightenment, ca 1680–1800 Ottomans besiege Vienna, 1683 Revocation of Edict of Nantes, 1685 Glorious Revolution in England, 1688

Period (CA 1700–1940)	Africa and the Middle East	The Americas
1700	Rise of Ashanti Empire, ca 1700 Decline of Safavid Empire under Nadir Shah, 1737–1747	Silver production quadruples in Mexico and Peru, ca 1700–1800 Spain's defeat in War of the Spanish Succession results in colonial dependence on Spanish goods, 1700s
1750	Selim III introduces administrative and military reforms, 1761–1808 British seize Cape Town, 1795 Napoleon's campaign in Egypt, 1798	"French and Indian Wars," 1756–1763 Quebec Act, 1774 American Revolution, 1775–1783 Comunero revolution, New Granada, 1781
1800	Muhammad Ali founds dynasty in Egypt, 1805–1848 Slavery abolished in British Empire, 1807 Peak year of African transatlantic slave trade, 1820	Latin American wars of independence, 1806–1825 Brazil wins independence, 1822 Monroe Doctrine, 1823 Political instability in most Latin American countries, 1825–1870 U.S.-Mexican War, 1846–1848
1850	Crimean War, 1853–1856 Suez Canal opens, 1869 European "scramble for Africa," 1880–1900 Battle of Omdurman, 1898 Boer War, 1899–1902	American Civil War, 1861–1865 British North America Act, 1867, for Canada Diaz controls Mexico, 1876–1911 United States practices "dollar diplomacy" in Latin America, 1890–1920s Spanish-American War, 1898
1900	Union of South Africa formed, 1910 French annex Morocco, 1912 Ottoman Empire dissolved, 1919; Kemal's nationalist struggle in Turkey	Massive immigration from Europe and Asia to the Americas, 1880–1914 Mexican Revolution, 1910 Panama Canal opens, 1914 Mexico adopts constitution, 1917
1920	Cultural nationalism in Africa, 1920s Turkish Republic recognized, 1923 Reza Shah leads Iran, 1925–1941	U.S. "consumer revolution," 1920s Stock market crash in United States; Great Depression begins, 1929
1930	African farmers organize first "cocoa holdups," 1930–1931 Iraq gains independence, 1932	Revolutions in six South American countries, 1930 New Deal begins in United States, 1933
1940	Arabs and Jews at war in Palestine; Israel created, 1948 Apartheid system in South Africa, 1948–1991	Surprise attack by Japan on Pearl Harbor, 1941 United Nations established, 1945 Perón rules Argentina, 1946–1953

East Asia	India and Southeast Asia	Europe
Height of Edo urban culture in Japan, ca 1700 Height of Qing Dynasty under Emperor Ch'ien-lung, 1736–1799	Decline of Mughal Empire, ca 1700–1800 Persian invaders loot Delhi, 1739 French and British fight for control of India, 1740–1763	War of Spanish Succession, 1701–1713 Treaty of Utrecht, 1713 Cabinet system develops in England, 1714–1742
Maximum extent of Qing Empire, 1759	Treaty of Paris gives French colonies in India to Britain, 1763 Cook in Australia, 1768–1771; first British prisoners to Australia, 1788 East India Act, 1784	Watt produces first steam engine, 1769 Outbreak of French Revolution, 1789 National Convention declares France a republic, 1792
Anglo-Chinese Opium War, 1839–1842 Treaty of Nanjing, 1842: Manchus surrender Hong Kong to British	British found Singapore, 1819 Java War, 1825–1830 British defeat last independent native state in India, 1848	Napoleonic Empire, 1804–1814 Congress of Vienna, 1814–1815 European economic penetration of non-Western countries, ca 1816–1880 Greece wins independence, 1830 Revolution of 1848
Taiping Rebellion, 1850–1864 Perry's arrival opens Japan to United States and Europe, 1853 Meiji Restoration in Japan, 1867 Adoption of constitution in Japan, 1890 Sino-Japanese War, 1894–1895 "Hundred Days of Reform" in China, 1898	Great Rebellion in India, 1857–1858 French seize Saigon, 1859 Indian National Congress formed, 1885 French acquire Indochina, 1893 United States gains Philippines, 1898	Second Empire and Third Republic in France, 1852–1914 Unification of Italy, 1859–1870 Bismarck controls Germany, 1862–1890 Franco-Prussian War, 1870–1871; foundation of the German Empire Reform Bill, Great Britain, 1867 Second Socialist International, 1889–1914
Boxer Rebellion in China, 1900–1903 Russo-Japanese War, 1904–1905 Chinese revolution; fall of Qing Dynasty, 1911 Chinese Republic, 1912–1949	Commonwealth of Australia, 1900 Muslim League formed, 1906 First calls for Indian independence, 1907 Amritsar massacre in India, 1919 Intensification of Indian nationalism, 1919–1947	Revolution in Russia; Tsar Nicholas II issues October Manifesto, 1905 Triple Entente (Britain, Russia, France), 1914–1918 World War I, 1914–1918 Treaty of Versailles, 1919
Kita Ikki advocates ultranationalism in Japan, 1923 Jiang Jieshi unites China, 1928	Gandhi launches nonviolent resistance campaign, 1920	Mussolini seizes power in Italy, 1922 Stalin takes power in U.S.S.R., 1927 Depths of Great Depression, 1929–1933
Japan invades China, 1931 Mao Zedong's Long March, 1934 Sino-Japanese War, 1937–1945	Gandhi's Salt March, 1930 Japan conquers Southeast Asia, 1939–1942	Hitler gains power, 1933 Civil War in Spain, 1936–1939 World War II, 1939–1945
United States drops atomic bombs on Hiroshima and Nagasaki, 1945 Chinese civil war, 1945–1949; Communists win	Philippines gain independence, 1946 India (Hindu) and Pakistan (Muslim) gain independence, 1947	Marshall Plan, 1947 NATO formed, 1949 Soviet Union and Red China sign 30-year alliance, 1949

Period (CA 1950–1990)	Africa and the Middle East	The Americas
1950	Egypt declared a republic; Nasser named premier, 1954 Morocco, Tunisia, Sudan, and Ghana gain independence, 1956–1957 French-British Suez invasion, 1956	Castro takes power in Cuba, 1959
1960	Mali, Nigeria, and the Congo gain independence, 1960 Biafra declares independence from Nigeria, 1967 Arab-Israeli Six-Day War, 1967	Cuban missile crisis, 1962 Military dictatorship in Brazil, 1964–1985 United States escalates war in Vietnam, 1964
1970	"Yom Kippur War," 1973 Islamic revolution in Iran, 1979 Camp David Accords, 1979	Military coup in Chile, 1973 U.S. Watergate scandal, 1974 Revolutions in Nicaragua and El Salvador, 1979
1980	Iran-Iraq War, 1980–1988 Reforms in South Africa, 1989 to present	U.S. military buildup, 1980–1988 Argentina restores civilian rule, 1983
1990	Growth of Islamic fundamentalism, 1990 to present Iraq driven from Kuwait by United States and allies, 1991 Israel and Palestinians sign peace agreement, 1993 Nelson Mandela elected president of South Africa, 1994	Canada, Mexico, and United States form free-trade area (NAFTA), 1994 Haiti establishes democratic government, 1994 Permanent extension of Treaty on the Non-Proliferation of Nuclear Weapons, 1995

East Asia	India and Southeast Asia	Europe
Korean War, 1950–1953 Japan begins long period of rapid economic growth, 1950 Mao Zedong announces Great Leap Forward, 1958	Vietnamese nationalists defeat French; Vietnam divided, 1954 Islamic Republic of Pakistan declared, 1956	Death of Stalin, 1953 Warsaw Pact, 1955 Revolution in Hungary, 1956 Common Market formed, 1957
Sino-Soviet split becomes apparent, 1960 Great Proletarian Cultural Revolution in China, 1965–1969	Indira Gandhi prime minister of India, 1966–1977, 1980–1984	Student revolution in France, 1968 Soviet invasion of Czechoslovakia, 1968
China pursues modernization, 1976 to present	India-Pakistan war, 1971 Communist victory in Vietnam War, 1975 Chinese invade Vietnam, 1979	Brandt's Ostpolitik, 1969–1973 Soviet invasion of Afghanistan, 1979
Japanese foreign investment surge, 1980–1992 China crushes democracy movement, 1989	Sikh nationalism in India, 1984 to present Corazón Aquino takes power in Philippines, 1986	Soviet reform under Gorbachev, 1985–1991 Communism falls in eastern Europe, 1989–1990
Birthrates keep falling Economic growth and political repression in China, 1990 to present	Vietnam embraces foreign investment, 1990 to present U.S. military bases closed in Philippines, 1991	Maastricht treaty proposes monetary union, 1990 Conservative economic policies, 1990s End of Soviet Union, 1991 Civil war in Bosnia, 1991 to present